A PRIMER OF **DRUG ACTION**

Abductor, 2006
leaves, photocollage, acrylic and resin on wood panel
96"x78"

Fred Tomaselli (born in 1956 in Santa Monica, California) has exhibited widely in the United States and abroad. His work is included in many private and public collections, including the Sintra Museum of Modern Art in Sintra, Portugal, and the Whitney Museum of American Art and the Museum of Modern Art in New York City. In the 1990s Tomaselli first gained attention for his collage-based paintings composed of painted lines and various forms of psychoactive drugs, pills, and marijuana leaves. He lives and works in Brooklyn, New York.

A PRIMER OF **DRUG ACTION**

A comprehensive guide to the actions, uses, and side effects of psychoactive drugs

ELEVENTH EDITION

ROBERT M. JULIEN M.D., PH.D.

Claire D. Advokat, Ph.D.
Louisiana State University

and Joseph E. Comaty, Ph.D., M.P.
Louisiana State Office of Mental Health

WORTH PUBLISHERS

Publisher: Catherine Woods
Acquisitions Editor: Erik Gilg
Executive Marketing Manager: Katherine Nurre
Project Editor: Penelope Hull
Art Director and Cover Designer: Barbara Reingold
Photo Editor: Bianca Moscatelli
Production Manager: Barbara Anne Seixas
Composition and Illustrations: TSI Graphics
Manufacturer: RR Donnelley

ISBN-13: 978-1-4292-0679-2
ISBN-10: 1-4292-0679-9

Printed in the United States of America

First printing 2007

Library of Congress Control Number: 2007936052

Worth Publishers
41 Madison Avenue
New York, NY 10010
www.worthpublishers.com

Contents

Selected

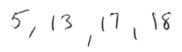

Preface

In the 33 years since the publication of the first edition of *A Primer of Drug Action*, there has been an explosion of knowledge about psychoactive drugs, the psychological disorders for which these drugs can be used, and the receptor substrates on which drugs act. Even in the three years since publication of the tenth edition, we have witnessed the introduction of new drugs for treating schizophrenia, depression, bipolar illness, Alzheimer's disease, parkinsonism, and other neurological and psychological disorders. New uses for existing drugs have extended our treatment of disorders such as persistent anxiety disorders, dysthymia, fibromyalgia, personality disorders, aggressive disorders, depression, and pain. We have witnessed marked increases in the prescription of medications for the treatment of psychological disorders of children and adolescents, and we have gained new understanding of the long-term adverse consequences of untreated psychological disorders. We have also recognized the need to develop augmentation and collaborative strategies to better treat mental health disorders. The use of currently available drugs for "off-label" use continues to expand, offering new hope for the treatment of psychological disorders and the prevention of substance abuse relapse.

In 1975, when the first edition of *A Primer of Drug Action* was published, we had few drugs to treat many of the psychological disorders discussed in the eleventh edition. We had little idea of the structure or roles of drug receptors. Child and adolescent psychopharmacology was embryonic, and most of the drugs presented in this edition had not even been conceived of. As the twenty-first century progresses, we have described the human genetic code and are beginning to explore the mechanisms by which gene expression can be modified by drugs. We will develop new and better drug delivery systems. We will develop remarkable new treatments for mental disorders, and we will see vast improvements in drug design and delivery and in the therapeutic uses of drugs as phenotype-specific agents. Drug abuse and dependence will undoubtedly continue to be problems; however, we will develop new medications to help people escape the ravages of drug dependency. We hope to see new treatments to prevent, delay, or ameliorate neuro-degenerative disorders and to protect neurons after injury or insult.

Each of the prior ten editions of *A Primer of Drug Action* has managed to mirror and document scientific and clinical advances. The eleventh edition continues to do so, presenting the general principles of each class of psychoactive drugs and providing specific information about each drug in the class. Also addressed are the mechanisms of action of each drug and drug class, current theories about the etiology of major psychological disorders and rationales for drug treatment, and the uses and limitations of psychopharmacology in patient care. Drugs of compulsive abuse are given equal time with drugs for therapeutic purposes. Often a drug of abuse has many and valid therapeutic uses. Theories of drug-induced behavioral reinforcement, comorbidity of substance abuse with other psychological disorders, and the treatment of substance abuse and relapse prevention are presented. In essence, the major changes that have occurred since the publication of the tenth edition in 2005 necessitated a continuing update.

Current research into the mechanism of action and pharmacology of psychoactive drugs is fully discussed and referenced. The pharmacological and psychotherapeutic treatments of psychological disorders are integrated, and the interface between psychopharmacotherapy and the mental health professions is addressed. The book emphasizes that both prescribing and nonprescribing mental health professionals should be knowledgeable about and conversant in the pharmacology of the drugs their clients are taking. This has become even more important since the publication of clinical practice guidelines for the treatment of major psychological disorders, so each chapter contains a brief discussion of the clinical interface between pharmacological and psychological treatments.

FEATURES OF THE ELEVENTH EDITION

In its first 30-plus years of publication, *A Primer of Drug Action* helped shape knowledge about psychopharmacology, drug abuse, and psychopharmacotherapy. For the eleventh edition, I welcome Claire Advokat, Ph.D., and Joseph Comaty, Ph.D., M.P., as contributors. Advokat is a professor in the Department of Psychology at Louisiana State University in Baton Rouge, and she holds an adjunct faculty appointment with the Alliant International University/California School of Professional Psychology. Comaty is chief psychologist, HIPAA privacy officer, and chief of the Bureau of Applied Research and Program Evaluation in the Division of Planning, Evaluation, and Information Technology of the Louisiana State Office of Mental Health, Department of Health and Hospitals, in Baton Rouge, Louisiana. He holds adjunct faculty appointments in the Department of Psychology, Louisiana State

University, and the Alliant International University/California School of Professional Psychology. Comaty is a clinical and medical psychologist, licensed to prescribe psychotherapeutic drugs in the state of Louisiana. Advokat and Comaty bring a unique viewpoint and unique contributions to the new edition.

The eleventh edition of *A Primer of Drug Action* is updated with the aim of keeping the position of the book as the most current, objective, and understandable introduction to the pharmacology of drugs that affect the mind and behavior. Each of the 21 chapters has been updated. Included in each presentation are not only the traditional and newly available drugs but also discussions of both current and future directions in drug research (including new drugs that are on the horizon but not yet available for clinical use). The two chapters devoted to child and adolescent psychopharmacology and to geriatric psychopharmacology include much new and important information about the use of medications in these populations.

It is my hope that the new edition of *A Primer of Drug Action* will serve the needs of readers who want a concise, clearly presented, and comprehensive introduction to psychopharmacology, drug education, and psychopharmacotherapy.

Robert M. Julien, M.D., Ph.D.
Portland, Oregon
drjulien.com

Available from the publisher is the *Test Bank* (ISBN 1-4292-0794-9) by Peter E. Simson, Miami University of Ohio. The new edition of the *Test Bank* contains approximately 850 items in multiple-choice, true-false, and short-answer formats. Each question is keyed to the page in the book on which the answer is located.

A PRIMER OF **DRUG ACTION**

Introduction to Psychopharmacology: How Drugs Interact with the Body and the Brain

Pharmacology is the science of how drugs affect the body. *Psychopharmacology* is a subdivision of pharmacology and is the study of how drugs affect specifically the brain and behavior. To understand the actions, behavioral uses, therapeutic uses, and abuse potentials of psychoactive drugs, we must necessarily understand how the body responds to the taking of a drug. This understanding involves the basic principles of drug absorption, distribution, metabolism, and excretion (collectively termed *pharmacokinetics*) as well as the interactions of a drug with its "receptor," or the structure with which the drug interacts to produce its effects (the area of study termed *pharmacodynamics*).

This book is specifically oriented to drugs that affect the brain and behavior. Therefore, it is an introduction to psychopharmacology, presenting not only drugs useful in treating psychological disorders but also drugs prone to compulsive use and abuse. This book begins with three chapters devoted to the fundamentals of drug action. Chapter 1 explores the area of pharmacokinetics, the movement of drug molecules into, through, and out of the body. It addresses such questions as the following: Once a drug arrives in the stomach (if taken orally), how and why does it gain access to the bloodstream? Once in the bloodstream, how is it distributed throughout the body? Is it distributed evenly? How is distribution reflected in the actions of the drug? Finally, how does the body eventually get rid of the drug?

Chapter 2 explores the area of pharmacodynamics. It examines the interaction between drugs and the receptors to which the drugs attach, as well as how the attachment results in alterations in cell function and behavior. Receptors are described both structurally and functionally, and how drugs alter receptor structure and function is discussed. Finally, the ways such actions underlie the therapeutic effects and the side effects of drugs are illustrated.

Chapter 3 applies knowledge about basic pharmacology to the specifics of drug action on the brain and behavior. For readers without background in neuroscience, the structure and function of the neuron are explained because psychoactive drugs act to produce their effects on various parts of neurons. We focus on the point of connection between two different neurons, an area called the *synapse*. By studying the process of synaptic transmission and specific neurotransmitters, we begin to understand the mode of action of psychoactive drugs as well as the complexity of brain functioning in both health and disease. Furthermore, this process of synaptic transmission is not a static process; rather, neurons have the ability to continually remodel themselves, a process called *synaptic plasticity*. Such a process is involved in learning and memory, as well in such disorders as anxiety and depression. A healthy, functioning brain is one that through this process of synaptic plasticity is continually remodeling itself in response to environment. Healthy neurons continually form new synaptic contacts, maintaining the beautiful architecture that exists through healthy interactions with millions of other neurons.

Pharmacokinetics: How Drugs Are Handled by the Body

When we have a headache, we take for granted that after taking some aspirin our headache will probably disappear within 15 to 30 minutes. We also take for granted that, unless we take more aspirin later, the headache may recur within 3 or 4 hours. This familiar scenario illustrates four basic processes in the branch of pharmacology called *pharmacokinetics*. Using the aspirin example, the four processes are as follows:

1. *Absorption* of the aspirin into the body from the swallowed tablet
2. *Distribution* of the aspirin throughout the body, including into a fetus, should a female patient be pregnant at the time the drug is taken
3. *Metabolism* (detoxification or breakdown) of the drug as the aspirin that has exerted its analgesic effect is broken down into metabolites (by-products or waste products) that no longer exert any effect
4. *Elimination* of the metabolic waste products, usually in the urine

The goal of this chapter is to explore these processes of pharmacokinetics, concluding with discussion about how pharmacokinetics can be used to determine the time course of action for drugs. The chapter also explores the steady-state maintenance of therapeutic blood levels of drugs in the body and the usefulness of therapeutic drug

monitoring. Finally, the chapter introduces the concepts of drug *tolerance* and drug *dependence.*

The understanding of pharmacokinetics, along with knowledge
about the *dosage* taken, allows determination of the concentration of a
drug at its *receptors* (sites of action) and the *intensity* of drug effect on the
receptors as a function of time. Thus, pharmacokinetics in its simplest
form describes the time course of a particular drug's actions—the time to
onset and the duration of effect. Usually, the time course simply reflects
the amount of *time* required for the rise and fall of the drug's concentration at the target site. Figure 1.1 illustrates the complexity of drug movement through the body and its equilibrium at its site of action.

The root *kinetics* in the word *pharmacokinetics* implies movement
and time. As each of the drugs in this book is discussed, the focus is first
on the time course of the drug's movement through the body, particu-

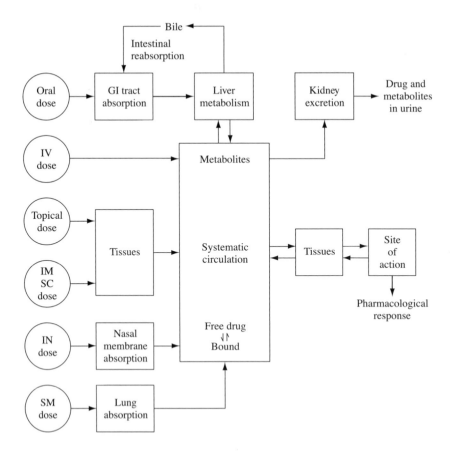

FIGURE 1.1 Schematic representation of the fate of a drug in the body. IM = intramuscular; IV = intravenous; IN = intranasal; SC = subcutaneous; SM = smoked.

larly its *half-life* and any complications that arise from alterations in its rate of metabolism. Knowledge of movement and time offers significant insight into the action of a drug. At the very least, it helps distinguish a particular drug from other related drugs. For example, the main difference between two benzodiazepines (Chapter 6), lorazepam (Ativan) and triazolam (Halcion) is in their pharmacokinetics.[1] Both these drugs depress the functioning of the brain, causing sedative and antianxiety effects. However, lorazepam persists for at least 24 hours in the body, while triazolam persists for only about 6 to 8 hours. If lorazepam is administered at bedtime for treatment of insomnia, daytime sedation the next day can be a problem, since lorazepam persists in the body through the next day. However, for longer, steady action (as might be useful in treating anxiety), lorazepam would be the superior agent to use.

The kinetic differences between lorazepam and triazolam are illustrated in Figure 1.2, which shows three ranges: an ineffective range (where not enough drug is present to produce either sedative or antianxiety effects), a therapeutic range, and a toxic range (where sedation becomes excessive). Triazolam reaches peak blood level rapidly and is of short duration. Lorazepam, on the other hand, reaches peak blood level later and persists longer in the therapeutic range. In essence, pharmacokinetic differences account for these results and allow two similar drugs to be used to achieve quite different therapeutic goals.

Drug Absorption

The term *drug absorption* refers to processes and mechanisms by which drugs pass from the external world into the bloodstream. For any drug, a route of administration, a dose of the drug, and a dosage form (liquid, tablet, capsule, injection, patch, spray, or gum) must be selected that will both place the drug at its site of action in a pharmacologically effective

---

[1]Most drugs used in medicine are known by two or even three names. The most complicated name for a drug is its *structural name*, which accurately describes its chemical structure in words. In this book, the chemical names for drugs are not used. The second name for a drug is its *generic name*, a somewhat easier-to-remember name given to the drug by its discoverer or manufacturer. After a drug's patent protection runs out (usually 17 years after the date of its patent registration by the manufacturer), any other generic drug manufacturer may legitimately sell the drug under this name. The third name is the drug's *trade name*, a unique name placed on the drug by its original patent holder. Only that manufacturer can ever sell the drug under that name, even after the patent runs out and others sell the drug under its generic name. For example, many companies sell aspirin, a generic name for acetylsalicylic acid, the structural name. However, only Bayer Pharmaceuticals (the original company that patented acetylsalicylic acid) can call it Bayer Aspirin. In this book, when a drug is introduced, the generic name is given first, and the generic name is not capitalized. The trade name follows in parentheses, is capitalized, and usually is not given again.

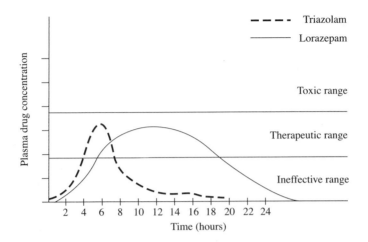

FIGURE 1.2 Theoretical blood levels of triazolam (a short-acting benzodiazepine) and lorazepam (a longer-acting benzodiazepine) over time following oral administration. Approximations for ineffective, therapeutic, and toxic blood levels are shown.

concentration and maintain the concentration for an adequate period of time. Drugs are most commonly administered in one of six ways:

- Orally (swallowed when taken by mouth)
- Rectally (drug embedded in a suppository, which is placed in the rectum)
- Parenterally (given in liquid form by injection with a needle and syringe)
- Inhaled through the lungs as gases, as vapors, or as particles carried in smoke or in an aerosol
- Absorbed through the skin (usually as a drug-containing skin patch)
- Absorbed through mucous membranes (from "snorting" or sniffing the drug, with the drug depositing on the oral or nasal mucosa)

Oral Administration

To be effective when administered orally, a drug must be soluble and stable in stomach fluid (not destroyed by gastric acids), enter the intestine, penetrate the lining of the stomach or intestine, and pass into the bloodstream. Because they are already in solution, drugs that are administered in liquid form tend to be absorbed more rapidly than those given in tablet or capsule form. When a drug is taken in solid form, both the rate at which it dissolves and its chemistry limit the rate of absorption.

After a tablet dissolves, the drug molecules contained within it are carried into the upper intestine, where they are absorbed across the intestinal mucosa by a process of *passive diffusion,* passing from an area of high concentration into an area of lower concentration. This process necessitates that the drug molecules, at least to some degree, be soluble in fat (be *lipid soluble*). In reality, even a small amount of lipid solubility allows for absorption after oral administration; the most lipid-soluble drugs are merely absorbed faster than less lipid-soluble drugs. In general, most psychoactive drugs have good solubility in the lipid linings of the stomach and intestine; therefore about 75 percent (or more) of the amount of an orally administered psychoactive drug is absorbed into the bloodstream within about 1 to 3 hours after its administration.

There are only rare exceptions to this general rule. One involves the antidepressant drug buspirone (BuSpar; Chapter 7). This drug has limited clinical efficacy, primarily because most of it is rapidly broken down (metabolized) by a drug-metabolizing enzyme located in the walls of the stomach lining. This enzyme (called CYP-3A4, discussed later) reduces the oral absorption of buspirone by over 90 percent. However, should buspirone be taken with grapefruit juice, a component in the juice (called "furanocoumarin") inhibits the buspirone-metabolizing enzyme, allowing the drug to be more completely absorbed (Figure 1.3), increasing its therapeutic utility (Lilja et al.,

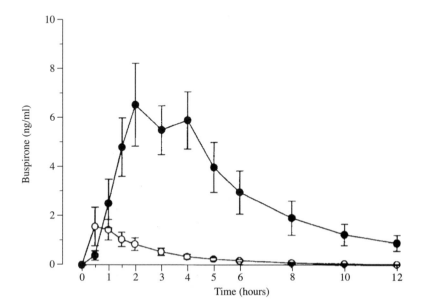

FIGURE 1.3 Plasma concentrations (mean and SEM) of buspirone (in nanograms per milliliter of plasma) in ten healthy volunteers after a single oral dose of 10 mg buspirone, after ingestion of 200 ml (about 7 oz) grapefruit juice (*solid circles*) or water (*open circles*) three times a day for 2 days, and on day 3 with buspirone administration 30 and 90 minutes later. [Data from Lilja et al. (1998).]

1998; Rheeders et al., 2006; Paine et al., 2006). Greenblatt and coworkers (2003) demonstrated increases in the absorption of the anti-anxiety drug diazepam (Valium) when taken with grapefruit juice, although the increase in diazepam absorption is not as great when it is taken with grapefruit juice as is the increase of absorption when buspirone is taken with grapefruit juice.

Although oral administration of drugs is common, it does have disadvantages. First, it may occasionally lead to vomiting and stomach distress. Second, although the amount of a drug that is put into a tablet or capsule can be calculated, how much of it will be absorbed into the bloodstream cannot always be accurately predicted because of genetic differences between individual people and because of differences in the manufacture of the drugs. Finally, the acid in the stomach destroys some orally administered drugs, such as the local anesthetics and insulin, before they can be absorbed. To be effective, those drugs must be administered by injection.

Rectal Administration

Although the primary route of drug administration is oral, some drugs are administered rectally (usually in suppository form) if the patient is vomiting, unconscious, or unable to swallow. However, absorption is often irregular, unpredictable, and incomplete, and many drugs irritate the membranes that line the rectum.

Administration by Inhalation

In recreational drug misuse and abuse, inhalation of drugs is a popular method of administration. Examples of drugs taken by this route include nicotine in tobacco cigarettes and tetrahydrocannabinol in marijuana, as well as smoked heroin, crack cocaine, crank methamphetamine, and the various inhalants of abuse, all of which are discussed at length later in the book. The popularity of inhalation as a route of administration follows from two observations:

1. Lung tissues have a large surface area through which large amounts of blood flow, allowing for rapid absorption of drugs from lung into the blood (often within seconds).
2. Drugs absorbed into pulmonary (lung) capillaries are carried in the pulmonary veins directly to the left side (arterial side) of the heart (Figure 1.4) and from there directly into the aorta and the arteries carrying blood to the brain.

As a result, drugs administered by inhalation may have an even faster onset of effect than drugs administered intravenously. If drugs

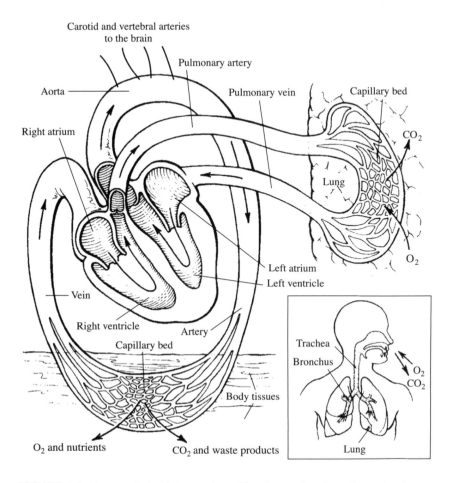

Carotid and vertebral arteries to the brain

Pulmonary artery

Aorta

Pulmonary vein

Capillary bed

Right atrium

CO_2

Lung

O_2

Left atrium

Left ventricle

Vein

Right ventricle

Artery

Capillary bed

Trachea

Bronchus

O_2

CO_2

Body tissues

O_2 and nutrients

CO_2 and waste products

Lung

FIGURE 1.4 Heart and circulatory system. Blood returning from the systemic venous circulation to the heart enters the right atrium and flows into the right ventricle. With contraction of the heart, this blood is pumped into the pulmonary arteries leading to the lungs. Once in the pulmonary capillaries, carbon dioxide (CO_2) is lost and replaced by oxygen. The oxygenated blood returns to the heart in the pulmonary veins, which empty into the left atrium. With heart contraction, the oxygenated blood is pumped from the left ventricle into the aorta and is carried to the body tissues and brain, where oxygen and nutrients are exchanged in the systemic capillary beds. Oxygen and nutrients are supplied to the body tissues through the walls of the capillaries; CO_2 and other waste products are returned to the blood. The CO_2 is eliminated through the lungs, and the other waste products are metabolized in the liver and excreted in the urine.

administered in this fashion are behaviorally reinforcing, intoxicating, and subject to compulsive abuse, the rapid onset of effect can be intense, to say the least.

Administration Through Mucous Membranes

Occasionally, drugs are administered through the mucous membranes of the mouth or nose. A few examples:

- A heart patient taking nitroglycerine places the tablet under the tongue, where the drug is absorbed into the bloodstream rapidly and directly.
- Cocaine powder, when sniffed, adheres to the membranes on the inside of the nose and is absorbed directly into the bloodstream. (Cocaine is discussed in Chapter 7.)
- Nasal decongestants are sprayed directly onto mucous membranes from which they are both absorbed and act locally to constrict the mucous membranes, relieving nasal congestion.
- Nicotine (Chapter 8) in snuff, nasal spray, or chewing-gum formulations (Chapter 6) is absorbed through the mucosal membranes directly into the bloodstream.
- Caffeine (Chapter 8) became available in 1999 in chewing-gum form; the caffeine is rapidly absorbed as the gum is chewed.
- For use before and after surgery on children, the opioid narcotic fentanyl (Sublimase; Chapter 15) became available in 1998 in lollipop form, so this pain-relieving drug can be provided without subjecting a child to a painful injection. As the lollipop is sucked, the drug is released and absorbed through the mucous membranes of the mouth. This form of administering fentanyl has also become popular for patients with disabling pain conditions when orally administered pain relievers are insufficient and injection of opioid narcotics is too painful.
- Recently introduced is a sublingual (placed under the tongue) combination of buprenorphine (an opioid narcotic) and naloxone (an opioid antagonist) for the office-based treatment of opioid dependency. The combination product is called Suboxone, and it is discussed in Chapter 15. The buprenorphine is absorbed through the mucous membranes, but the antagonist, naloxone, is not. Used in this fashion, the desired narcotic effect is achieved. However, should the pill be crushed, dissolved, and injected, the antagonist, naloxone, precipitates drug withdrawal. This effect tends to discourage abuse of the buprenorphine and reduce illicit use. It is yet another example of how knowledge of pharmacokinetics can be used to therapeutic benefit in special circumstances.

Administration Through the Skin

Over the past several years, several prescribed medications have been incorporated into *transdermal patches* that adhere to the skin. This is a unique bandage-like therapeutic system that provides continuous, controlled release of a drug from a reservoir through a semipermeable membrane (Figure 1.5). The drug is slowly absorbed into the bloodstream at the area of contact. Some examples of drug-containing patches:

- Nicotine (used to deter smoking behaviors)
- Fentanyl (used to treat chronic pain)
- Nitroglycerine (used to prevent the symptoms of angina pectoris in patients with coronary artery disease)
- Clonidine (used to treat hypertension)
- Estrogen (used to replace reduced hormones in postmenopausal women)
- Scopolamine (used to prevent motion sickness)
- Selegiline (Eldapryl; used to treat depression; Chapter 9)
- Methylphenidate (Daytrana, a 9-hour patch used to treat attention deficit/hyperactivity disorder in children)

All these transdermal skin patches allow for slow, continuous absorption of drug over hours or even days, potentially minimizing side effects associated with rapid rises and falls in plasma concentrations of the drug contained in the patch. In all cases, the drug is slowly, predictably,

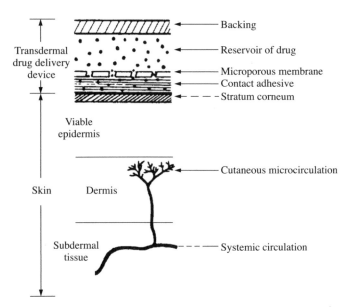

FIGURE 1.5 Diagrammatic representation of a transdermal "patch" delivery system placed on the skin.

and continuously released from the liquid in the patch and absorbed into the systemic circulation, allowing the levels of drug in the plasma to remain relatively constant over the time of absorption.

Administration by Injection

Administration of drugs by injection can be *intravenous* (directly into a vein), *intramuscular* (directly into a muscle), or *subcutaneous* (just under the skin). Each of these routes of administration has its advantages and disadvantages (Table 1.1), but all share some features. In general, administration by injection produces a more prompt response than does oral administration because absorption is faster. Also, injection permits a more accurate dose because the unpredictable processes of absorption through the stomach and intestine are bypassed.

Administration of drugs by injection, however, has several drawbacks. First, the rapid rate of absorption leaves little time to respond to an unexpected drug reaction or accidental overdose. Second, administration by injection requires the use of sterile techniques. Hepatitis and AIDS are examples of diseases that can be transmitted as a drastic consequence of unsterile injection techniques. Third, once a drug is administered by injection, it cannot be recalled.

Intravenous Administration.   In an intravenous injection, a drug is introduced directly into the bloodstream. This technique avoids all the variables related to oral absorption. The injection can be made slowly, and it can be stopped instantaneously if untoward effects develop. In addition, the dosage can be extremely precise, and the practitioner can dilute and administer in large volumes drugs that at higher concentrations would be irritants to the muscles or blood vessels.

The intravenous route is the most dangerous of all routes of administration because it has the fastest speed of onset of pharmacological action. Too-rapid injection can be catastrophic, producing life-threatening reactions (such as collapse of respiration or of heart function). Also, allergic reactions, should they occur, may be extremely severe. Finally, drugs that are not completely solubilized before injection cannot usually be given intravenously because of the danger of blood clots or emboli forming. Infection and transmission of infectious diseases are an ever-present danger when sterile techniques are not employed.

Intramuscular Administration.   Drugs that are injected into skeletal muscle (usually in the arm, thigh, or buttock) are generally absorbed fairly rapidly. Absorption of a drug from muscle is more rapid than absorption of the same drug from the stomach but slower than absorption of the drug administered intravenously. The absolute rate of absorption of a drug from muscle varies, depending on the rate of

TABLE 1.1 Some characteristics of drug administration by injection

Route	Absorption pattern	Special utility	Limitations and precautions
Intravenous	Absorption circumvented Potentially immediate effects	Valuable for emergency use Permits titration of dosage Can administer large volumes and irritating substances when diluted	Increased risk of adverse effects Must inject solutions slowly as a rule Not suitable for oily solutions or insoluble substances
Intramuscular	Prompt action from aqueous solution Slow and sustained action from repository preparations	Suitable for moderate volumes, oily vehicles, and some irritating substances	Precluded during anticoagulant medication May interfere with interpretation of certain diagnostic tests (e.g., creatine phosphokinase)
Subcutaneous	Prompt action from aqueous solution Slow and sustained action from repository preparations	Suitable for some insoluble suspensions and for implantation of solid pellets	Not suitable for large volumes Possible pain or necrosis from irritating substance

blood flow to the muscle, the solubility of the drug, the volume of the injection, and the solution in which the drug is dissolved and injected.

Intramuscular injections are of two types: (1) fairly rapid onset and short duration of action and (2) slow onset and prolonged action. In the former situation, the drug is dissolved in an aqueous (water) solution. Following injection, the water and dissolved drug are quite rapidly absorbed, with complete absorption occurring over a very few hours. In the latter situation, classically the drug is suspended in an oily solution. The oil and dissolved drug solution is only slowly absorbed and complete absorption can take days or weeks. More recently, space-age manufacture has placed the drug in bioabsorbable polymer microspheres, and a constant amount of drug is released each day for a period of a week or more (Risperdol Consta; Chapter 9). Similarly, the opioid narcotic antagonist naltrexone suspended in injected microcapsules releases a constant amount of drug into blood over a period of several weeks. This new product is marketed under the trade name Vivitrol and is indicated in the treatment of opioid-dependent patients.

Subcutaneous Administration. Absorption of drugs that have been injected under the skin (subcutaneously) is rapid. The exact rate depends mainly on the ease of blood vessel penetration and the rate of blood flow through the skin. Irritating drugs should not be injected subcutaneously because they may cause severe pain and damage to local tissue. The usual precautions to maintain sterility should be applied.

Drug Distribution

Once absorbed into the bloodstream, a drug is distributed throughout the body by the circulating blood, passing across various barriers to reach its site of action (its receptors). At any given time, only a very small portion of the total amount of a drug that is in the body is actually in contact with its receptors (see Figure 1.1). Most of the administered drug is found in areas of the body that are remote from the drug's site of action. For example, in the case of a psychoactive drug, most of the drug circulates outside the brain and therefore does not contribute directly to its pharmacological effect. This wide distribution often accounts for many of the side effects of a drug. *Side effects* are results that are different from the primary, or therapeutic, effect for which a drug is taken.

Action of the Bloodstream

Every minute in the average-size adult, the heart pumps a volume of blood that is roughly equal to the total amount of blood in the circulatory system. Thus, the entire blood volume circulates in the body about once every minute. Once absorbed into the bloodstream, a drug is rapidly (usually within the 1-minute circulation time) distributed throughout the circulatory system.

A schematic diagram of the circulatory system is presented in Figure 1.4. Blood returning to the heart through the veins is first pumped into the pulmonary (lung) circulation system, where carbon dioxide is removed and replaced by oxygen. The oxygenated blood then returns to the heart and is pumped into the great artery (the aorta). From there blood flows into the smaller arteries and finally into the capillaries, where nutrients (and drugs) are exchanged between the blood and the cells of the body. After blood passes through the capillaries, it is collected by the veins and returned to the heart to circulate again. Psychoactive drugs quite quickly become evenly distributed throughout the bloodstream, diluted not only by blood but also by the total amount of water in the body.

If a drug is taken orally, it passes through the cells lining the gastrointestinal (GI) tract and then through the liver; from there the drug enters the central circulation and is carried to the heart to be distributed throughout the body. Occasionally, drug-metabolizing enzymes in either the cells of the GI tract or the liver can markedly reduce the amount of drug that reaches the bloodstream. This process is called *first-pass metabolism.* Examples of first-pass metabolism of the drugs buspirone and diazepam were presented earlier in this chapter. Another example involves ethyl alcohol and the enzyme that metabolizes the alcohol. This enzyme is called *alcohol dehydrogenase.* It is found in the cells lining the GI tract and in cells of the liver. As we will see in Chapter 4, women have less of this enzyme in the GI tract cells and therefore exhibit higher blood alcohol levels for a given amount of alcohol ingested (corrected for body weight) than do men.

Injected (by whatever route), absorbed transdermally, or absorbed from mucous membranes, a drug bypasses intestinal absorption, rapidly enters veins, and is carried in blood to the right side of the heart (with minimal amounts passing initially through the liver). The drug is then circulated through the pulmonary vessels, returns to the left side of the heart, and finally travels through the aorta to the brain and the body. Sodium pentothal is an example of an injected general anesthetic. Injected intravenously, it circulates to the heart, then the lungs, and then the brain (see Figure 1.4). After injection, consciousness is lost within about 30 seconds.

Inhaled drugs are absorbed from the lungs and carried in pulmonary veins directly to the left side of the heart and from there, rapidly to the brain. The effects of smoked tobacco or smoked marijuana are felt within a breath or two.

Body Membranes That Affect Drug Distribution

Four types of membranes in the body affect drug distribution: (1) cell membranes, (2) walls of the capillary vessels in the circulatory system, (3) blood-brain barrier, and (4) placental barrier.

Cell Membranes. To be absorbed from the intestine or to gain access to the interior of a cell, a drug must penetrate the cell membranes. The structure and properties of cell membranes determine their permeability to drugs. In Figure 1.6, the two layers of circles represent the water-soluble head groups of complex lipid molecules called *phospholipids.* The phospholipid heads form a rather continuous layer on both the inside and the outside of the cell membrane. The wavy lines that extend

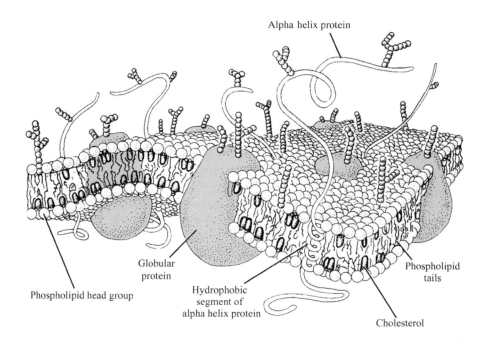

Alpha helix protein

Globular protein

Phospholipid head group

Hydrophobic segment of alpha helix protein

Phospholipid tails

Cholesterol

FIGURE 1.6 Diagrammatic representation of a cell membrane, a phospholipid bilayer in which cholesterol and protein molecules are embedded. Both globular and helical kinds of protein traverse the bilayer. Cholesterol molecules tend to keep the tails of the phospholipids relatively fixed and orderly in the regions closest to the hydrophilic phospholipid heads; the parts of the tails closer to the core of the membrane move about freely. [From M. S. Bretscher, "The Molecules of the Cell Membrane," *Scientific American* 253 (1985): 104.]

from the heads into the membrane are the lipid chains of the phospholipid molecules. Therefore, for our present purposes, the interior of the cell membrane can be considered to consist of a sea of lipid in which large proteins are suspended.

Cell membranes, consisting of protein and fat, provide a physical barrier that is permeable to small, lipid-soluble drug molecules but is impermeable to large, lipid-insoluble drug molecules. Cell membranes (as barriers to the absorption and distribution of drugs) are important for the passage of drugs (1) from the stomach and intestine into the bloodstream, (2) from the fluid that closely surrounds tissue cells into the interior of cells, (3) from the interior of cells back into the body water, and (4) from the kidneys back into the bloodstream.

Capillaries. Within a minute or so of entering the bloodstream, a drug is distributed fairly evenly throughout the entire blood volume. From there, drugs leave the bloodstream and are exchanged (in equilibrium)

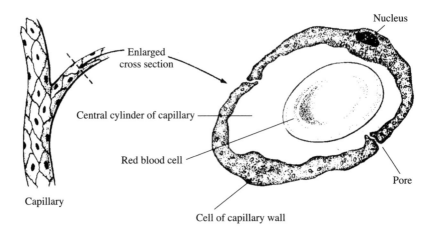

FIGURE 1.7 Cross section of a blood capillary. Within the capillary are the fluids, proteins, and cells of the blood, including the red blood cells. The capillary itself is made up of cells that completely surround and define the central cylinder (or lumen) of the capillary. Water-filled pores form channels, allowing free flow of blood plasma and extracellular fluid.

between blood capillaries and body tissues. Figure 1.7 is a cross-sectional diagram of a capillary. Capillaries are tiny, cylindrical blood vessels with walls that are formed by a thin, single layer of cells packed tightly together. Between the cells are small pores that allow passage of small molecules between blood and the body tissues. The diameter of these pores is between 90 and 150 angstroms (Å), which is larger than most drug molecules. Thus, most drugs freely leave the blood through these pores in the capillary membranes, passing along their concentration gradient until equilibrium is established between the concentrations of drug in the blood and in body tissues and water.

The transport of drug molecules between plasma and body tissues is independent of lipid solubility because the membrane pores are large enough for even fat-insoluble drug molecules to penetrate. However, the pores in the capillary membrane are not large enough to permit the red blood cells and the plasma proteins to leave the bloodstream. Thus, the only drugs that do not readily penetrate capillary pores are drugs that bind to plasma proteins. The rate at which drug molecules enter specific body tissues depends on two factors: the rate of blood flow through the tissue and the ease with which drug molecules pass through the capillary membranes.

Because blood flow is greatest to the brain and much less to the bones, joints, and fat deposits, drug distribution generally follows a similar pattern (Figure 1.8). An example might be appropriate. When marijuana is smoked, the active drug, tetrahydrocannabinol

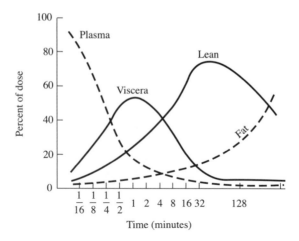

FIGURE 1.8 Diagrammatic representation of the distribution of a lipid-soluble drug (thiopental, a barbiturate discussed in Chapter 5) in blood plasma, body fat, lean body mass (muscle), and visceral tissues at various times after intravenous injection of the drug. Time scales (in minutes) progress geometrically.

(THC; Chapter 18) achieves plasma concentrations of about 10 to 20 nanograms of drug per milliliter of plasma (ng/ml) soon after initiation of smoking. Within about 30 minutes, it achieves levels of about 50 to 100 ng/ml, which falls off within 1 hour to less than 5 to 10 ng/ml because the drug is rapidly taken up into body fat. From there, it slowly returns to plasma and is metabolized to an inactive metabolite (carboxy-THC) that is excreted in the urine.

Blood-Brain Barrier. The brain requires a protected environment in which to function normally, and a specialized structural barrier, called the *blood-brain barrier* (BBB), plays a key role in maintaining this environment. The BBB involves specialized cells in the brain that affect nearly all its blood capillaries (Figure 1.9). In most of the rest of the body, the capillary membranes have pores; in the brain, however, the capillaries are tightly joined together and covered on the outside by a fatty barrier called the *glial sheath,* which arises from nearby astrocyte cells.

Thus, to reach the cells in the brain, a drug leaving the capillaries in the brain has to traverse both the wall of the capillary itself (because there are no pores to pass through) and the membranes of the astrocyte cells. Therefore, as a general rule, the rate of passage of a drug into the brain is determined by two factors: (1) the size of the drug molecule and (2) its lipid (fat) solubility. Large, highly ionized drugs penetrate poorly, while small, fat-soluble drugs penetrate rapidly. The molecules of almost all psychoactive drugs are small enough and sufficiently lipid

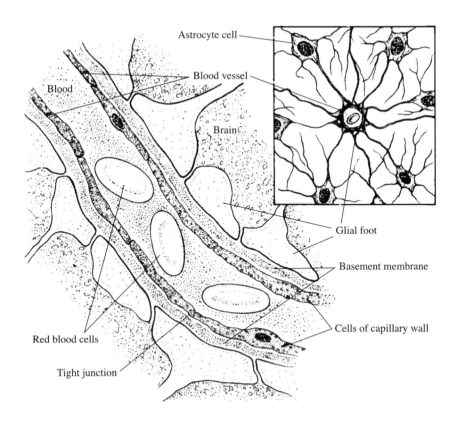

Astrocyte cell

Blood vessel

Blood

Brain

Glial foot

Basement membrane

Cells of capillary wall

Red blood cells

Tight junction

FIGURE 1.9 Blood-brain barrier. Blood and brain are separated by capillary cells packed tightly together and by a fatty barrier called the glial sheath, which is made up of extensions (glial feet) from nearby astrocyte cells (*inset*). A drug diffusing from blood to brain must move through the cells of the capillary wall because there are tight junctions rather than pores between the cells; the drug must then move through the fatty glial sheath.

soluble to cross the blood-brain barrier, exerting their actions on neurons in the brain. Drugs that cannot cross the BBB are restricted in action to structures located outside the central nervous system (CNS). These drugs do not act on the brain. Penicillin is an example of such a drug. It does not cross the BBB and is not of use in treating infections located in the CNS: its effectiveness as an antibiotic is restricted to infections located outside the brain. Pardridge (2003) discusses the difficulties that the blood-brain barrier presents in attempts to develop new drugs for CNS diseases:

> Only a small class of drugs—small molecules with high lipid solubility and a low molecular mass—actually cross the BBB. There are only a few diseases that consistently respond to this category of

small molecules and these include depression, affective disorders, schizophrenia, chronic pain, and epilepsy. In contrast, many serious disorders of the brain do not respond to the conventional lipid-soluble small-molecule model and these include Alzheimer disease, stroke/neuroprotection, brain and spinal cord injury, brain cancer, HIV infections of the brain, various ataxia-producing disorders, amyotropic lateral sclerosis, multiple sclerosis, Huntington disease, and childhood inborn genetic errors of the brain. (p. 91)

Pardridge concluded that the development of new therapeutic modalities for brain diseases is hampered by our inability to solve the problems of drug transport across the BBB and that the absence of an academic research infrastructure is the single most important limiting factor on the future of brain drug development.

Placental Barrier.   Among all the membrane systems of the body, the placental membranes are unique, separating two distinct human beings with differing genetic compositions and differing sensitivities to drugs. The fetus obtains essential nutrients and eliminates metabolic waste products through the placenta without depending on its own organs, many of which are not yet functioning. The dependence of the fetus on the mother places the fetus at the mercy of the placenta when foreign substances (such as drugs or toxins) appear in the mother's blood (Gilstrap and Little, 1998). The placental barrier is discussed further in the discussions of individual drugs.

A schematic representation of the placental network, which transfers substances between the mother and the fetus, is shown in Figure 1.10. In general, the mature placenta consists of a network of vessels and pools of maternal blood into which protrude treelike or fingerlike villi (projections) that contain the blood capillaries of the fetus. Oxygen and nutrients travel from the mother's blood to that of the fetus, while carbon dioxide and other waste products travel from the blood of the fetus to the mother's blood.

The membranes that separate fetal blood from maternal blood in the intervillous space resemble, in their general permeability, the cell membranes that are found elsewhere in the body. In other words, drugs cross the placenta primarily by passive diffusion. Fat-soluble substances (including all psychoactive drugs) diffuse readily, rapidly, and without limitation. The view that the placenta is a barrier to drugs is inaccurate. A more appropriate approximation is that the fetus is to at least some extent exposed to essentially all drugs taken by the mother.

As a general rule, all psychoactive drugs (all those discussed in this book) will be present in the fetus at a concentration quite similar to that in the mother's bloodstream. However, the presence of the drug in

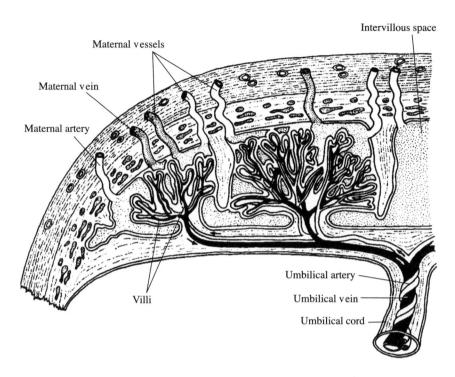

Intervillous space

Maternal vessels

Maternal vein

Maternal artery

Umbilical artery

Villi

Umbilical vein

Umbilical cord

FIGURE 1.10 Placental network separating the blood of mother and fetus. Note the close relationship between fetal and maternal blood in the villus.

the fetus is not necessarily detrimental to the fetus. Some drugs certainly are detrimental and their use should be avoided in women who are or who might become pregnant. Ethyl alcohol is an obvious example. Many psychoactive medicines have been shown to be relatively safe to fetal growth and development when taken by a pregnant female. The effects of specific drugs on the fetus will be presented as each drug is discussed in this book.

Termination of Drug Action

Routes through which drugs can leave the body include (1) the kidneys, (2) the lungs, (3) the bile, and (4) the skin. Excretion through the lungs occurs only with highly volatile or gaseous agents, such as the general anesthetics and, in small amounts, alcohol ("alcohol breath"). Drugs that are passed through the bile and into the intestine are usually reabsorbed into the bloodstream from the intestine. Also, small amounts of a few drugs can pass through the skin and be excreted in sweat (perhaps 10 to 15 percent of the total amount of the drugs).

However, most drugs leave the body in urine, either as the unchanged molecule or as a broken-down *metabolite* of the original drug. More correctly, *the major route of drug elimination from the body is renal (urinary) excretion of drug metabolites produced by the hepatic (liver) biodegradation of the drug.*[2]

Psychoactive drugs are usually too lipid soluble to be excreted passively with the excretion of urine. They have to be transformed into metabolites that are more water soluble, bulkier, less lipid soluble, and (usually) less biologically active (even inactive) when compared with the parent molecule (the molecule that was originally ingested and absorbed).[3] Thus, for a lipid-soluble drug to be eliminated, it must be metabolically transformed (by enzymes located in the liver) into a form that can be excreted rapidly and reliably. This biotransformation relieves the body of the burden of foreign chemicals and is essential to our survival. Such mechanisms are not new. Biotransformation of foreign substances probably originated millions of years ago when humans invented fire and began to eat the char of barbecued meat, ingesting and absorbing substances that were foreign and potentially toxic to the body.

Role of the Kidneys in Drug Elimination

Physiologically, our kidneys perform two major functions. First, they excrete most of the products of body metabolism; second, they closely regulate the levels of most of the substances found in body fluids. The kidneys are a pair of bean-shaped organs that lie at the rear of the abdominal cavity at the level of the lower ribs. The outer portion of the kidney is made up of more than a million functional units, called *nephrons* (Figure 1.11). Each nephron consists of a knot of capillaries (the *glomerulus*) through which blood flows from the renal artery to the renal vein. The glomerulus is surrounded by the opening of the nephron (*Bowman's capsule*), into which fluid flows as it filters out of the capillaries. Pressure of the blood in the glomerulus causes fluid to leave the capillaries and flow into the Bowman's capsule, from which it

---

[2]When evaluating urine for the presence of drugs of abuse, inactive drug metabolites rather than active drug are found in the urine. It is often unclear whether there is correlation between the presence of the metabolite in urine and active drug in plasma *at the time the urine sample was taken.*

[3]Some drugs are exceptions: an administered drug may be metabolized into an "active" metabolite, which is at least as active and possibly more active and may have a longer duration of action than the parent drug. Examples in psychopharmacology include diazepam (Valium; Chapter 6), which is metabolized to nordiazepam, and fluoxetine (Prozac; Chapter 7), which is metabolized to norfluoxetine. In both cases, the parent drug has an effect that lasts for two or three days, while the metabolite is active for over a week, until it is eventually biotransformed to an inactive compound that can be excreted.

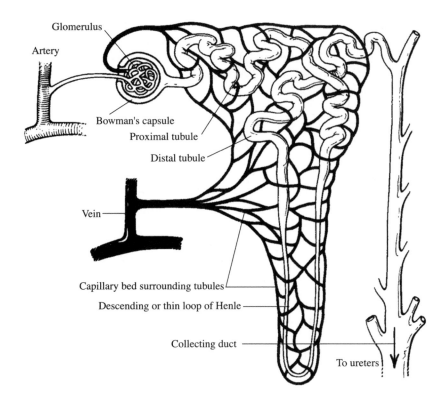

Glomerulus

Artery

Bowman's capsule
Proximal tubule
Distal tubule

Vein

Capillary bed surrounding tubules
Descending or thin loop of Henle

Collecting duct

To ureters

FIGURE 1.11 Nephron within a kidney. Note the complexity of the structure and the intimate relation between the blood supply and the nephron. Each kidney is composed of more than a million nephrons.

flows through the tubules of the nephrons into a duct that collects fluid from several nephrons. The fluid from the collecting ducts is eventually passed through the ureters and into the urinary bladder, which is emptied periodically.

In an adult, about 1 liter (1000 cubic centimeters) of plasma is filtered into the nephrons of the kidneys each minute. Left behind in the bloodstream are blood cells, plasma proteins, and the remaining plasma. As the filtered fluid (water) flows through the nephrons, most of it is reabsorbed into the plasma. By the time fluid reaches the collecting ducts and bladder, only 0.1 percent remains to be excreted. Because about 1 cubic centimeter per minute of urine is formed, 99.9 percent of filtered fluid is therefore reabsorbed.

Lipid-soluble drugs can easily cross the membranes of renal tubular cells, and they are reabsorbed along with the 99.9 percent of reabsorbed water. Drug reabsorption occurs passively, along a developing concentration gradient—the drug becomes concentrated inside the

nephrons (as a result of water reabsorption), and the drugs are themselves reabsorbed with water back into plasma. Thus, the kidneys
alone are not capable of eliminating psychoactive drugs from the body;
some other mechanism must overcome this process of passive renal reabsorption of the drug.

Role of the Liver in Drug Metabolism

Since the kidneys are not capable of ridding the body of drugs, the reabsorbed drug is eventually picked up by liver cells (*hepatocytes*) and
enzymatically biotransformed (by enzymes located in these hepatocytes) into metabolites that are usually less fat soluble, less capable of
being reabsorbed, and therefore capable of being excreted in urine. As
the drug is carried to the liver (by blood flowing in the hepatic artery
and portal vein), a portion is cleared from blood by the hepatocytes
and metabolized to by-products that are then returned to the bloodstream (Figure 1.12). The metabolites are then carried in the bloodstream to the kidneys, filtered into the renal tubules, and are poorly
reabsorbed, remaining in the urine for excretion. Mechanisms involved in drug metabolism by hepatocytes are complex, but they have
gained increased importance in psychopharmacology because of recently described drug interactions involving certain antidepressant
drugs (Chapter 7) (Greenblatt et al., 1999).

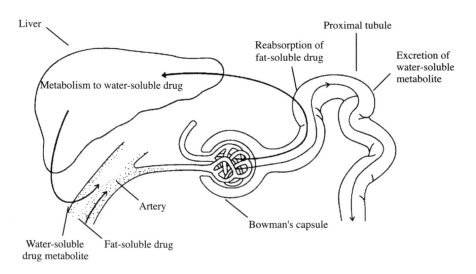

FIGURE 1.12 How the liver and kidneys interact to eliminate drugs from the body.
Drugs may be filtered into the kidney, reabsorbed into the bloodstream, and carried
to the liver for metabolic transformation to a more water-soluble compound that,
having been filtered into the kidney, cannot be reabsorbed and is therefore excreted
in urine.

The *cytochrome P450 enzyme family,* physically located in hepatocytes (with a few located in the cells lining the GI tract), is the major system involved in drug metabolism. This gene family originated more than 3.5 billion years ago and has diversified to accomplish the metabolism (detoxification) of environmental chemicals, food toxins, and drugs—all foreign to our needs. Thus, the cytochrome P450 enzyme system (of which hundreds exist and about 50 of which are functionally active in humans) can detoxify a chemically diverse group of foreign substances. Several P450 enzyme families can be found within any given hepatocyte.

A few of these enzyme families, particularly cytochrome families 1, 2, and 3 (designated *CYP-1, CYP-2,* and *CYP-3*), encode enzymes involved in most drug biotransformations. By definition, since these three families promote the breakdown of numerous drugs and toxins, enzyme specificity is low (the enzymes are nonspecific in action). Thus, the body is enzymatically capable of metabolizing multiple different drugs.

CYP-3A4 (a subfamily of CYP-3) catalyzes about 50 percent of drug biotransformations (Figure 1.13); this variant is found not only in liver but also in the GI tract, as we saw with the metabolism of buspirone. CYP-2D6 catalyzes about 20 percent of drugs, and CYP-2C variants catalyze an additional 20 percent. Other CYP enzyme variants are responsible for metabolizing the remaining 10 percent of drugs.

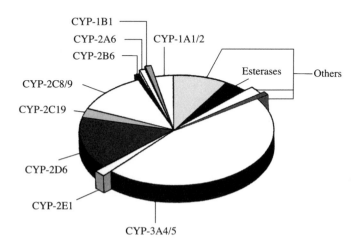

FIGURE 1.13 The approximate proportion of drugs metabolized by the major hepatic CYP enzymes. The relative size of each pie section indicates the estimated percentage of metabolism that each enzyme contributes to the metabolism of drugs.

Factors Affecting Drug Biotransformation

Several different factors can alter the rate at which drugs are metabolized, either increasing or decreasing the rate of drug elimination from the body. In general, *genetic, environmental, cultural,* and *physiological factors* can be involved (Lin et al., 2001).

First, it is now becoming apparent that genetic variations may affect how different people respond to medications. Recently, it has been shown that genetic variations are susceptible to clinical testing. Two laboratories now offer testing kits that other laboratories can purchase to process pharmacogenetic tests. Other laboratories can process DNA samples and interpret the results for the clinician. Psychogenetic testing allows prescribers to consider genetic information from patients in selecting medications and doses for certain psychiatric disorders.[4] As one example, the AmpliChip CYP-450 test screens for variations of two genes, CYP-2D6 and CYP-2C19 (deLeon et al, 2006; deLeon, 2006). Several drugs discussed in this text are affected by the enzymes on the AmpliChip CYP-450 (Table 1.2). Other DNA test kits will follow, the next probably being one for the serotonin transporter, variations of which influence the efficacy, tolerability, and adverse reactions to antidepressants (Murphy et al., 2004; Kim et al., 2006).

A simple example may be in order. Genetic DNA testing can now identify how a person may metabolize several drugs of different therapeutic classes, including antidepressants, analgesics, and antipsychotic

---

[4]For an introductory Web-based video presentation on this topic prepared by Genelex Corporation, see www.healthanddna.com

---

TABLE 1.2 Some drugs that inhibit, induce, or are metabolized by enzymes on the AmpliChip.

CYP-2D6	CYP-2C19
Bupropion	Barbiturates
Amitriptyline	Carbamazepine
Desipramine	Fluoxetine
Fluoxetine	Fluvoxamine
Fluvoxamine	Paroxetine
Fluphenazine	Sertraline
Halperidol	Topiramate
Paroxetine	Thioridazine
Perphenazine	

From *Brown University Psychopharmacology Update,* Vol. 16 (February 2005), p. 5.

TABLE 1.3 Significance of genetic testing in the determination of drug dosage

	Normal metabolizer	Slow metabolizer	Fast metabolizer
Genetic variation	Your genes produce a typical amount of enzyme.	Your genes produce too little enzyme.	Your genes produce too much enzyme.
Effects on you	The antidepressant helps your depression and causes few side effects.	The antidepressant builds up in your body, causing intolerable side effects.	The antidepressant is eliminated too quickly, providing little or no improvement in depression.
Treatment options	Follow the recommended dosage.	Switch antidepressants or reduce your dosage.	Switch antidepressants or increase your dosage.

drugs. In general, DNA testing using a simple mouth swab can identify whether a person is a normal metabolizer of a specific drug, a slow metabolizer, or a fast metabolizer. Results provide a scientific basis for understanding why a person might become unexpectedly toxic after therapeutic doses of a drug or, on the other hand, might fail to respond to what was thought to be a therapeutic dose (Table 1.3).[5]

Second, if more than one drug is present in the body, the drugs may interact with one another either in a therapeutically beneficial way or in a way that can adversely affect the patient. Beneficially, two drugs can have additive therapeutic effects; for example, improving antidepressant or antianxiety treatment. In the liver, however, one drug can either increase or reduce the rate of metabolism of a second drug, reducing or increasing the blood level of the second drug. For example, *carbamazepine* (Tegretol; Chapter 8) is particularly effective in stimulating the production of the drug-metabolizing enzyme CYP-3A3/4 in the liver (a process called *enzyme induction*), inducing an apparent *metabolic tolerance* to other drugs metabolized by CYP-3A3/4. In essence, in the presence of carbamazepine, the rate at which all drugs metabolized by the CYP-3A3/4 enzymes increases. Therefore, drug *tolerance* develops as the blood level of drug for a given amount taken falls more rapidly than would be expected if tolerance had not developed. Thus, increasing doses of a drug

[5]For a Web-based introduction to genetic DNA testing for drug metabolism, see www.genemedrx.com and click "Clinical Pharmacogenetics in the Practice of Medicine."

must be administered to maintain the same level of drug in the plasma and to produce the same effect produced by previously administered smaller doses. In essence, the second drug becomes less effective because it is metabolized more rapidly. The phenomenon of the association of tolerance to one drug with apparent tolerance to another is termed *cross-tolerance*.

In contrast to carbamazepine (which increases the rate of metabolism of other drugs), some psychoactive drugs *depress* the activity of the CYP enzyme that metabolizes other drugs metabolized by the same enzyme. This process serves to *increase* the blood level of the other drugs and unexpectedly increase their toxicity. For example, SSRI-type antidepressants, such as fluoxetine (Prozac; Chapter 7), inhibit the enzymes CYP-1A2 and CYP-2C, increasing the toxicity of several other types of antidepressants and certain antipsychotic drugs, as well as caffeine (perhaps inducing caffeinism; Chapter 14). Similarly, the antibipolar drug *valproic acid* (Chapter 8) inhibits the metabolism of lamotrigine (Lamictal, another antibipolar drug), increasing the plasma level of lamotrigine and thus potentially increasing its toxicity. Such drug interactions are potentially severe and have been known to produce fatalities. As an interesting aside, the pain-relieving drug codeine (Chapter 16) needs to be metabolized by CYP-2D6 into morphine, which is codeine's active metabolite responsible for its analgesic effect. Some SSRIs (for example, fluoxetine and paroxetine) block this metabolic conversion of codeine to morphine, and for patients taking SSRIs codeine is ineffective as a pain-relieving agent.

Preskorn and Flockhart (2006) present a recent review of psychiatric drug interactions. Spina and Perucca (2002) discuss the pharmacokinetic interactions between widely used psychotropic medications. DeVane (2006) and Preskorn and Werder (2006) debate the significance of drug interactions involving antidepressant drugs.

Other Routes of Drug Elimination

Other routes for excreting drugs include the air we exhale, bile, sweat, saliva, and breast milk. Many drugs and drug metabolites may be found in these secretions, but their concentrations are usually low, and these routes are not usually considered primary paths of drug elimination. Perhaps clinically significant, however, is the transfer of psychoactive drugs (such as nicotine) from mothers to their breast-fed babies.

Time Course of Drug Distribution and Elimination: Concept of Drug Half-Life

Knowledge about the relationship between the time course of drug action in the body is essential for (1) predicting the optimal dosages and dose intervals needed to reach a therapeutic effect, (2) maintaining a therapeutic drug level for the desired period of time, and (3) determining the time needed to eliminate the drug. The relationship between the pharmacological response to a drug and its concentration in blood is fundamental to pharmacology. With psychoactive drugs, the level of drug in the blood closely approximates the level of drug at the drug's site of action in the brain.

Figure 1.14 illustrates the time-concentration relationship for a drug that is injected intravenously and therefore reaches peak plasma concentration immediately. For our purposes here, intravenous injection removes the variability involved with oral absorption and slow attainment of peak blood levels. Note that after the immediate peak in the plasma concentration, the concentration appears to fall very rapidly, followed by a slower decline in concentration. The rapid fall reflects the rapid redistribution of the drug out of the bloodstream into body tissues. This process of *redistribution* takes only minutes to spread a drug nearly equally throughout the major tissues of the body. The upper left portion of the curve in Figure 1.14 represents the rapid-distribution phase, which lasts only a few minutes. The shallower part of the curve

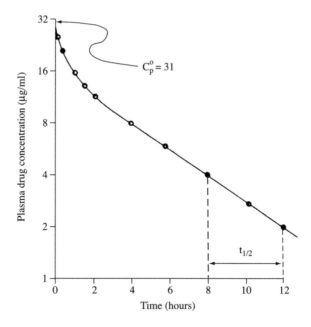

FIGURE 1.14 Plasma concentration time curve following intravenous injection of a drug. In this example, drug concentrations are measured in plasma every 30 minutes for the first 2 hours following drug injection, then every 2 hours until 12 hours after injection. Over the first 2 hours, redistribution exists as the drug leaves plasma and enters body tissues and equilibrates with those tissues. After redistribution, the fall in plasma level is linear, exhibiting a metabolic half-life of 4 hours, regardless of the plasma concentration of the drug.

represents the slower, prolonged decrease in the level of drug in the blood required for the body to detoxify the drug by hepatic metabolism. (The plasma concentration of the drug metabolites is not illustrated.) The calculated elimination half-life is a measure of this process, and it allows the time course of drug action to be calculated.

Figure 1.14 shows that the elimination half-life of the drug is about 4 hours (the time for the blood level to fall from 4 µg/ml to 2 µg/ml). The 4-hour half-life then remains constant over time. In other words, it takes the same amount of time for the blood level to fall from 8 µg/ml to 4 µg/ml as it does to fall from 4 µg/ml to 2 µg/ml or from 2 µg/ml to 1 µg/ml. Thus, a different absolute amount of drug is metabolized within each half-life; the time interval remains constant.

The knowledge of a drug's half-life is important because it tells us how long a drug remains in the body. As shown in Table 1.4, it takes four half-lives for 94 percent of a drug to be eliminated by the body and six half-lives for 98 percent of the drug to be eliminated. At that point, a person is, for most practical purposes, drug free. It is important to remember that even though the blood level of the drug is reduced by 75 percent after two half-lives, the drug persists in the body at low levels for at least six half-lives. The so-called drug hangover is a result.

Throughout this book, drug half-lives are cited to describe the duration of action of psychoactive drugs in the body and allow comparisons between drugs with similar actions but differing half-lives. Most drug half-lives are measured in hours; others are measured in days, and recovery from the drug may take a week or more. For example, the elimination half-life of diazepam (Valium; Chapter 6) is about 30 hours in a healthy young adult (Figure 1.15), much longer in the elderly. The half-life of its active metabolite (nordiazepam, not illustrated in Figure 1.15) is even longer, on the order of several days to a week. The elderly exhibit

TABLE 1.4 Half-life calculations

	Amount of drug in the body	
Number of half-lives	Percent eliminated	Percent remaining
0	0	100
1	50	50
2	75	25
3	87.5	12.5
4	93.8	6.2
5	96.9	3.1
6	98.4	1.6

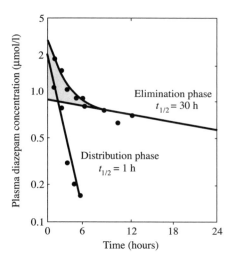

FIGURE 1.15 Plasma levels of diazepam (Valium, a benzodiazepine) following a single intravenous dose. The fast (distribution) phase has a half-life of about 1 hour. The slower, metabolic elimination phase shows a half-life of 30 hours. The long half-life of the active diazepam metabolite nordiazepam is not shown.

even more prolongation of the half-lives of both diazepam and nordiazepam; the duration of action can be 4 weeks or even longer.

Note that drug half-life is the *time* for the plasma level of drug to fall by 50 percent. Thus, half-life is independent of the absolute level of drug in blood: the level falls by 50 percent every half-life, regardless of how many molecules of drug were actually metabolized during that time. Therefore, a varying amount of drug is metabolized with each half-life (fewer actual molecules are metabolized per half-life as the plasma level of drug falls).

One of the rare exceptions to this concept is the metabolism of ethyl alcohol by the enzyme alcohol dehydrogenase. Here, a constant amount of alcohol is metabolized per hour, regardless of the absolute amount of alcohol present in blood, and the blood level falls in a straight line.[6] (The metabolism of alcohol is discussed in Chapter 4.)

Drug Half-Life, Accumulation, and Steady State

The biological half-life of a drug is not only the time required for the drug concentration in blood to fall by one-half, but it is also the determinant of the length of time necessary to reach a steady-state

---

[6]Usually, about 10 cubic centimeters (cc) of absolute alcohol are metabolized per hour, regardless of blood level. The significance of this rate is discussed in Chapter 4.

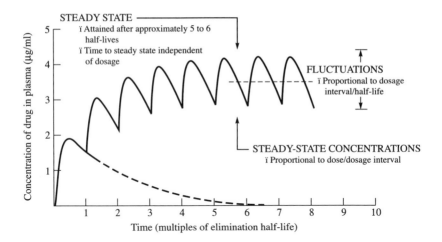

FIGURE 1.16 Plasma drug concentrations during repeated oral administration of a drug at intervals equal to its elimination half-life. The heavy dashed curve illustrates elimination if only a single dose is given. Because only 50 percent of each dose is eliminated before the next dose is given, the drug accumulates, reaching steady-state concentration in five to six half-lives. The sinusoidal curve shows the maximal and minimal drug concentrations at the beginning and end of each dosage interval, respectively. The light dashed line illustrates the average concentration achieved at steady state.

concentration (Figure 1.16). If a second full dose of drug is administered before the body has eliminated the first dose, the total amount of drug in the body and the peak level of the drug in the blood will be greater than the total amount and peak level produced by the first dose. For example, if 100 milligrams (mg) of a drug with a 4-hour half-life were administered at 12 noon, 50 mg of drug would remain in the body at 4 P.M. If an additional 100 mg of the drug were then taken at 4 P.M., 75 mg of drug would remain in the body at 8 P.M. (25 mg of the first dose and 50 mg of the second). If this administration schedule were continued, the amount of drug in the body would continue to increase until a plateau (steady-state) concentration was reached.

In general, the time to reach *steady-state concentration* (the level of drug achieved in blood with repeated, regular-interval dosing) is about six times the drug's elimination half-life and is independent of the actual dosage of the drug. In one half-life, a drug reaches 50 percent of the concentration that will eventually be achieved. After two half-lives, the drug achieves 75 percent concentration; at three half-lives, the drug achieves the initial 50 percent of the third dose, the next 25 percent from the second dose, plus half of the remaining 25 percent from the first dose. At 98.4 percent (the concentration achieved after six half-lives), the drug concentration is essentially at steady state. This is the rationale behind the general rule. The steady-state concentration is achieved when the amount administered per unit time equals the amount eliminated per unit time. The interdependent variables that determine the ultimate concentration (or steady-state blood level of drug) are the dose (which determines the blood level but not the time to steady state), the dose interval, the half-life of the drug, and other, and more complex factors that can affect drug elimination.

In summary, steady, regular-interval dosing leads to a predictable accumulation, with a steady-state concentration reached after about six half-lives; the magnitude of the concentration is proportional to dose and dosage interval. Clinically, these factors guide drug therapy when blood levels of the drug are monitored and correlated with therapeutic results.

Therapeutic Drug Monitoring

Therapeutic drug monitoring (TDM) can aid a clinician in making critical decisions in therapeutic applications. In psychopharmacology, TDM can dramatically improve the prognosis of psychological disorders, making previously difficult-to-treat disorders much more treatable. The basic principle underlying TDM is that a threshold plasma concentration of a drug is needed at the receptor site to initiate and maintain a pharmacological response. Critically important is that plasma concentrations of psychoactive drugs correlate well with tissue or receptor concentrations. Therefore, TDM is an indirect although usually quite accurate measurement of drug concentration at the receptor site. To make the correlation between TDM, dosage, and therapeutic response, large-scale clinical trials are performed, and blood samples are drawn at several time periods during both acute (short-term) and chronic (long-term) therapy. Statistical correlation is made between the level of drug in plasma and the degree of therapeutic response. A dosage regimen can then be designed to achieve the appropriate blood level of a drug.

The goals of TDM are many. One goal is to assess whether a patient is taking medication as prescribed; if plasma levels of the drug are below the therapeutic level because the patient has not been taking the required medication, therapeutic results will be poor. Another goal is to avoid toxicity; if plasma levels of the drug are above the therapeutic level, the dosage can be lowered, effectiveness maintained, and toxicity minimized. A third goal is to enhance therapeutic response by focusing not on the amount of drug taken but on the measured amount of drug in the plasma. Other goals include possible reductions in the cost of therapy (since a patient's illness is better controlled) and the substantiation of the need for unusually high doses in patients who require higher-than-normal intake of prescribed medication to maintain a therapeutic blood level of a drug.

Winek and coworkers (2001) and Baselt (2002) present blood level data for numerous medications, including most psychopharmacology agents.

Drug Tolerance and Dependence

Drug tolerance is defined as a state of progressively decreasing responsiveness to a drug. A person who develops tolerance requires a larger dose of the drug to achieve the effect originally obtained by a smaller dose. At least three mechanisms are involved in the development of drug tolerance—two are pharmacological mechanisms, one is a behavioral mechanism.

In *metabolic tolerance,* the first of the two classically described types of pharmacological tolerance, more enzyme is available to metabolize a drug and, as a result, more drug must be administered to maintain the same level of drug in the body. *Cellular-adaptive,* or *pharmacodynamic, tolerance* is the second type of pharmacological tolerance. Receptors in the brain adapt to the continued presence of the drug, with neurons adapting to excess drug either by reducing the number of receptors available to the drug or by reducing their sensitivity to the drug. Such reduction in numbers or sensitivity is termed *down regulation,* and higher levels of drug are necessary to maintain the same biological effect.

Behavioral conditioning processes are the third type of drug tolerance. The exposure of drugs to receptors does not account for the substantial degree of tolerance that many people acquire to opioids, barbiturates, ethyl alcohol, and other drugs. Instead, tolerance can be demonstrated when a drug is administered in the context of usual predrug cues but not in the context of alternative cues. Poulos and Cappell (1991) proposed a *homeostatic theory* of drug tolerance. They found that, with morphine analgesia, testing in an environment in which tolerance had developed affected the manifestation of tolerance, and an environmental cue could maintain the tolerance. This *contingent tolerance* is pervasive and represents a general process underlying the development of all forms of systemic tolerance.

The environmental cues routinely paired with drug administration will become conditioned stimuli that elicit a conditioned response that is opposite in direction to or compensation for the direct effects of the drug. Over conditioning trials, the compensatory conditioned response grows in magnitude and counteracts the direct drug effects; that is, tolerance develops.

Physical dependence is an entirely different phenomenon from tolerance, even though the two are often associated temporally. A person who is physically dependent needs the drug to avoid withdrawal symptoms if the drug is not taken. The state is revealed by withdrawing the drug and noting the occurrence of physical and/or psychological changes (withdrawal symptoms). These changes are referred to as an *abstinence syndrome.* Readministering the drug can relieve the symptoms of withdrawal.

Because physical dependence is often manifested following cessation of use of drugs of abuse such as alcohol and heroin, the term has been linked with "addiction," implying that withdrawal signs are "bad" and observed only with drugs of abuse. This conclusion is far from the truth: rather severe withdrawal signs can follow cessation of such therapeutic drugs as the SSRI type of clinical antidepressants (Chapter 9).[7] Therefore, the occurrence of withdrawal signs after drug removal is not necessarily a sign of drug "addiction" that is usually associated with "bad" drugs such as heroin. Rather, physical dependence is an indication that brain and body functions were altered by the presence of a drug and that a different homeostatic state must be initiated at drug withdrawal. It takes time (from a few days to about two weeks) for the brain and the body to adapt to the new state of equilibrium where drug is absent.

STUDY QUESTIONS

1. What is meant by the term *pharmacokinetics?*

2. Why must a psychoactive drug be altered metabolically in the body before it can be excreted?

3. Discuss the advantages and disadvantages of the various methods of administering drugs.

4. List the various membrane barriers that may affect drug distribution.

5. Discuss the blood-brain barrier as a limitation to drug transport.

6. Discuss the placental barrier as it affects the distribution of psychoactive drugs. What are the cautions for the use of psychotropic medication during pregnancy?

7. If a drug has an elimination half-life of 6 hours, how long does it take for the drug to be effectively eliminated from the body after administration of a single dose?

8. What is drug tolerance and why does it occur? Discuss three mechanisms underlying the development of tolerance.

---

[7]Removal of SSRI-type antidepressants is followed in many patients by withdrawal signs that can be organized into five core somatic symptoms: (1) disequilibrium (dizziness, vertigo, ataxia), (2) GI symptoms (nausea, vomiting), (3) flulike symptoms (fatigue, lethargy, myalgias, chills), (4) sensory disturbances (paresthesias, sensation of electric shocks), and (5) sleep disturbances (insomnia, vivid dreams).

9. What are the various routes through the body whereby a drug can be eliminated?

10. Define *half-life*. How does *half-life* apply to steady state?

11. What is meant by the term *therapeutic drug monitoring?* In what instances might it be of value?

REFERENCES

Baselt, R. C. (2002). "Disposition of Toxic Drugs and Chemicals in Man." Foster City, CA: Biomedical Publications.

deLeon, J. (2006). "AmpliChip CYP450 Test: Personalized Medicine Has Arrived in Psychiatry." *Expert Reviews in Molecular Diagnostics* 6: 277–286.

deLeon, J., et al. (2006). "The AmpliChip CYP450 Genotype Test: Integrating a New Clinical Tool." *Molecular Diagnostic Therapeutics* 10: 135–151.

DeVane, C. L. (2006). "Antidepressant-Drug Interactions Are Potentially but Rarely Clinically Significant." *Neuropsychopharmacology* 31: 1594–1604.

Gilstrap, L. C., and B. B. Little (1998). *Drugs and Pregnancy,* 2nd ed. New York: Chapman & Hall.

Greenblatt, D. J., et al. (1999). "Human Cytochromes and Some Newer Antidepressants: Kinetics, Metabolism, and Drug Interactions." *Journal of Clinical Psychopharmacology* 19, Supplement 1: 23S–35S.

Greenblatt, D. J., et al. (2003). "Time Course of Recovery of Cytochrome P450 3A Function After Single Doses of Grapefruit Juice." *Clinical Pharmacology and Therapeutics* 74: 121–129.

Kim, D. K., et al. (2006). "Monoamine Transporter Gene Polymorphisms and Antidepressant Response in Koreans with Late-Life Depression." *Journal of the American Medical Association* 296: 1609–1618.

Lilja, J. J., et al. (1998). "Grapefruit Juice Substantially Increases Plasma Concentrations of Buspirone." *Clinical Pharmacology and Therapeutics* 64: 655–660.

Lin, K. M., et al. (2001). "Culture and Psychopharmacology." *Psychiatric Clinics of North America* 24: 523–538.

Murphy, G. M., Jr., et al. (2004). "Effects of the Serotonin Transporter Gene Promoter Polymorphism on Mirtazepine and Paroxetine Efficacy and Adverse Effects in Geriatric Major Depression." *Archives of General Psychiatry* 61: 1163–1169.

Paine, M. F., et al. (2006). "A Furanocoumarin-Free Grapefruit Juice Establishes Furanocoumarins as the Mediators of the Grapefruit Juice-Felodipine Interaction." *American Journal of Clinical Nutrition* 84: 1097–1105.

Pardridge, W. M. (2003). "Blood-Brain Barrier Drug Targeting: The Future of Brain Drug Development." *Molecular Interventions* 3: 90–105.

Poulos, C. X., and H. Cappell (1991). "Homeostatic Theory of Drug Tolerance: A General Model of Physiological Adaptation." *Psychological Reviews* 98: 390–408.

Preskorn, S. H., and Werder, S. (2006). "Detrimental Antidepressant Drug-Drug Interactions: Are They Clinically Relevant?" *Neuropsychopharmacology* 31: 1605–1612.

Rheeders, M., et al. (2006). "Drug-Drug Interactions after Single Oral Doses of the Furanocoumarin Methoxsalen and Cyclosporine." *Journal of Clinical Pharmacology* 46: 768–775.

Spina, E., and E. Perucca (2002). "Clinical Significance of Pharmacokinetic Interactions Between Antiepileptic and Psychotropic Drugs." *Epilepsia* 43, Supplement 2: 37–44.

Winek, C. L., et al. (2001). "Winek's Drug & Chemical Blood Level Data 2001." *Forensic Science International* 122: 107–123.

Chapter 2

Pharmacodynamics: How Drugs Act

While the body is trying to rid itself of an ingested psychoactive drug, the drug is exerting effects by attaching to receptors in cells in both the brain and the body. As a result of the interactions, the body experiences effects that are characteristic for the drug.

It is a basic principle of pharmacology that the pharmacological, physiological, or behavioral effects induced by a drug follow from their interaction with receptors.

The study of the interactions is termed *pharmacodynamics* and involves exploring the mechanisms of drug action that occur at the molecular level. While *pharmacokinetics* is the study of what the body does to a drug, *pharmacodynamics* is the study of what the drug does to the body. The two studies provide the basis for both the rational therapeutic use of a drug and the design of new and superior therapeutic agents.

To produce an effect, a drug must bind to and interact with specialized receptors, usually located on cell membranes. In the case of psychoactive drugs, these receptors are usually located on the surface of neurons in the brain. The occupation of a receptor by a drug (*drug-receptor binding*) leads to a change in the functional properties of the neuron, resulting in the drug's characteristic pharmacological response. In most instances, drug-receptor binding is both *ionic* and *reversible* in nature, with positive and negative charges on various portions of the drug molecule and the receptor protein attracting one to the other.[1] The strength of ionic attachment is determined by the fit of the three-dimensional structure of the drug to the three-dimensional site on the receptor.

Importantly, when a psychoactive drug binds to a receptor and thereby alters (activates or blocks) the normal functions of that receptor, the neuronal response to the drug is one of two types: (1) an immediate response to the presence of the drug on the receptor, or (2) when the drug is given over a longer period of time, long-term changes in the properties of the receptors resulting in long-term changes in neuronal, brain, and behavioral functioning.[2]

Immediate responses follow from the acute binding of a drug to its receptor with initiation of an immediate neuronal (and behavioral) response. For example, drinking a cup of coffee (containing the drug caffeine), smoking a cigarette (containing nicotine), or smoking illicit cocaine or methamphetamine results in release of the neurotransmitter dopamine; dopamine activates our reward system and a stimulant or pleasurable feeling can follow. With respect to medications, ingestion of methylphenidate (Ritalin) can rapidly relieve the symptoms of attention deficit/hyperactivity disorder, potent opioid analgesia can rapidly relieve severe pain, and certain sedatives can rapidly induce drowsiness and be used in the treatment of insomnia. Such actions are all thought to follow an acute agonist action at specific receptors. Similarly, many of the side effects of drugs (such as dry mouth, unwanted sedation, blurred vision, and so on) follow from acute actions at other receptors, often distinct from those responsible for the desired drug action.

Longer-term responses to a drug require that a drug be taken continually over a period of time. Here, the drug is in contact with its receptors for days to months. As a result, neurons "adapt" to the presence of drug, resulting in long-term changes in neuronal functioning. In the case of long-term antidepressant drug therapy, neurons adapt by becoming more "healthy," and this reaction can be followed by relief of depression (Chapter 7). The same principle probably applies to medication therapy for bipolar illness and various anxiety disorders.

[1]Reversible ionic binding is contrasted with the formation of a permanent, irreversible, covalent bond between a drug and a receptor. One of the rare instances in psychopharmacology where an irreversible covalent bond forms is between certain antidepressant drugs and the enzyme monoamine oxidase (Chapter 9).

[2]When a drug binds to a receptor and exerts an action like that exerted by the normal neurotransmitter, the action is termed an *agonistic* action and the drug is called an *agonist* for that receptor. Conversely, when the drug binds to a receptor and exerts no agonist action but merely blocks access of the transmitter to its receptor, the drug is called an *antagonist* for the receptor.

Some long-term adaptations to the presence of drug can be harmful. For example, drug "dependency" can follow long-term use of certain sedatives, stimulants, opioid narcotics, and even (although this is debated) antidepressants. In all these cases, withdrawal symptoms are observed after drug discontinuation. The exact responses vary with each type of drug and are discussed in the appropriate chapter of this book.

Receptors for Drug Action

Drugs exert their effects by forming reversible ionic bonds with specific receptors. A *receptor* is a fairly large molecule (usually a protein[3]) that is present on the surface of or within a cell that furnishes the site or sites where biologically active, naturally occurring, endogenous compounds (called *transmitters or modulators)* induce their normal biological effects. Literally hundreds of different types of receptors are known (each being a unique protein molecule), and the ability to recognize one specific neurotransmitter characterizes each one (Feldman et al., 1997, p. 13). Thus, only one neurotransmitter might be specific enough to fit or bind to a specific receptor protein. For example, if only serotonin binds to a specific protein receptor, the protein is called a serotonin receptor. But although the receptor is specific for serotonin, serotonin (as a neurotransmitter) also binds to other, structurally different receptors.

To date, more than 15 different serotonin receptor proteins have been identified.[4] In pharmacology, this diversity makes it possible to develop closely related drugs, each with a slightly different degree of affinity (strength of attachment) for the different serotonin receptors. For example, a specific drug might have affinity for a serotonin 1 receptor but not for any other serotonin receptor. Until recently it was not possible to develop such a drug. However, with the understanding that drug receptors are proteins, it became possible to isolate a specific receptor protein from the rest of the brain, purify it, deter-

---

[3]A protein is a complex chain of various amino acids. Proteins are essential to life, functioning, among other things, as metabolic enzymes and receptors.

[4]Each receptor protein that binds serotonin, for example, has a slightly different amino acid composition; nevertheless, their three-dimensional structures are similar enough that serotonin, for example, still fits a "slot" (like a lock-and-key arrangement) and ionically binds to the protein. Pharmacologists have named these different protein receptors serotonin 1, serotonin 2, serotonin 3, and so on; in earlier years, multiple receptors for a single neurotransmitter were given more exotic names (for example, muscarinic and nicotinic for acetylcholine receptors, alpha and beta for adrenergic receptors, and mu, delta, and kappa for opioid receptors).

mine its amino acid sequence, isolate the portion of DNA responsible for making the protein, and clone the protein receptor to produce sufficient quantities of receptor against which drugs could be screened for affinity and activity. This is the pharmacology of the twenty-first century!

It is now known that a given drug may be more specific for a given set of receptors than is the endogenous neurotransmitter. Serotonin, for example, must necessarily attach to all its more than 15 different serotonin receptors (it has to because it is the endogenous neurotransmitter at each receptor). However, a given drug might attach to only one receptor. For example, buspirone (BuSpar) attaches to serotonin 1_A receptors, which results in antianxiety and antidepressant actions. It has no affinity for other serotonin receptors.

Figures 2.1 through 2.4 demonstrate six important points about drug-receptor interactions:

1. A receptor is usually a membrane-spanning protein (Figure 2.1) that has binding sites for an endogenous neurotransmitter and appropriate drug molecules.

2. This membrane-spanning protein is not a simple globule (as suggested by Figure 2.1) but a continuous series of either 5, 7, or 12 alpha helical coils (loops of amino acids) embedded in the membrane (Figure 2.2).

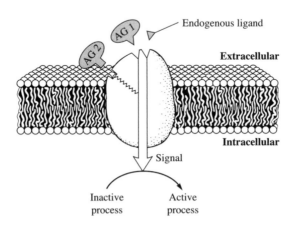

FIGURE 2.1 Diagrammatic representation of the classical concept of a receptor. One type of agonist (AG 1) fits the receptor site for an endogenous neurotransmitter and mimics the action of the neurotransmitter. Another type of agonist (AG 2) binds to an adjacent receptor site, thereby influencing (amplifying) signal transmission. Signal transmission activates intracellular processes that are inactive without receptor activation.

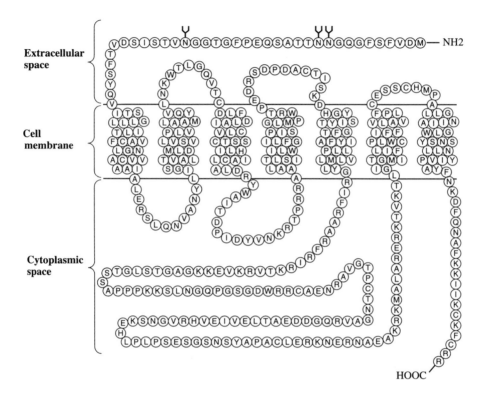

FIGURE 2.2 Schematic representation of the primary structure of the serotonin 1$_A$ postsynaptic receptor. Each circle represents an individual amino acid; the letter is the initial of the name of the amino acid. This receptor is one member of a large "family" of postsynaptic neurotransmitter receptors containing 7-transmembrane alpha helical coils.

3. The endogenous neurotransmitter (and presumably drugs also) attaches inside the space between these coils (Figure 2.3) and is held in place by ionic attractions.

4. This reversible ionic binding of the neurotransmitter that is specific for the receptor may activate the receptor, usually by changing the structure of the protein (Figure 2.4). This change allows a "signal," or "information," to be transmitted through the receptor to the inside of the cell. Ultimately, receptor alterations change enzyme activity in the neuron, thus altering neuronal function.

5. The intensity of the resulting transmembrane signal is thought to be at least partly determined by the percentage of receptors that are occupied by molecules of neurotransmitter.

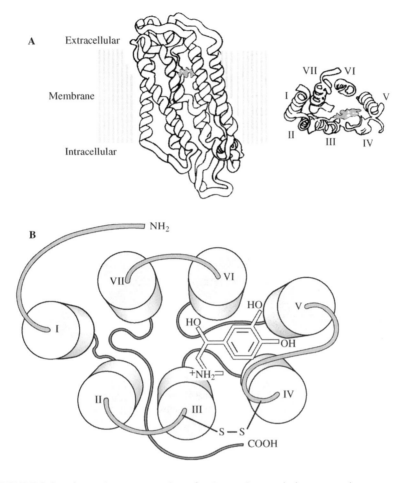

FIGURE 2.3 Schematic representation of a G protein-coupled transmembrane receptor, with a molecule of neurotransmitter (norepinephrine) lying in its binding site. Note the arrangement of the 7-transmembrane helical coils and the site of the transmitter attachment deep within the structure. The ionic interactions between the transmitter and particular amino acid side chains are not illustrated. In **A,** the membrane and continuous coils are shown. In **B,** the helical coils are represented as cylinders with the molecule of norepinephrine interacting with four of the coils.

6. A drug can affect the transmembrane signal by binding either to the specific receptor site for the endogenous neurotransmitter or to a nearby site.

   Binding of a drug to a receptor results in one of three actions:

• Binding to a receptor site normally occupied by the endogenous neurotransmitter can initiate a cellular response similar or

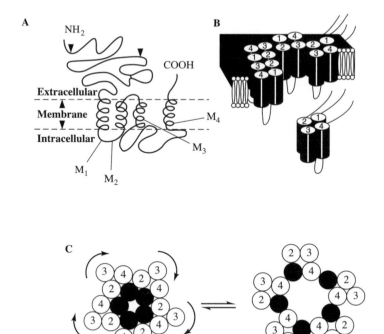

FIGURE 2.4 Presumed topology of the GABA_A receptor. **A**. Single subunit with its large extracellular terminal part, and four transmembrane helical coils. **B**. Arrangement of the transmembrane domains of five subunits to form a central channel. **C**. Transmembrane domain in a transverse section through the membrane when the channel is closed (*left*) and open (*right*).

identical to that exerted by the transmitter. As discussed earlier, the drug thus mimics the action of the transmitter. This is called an *agonistic action* and the drug is termed an *agonist* for that transmitter.

• Binding to a site near the binding site for the endogenous transmitter can facilitate transmitter binding. This is also an agonistic action. Such a facilitative effect is termed an "allosteric" action.

• Binding to a receptor site normally occupied by a neurotransmitter but not initiating a transmitterlike action blocks access of the transmitter to its binding site, which inhibits the normal physiological action of the transmitter. This is called an *antagonistic action* and the drug is termed an *antagonist* for that neurotransmitter or receptor site.

It is also a general rule of psychopharmacology that drugs do not create any unique effects; they merely modulate normal neuronal functioning, mimicking or antagonizing the actions of a specific neurotransmitter. Binding accompanied by drug-induced mimicry or facilitation of neurotransmitter action is an agonistic action.[5] Drug occupation of a receptor that is not accompanied by neurotransmitter-like activation blocks the access of the neurotransmitter to the receptor and is an antagonistic action.[6]

Receptor Structure

What does a receptor look like? As stated earlier, most receptors are membrane-spanning proteins, each having 5, 7, or 12 alpha helical coils. Although there are several different configurations of proteins that may serve a receptor function, the following is a brief summary of the major types most relevant to the action of drugs.

Ion Channel Receptors. (Ion channel receptors are also called *ionotropic receptors.*) The first type of membrane-spanning receptor is the kind that forms an *ion channel.* That is, the central portion of the receptor forms a pore that spans the membrane of the neuron, which enlarges in size when either an endogenous neurotransmitter or exogenous drug attaches to the receptor-binding site. The attachment allows flow of a specific *ion* (such as chloride ion) through the enlarged pore.

Figures 2.4 and 2.5 illustrate the neurotransmitter gamma aminobutyric acid (GABA) and a drug (a benzodiazepine) opening a channel and allowing inward flow of chloride ions through an enlarged pore within a GABA-activated receptor. Benzodiazepines (Chapter 6) serve as agonists at this site by binding to a site near the GABA-binding site and by facilitating the action of GABA. This action allows flow of chloride ions into the neuron, hyperpolarizing the neuron and inhibiting neuronal function. This action underlies the use of benzodiazepines as sedative, antianxiety, amnestic, and antiepileptic agents.

In contrast, the drug flumazenil (Romazicon) attaches to the benzodiazepine-binding site but does not facilitate the action of GABA. It does, however, compete with any benzodiazepine that is

---

[5]Example: Buspirone attaches to the serotonin 1_A receptor and activates it, mimicking serotonin action on the receptor, which results in an antianxiety action of clinical significance.

[6]Example: All the drugs developed to treat schizophrenia (antipsychotic drugs; Chapter 9) are antagonists at dopamine-2 receptors. By attaching to this subtype of dopamine receptor, they prevent endogenous dopamine molecules from attaching, activating, and producing an effect at these sites.

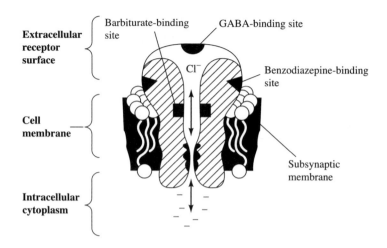

FIGURE 2.5 GABA_A receptor in a perpendicular section through the membrane. The localization of the various binding sites is purely hypothetical. [From W. E. Haefley et al., "The Multiplicity of Actions of Benzodiazepine Receptor Ligands," *Canadian Journal of Psychiatry* 38, Supplement 4 (1993): 5102–5107.]

present, displacing the benzodiazepine from the receptor and reversing the actions of the benzodiazepine. Flumazenil is classified pharmacologically as a benzodiazepine antagonist and is used clinically to treat benzodiazepine overdoses.[7]

G Protein-Coupled Receptors.   A second type of membrane-spanning receptor protein is called a *G protein-coupled receptor*. These receptors may also be called "metabotropic" receptors. The activation of these receptors induces the release of an attached intracellular protein (a *G protein*) that, in turn, controls enzymatic function within the postsynaptic neuron. Figure 2.2 illustrates the structure of one of the more than 15 such receptors for serotonin (here, the serotonin 1_A receptor). Figure 2.6 illustrates some of the intracellular alterations that can be induced as a result of activation of this receptor.

G protein-coupled receptors (sometimes abbreviated as GPCRs) are discussed throughout this book because they are involved in the synaptic effects of many neurotransmitters, such as acetylcholine, norepinephrine,

---

[7]Also shown in Figure 2.5 is a barbiturate-binding site on the GABA receptor complex. Barbiturates (Chapter 5) act like benzodiazepines in increasing the effect of GABA on the chloride channel within the GABA receptor. Thus, with a site and mechanism of action similar to that exerted by benzodiazepines, the two classes of drugs might be expected to demonstrate similar clinical and behavioral effects. In general, they do.

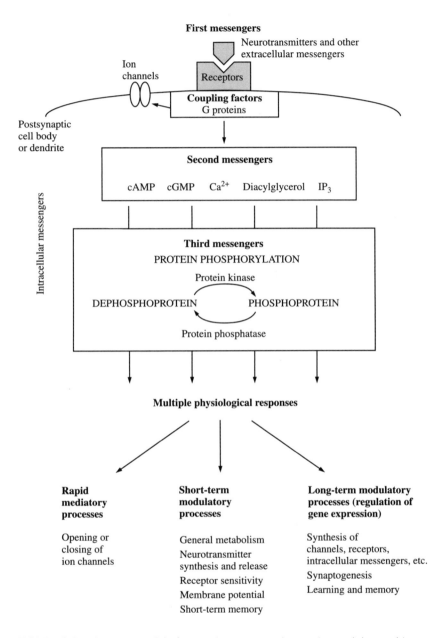

FIGURE 2.6 Schematic model of transmitter-receptor interaction and the resulting second-messenger action. Second messengers are intracellular proteins, molecules, or ions that are regulated by transmitter-receptor activation. The neurotransmitter is the first messenger, and binding is a recognition action. Receptor alteration with G protein release represents transduction of first-messenger binding. As shown here, second messengers amplify the signal and serve to turn on or turn off numerous rapid and long-term physiological responses.

dopamine, serotonin, and opioid endorphins, all of which are involved in the action of psychoactive drugs. The molecular structure of G protein-coupled receptors (more than 50 have been identified, and more keep coming!) consists of a single protein chain of 400 to 500 amino acids possessing seven transmembrane alpha helices (see Figure 2.2). Both the extracellular and the intracellular terminal portions of the protein chain vary in length and in amino acid composition. G protein-coupled receptors are the middlemen, able to communicate between the neurotransmitter-receptor complex and intracellular enzymes (the *second messenger*[8]) or adjacent ion channels (see Figure 2.6). The G protein consists of three functional subunits, which taken together have historically been called G protein because they interact with guanine nucleotides within the cell. Metabotropic receptors control many cellular processes, such as ion channel function, energy metabolism, cell division and differentiation, and neuronal excitability.

In addition to the ionotropic and metabotropic types of receptor proteins, there are two other types of proteins that function in a similar manner and that are crucial to understanding drug mechanisms.

Carrier Proteins.   The third type of membrane-spanning protein is a *carrier* (or *transport*) *protein*. This type of receptor transports small organic molecules (such as neurotransmitters) across cell membranes against concentration gradients. Important in psychopharmacology are the *presynaptic* carrier proteins that function to bind dopamine, norepinephrine, or serotonin (and other neurotransmitters) in the synaptic cleft and transport them back into the presynaptic nerve terminal, terminating the synaptic transmitter action of these neurotransmitters. Many drugs discussed in this book (both therapeutic and abused) exert their actions by blocking the carrier protein that is specific for transporting a specific neurotransmitter. Until recently, little was known about these transporters except that they genetically encoded chains of amino acids (proteins) arranged as 12 helical arrays of amino acids embedded in the membrane of the presynaptic nerve terminal (contrasted with the 7-helical array present in the postsynaptic serotonin receptor shown in Figure 2.2). An example is that of the dopamine transporter protein shown in Figure 2.7.

Recent work by Gouaux and coworkers (Yernool et al., 2004; Gouaux and MacKinnon, 2005; Armstrong et al., 2006) has added considerably to our knowledge of these transporters. They carry molecules of neurotransmitter across membranes of presynaptic nerve terminals, even against a concentration gradient (therefore more than passive diffusion). To do so, the transporters must exist in at least

---

[8]The endogenous neurotransmitter is the first messenger, carrying information between presynaptic and postsynaptic neurons across the synaptic cleft (Chapter 3).

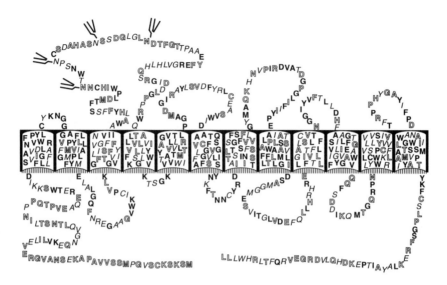

FIGURE 2.7 Schematic representation of the dopamine transporter showing proposed orientation in the presynaptic membrane. [From S. Shimada et al., "Cloning and Expression of a Cocaine-Sensitive Dopamine Transporter Complimentary DNA," *Science* 254 (1991): 576–578.

three ionic states: open to the synapse, occluded with the transmitter "trapped" inside, and open to the cytoplasm of the presynaptic neuron (Figure 2.8). It now appears that the transporter is a bowl-shaped structure with a fluid-filled basin (open to the synaptic cleft) extending halfway across the membrane of the presynaptic nerve terminal (Figure 2.9). At the bottom of the basin are three binding sites for the neurotransmitter, each cradled by two helical "hairpins" reaching from opposite sides of the membrane. In the resting state, the bowl is open to the synaptic cleft. It traps one or more molecules of released transmitter per "cycle," allowing floods of molecules to move from the synaptic cleft into the presynaptic terminal and become available for rerelease. It seems that the transport of transmitter is achieved by movements of the hairpins that allow alternating access to either side of the membrane (for example, the outer layer closes, trapping the transmitter, and then the inner layer opens, ejecting the transmitter into the cytoplasm of the presynaptic terminal).[9]

[9]In the case of glutamate transport, Armstrong and coworkers (2006) state: "Activation of the glutamate receptor involves binding of glutamate to the agonist-binding domain clamshell, followed by closure of the clamshell by approximately 21 degrees. Because the ligand-binding domains are braced against each other in a back-to-back fashion, this simple domain closure is transduced to the ion channel domain, leading to opening of the conductive pore (to the interior of the neuron)."

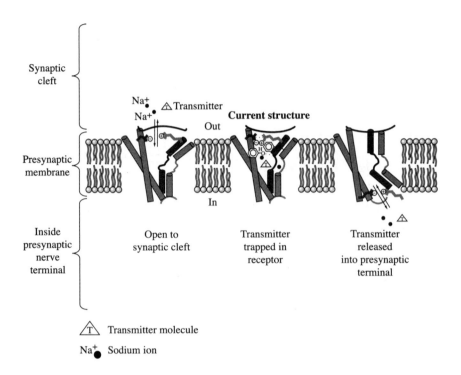

Synaptic cleft

Presynaptic membrane

Inside presynaptic nerve terminal

Na⁺ △ Transmitter

Na⁺

Current structure

Out

In

Open to synaptic cleft

Transmitter trapped in receptor

Transmitter released into presynaptic terminal

△ Transmitter molecule
T

Na⁺• Sodium ion

FIGURE 2.8 Schematic drawing of a proposed conformational change involving transport of transmitter and sodium ions across the membrane of the presynaptic nerve terminal. *Left:* Transporter open to the synaptic cleft. *Center:* Transmitter "trapped" inside the transporter. *Right:* Inward-facing state with transmitter "released" into the cytoplasm of the neuron. [From A. Yamashita et al., "Crystal Structure of a Bacterial Homologue of Na⁺/Cl⁻-Dependent Neurotransmitter Transporters," *Nature* 437 (2005), Figure 6, p. 221.]

Enzymes. A fourth type of receptor protein for psychoactive drugs is *enzymes*—in particular, enzymes that regulate the synaptic availability of certain neurotransmitters. These enzymes function to break down neurotransmitters and their inhibition by drugs increases transmitter availability. Following are two examples: *acetylcholine esterase*, the enzyme that breaks down acetylcholine within the synaptic cleft (Chapter 3), and *monoamine oxidase*, the enzyme that breaks down norepinephrine and dopamine within presynaptic nerve terminals, controlling the amount available for release (Chapters 3 and 7).

Drugs known as *irreversible acetylcholine esterase inhibitors* form covalent bonds with the enzyme and have been used as insecticides and as lethal "nerve gases." Drugs that *reversibly* inhibit the enzyme *acetylcholine esterase* are used clinically as cognitive enhancers, delaying the onset of Alzheimer's disease (Chapter 11).

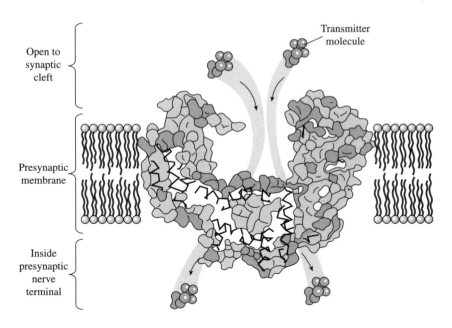

Open to
synaptic
cleft

Presynaptic
membrane

Inside
presynaptic
nerve
terminal

Transmitter
molecule

FIGURE 2.9 Schematic drawing of the proposed movement of neurotransmitter molecules through a transporter protein and into the presynaptic nerve terminal. The drawing illustrates the total movement and summarizes the three-step outline in Figure 2.8. The deep aqueous basin reaches halfway across the membrane. [Adapted from Yernool et al. (2004).]

Drugs that irreversibly inhibit the enzyme *monoamine oxidase* are called monoamine oxidase inhibitors (MAOIs) and are used primarily as antidepressants (Chapter 7).

Drug-Receptor Specificity

As discussed, receptors exhibit high specificity both for one particular neurotransmitter and for certain drug molecules. Making only modest variations in the chemical structure of a drug may greatly alter the intensity of a receptor's response to it. For example, amphetamine and methamphetamine (Chapter 13) are both powerful psychostimulants. Although their chemical structures are very close, they differ by the simple addition of a methyl ($-CH_3$) group to amphetamine, forming methamphetamine. Methamphetamine produces much greater behavioral stimulation at the same milligram dosage. Both drugs attach to the same receptors in the brain, but methamphetamine exerts a much more powerful action on them, at least in milligrams. The drug molecule with the "best fit" to the receptor (methamphetamine, in this example) elicits the greatest response from the cell. In pharmacological terms, methamphetamine is more *potent* than amphetamine because a lower absolute dose achieves the same level of response as a higher dose of amphetamine. But as we will see next, a more *potent* drug is not necessarily a more *effective* drug. It merely produces its effects at a somewhat lower dose.

As a consequence of drug binding to a receptor, cellular function is altered, resulting in observable effects on physiological or psychological functioning. The total action of the drug in the body results from drug actions either (1) on one specific type of receptor or (2) at different types of receptors. In either case, whether the drug is used for therapeutic or recreational purposes, the total action will produce additional responses, called *side effects*.

As an example of the side effects produced by the first mechanism, fluoxetine-induced blockade of presynaptic serotonin reuptake increases serotonin availability at all postsynaptic serotonin receptors. This single action results not only in relief of depression but also in such side effects as anxiety, insomnia, and sexual dysfunction (Chapter 7).

As an example of the side effects produced by the second mechanism, certain other antidepressants (the tricyclic antidepressants; Chapter 7) increase both serotonin and norepinephrine availability (reducing depression). But, in addition, they also produce sedation as a result of their blocking acetylcholinergic receptors; dry mouth and blurred vision can result. A balance between wanted effects and inevitable but unwanted side effects is always desirable.

Dose-Response Relationships

One way of quantifying drug-receptor interactions is to use *dose-response curves*. In Figure 2.10, two different types of dose-response curves are illustrated. In graph A, the dose is plotted against the

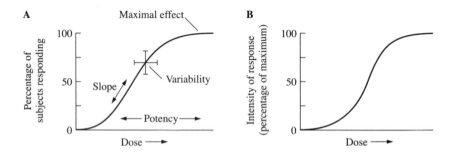

FIGURE 2.10 Two types of dose-response curves. **A.** Curve obtained by plotting the dose of drug against the percentage of subjects showing a given response at any given dose. **B.** Curve obtained by plotting the dose of drug against the intensity of response observed in any single person at a given dose. The intensity of response is plotted as a percentage of the maximum obtainable response.

percentage of people (from a given population) who exhibit a characteristic effect at a given dosage. In graph B, the dose is plotted against the intensity, or magnitude, of the response in a single person. These curves indicate that a dose exists that is low enough to produce little or no effect; at the opposite extreme, a dose exists beyond which no greater response can be elicited. Dose-response curves demonstrate several important characteristics:

- *Potency* refers to the absolute number of molecules of drug required to elicit a response, a measurement of the dose required.
- *Efficacy* refers to the maximum effect obtainable, with additional doses producing no more effect.
- *Variability* and *slope* refer to individual differences in drug response; some patients respond at very low doses and some require much more drug.

The location of the dose-response curve along the horizontal axis reflects the potency of the drug. If two drugs produce an equal degree of stimulation, but one exerts this action at half the dose level of the other, the first drug is considered to be *twice* as *potent* as the second drug (Figure 2.11). As stated, however, potency is a relatively unimportant characteristic of a drug, because it makes little difference whether the effective dose of a drug is 1.0 milligram or 100 milligrams as long as the drug is administered in an appropriate dose with no undue toxicity.

Slope refers to the more or less linear central portion of the dose-response curve. A steep slope on a dose-response curve implies that there is only a small difference between the dose that produces a

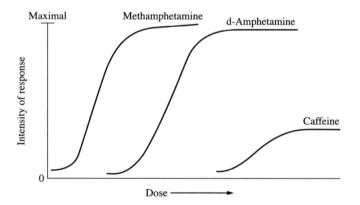

FIGURE 2.11 Theoretical dose-response curves for three psychostimulants to illustrate equal efficacy of methamphetamine and dextroamphetamine, increased potency of methamphetamine, and reduced potency and efficacy of caffeine.

barely discernible effect and the dose that causes a maximal effect. The steeper the slope, the smaller is the increase in dose required to go from a minimum response to a maximum effect. This can be good, as it may indicate that there is little biological variation in the response to the drug. Conversely, it may be a disadvantage if it indicates that untoward toxicity occurs with only minimal increases in dose.

The *peak* of the dose-response curve indicates the maximum effect, or efficacy, that can be produced by a drug, regardless of further increases in dose. Not all psychoactive drugs can exert the same level of effect. For example, caffeine, even in massive doses, cannot exert the same intensity of central nervous system (CNS) stimulation as amphetamine (see Figure 2.11). Similarly, aspirin can never achieve the greater analgesic effect of morphine. Thus, the maximum effect is an inherent property of a drug and is one measure of a drug's efficacy.

Most psychoactive drugs are not used to the point of their maximum effect because side effects and toxicities limit the upper range of dosage, regardless of whether the drug is administered for a therapeutic purpose or taken for recreational use. Therefore, the usefulness of a compound is correspondingly limited, even though the drug may be inherently capable of producing a greater or more intense effect.

Drug Safety and Effectiveness

For a drug to be approved by the federal Food and Drug Administration (FDA), its manufacturer must demonstrate both that the drug is *effective* for the claimed therapeutic use and that it is *safe* to use in a wide population. Effectiveness is determined in animal experiments and in human trials. Effectiveness is further assessed as the drug undergoes wider use in the general population. Safety refers to the potential for the drug to cause adverse effects, effects that vary from predictable and tolerable side effects to serious and unpredictable toxicities such as serious, unpredictable, and unrecognized allergic reactions to the drug. Also, when a drug is introduced into a general population, there is variability in response because of genetic or other population variances. Drug-drug interactions are also a common and important type of adverse effect, often predictable and often underappreciated during clinical trials (Jurrlink et al., 2003; al-Khatib et al., 2003).

Variability in Drug Responsiveness

The dose of a drug that produces a specific response varies considerably among patients. Variability among patients can result from differences in rates of drug absorption and metabolism, previous experience with drug use, various physical, psychological, and emotional states, and so on. Despite the etiology of the variability, any population will have a few subjects who are remarkably sensitive to the effects (and side effects) of a drug and a few who will exhibit remarkable drug tolerance, requiring quite large doses to produce therapeutic results. The variability, however, usually follows a predictable pattern, resembling a Gaussian distribution (Figure 2.12). In a few instances, however, a specific population (following a genetically predetermined pattern) will skew this distribution by exhibiting a unique pattern of responsiveness, usually due to genetic alterations in drug metabolism.

From Figure 2.12, it is obvious that, although the average dose required to elicit a given response can be calculated easily, some people respond at very much lower doses than the average and others respond only at very much higher doses . Thus, it is extremely important that the dose of any drug be individualized. Generalizations about "average doses" are risky at best.

The dose of a drug that produces the desired effect in 50 percent of the subjects is called the ED_{50}, and the lethal dose for 50 percent of the subjects is called the LD_{50}. The LD_{50} is calculated in exactly the same way as the ED_{50}, except that the dose of the drug is plotted against the number of experimental animals that die after being administered various doses of the compound. Both the ED_{50} and the LD_{50} are determined in several species of animals to prevent accidental drug-induced toxicity in humans. The ratio of the LD_{50} to the ED_{50} is used as an index of the relative safety of the drug and is called the *therapeutic index.*

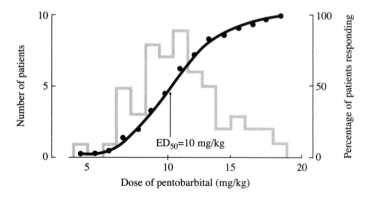

FIGURE 2.12 Example of biological variation. Histogram (*left ordinate*) and cumulative frequency histogram (*right ordinate*) following intravenous administration of pentobarbital, used to cause drowsiness in hospitalized patients. An ED_{50} of about 10 mg/kg body weight is shown. Note, however, that some patients exhibited sedation at about 4 mg/kg, while others required a dose of about 18 mg/kg The stair-step bars illustrate the data behind the dose-response curve.

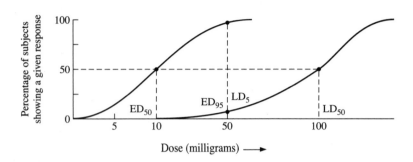

FIGURE 2.13 Two dose-response curves. *Left:* Dose of drug required to induce a given response. *Right:* Lethal dose of the compound. See text for discussion.

To illustrate, two dose-response curves are shown in Figure 2.13. The curve at the left illustrates the dose of drug necessary to induce sleep in a population of mice, and the one at the right illustrates the dose of drug necessary to kill a similar population. In this example, the $LD_{50}:ED_{50}$ ratio is seen to be 100:10, or 10. This may seem like a rather large margin, but note that at a dose of 50 milligrams, 95 percent of the mice sleep while 5 percent of the mice die. This overlap demonstrates both the difficulty in assessing the relative safety of drugs for use in large populations and the biological variation in individual responses to drugs. With this particular compound, a dose cannot be administered that will guarantee that 100 percent of the mice will sleep and none will die. Thus, a more useful indication of the margin of safety is a ratio of the lethal dose for 1 percent of the population to the effective dose for 99 percent of the population ($LD_1:ED_{99}$). A sedative drug with an $LD_1:ED_{99}$ of 1 would be a safer compound than the drug shown in Figure 2.13. Note that the clinical usefulness of indices obtained from laboratory animals is limited because these indices do not reflect the occasional unexpected response (from the causes listed earlier) that can seriously harm a patient.

Drug variability is also intimately associated with drug toxicity. Therefore, the side effects that are invariably associated with a drug, as well as its more serious toxicities (including those that can be fatal), must always be considered.

Drug Interactions

The effects of one drug can be modified by the concurrent administration of another drug. Understanding drug interactions is vital to understanding psychopharmacology as well as psychotherapeutics (the use of drugs to treat psychological disorders). First, it is important to state that some drug interactions are "good" and some are "bad." Interactions are beneficial when two drugs used together achieve therapeutic benefit when a single drug alone is insufficient. For example, combining two drugs with antidepressant properties may afford relief from depression that was unattainable with either drug alone. On the other hand, drug interaction can be detrimental. Detrimental actions can have either a pharmacokinetic or a pharmacodynamic basis.

Chapter 1 explained how certain drugs might either increase or decrease the rate of hepatic metabolism of other drugs and how this interaction affected the plasma levels of other drugs metabolized by the same enzymes. For example, carbamazepine increases the rate of metabolism of certain other medicines, reducing the blood concentration of the second drug and reducing its effectiveness. Conversely, valproic acid can inhibit the metabolism of other drugs, such as lamotrigine, increasing its blood concentrations and potentially increasing its toxicity or side effects.

In a pharmacodynamic interaction, drugs can interact through an adverse *additive mechanism,* where the effects of one drug potentiate the side effects of a second drug. For example, alcohol taken after a benzodiazepine tranquilizer has been ingested or after smoking marijuana increases sedation and loss of coordination. This action may have little consequence if the doses of each drug are low, but higher doses of either or both drugs can be dangerous both to the user and to others. Even though a person may normally be able to ingest a limited amount of alcohol and still drive a car without significant loss of control or coordination, the concurrent use of tranquilizers or marijuana may profoundly impair driving performance, endangering the driver, passengers, and other motorists. Ramaekers et al. (2000) document the adverse interaction between alcohol and marijuana on driving performance.

Drug Toxicity

All drugs can produce harmful effects as well as beneficial ones. Unwanted effects fall into one of two categories:

1. Effects that are related to the principal and predictable pharmacological actions of a drug (for example, the sedation caused by drinking alcohol or the dry mouth experienced while taking certain antidepressants)

2. Effects that are unrelated to the expected actions of a drug (for example, a severe allergic reaction to a drug)

It is important to categorize harmful effects of drugs in terms of their severity and to distinguish between effects that cause a temporary inconvenience or discomfort and effects that can lead to organ damage, permanent disability, or even death.

Most drugs exert effects on several different body functions. To achieve the desired therapeutic effect or effects, some side effects often must be tolerated. Toleration is possible if the side effects are minor, but if they are more serious, they may be a limiting factor in the use of the drug. The distinction between therapeutic effects and side effects is relative and depends on the purpose for which the drug is administered: one person's side effect may be another person's therapeutic effect. For example, in one patient receiving morphine for its pain-relieving properties, the intestinal constipation that morphine induces may be an undesirable side effect that must be tolerated. For a second patient, however, morphine may be used to treat severe diarrhea, in which case the constipation induced is the desired therapeutic effect and relief of pain is a side effect.

In addition to side effects that are merely irritating, some drugs may cause reactions that are very serious, including serious allergies, blood disorders, liver or kidney toxicity, or abnormalities in fetal development. Fortunately, the incidence of serious toxic effects is quite low. As specific drugs are discussed in later chapters, both side effects and more serious toxicities are presented for each drug.

Allergies to drugs may take many forms, from mild skin rashes to fatal shock. Allergies differ from normal side effects, which can often be eliminated or at least made tolerable by a simple reduction in dosage. However, a reduction in the dose of a drug may have no effect on a drug allergy because exposure to any amount of the drug can be hazardous and possibly catastrophic for the patient.

Damage to the liver and kidneys results from the role of these organs in concentrating, metabolizing, and excreting toxic drugs. Examples of drug-induced liver damage include damage caused by alcohol and damage caused by certain of the inhalants of abuse (Chapter 4). Some of the major tranquilizers (for example, the phenothiazines) may induce jaundice by increasing the viscosity of bile in the liver (Chapter 9).

The toxicity to a fetus of both socially abused and some therapeutic drugs should be mentioned. Data quite clearly show the adverse effects of nicotine and ethyl alcohol on the fetus. Similarly, the effects of cocaine and other stimulant drug abuse on the fetus have received much attention. These drugs are responsible for a majority of preventable fetal toxicities and are some of the major health hazards in the country today.

Placebo Effects

As stated by Nies (2001):

> The net effect of drug therapy is the sum of the pharmacological effects of the drug and the nonspecific placebo effects associated with the therapeutic effort. Although identified specifically with

administration of an inert substance in the guise of medication, placebo effects are associated with the taking of any drug, active or inert. (p. 57)

About 1950, so-called *double-blind, randomized, controlled clinical trials* of medications became the gold standard for studying drug effects in humans. Controlled trials were intended to remove the bias, expectations, and even fraud associated with clinical studies in which uncontrolled variables led to much subjective and presumably biased outcomes (Lakoff, 2002). This book refers throughout to the results obtained from recent drug trials that continue to use the double-blind, randomized, placebo-controlled trial design.

Recently, however, the placebo effect of drugs has come under scrutiny, especially in trials of antidepressant medication. Indeed, recent papers confirm that placebo effects, even in double-blind, randomized, controlled trials, are significant and are increasing at a rate of about 7 percent per decade (Figure 2.14). As summarized by Walsh and coworkers (2002), in the analysis of double-blind, randomized,

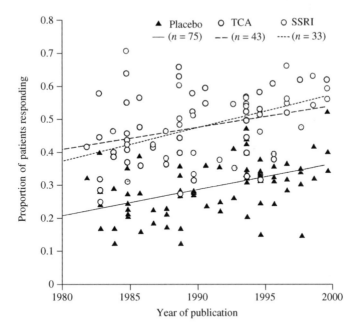

FIGURE 2.14 Proportion of patients assigned to placebo, tricyclic antidepressants (TCAs), and selective serotonin reuptake inhibitor antidepressants (SSRIs) who showed a 50 percent or greater improvement in their depression as measured by the Hamilton Rating Scale for Depression Score by the year of publication of results of clinical trials. [From Walsh et al. (2002), p. 1843.]

controlled clinical trials of drugs used to treat depression, about 28 percent of patients treated with placebo respond positively and significantly. This compares with 50 percent of patients who respond similarly when treated with active medication, illustrating that placebo effects contribute significantly (perhaps half) to the clinical response.

What then is a placebo? Commonly it is a sugar pill (a dummy pill), although this is only one type of placebo responsible for beneficial effects. Hrobjartsson and Gotzsche (2001) state, "A placebo could be pharmacological (e.g., a tablet), physical (e.g., a manipulation), or psychological (e.g., a conversation)" (p. 1594). It may also be as simple as altering the therapeutic environment (Mayberg et al., 2002). Obviously then, placebo is active treatment, whether it is administration of a sugar pill, manipulating or touching a patient, or talking to or otherwise counseling a patient. In clinical trials of medication, placebo treatment should be controlled, and often it is not. For example, in a recent study of placebo effects on brain function in depressed people, patients who received placebo pills also received "brief sessions of supportive psychotherapy with a research nurse," presumably to avoid relapse to depression when active medication was withheld (Leuchter et al., 2002, p.123).

Placebos seem to work best on symptoms or diseases that vary (wax and wane) over time. Perhaps the most prominent examples are major depression and chronic pain. The placebo action is independent of any chemical property of the drug; it arises largely because of what the patient or the prescriber expects or desires or from the complex interactions associated with the therapeutic alliance. A placebo response may result from either the patient's or the physician's mental set or from the entire environmental context in which the drug is taken. Placebos can therapeutically empower patients to stimulate their psychophysiological self-regulation abilities.

Certainly, both prescriber and patient expectations of drug efficacy have a major influence on the placebo response to medication. Expectations guide the search for information and organize information obtained from the search. Both the patient and the prescriber may have expectations regarding anticipated benefits possibly resulting from drug administration. In therapeutics, expectations of improvement at the start of drug therapy can predict subsequent therapeutic effectiveness and response. Perhaps even the "feeling" of side effects serves to verify the expectation that the drug is "working." Lakoff (2002) and Faries and coworkers (2001) describe a double-blind placebo run-in period as perhaps the best way to reduce the placebo effect in drug trials. Placebo pills are administered, unbeknownst to either the doctor or the patient, for a week and then patients who responded positively are eliminated from the trial. In studies using a single-blind run-in period (the doctor knew a placebo was being given), only 5 percent of subjects exhibited a placebo response and were eliminated from the study, compared to 28 percent of patients responding positively to placebo when neither the doctor nor the patient knew that only placebo was being given. Thus, the double-blind run-in before drug treatment may be a better model for reducing placebo response rates. Unfortunately, this technique has not been used in reported drug trials to date (it is a new model). It may become a model for the future. At least, however, these results demonstrate that the health care practitioner is an important contributor to the placebo response. It is not just inherent in the patient.

STUDY QUESTIONS

1. What is meant by the term *pharmacodynamics?*

2. What is a receptor? What is a drug receptor?

3. Discuss the structure of a drug receptor.

4. Distinguish between *agonist* and *antagonist* as they relate to drug-receptor interactions.

5. Compare and contrast a presynaptic receptor and a postsynaptic receptor.

6. List the four types of receptors discussed in this chapter.

7. Discuss drug-receptor specificity. Can a drug ever be more specific for a receptor than is the endogenous neurotransmitter? Explain.

8. What is meant by a dose-response relationship? Draw a hypothetical example of a dose-response relationship.

9. Discuss the factors that influence the time course of drug action in the body.

10. Discuss how two drugs might interact with each other in the body.

11. Which factors contribute to the intensity of drug effects?

12. What are two important functions of neuronal receptors? How do drugs affect receptors?

13. Discuss the placebo response as it relates to drug trials and to therapeutic response and the therapeutic alliance between patient and health care worker.

REFERENCES

Armstrong, N., et al. (2006). "Measurement of Conformational Changes Accompanying Desensitization in an Ionotropic Glutamate Receptor." *Cell* 127: 85–97.

Faries, D. E., et al. (2001). "The Double Blind Variable Placebo Lead-In Period: Results from Two Antidepressant Clinical Trials." *Journal of Clinical Psychopharmacology* 21: 561–568.

Feldman, R. S., J. S. Meyer, and L. F. Quenzer (1997). *Principles of Neuropsychopharmacology.* Sunderland, MA: Sinauer.

Gouaux, E., and R. MacKinnon. (2005). "Principles of Selective Ion Transport in Channels and Pumps." *Science* 310: 1461–1465.

Hrobjartsson, A., and P. C. Gotzsche (2001). "Is the Placebo Powerless? An Analysis of Clinical Trials Comparing Placebo with No Treatment." *New England Journal of Medicine* 344: 1594–1602.

Jurrlink, D. N., et al. (2003). "Drug-Drug Interactions Among Elderly Patients Hospitalized for Drug Toxicity." *Journal of the American Medical Association* 289: 1652–1658.

Khatib, S. M. al-, et al. (2003). "What Clinicians Should Know About the QT Interval." *Journal of the American Medical Association* 289: 2120–2127.

Lakoff, A. (2002). "The Mousetrap: Managing the Placebo Effect in Antidepressant Trials." *Molecular Interventions 2:* 72–76.

Leuchter, A. F., et al. (2002). "Changes in Brain Function of Depressed Subjects During Treatment with Placebo." *American Journal of Psychiatry* 159: 122–129.

Mayberg, H. S., et al. (2002). "The Functional Neuroanatomy of the Placebo Effect." *American Journal of Psychiatry* 159: 728–737.

Nies, A. S. (2001). "Principles of Therapeutics." In J. G. Hardman, L. E. Limbird, and A. G. Gilman, eds., *Goodman and Gilman's The Pharmacological Basis of Therapeutics,* 10th ed. (pp. 45–66). New York: McGraw-Hill.

Ramaekers, J. G. (2000). "Marijuana, Alcohol, and Actual Driving Performance." *Human Psychopharmacology* 15: 551–558.

Walsh, B. T., et al. (2002). "Placebo Response in Studies of Major Depression: Variable, Substantial, and Growing." *Journal of the American Medical Association* 287: 1840–1847.

Yernool, D., et al. (2004). "Structure of a Glutamate Transporter Homologue from *Pyrococcus horikoshii.*" *Nature* 431: 811–818.

Chapter 3

The Neuron, Synaptic Transmission, and Neurotransmitters

All our thoughts, actions, memories, and behaviors result from biochemical interactions that take place in and between *neurons*. Drugs that affect these processes are, in general, called *psychoactive drugs*. In essence, psychoactive drugs are chemicals that alter (mimic, potentiate, disrupt, or inhibit) the normal neuronal processes associated with neuronal function or communication between neurons. To understand the actions of psychoactive drugs, therefore, it is necessary to have some idea of what a neuron is and how neurons interact with each other.

Overall Organization of the Brain

The human brain consists of perhaps 90 billion individual neurons located in the skull and the spinal canal. The *spinal cord* extends from the lower end of the medulla to the sacrum. The spinal cord consists of neurons and fiber tracts involved in the following:

- Carrying sensory information from the skin, muscles, joints, and internal body organs to the brain
- Organizing and modulating the motor outflow to the muscles (to produce coordinated muscle responses)

- Modulating sensory input (including pain impulses)
- Providing autonomic (involuntary) control of vital body functions

The lower part of the brain, attached to the upper part of the spinal cord, is the *brain stem* (Figure 3.1). It is divided into three parts: the *medulla*, the *pons*, and the *midbrain*. All impulses that are conducted in either direction between the spinal cord and the brain pass through the brain stem, which is also important in the regulation of vital body functions, such as respiration, blood pressure, heart rate, gastrointestinal functioning, and the states of sleep and wakefulness. The brain stem is also involved in behavioral alerting, attention, and arousal responses. Depressant drugs, such as the barbiturates (Chapter 5), depress the brain-stem activating system; this action probably underlies much of their hypnotic action.

Behind the brain stem is a large, bulbous structure—the *cerebellum*. A highly convoluted structure, the cerebellum is connected to the brain stem by large fiber tracts. The cerebellum is necessary for the proper integration of movement and posture. Drunkenness, which is

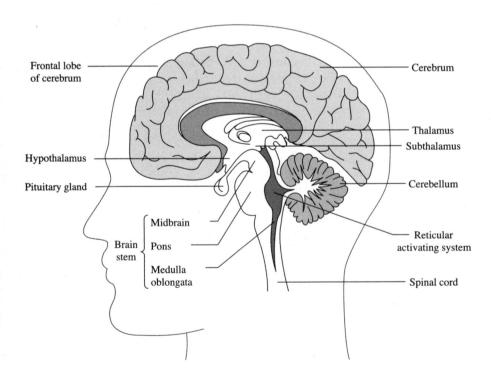

FIGURE 3.1 Midline section of the brain illustrating several structures lying below the cerebral cortex.

characterized by ataxia (loss of coordination and balance, staggering, and other deficits), appears to be caused largely by an alcohol-induced depression of cerebellar function.

The area immediately above the brain stem and covered by the cerebral hemispheres is the *diencephalon*. This area includes the hypothalamus, pituitary gland, various fiber tracts (bundles of axons that travel as a group from one area to another), subthalamus, and thalamus. Three of these areas are discussed here: the subthalamus, the hypothalamus, and the limbic system.

The *subthalamus* is a small area underneath the thalamus and above the midbrain. It contains a variety of small structures that, together with the basal ganglia, constitute one of our motor systems, the *extrapyramidal system*. Patients who have Parkinson's disease (Chapter 11) have a deficiency of the neurotransmitter dopamine in the terminals of their nerve axons, which originate in cell bodies in the substantia nigra (one of the subthalamic structures).

The *hypothalamus* is a collection of neurons in the lower portion of the brain near the junction of the midbrain and the thalamus. It is located near the base of the skull, just above the pituitary gland (the function of which it largely modulates). The hypothalamus is the principal center in the brain responsible for the integration of our entire autonomic (involuntary or vegetative) nervous system. Thus, it helps control such vegetative functions as eating, drinking, sleeping, regulation of body temperature, sexual behavior, blood pressure, emotion, and water balance. In addition, the hypothalamus closely controls hormonal output of the pituitary gland. Neurons in the hypothalamus produce substances called *releasing factors*, which travel to the nearby pituitary gland, inducing the secretion of hormones that regulate fertility in females and sperm formation in males. The hypothalamus is a site of action for many psychoactive drugs, either a site for the primary action of the drug or a site responsible for side effects associated with the use of a drug.

Closely associated with the hypothalamus is the *limbic system*, the major components of which are the *amygdala* and the *hippocampus*. These structures integrate memory (hippocampus), emotion (amygdala), and reward with behavioral motor, and autonomic functions. Because the limbic system and the hypothalamus interact to regulate emotion and emotional expression, these structures are logical sites for the study of psychoactive drugs that alter mood, affect, emotion, or responses to emotional experiences.

The hypothalamic and limbic areas contain structures important in psychopharmacology and the abuse potential of drugs. Included here are the dopamine-rich reward centers that involve the *ventral tegmental area*, the *median forebrain bundle*, and the *nucleus accumbens*. Throughout this text, this reward system is discussed as a site of the behavior-reinforcing action of psychoactive drugs that are subject to compulsive abuse.

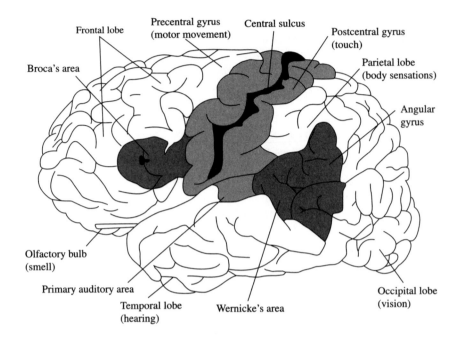

Frontal lobe
Precentral gyrus
(motor movement)
Central sulcus
Postcentral gyrus
(touch)
Broca's area
Parietal lobe
(body sensations)
Angular gyrus
Olfactory bulb
(smell)
Primary auditory area
Temporal lobe
(hearing)
Wernicke's area
Occipital lobe
(vision)

FIGURE 3.2 Surface structure of the brain showing major areas of the cerebral cortex.

Almost completely covering the brain stem and the diencephalon is the *cerebrum*. In humans the cerebrum is the largest part of the brain. It is separated into two distinct hemispheres, left and right, with numerous fiber tracts connecting the two. Because skull size is limited and the cerebrum is so large, the outer layer of the cerebrum, the *cerebral cortex*, is deeply convoluted and fissured. Like other parts of the brain, the cerebral cortex is divided by function; it contains centers for vision, hearing, speech, sensory perception, and emotion. The various regions of the cerebral cortex can be classified in several ways, among them, the type of function or sensation that is processed. Figure 3.2 illustrates some of this categorization.

The Neuron

The neuron is the basic component of the central nervous system (CNS), and each neuron shares common structural and functional characteristics (Figure 3.3). A typical neuron has a *soma* (cell body), which contains the nucleus (within which is the genetic material of the cell). Extending from the soma in one direction are many short fibers, called *dendrites* (hundreds of widely branched extensions), that receive input from other neurons through *receptors* located on the dendritic

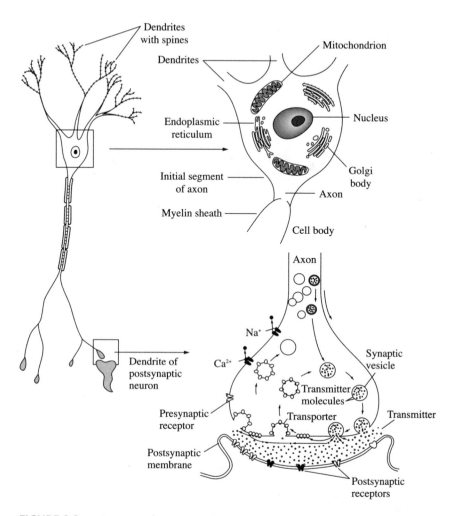

FIGURE 3.3 Major parts of a neuron. The genetic material (DNA) is contained in the nucleus, and several specialized organelles are present in the cytoplasm, the material of the cell outside the nucleus. The cell is covered by a thin wall, or membrane. Mitochondria are present in the cell body, the fibers, and the terminals. The terminals also contain small, round vesicles that contain neurotransmitter chemicals. Synaptic connections from the fibers of other neurons cover the cell body and dendrites. In many neurons the synapses on dendrites can be seen as little spines. The axon itself has no synapses on it except sometimes at its synaptic terminals, where other neuron axon terminals may form synapses on synapses.

membrane. On receipt of a signal from another cell, current is generated and travels down the dendrite to the soma. Extending in another direction from the soma is a single elongated process called an *axon*, which varies in length from as short as a few millimeters to as long as a meter (meter-length examples are the axons that run from the motor neurons of the spinal cord out to the muscles that they innervate). The axon, in essence, transmits electrical activity (in the form of *action potentials*) from the soma to other neurons or to muscles, organs, or glands of the body. Normally, the axon conducts impulses in only one direction—from the soma down the axon to a specialized structure that, together with one or more dendrites from another neuron, forms a complex microspace called *a synapse* (Figure 3.4).

A given neuron in the brain may receive several thousand synaptic connections from other neurons. Hence if the human brain has 10^{11} neurons, then it has at least 10^{14} (or many trillions of) synapses (Hyman, 2005). The number of possible different combinations of synaptic connections among the neurons in a single human brain is larger than the total number of atomic particles that make up the known universe. Hence the diversity of the interconnections in a human brain seems almost without limit.

It was once thought that the brain has the maximal number of neurons at birth; once a neuron dies, it is not replaced. This concept has been debunked as we now realize that new neurons form every day (a process called *neurogenesis*) and existing neurons need to be maintained in a state of health (Kempermann et al., 2004; Schaffer and

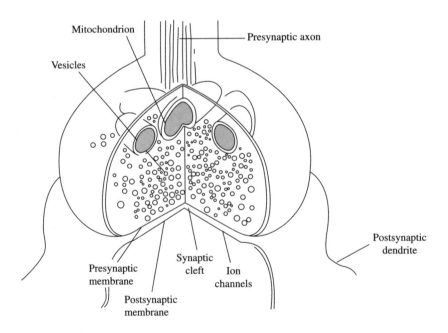

FIGURE 3.4 Three-dimensional drawing of a synapse. The axon terminal is the top knoblike structure, and the spine of the receiving neuron is the bottom one. Note the space (synaptic cleft) between the presynaptic terminal membrane and the postsynaptic cell membrane.

Gage, 2004). All during our lifetime, the number and pattern of synaptic connections continue to develop, and the connections are continually being reshaped, resynthesized, and "sculpted" by experience. The synaptic connections appear to form the anatomical basis of memory and the maintenance of a normal state of mood (Sutton and Schuman, 2006; Ashraf and Kunes, 2006). This continual reshaping and remodeling of neurons is associated with the process of synaptic plasticity (Thomas and Davies, 2005). The synaptic contacts between neurons are continually being reshaped and the axon terminals as well as the dendrites are continually reforming new synaptic connections while losing old ones. This remodeling probably begins even before birth and continues all our lives. (The relationship between neuronal "health" and depression is discussed in Chapter 7.)

A synapse is the point of functional contact between an axon terminal and another cell (see Figure 3.4). A synapse consists of a minute space (the *synaptic cleft*) between the presynaptic membrane (which is the axon terminal) of one neuron and the postsynaptic membrane of the receiving neuron. The presynaptic terminal contains numerous structural elements, the most important of which (for our purposes) are the small synaptic vesicles, each of which contains several thousand molecules of neurotransmitter chemical (the *first messenger*) that transmits information from one neuron to another). These vesicles store the transmitter, which is available for release (Figure 3.5). Through a process called *exocytosis* and under the influence of calcium ions, vesicles fuse with the presynaptic membrane and molecules of transmitter are released into the synaptic cleft. The transmitter substance diffuses across the synaptic cleft and attaches to various types of receptors on the postsynaptic membrane of the next neuron, transmitting information chemically from one neuron to another. The neurons do not physically touch each other; synaptic transmission is a chemical rather than an electrical process.

The process of synaptic transmission takes a remarkably short time. In the case of *ion channel receptors,* the entire process may occur over a time span as short as a millisecond for transmitter release (from presynaptic vesicles), diffusion (across the cleft), receptor attachment, channel opening, and ion influx. *G protein-coupled receptors* are slow-response receptors—they produce activation responses that may last from hundreds of milliseconds to perhaps many seconds. These responses are generally thought to be modulatory; the neurotransmitter either dampens or enhances intracellular enzymatic functions. Through release of the intracellular *second messenger* (Chapter 2), slow-response receptors trigger the cell's internal machinery, leading to effects as diverse as modulation of ion channel activity to protein transcription from genetic material (a process described later as being involved in mechanisms of long-term memory formation in glutamate-releasing neurons).

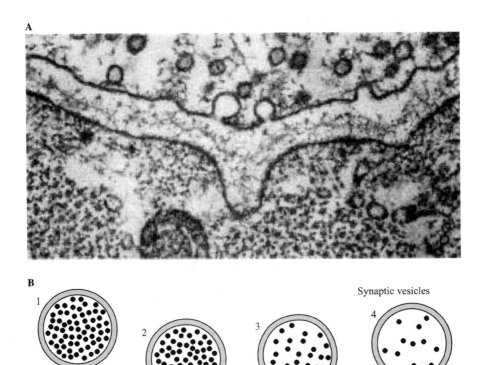

FIGURE 3.5 A. Photomicrograph of a synapse in action, taken with the electron microscope. Vesicles are releasing their transmitter chemical into the synaptic cleft. **B.** Schematic of the process.

Termination of Synaptic Transmission

As discussed, the arrival of an action potential at the synapse induces release of a neurotransmitter into the synaptic cleft, and the transmitter then reversibly binds to its receptors. Certain mechanisms must be present to get rid of neurotransmitter; otherwise transmitter would remain in the synaptic cleft and continually bind to the postsynaptic receptors. Every synapse is able to accomplish the removal of transmitter from the synaptic cleft. In most cases, transmitter removal occurs through either of three mechanisms:

1. An enzyme present in the synaptic cleft breaks down any neuro-transmitter lingering within the synapse.

2. The transmitter is taken back into the presynaptic cell through the 12-helix reuptake transporter receptor present on the presynaptic membrane (see Figure 2.8).

3. In the case of glutamate neurotransmission, after release the gluta-mate is taken up into an adjacent glial cell, reprocessed, and re-turned to the presynaptic nerve terminal.

Examples of neurotransmitters removed by the second mechanism (presynaptic reuptake) include the following:

• Norepinephrine, presynaptic reuptake of which is blocked by the *tri-cyclic antidepressants* and *atomoxetine* (Strattera)

• Serotonin, presynaptic reuptake of which is blocked by the *selective serotonin reuptake inhibitor* (SSRI) *antidepressants*

• Dopamine, presynaptic reuptake of which is blocked by *bupropion* (Wellbutrin) and by *cocaine*

These neurotransmitters will be described in this book. In the case of the neurotransmitter acetylcholine, the enzyme *acetylcholine esterase* breaks down the transmitter into acetate and choline, which are then taken up into the nerve terminal and the acetylcholine resynthesized.

Receptor Specificity

It would be nice if there were a single receptor type for each specific neurotransmitter. In actuality, virtually every transmitter binds to sev-eral distinct receptor subtypes. For example, norepinephrine, serotonin, and dopamine bind to (have affinity for) multiple postsynaptic recep-tors as well as their specific presynaptic transporter. On the postsynap-tic membrane, a neurotransmitter may bind to both fast-response (ion channel) receptors and slow-response (G protein-coupled) receptors. A transmitter may bind to different types of G protein-coupled receptors, each initiating different intracellular processes. For example, for sero-tonin receptors, at least 15 different subtypes of receptors have been de-scribed. All this leads to immense opportunity for the development of drugs with incredible specificity—for example, for blocking one specific subtype of postsynaptic serotonin receptor, reducing or eliminating the side effects that limit the clinical usefulness of existing psychotherapeu-tic agents. Table 3.1 lists a few of the commonly recognized neurotrans-mitters, some of the receptor subtypes that have been identified, and some of the brain functions thought to be under the control of each transmitter. Besides these substances, many lipids and proteins (pep-tides) have also been implicated in synaptic transmission (Hyman, 2005). Several will be discussed in this text.

TABLE 3.1 Selected neurotransmitters in the CNS

Neurotransmitter	Receptors	Function
Acetylcholine (ACh)	Muscarinic (M_1 through M_5) Nicotinic (N_N and N_M)	Memory function, sensory processing, motor coordination, neuromuscular junction neurotransmission, and autonomic nervous system
Norepinephrine (NE)	Alpha$_1$ and alpha$_2$; beta$_1$, beta$_2$, and beta$_3$	CNS sensory processing, cerebellar function, sleep, mood, learning, memory, anxiety, and sympathetic nervous system
Dopamine (DA)	D_1 through D_5 in two families designated D_1 and D_2	Motor regulation, reinforcement, olfaction, mood, concentration, hormone control, and hypoxic drive
Serotonin (5-HT)	Currently 18 receptors have been identified and broken into 8 families designated 5-HT$_1$ through 5-HT$_8$	Emotional processing, mood, appetite, sleep, pain processing, hallucinations, and reflex regulation
Glutamate (Glu)	NMDA, non-NMDA, and metabotropic	Long-term potentiation, memory, major excitatory function within the CNS and PNS
Gamma amino-butyric acid (GABA)	GABA$_A$ and GABA$_B$	Major inhibitory neurotransmitter in the CNS
Histamine (H)	H_1 and H_2	Sleep, sedation, and temperature regulation
Glycine (Gly)		Major inhibitory function within the spinal cord

From P. M. Carvey, *Drug Action in the Central Nervous System* (Oxford: Oxford University Press, 1988), p. 7.

The Soma

Present in all cells of the body (except red blood cells), the soma has a *nucleus* that contains the basic genetic material (the DNA) for the cell (see Figure 3.3). Because the neuron is a specialized type of cell, its DNA expresses a subset of genes that encode the special structural and enzymatic proteins that endow the neuron with its size, shape, location, and other functional characteristics (Cooper et al., 2003). Also located in the soma are the *mitochondria*, which provide the biological energy for the neuron. This energy, in the form of *adenosine triphosphate* (ATP), is made available for all the various chemical reactions carried out in the cell (such as neurotransmitter synthesis, storage, release, and reuptake).

In response to stimuli (perhaps initiated by a second-messenger action), the DNA in the nucleus is transcribed into a second similar molecular form as strands of ribonucleic acid (RNA), which is then "edited" by several rapid steps and exported from the nucleus to the cytoplasm of the soma. The edited RNA is called *messenger RNA*, and this nuclear material is then translated from the nucleic acid code of the RNA into the amino acid sequence of the protein that is to be expressed (Figure 3.6).

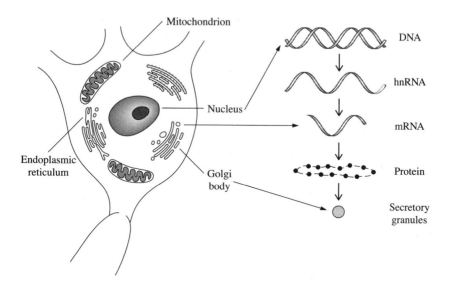

FIGURE 3.6 Formation of transmitter substances and "packaging" in vesicles from genetic material in the nucleus. DNA-encoded information is transcribed in the nucleus to a primary transcript form (hnRNA), which is edited and exported from the nucleus to the cytoplasm as messenger RNA (mRNA). The information is then translated from the genetic nucleic acid code of RNA into the amino acid sequence of the protein that is to be expressed. Within the Golgi body portion of the endoplasmic reticulum, the transmitter is packaged into secretory organelles for transport down the axon to the neuron terminals.

Expression, or translation, occurs on the *endoplasmic reticulum,* where the neurotransmitters are synthesized and then "packaged" into vesicles that are then transported in specialized *microtubules* down the axon to the synaptic terminals, where they await release (Figure 3.7). Even the presynaptic receptors (such as the dopamine transporter) are made in the soma and carried down the axon, embedding in the cell membrane where they exert their synaptic functions.

Specific Neurotransmitters

Neurons release specific chemical substances from their presynaptic nerve terminals, and it is the interaction between psychoactive drugs and these chemicals (and the receptors on which they act) that underlies the actions of the drugs. Therefore, it is important to introduce these chemicals as neurotransmitters. The earliest chemicals identified as CNS neurotransmitters were acetylcholine and norepinephrine, largely because of their established roles in the peripheral nervous system. In the 1960s, serotonin, epinephrine, and dopamine were added. In the 1970s, gamma aminobutyric acid (GABA), glycine, glutamate, and certain neuropeptides (such as the endorphins) were identified. In the late 1980s, the lipid amide anandamide was identified as the endogenous transmitter for the tetrahydrocannabinol receptor. Today, dozens (perhaps hundreds) of neurotransmitters are recognized (Snyder, 2002).

Acetylcholine

Acetylcholine (ACh) was identified as a transmitter chemical first in the peripheral nervous system and later in brain tissue. Deficiencies in acetylcholine-secreting neurons have classically been associated with the dysfunctions seen in Alzheimer's disease. Certainly drugs that either potentiate or inhibit the central action of acetylcholine exert profound effects on memory. For example, scopolamine is a psychedelic drug (Chapter 18) that blocks central cholinergic receptors and as a result produces amnesia. Conversely, drugs that increase the amount of acetylcholine in the brain appear to improve memory function and are used to delay the onset of Alzheimer's disease (Chapter 11).

ACh is synthesized in a one-step reaction from two precursors (choline and acetyl-CoA) and then is stored within synaptic vesicles for later release. This reaction and the dynamics of ACh release, metabolism, and resynthesis are shown in Figure 3.8. Like other neurotransmitters, ACh is released into the synaptic cleft, rapidly diffuses across the cleft, and reversibly binds to postsynaptic receptors. Once ACh has exerted its effect on postsynaptic receptors, its action is terminated by *acetylcholine esterase* (AChE).

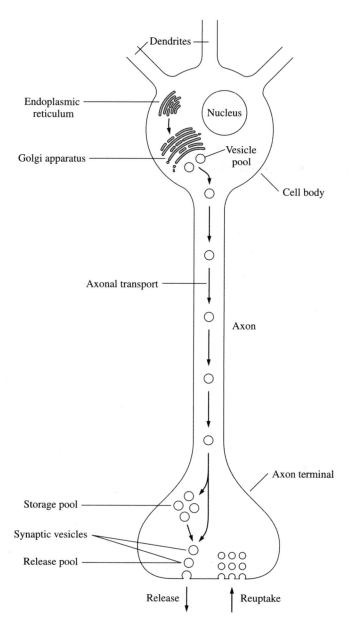

FIGURE 3.7 Axon transport. Chemicals travel from the cell body to the terminals. It is believed that they move along the axon in microtubules that fill the axon.

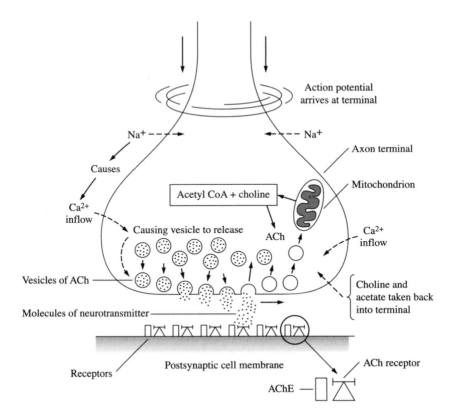

FIGURE 3.8 Chemical synapse. Acetylcholine (ACh) is used as the example. It is made in the axon terminal from acetyl coenzyme A (acetyl CoA) and choline, stored in vesicles, and released. When the action potential arrives at the terminal, closed calcium channels in the terminal are opened and Ca^{2+} rushes into the terminal, triggering vesicles to fuse with the membrane and release ACh molecules into the synaptic cleft. They attach to ACh receptors on the postsynaptic membrane and trigger the opening of Na^+ channels. ACh is immediately broken down at the receptors by acetylcholine esterase (AChE) into choline and acetate, which are taken back up by the terminal and reused.

The enzymatic reaction that degrades ACh is important not only in the treatment of Alzheimer's disease but in agriculture and in the military. Drugs that inhibit the action of AChE are referred to as *AChE inhibitors* and include both "reversible" AChE inhibitors and "irreversible" AChE inhibitors. *Irreversible AChE inhibitors* form a permanent covalent bond with the enzyme and totally inhibit enzyme function. Usually administered in "toxic" doses, the result is usually fatal. Some of these toxic drugs (such as *malathion* and *parathion)* are exploited in gardening and agriculture as insecticides because they kill insects on contact. Other irreversible AChe inhibitors (such as *Sarin* and *Soman*) have been used in the military as lethal nerve gases.

Less toxic and shorter acting are the *reversible AChE inhibitors,* used to more modestly increase ACh levels in the brain. They increase ACh levels and clinically are used as cognitive enhancers, delaying the decline in cognitive function in patients with Alzheimer's disease. Individual agents are discussed in Chapter 11.

ACh is distributed widely in the brain (Figure 3.9). The cell bodies of cholinergic neurons in the brain lie in two closely related regions. One involves the *septal nuclei* and the *nucleus basalis.* The axons of these neurons project to forebrain regions, particularly the hippocampus and cerebral cortex. The second originates in the midbrain region and projects anteriorly to the thalamus, basal ganglia, and diencephalon and posteriorly to the reticular formation, pons, cerebellum, and cranial nerve nuclei. In addition to its generally agreed-on role in learning and memory, the diffuse distribution of ACh is consistent with suggestions that ACh is involved in circuits

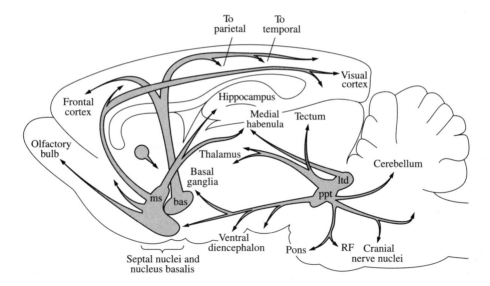

FIGURE 3.9 Representation of the cholinergic systems in the rat brain. As illustrated, central cholinergic neurons exhibit two basic organizational schemata: (1) local circuit cells (those that morphologically are arrayed wholly within the neural structure in which they are found) exemplified by the interneurons of the caudate-putamen nucleus; (2) projection neurons (those that connect two or more different regions). Of the cholinergic projection neurons that interconnect central structures, two major subconstellations have been identified: (1) the forebrain cholinergic complex composed of neurons in the medial septal nucleus (ms) and nucleus basalis (bas) and projecting to the entire nonstriatal telencephalon; (2) the pontomesencephalotegmental cholinergic complex, composed of cells in the pendunculopontine (ppt) and laterodorsal (ltd) tegmental nuclei and projecting ascendingly to the thalamus and other diencephalic loci and descendingly to the pontine and medullary reticular formation (RF), cerebellum, and cranial nerve nuclei.

that modulate sensory reception; in mechanisms related to behavioral arousal, attention, energy conservation, and mood, and in REM activity during sleep.

Catecholamine Neurotransmitters: Dopamine and Norepinephrine

The term *catecholamine* refers to compounds that contain a catechol nucleus (a benzene ring with two attached hydroxyl groups) to which is attached an amine group (Figure 3.10). In the CNS, the term usually refers to the transmitters *dopamine* (DA) and *norepinephrine* (NE). In the peripheral nervous system, *epinephrine* ("adrenaline") is a third catecholamine transmitter. In the brain, a large number of psychoactive drugs (both licit and illicit, therapeutic and abused) exert their effects by altering the synaptic action of NE and DA.

The chemical synthesis of DA is illustrated in Figure 3.10. NE is produced by an additional step that involves oxidation of the proximal carbon of the ethyl side chain. Biosynthesis of the catecholamines begins with the amino acid tyrosine and is a complicated process involving genetic and enzymatic regulation. Following synthesis, the transmitter is stored in vesicles for release into the synaptic space. This release is controlled by *presynaptic receptors* (autoreceptors) that serve as a negative feedback mechanism. When stimulated by transmitter, these receptors reduce the synthesis and release of transmitter. Thus, when large amounts of transmitter are present in the synaptic cleft, excess transmitter acts on the autoreceptors to reduce further production and release. Conversely, if an autoreceptor is blocked by an antagonist (for example, mirtazepine; Chapter 7), synthesis and release of transmitter is increased.

Following release, NE and DA attach to postsynaptic receptors. As discussed earlier, inactivation in the synaptic cleft occurs primarily by reuptake of the transmitter from the synaptic cleft into the presynaptic nerve terminal. Within the nerve terminal, catecholamines can be inactivated by enzymes, such as monoamine oxidase (MAO). The products of inactivation are further metabolized and eliminated from the body through the urine. The class of antidepressants referred to as MAO inhibitors (Chapter 7) acts by inhibiting MAO, thereby increasing the amounts of DA and NE available for synaptic release.

Postsynaptic Catecholamine Receptors.   Unlike transmitters such as ACh and GABA, which affect ion channels, postsynaptic binding of DA or NE triggers a sequence of chemical events in the postsynaptic cell membrane, eventually affecting either ion channels or intracellular metabolic activity. It is likely that the slow onset of action of antidepressant drugs (several weeks to achieve a therapeutic effect) follows the down regulation of postsynaptic catecholamine receptors as an adaptation to the presence of increased amounts of transmitter present

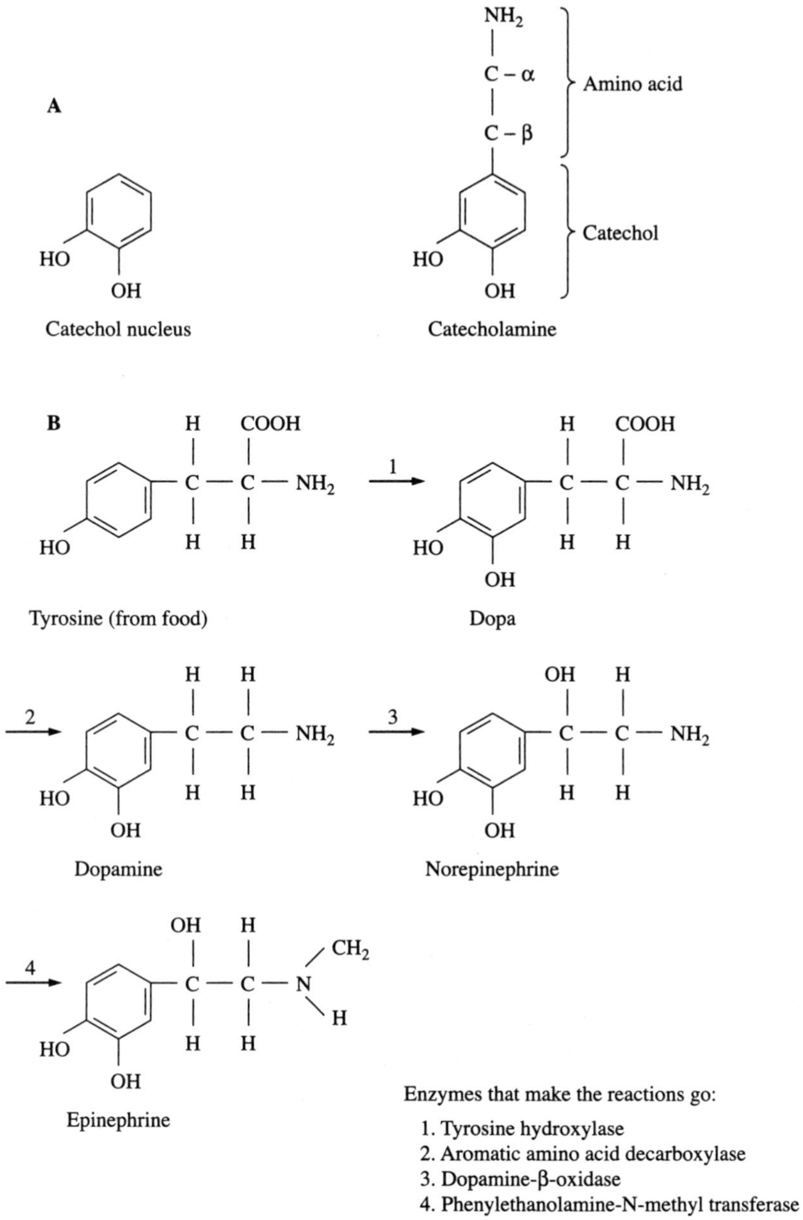
A
Amino acid
Catechol
Catechol nucleus
Catecholamine
B
Tyrosine (from food)
Dopa
Dopamine
Norepinephrine
Epinephrine
Enzymes that make the reactions go:
1. Tyrosine hydroxylase
2. Aromatic amino acid decarboxylase
3. Dopamine-β-oxidase
4. Phenylethanolamine-N-methyl transferase

FIGURE 3.10 A. Catechol and catecholamine structure. All catecholamines share the catechol nucleus, a benzene ring with two adjacent hydroxyl (OH) groups. **B.** Structures and synthesis of the catecholamines. Tyrosine, an amino acid found in foods, is converted into dopa, then into dopamine, next into norepinephrine, and finally (in the peripheral nervous system) into epinephrine, depending on which enzymes (1–4) are present in the cell.

in the synaptic cleft (because the reuptake elimination of the transmitter was blocked by the drug).

Each catecholamine transmitter exerts effects on a number of different postsynaptic receptors. Norepinephrine and epinephrine exert effects at two primary types of receptors (alpha and beta), each of which has at least two subtypes. Dopamine exerts postsynaptic effects on at least six receptors, divided into two families (D_1 and D_2). Confusingly, D_1 receptors are subdivided into two subtypes—D_1 and D_5—and D_2 receptors into four subtypes—D_{2A}, D_{2B}, D_3, and D_4. Postsynaptic dopamine receptors of the D_2 family are responsible for at least part of the antipsychotic activity of the drugs discussed in Chapter 9. Alterations in dopamine receptor function have been implicated in numerous diseases and behavioral states including schizophrenia, Parkinsonism, Huntington's chorea, affective disorders, sexual activity, reward, attention deficit hyperactivity disorder, and others.

Norepinephrine Pathways. The cell bodies of NE neurons are located in the brain stem, mainly in the locus coeruleus (Figure 3.11). From there, axons project widely throughout the brain to nerve terminals in

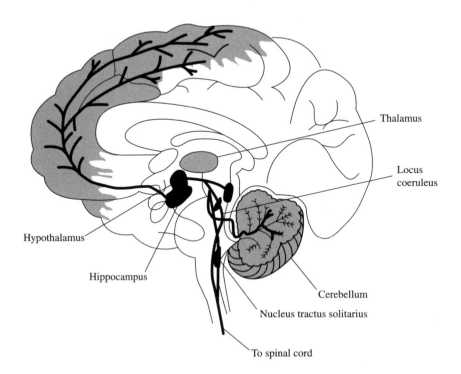

FIGURE 3.11 NE projection system in the human brain. The cell bodies are in the locus coeruleus and adjacent regions of the brain stem and project widely to the forebrain and cerebellum and to the brain stem and spinal cord.

the cerebral cortex, the limbic system, the hypothalamus, and the cerebellum. Axonal projections also travel to the dorsal horns of the spinal cord, where they exert an analgesic action (Chapter 16). The release of NE produces an alerting, focusing, orienting response, positive feelings of reward, and analgesia. NE release may also be involved in basic instinctual behaviors, such as hunger, thirst, emotion, and sex.

Dopamine Pathways. Dopamine pathways in the brain originate in the brain stem, sending axons both rostral to the brain and caudal to the spinal cord. Three dopamine circuits are classically described (Figure 3.12):

1. Cell bodies in the hypothalamus send short axons to the pituitary gland. These neurons are believed to function in the regulation of certain hormones. Alterations in hormone function are commonly seen in people with schizophrenia taking various antipsychotics, which block these dopamine receptors (Chapter 9).

2. Cell bodies in the brain-stem structure called the substantia nigra project to the basal ganglia, playing a major role in the regulation of movement. Parkinsonism, its treatment with l-DOPA (Chapter 11), and antipsychotic-induced extrapyramidal side effects (Chapter 9) all involve this pathway.

3. Cell bodies in the midbrain (ventral tegmentum), near the substantia nigra, project to higher brain regions including the cerebral cortex (especially the frontal cortex) and the limbic system, including

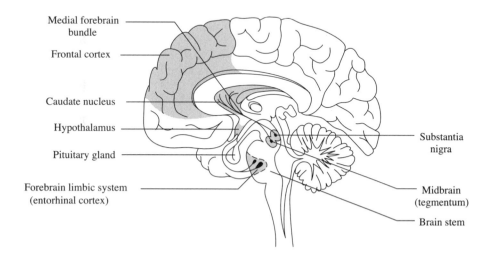

FIGURE 3.12 The three dopamine systems in the brain. One is a local circuit in the hypothalamus; another is the pathway from the substantia nigra to the caudate nucleus of the basal ganglia, which is involved in motor functions and Parkinson's disease; the third consists of cell bodies in the brain stem and midbrain (tegmentum) that project widely to the cerebral cortex and forebrain limbic system (entorhinal cortex).

the limbic cortex, nucleus accumbens, amygdaloid complex, and the entorhinal cortex; the entorhinal cortex is the major source of neurons projecting to the hippocampus. Alterations in the development of this pathway may be involved in the pathogenesis of schizophrenia and its amelioration by neuroleptic drugs. In addition, this dopaminergic pathway involving the ventral tegmentum, nucleus accumbens, and frontal cortex appears to underlie our "central reward pathway" (Figure 3.13), augmentation of which appears necessary to induce compulsive abuse and sustain continued use of most drugs of abuse (Chapter 21).

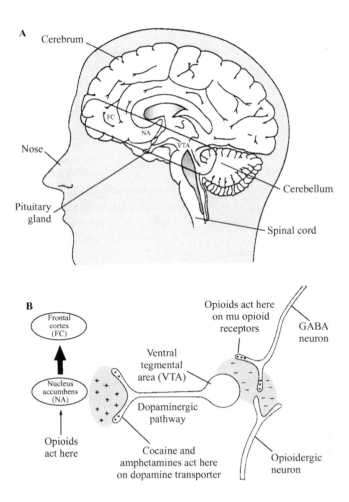

FIGURE 3.13 The limbic dopaminergic reward pathway. **A.** Human brain sliced open lengthwise, showing the relevant midbrain and forebrain area, outlined by an oval. VTA = ventral tegmental area; NA = nucleus accumbens; FC = frontal cortex. **B.** Diagram of the area outlined in **A.** Heavy dots = stored neurotransmitter at nerve endings; + = excitatory neurotransmitter; – = inhibitory neurotransmitter.

Serotonin

Serotonin (5-hydroxytryptamine, 5-HT) was first investigated as a CNS neurotransmitter in the 1950s when lysergic acid diethylamide (LSD) was found to structurally resemble serotonin and block the contractile effect of serotonin on the gastrointestinal tract. At that time, it was hypothesized that LSD-induced hallucinations might be caused by alterations in the functioning of serotonin neurons and that serotonin might be involved in abnormal behavioral functioning. Today, drugs that potentiate the synaptic actions of serotonin are widely used as antidepressants and as antianxiety agents useful in treating such disorders as obsessive-compulsive disorder, panic disorder, and phobias. Some of these *serotonerigic drugs* fall under the category of *selective serotonin reuptake inhibitors* (SSRIs; Chapter 7). Serotonin plays a role in depression and other affective states, sleep, sex, and the regulation of body temperature; use of an SSRI to treat depression can be associated with such side effects as insomnia, anxiety, and loss of libido.

Significant amounts of serotonin are found in the upper brain stem, particularly in the pons and the medulla (areas that are collectively called the *raphe nuclei*). Rostral projections from the brain stem terminate diffusely throughout the cerebral cortex, hippocampus, hypothalamus, and limbic system (Figure 3.14). Serotonin projections largely parallel those of DA, although they are not as widespread. Serotonin seems to have an effect that is opposite that of DA, and altered serotonin function has been postulated to augment the behavioral stimulant actions of cocaine (Rocha et al., 1998a); serotonin receptors have been postulated to modulate the activity of dopaminergic reward pathways and thus the effects of various drugs of abuse (Rocha et al., 1998b). Axons of serotonin neurons projecting to the spinal cord from cell bodies located in the raphe nuclei may be involved in the modulation of both pain (Chapter 16) and spinal reflexes.

In addition to the presynaptic serotonin transporter (blocked by SSRIs), several chemically distinct postsynaptic serotonin (5-HT) receptors have been identified.[1] They have been classified in families (designated by a number) and subtypes within a family (designated by a letter). Note that this is a different type of designation than the one for dopamine. The main families of 5-HT receptors are designated $5\text{-}HT_1$, $5\text{-}HT_2$, $5\text{-}HT_3$, and $5\text{-}HT_4$. The $5\text{-}HT_3$ receptor is an ion channel; the others use a G protein-coupled second-messenger system.

Throughout this book, reference is made to drugs that affect serotonin neurotransmission by acting at one or more receptors for serotonin. These drugs range from anxiolytics and antidepressants to psychedelics.

---

[1]The symbol "5-HT" refers to 5-hydroxytryptamine, the structural name for serotonin. The terms 5-HT and serotonin are used interchangeably.

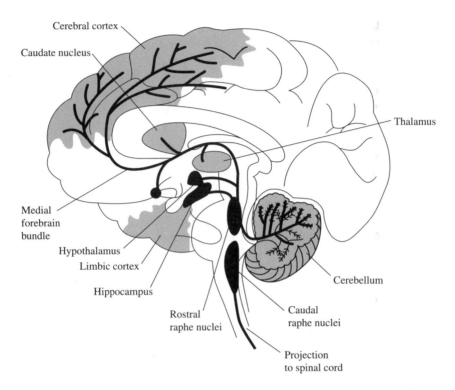

FIGURE 3.14 Serotonin pathways in the human brain. Cell bodies and fiber tracts (axonal projections) are shown in black. Serotonergic terminals are represented by the shaded areas.

Amino Acid Neurotransmitters

The "classical" neurotransmitters (ACh, NE, DA, and serotonin), although important in behavioral regulation and in the actions of psychotropic drugs, are nevertheless used by only a small proportion of the neurons in the brain (Snyder, 2002). Dozens, if not hundreds, of other neurotransmitters exist in the brain, and many of them have been implicated in the actions of psychoactive drugs. Many of these transmitters are discussed, as appropriate, throughout this book. Examples include *endorphins* and their receptors, involved in the action of opioid narcotics (Chapter 16), and *anandamide* and its receptors, involved in the action of tetrahydrocannabinol (Chapter 17). Snyder (2002) reviews the history of the development of our concepts of synaptic transmission.

Here we introduce two amino acid neurotransmitters that are widely distributed in the brain. The first, *glutamic acid* (or *glutamate*), is the major universally excitatory neurotransmitter, present on virtually all neurons within the brain. The second is *gamma aminobutyric acid* (GABA), which is the major inhibitory neurotransmitter in the brain. Most other amino acids in the brain do not serve as neurotransmitters (with the exception of aspartate and glycine) but function as precursor molecules for the biosynthesis of other transmitters (for example, tyrosine for catecholamines and tryptophan for serotonin).

Both glutamate and GABA function to modulate a number of ion channels and G protein-coupled receptors, maintaining a balance between excitation and inhibition in the brain. This balance is vital to behavioral control mechanisms. The following sections focus on glutamate and GABA as they are involved in the actions of several psychoactive drugs ranging from the benzodiazepine antianxiety agents (Chapter 6) to the mood stabilizers (Chapter 8).

Glutamate. Glutamate is a major excitatory neurotransmitter in the brain. Glutamate receptors are found on the surface of virtually all neurons. Glutamate is also the precursor for the major inhibitory neurotransmitter GABA. GABA is formed from glutamate under control of the enzyme *glutamic acid decarboxylase.*

Glutamate neurotransmission plays a critical role in cortical and hippocampal cognitive function, pyramidal and extrapyramidal motor function, cerebellar function, and sensory function. Research is focusing on the importance of glutamate dysfunction in the pathogenesis of schizophrenia, especially the negative symptoms, and the cognitive dysfunction associated with the disorder (Chapter 9). Glutamate also plays an important role in "synaptic plasticity" and is involved in the molecular processes that underlie learning and memory. However, glutamate excesses can be a potent neuronal "excitotoxin," triggering either rapid or delayed death of neurons. This excitotoxicity may play a role in the neuronal injury that accompanies alcoholism (Chapter 4), Alzheimer's disease (Chapter 11), head injury, and a variety of other disorders as reviewed by Weeber and coworkers (2002).

Glutamate is a nonessential amino acid, meaning that it is easily synthesized in the body and is not required in the diet. It does not readily penetrate the blood-brain barrier, and it is produced locally by specialized neuronal mechanisms (Figure 3.15). It can be synthesized by a number of different chemical reactions, among which is the normal breakdown of glucose. A second reaction is synthesis from glutamine. In this mechanism (which might be the more important for neuronal glutamate), there is a glutamine cycle in which synaptically inactive glutamine serves as a reservoir of glutamate. In this cycle, after glutamate is released from a neuron and exerts its excitatory effect, it is transported (taken up) into astrocytes (neighboring support cells in the brain) and converted to glutamine, which is stored in the astrocytes. Eventually, the glutamine diffuses out of the astrocytes and enters the presynaptic nerve terminals, where it is

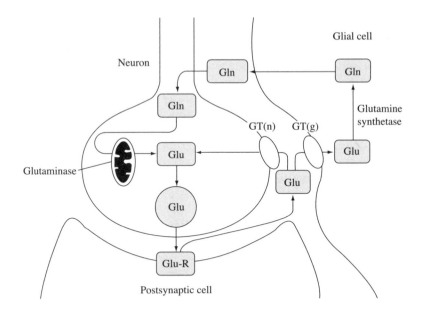

FIGURE 3.15 Pathways for glutamine release, reuptake, and reutilization. Glutamate (Glu) is released into the synapse and recaptured by a glutamate transporter located on adjacent glial cells. Within the glial cells, glutamate is converted to glutamine (Gln) by the enzyme *glutamine synthetase.* Gln then returns to the cerebrospinal fluid where it is present in high concentrations. It diffuses into neuronal terminals to replenish the Glu after conversion to Glu from Gln by the enzyme *glutaminase.* [From Cooper et al. (2003), p. 133].

converted to glutamate, the active neurotransmitter. The cycle then repeats (Feldman et al., 1997).

Postsynaptic glutamate receptors are many and can be subdivided into two major types: *ionotropic receptors* (directly coupled to membrane ion channels permeable to sodium and/or calcium) and *metabotropic receptors* (coupled to G proteins). The ionotropic receptor subtypes can be further divided into three: NMDA, kainate, and AMPA (the latter two are sometimes referred to as "non-NMDA" receptors; Figure 3.16). In the adult human brain, NMDA and AMPA receptors are colocalized in about 70 percent of their synapses. These receptors mediate rapid excitation of postsynaptic neurons, with especially high concentrations in the cerebral cortex, hippocampus, striatum, septum, and amygdala.

NMDA receptors are activated by glutamate in the presence of another amino acid, either glycine or serine. At resting potential, the NMDA ion channel is blocked by magnesium ions (Mg^+). Only when the membrane is depolarized (by the activation of AMPA or kainate receptors on the same postsynaptic neuron) is the Mg^+ blockade of the

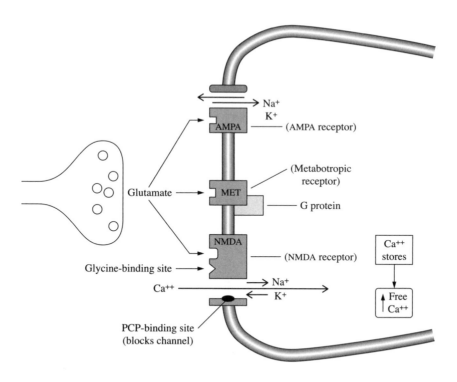

FIGURE 3.16 Glutamate receptor family. The AMPA receptor controls fast sodium and potassium channels; the NMDA receptor controls calcium channels; the metabotropic receptor controls a second-messenger system via a G protein that acts on the intracellular machinery of the cell. (PCP is discussed in Chapter 18.)

ion channel relieved. Then the NMDA receptor channel opens and permits the entry of both sodium and calcium ions (see Figure 3.16). Within the NMDA receptor ion channel is a binding site for phencyclidine and ketamine (two "psychedelic" drugs discussed in Chapter 18). These two drugs are noncompetitive antagonists at this NMDA receptor: they inhibit NMDA functioning. Other nonpsychedelic drugs of this type have neuroprotective and antidepressant properties.

NMDA receptors also play a critical role in regulating synaptic plasticity and play vital roles in learning, memory, and cognitive ability. To form memory, high-frequency presynaptic activity in cerebral cortical and limbic neurons leads to the presynaptic release of glutamate, which activates a host of glutamate receptors on the postsynaptic dendritic spines (Figure 3.17). This activity produces a large postsynaptic depolarization, which allows for activation of NMDA ionoptropic receptors, ultimately leading to calcium ion influx into the neuron. The high levels of glutamate also activate metabotropic receptors, which are coupled via a phospholipase enzyme to a cascade

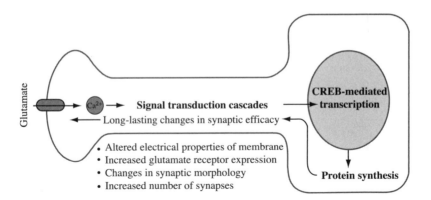

FIGURE 3.17 Processes involved in memory formation. Formation of memory is a complex process that requires several aspects of neuronal function. Memory formation begins with activation of NMDA-type glutamate receptors, allowing Ca++ to flow into the cell. The Ca++ flux activates several intracellular second-messenger signaling cascades. The signaling processes activate the transcription factor CREB, which leads to the modulation of several genes required for consolidation of long-term memory. Translation of newly synthesized mRNAs leads to production of proteins required to affect long-term changes in neuronal physiology. [From Weeber et al. (2002), p. 377.]

of signal transduction pathways, terminating in activation of a cyclic AMP response-element-binding protein (CREB), which in turn is vital in initiating transcription of new proteins involved in the formation of long-term memory. These new memory proteins are carried out of the nucleus and are translated into functional proteins that effect lasting changes in synaptic strength by altering the electrical properties of the synaptic membrane. These memory proteins do so by "increasing the responsiveness to neurotransmitter, and even changing the number and size of synapses" (Weeber et al., 2002, pp. 377–378). Disruption of this process can be deleterious; disruption can be expressed as deficits in memory formation (Chapter 11) or as depression (Chapter 7).

Although NMDA activity plays an important role in synaptic plasticity (neuronal "health"), excessive glutaminergic signaling is also involved in neuronal toxicity. For example, ethanol (Chapter 4) reduces glutamate activity, and alcohol withdrawal markedly increases glutamate release from neurons; excesses of glutamate can lead to neuronal destruction through overactivity of NMDA receptors. Attempts to treat alcoholism aim to prevent such neuronal injury by preventing repeated relapses and withdrawals (Chapter 4). Also, traumatic head injury results in massive release of glutamate, and attempts to provide "brain protection" after head injury are aimed at preventing glutaminergic overactivity. Anoxia and hypoglycemia are other glutamate-releasing events that can lead to neuronal damage. Apparently, the entry of large excesses of calcium ions into cells via the NMDA receptors is an important step in the rapid cell death that occurs with excitotoxicity. Finally, new treatments to prevent the progression of Alzheimer's disease and other dementias are aimed at protecting neurons through blockage of NMDA receptor activity (Chapter 11). In 2004, the first anti-Alzheimer's drug that acts through a glutaminergic mechanism became available for clinical use (Chapter 11).

Gamma Aminobutyric Acid   Gamma aminobutyric acid (GABA), a universally inhibitory transmitter, is found in high concentrations in the brain and spinal cord. Two different types of GABA receptors are described, GABA$_A$ and GABA$_B$.

GABA$_A$ receptors are fast receptors and have four transmembrane helical complexes that join to form an ion channel receptor for chloride ions (see Figure 2.4). Activation of this receptor by GABA opens the channel and leads to an influx of chloride into the cell, hyperpolarizing the cell and reducing its excitability. Barbiturate and benzodiazepine binding to this receptor facilitates the action of GABA (Chapters 5 and 6). This action is associated with the anxiolytic, amnestic, and anesthetic effects of these sedative drugs (Tomlin et al., 1999). GABA$_A$ receptors are found in high density in the cerebral cortex, hippocampus, and cerebellum.

Important for future pharmacologic research, about ten different subtypes of the GABA$_A$ receptor occur, allowing for the development of agonists and antagonists of specific GABA$_A$ receptor subtypes (Chapter 6). Such drugs might be novel antianxiety agents, anticonvulsants, or cognitive enhancers. Buggy and colleagues (2000) reported that certain anesthetic drugs exert their sedative and amnestic actions by activating GABA$_A$ neurons that in turn reduce the functioning of glutamate neurons on which they synapse.

GABA$_B$ receptors are slow-response receptors of the G protein-coupled type. Activation of GABA$_B$ receptors in the amygdala is associated with the membrane-stabilizing, antiaggressive properties of valproic acid, a drug widely used to treat bipolar disorder (Chapter 8).

Peptide Neurotransmitters

Most of the newly identified neurotransmitters are peptides, which are small proteins (chains of amino acid molecules attached in a specific order). Peptide transmitters can be classified into several groups; one important group is the opioid-type peptides. Other groups include the hypothalamic-releasing hormones, the pituitary hormones, and the so-called gut-brain peptides. Feldman and colleagues (1997) and Cooper and colleagues (2003) discuss these peptides and their possible implications in psychopharmacology.

In this book, one peptide transmitter of interest is the type involved in the actions of the opioids, such as morphine. *Opioid peptides* include the *endorphins* (about 16 to 30 amino acids in length) and the shorter-chain *enkephalins* (5 amino acids in length). These substances are formed from a larger protein produced elsewhere in the body. The endorphins may be involved in a wide variety of emotional states, including pain perception, reward, emotional stability, and energy "highs," and in acupuncture. Narcotics such as morphine, codeine, and heroin activate (are agonists at) receptors for endorphins and enkephalins (Chapter 16).

Opioid receptors are termed *mu, kappa,* and *delta;* the mu receptor mediates most of the analgesic and reinforcing properties of morphine and other narcotics. These receptors are the usual 7-transmembrane-spanning proteins, consisting of about 370 to 400 amino acids. They are G protein-coupled receptors; activation of the receptor by a neurotransmitter or an exogenous opioid serves to either activate adjacent ion channels (increasing potassium conductance or decreasing calcium conductance) or inhibit the intracellular function of the enzyme adenylate cyclase. From here, the intracellular consequences become quite complicated (see Cooper et al., 2003).

Another peptide transmitter of interest in this book is *substance P,* a *gut-brain peptide* (11 amino acids in length) that plays an important role as a sensory transmitter, especially for pain impulses that enter the spinal cord and brain from a peripheral site of tissue injury. Opioids, serotonin agonists, and norepinephrine agonists exert much of their analgesic effect by acting on substance P nerve terminals to limit the release of this pain-inducing peptide. Substance P antagonists are also being developed as antidepressant drugs.

Receptors for substance P appear to be G protein-coupled receptors; activation appears to result in inhibition of adjacent potassium channels and activation of intracellular second messengers (phospholipase C or adenylate cyclase). The role of substance P in pain transmission is discussed in Chapter 16.

STUDY QUESTIONS

1. Define a psychoactive drug.

2. What are some of the functions of the spinal cord?

3. What is a neuron? Describe the following parts of a neuron: dendrites, soma, axon, synaptic terminal.

4. What is a synapse? How does it function?

5. How is the synaptic transmitter action of a released chemical terminated? Give two examples.

6. Name a drug that blocks the action of acetylcholine as a neurotransmitter. What are the consequences of the blockade? Name a drug that potentiates the action of acetylcholine as a transmitter. What might such a drug be used for?

7. Name three catecholamine neurotransmitters. How is their neurotransmitter action terminated? What drugs block this process?

8. Describe the various types of serotonin receptors. What drugs might either stimulate or block them? How might these drugs be applied for therapeutic benefit?

9. Name two amino acid neurotransmitters. Describe any drugs that might potentiate or block the actions of each one. How might these drugs be used therapeutically?

10. What is substance P? How does it relate to neuropharmacology?

REFERENCES

Ashraf, S. I., and Kunes, S. (2006). "A Trace of Silence: Memory and MicroRNA at the Synapse." *Current Opinions in Neurobiology* 16: 535–539.

Buggy, D. J., et al. (2000). "Effects of Intravenous Anesthetic Agents on Glutamate Release: A Role for $GABA_A$ Receptor-Mediated Inhibition." *Anesthesiology* 92: 1067–1073.

Cooper, J. R., et al. (2003). *The Biochemical Basis of Neuropharmacology,* 8th ed. New York: Oxford University Press.

Cummings, J. L. (2000). "Cholinesterase Inhibitors: A New Class of Psychotropic Compounds." *American Journal of Psychiatry* 157: 4–15.

Feldman, R. S., et al. (1997). *Principles of Neuropsychopharmacology.* Sunderland, MA: Sinauer.

Hyman, S. E. (2005). "Neurotransmitters." *Current Biology* 15: R154–R158.

Kempermann, G., et al. (2004). "Functional Significance of Adult Neurogenesis." *Current Opinions in Neurobiology* 14: 186–191.

Rocha, B. A., et al. (1998a). "Cocaine Self-Administration in Dopamine-Transporter Knockout Mice." *Nature Neuroscience* 1: 132–137.

Rocha, B. A., et al. (1998b). "Increased Vulnerability to Cocaine in Mice Lacking the Serotonin-1B Receptor." *Nature* 393: 175–178.

Schaffer, D. V., and Gage, F. H. (2004). "Neurogenesis and Neuroadaptation." *Neuromolecular Medicine* 5: 1–9.

Snyder, S. H. (2002). "Forty Years of Neurotransmitters: A Personal Account." *Archives of General Psychiatry* 59: 983–994.

Sutton, M. A., and Schuman, E. M. (2006). "Dendritic Protein Synthesis, Synaptic Plasticity, and Memory." *Cell* 127: 49–58.

Thomas, K., and Davies, A. (2005). "Neurotropins: A Ticket to Ride for BDNF." *Current Biology* 15: R262–R264.

Tomlin, S. L., et al. (1999). "Preparation of Barbiturate Optical Isomers and Their Effects on GABA$_A$ Receptors." *Anesthesiology* 90: 1714–1722.

Weeber, E. J., et al. (2002). "Molecular Genetics of Human Cognition." *Molecular Interventions* 2: 376–390

Drugs That Depress Brain Function: Sedative-Hypnotic Drugs

The sedative-hypnotic drugs (or central nervous system—CNS—depressants) are drugs that affect neurons so that the functioning of the brain is depressed, resulting in a behavioral state of calm, relaxation, disinhibition, drowsiness, and sleep as doses of drug increase. These agents were classically ingested to ease anxiety, tension, and agitation and to induce a soporific state. Behaviorally, what is observed is a dose-related state of increasing intoxication with release from inhibitions, sedation, sleep, unconsciousness, general anesthesia, coma, and, eventually, death from respiratory and cardiac depression. Increasing cognitive and psychomotor impairments are induced as the dose of these drugs is increased. Drugs classified as nonselective CNS depressants are not specific treatments for anxiety, despite hundreds of years of use for this disorder. Nor are these drugs either analgesic or antidepressant.

Drugs classified as nonselective CNS depressants include ethyl alcohol and the inhalants of abuse (Chapter 4), the barbiturates and their variants, general anesthetics and antiepileptic drugs (all covered in Chapter 5), as well as the benzodiazepines, their variants, and several newer antiinsomnia drugs (all covered in Chapter 6). Compared with alcohol and the barbiturates, the benzodiazepines and newer sedative-hypnotics have a lesser capacity to produce potentially fatal CNS depression. Because of this improved margin of safety, these drugs have replaced the barbiturates for the treatment of insomnia. Finally, within the past 15 to 20 years, newer and more specific anxiolytic-antidepressant drugs (Chapter 7) have replaced benzodiazepines in the treatment of anxiety disorders. Specific medical indications for nonselective CNS depressants are therefore rapidly diminishing. Medically, these drugs are still used to induce amnesia (such as for the performance of invasive medical procedures) and occasionally for the short-term treatment of severe anxiety disorders.

Socially, sedative-hypnotic drugs (including alcohol) are used as drugs of abuse to induce a state of diminished awareness, diminished capacity, and intoxication.

The terms *sedative, tranquilizer,* and *hypnotic* can be applied to any CNS depressant. These drugs, including alcohol, diminish environmental awareness, reduce response to sensory stimulation, depress cognitive functioning, decrease spontaneity, and reduce physical activity. Higher doses produce increasing drowsiness, lethargy, clouding of consciousness with amnesia, hypnosis, and unconsciousness. Because sedative drugs can produce amnesia ("blackout") in people who may be otherwise awake (although "intoxicated"), some (including alcohol) have been implicated as "date rape" drugs.

The uniformity of action of all CNS depressants correctly implies that the effects of any CNS depressant potentiate the effects of any other CNS depressant. For example, alcohol exaggerates the depression induced by benzodiazepines, and benzodiazepines intensify the impairment of driving ability in a person who has been drinking alcohol. The depressant effects of sedative drugs are additive; frequently they are supra-additive. Thus, the depression that is observed in a person who has taken more than one drug is greater than would be predicted if the person had taken only one. Such intense depression is often unpredictable and unexpected, and it can lead to dangerous or even fatal consequences. Depressant drugs should not be used in combination, especially if one of the drugs is ethyl alcohol.

All the CNS sedative-hypnotic agents carry the risk of inducing physiological dependence, psychological dependence, and tolerance. *Physiological dependence* is characterized by the occurrence of withdrawal signs and symptoms when the drug is not taken. Signs and symptoms range from sleep disturbances (rebound insomnia, for example) to life-threatening withdrawal convulsions. *Psychological dependence* follows from the positive reinforcement effects of the drugs. *Tolerance* occurs as a result of both the induction of drug-metabolizing enzymes in the liver and the adaptation of cells in the brain to the continuous presence of drug. In addition, a remarkable degree of *cross-tolerance* may occur: tolerance to one drug results in a lessened response to another drug. *Cross-dependence* also may be exhibited, in which one drug can prevent the withdrawal symptoms that are associated with physical dependence on a different drug.

Chapter 4

Ethyl Alcohol and the Inhalants of Abuse

ETHYL ALCOHOL

The term *alcohol* socially applies to *ethyl alcohol* (ethanol)—a psychoactive drug that is similar in most respects to all the other sedative-hypnotic compounds that are discussed in Chapters 5 and 6. The main difference from the other depressants is that ethanol is used primarily for recreational rather than medical purposes. Because ethanol is the second most widely used psychoactive substance in the world (after caffeine), its use as a sedative and intoxicant has created special problems for both individual users and society in general.

Pharmacology of Alcohol

Ethyl alcohol is not merely a recreational beverage; it is a drug that, like any other psychoactive agent, affects the brain and behavior. Therefore, in discussing alcohol, we need to address its basic pharmacology (pharmacokinetics and pharmacodynamics) as well as its side effects, teratogenic effects, and toxicities. In addition, since alcohol ingestion is widely associated with drug dependence, treatment of alcohol dependence must be addressed.

Pharmacokinetics

Since alcohol is so rapidly and well absorbed orally, its major route of administration is the drinking of beverages containing the drug. Alcoholic beverages include beer, wine, and hard liquors; hard liquors, such as gin and whiskey, are fortified to alcohol levels beyond those achievable with fermentation.

Absorption. Ethyl alcohol is a simple two-carbon molecule (Figure 4.1). It is rarely drunk in its pure form; rather, it is found in 12 to 14 percent concentrations in wines, usually about 5 percent in beers (as much as 7 to 10 percent in some "microbrews"[1]), and 40 to 50 percent in "hard" liquors. In the latter, concentration is usually expressed as alcohol "proof," which is twice the percent concentration (for example, 80 proof = 40 percent ethanol). The appendix at the end of this chapter addresses the amount of alcohol that is present in many different forms of alcohol-containing beverages.

Alcohol is soluble in both water and fat, and it diffuses easily across all biological membranes. Thus, after it is drunk, alcohol is rapidly and completely absorbed from the entire gastrointestinal tract, although most is absorbed from the upper intestine because of its large surface area. The time from the last drink to maximal concentration in blood ranges from 30 to 90 minutes. In a person with an empty stomach, approximately 20 percent of a single dose of alcohol is absorbed directly from the stomach, usually quite rapidly. The remaining 80 percent is absorbed rapidly and completely from the upper intestine; the only limiting factor is the time it takes to empty the stomach.

It now appears that women absorb more ethanol than do men. Because of this, women become more impaired than men after drinking equivalent amounts of alcohol and may suffer more alcohol-related organ damage (Agartz et al., 2003; Hommer et al., 2001) and more traumas resulting from traffic crashes and interpersonal violence (Mumenthaler et al., 2003). This phenomenon appears to result mainly from a lower amount of drug-metabolizing enzyme in the wall of the stomach of the female.

---

[1]Micobrewed beers contain anywhere from 4.5 to 10 percent alcohol, depending on the product. Lighter brews contain about 4.5 to 6 percent; heavier bocks and porters may contain 7 to 9 percent alcohol; specialty products, triple beers, and barley wines may contain 10 percent or even more alcohol. Thus, some microbrewed beers may easily contain twice (or three times) as much alcohol as ordinary 3.2 percent beers. See the appendix at the end of this chapter for more information.

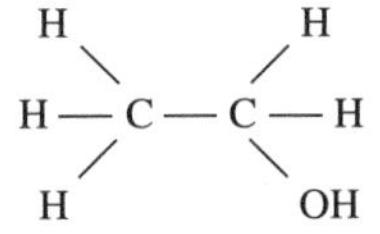

FIGURE 4.1 Structure of ethanol (CH_3CH_2OH).

Distribution. After absorption, alcohol is evenly distributed through-out all body fluids and tissues. The blood-brain barrier is freely perme-able to alcohol. When alcohol appears in the blood and reaches a person's brain, it crosses the blood-brain barrier almost immediately. Alcohol is also freely distributed across the placenta and easily enters the brain of a developing fetus. Fetal blood alcohol levels are essen-tially the same as those of the drinking mother.

Metabolism and Excretion. Approximately 95 percent of the alcohol a person ingests is enzymatically metabolized by the enzyme *alcohol dehy-drogenase.* The other 5 percent is excreted unchanged, mainly through the lungs.[2] About 85 percent of the metabolism of alcohol occurs in the liver. Up to 15 percent of alcohol metabolism is carried out by a gastric al-cohol dehydrogenase enzyme, located in the lining of the stomach, which can decrease the blood level of alcohol by about 15 percent, obviously at-tenuating alcohol's systemic toxicity. The metabolism of alcohol by gas-tric alcohol dehydrogenase is part of what was called *first-pass metabolism* in Chapter 1. Rapid gastric emptying (as by drinking on an empty stomach) reduces the time that alcohol is susceptible to first-pass metabolism and results in increased blood levels. Drinking on a full stomach retains alcohol in the stomach, increases its exposure to gastric alcohol dehydrogenase, and reduces the resulting blood level of the drug.

Several years ago, Frezza and coworkers (1990) reported that whenever women and men consume comparable amounts of alcohol (after correction for differences in body weight), women have higher blood ethanol concentrations than men (Figure 4.2). The reasons appear to be threefold:

- Women have about 50 percent less gastric metabolism of alcohol than men because women, whether alcoholic or nonalcoholic, have a lower level of gastric alcohol dehydrogenase enzyme. Since the gastric en-zyme metabolizes about 15 percent of ingested alcohol, the blood al-cohol concentration (BAC) is increased by about 7 percent over that in a male drinking the same weight-adjusted amount of alcohol.

- Men may have a greater ratio of muscle to fat than do women. Men thus have a larger vascular compartment (fat has little blood supply). Therefore alcohol is somewhat more diluted in men, again decreasing blood alcohol levels in men compared to women.

---

[2]Small amounts of alcohol are excreted from the body through the lungs; most of us are familiar with "alcohol breath." This excretion forms the basis for the breath analysis test because alcohol equilibrates rapidly across the membranes of the lung. In the "breathalyzer" test, a ratio of 1:2300 exists between alcohol in exhaled air and alcohol in venous blood. The blood alcohol concentration is easily extrapolated from the alcohol concentration in the expired air.

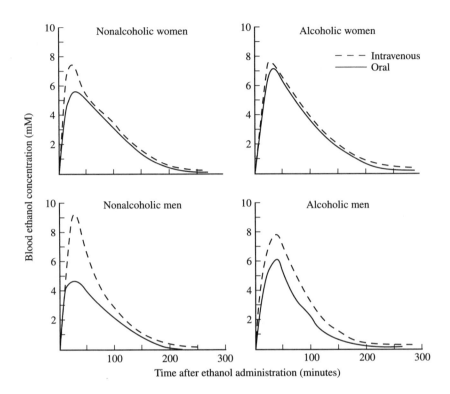

FIGURE 4.2 Effects of route of administration and gender on BAC. Ethanol was administered in a dose of 0.3 milligram per kilogram of body weight either by intravenous injection (dashed lines) or orally (solid lines) to nonalcoholic and alcoholic men and women. The higher BAC after oral alcohol intake by women compared with men shows that first-pass metabolism (in the stomach) is lower in women than in men. This is especially noticeable in alcoholic women compared with all other groups of men and women. [Modified from Frezza et al. (1990), p. 97.]

- Women, with higher body fat than men (fat contains little alcohol), concentrate alcohol in plasma, drink for drink, more than men, raising the apparent blood level.

The metabolism of alcohol by alcohol dehydrogenase is only the first step in a three-step metabolic process involved in the breakdown of alcohol (Figure 4.3):

1. Alcohol dehydrogenase functions to convert alcohol to acetaldehyde. A coenzyme called *nicotinamide adenine dinucleotide* (NAD) is required for the activity of this enzyme. The availability of NAD is the rate-limiting step in this reaction; enough is present so that the maximum amount of alcohol that can be metabolized in 24 hours is about 170 grams.

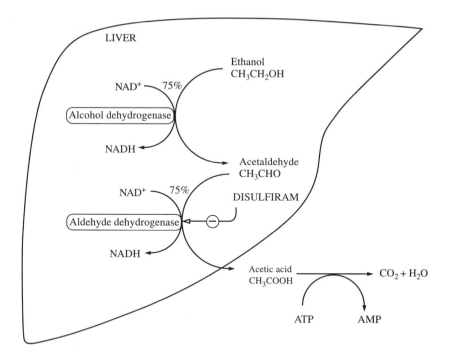

FIGURE 4.3 Metabolism of ethanol. Ethanol is oxidated by the enzyme alcohol de-hydrogenase using NAD^+ (nicotinamide adenine dinucleotide) as a cofactor to form acetaldehyde. A second oxidative step converts acetaldehyde to acetic acid, which, in turn, is broken down to carbon dioxide and water. The first step involving alcohol dehydrogenase is the rate-limiting step. The drug disulfiram (Antabuse) blocks the second step by blocking the activity of aldehyde dehydrogenase. ATP = adenosine phosphate; AMP = adenosine monophosphate.

2. The enzyme *aldehyde dehydrogenase* converts acetaldehyde to acetic acid. The drug *disulfiram* (Antabuse) irreversibly inhibits this enzyme.

3. Acetic acid is broken down into carbon dioxide and water, thus releasing energy (calories).

The average person metabolizes 7 to 8 grams (about 10 milliliters) of 100 percent alcohol per hour, independent of the blood level of alcohol. This rate is fairly constant for different people.[3] Thus, it would take an adult 1 hour to metabolize the amount of alcohol that is contained

---

[3]In biochemical terms, this is called zero-order metabolism. Virtually all other drugs are metabolized by first-order metabolism, which means that the amount of drug metabolized per unit time depends on the amount (or concentration) of drug in blood (see Chapter 1). Perhaps zero-order metabolism occurs because the amount of enzyme (or a cofactor required for activity of the enzyme) is limited and becomes saturated with only small amounts of alcohol in the body.

in a 1-ounce glass of 80 proof (40 percent) whiskey, a 3.5-ounce glass of 12 percent wine, a 12-ounce bottle of 3.2 percent beer, or a 6-ounce glass of 7 percent microbrew. Consumption of 3.5 ounces of wine, 12 ounces of 3.2 percent beer, 8 ounces of 5 percent beer, or 1 ounce of 80 proof whiskey per hour would keep the blood levels of alcohol in a person fairly constant. If a person ingests more alcohol in any given hour than is metabolized, his or her blood concentrations increase. Consequently, there is a limit to the amount of alcohol a person can consume in an hour without becoming drunk.

So what is a drink equivalent? Once, beers contained 3.2 percent alcohol and a 12-ounce beer, containing about 10 cc of absolute alcohol, was considered to be a drink equivalent. Today, only a couple of states are 3.2 percent beer states; most allow 4.5 percent to 5.2 percent beers, more in "ice" beers and certain microbrews. Fortified beers and some microbrewed beers contain about 8 to 9 percent ethanol. A 12-ounce 5 percent beer therefore is 1.5 drink equivalents. A 16-ounce 5 percent beer is almost 2 drink equivalents. A 12-ounce, 5.5 percent "ice" beer is 1.7 drink equivalents. Often, alcoholic beverage products do not list the alcohol percentage on their label, undoubtedly a flaw in our system. It is incumbent on both the server and the imbiber to know the concentration of alcohol in the product being drunk because a person metabolizes one drink equivalent per hour. Ingesting more per hour results in drug accumulation, which results in a rise in blood alcohol concentration. The appendix at the end of this chapter expands on the topic of drink equivalents.

These kinetics permit not only estimation of BAC after drinking a known amount of alcoholic beverage but also estimation of the fall in blood concentration over time after drinking ceases. The following may serve to explain the relationship between the amounts of alcohol consumed, the resulting BAC, and the impairment of motor and intellectual functioning (here, driving ability). Most states define a BAC of 0.08 gram percent (grams%)[4] as intoxication, and a person who drives with a BAC above this amount can be charged with driving while under the influence of alcohol. Thus, one might assume that a level of 0.07 grams% is acceptable but a level of 0.09 grams% is not. However, the behavioral effects of alcohol are not all or none; alcohol (like all sedatives) progressively impairs a person's ability to function. Thus, the 0.08 grams% blood level is only a legally established, arbitrary value. A person whose BAC is under 0.08 grams% yet functions with impairment detrimental to operation of a motor vehicle can still suffer criminal penalties. Driving ability is minimally impaired at a BAC of

---

[4]Grams% is the number of grams of ethanol that would be contained in 100 milliliters of blood.

0.01 grams%, but at 0.04 to 0.08 grams%, a driver has increasingly impaired judgment and reactions and becomes less inhibited. As a result, the risk of an accident quadruples. The deterioration of a person's driving ability continues at a BAC of 0.10 to 0.14 grams%, leading to a sixfold to sevenfold increase in the risk of having an accident. At 0.15 grams% and higher, a person is 25 times more likely to become involved in a serious accident.

Figure 4.4 illustrates the correlation between the number of drink equivalents imbibed, gender, body weight, and the resulting blood alcohol concentration. First choose the correct chart (male or female). Then find the number that is closest to your body weight in pounds. Look down the left column to find the number of drinks consumed. BAC is found by matching body weight with number of drinks ingested. Then note that BAC falls about 0.015 percent every hour since the first drink was ingested. From the total number of drinks ingested, subtract the amount of alcohol that has been metabolized over the number of hours since drinking began (remember that approximately 1 drink equivalent is metabolized in 1 hour). The final figure is the approximate BAC. By calculating this number, the degree to which driving ability is impaired can be predicted.

Some agencies and organizations have even more stringent BAC standards than the states. For example, the Federal Department of Transportation regulations test and prevent truck drivers from driving at 0.04 grams% and airline pilots from flying at 0.02 grams% after 24 hours of abstinence.

Factors that may alter the predictable rate of metabolism of alcohol are usually not clinically significant. With long-term use, however, alcohol can induce drug-metabolizing enzymes in the liver, increasing the liver's rate of metabolizing alcohol (and so inducing *tolerance)* as well as its rate of metabolizing other compounds that are similar to alcohol (termed *cross-tolerance).*

Pharmacodynamics

Identifying the mechanism of the action of alcohol continues to be difficult. For many years, it was presumed that alcohol acted through a general depressant action on nerve membranes and synapses. Because it is both water soluble and lipid soluble, ethanol dissolves into all body tissues. This property led to a unitary hypothesis of action—that the drug dissolves in nerve membranes, distorting, disorganizing, or "perturbing" the membrane similar to the action of general anesthetics (Chapter 5). The result is a nonspecific and indirect depression of neuronal function. This mechanism would account for the nonspecific and generalized depressant behavioral effects of the drug. The hypothesis, however, does not explain the evidence that alcohol may disturb both

Blood Alcohol Concentration —A Guide

One drink equals 1 ounce of 80 proof alcohol; 12-ounce bottle of beer; 2 ounces of 20% wine; 3 ounces of 12% wine.

Men

Drinks	Approximate blood alcohol percentage (grams%)								
	Body weight (pounds)								
	100	120	140	160	180	200	220	240	
0	.00	.00	.00	.00	.00	.00	.00	.00	Only safe driving limit
1	.04	.03	.03	.02	.02	.02	.02	.02	Impairment begins
2	.08	.06	.05	.05	.04	.04	.03	.03	Driving skills significantly affected
3	.11	.09	.08	.07	.06	.06	.05	.05	
4	.15	.12	.11	.09	.08	.08	.07	.06	Possible criminal penalties
5	.19	.16	.13	.12	.11	.09	.09	.08	
6	.23	.19	.16	.14	.13	.11	.10	.09	
7	.26	.22	.19	.16	.15	.13	.12	.11	Legally intoxicated
8	.30	.25	.21	.19	.17	.15	.14	.13	
9	.34	.28	.24	.21	.19	.17	.15	.14	
10	.38	.31	.27	.23	.21	.19	.17	.16	Criminal penalties

Alcohol is "burned up" by the body at .015 grams% per hour, as follows:

Number of hours since starting first drink	1	2	3	4	5	6
Percent alcohol burned up	.015	.030	.045	.060	.075	.090

Calculate BAC

Example:
180 lb. man? – 6 drinks in 4 hours
BAC = .130 grams% on chart
Subtract .060 grams% metabolized in 4 hours
BAC = .070 grams%   DRIVING IMPAIRED

Women

Drinks	Approximate blood alcohol percentage (grams%)									
	Body weight (pounds)									
	90	100	120	140	160	180	200	220	240	
0	.00	.00	.00	.00	.00	.00	.00	.00	.00	Only safe driving limit
1	.05	.05	.04	.03	.03	.03	.02	.02	.02	Impairment begins
2	.10	.09	.08	.07	.06	.05	.05	.04	.04	Driving skills significantly affected
3	.15	.14	.11	.10	.09	.08	.07	.06	.06	
4	.20	.18	.15	.13	.11	.10	.09	.08	.08	
5	.25	.23	.19	.16	.14	.13	.11	.10	.09	Criminal penalties
6	.30	.27	.23	.19	.17	.15	.14	.12	.11	
7	.35	.32	.27	.23	.20	.18	.16	.14	.13	Legally intoxicated
8	.40	.36	.30	.26	.23	.20	.18	.17	.15	
9	.45	.41	.34	.29	.26	.23	.20	.19	.17	
10	.51	.45	.38	.32	.28	.25	.23	.21	.19	Criminal penalties

Alcohol is "burned up" by the body at .015 grams% per hour, as follows:

Number of hours since starting first drink	1	2	3	4	5	6
Percent alcohol burned up	.015	.030	.045	.060	.075	.090

Calculate BAC

Example:
140 lb woman – 6 drinks in 4 hours
BAC = .190 grams% on chart
Subtract .060 grams% metabolized in 4 hours
BAC = .130 grams% — LEGALLY INTOXICATED

FIGURE 4.4 Relation between blood alcohol concentration, body weight, and the number of drinks ingested for men and women. See text for details.

the synaptic activity of various neurotransmitters, especially major excitatory (glutamate) and inhibitory (GABA) systems, and various intracellular transduction processes.

Glutamate Receptors. Ethanol is a potent inhibitor of the function of the NMDA subtype of glutamate receptors. Ethanol disrupts glutaminergic neurotransmission by depressing the responsiveness of NMDA receptors to released glutamate. This attenuation of glutamate responsiveness may be exacerbated by its known enhancement of inhibitory GABA neurotransmission. With chronic alcohol intake and persistent glutaminergic suppression, there is a compensatory up regulation of NMDA receptors. Thus, on removal of ethanol's inhibitory effect (as would occur during alcohol withdrawal), these excess excitatory receptors would result in withdrawal signs, including seizures. Excess glutamate release during withdrawal may also be responsible for excitatory neuronal nerve damage and loss (Heinz, 2006).

The drug *acamprosate*, a structural analogue of glutamate (Figure 4.5), is an anticraving drug used to maintain abstinence in alcohol-dependent patients, an action postulated to be produced by interaction with glutaminergic NMDA receptors, attenuating neuronal hyperexcitability induced by chronic alcohol ingestion and withdrawal. The use of acamprosate in the treatment of alcoholism is discussed later in this chapter.

GABA Receptors. Ethanol activates the GABA-mediated increase in chloride ion flows, resulting in neuronal inhibition. The behavioral results of this inhibition include sedation, muscle relaxation, and inhibition of cognitive and motor skills. A GABAergic antianxiety effect was

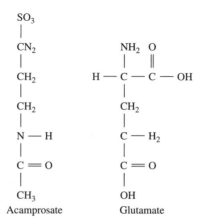

FIGURE 4.5 Structures of acamprosate and glutamate.

illustrated by Kushner and coworkers (1996), who demonstrated that low doses of ethanol act acutely to reduce both panic and the anxiety surrounding panic. This finding lends support to the view that drinking by those with panic disorder, stress, and anxiety is reinforced by this GABAergic agonistic effect. Thus, the use of alcohol to self-medicate one's panic or anxiety disorder may contribute to the high rate at which alcohol-use disorders occur with anxiety and panic disorders. Matsuzawa and Suzuki (2002) discuss the interaction between ethanol and stress in the mechanism of psychological dependence on ethanol. They invoke a mechanism in which GABAergic inhibition results in activation of opioid receptors that ultimately activates behaviorally rewarding dopaminergic neurons. Boehm et al. (2002) demonstrate that alcohol's behavioral effects may be exerted through modulation of GABA receptors on dopamine cell bodies in the ventral tegmental area. Johnson and colleagues (2005) review the role of GABAergic actions in the pharmacology of alcohol.

Ethanol binds to a different subunit on the $GABA_A$ receptor than do other GABA agonists. A chronic adaptive effect seems to involve changes in intracellular mRNA, suggesting that chronic alcoholism can affect gene expression. As a result of the GABAergic agonistic action, the activity of other transmitter systems is affected. The GABA agonist action of ethanol has been linked to the positive reinforcing effects of the drug (Matsuzawa and Suzuki, 2002). The abuse potential of alcohol follows from an ultimate action to augment dopamine neurotransmitter systems, particularly the dopaminergic projection from the ventral tegmental area to the nucleus accumbens and to the frontal cortex (Chapter 3). This action is probably an indirect effect rather than a direct action exerted on dopamine-secreting neurons.

Opioid Receptors. Wand and coworkers (1998) present data consistent with a dysfunctional brain opioid system as part of a neurocircuitry involved in heavy alcohol drinking and alcohol dependence. Alcohol-dependent people and their offspring may have a deficit in brain opioid activity. Ethanol may induce opioid release, which in turn triggers dopamine release in the brain reward system. Administration of *naltrexone* (ReVia, Vivatrol) blocks opioid release and may reduce alcohol craving. Naltrexone is FDA-approved for the treatment of alcohol dependency; its use in treating alcohol dependence is discussed later in this chapter.

Serotonin Receptors. There is some literature on the role of serotonin in the actions of alcohol. Chronic alcohol consumption results in augmentations in serotoninergic activity, and serotonin dysfunction has been postulated to play a role in the pathogenesis of some types of alcoholism. Today, emphasis is on the role of serotonin

5-HT$_2$ and 5-HT$_3$ receptors in the central effects of ethanol; these receptors are located on dopaminergic neurons in the nucleus accumbens. Serotonin reuptake-inhibiting antidepressants such as *sertraline* (Zoloft, Chapter 7) reduce alcohol drinking in alcoholics of lower risk and/or severity (Dundon et al., 2004). Interestingly, sertraline is more effective in reducing alcoholic behaviors in lower-risk alcohol-dependent males than in lower-risk alcohol-dependent females (Pettinati et al., 2004). The effectiveness of sertraline is discussed later in this chapter.

Cannabinoid Receptors. Within the past few years, important information has been gathered on the probable role of cannabinoid receptors (Chapter 17) in the actions of alcohol, especially in post-withdrawal cravings and in the relapse to drinking. Chronic ingestion of ethanol stimulates the formation of the endogenous neurotransmitter for cannabinoid receptors, a substance called *anandamide*. This neurotransmitter activates the cannabinoid receptors and, with continued ethanol ingestion, eventually leads to down regulation of these receptors. Down regulation then disinhibits the nucleus accumbens, our endogenous reward system. Removal of ethanol by cessation of drinking leads to a hyperactive endocannabinoid reaction, which appears to result in a craving for alcohol and a return to drinking.

Mice that are genetically inbred to lack cannabinoid receptors do not voluntarily consume alcohol and also lack alcohol-induced dopamine-mediated reward responses in the nucleus accumbens (Hungund et al., 2003). Similarly, administration of drugs that block cannabinoid receptors (cannabinoid antagonists) prevents relapse to alcohol ingestion (Serra et al., 2002). Therefore, it now appears that ethanol and cannabinoid agonists (for example, tetrahydrocannabinol in marijuana) activate the same reward system. Down regulation of cannabinoid receptors may be involved in the development of tolerance to and dependence on ethanol, and an active response from cannabinoid receptors after alcohol detoxification may lead to alcohol craving and eventual compulsion to relapse (Wang et al., 2003). The effects of the cannabinoid antagonists such as rimonobant (Acomplia) are discussed later in this chapter.

Pharmacological Effects

The graded, reversible depression of behavior and cognition is the primary pharmacological effect of alcohol. Respiration is transiently stimulated at low doses, but as blood concentrations of alcohol increase, respiration becomes progressively depressed; at very high, doses, respiration ceases, causing death. Alcohol is also anticonvulsant, although it is not clinically used for this purpose. On the other hand, withdrawal from alcohol ingestion is accompanied by a prolonged period of hyperexcitability, and seizures can occur; seizure activity peaks approximately 8 to 12 hours after the last drink.

In the CNS, the effects of alcohol are additive with those of other sedative-hypnotic compounds, resulting in more sedation and greater impairment of motor and cognitive abilities. Other sedatives (especially the benzodiazepines) and marijuana are the sedative-hypnotic drugs most frequently combined with alcohol, and they increase its deleterious effects on motor and intellectual skills (for example, driving ability) as well as alertness. Patients suffering from insomnia find alcohol to be an effective hypnotic agent.

Alcohol also affects the circulation and the heart. Alcohol dilates the blood vessels in the skin, producing a warm flush and a decrease in body temperature. Thus, it is pointless and possibly dangerous to drink alcohol to keep warm when one is exposed to cold weather. Long-term use of high doses of alcohol is associated with diseases of the heart muscle, which can result in heart failure. However, recent observations have demonstrated that *low* doses of alcohol consumed daily (up to 2 drink equivalents per day for men and 0.5 to 1.0 daily drink equivalent for women) *reduce* the risk of coronary artery disease (Mukamal et al., 2003) and peripheral artery disease (Djousse et al., 2000). This protective effect on coronary and peripheral blood vessels occurs because of an alcohol-induced increase in high-density lipoprotein in blood with a corresponding decrease in low-density lipoprotein. (The higher the concentration of high-density lipoprotein and the lower the concentration of low-density lipoprotein, the lower is the incidence of development of arteriosclerosis and occlusive vascular disease.) Unfortunately, the cardioprotective effect of low doses of alcohol is lost on people who also smoke cigarettes.

Light to moderate doses of alcohol have also been shown to reduce the incidence of ischemic strokes (Figure 4.6). Ischemic strokes are strokes due to loss of oxygen delivery to specific areas of the brain. This protective action can reduce the risk of dementia among older adults (Solfrizzi et al., 2007). The mechanisms responsible for the protective effect of low doses of alcohol on ischemic stroke appear to involve alcohol-induced increases in (protective) high-density cholesterol and an aspirinlike decrease in platelet aggregation. Higher amounts of alcohol (more than 14 drinks per week) were associated with an increased risk of stroke.

Alcohol (like all depressant drugs) is not an aphrodisiac. The behavioral disinhibition induced by low doses of alcohol may appear to cause some loss of restraint, but alcohol depresses body function and interferes with sexual performance. As Shakespeare says in *Macbeth:* "It provokes the desire, but it takes away the performance."

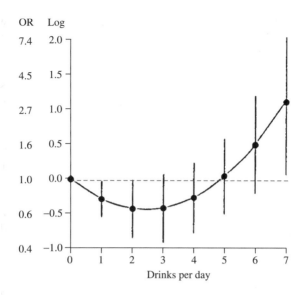

FIGURE 4.6 Relationship between alcohol and stroke. The reference group (indicated by the dashed horizontal line) is those not drinking during the past year. Analysis is matched for age, sex, and race/ethnicity and adjusted for hypertension, diabetes, heart disease, cigarette use, and education. OR = odds ratio for having a stroke. Log = logarithmic scale of stroke incidence. Vertical lines indicate 95 percent confidence intervals. [From R. L. Sacco et al., "The Protective Effect of Moderate Alcohol Consumption on Ischemic Stroke," *Journal of the American Medical Association* 281 (1999), p. 57.]

Psychological Effects

The short-term psychological and behavioral effects of alcohol are primarily restricted to the CNS, where a mixture of stimulant and depressant effects is seen after low doses of the drug. Figure 4.7 correlates the effects of alcohol with levels of the drug measured in the blood. The behavioral reaction to disinhibition, which occurs at low doses, is largely determined by the person, his or her mental expectations, and the environment in which drinking occurs. In one setting a person may become relaxed and euphoric; in another he or she may become withdrawn or violent. Mental expectations and the physical setting become progressively less important at increasing doses because the sedative effects increase and behavioral activity decreases.

As doses increase, a person may still function (although with less coordination) and attempt to drive or otherwise endanger self and others. Perceptual speed is an important component of task performance and is markedly impaired by ethanol (Schweizer et al., 2004). At BAC values of about 0.05 to 0.09 grams%, some common clinical symptoms

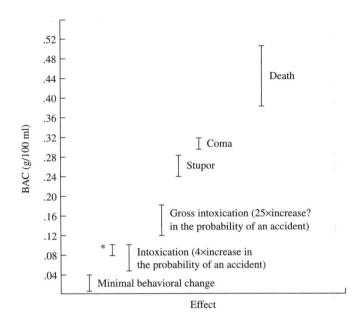

FIGURE 4.7 Correlation of the blood level of ethanol with degrees of intoxication. The legal level of intoxication (*) varies according to state law; the range of BAC values is shown. BAC = blood alcohol concentration.

are sociability, talkativeness, decreased inhibitions, diminution of attention, judgment, and control, slowed information processing, and loss of efficiency in critical performance testing. As the BAC increases, the drinker becomes progressively more incapacitated. Memory, concentration, and insight are progressively dulled and lost. At a BAC of about 0.25 grams%, the ability to transcribe (form) memory proteins from genetic material (Chapter 3) is lost and "blackout"—a state closely related to organic dementia with severe cognitive dysfunction—occurs.

Alcohol intoxication, with its resulting disinhibition, plays a major role in a large percentage of violent crimes, including fighting, rape, sexual assault, and certain kinds of deviant behaviors. Alcohol is implicated in more than half of all homicides and assaults; about 40 percent of violent offenders in jail were drinking at the time of the offense for which they were incarcerated. Many of these offenses probably would not have occurred if the offender, the victim, or both had not been intoxicated (McClelland and Teplin, 2001). Martin (2001) studied how alcohol use by men affects intimate-partner violence. She states that alcohol intoxication may contribute to aggressive and criminal behavior through its mediating effects on the physiological, cognitive, affective, or behavioral functioning of the drinker. Through effects on the GABA system, alcohol reduces the anxiety about the consequences of aggressive behavior. Through dopaminergic activation, impulse control is reduced, which increases the likelihood of aggression. Through glutamate depression, cognitive functioning is impaired, reducing the drinker's ability to find peaceful (nonviolent) solutions to difficult situations. Many drinkers develop a type of "alcohol myopia," defined as shortsightedness in which superficially understood, immediate aspects of experience have a disproportionate influence on behavior and emotion. Cognitive and attentional deficits cause a focus on the present, reduce fear and anxiety, and impair problem solving. Finally, alcohol use increases concerns with power and dominance, linked to male violence generally and to intimate-partner interactions in particular. The effect can be an inappropriate sense of mastery, control, or power (Abbey et al., 2002). This issue of violence and crime applies to women as well as to men (Martin and Bryant, 2001). In fact, the effects of ethanol on aggression and violence, in the absence of cocaine, are more then three times as great for female as for male arrestees.

Hindson and coworkers (2001) surveyed 42,000 adults as part of a U.S. Census Bureau survey about alcohol use/abuse and physical fighting. Relative to those who did not begin drinking until age 21 or older, those who started drinking before age 17 were three to four times more likely ever in their lives and at least three times more likely in the past year to have been in a fight after drinking. Thus, early-age onset of drinking is associated with alcohol-related violence not only among people under 21 but among adults as well.

More than 50 percent of all motor vehicle highway accidents are alcohol related, a number that has changed little in 20 years. More than 10 million people in the United States currently suffer the consequences of their alcohol abuse, which include arrests, traffic accidents, occupational injuries, violence, and health and occupational losses. This number does not include the 10 million people considered to be alcohol dependent (and suffering their own negative consequences). About 10 percent of our society is personally afflicted with (or suffers the consequences of) another's alcohol use. Untreated alcohol problems lead to death, disability, and $185 billion each year in avoidable health, business, and criminal justice costs.

Noel and colleagues (2001) studied 30 recently detoxified male alcoholics (with matched controls) to assess "frontal lobe" or "executive" functioning and the vulnerability of the frontal lobes to alcohol abuse. In all tests of executive function, nondrinking alcoholics performed poorly compared with controls. The researchers stated:

> Chronic alcohol consumption is associated with severe executive function deficits, still present after a protracted period of alcohol abstinence. This supports the idea that cognitive deficit in detoxified, sober alcoholics is due, at least partly, to frontal lobe dysfunction. (p. 1152)

Furthermore:

> These findings could have important implications, particularly con-
> cerning relapse. Since drug use is largely controlled by automatic
> processes, executive functions are needed to block this and maintain
> abstinence. Thus, the existence of persistent executive function
> deficits could affect the capacity to maintain abstinence. (p. 1152)

Persistent alcohol use harms adolescents. Brown and coworkers
(2000) studied alcohol-dependent adolescents (who developed dependency in early adolescence) and found that recent detoxification was
associated with poor visuospatial functioning (as might be expected),
whereas alcohol withdrawal early in life was associated with persistence of poor retrieval of verbal and nonverbal information. This finding reflects long-term effects on working memory.

Long-term effects of alcohol may also involve many different organs of a person's body. Long-term ingestion of only moderate
amounts of alcohol seems to produce few physiological alterations. As
noted earlier, low to moderate doses can even be protective to the heart
and vascular system. On the down side, long-term ingestion of larger
amounts of alcohol leads to a variety of serious neurological, mental,
and physical disorders. These disorders are described in the section on
alcoholism and its pharmacological treatment.

Alcohol is quite caloric but has little nutritional value; consumption of a high-alcohol diet (and little else!) slowly leads to vitamin deficiencies and nutritional diseases, which may result in physical
deterioration. Alcohol abuse has been suggested as the most common
cause of vitamin and trace element deficiencies in adults.

Tolerance and Dependence

The patterns and mechanisms for the development of tolerance to,
physical dependence on, and psychological dependence on alcohol are
similar to those for other CNS depressants (Chapter 5). The extent of
tolerance depends on the amount, pattern, and extent of alcohol ingestion. People who ingest alcohol only intermittently on sprees or more
regularly but in moderation develop little or no tolerance. People who
regularly ingest large amounts of alcohol develop marked tolerance.
The tolerance is of three types:

1. *Metabolic tolerance,* where the liver increases its amount of drug-
   metabolizing enzyme. This type accounts for at most 25 percent of
   the tolerance to alcohol.

2. *Tissue, or functional, tolerance,* where neurons in the brain adapt
   to the amount of drug present. Drinkers who develop this type of

tolerance characteristically display blood alcohol levels about twice those of nontolerant drinkers at a similar level of behavioral intoxication. Note, however, that despite behavioral adaptation, impairments in cognitive function are similar at similar blood levels in both tolerant and nontolerant drinkers. In other words, at a BAC of 0.15 grams%, both tolerant and nontolerant drinkers display marked deficits in insight, judgment, cognition, and other executive functions. The tolerant person may just *appear* less intoxicated. As discussed, memory formation and severe cognitive impairments occur at a BAC of about 0.25 grams%. A "tolerant" person does not develop tolerance to these memory/cognitive effects but behaviorally may appear to function reasonably normally (for example, be able to drive home in a "blackout," although this activity is illegal).

3. *Associative, contingent, or homeostatic tolerance.* A variety of environmental manipulations can counter the effects of ethanol, and counterresponses are a possible mechanism of tolerance.

When physical dependence develops, withdrawal of alcohol results, within several hours, in a period of rebound hyperexcitability that may eventually lead to convulsions. Alcohol abuse is one of the most common causes of adult-onset seizures; seizures occur in about 10 percent of adults during alcohol withdrawal. Alcohol withdrawal seizures are a life-threatening consequence of alcohol cessation in alcoholics. The period of seizure activity is relatively short, usually 6 hours or less, but seizures can be very severe. Blocking seizure activity during withdrawal is a major goal of detoxification and usually involves two classes of agents: the benzodiazepines and the anticonvulsants. As early as 1978, Ballenger and Post noted that the severity of alcohol withdrawal seizures is correlated with the number of years of alcohol abuse and perhaps with the number of detoxifications.

A "kindling" model of alcohol withdrawal seizures suggests that repeated alcohol withdrawals may lead to an increase in the severity of subsequent withdrawals and a greater likelihood of withdrawal seizures with each detoxification. Indeed, the number of detoxifications is an important variable in the predisposition to withdrawal seizures (Figure 4.8). Malcolm and coworkers (2000) applied this concept to a postulate that holds that repeated detoxifications might also cause neurobehavioral alterations that may affect alcohol craving. Patients who had experienced multiple detoxifications had higher scores on tests that measure obsessive thoughts about alcohol, drink urges, and drinking behaviors. Thus, recurrent detoxifications may lead to increased rates of relapse due to a "kindling" of behaviors and thoughts leading to a compulsion to return to drinking. The researchers added that the kindling effect persists despite treatment with benzodiazepines or other traditional sedative-hypnotic drugs. In fact,

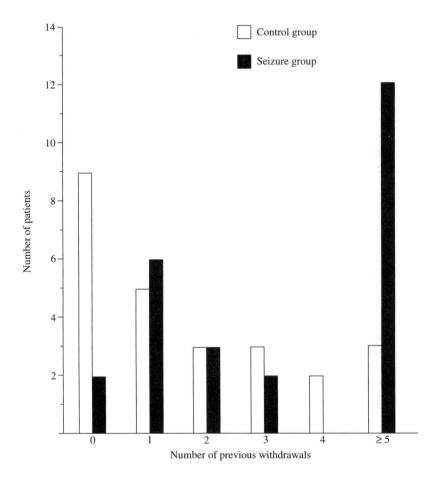

FIGURE 4.8 Number of previous withdrawals (prior detoxifications) in two groups of alcoholics. Fifty male alcoholics were divided into two groups. The control group had not experienced alcohol withdrawal seizures, and the seizure group comprised subjects who had experienced one or more withdrawal seizures in their past history. This figure demonstrates that 12 of the 25 alcoholics with a history of withdrawal seizures had undergone five or more detoxifications, compared to only 3 of the 25 in the control group. [From M. E. Brown et al., "Alcohol Detoxification and Withdrawal Seizures: Clinical Support for a Kindling Hypothesis," *Biological Psychiatry* 23 (1988), p. 511.]

the medical management of alcohol detoxification may be better achieved with anticonvulsant "mood stabilizers" (Chapter 8) than with benzodiazepines (Becker et al., 2006).

In addition to withdrawal seizures and cravings, the alcohol withdrawal syndrome can consist of a period of tremulousness, with hallucinations, psychomotor agitation, confusion and disorientation, sleep disorders, and a variety of associated discomforts—a syndrome that is sometimes referred to as *delirium tremens* (DTs).

Fadda and Rossetti (1998) reviewed withdrawal as a sign of alcohol-induced neuroadaptation and the neurodegeneration that may play a role in the persistent cognitive deficits that result from alcohol dependence. Markianos and coworkers (2000) assessed dopamine receptor responsiveness in alcoholic patients during their usual alcohol consumption and after detoxification. Detoxification was characterized by slow recovery of dopamine receptor responsiveness. The Markianos team postulated that the dopamine system is involved in alcohol dependence and withdrawal.

Side Effects and Toxicity

Many side effects and toxicities associated with alcohol have already been mentioned; following is a summary and expansion. In acute use, a *reversible drug-induced dementia* is induced. This syndrome is manifested as a clouded sensorium with disorientation, impaired insight and judgment, anterograde amnesia (blackouts), and diminished intellectual capabilities. Some mental impairments begin at low levels of alcohol. As levels approach about 0.20 grams%, memory becomes severely affected, and by a BAC of about 0.25 grams%, the ability to form memory is virtually absent and blackout becomes quite complete. John and Prichep (2005) discuss the different mechanisms probably involved at doses of sedatives required to produce amnesia; loss of consciousness occurs at much higher doses, and "anesthesia" occurs only following very much larger doses. In other words, a person who has ingested a large quantity of alcohol can be amnestic in the presence of consciousness, a concept that will be discussed further in Chapter 6.

With increasing doses (or blood levels) of alcohol, a person's affect may be labile, with emotional outbursts precipitated by otherwise innocuous events. With high doses of alcohol, delusions, hallucinations, and confabulations may occur. In social functioning, these alterations result in unpredictable states of disinhibition (drunkenness), alterations in driving performance, and uncoordinated motor behavior. As stated earlier, only at very high doses (perhaps at BACs greater than 0.35–0.4 grams%) is consciousness lost and a state of "anesthesia" with immobilization begun. At this point, respiration becomes shallow and fatalities can result.

Liver damage is a serious physiological long-term consequence of excessive alcohol consumption. Irreversible changes in both the structure and the function of the liver are common. For example, ethanol produces active oxidants during its metabolism by hepatocytes, which results in oxidative stress on liver cells. The significance of alcohol-induced liver dysfunction is illustrated by the fact that 75 percent of all deaths attributed to alcoholism are caused by cirrhosis of the liver, and cirrhosis is the seventh most common cause of death in the United States.

Long-term alcohol ingestion may irreversibly cause the *destruction of nerve cells,* producing a permanent brain syndrome with dementia (Korsakoff's syndrome). More subtle and persistent cognitive deficits may be present whether or not a diagnosis of Korsakoff's syndrome is made. This condition is termed *alcohol dementia,* and it can involve long-term problems with memory, learning, and other cognitive skills. The *digestive system* may also be affected. *Pancreatitis* (inflammation of the pancreas) and *chronic gastritis* (inflammation of the stomach), with the development of peptic ulcers, may occur.

A great deal of epidemiological evidence now shows that chronic excessive alcohol consumption is a major risk factor for *cancer* in humans. Although ethanol alone may not be carcinogenic, it is a cocarcinogen, or a tumor promoter. The metabolism of ethanol leads to the generation of acetaldehyde and free radicals. Acetaldehyde has been shown to promote tumor growth, promoting cancers of the oral pharynx, stomach, and intestine. Statistically, heavy drinking increases a person's risk of developing cancer of the tongue, mouth, throat, voice box, and liver. The risk of head and neck cancers for heavy drinkers who smoke is 6 to 15 times greater than for those who abstain from both. The risk of throat cancer is 44 times greater for heavy users of both alcohol and tobacco than for nonusers.

Although the finding is controversial, ethanol may increase the risk for breast cancer by still unidentified means; it may produce free radicals that cause oxidative stress to cells in breast tissue (Hamajima et al., 2002). Alcohol-associated breast cancers appear with highest frequency in postmenopausal women who report regular consumption of alcohol before the age of 40 years (Lenz et al., 2002). The increased risk of breast cancer may offset the beneficial effects of moderate alcohol consumption on cardiovascular disease.

Teratogenic Effects

For years we have known that alcohol is both a physical and a behavioral teratogen. Drug-induced alterations occur in brain structure and/or function. *Fetal alcohol syndrome* (FAS) is a devastating developmental disorder that occurs in the offspring of mothers who have high blood levels of alcohol during critical stages of fetal development; it affects as many as 30 to 50 percent of infants born to alcoholic women (Little et al., 1998). The rate of FAS is about 3 to 5 per 1000 live births. Clearly, a relatively large number of otherwise biologically normal infants may be irreversibly damaged by maternal alcohol abuse during pregnancy, and alcohol abuse during pregnancy appears to be the most frequent known teratogenic cause of mental retardation.

It is generally accepted that more than 3 ounces of absolute alcohol daily, especially in conjunction with binge drinking, poses a special risk of FAS to the fetus. Even very low daily doses of alcohol taken early in pregnancy can be associated with smaller body size (height and weight) in offspring even as late as their teenage years (Day et al., 2002). Whether neurodevelopmental alterations accompany this long-term effect is unknown at this time. Because subtle intellectual and behavioral effects of low-level alcohol consumption may go unnoticed, no safe level of alcohol intake during pregnancy has been established.

Features of the full fetal alcohol syndrome include the following:

- CNS dysfunction, including low intelligence and microcephaly (reduced cranial circumference), mental retardation, and behavioral abnormalities (often presenting as hyperactivity and difficulty with social integration)
- Retarded body growth rate (fetal growth retardation)
- Facial abnormalities (short palpebral fissures, short nose, wide-set eyes, and small cheekbones)
- Other anatomical abnormalities (for example, congenital heart defects and malformed eyes and ears) (Sampson et al., 1997, p. 317)

In the United States, an estimated 2.6 million infants are born annually following significant in utero alcohol exposure. Many display the full features of FAS, and about one newborn out of every hundred live births displays a "lesser degree of damage, termed *fetal alcohol effects,*" perhaps more correctly termed *alcohol-related neurodevelopmental disorder* (ARND) (Sampson et al., 1997). Taken together, the combined rate of FAS and ARND is estimated to be at least 9 per 1000 live births. Alcohol ingestion is thus the third leading cause of birth defects with associated mental retardation; it is the only one that is preventable.

Perhaps a new term should be utilized to encompass the full spectrum of fetal damage that can follow ingestion of ethanol by pregnant women. "Fetal alcohol spectrum disorder" would include both fetal alcohol syndrome and fetal alcohol effects, covering that gray line between infants with facial abnormalities and infants with "milder" effects, such as hyperactivity and aggressive behaviors.

Although the structural abnormalities and growth retardation of FAS are well described, the behavioral and cognitive effects of alcohol exposure are less appreciated. Affected and subject to deficits are intelligence (IQ), attention, learning, memory, language, and motor and visuospatial activities in children prenatally exposed to varying amounts of alcohol (Willford et al., 2004). Also present can be sensory problems involving ocular, auditory, vestibular, and speech and language development. Carmichael and coworkers (1997) studied a cohort of 500 children, 250 of whom were infants of "heavier" drinkers who typically drank at "social drinking levels." The other 250 children were infants of infrequent drinkers and abstainers. There were significant alcohol-related differences in behavioral and learning difficulties during adolescence. Exposure to alcohol during pregnancy was associated "with a profile of adolescent antisocial behavior, school problems, and self-perceived learning difficulties." Thus, brain function can be markedly affected in offspring of alcohol-drinking mothers in the absence of the observable structural abnormalities.

In a study in Finland, Autti-Ramo (2000) followed 70 children with fetal alcohol exposure (42 with recognized cognitive and other deficits, 10 with physical growth restrictions only, and 18 classified as normal). They were assessed at age 12 years for psychosocial well-being. The longer the alcohol exposure during pregnancy, the more likely the child was to have significant cognitive and social impairments. Of the 42 children with early recognition of cognitive deficits, 29 (69 percent) were in permanent foster or institutional care. Even among the children in the normal and growth-restricted groups, 10 (36 percent) were temporarily or permanently in alternative care. Behavioral problems were significant. Thus, alcohol exposure in utero can be associated with social disadvantages, including alternative care and behavioral problems.

Baer and coworkers (2003) reported results of a 21-year longitudinal study in which they followed offspring of 500 women who, in 1974–1975, drank during their pregnancy (30 percent binge drank). Offspring of 2 women displayed FAS and 31 offspring were identified as having components of ARND. When offspring attained the age of 21 years, 21 percent of their fathers and 11 percent of their mothers were identified as having had a history of alcohol problems. The offspring of mothers who binge drank during pregnancy exhibited three times the likelihood of at least mild alcohol dependence (14.1 percent versus 4.5 percent).

The mechanisms responsible for the production of FAS and ARND are unclear. Ikonomidou and coworkers (2000) reported that ethanol-treated rats had reduced neuronal densities in their developing forebrain; the effects occurred during the time period of synaptogenesis. The authors postulated that the neurodegeneration followed from both NMDA receptor blockade and positive $GABA_A$ receptor activation.

The prevention of FAS and ARND obviously involves abstinence from alcohol by women who are, plan to become, or are capable of becoming pregnant. Screening questionnaires may be effective in helping to protect not only the unborn infant but also the long-term health of the mother. Because alcohol screening can effectively identify women and infants at risk, it is recommended for women during prenatal visits.

Alcoholism and Its Pharmacological Treatment

The recognition of alcoholism as a multifaceted disease and behavioral process is relatively recent. In 1935, Alcoholics Anonymous was founded on a *moral model* of alcoholism; it offered a spiritual and behavioral framework for understanding, accepting, and recovering from the compulsion to use alcohol. In the late 1950s, the American Medical Association recognized the syndrome of alcoholism as an illness. In the mid-1970s, alcoholism was redefined as a *chronic, progressive, and potentially fatal disease.* In 1992, the description was expanded as follows:

> Alcoholism is a primary, chronic disease with genetic, psychosocial, and environmental factors influencing its development and manifestations. The disease is often progressive and fatal. It is characterized by impaired control over drinking, preoccupation with the drug alcohol, use of alcohol despite adverse consequences, and distortions in thinking, most notably denial. Each of these symptoms may be continuous or periodic. (Morse and Flavin, 1992, p. 1012)

In this definition, "adverse consequences" involve impairments in physical health, psychological functioning, interpersonal functioning, and occupational functioning, as well as legal, financial, and spiritual problems. "Denial" refers broadly to a range of psychological maneuvers that decrease awareness of the fact that alcohol use is the cause of problems rather than a solution to problems. Denial becomes an integral part of the disease and is nearly always a major obstacle to recovery.

Feldman and colleagues (1997) discussed a *behavioral model* of alcoholism:

- Alcohol consumption ranges from complete abstention to levels that induce chronic intoxication, and drinkers can move up and down the continuum of intoxication as a function of varying circumstances.
- The consequences of alcohol ingestion (at least in the short term) are behaviorally reinforcing.
- Alcohol drinking is subject to the same control mechanisms that govern other reinforced behaviors.
- Alcoholism is a learned but maladaptive behavior pattern.
- This behavior pattern can be altered by appropriate reinforcement contingencies, allowing for the possibility of controlled drinking in former alcoholics.

To this behavioral model must be added inherent genetic factors that confer heightened vulnerability to alcoholism in some people. Prescott and Kendler (1999) provide data and review the evidence for the strong role of genetic factors in the development of alcoholism among males; environmental factors seem to be much less important.

Regardless of a genetic, behavioral, or medical cause of alcoholism, it is now obvious that the *age of onset* of drinking behaviors markedly affects long-term outcomes and societal functioning. Heavy users of alcohol at early ages have, as might be predicted, the poorest outcomes as adults. Heavy drinking as early as age 13 years predicts a high risk for subsequent alcohol dependency, low levels of academic achievement, and poor interactions in family and social activities. Binge drinking at age 15 years and continuing through age 18 results in an even higher rate of alcohol dependency (Hill et al., 2000).

Rohde and coworkers (2001) followed a large cohort of adolescents (14 to 18 years old) through age 24 years. Approximately three-quarters of the adolescents at initial interview had tried alcohol; those who drank often consumed large quantities of alcohol. Problematic alcohol use occurred in 23 percent. Of the latter group, 80 percent had some form of comorbidity with alcohol use: increased rates of depression, disruptive behavior, drug use disorders, and daily tobacco use. By age 24, problem-drinking adolescents exhibited increased rates of substance abuse disorders, depression, and antisocial and borderline personality disorders. Therefore, early adolescent excessive alcohol use is not a benign condition that resolves over time.

In many cases, alcohol may (at least at first) be ingested in an attempt at *self-medication* of psychological distress. A person who, before drinking alcohol, experiences anxiety, depression, bipolar, or other responsive psychological disorders may find the symptomatology alleviated by ethanol. This then leads to unregulated and unmonitored drug ingestion (the drug is not taken under a physician's supervision). Either the positive reinforcing effects of the drug or drinking to avoid the unpleasantness of withdrawal then trap the person. In support of this concept, Goodwin and Gabrielli (1997) state:

> A good deal of evidence now indicates that many and perhaps most alcoholics do *not* have primary alcoholism. Their alcoholism *is* associated with other psychopathology, including addiction to other drugs, depression, manic-depressive illness, anxiety disorder, or antisocial personality. (p. 144)

They further state that 30 to 50 percent of alcoholics meet criteria for major depression; 33 percent have a coexisting anxiety disorder; many have antisocial personalities; some are schizophrenic; and many (36 percent) are addicted to other drugs. Some, if not many, alcoholics may have first used alcohol and become psychologically dependent on the drug as a self-prescribed medication to treat their primary disorder.

Lapham and coworkers (2001) studied psychiatric diagnoses in over 1000 males and females aged 23 to 54 years who were convicted of driving while impaired. Eighty-five percent of female and 91 percent of male offenders reported a lifetime alcohol use disorder; 32 percent of female and 38 percent of male offenders had a drug use disorder. Fifty percent of female and 33 percent of male offenders had at least one additional psychiatric disorder, mainly posttraumatic stress disorder or major depression. Woody (2001) discussed the implications and need to implement treatment interventions for these offenders. Court and diversionary programs focus on alcohol use, not on drug use and other psychological problems. The costs of treatment are high, and most offenders are unwilling to enter treatment (usually denial is present). Psychological assessments are rare, and education is ineffective. Rearrest rates are high. New incentives are needed, including biweekly urine and blood tests as a condition for driving. Kushner and coworkers (1999) demonstrate that in a college-age population,

> cross-sectionally, the odds of having either an anxiety disorder or an alcohol use disorder were two- to fivefold greater when the other condition was present. . . . Alcohol use disorders (especially alcohol dependence) and anxiety disorders demonstrate a reciprocal causal relationship over time, with anxiety disorders leading to alcohol dependence and vice versa. (p. 723)

Lejoyeux and coworkers (1999) noted that 38 percent of alcohol-dependent patients presented had an impulse-control problem. The co-occurrence of pathologic gambling (one type of impulse-control disorder) was associated with a younger age of onset of alcohol dependence, a higher number of detoxifications, and a longer duration of dependence. Both alcohol dependence and pathologic gambling are pleasure-seeking dependencies, and alcohol use may provide much the same reinforcement as gambling. Frye et al. (2003) discuss the co-occurrence of alcoholism and bipolar disorder. An overwhelmingly positive association exists between alcohol use disorder and personality disorders, especially antisocial, histrionic, and dependent disorders (Grant et al., 2004). *Dual diagnosis* (or *comorbid illness*) must always be presumed (until proven otherwise).

Dawson and coworkers (2007) studied the relationship between early-onset drinking (age 14 or younger) and life's stressors. They found that initiation of drinking at ages 14 or younger increased the association between the number of stressors and the average daily volume of alcohol ingested. Early-onset drinking thus appears to increase stress-reactive alcohol consumption. In other words, early-onset ethanol drinkers are more likely to use alcohol as a "stress reducer" than are drinkers who begin drinking at a later age. For example, early-onset drinkers increase their alcohol consumption (even in later life) 19 percent with each stressful event, compared with only a 3 percent increase by older-onset drinkers. Thus, early-onset drinkers grow into adults who rely on alcohol to cope more than do older-onset drinkers of similar age.

Alcoholism is a major public health problem. Of the 160 million Americans who are old enough to drink legally, 112 million do so. As many as 14 million Americans may have serious alcohol problems, and about half that number are considered to be alcoholic. Alcoholism costs about 100,000 Americans lives each year and in excess of $166 billion annually in direct and indirect health and societal costs. Older people who drink are at risk for their own set of problems.

In 2005, the National Institute on Alcohol Abuse and Alcoholism published a new clinician's guide asking all clinicians and mental health workers to screen for alcohol use patterns that place a person at risk for alcohol-related problems. This guide, titled *Helping Patients Who Drink Too Much* was updated in 2007 (National Institute on Alcohol Abuse and Alcoholism, 2007). Men who drink 5 or more standard drinks in a day (or 15 or more per week) and women who drink 4 or more in a day (or 8 or more per week) are at increased risk for alcohol-related problems (Dawson et al., 2005). The guide asks practitioners to utilize a simple, single question pre-screen: "Do you sometimes drink beer, wine, or other alcoholic beverages?" A "yes" answer leads to two additional questions to determine a weekly average number of drinks ingested as well as determination of a maladaptive pattern of alcohol use. This guide can be down-loaded at www.niaaa.nih.gov.

Although widely recommended, brief interventions have proven efficacy in decreasing alcohol consumption only in unhealthy drinkers without alcohol dependence and in outpatient settings. Saitz and coworkers (2007) recently demonstrated that brief interventions are insufficient for the treatment of persons with alcohol dependence. More extensive, tailored interventions are necessary.

Pharmacotherapies for Alcohol Abuse and Dependence

Because alcoholism involves the ingestion of alcohol, eliminating the ingestion of alcohol is an obvious therapeutic strategy. Achieving success, however, is an extremely difficult task. Vaillant (1996) performed a remarkable 50-year follow-up of two cohorts of men who abused alcohol at an early age. One group consisted of university undergraduates and the second consisted of nondelinquent inner-city adolescents. By 60 years of age, 18 percent of the college alcohol abusers had died, 11 percent were abstinent, 11 percent were controlled drinkers, and 60 percent were still abusing alcohol. By 60 years of age, 28 percent of the inner-city alcohol abusers had died, 30 percent were abstinent, 12 percent were controlled drinkers, and 30 percent were still abusing alcohol. As alcohol abuse after age 60 can be devastating, the greater levels of abuse by college-educated males need to be addressed. Barrick and Connors (2002) discuss approaches to the treatment of older adults with alcohol use disorders.

The ideal goals of pharmacotherapy for alcohol dependence and abuse include the following:

- Reversal of the acute pharmacologic effects of alcohol
- Treatment and prevention of withdrawal symptoms and complications
- Maintenance of abstinence and prevention of relapse with agents that decrease craving for alcohol or the loss of control over drinking or make it unpleasant to ingest alcohol
- Treatment of coexisting psychiatric disorders that complicate recovery
- Limitation of neuronal injury during detoxification by blocking withdrawal-induced glutaminergic activation and glutamate receptor up regulation (Krupitsky et al., 2007)

Can these goals be met? First, at this time, no agent that can reverse the acute pharmacologic effects of alcohol is available. Some feel that caffeine can antagonize alcohol intoxication and increase alertness. This is not true, as a behavioral stimulant can only increase activity, not reverse the motor, cognitive, or other dysfunctions induced by alcohol. Therefore, acute alcohol intoxication is usually treated with supportive care to protect both the intoxicated person and others placed at risk of injury.

Pharmacotherapies are available for four interventions:

1. To treat and prevent withdrawal symptoms
2. To reduce relapse to drinking behaviors
3. To treat complications in alcohol-dependent people who are decreasing or discontinuing alcohol
4. To reduce glutamate release and glutamate receptor up regulation with subsequent neuronal damage

Medications can also effectively prevent and treat the symptoms, seizures, and DTs associated with withdrawal. In addition, medications are available to help address and treat the comorbidities observed in alcohol-dependent people. Medications include anxiolytics, antidepressants, and mood stabilizers. However, pharmacological agents are less effective in reducing the rates of relapse to renewed drinking.

Currently, three oral medications (naltrexone, acamprosate, and disulfiram) and one injectable medication (extended-release injectable naltrexone) are FDA-approved for treating alcohol dependence (Table 4.1). The expected introduction of orally administered rimonobant (a cannabinoid receptor antagonist; Chapter 17) will provide another important option. However, rimonobant probably will not be approved by the FDA for this use; it is likely to be used "off-label" for the treatment of alcoholism. In addition, mood stabilizer anticonvulsants currently available have therapeutic efficacy as both detoxification and antirelapse agents.

TABLE 4.1 Drugs used to decrease alcohol consumption, reduce craving, maintain abstinence, or prevent relapse in alcohol-dependent individuals

Drug	Mechanism	Comments
Disulfiram	Inhibits aldehyde dehydrogenase to allow acetaldehyde accumulation	Clinical efficacy in question as a result of controlled trials. Effective in special situations.
Calcium carbimide	Same as disulfiram	May have fewer side effects than disulfiram. Available in Canada, not in USA.
Naltrexone	Endogenous opioid antagonist	Approved by FDA for treating alcohol dependence. Reduces consumption in heavy drinkers.
Acamprosate	NMDA and GABA$_A$ receptor modulator	Reduces unpleasant effects of alcohol abstinence, reduces craving. May have adverse fetal effects.
Fluoxetine and other serotonin antidepressants	SSRI-type serotonin agonist	Reduces depression and anxiety comorbid with alcohol dependency.
Buspirone	Serotonin 5-HT$_{1A}$ agonist	Little demonstrable efficacy may be due to inadequate amounts in blood.
Ondansetron, Ritanserin	Serotonin 5-HT$_3$ antagonists	May reduce craving. Poorly demonstrated efficacy.
Carbamazepine	Mood stabilizer, anticonvulsant	Can reduce unpleasant withdrawal effects.
Gamma-hydroxy-butyrate (GHB)	NMDA antagonist	Sedative-euphoriant. Can alleviate withdrawal symptoms. Subject to abuse.
Bromocriptine	Dopamine agonist	Can reduce craving. Little documented efficacy in reducing relapse.
Rimonobant	Cannabinoid receptor antagonist	Reduces desire to drink

Pharmacotherapies for Management of Alcohol Withdrawal

At its simplest, if taking alcohol reduces glutamate activity and increases GABA activity in the brain, alcohol withdrawal results in the opposite: reduced GABA activity and increased glutamate activity. These changes result in uncontrolled excitation and can damage cognitive functioning (Duka et al., 2003). The major therapeutic goal of managing acute alcohol withdrawal or detoxification is to prevent uncontrolled excitation by either reducing glutamate activity or increasing GABA activity.

Benzodiazepines. Increasing GABA activity is the mechanism underlying the use of the benzodiazepines as current drugs of choice for the treatment of acute alcohol withdrawal; they ameliorate the symptoms of withdrawal and also prevent seizures and DTs (Daeppen et al., 2002). It may not seem logical to substitute one potentially addictive drug (a benzodiazepine) for another (ethanol). An explanation follows. The short duration of the action of alcohol and its narrow range of safety make it an extremely dangerous drug from which to withdraw. When alcohol ingestion is stopped, withdrawal symptoms begin within a few hours. Substituting a long-acting drug prevents or suppresses the withdrawal symptoms. The longer-acting benzodiazepine is then either maintained at a level low enough to allow the person to function or is withdrawn gradually. Preferred drugs are the benzodiazepines with long-acting active metabolites—chlordiazepoxide (Librium) or diazepam (Valium). Acute seizure activity is well controlled with the faster-onset, shorter-acting benzodiazepine lorazepam. The pharmacology of the benzodiazepines is discussed in Chapter 6.

Anticonvulsant Mood Stabilizers. Malcolm and coworkers (2001) reviewed several studies relevant to the use of anticonvulsants in acute alcohol withdrawal and dependence. They note the limitations of benzodiazepines for this use: sedation, psychomotor deficits, and additive interactions with alcohol, and abuse and dependence liabilities. While older anticonvulsants have significant limitations that can be deleterious in alcoholics (contributing to liver and pancreatic problems, for example), they have historically been demonstrated to be effective. For example, carbamazepine (Tegretol) and valproic acid (Depakote) have been successfully used in place of benzodiazepines, despite potentially significant adverse side effects (Malcolm et al., 2002; Salloum et al., 2005). Newer anticonvulsants—for example, gabapentin (Neurontin), oxcarbazepine (Trileptal), lamotrigine (Lamictal) and topiramate (Topamax)—have significant potential and are less toxic than carbamazepine and valproic acid, which may make them a better choice than benzodiazepines for the treatment of alcohol withdrawal.

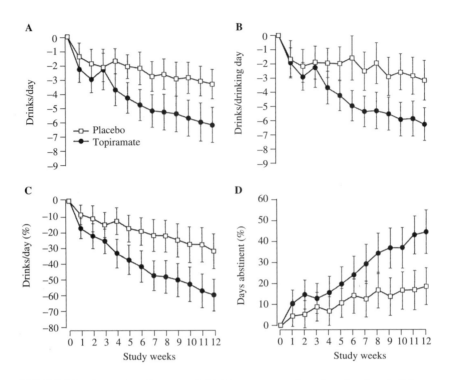

FIGURE 4.9 Change in self-reported drinking outcomes from baseline (week 0) forward for 12 weeks. **A.** Absolute reductions in drinks per day. **B.** Absolute reductions in drinks per drinking day. **C.** Percentage reduction in heavy drinking days. **D.** Percentage of days abstinent. The number of participants for each value varied from 48 to 75. Topiramate positively affected all four measurements. [From Johnson et al. (2003), p. 1681.]

Komanduri (2003) and Johnson and coworkers (2003) have demonstrated the efficacy and safety of topiramate (Topamax) in the treatment of alcohol dependency (Figure 4.9). Croissant and coworkers (2006) demonstrated the efficacy of oxcarbazepine (Trileptal) in alcohol-dependent patients. Therefore, with these demonstrations of efficacy, topiramate and oxcarbazepine are now two of the very few effective drugs currently available for treating alcohol dependence, even though such use is not FDA approved (it is "off-label").

Recently, Rubio and coworkers (2006) and Krupitsky and coworkers (2007) reported on the efficacy of lamotrigine (Lamictal) to improve mood, alcohol craving, and alcohol consumption while reducing glutamate release and presumably exerting "brain protection" during alcohol withdrawal in patients with alcoholism. The pharmacology of anticonvulsants is presented in Chapters 5 and 8, where they are discussed as mood stabilizers for the treatment of bipolar disorder.

Pharmacotherapies to Help Maintain Abstinence and Prevent Relapse

Numerous drugs to decrease daily consumption of ethanol and prevent clinical relapse to continued drinking have been tried; many are listed in Table 4.1. Some have been successful and many are of limited use.

Alcohol-Sensitizing Drugs. Among others, disulfiram (Antabuse) and calcium carbimide (Temposil, available in Canada only) are used to deter a patient from drinking alcohol by producing an aversive reaction if the patient drinks. These drugs alter the metabolism of alcohol, allowing acetaldehyde to accumulate. If the patient ingests alcohol within several days of taking the aversive drug, the accumulation results in an acetaldehyde syndrome, characterized by flushing, throbbing headache, nausea, vomiting, chest pain, and other severe symptoms. It is felt that calcium carbimide may have fewer side effects than does disulfiram. If taken daily, aversive agents can result in total abstinence in many patients. However, controlled trials of disulfiram therapy to reduce alcohol consumption have been disappointing, demonstrating that often disulfiram fares little better than placebo treatment.

Opioid Antagonists. Naltrexone was approved by the FDA in 1994 for use in the treatment of alcohol dependence to reduce the craving for alcohol, even though the effect was small. The hypothesis of action is that the reinforcing properties of alcohol involve the opioid system; blockade of the opioid system by naltrexone should reduce craving by reducing the positive reinforcement associated with alcohol use. Initial studies with naltrexone were encouraging; however, subsequent studies determined that the efficacy of orally administered naltrexone in the prevention of alcohol relapse is much more modest (Pettinati et al. (2006).

Preparations of naltrexone available for clinical use include oral naltrexone (ReVia), with once-daily dosing, and a new, extended-release injectable naltrexone (Vivitrol), given as a once-per-month injection (Swainstrom-Harrison et al., 2006). Compliance has always been a problem with naltrexone therapy. It is hoped that the long-acting injectable formulation will facilitate patient compliance by providing therapy over a period of one month per injection (Johnson et al., 2004; Johnson, 2007).

Mason and coworkers (1999) studied a related opioid antagonist, nalmefene (Revex). In an initial study in 105 adults with alcohol dependence, orally administered nalmefene was effective in preventing relapse to heavy drinking compared with placebo therapy (Figure 4.10); no medically serious side effects were observed. Subsequent studies (Anton et al., 2004) have been less enthusiastic. The pharmacology of naltrexone, nalmefene, and other opioid antagonists is discussed further in Chapter 16.

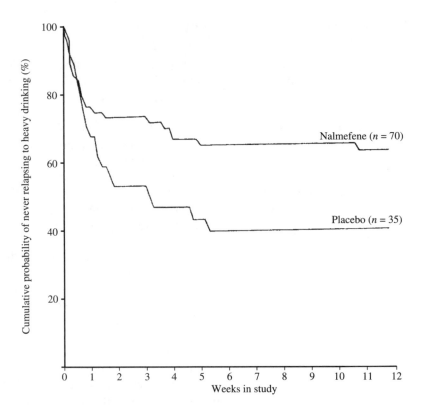

FIGURE 4.10 Rates of never relapsing to heavy drinking from randomization (week 0) through the end of double-blind treatment. [From Mason et al. (1999), p. 722.]

Acamprosate. Acamprosate (Campral) has recently become FDA approved for use in the treatment of alcoholism in the United States. Acamprosate was the first pharmacologic agent specifically designed to maintain abstinence in ethanol-dependent people after detoxification. With a chemical structure similar to that of GABA (see Figure 4.5), acamprosate is thought to exert both a GABA-agonistic action at GABA receptors and an inhibitory action at glutaminergic NMDA receptors, actions similar to those exerted by ethanol. The drug is poorly absorbed orally and therefore is given in relatively high doses (about 2 grams per day). Acamprosate has a half-life of about 18 hours, and it is excreted unchanged by the kidneys; it is not metabolized before excretion.

In early human studies, acamprosate was thought to be about three times as effective as placebo, with drinking frequency reduced by 30 to 50 percent. Today, it is thought to perhaps be comparable to naltrexone, with efficacy increased by adding the drug to established, abstinence-based, cognitive-behavioral rehabilitation programs (Feeney et al., 2002) or by combining the drug with naltrexone (Kiefer et al., 2003)

(Figure 4.11). In both situations, naltrexone and acamprosate, although less than impressive individually, can be effective used together and/or added to intensive psychotherapies. Since combination therapy may be important, Mason and coworkers (2002) studied the pharmacokinetic interaction between acamprosate and naltrexone. Coadministration of the two drugs significantly increased the rate and extent of absorption of acamprosate, as indicated by an average 33 percent increase in acamprosate blood level and a 33 percent reduction in time to peak blood level. Acamprosate did not affect the pharmacokinetics of naltrexone. Thus, when using the two drugs in combination, the dose of acamprosate, although poorly absorbed orally, can be reduced by 33 percent. This pharmacokinetic interaction was not utilized in the combination study reported by Kiefer and coworkers: they used a dose of 2 grams per day with or without naltrexone. How this interaction might have affected their results is unknown. Acamprosate, used alone in the treatment of alcohol dependence has had unremarkable effects, usually faring little better than placebo (Feeney et al, 2006; Doggrell, 2006; Morley et al., 2006). This relative lack of efficacy was verified in the COMBINE study discussed later.

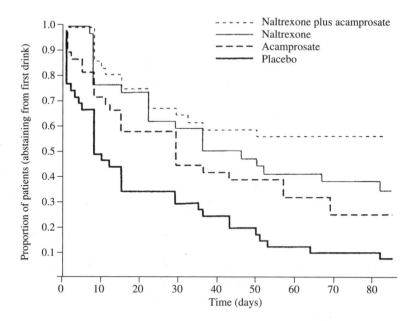

FIGURE 4.11 Time in days to relapse to drinking following a 2-week period of detoxification, followed by initiation of therapy with one of four regimens: placebo therapy, acamprosate (2 grams per day), naltrexone (50 milligrams per day), or combined acamprosate/naltrexone. Each group consisted of 40 patients. The three medication groups were significantly different from the placebo group in preventing or delaying relapse. In addition, the effects of combined medication were significantly different from the effects of either medication used alone. [From Kiefer et al. (2003), p. 96.]

Dopaminergic Drugs.   *Dopaminergic drugs,* such as *bupropion* (Wellbu-trin), have theoretical use in maintaining abstinence because (1) the posi-tive reinforcement associated with alcohol attractiveness appears to involve the dopaminergic reward system; (2) withdrawal may be accom-panied by hypofunction of this reward system; and (3) depression is often comorbid with alcohol dependency. Since bupropion acts as an antide-pressant at least partly through a dopaminergic action, patients with co-morbid depression and alcohol dependence might be candidates for treatment with this drug. Further study in this area is probably warranted.

Serotoninergic Drugs.   *Serotoninergic drugs* have been studied as agents for treating alcohol dependence. The research follows from the concept that there may be a relationship between serotonin function and alcohol consumption. In addition, different subtypes of alcoholics may be differentiated by the type or complexity of their serotonin dys-function (Pettinati et al., 2003). Beyond excessive drinking, behaviors that are indicators of serotonin dysregulation include depression, anxi-ety, impulsiveness, and early-onset drinking.

Three classes of drugs that affect serotonin function have been evaluated:

1. Selective serotonin reuptake inhibitors (SSRIs), such as *fluoxetine* (Prozac) and *sertraline* (Zoloft)

2. A serotonin 5-HT$_{1A}$ agonist, *buspirone* (BuSpar)

3. A serotonin 5-HT$_3$ antagonist, *ondansetron* (Zofran)

SSRIs and buspirone are FDA-approved for treating depression and anxiety disorders (Chapter 7). SSRIs have also been evaluated for treating alcohol dependence, especially when alcoholic patients exhibit comorbid mood or anxiety disorders. In general, the results have been inconsistent. However, some progress has been made and efficacy can be differentiated in Type A and Type B alcoholics (Cornelius et al., 2000). Type B alcoholics are characterized by early-age onset of drinking (ages 13 to 14 years), high levels of premorbid vulnerability, high levels of alcohol and other drug use severity, and high levels of comorbid psychopathology. Type B alcoholics respond poorly to treatment with SSRIs. Type A alcoholics have a later onset of heavy drinking (usually after the age of 20 years), lower levels of risk/severity of alcoholism, and lower levels of comorbid psychopathology. Type A alcoholics are relatively uncomplicated in their history and clinical presentation, despite high levels of alcohol consump-tion (Randall et al., 2001) (Figure 4.12). Both drinking behaviors and af-fective dysregulation (for example, depression) may be positively affected. The efficacy of buspirone has been disappointing.

The serotonin 5-HT$_3$ antagonist ondansetron has been shown to reduce drinking behaviors in patients with early-onset alcoholism.

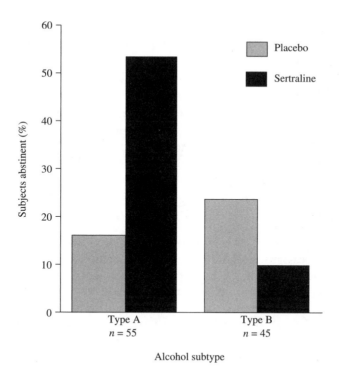

FIGURE 4.12 Proportion of alcohol-dependent subjects who maintained complete abstinence over a 14-week treatment period with respect to receiving either placebo or sertraline (an SSRI-type antidepressant) in double-blind fashion. Type A people were of the later-onset, lower-risk/severity class of alcoholics. Type B people were of the earlier-onset, higher-risk/severity class of alcoholics. There was a significantly different response to sertraline in Type A alcoholics but not in subjects with Type B alcoholism. [From H. M. Pettinati et al., "Sertraline Treatment for Alcohol Dependence: Interactive Effects of Medication and Alcoholic Subtype," *Alcoholism: Clinical and Experimental Research* 16 (2000), p. 1044.]

Patients with later-onset alcoholism were not benefited (Johnson et al., 2000). Ait-Daoud and coworkers (2001) reported potentiation of the action of ondansetron combined with naltrexone.

Nicotinic Mechanism. Chapter 14 discusses a new treatment for cigarette (nicotine) dependence. Varenicline (Chantix) is a "partial nicotinic agonist," reducing the reinforcing effect of nicotine. Early data indicate that it reduces the rate of relapse in people with alcohol dependence (Steensland et al., 2007). More should be forthcoming in this interesting area.

Cannabinoid Mechanisms. As discussed, we are just learning about a cannabinoid mechanism underlying alcohol craving and relapse (Basavarajappa and Hungund, 2002). Early data demonstrate that cannabinoid receptor antagonists such as rimonabant (Acomplia) can effectively moderate consumption of alcohol (Lopez-Moreno et al.,

2006; Fattore et al., 2007; Nowak et al., 2006; Maldonado et al., 2006) and may be a new generation of compounds for treating drug and alcohol dependence.

COMBINE Study

Treatment for alcohol dependence may include medications, behavioral therapies, or both. To understand how combining these treatments may impact effectiveness, a large, placebo-controlled study (1383 recently alcohol-abstinent volunteers in 11 treatment sites) was designed—the Combined Pharmacotherapies and Behavioral Interventions for Alcohol Dependence, or COMBINE, study. In different combinations, two medications (oral naltrexone and acamprosate) and two behavioral interventions (medical management, or MM, and combined behavioral intervention, or CBI) were employed. MM employed a series of brief counseling sessions to enhance medication compliance and abstinence from alcohol. CBI was a more intensive treatment similar to that used by trained psychotherapists working in alcoholism treatment facilities.

All treatment groups showed substantial reductions in drinking (Anton et al., 2006; Doggrell, 2006). Unexpectedly, acamprosate showed no evidence of efficacy; it reduced drinking no better than placebo. MM with naltrexone, CBI, or both fared better than placebo or acamprosate on drinking outcomes (percent days abstinent from alcohol and time to first heavy drinking day). No combination produced better efficacy than naltrexone or CBI alone in the presence of medical management. Placebo pills and MM had a positive effect above that of CBI alone. The authors concluded that "Naltrexone with MM could be delivered in health care settings, thus serving alcohol-dependent patients who might otherwise not receive treatment."

Pharmacotherapies to Help Treat Comorbid Psychological Conditions

Relapse to drinking behaviors and untreated comorbid psychological disorders are closely intertwined. Addictive behaviors and cravings as well as affective psychopathology (anxiety, depression, irritability, anger, insomnia, and so on) involve complex and poorly understood interactions between the opioid, dopaminergic, and serotonergic systems. Opioid and dopaminergic systems are probably involved in mechanisms of craving, and serotonergic dysfunction is at a minimum involved in affective dysregulation. Heinz and coworkers (2001) discuss the relationship between serotonergic dysfunction, negative mood states, aggressive behavior, and excessive alcohol intake.

When alcohol abuse and aggressive behaviors occur comorbidly, with or without abuse of other drugs, psychosocial and behavioral therapies are essential. Pharmacological treatments are not (and probably never will be) effective without the addition of intensive psychological therapies in all their various forms. In the treatment of affective disorders that occur comborbidly with alcohol dependence, antidepressants (Chapter 7) may be useful. Anticonvulsant mood stabilizers (drugs such as pregabalin or topiramate) may be of use in the control of emotional states such as anger, aggression, insomnia, and emotional outbursts (Chapter 8).

INHALANTS OF ABUSE

Inhalants are breathable chemical vapors that produce psychoactive (mind-altering) effects. They are among the most toxic and lethal of substances that can be abused.[5] Although other abused substances can be inhaled (for example, nicotine, THC, cocaine, methamphetamine), the term "inhalants" is used to describe a variety of substances whose main common characteristic is that they are rarely, if ever, taken by any route other than inhalation. A variety of products commonplace in the home and in the workplace contain substances that can be inhaled. A few were developed as general anesthetics (Chapter 5). Examples include nitrous oxide and halothane. These anesthetics were never meant to be used to achieve a "recreational" intoxicating effect. Likewise, other agents were developed for home and industrial use and were never intended to be used to affect the mind. Household inhalants include such products as nail polish remover, spray paint, glues, lighter fluid, hair and deodorant sprays, cleaning fluids, and pressurized whipped cream. Common industrial agents include gasoline, dry cleaning fluids, paint thinner, and paint remover. Table 4.2 lists many of the commonly encountered inhalants of abuse.

Not included in Table 4.2 are the *nitrites*, a special class of inhalants. Although other inhalants are used to alter mood, the nitrites are used primarily as sexual enhancers. Formerly, one nitrite (amyl nitrite) was used to dilate veins and reduce the workload of the heart; it relieved chest pain associated with coronary artery disease. Today, amyl nitrite is infrequently used for this purpose. Other nitrites (isobutyl nitrite and butyl nitrite) are sold as video head cleaners, leather cleaners, and so on. These nitrites produce vasodilatation and a "flush" with reduction in blood pressure that is claimed to increase sexual satisfaction.

Inhalant abuse (also known as *huffing* or *bagging*) is the intentional inhalation of a volatile substance for the purpose of achieving a euphoric state. Inhalant abuse disproportionately affects young people. Inhalants are frequently the first mind-altering drugs used by children, occasionally as young as 3 or 4 years of age. Inhalant abuse reaches its peak at some point during the seventh to ninth grades, with eighth graders regularly showing the highest rates of abuse (Figure 4.13). In 2004, eighth-grade girls reported more inhalant abuse than eighth-grade

[5]See www.inhalants.com

TABLE 4.2 Chemicals commonly found in inhalants

	Inhalant	Chemical
Adhesives	Airplane glue	Toluene, ethyl acetate
	Other glues	Hexane, toluene, methyl chloride, acetone, methyl ethyl ketone, methyl butyl ketone
	Special cements	Trichloroethylene, tetrachloroethylene
Aerosols	Spray paint	Butane, propane (U.S.), fluorocarbons, toluene, hydrocarbons, "Texas shoe shine" (a spray containing toluene)
	Hair spray	Butane, propane (U.S.), CFCs
	Deodorant, air freshener	Butane, propane (U.S.), CFCs
	Analgesic spray	Chlorofluorocarbons (CFCs)
	Asthma spray	Chlorofluorocarbons (CFCs)
	Fabric spray	Butane, trichloroethane
	PC cleaner	Dimethyl ether, hydrofluorocarbons
Anesthetics	Gas	Nitrous oxide
	Liquid	Halothane, enflurane
	Local	Ethyl chloride
Cleaning agents	Dry cleaning	Tetrachloroethylene, trichloroethane
	Spot remover	Xylene, petroleum distillates, chlorohydrocarbons
	Degreaser	Tetrachloroethylene, trichloroethane, trichloroethylene
Solvents and gases	Nail polish remover	Acetone, ethyl acetate
	Paint remover	Toluene, methyl chloride, methanol acetone, ethyl acetate
	Paint thinner	Petroleum distillates, esters, acetone
	Correction fluid and thinner	Trichloroethylene, trichloroethane
	Fuel gas	Butane, isopropane
	Lighter fluid	Butane, isopropane
	Fire extinguisher	Bromochlorodifluoromethane
Aerosol whipped cream canisters		Nitrous oxide
"Room odorizers"	Locker Room, Rush, poppers	Isoamyl, isobutyl, isopropyl or butyl nitrate (now illegal), cyclohexyl

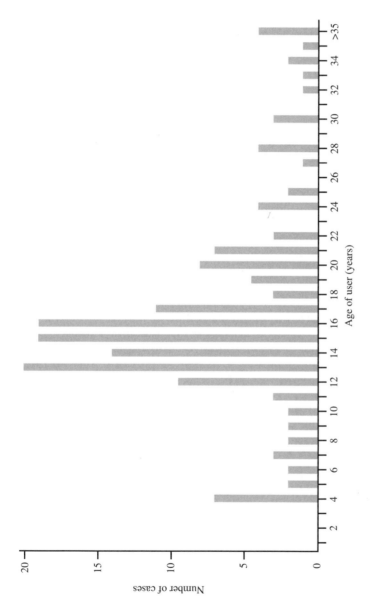

FIGURE 4.13 Bar graph of the ages of inhalant abusers who presented to the emergency room (total number = 165). The youngest inhalant abusers were age 4 years. The peak incidence was at 12 to 16 years. [From H. A. Spiller and E. P. Krenzelok, "Epidemiology of Inhalant Abuse Reported in Two Regional Poison Centers," *Journal of Toxicology—Clinical Toxicology* 35 (1997), p. 170.]

boys (10.5 percent versus 8.8 percent) using inhalants during the past year. By the twelfth grade, more boys than girls abuse inhalants (4.8 percent versus 3.4 percent). Inhalants are popular with youth because of peer influence, low cost, availability, and rapid onset of effect. When inhaled, they produce euphoria, delirium, intoxication, and alterations in mental status, resembling alcohol intoxication or a "light" state of general anesthesia. Users are usually not aware of the potentially serious health consequences that can result. Especially in children, inhalant abuse is an underrecognized form of substance abuse with significant morbidity and mortality.

Why Inhalants Are Abused and Who Abuses Them

Inhalant abuse goes back at least a hundred years, when ether, nitrous oxide, and chloroform were introduced into medicine as general anesthetics. Concomitant with their discovery as anesthetics was their discovery as intoxicating agents, leading to nitrous oxide and ether parties. Today, inhalant abuse is one of the most pervasive yet least recognized drug problems (Brouette and Anton, 2001). In the United States, the prevalence of inhalant abuse among adolescent youths is exceeded only by the use of marijuana, alcohol, and tobacco. More than 12 million Americans have abused inhalants at least once in their lives. Inhalant abuse is on the rise, with 1.8 million new users ages 12 to 17 years in a recent three-year period. A few users continue their abuse of inhalants into adulthood, usually as part of a polysubstance abuse pattern (see Figure 4.13). Patterns of abuse resemble patterns seen in abuse of other types of substances: there are experimenters, intermittent users, and chronic inhalant abusers.

Although injuries are associated with the frequency of use, the so-called sudden sniffing death syndrome can occur in first-time users. Brown and coworkers (1999) reviewed deaths from inhalant abuse in the state of Virginia over the ten-year period 1987–1996. The 39 deaths accounted for 0.3 percent of all deaths in males aged 13 to 22 years. Age of death ranged from 13 to 42 years; 70 percent of deaths occurred at 22 years of age or younger. Ninety-five percent of the deaths occurred in males. Gasoline fuels accounted for 46 percent of the fatalities. Butane and propane sniffing is also associated with "sudden sniffing death" due to production of rapid-onset, potentially fatal cardiac arrhythmias.

Medical Consequences of Inhalant Abuse

Most inhaled vapors produce rapid onset of a state of intoxication (or "drunkenness") that resembles alcohol intoxication, with slurred speech, impaired judgment, euphoria, and dizziness. Most inhalants produce intoxication that lasts only a few minutes. Therefore, abusers frequently try to prolong the high by continuing to inhale repeatedly over a course of several hours. This practice can be very dangerous for several reasons, including lack of oxygen (hypoxia) and asphyxiation, as well as the organ toxicities to be discussed. With increasing intoxication, the user experiences ataxia (staggering), dizziness, delirium, and disorientation. With severe intoxication come muscle weakness, lethargy, and signs of light to moderate general anesthesia. Even without hypoxia itself, hallucinations and behavioral changes may occur.

Toluene is a common ingredient in a number of the substances sought out for inhalant abuse, apparently for its euphorigenic, hallucinogenic, and behaviorally rewarding effects. Therefore, within the past few years several researchers have explored the effects of toluene on the brain (Bespalov et al., 2003; Gerasimov et al., 2002; Riegel and French, 2002). To summarize, toluene is taken up into and activates the central reward centers, including the mesolimbic dopaminergic reward centers and the frontal cortex, and this effect is accompanied by rewarding behaviors.

Not all inhalants exert this action on central dopaminergic reward centers, but many do. With some agents (particularly the *nitrites*), vasodilation and muscle relaxant effects appear to underlie use. With anesthetics, such as *nitrous oxide,* a state of light general anesthesia is induced, although reward activation may occur at low doses. With the *volatile solvents* and *fuels,* conclusions are difficult to draw, but their profile of acute behavioral and pharmacological effects is similar to that observed with subanesthetic concentrations of clinically used volatile anesthetics.

Although death is relatively rare during acute intoxication, when it does occur, it usually follows from lack of oxygen to the brain (anoxia), cardiac arrhythmias, aspiration of vomitus, or trauma (Kurtzman et al., 2001; Zvosec et al., 2001). S*udden sniffing death syndrome* may account for 50 percent of fatalities from acute intoxication. Volatile hydrocarbons sensitize the heart to serious arrhythmias when a person is startled or becomes excited during intoxication. The sudden surge of adrenaline acts on the sensitized heart to set off serious and life-threatening arrhythmias. This kind of episode can occur during initial experimentation and during any episode of abuse.

With *chronic abuse* of inhalants, serious complications can include peripheral and central nervous system dysfunction (peripheral neuropathies and encephalopathy), liver and/or kidney failure, dementia, loss of cognitive and other higher functions, gait disturbances, and loss of coordination. In a study of 55 inhalant abusers with an average 10 years of abusing, Rosenberg and coworkers (2002) administered a battery of cognitive tests as well as performing magnetic resonance imaging (MRI). This group was compared with a group of 61 cocaine abusers. Both groups displayed scores below general population averages on tests of cognitive functioning, but inhalant abusers consistently scored even below the cocaine abusers on tests involving working memory, planning, and problem solving. Almost half of the inhalant abusers had abnormalities in their MRI scans (compared to 25 percent of the cocaine abusers). Most marked was diffuse white matter degeneration in several brain areas.

Many people who abuse inhalants for prolonged periods over many days feel a strong need to continue abusing them, implying compulsive abuse. A mild withdrawal syndrome can follow long-term abuse, perhaps similar to withdrawal from any of many sedative-hypnotic drugs. Long-term inhalant abusers exhibit symptoms including weight loss, muscle weakness, disorientation, incoordination, irritability, depression, and neurocognitive deficits.

Treatment of acute inhalant intoxication is primarily supportive with the administration of supplemental oxygen. Treatment of chronic inhalant abuse is much more difficult. Results of a recent survey of 550 drug treatment program directors indicate that most inhalant abusers have a pessimistic attitude about the treatment effectiveness and hopes for long-term recovery (Beauvais et al., 2002). The surveyed directors perceived that a great deal of neurological damage results from inhalant use and that education, preventive efforts, and treatments are inadequate. Early identification of abusers and rapid intervention are essential in preventing both short-term and long-term consequences.

Standard approaches are generally ineffective for inhalant abusers because of the need for long-term detoxification and adverse effects on cognitive function. Talk therapies are inappropriate for many patients with neurological dysfunction, and the short attention span and poor impulse control that many patients have makes group therapy a poor choice as well. Instead, special treatment approaches for habitual users might include the following:

- Detoxification
- Medical and neurological evaluation
- Neurocognitive assessment
- Neurocognitive rehabilitation for patients who are impaired
- Academic programs to ensure participation in school
- Team approach with medical, neurological, psychological, occupational, psychomotor rehabilitation, and educational components
- Occupational and physical therapy where indicated
- Restriction or elimination of access to inhalable substances
- Aftercare that takes easy availability of inhalants into account, as well as residual cognitive impairment and poor social functioning

The best treatment is prevention. It must come from everyone involved in a child's life: parents, educators, school nurses, school bus drivers, and school cafeteria workers.

STUDY QUESTIONS

1. Pharmacologically, what is ethyl alcohol?

2. Describe the metabolism of alcohol. What enzymes are involved? What drug blocks one of these enzymes?

3. How do women and men differ in their metabolism of alcohol?

4. How does the kinetics of alcohol metabolism differ from that of most other drugs?

5. How long does it take for an adult to metabolize the alcohol in a 1-ounce glass of 80 proof whiskey? A 4-ounce glass of wine? A 12-ounce bottle of beer? A pint of 7 percent microbrew?

6. What BAC is defined in most states as "intoxication"?

7. Describe how alcohol exerts its effects on the CNS.

8. Why might a person who has developed a physical dependence on alcohol be treated with a benzodiazepine as a substitute for the alcohol?

9. Summarize some of the drugs and techniques used in treating alcoholism. What medications might be used to ameliorate alcohol withdrawal? Differentiate alcohol withdrawal from alcoholism. Discuss in terms of the COMBINE report.

10. Describe the disease concept of alcoholism. Discuss the comorbidity of alcohol dependence with other psychological disorders.

11. Describe some of the fetal effects of alcohol. Is there a "safe" level of drinking during pregnancy?

12. Summarize some of the problems associated with inhalant abuse.

REFERENCES

Abbey, A., et al. (2002). "How Does Alcohol Contribute to Sexual Assault? Explanations from Laboratory and Survey Data." *Alcoholism: Clinical and Experimental Research* 26: 575–581.

Agartz, I., et al. (2003). "CSF Monoamine Metabolites and MRI Brain Volumes in Alcohol Dependence." *Psychiatry Research* 122: 21–35.

Ait-Daoud, N., et al. (2001). "Combining Ondansetron and Naltrexone Reduces Craving Among Biologically Predisposed Alcoholics: Preliminary Clinical Evidence." *Psychopharmacology* 154: 23–27.

Anton, R. F., et al. (2004). "A Multi-Site Dose Ranging Study of Nalmefene in the Treatment of Alcohol Dependence." *Journal of Clinical Psychopharmacology* 24: 421–428.

Anton, R. F. et al. (2006). "Combined Pharmacotherapies and Behavioral Interventions for Alcohol Dependence: The COMBINE Study: A Randomized Controlled Trial." *Journal of the American Medical Association* 295: 2003–2017.

Autti-Ramo, I. (2000). "Twelve-Year Follow-Up of Children Exposed to Alcohol in Utero." *Developmental Medicine and Child Neurology* 42: 406–411.

Baer, J. S., et al. (2003). "A 21-Year Longitudinal Analysis of the Effects of Prenatal Alcohol Exposure on Young Adult Drinking." *Archives of General Psychiatry* 60: 377–385.

Ballenger, J. C., and R. M. Post (1978). "Kindling as a Model for Alcohol Withdrawal Syndromes." *British Journal of Psychiatry* 133: 1–14.

Barrick, C., and G. J. Connors (2002). "Relapse Prevention and Maintaining Abstinence in Older Adults with Alcohol-Use Disorders." *Drugs and Aging* 19: 583–594.

Basavarajappa, B. S., and B. L. Hungund (2002). "Neuromodulatory Role of the Endocannabinoid Signaling System in Alcoholism: An Overview." *Prostaglandins, Leukotrienes and Essential Fatty Acids* 66: 287–299.

Beauvais, F., et al. (2002). "A Survey of Attitudes Among Drug Use Treatment Providers Toward the Treatment of Inhalant Users." *Substance Use and Abuse* 37: 1391–1410.

Becker, H. C., et al. (2006). "Pregabalin Is Effective Against Behavioral and Electrographic Seizures During Alcohol Withdrawal." *Alcohol and Alcoholism* 24: 399–406.

Bespalov, A., et al. (2003). "Facilitation of Electrical Brain Self-Stimulation Behavior by Abused Solvents." *Pharmacology and Biochemistry of Behavior* 75: 199–208.

Boehm, S. L. et al. (2002). "Ventral Tegmental Area Region Governs GABA(B) Receptor Modulation of Ethanol-Stimulated Activity in Mice." *Neuroscience* 115: 185–200.

Brouette, T., and R. Anton (2001). "Clinical Review of Inhalants." *American Journal on Addictions* 10: 79–94.

Brown, S. A., et al. (2000). "Neurocognitive Functioning of Adolescents: Effects of Protracted Alcohol Use." *Alcoholism: Clinical and Experimental Research* 24: 164–171.

Brown, S. E., et al. (1999). "Deaths Associated with Inhalant Abuse in Virginia from 1987 to 1996." *Drug and Alcohol Dependence* 53: 239–245.

Carmichael, H., et al. (1997). "Association of Prenatal Alcohol Exposure with Behavioral and Learning Problems in Early Adolescence." *Journal of the American Academy of Child and Adolescent Psychiatry* 36: 1187–1194.

Cornelius, J. R., et al. (2000). "Fluoxetine Versus Placebo in Depressed Alcoholics: A 1-Year Follow-Up Study." *Addiction Behavior* 25: 307–310.

Croissant et al. (2006). "A Pilot Study of Oxcarbazepine Versus Acamprosate in Alcohol-Dependent Patients." *Alcoholism: Clinical and Experimental Research* 30: 630–635.

Daeppen, J.-P., et al. (2002). "Symptom-Triggered v. Fixed-Schedule Doses of Benzodiazepine for Alcohol Withdrawal: A Randomized Treatment Trial." *Archives of Internal Medicine* 162: 1117–1121.

Dawson, D. A. et al. (2005). "Quantifying the Risks Associated with Exceeding Recommended Drinking Limits." *Alcoholism: Clinical and Experimental Research* 29: 902–908.

Dawson, D. A. et al. (2007). "Impact of Age at First Drink on Stress-Reactive Drinking." *Alcoholism: Clinical and Experimental Research* 31: 69–77.

Day, N. L., et al. (2002). "Prenatal Alcohol Exposure Predicts Continued Deficits in Offspring Size at 14 Years of Age." *Alcoholism: Clinical and Experimental Research* 26: 1584–1591.

Djousse, L., et al. (2000). "Alcohol Consumption and Risk of Intermittent Claudication in the Framingham Heart Study." *Circulation* 102: 3092–3097.

Doggrell, S. A. (2006). "Which Treatment for Alcohol Dependence: Naltrexone, Acamprosate, and/or Behavioral Intervention? *Expert Opinion in Pharmacotherapy* 7: 2169–2173.

Duka, T., et al. (2003). "Impairment in Cognitive Functions After Multiple Detoxifications in Alcoholic Inpatients." *Alcoholism: Clinical and Experimental Research 27:* 1563–1572.

Dundon, W. et al. (2004). "Treatment Outcomes in Type A and B Alcohol Dependence 6 Months After Serotonergic Pharmacotherapy." *Alcoholism: Clinical and Experimental Research* 28: 1065–1073

Fadda, F., and Z. L. Rossetti (1998). "Chronic Ethanol Consumption: From Neuroadaptation to Neurodegeneration." *Progress in Neurobiology* 56: 385–431.

Fattore, L. et al (2007). "An Endocannabinoid Mechanism in Relapse to Drug Seeking: A Review of Animal Studies and Clinical Perspectives." *Brain Research Brain Research Review* 53: 1–16.

Feeney, G. F., et al. (2002). "Cognitive Behavioural Therapy Combined with the Relapse-Prevention Medication Acamprosate: Are Short-Term Treatment Outcomes for Alcohol Dependence Improved?" *Australian and New Zealand Journal of Psychiatry* 36: 622–628.

Feeney, G. F., et al. (2006). "Is Acamprosate Use in Alcohol Dependence Treatment Reflected in Improved Subjective Health Status Outcomes Beyond Cognitive Behavioral Therapy Alone?" *Journal of Addictive Diseases* 25: 49–58.

Feldman, R. S., J. S. Meyer, and L. F. Quenzer (1997). *Principles of Neuropsychopharmacology* (p. 627). Sunderland, MA: Sinauer.

Frezza, M., et al. (1990). "High Blood Alcohol Levels in Women: The Role of Decreased Gastric Alcohol Dehydrogenase Activity and First-Pass Metabolism." *New England Journal of Medicine* 322: 95–99.

Frye, M. A., et al. (2003). "Gender Differences in Prevalence, Risk, and Clinical Correlates of Alcoholism Comorbidity in Bipolar Disorder." *American Journal of Psychiatry* 160: 883–889.

Gerasimov, M. R., et al. (2002). "Study of Brain Uptake and Biodistribution of [11C] Toluene in Non-Human Primates and Mice." *Life Sciences* 70: 2811–2828.

Goodwin, D. W., and W. F. Gabrielli (1997). "Alcohol: Clinical Aspects." In J. H. Lowinson, P. Ruiz, R. B. Millman, and J. G. Langrod, eds., *Substance Abuse: A Comprehensive Textbook*, 3rd ed. (pp. 142–148). Baltimore: Williams & Wilkins.

Grant, B. F., et al. (2004). "Co-occurence of 12-Month Alcohol and Drug Use Disorders and Personality Disorders in the United States." *Archives of General Psychiatry* 61: 361–368.

Hamajima, N., et al. (2002). "Alcohol, Tobacco, and Breast Cancer— Collaborative Reanalysis of Individual Data from 53 Epidemiological Studies, Including 58,515 Women with Breast Cancer and 95,067 Women Without the Disease." *British Journal of Cancer* 87: 1234–1245.

Heinz, A., et al. (1998). "In Vivo Association Between Alcohol Intoxication, Aggression, and Serotonin Transporter Availability in Nonhuman Primates." *American Journal of Psychiatry* 155: 1023–1028.

Heinz, A., et al. (2001). "Serotonergic Dysfunction, Negative Mood States, and Response to Alcohol." *Alcoholism: Clinical and Experimental Research* 25: 487–495.

Heinz, A., et al. (2006). "Neurobiological Correlates of the Disposition and Maintenance of Alcoholism." *Pharmacopsychiatry* 36 (Supplement 3): S255–S258.

Hill, K. G., et al. (2000). "Early Adult Outcomes of Adolescent Binge Drinking: Person- and Variable-Centered Analysis of Binge Drinking Trajectories." *Alcoholism: Clinical and Experimental Research* 24: 892–901.

Hindson, R., et al. (2001). "Age of Drinking Onset and Involvement in Physical Fights After Drinking." *Pediatrics* 108: 872–877.

Hommer, D., et al. (2001). "Evidence for a Gender-Related Effect of Alcoholism on Brain Volumes." *American Journal of Psychiatry* 158: 198–204.

Hungund, B. L., et al. (2003). "Cannabinoid CB1 Receptor Knockout Mice Exhibit Markedly Reduced Voluntary Alcohol Consumption and Lack Alcohol-Induced Dopamine Release in the Nucleus Accumbens." *Journal of Neurochemistry* 84: 698–704.

Ikonomidou, C., et al. (2000). "Ethanol-Induced Apoptotic Neurodegeneration and Fetal Alcohol Syndrome." *Science* 287: 1056–1060.

John, E. R., and L. S. Prichap (2005). "The Anesthetic Cascade: A Theory of How Anesthesia Suppresses Consciousness." *Anesthesiology* 102: 447–471.

Johnson, B. A. (2007). "A Synopsis of the Pharmacological Rationale, Properties, and Therapeutic Effects of Depot Preparations of Naltrexone for Treating Alcohol Dependence." *Expert Opinion on Pharmacotherapy* 7: 1065–1073.

Johnson, B. A., et al. (2000). "Ondansetron for Reduction of Drinking Among Biologically Predisposed Alcoholic Patients: A Randomized Controlled Trial." *Journal of the American Medical Association* 284: 963–971.

Johnson, B. A., et al. (2003). "Oral Topiramate for Treatment of Alcohol Dependence: A Randomized Controlled Trial." *Lancet* 361: 1677–1685.

Johnson, B. A., et al. (2004). "A Pilot Evaluation of the Safety and Tolerability of Repeat Dose Administration of Long-Acting Injectable Naltrexone (Vivitrex) in Patients with Alcohol Dependence." *Alcoholism: Clinical and Experimental Research* 28: 1356–1361.

Johnson, B. A. et al. (2005). "Safety and Efficacy of GABAergic Medications for Treating Alcoholism." *Alcoholism: Clinical and Experimental Research* 29: 248–254.

Kiefer, F., et al. (2003). "Comparing and Combining Naltrexone and Acamprosate in Relapse Prevention of Alcoholism: A Double-Blind, Placebo-Controlled Study." *Archives of General Psychiatry* 60: 92–99.

Komanduri, R. (2003). "Two Cases of Alcohol Craving Curbed by Topiramate." *Journal of Clinical Psychiatry* 64: 612.

Krupitsky, E. M., et al. (2007). "Antiglutamatergic Strategies for Ethanol Detoxification: Comparison with Placebo and Diazepam." *Alcoholism: Clinical and Experimental Research* 31: 604-611.

Kurtzman, T. L., et al. (2001). "Inhalant Abuse by Adolescents." *Journal of Adolescent Health* 28: 170–180.

Kushner, M. G., et al. (1996). "The Effects of Alcohol Consumption on Laboratory-Induced Panic and State Anxiety." *Archives of General Psychiatry* 53: 264–270.

Lapham, S. C., et al. (2001). "Prevalence of Psychiatric Disorders Among Persons Convicted of Driving While Impaired." *Archives of General Psychiatry* 58: 943–949.

Lejoyeux, M., et al. (1999). "Study of Impulse-Control Disorders Among Alcohol-Dependent Patients." *Journal of Clinical Psychiatry* 60: 302–305.

Lenz, S. K., et al. (2002). "Association Between Alcohol Consumption and Postmenopausal Breast Cancer: Results of a Case-Control Study in Montreal, Quebec, Canada." *Cancer Causes and Control* 13: 701–710.

Little, B. B., et al. (1998). "Alcohol Use During Pregnancy and Maternal Alcoholism." In L. C. Gilstrap and B. B. Little, eds., *Drugs and Pregnancy*, 2nd ed. (pp. 395–404). New York: Chapman & Hall.

Lopez-Moreno, J. A., et al. (2006). "The CB1 Cannabinoid Receptor Antagonist Rimonabant Chronically Prevents the Nicotine-Induced Relapse to Alcohol." *Neurobiological Disease* 25: 274–283.

Malcolm, R., et al. (2000). "Recurrent Detoxification May Elevate Alcohol Craving as Measured by the Obsessive Compulsive Drinking Scale." *Alcohol* 20: 181–185.

Malcolm, R., et al. (2001). "Update on Anticonvulsants for the Treatment of Alcohol Withdrawal." *American Journal on Addictions* 10, Supplement: 16–23.

Malcolm, R., et al. (2002). "Differential Effects of Medication on Mood, Sleep Disturbance, and Work Ability in Outpatient Alcohol Detoxifications." *American Journal on Addictions* 11: 141–150.

Maldonado, R., et al. (2006). "Involvement of the Endocannabinoid System in Drug Addiction." *Trends in Neuroscience* 29: 225–232.

Markianos, M., et al. (2000). "Dopamine Receptor Responsivity in Alcoholic Patients Before and After Detoxification." *Drug and Alcohol Dependence* 57: 261–265.

Martin, S. E. (2001). "The Links Between Alcohol, Crime and the Criminal Justice System: Explanations, Evidence and Interventions." *American Journal on Addictions* 10: 136–158.

Martin, S. E., and K. Bryant (2001). "Gender Differences in the Association of Alcohol Intoxication and Illicit Drug Abuse Among Persons Arrested for Violent and Property Offenses." *Journal of Substance Abuse* 3: 563–581.

Mason, B. J., et al. (1999). "A Double-Blind, Placebo-Controlled Study of Oral Nalmefene for Alcohol Dependence." *Archives of General Psychiatry* 56: 719–724.

Mason, B. J., et al. (2002). "A Pharmacokinetic and Pharmacodynamic Drug Interaction Study of Acamprosate and Naltrexone." *Neuropsychopharmacology* 27: 596–606.

Matsuzawa, S., and T. Suzuki (2002). "Psychological Stress and Rewarding Effect of Alcohol." *Nihon Arukor Yakubutsu Igakkai Zasshi* 37: 143–152.

McClelland, G. M., and L. A. Teplin (2001). "Alcohol Intoxication and Violent Crime: Implications for Public Policy." *American Journal on Addictions* 10: 70–85.

Morley, K. C., et al. (2006). "Naltrexone Versus Acamprosate in the Treatment of Alcohol Dependence: A Multi-Centre, Randomized, Double-Blind, Placebo-Controlled Trial." *Addiction* 101: 1451–1462.

Morse, R. M., and D. K. Flavin (1992). "The Definition of Alcoholism." *Journal of the American Medical Association* 268: 1012–1014.

Mukamal, K. J., et al. (2003). "Roles of Drinking Pattern and Type of Alcohol Consumed in Coronary Heart Disease in Men." *New England Journal of Medicine* 348: 109–118.

Mumenthaler, J. T., et al. (2003). "Gender Differences in Moderate Drinking Effects." *Alcohol Research and Health* 23: 55–64. Published online at niaaa.nih.gov/publications/arh23-1/55-64.

Myrick, H., et al. (2001). "New Developments in the Pharmacotherapy of Alcohol Dependence." *American Journal on Addictions* 10, Supplement: 3–15.

National Institute on Alcohol Abuse and Alcoholism (2007). "Helping Patients Who Drink Too Much." NIAAA Publications Distribution Center, P. O. Box 10686, Rockville, MD 20849-0686. Downloadable at www.niaaa.nih.gov.

Noel, X., et al. (2001). "Supervisory Attentional System in Nonamnestic Alcoholic Men." *Archives of General Psychiatry* 58: 1152–1158.

Nowak, K. L., et al. (2006). "Pharmacological Manipulation of CB1 Receptor Function Alters Development of Tolerance to Alcohol." *Alcohol and Alcoholism* 41: 24–32.

Pettinati, H. M., et al. (2003). "The Status of Serotonin-Selective Pharmacotherapy in the Treatment of Alcohol Dependence." *Recent Developments in Alcoholism* 16: 247–262.

Pettinati, H. M., et al. (2004). "Gender Differences in Responses to Sertraline Pharmacotherapy in Type A Alcohol Dependence." *American Journal of the Addictions* 13: 236–247.

Pettinati, H. M., et al. (2006). "The Status of Naltrexone in the Treatment of Alcohol Dependence: Specific Effects on Heavy Drinking." *Journal of Clinical Psychopharmacology* 26: 610–625.

Prescott, C. A., and K. S. Kendler (1999). "Genetic and Environmental Contributions to Alcohol Abuse and Dependence on a Population-Based Sample of Male Twins." *American Journal of Psychiatry* 156: 34–40.

Randall, C. L., et al. (2001). "Paroxetine for Social Anxiety and Alcohol Use in Dual-Diagnosed Patients." *Depression and Anxiety* 14: 255–262.

Riegel, A. C., and E. D. French (2002). "Abused Inhalants and Central Reward Pathways: Electrophysiological and Behavioral Studies in the Rat." *Annals of the New York Academy of Sciences* 965: 281–291.

Rohde, P., et al. (2001). "Natural Course of Alcohol Use Disorders from Adolescence to Young Adulthood." *Journal of the American Academy of Child and Adolescent Psychiatry* 40: 83–90.

Rosenberg, N. L., et al. (2002). "Neuropsychologic Impairment and MRI Abnormalities Associated with Chronic Solvent Abuse." *Journal of Toxicology— Clinical Toxicology* 40: 21–34.

Rubio, G., et al. (2006). "Effects of Lamotrigine in Patients with Bipolar Disorder and Alcohol Dependence." *Bipolar Disorder* 8: 289–293.

Saitz, R., et al. (2007). "Brief Intervention for Medical Inpatients with Unhealthy Alcohol Use: A Randomized, Controlled Trial." *Annals of Internal Medicine* 146: 167–176.

Salloum, I. M., et al. (2005). "Efficacy of Valproate Maintenance in Patients with Bipolar Disorder and Alcoholism." *Archives of General Psychiatry* 62: 37–45.

Sampson, P. D., et al. (1997). "Incidence of Fetal Alcohol Syndrome and Prevalence of Alcohol-Related Neurodevelopmental Disorder." *Teratology* 56: 317–326.

Schweizer, T. A., et al. (2004). "Fast, but Error-Prone, Responses During Acute Alcohol Intoxication: Effects of Stimulus-Response Mapping Complexity." *Alcoholism: Clinical and Experimental Research* 28: 643–649.

Serra, S., et al. (2002). "Blockade by the Cannabinoid CB(1) Receptor Antagonist, SR 141716, of Alcohol Deprivation Effect in Alcohol-Preferring Rats." *European Journal of Pharmacology* 443: 95–97.

Solfrizzi, V., et al. (2007). "Alcohol Consumption, Mild Cognitive Impairment, and Progression to Dementia." *Neurology* 68: 1790–1799.

Steensland, P., et al. (2007). "Varenicline, an $\alpha 4 \beta 2$ Nicotinic Acetylcholine Receptor Partial Agonist, Selectively Decreases Ethanol Consumption and Seeking." *Proceedings of the National Academy of Sciences* 104: 12518–12523.

Swainstron-Harrison, T. "Extended-Release Intramuscular Naltrexone." *Drugs* 66: 1741–1751.

Vaillant, G. E. (1996). "A Long-Term Follow-Up of Male Alcohol Abuse." *Archives of General Psychiatry* 53: 243–249.

Wand, G. S., et al. (1998). "Family History of Alcoholism and Hypothalamic Opioidergic Activity." *Archives of General Psychiatry* 55: 1114–1119.

Wang, L., et al. (2003). "Endocannabinoid Signaling via Cannabinoid Receptor 1 Is Involved in Ethanol Preference and Its Age-Dependent Decline in Mice." *Proceedings of the National Academy of Sciences of the United States of America* 100: 1393–1398.

Willford, J. A., et al. (2004). "Verbal and Visuospatial Learning and Memory Function in Children with Moderate Prenatal Alcohol Exposure." *Alcoholism: Clinical and Experimental Research* 28: 497–507.

Woody, G. E. (2001). "More Reasons to Buckle Your Seat Belt." *Archives of General Psychiatry* 58: 950–951.

Zvosec, D. L., et al. (2001). "Adverse Effects, Including Death, Associated with the Use of 1,4-Butanediol." *New England Journal of Medicine* 344: 87–94.

What Is a Drink?
How Much Alcohol Is in My Drink?

One drink equivalent is the amount of alcohol that contains 10 cubic centimeters (1/3 ounce) of 100 percent ethanol. This is the amount of ethanol that the body metabolizes in 1 hour and that reduces the blood alcohol concentration (BAC) by 0.015 grams%.

This amount of alcohol is contained in about 1 ounce of 40 percent (80 proof) liquor, 3 ounces of 12 percent wine, a 12-ounce bottle of 3.2 percent beer, or 7 ounces of 5 percent beer. Most beers currently available are in the 5 percent range. Currently, there are only two 3.2 percent beer states in the country. All others allow higher alcohol contents.

The following beverages are converted to their calculated drink equivalents and the number of drink equivalents can be used with Figure 4.4 to estimate your BAC.

If you consume	You have consumed about
One 12-oz Budweiser (5% alcohol)	1.5 drink equivalents
One 6-pack of 12-oz Budweiser	9 drink equivalents
Short case (12 bottles) of 12-oz Budweiser	18 drink equivalents
One 16-oz Budweiser	1.9 (about 2) drink equivalents
One 24-oz Budweiser	3 drink equivalents
One 40-oz Budweiser	5 drink equivalents
One 12-oz Bud Light (4.2%)	1.25 drink equivalents
One 12-oz Bud-Ice (5.5%)	1.9 (almost 2) drink equivalents
One 16-oz Old English 800 (8%)	3.8 (almost 4) drink equivalents
One 40-oz Old English 800	9 drink equivalents
Two 40-oz Old English 800	18 drink equivalents (2/3 pint of whiskey)
One 16-oz Rainier Ale (7.2%)	3.5 drink equivalents
One 40-oz St. Ides Malt (7.3%)	8 drink equivalents
One 16-oz microbrew (5% to 7%)	2.2 to 3.4 drink equivalents
One 64-oz pitcher of microbrew	9.5 to 13 drink equivalents
One 12-oz Hornsby Draft Cider (6%)	2 drink equivalents
One 16-oz barley wine (10%)	4.8 drink equivalents
One 12-oz Zima cooler (4.6%)	1.6 drink equivalents
One 12-oz Mike's Hard Lemonade (5%)	1.8 drink equivalents

Comments

Budweiser and the other brand names are used for illustration only. Other beers are similar, with modest differences. Their alcohol concentration may or may not be listed on the label or package. Coors beer, another popular beer, is 4.9 percent alcohol; Coors Light is 4.2 percent. Busch beer is 4.5 percent; Henri Weinhard Private Reserve is 4.6 percent; Red Dog is 5 percent alcohol.

Ice beers are made by slightly freezing the brew and removing some of the ice, increasing the alcohol content. Most are 5.9 percent alcohol (12-oz bottle = 2 drink equivalents).

Wine coolers are classified as malt beverages and have alcohol contents from 4.6 percent to 7 percent. They are considered to be 1.5 to 2 drink equivalents per bottle.

A tavern can sell beer, ale, and malt liquor up to 14 percent alcohol, hard cider up to 10 percent alcohol, and wine up to 14 percent alcohol. Taverns and pubs often serve beer and ale in pitchers that contain from 60 to 72 ounces. If the pitcher contains regular draft beer at about 5 percent alcohol, a 64-ounce pitcher contains about 9.5 drink equivalents of ethanol.

Chapter 5

Barbiturates, General Anesthetics, Gamma Hydroxybutyrate (GHB), and Antiepileptic Drugs

Discussion of drugs that depress the functioning of the CNS began in Chapter 4 with ethyl alcohol. We continue the discussion by introducing the historically important drugs that were used as sedatives, sleeping aids (hypnotics), and antianxiety nostrums. Prior to the appearance of the third edition of the *Diagnostic and Statistical Manual of Mental Disorders* (DSM-III) in 1980, all anxiety disorder subtypes (as we know them today) were lumped under the single diagnostic entity, "anxiety neurosis." To treat anxiety neurosis, barbiturates and several older non-barbiturate sedatives, as well as the benzodiazepines (introduced in about 1960), were considered appropriate. Sedative-hypnotic drugs were also used to treat epilepsy and to produce general anesthesia for surgical procedures. These drugs are discussed in this chapter. Chapter 6 covers the pharmacology of today's most widely used sedatives: the benzodiazepines, their variants, and medicines currently indicated for use in the management of insomnia.

Historical Background

From time immemorial, human beings have sought ways and means of achieving release from distressing and disabling anxiety and of inducing sleep to counteract debilitating insomnia. *Alcohol* is undoubtedly the oldest drug used for these purposes. *Opium* (which contains *morphine* as its major active ingredient) has similarly been used to induce a somnolent stupor for relief from anxiety and to bring on sleep. The addiction potential of morphine and other "narcotics" limits this use. In the middle of the nineteenth century, *bromide* and *chloral hydrate* became available as safer, more reliable alternatives to alcohol and opium as sedative agents. Then, in 1912, *phenobarbital* was introduced into medicine as a sedative drug, the first of the structurally classified group of drugs called *barbiturates* (Figure 5.1). Between 1912 and 1950, hundreds of barbiturates were tested and approximately 50 were marketed commercially. The barbiturates so dominated the stage that

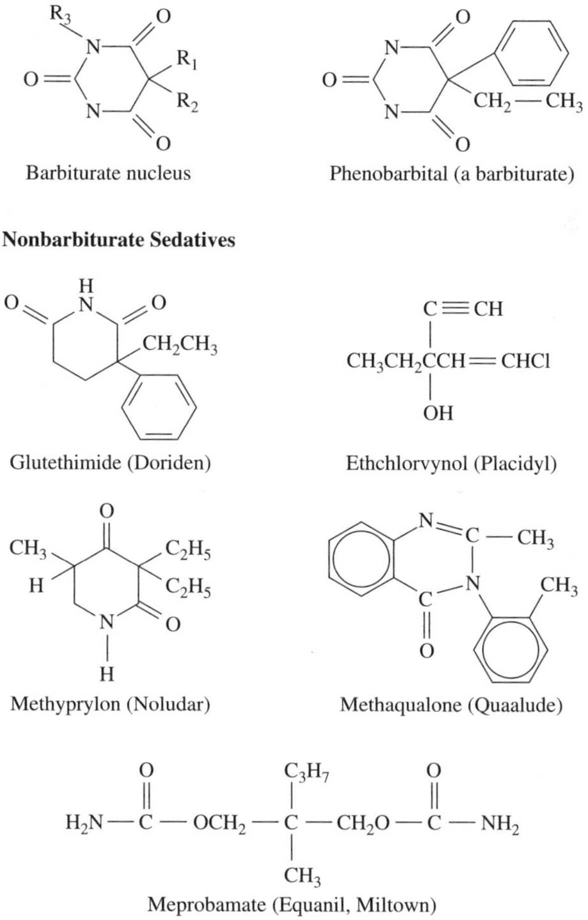

Barbiturate nucleus

Phenobarbital (a barbiturate)

Nonbarbiturate Sedatives

Glutethimide (Doriden)

Ethchlorvynol (Placidyl)

Methyprylon (Noludar)

Methaqualone (Quaalude)

Meprobamate (Equanil, Miltown)

FIGURE 5.1 Chemical structures of classical sedatives. Barbiturates are defined by containing the barbiturate nucleus. Nonbarbiturate sedatives do not have this basic structure.

few structurally different sedatives were successfully marketed before 1960, when *chlordiazepoxide* (Librium; Chapter 6) became the first available *benzodiazepine* tranquilizer, heralding a new era in the treatment of anxiety and insomnia.

When the barbiturates were discovered, researchers had no idea of the mechanisms through which they might exert their sedative actions. Therefore, they classified them instead by their chemical structure. All drugs that share this basic structure were classified as barbiturates and all shared the same spectrum of actions.

Sites and Mechanisms of Action

Historically, the sedative and hypnotic actions of the barbiturates and other sedatives have been perceived to result from a unique sensitivity of neurons in the CNS to nonselective neuronal depression that follows administration of these drugs. These compounds were presumed to depress diffuse neuronal pathways both in the brain stem and in the cerebral cortex. Brain-stem depression would continue as dosage was increased, accounting for the deep coma, cessation of respiration, and death that can follow drug overdosage.

Today, the mechanisms involved in the action of the barbiturates are perceived as both complex and controversial (Dickinson et al., 2002). Barbiturates and other sedatives reduce electrical and metabolic activity of the brain, and the reductions are accompanied by decreases in whole-brain glucose metabolism. The reductions may follow from either reduction of excitatory activity or augmentation in inhibitory activity.

As discussed in Chapter 3, *glutamate* is the predominant excitatory neurotransmitter in the brain, while *GABA* is the predominant inhibitory neurotransmitter. Twenty years ago, anesthetic doses of a barbiturate were demonstrated to attenuate glutamate neurotransmission, providing not only sedation but also a degree of "brain protection" following something like head injury. Jevtovic-Todorovic and coworkers (1998) reported that the anesthetic gas *nitrous oxide* is an antagonist at glutamate-NMDA receptors, as is the psychedelic anesthetic *phencyclidine* (Chapter 19). They postulated that the amnestic properties of sedative drugs might result from glutamate antagonism, as memory formation is highly dependent on the activity of glutamate neurons. Wu and coworkers (2004) demonstrated that the anesthetic drug isoflurane depresses glutamate neurotransmission by reducing the amplitude of action potentials in the presynaptic nerve terminals of glutamate neurons. Veselis and coworkers (2002) demonstrated that the amnestic effects of propofol (an injectable general anesthetic) occur concomitantly with reductions in cerebral blood flow to areas of the brain associated with working memory processes (right-sided prefrontal and posterior parietal brain regions). It is quite likely that the sedative, anxiolytic, and anesthetic effects lie elsewhere.

"Elsewhere" now appears to involve augmentation of GABA neurotransmission. Recalling the discussion of the $GABA_A$ receptor in Chapter 3, barbiturates and benzodiazepines bind to areas next to this receptor, each drug at its own specific site, serving to facilitate binding of GABA to its receptor. Tomlin and colleagues (1999) reported the effects of barbiturates on $GABA_A$ receptors and concluded:

> There seems to be little doubt that the barbiturates exert their effects by binding to specific sites on the $GABA_A$ receptor, and that these effects play a major role in the anesthetic properties of these agents. (p. 714)

A similar action on the $GABA_A$ receptor underlies the anesthetic action of the drug *etomidate* (Amidate). Examining other anesthetics, Nishikawa and Harrison (2003) noted that several *volatile anesthetic agents* (sevoflurane, isoflurane, and desflurane) bind directly to the alpha subunit of the $GABA_A$ receptor and that the bond may underlie their general anesthetic action. In 2002, Dickinson and coworkers demonstrated that *thiopental* (Pentothal, an ultrashort-acting barbiturate) specifically enhanced inhibitory GABA transmission in the absence of any action of glutaminergic neurotransmission. They concluded that inhibition of excitatory neurotransmission is not an important factor, at least in producing unconsciousness and a state of anesthesia. Therefore, it now appears that binding to GABA receptors results in facilitation of GABA-induced neurotransmission (channel opening with increased influx of chloride ions and cellular hyperpolarization) and accounts for the sedative-hypnotic and anesthetic actions of barbiturates, benzodiazepines, anesthetics, and similar "depressant" drugs (John and Prichep, 2005).

Barbiturates bind to the $GABA_A$ receptor and facilitate GABA binding, and they are also capable of opening the chloride channel in the absence of GABA. This independent action is thought to account for the increased toxicity of barbiturates (including fatalities in overdosage) when compared with the relative absence of overdose toxicity seen with the benzodiazepines. As we will see in Chapter 6, the benzodiazepines have a ceiling effect on CNS depression since they enhance only the effects of GABA; they do not open chloride ion channels independently of GABA availability.

Sedative-Induced Brain Dysfunction

Chapter 4 introduced the concept of a "blackout" that results from high levels of ethyl alcohol in the blood (e.g., a blood alcohol level of about 0.25 grams% or higher). A blackout is a state of *anterograde amnesia,* resulting in loss of memory for current events or actions at a certain blood level of alcohol that persists until the level of alcohol drops again below the amnestic level. More correctly, ethyl alcohol blackout is a manifestation of a *drug-induced, reversible, organic brain syndrome* (or state of dementia) that can follow use of any sedative. Therefore, any sedative, in high enough doses, can produce amnesia and a state of dementia. This action is distinct from the effect of higher doses to produce unconsciousness (John and Prichep, 2005).

This state of dementia (whether drug-induced or organic) produces characteristic behavioral, intellectual, and cognitive deficits. One way to diagnose drug-induced dementia is to perform a *mental status examination* while the patient is under the influence of the drug. The examination evaluates 12 areas of mental functioning (Table 5.1). When a person is in a demented state, 5 of the 12 components of the mental status examination are particularly altered (sensorium, affect, mental content, intellectual function, and insight and judgment). The sensorium becomes clouded, which causes disorientation in time and place; memory becomes impaired, which is manifested by forgetfulness and loss of short-term memory (the blackout); the intellect becomes depressed; judgment is altered. Affect becomes shallow and labile; that is, the person becomes extremely vulnerable to external

TABLE 5.1 Mental status examination: Twelve areas of mental functioning

   1. General appearance
* 2. Sensorium
      a. Orientation to time, place, and person
      b. Clear vs. clouded thinking
   3. Behavior and mannerisms
   4. Stream of talk
   5. Cooperativeness
   6. Mood (inner feelings)
* 7. Affect (surface expression of feelings)
   8. Perception
      a. Illusions (misperception of reality)
      b. Hallucinations (not present in reality)
   9. Thought processes: logical vs. strange or bizarre
* 10. Mental content (fund of knowledge)
* 11. Intellectual function (ability to reason and interpret)
* 12. Insight and judgment

* Characteristically altered in both organic dementia and reversible, drug-induced dementia.

stimuli and may be sullen and moody one moment and exhibit mock anger or rage the next. This kind of mental status is diagnosed as a "brain syndrome" caused by depressed nerve cell function. This state of anterograde amnesia is the reason these sedative drugs are called "date rape" drugs, as the person who takes the drug does not remember what happened during the period of intoxication.

Certain people (such as the elderly) who already have some natural loss of nerve cell function are adversely affected by these drugs; they experience increased disorientation and further clouding of consciousness. Frequently these people exhibit a state of drug-induced paradoxical excitement, which is characterized by a labile personality with marked anger, delusions, hallucinations, and confabulations, all part of the brain syndrome. Treating drug-induced dementia requires that administration of the sedative drug be stopped.

SPECIFIC DEPRESSANTS

Barbiturates

Barbiturates were the mainstays in treating anxiety and insomnia from 1912 to about 1960. During that period, they were associated with thousands of suicides, deaths from accidental ingestion, widespread dependency and abuse, and many serious interactions with other drugs and alcohol. They are now rarely used; however, they remain the classic prototype of sedative-hypnotic drugs.

Pharmacokinetics. Barbiturates are all of similar structure, and classification of individual drugs is by their individual pharmacokinetics. As shown in Table 5.2, their half-lives can be quite short (3-minute redistribution half-life for thiopental), longer (up to 48-hour elimination half-life for amobarbital, pentobarbital, and secobarbital), or very long (24- to 120-hour elimination half-life for phenobarbital). The hypnotic action of ultrashort-acting barbiturates (such as thiopental) is terminated by redistribution, while the action of other barbiturates is determined by their rate of metabolism by enzymes in the liver.

Taken orally, barbiturates are rapidly and completely absorbed and are well distributed to most body tissues. The ultrashort-acting barbiturates are exceedingly lipid soluble, cross the blood-brain barrier rapidly, and induce sleep within seconds following their intravenous injection. Because the longer-acting barbiturates are more water soluble, they are slower to penetrate the CNS. Sleep induction with these compounds, therefore, is delayed for 20 to 30 minutes, and residual hangover is prominent (since the plasma half-lives of most barbiturates vary from 10 to more than 48 hours).

TABLE 5.2 Half-lives and uses of some barbiturates

Drug name							Uses		
Trade	Generic	R_1[a]	R_2[a]	R_3[a]	Distribution (min)	Elimination (h)	Insomnia	Anesthesia	Epilepsy
Amytal	Amobarbital	Ethyl	Isopentyl	H		10–40	X		
Alurate	Aprobarbital	Allyl	Isopentyl	H		12–34	X		
Butisol	Butabarbital	Athyl	*sec*-Butyl	H		34–42	X		
Mebaral	Mephobarbital	Ethyl	Phenyl	CH_3		50–120			X
Brevital	Methohexital	Allyl	1-Methyl, 2-Pentynyl	CH_3		1–2		X	
Nembutal	Pentobarbital	Ethyl	Methyl butyl	H		15–50	X		
Luminal	Phenobarbital	Ethyl	Phenyl	H		24–120	X		X
Seconal	Secobarbital	Allyl	Methyl butyl	H		15–40	X		
Lotusate	Talbutal	Allyl	*sec*-Butyl	H			X		
Surital	Thiamylal	Allyl	Methyl butyl	H				X	
Pentothal	Thiopental	Ethyl	Methyl butyl	H	3	3–6		X	

[a] Symbols R_1, R_2, and R_3 refer to chemical substitution at these positions on the barbiturate nucleus shown in Figure 5.1.

Urinalysis is used to screen for the presence of barbiturates as well as other psychoactive drugs of abuse. Depending on the specific barbiturate, tests are positive for as short as 30 hours or as long as several weeks after the drug is ingested. When urinalysis is positive for barbiturates, more specific confirmation is needed to determine the exact drug that was taken.

Pharmacological Effects. Like ethyl alcohol, barbiturates have a low degree of selectivity, and it is not possible to achieve anxiolysis without evidence of sedation. Barbiturates are not analgesic; they cannot be relied on to produce sedation or sleep in the presence of even moderate pain.

Sleep patterns are decidedly affected by barbiturates; rapid eye movement (REM) sleep is markedly suppressed. Because dreaming occurs during REM sleep, barbiturates suppress dreaming. During drug withdrawal, dreaming becomes vivid and excessive. Such rebound increase in dreaming during withdrawal (termed REM rebound) is one example of a withdrawal effect following prolonged periods of barbiturate ingestion. The vivid nature of the dreams can lead to insomnia, which can be clinically relieved by restarting the drug, negating the attempt at withdrawal.

Since barbiturates are sedatives and depress memory functioning, they are *cognitive inhibitors.* Drowsiness and more subtle alterations of judgment, cognitive functioning, motor skills, physical coordination, and behavior may persist for hours or days until the barbiturate is completely metabolized and eliminated. Sedative doses of barbiturates have minimal effect on respiration, but overdoses (or combinations of barbiturates and alcohol) can result in death. Barbiturate-alcohol combinations have been responsible for both accidental and intentional suicides.

Barbiturates exert few significant effects on the cardiovascular system, the gastrointestinal tract, the kidneys, or other organs until toxic doses are reached. In the liver, barbiturates stimulate the synthesis of enzymes that metabolize barbiturates as well as other drugs, an effect that produces significant tolerance to the drugs.

Psychological Effects. The behavioral, motor, and cognitive inhibitions caused by barbiturates are similar to those caused by alcohol-induced inebriation and may even be indistinguishable from it. A person may respond to low doses either with relief from anxiety (the expected effect) or with withdrawal, emotional depression, or aggressive and violent behavior. Higher doses lead to more general behavioral depression and sleep. Mental set and physical or social setting can determine whether relief from anxiety, mental depression, aggression, or another unexpected or unpredictable response is experienced. Driving skills, judgment, insight, and memory all become severely impaired during the period of intoxication.

Clinical Uses.   Use of barbiturates has declined rapidly in recent years for several reasons: (1) they are lethal in overdose, (2) they have a narrow therapeutic-to-toxic range, (3) they have a high potential for inducing tolerance, dependence, and abuse, and (4) they interact dangerously with many other drugs. Despite these disadvantages, the barbiturates have occasional use as anticonvulsants, as intravenous anesthetics, to provide "brain protection" after head injury, and, in psychiatry, to sedate for an "amytal interview." Their use as anxiolytics is relatively obsolete.

Adverse Reactions.   Drowsiness is one of the primary effects induced by barbiturates; it is an inescapable accompaniment to the anxiolytic effect and is often the effect sought if the drug is intended to produce either daytime sedation or nighttime sleep. Barbiturates significantly impair motor and intellectual performance and judgment. It should be emphasized that all sedatives are equivalent to alcohol in their effects, that all are additive in their effects with alcohol, and that their effects persist longer than might be predicted. There are no specific antidotes with which one can treat barbiturate overdosage. Treatment is aimed at supporting the respiratory and cardiovascular system until the drug is metabolized and eliminated.

Tolerance.   The barbiturates can induce tolerance by either of two mechanisms: (1) the induction of drug-metabolizing enzymes in the liver and (2) the adaptation of neurons in the brain to the presence of the drug. With the latter mechanism, tolerance develops primarily to the sedative effects, much less to the brain-stem depressant effects on respiration. Thus, the margin of safety for the person who uses the drug decreases.

Physical Dependence.   Normal clinical doses of barbiturates can induce a degree of physical dependence, usually manifested by sleep difficulties during attempts at withdrawal. Withdrawal from high doses of barbiturates may result in hallucinations, restlessness, disorientation, and even life-threatening convulsions.

Psychological Dependence.   Psychological dependence refers to a compulsion to use a drug for a pleasurable effect. All CNS depressants, including barbiturates, can have such an effect and are known to be abused compulsively. Because they can relieve anxiety, induce sedation, and produce a state of euphoria, these drugs may be used to achieve a variety of pleasurable psychological states in a variety of abuse situations.

Effects in Pregnancy.   Barbiturates, like all psychoactive drugs, are freely distributed to the fetus. Data are limited on whether deleterious fetal abnormalities occur as a result of a pregnant woman taking barbiturates, although there is a suggestion that developmental abnormalities occur. This possibility can be a concern for pregnant women who are epileptic and must take a barbiturate to prevent seizures. As reviewed by Ramin and colleagues (1998):

> The risk for the pregnant woman treated with phenobarbital and other antiseizure medications of having an infant with congenital malformations is two to three times greater than that of the general population. It is not entirely clear whether this increased risk is secondary to the anticonvulsants, genetic factors, the seizure disorder itself, or possibly a combination of these factors, although . . . evidence exists for the implication of anticonvulsants as the etiology. (p. 172).

Other studies report reduced Wechsler IQ scores in adult males whose mothers used phenobarbital.

These studies imply that barbiturate exposure during pregnancy might result in deleterious cognitive effects in offspring. They do not imply that barbiturates might have a teratogenic potential. A conservative conclusion would be that barbiturates have the *potential* to result in adverse neonatal outcomes in offspring of mothers taking the drugs. It would be best to avoid taking them while pregnant, but they do not appear to be contraindicated (necessarily avoided) during pregnancy should they be medically necessary, for example, to prevent seizures in the mother (seizures that might also harm the fetus).

Nonbarbiturate Sedative-Hypnotic Drugs

In the early 1950s, three "nonbarbiturate" sedatives—*glutethimide* (Doriden), *ethchlorvynol* (Placidyl), and *methyprylon* (Noludar)—were introduced as anxiolytics, daytime sedatives, and hypnotics. They structurally resembled the barbiturates (see Figure 5.1), but they did not have the exact barbiturate nucleus and were structurally not barbiturates, despite being pharmacologically interchangeable. These drugs offered no advantages over the barbiturates. Now considered obsolete for use in medicine, they are occasionally encountered as drugs of abuse.

Meprobamate (Equanil, Miltown) was marketed in 1955 as an alternative to the barbiturates for daytime sedation and anxiolysis. Around it developed the term *tranquilizer* in a marketing attempt to distinguish it from the barbiturates, a distinction that was not borne out in reality. Like barbiturates, meprobamate produces long-lasting daytime sedation, mild euphoria, and relief from anxiety. Meprobamate is not as potent a respiratory depressant as the barbiturates; attempted suicides from overdosage are seldom successful unless the drug is mixed with opioid narcotics such as morphine or oxycodone (Chapter 16). Despite a continuing reduction in clinical use, abuse and dependency continue and are difficult to treat. There is a possibility that use of meprobamate during pregnancy may be associated with an increased frequency of congenital malformations.

Carisoprodol (Soma) is a precursor compound to meprobamate; after it is absorbed, it is rapidly metabolized to meprobamate, which is the active form of the drug. Currently, carisoprodol, as an intoxicant, is increasingly encountered as a drug of abuse.

Methaqualone (Quaalude) was another nonbarbiturate sedative that had little to justify its widespread use. During the late 1970s and early 1980s, its popularity rivaled that of marijuana and alcohol in its level of abuse. The attention was due to an undeserved reputation as an aphrodisiac (as a sedative, it was actually an *anaphrodisiac*, much like alcohol). It was, however, a "date rape" drug since, like all these drugs, the amnestic effect occurred at doses lower than the dose required to produce incapacitation or unconsciousness. Extensive illicit use and numerous deaths led to its ban from sale in the United States in 1984, although illicit supplies occasionally emerge as a drug of abuse.

Chloral hydrate (Noctec) is yet another drug of historical interest, having been available clinically since the late 1800s. It is rapidly metabolized to *trichlorethanol* (a derivative of ethyl alcohol), which is a nonselective CNS depressant and the active form of chloral hydrate. The drug is an effective sedative-hypnotic, with a plasma half-life of about 4 to 8 hours. Next-day hangover is less likely to occur than with compounds having longer half-lives. Its liability in producing tolerance and dependence is similar to that of the barbiturates. Withdrawal of the drug may be associated with disrupted sleep and intense nightmares. One interesting aside is that the combination of chloral hydrate with alcohol can produce increased intoxication, stupor, and amnesia. This mixture was called a *Mickey Finn* and was an early example of a "date rape" drug combination.

Paraldehyde, introduced into medicine before the barbiturates, is a polymer of acetaldehyde, an intermediate by-product in the body's metabolism of ethyl alcohol. Administered either rectally or orally, paraldehyde was historically used to treat delirium tremens (DTs) in alcoholics undergoing detoxification. Paraldehyde is rapidly absorbed (from both rectal and oral routes), sleep ensues within 10 to 15 minutes after hypnotic doses, and the drug is metabolized in the liver to acetaldehyde and eventually to carbon dioxide and water. Some paraldehyde is eliminated through the lungs, producing a characteristic breath odor. People dependent on paraldehyde (usually people who received paraldehyde as a treatment for alcoholism) suffer a variety of toxicities, primarily to the stomach, liver, and kidneys.

GENERAL ANESTHETICS

General anesthetics are potent CNS depressants that produce unconsciousness for surgical procedures. General anesthesia is therefore the most severe state of intentional drug-induced CNS depression. The agents that are used as general anesthetics are of two types: (1) those that are administered by inhalation through the lungs and (2) those that are injected directly into a vein.

The inhalation anesthetics in current use include one gas (nitrous oxide) and five volatile liquids (isoflurane, halothane, desflurane, enflurane, and sevoflurane). These drugs produce a dose-related depression of all functions of the CNS—an initial period of sedation followed by the onset of sleep. As anesthesia deepens, the patient's reflexes become progressively depressed and both amnesia and unconsciousness are induced. Adding an opioid narcotic (such as morphine) to a volatile anesthetic induces a state of unconsciousness and analgesia.

Occasionally, the inhaled anesthetic agents are subject to misuse. *Nitrous oxide,* a gas of low anesthetic potency, is an example. Currently used not only in anesthesia but also as a carrier gas in whipped cream charger cans (for example, Whippets), nitrous oxide induces a state of behavioral disinhibition, analgesia, and mild euphoria. Since the inhalation of nitrous oxide dilutes the air that a person is breathing, extreme caution must be exercised to prevent hypoxia. If the nitrous oxide were mixed only with room air, hypoxia would result, which could produce irreversible brain damage. Other inhaled anesthetics are similarly abused, presuming that the drug abuser can find a supply. Inhaled as vapors, these drugs produce intoxication, delirium, and eventually unconsciousness, which can be fatal should one lose the ability to breath while under the influence of the drug. Other forms of inhalant abuse were discussed in Chapter 4.

Several *injectable anesthetics* are available. *Thiopental* (Pentothal) and *methohexital* (Brevital) are ultrashort-acting barbiturates. *Propofol* (Diprovan) and *etomidate* (Amidate) are structurally unique; propofol structurally resembles the neurotransmitter GABA (Figure 5.2). The mechanism of action of all these anesthetics probably involves intense CNS depression produced secondary to facilitation of $GABA_A$ receptor activity and perhaps to depression of excitatory glutamate synaptic transmission. These drugs have little or no analgesic or euphoriant activity because their onset of unconsciousness and amnesia is immediate.

The injectable anesthetic *ketamine* is discussed in Chapter 18, Ketamine is unique as an anesthetic drug because it can induce unconsciousness and amnesia along with analgesia and psychedelic hallucinations. Because of the latter property, it is frequently encountered as

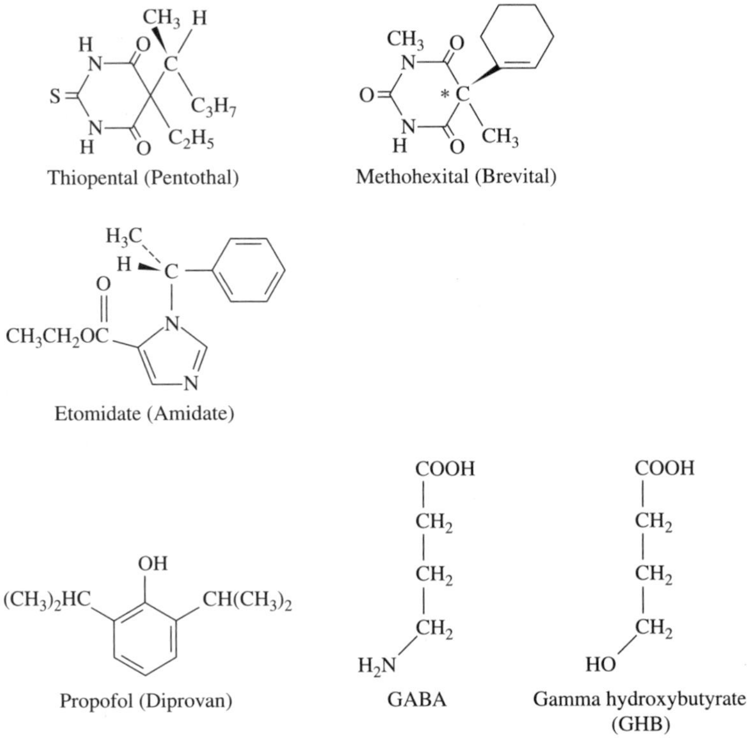

FIGURE 5.2 Chemical structures of intravenously administered "induction" anesthetics. Illustrated are two barbiturates (thiopental and methohexital) and two newer agents. Also illustrated are the structures of GABA and GHB. Propofol is structurally similar to GABA, as is GHB.

a drug of abuse. In anesthesia, ketamine is occasionally used because it induces amnesia and unconsciousness in the absence of reduction in blood pressure, an important consideration in conducting anesthesia in critically ill surgical patients.

GAMMA HYDROXYBUTYRATE

Gamma hydroxybutyric acid (gamma hydroxybutyrate, GHB, sodium oxybate; Xyrem) is a potent CNS depressant used in some countries (but not the United States) as an intravenous general anesthetic (Drasbek, et al, 2006). It is also a popular drug of abuse (Nicholson and Balster, 2001). GHB is a naturally occurring four-carbon molecule (see Figure 5.2) with a structure similar to GABA. GHB is an endogenous constituent of mammalian brains, synthesized locally from

GABA. It freely crosses the blood-brain barrier and, in the United States, is FDA-approved for use as a hypnotic in patients suffering from a sleep disorder called narcolepsy.

Since GHB is a sedative-hypnotic drug, it has euphoriant properties and has been purported (like ethanol) to have use for sexual enhancement. Therefore, it has significant abuse potential as an aphrodisiac and as a euphoriant. It has been available from foreign sources through a variety of venues and can be made at home. It has been sold illicitly under such names as RenewTrient, Revivarant, Blue Nitro, Remiforce, GH Revitalize, and Gamma G. It has been called "Nature's Quaalude," among a variety of other names.

GHB has been widely implicated as an illicit "date rape" drug, similar to chloral hydrate, methaqualone, and the various benzodiazepines (such as Rohypnol). Often one of these drugs is added to alcohol to potentiate the sedative/intoxicant/amnestic actions of the alcohol. There is no evidence that GHB aids sexual performance: it is a potent sedative and depressant. Like any depressant, it can produce a state of disinhibition, excitement, drunkenness, and amnesia.

Because of GHB's notorious reputation and abuse, the FDA classified GHB as a Schedule I controlled substance, implying high propensity for abuse and no therapeutic use. (The FDA also classifies heroin and marijuana as Schedule I drugs.) In 2003, although the drug was still scheduled in this manner, it was also FDA classified as Schedule III because of its new clinical indication for the treatment of narcolepsy. This was the first time that one drug had been scheduled under two FDA categories of control, depending on the intent for use and the manner in which it is used or abused. It is to be hoped that dual classification will again be used by the FDA to make available for controlled therapeutic use Schedule I substances such as tetrahydrocannabinol in marijuana for, for example, the relief of pain associated with multiple sclerosis.[1]

Pharmacokinetics. Available only in liquid form, GHB is rapidly absorbed after oral administration. Plasma level reaches a peak in about 30 to 75 minutes, longer if taken with a high-fat meal. The drug is rapidly metabolized to inactive metabolites and ultimately to carbon dioxide and water. The elimination half-life is about 30 minutes to an hour. GHB is virtually undetectable in urine. Food in the stomach markedly affects the rate of drug absorption, but nocturnal administration several hours after the last meal of the day offsets this effect (Borgen et al., 2003).

---

[1] A Schedule I classification means that to the FDA a drug has a high potential for abuse with no therapeutic use. Schedules II through V allow for therapeutic use under varying degrees of prescription regulation.

Adverse Effects. The toxicity of GHB stems from dose-dependent CNS depression by $GABA_B$ potentiation (Drasbek et al, 2006). Therefore, GHB overdoses are characterized by stupor, delirium, unconsciousness, coma, and death (Zvosec et al., 2001). Seizures, respiratory depression, and vomiting are common. Combined with alcohol, the toxic potential is greatly magnified. Nonfatal overdoses are characterized by an unarousable coma that lasts 1 to 2 hours. There are no antidotes for treating overdoses: treatment is "supportive" until the drug is eliminated. Acute withdrawal in a GHB-dependent person results in rapid onset of a withdrawal syndrome that includes insomnia, anxiety, and tremors. Withdrawal symptoms usually resolve in about 3 to 10 days.

Uses. Historically, GHB was used intraveneously (in Europe) for the induction of general anesthesia. Its use as an anesthetic has been supplanted by superior anesthetics. However, its use in treating narcolepsy remains (Medical Letter, 2002). Narcolepsy is a lifelong disorder characterized by fragmented sleep during the night, altered sleep patterns, and excessive sleepiness during the day. One bothersome daytime symptom is cataplexy (sudden loss of muscle tone) during the day. Cataplexy occurs in 60 to 75 percent of patients with narcolepsy, often precipitated by laughter, anger, surprise, or excitement. GHB is taken at bedtime and then 2.5 to 4 hours later, even if the patient has to be wakened to take the medicine. Taken in this fashion, the drug improves sleep and markedly reduces the number of daytime cataplexy attacks. Currently, because of its abuse potential, it must be registered with the FDA, and other restrictions govern its availability and distribution.

ANTIEPILEPTIC DRUGS

Seizures are manifestations of electrical disturbances in the brain. The term *epilepsy* refers to CNS disorders characterized by relatively brief, chronically recurring seizures that have a rapid onset. Epileptic seizures are often associated with focal (or localized) lesions in the brain. In laboratory animals, epileptic seizures can be induced by a variety of techniques, including "kindling" (repeated low-voltage electrical stimulation of the amygdala or hippocampus to increase the sensitivity of neurons therein). Post and Weiss (1989) associate kindling not only with antiepileptic drug action but also with the treatment of *bipolar disorders*. Indeed, in recent years, antiepileptic drugs have become a mainstay for the treatment of bipolar disorder (Chapter 8). In addition, certain of the antiepileptic drugs have been reported to be efficacious in treating a variety of *explosive be-*

havioral disorders in children, adolescents, and adults, in managing alcohol withdrawal and cravings, in treating certain *pain* states, including *peripheral neuropathies* that result from injury to peripheral nerves, and in the management of certain anxiety disorders such as posttraumatic stress disorder, generalized anxiety disorder, and even certain components of borderline personality disorder. (The variety of uses of anticonvulsants is discussed throughout this text, especially in Chapter 8.)

Perhaps this multitude of actions necessitates a new term for these agents, a term such as *neuromodulators* (Myrick et al., 2001).[2] In this book, these drugs are introduced for their original indication: antiseizure agents or anticonvulsants. The plasma half-lives and therapeutic blood levels of available antiepileptic drugs are listed in Table 5.3. LaRoche and Helmers (2004) review the newer antiepileptic drugs.

Relationships Between Structure and Activity

The original antiepileptic drugs belong to one of two chemically similar classes, *barbiturates* or *hydantoins* (Figure 5.3). More recently introduced drugs do not bear structural resemblance to classic drugs; rather, they were developed for antiepileptic potential because they either resembled GABA (Figure 5.4) or acted on GABA receptors to potentiate GABA neurotransmission. Development of newer drugs began in about 1980 with the introduction of *carbamazepine* (Tegretol) and *valproic acid* (Depakene) and has continued since with the introduction of several other agents that have clinical uses in addition to use as anticonvulsants.

Specific Agents

Among the *barbiturates*, phenobarbital was the first widely effective antiepileptic drug, replacing the more toxic agent, *bromide*, which had been used during the nineteenth century. *Mephobarbital* (Mebaral) is another barbiturate occasionally used for treating epilepsy. Because of their sedative effects, these two barbiturates are rarely used; equally effective, more specific, and less sedating antiepileptic agents are available. Epileptic children given barbiturates can display adverse neuropsychological reactions (behavioral

---

[2] This term removes the implication that a person with mania, behavioral disorders, alcohol dependence, or chronic pain is being treated as if he or she had a seizure disorder. *Neuromodulators* act to "stabilize" neuronal membranes either by facilitating inhibition or by limiting excitation. The mechanism of neuronal stabilization is not known, although Suzuki and coworkers (2002) postulate that the effect might be exerted through drug-induced modulation of the genetic expression of an enzyme (type II nitric oxide synthetase) that controls the levels of nitric oxide in the brain.

TABLE 5.3 Antiepileptic drugs available in the United States

Year introduced	Generic name	Trade name	Half-life (hours)	Therapeutic blood level (mcg/ml) [a]
1912	Phenobarbital	Luminal	50+	15–40
1935	Mephobarbital	Mebaral	—[b]	—
1938	Phenytoin	Dilantin	18+	5–20
1946	Trimethadione	Tridione	6–13	>700
1947	Mephenytoin	Mesantoin	95	—
1949	Paramethadione	Paradione	—	—
1951	Phenacemide	Phenurone	—	—
1952	Metharbital	Gemonil	—	—
1953	Phensuximide	Milontin	8	—
1954	Primidone	Mysoline	5–20	5–40
1957	Methsuximide	Celontin	2–40	—
1957	Ethotoin	Peganone	4–9	15–50
1960	Ethosuximide	Zarontin	30+	40–400
1968	Diazepam	Valium	20–50	—
1974	Carbamazepine	Tegretol	18–50	4–12
1975	Clonazepam	Klonopin	18–60	20–80
1978	Valproic acid	Depakene	5–20	50–150
1981	Clorazepate	Tranxene	30–100	—
1981	Lorazepam	Ativan	14	—
1993	Felbamate	Felbatol	22	—
1994	Gabapentin	Neurontin	5–7	—
1995	Lamotrigine	Lamictal	33	1–5
1998	Topiramate	Topamax	19–23	—
1998	Tiagabine	Gabatril	6–9	—
1999	Levetiracetam	Keppra	7	10
2000	Zonisamide	Zonegran	60	—

[a]mcg/ml = micrograms of drug per milliliter of blood
[b]— = data not available

hyperactivity and interference with learning ability). *Primidone* (Mysoline), an antiepileptic agent structurally similar to phenobarbital, is metabolized to phenobarbital, which might well be the major active form of the drug.

Phenytoin (Dilantin) remains a commonly used *hydantoin* anticonvulsant, producing less sedation than do the barbiturates.

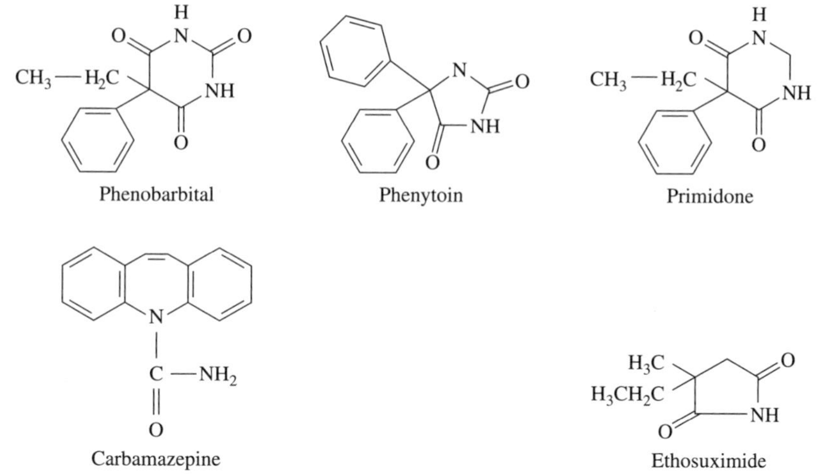

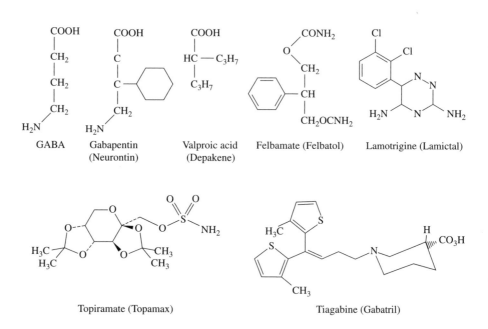

FIGURE 5.3 Chemical structures of several classic drugs used to treat epilepsy.

FIGURE 5.4 Chemical structures of several GABAergic drugs used to treat epilepsy. Most are also effective in treating bipolar disorder.

Phenytoin has a half-life of about 24 hours; thus, daytime sedation can be minimized if the patient takes the full daily dose at bedtime. Many bothersome side effects currently limit its use.

Benzodiazepines (Chapter 6) possess antiepileptic properties, although they are now only occasionally used for this purpose. When benzodiazepines are used in children, drug-induced personality changes and learning disabilities must be carefully monitored.

Valproic acid (valproate, divalproex; Depakene, Depakote, Depacon) is effective and widely used in treating seizure disorders in children. It acts by augmenting the postsynaptic action of GABA. Valproic acid has a short half-life (about 6 to 12 hours); it must be administered 2 or 3 times a day. About 75 percent of epileptic patients receiving valproic acid respond favorably. Serious side effects are rare, but liver failure has been reported. Like many of the newer anticonvulsants, valproic acid possesses GABAergic actions, so it is not surprising that the drug is highly effective in people with bipolar disorder, posttraumatic stress disorder, borderline personality disorder, aggressive behaviors, schizophrenia, and alcohol and cocaine dependence.

Carbamazepine (Tegretol) is an antiepileptic drug with a sedative effect that is perhaps less intense than that of the other antiepileptic agents. The primary limitations of carbamazepine include rare but potentially serious alterations in the cellular composition of blood (reduced numbers of white blood cells), presumably secondary to a depressant effect on bone marrow. For nonepileptic use, carbamazepine is used in the treatment of bipolar disorder, explosive behavioral disorders, pain syndromes, and alcohol withdrawal (Malcolm et al., 2002).

Gabapentin (Neurontin), a structural analogue of GABA (see Figure 5.4), was synthesized as a specific GABA-mimetic antiepileptic drug. Gabapentin appears to act by promoting the release of GABA from presynaptic nerve terminals. In 1995, gabapentin was reported effective in treating both an anxiety disorder (phobia) and pain (reflex sympathetic dystrophy). Since then, gabapentin has been tried in a variety of chronic pain states and psychiatric disorders, including bipolar disorder, and in the demented elderly to treat agitation and aggressive behavior. Gabapentin has also been reported to be effective in treating alcohol withdrawal and for prevention of relapse.

Lamotrigine (Lamictal), introduced into medicine in 1995, acts by inhibiting ion fluxes through sodium channels, stabilizing neuronal membranes, and inhibiting the presynaptic release of neurotransmitters, principally glutamate (Conroy et al., 1999). First introduced as an antiepileptic drug, it has beneficial effects on mood, on mental alertness, and on social interactions in some epilepsy patients.

Interestingly, in the treatment of head injury, release of glutamate has been associated with permanent neuronal damage. Lamotrigine and some other (but not all) anticonvulsants have been reported to inhibit hypoxia-induced or ischemia-induced release of glutamate; perhaps the drug may be clinically useful in providing brain protection following hypoxic insult (Rekling, 2003). Its use in treating alcoholism was discussed in Chapter 4.

Oxcarbazepine (Trileptal) is a structural derivative of carbamazepine. It differs in two ways: first, it is rapidly metabolized by a process called *reduction* to an active molecule and second, it has not been associated with the white blood cell toxicity associated with carbamazepine. Oxcarbazepine is being increasingly used to treat bipolar illness (Hellewell, 2002) and other disorders for which carbamazepine is also effective (Gentry et al., 2002).

Tiagabine (Gabitril) became clinically available in 1998 as another antiepileptic drug. The drug acts by inhibiting neuronal and glial uptake of GABA, secondary to its irreversibly inhibiting one of the GABA reuptake transporters located on the presynaptic nerve terminals of GABA-releasing neurons. This action serves to prolong GABA's synaptic action. Tiagabine appears to be less useful in the treatment of bipolar illness than are other antiepileptic drugs.

Several other new antiepileptic drugs have found use in the treatment of bipolar illness: *topiramate* (Topamax) (Marcotte, 1998), *levetiracetam* (Keppra) (Grunze and Walden, 2002), and zonisamide (Zonegran) (Tidwell and Swims, 2003). Topiramate was discussed in Chapter 4 for its use in treating alcoholism. Zonisamide has been shown to be effective as an antiobesity agent when combined with a balanced low-calorie diet (Gadde et al., 2003). It has also been used to treat binge-eating disorder (McElroy et al., 2004).

Antiepileptic Drugs in Pregnancy

Rates of stillbirth and infant mortality are higher for mothers with epilepsy. Children of epileptic mothers who received antiseizure medication during the early months of pregnancy have an increased incidence of a variety of birth defects. The risk is approximately 7 percent, compared with 2 to 3 percent for the general population. Pitting this fact against the obvious necessity to control seizures is a therapeutic dilemma in treating pregnant women who have epilepsy. In general, women with epilepsy of childbearing age should be advised of teratogenic potential. Before a woman becomes pregnant, it should be determined whether drugs can be tapered off and discontinued. If termination cannot be done safely, one approach is to use a single medication at the lowest possible dose that will control seizures. Divided daily doses may decrease the peak levels in plasma while maintaining an adequate steady-state level of the drug in the blood.

Cantrell and colleagues (1998) concluded that with proper management, 90 percent of women with epilepsy will have uneventful pregnancies and normal children.

STUDY QUESTIONS

1. List the various classes of CNS depressants and give examples of each class. What are common terms for CNS depressants?

2. What are the consequences of the drug blockade of glutamate receptors? Of GABA receptors?

3. Describe the gradation of action that occurs in a person as a result of taking progressively increasing doses of a nonselective CNS depressant.

4. What is meant by cross-tolerance of CNS depressants? By cross-dependence?

5. Describe what is meant by *supra-additive CNS depression.* How does potentiation work?

6. What is meant by the term *drug-induced reversible brain syndrome?*

7. What mechanisms are responsible for the differing durations of action of various barbiturates?

8. What are the oldest CNS depressants? The newest?

9. Describe the effects of barbiturates on sleep patterns both acutely and during drug withdrawal.

10. Compare the effects of barbiturates and chloral hydrate on the elderly.

11. How does paraldehyde resemble ethyl alcohol?

12. What are the particular dangers of use of CNS depressants in the elderly? In the young?

13. Describe the use and abuse of GHB.

14. Can GHB be used in the treatment of alcohol dependence? What are the disadvantages?

15. Which antiepileptic drugs are also used in the treatment of bipolar disorder? Why might they work?

16. Why might antiepileptic drugs be considered for use in nonepileptic, psychological disorders?

17. What are some of the disorders for which antiepileptic "neuro-modulators" might be used?

REFERENCES

Borgen, L., et al. (2003). "The Influence of Gender and Food on the Pharmacokinetics of Sodium Oxybate Oral Solution in Healthy Subjects." *Journal of Clinical Pharmacology* 43: 59–65.

Cantrell, D. T. C., et al. (1998). "Anticonvulsant Drugs During Pregnancy." In L. C. Gilstrap and B. B. Little, eds., *Drugs and Pregnancy*, 2nd ed. (pp. 137–147). New York: Chapman & Hall.

Conroy, B. P., et al. (1999). "Lamotrigine Attenuates Cortical Glutamate Release During Global Cerebral Ischemia in Pigs on Cardiopulmonary Bypass." *Anesthesiology* 90: 844–854.

Dickinson, R., et al. (2002). "Selective Synaptic Actions of Thiopental and Its Enantiomers." *Anesthesiology* 96: 884–892.

Drasbek, K. R., et al. (2006). "Gamma-Hydroxybutyrate: A Drug of Abuse." *Acta Neurologica Scandinavia* 114: 145–156.

Gadde, K. M., et al. (2003). "Zonisamide for Weight Loss in Obese Adults: A Randomized Controlled Trial." *Journal of the American Medical Association* 289: 1820–1825.

Gentry, J. R., et al. (2002). "New Anticonvulsants: A Review of Applications for the Management of Substance Abuse Disorders." *Annals of Clinical Psychiatry* 14: 233–245.

Grunze, H., and J. Walden (2002). "Relevance of New and Recently Discovered Anticonvulsants for Atypical Forms of Bipolar Disorder." *Journal of Affective Disorders* 72, Supplement: S15–S21.

Hellewell, J. S. (2002). "Oxcarbazepine (Trileptal) in the Treatment of Bipolar Disorders: Review of Efficacy and Tolerability." *Journal of Affective Disorders* 72, Supplement: S23–S34.

Jevtovic-Todorovic, V., et al. (1998). "Nitrous Oxide (Laughing Gas) Is an NMDA Antagonist, Neuroprotectant and Neurotoxin." *Nature Medicine* 4: 460–463.

John, E. R., and Prichap, L. S. (2005). "The Anesthetic Cascade: A Theory of How Anesthesia Suppresses Consciousness." *Anesthesiology* 102: 447–471.

LaRoche, S. M., and S. L. Helmers (2004). "The New Antiepileptic Drugs." *Journal of the American Medical Association* 291: 605–620.

Malcolm, R., et al. (2002). "The Effects of Carbamazepine and Lorazepam on Single Versus Multiple Previous Alcohol Withdrawals in an Outpatient Randomized Trial." *Journal of General and Internal Medicine* 17: 349–355.

Marcotte, D. (1998). "Use of Topiramate, a New Anti-Epileptic, as a Mood Stabilizer." *Journal of Affective Disorders* 50: 245–251.

McElroy, S. L., et al. (2004). "Zonisamide in the Treatment of Binge-Eating Disorder: An Open-Label, Prospective Trial." *Journal of Clinical Psychiatry* 65: 50–56.

Medical Letter on Drugs and Therapeutics (2002). "Gamma Hydroxybutyrate (Xyrem) for Narcolepsy." *Medical Letter* 44: 103–105.

Myrick, H., et al. (2001). "New Developments in the Pharmacology of Alcohol Dependence." *American Journal of Addictions* 10, Supplement: 3–15.

Nicholson, K. L., and R. L. Balster (2001). "GHB: A New and Novel Drug of Abuse." *Drug and Alcohol Dependence* 63: 1–22.

Nishikawa, K., and N. L. Harrison (2003). "The Actions of Sevoflurane and Desflurane on the Gamma-Aminobutyric Acid Receptor Type A: Effects of TM2 Mutations in the Alpha and Beta Subunits." *Anesthesiology* 99: 678–684.

Post, R. M., and S. R. B. Weiss (1989). "Sensitization, Kindling, and Anticonvulsants in Mania." *Journal of Clinical Psychiatry* 50, Supplement 12: 23–30.

Ramin, S. M., et al. (1998). "Psychotropics in Pregnancy." In L. C. Gilstrap and B. B. Little, eds., *Drugs and Pregnancy*, 2nd ed. (pp. 172–175). New York: Chapman & Hall.

Rekling, J. C. (2003). "Neuroprotective Effects of Anticonvulsants in Rat Hippocampal Slice Cultures Exposed to Oxygen/Glucose Deprivation." *Neuroscience Letters* 335: 167–170.

Suzuki, E., et al. (2002). "Antipsychotic, Antidepressant, Anxiolytic, and Anticonvulsant Drugs Induce Type II Nitric Oxide Synthetase mRNA in Rat Brain." *Neuroscience Letters* 333: 217–219.

Tidwell, A., and M. Swims (2003). "Review of the Newer Antiepileptic Drugs." *American Journal of Managed Care* 9: 253–276.

Tomlin, S. L., et al. (1999). "Stereoselective Effects of Etomidate Optical Isomers on Gamma-Aminobutyric Acid Type A Receptors and Animals." *Anesthesiology* 88: 708–717.

Veselis, R. A., et al. (2002). "A Neuroanatomical Construct for the Amnestic Effects of Propofol." *Anesthesiology* 97: 329–337.

Wu, X.-S., et al. (2004). "Isoflurane Inhibits Transmitter Release and the Presynaptic Action Potential." *Anesthesiology* 100: 663–670.

Zvosec, D. L., et al. (2001). "Adverse Events, Including Death, Associated with the Use of 1,4-Butanediol." *New England Journal of Medicine* 344: 87–94.

Chapter 6

Benzodiazepines and Related Anxiolytic Medications

Anxiety and sleep disorders have long plagued mankind. Both have been the object of drug therapy, probably since the discovery of alcohol as a product of fermentation. The modern treatment of these disorders began with the introduction of the benzodiazepine tranquilizers in the 1960s. Recognizing the limitations and complications of the benzodiazepines, present treatment of anxiety is accomplished with serotonin-type antidepressants (Chapter 7) and mood stabilizers (Chapter 8). Nevertheless, benzodiazepines continue in wide use for the treatment of anxiety. Sleep disorders (for example, insomnia) are widely treated with newer drugs (for example, Ambien, Lunesta) that exert actions on the same receptors on which benzodiazepines act. This chapter focuses on the pharmacology of drugs used to treat anxiety and insomnia. It emphasizes limitations and complications and includes such topics as sedative-induced sleep driving.

Anxiety disorders are the most frequent psychological disorders and are associated with substantial social and vocational impairments and adverse health behaviors, such as smoking and sedentary lifestyle, which may contribute to high levels of medical and psychiatric comorbidity (Katon and Roy-Byrne, 2007). The most common anxiety disorders are generalized anxiety disorder, panic disorder, social anxiety disorder, and posttraumatic stress disorder. Despite the substantial disability associated with each of these disorders, only a minority of persons with an anxiety disorder (15 to 36 percent) are in treatment (Kroenke et al., 2007). Similarly, insomnia affects millions of people, as many as 30 percent of the general population. Pharmacological treatments for insomnia, their benefits and limitations, are discussed in this chapter. It should be noted, however, that collaborative care engaging both pharmacotherapy and psychological therapies is the most efficacious treatment for both anxiety and sleep disorders (Rollman, et al., 2005; Roy-Byrne, et al., 2005).

Benzodiazepines

Benzodiazepines have anxiolytic (antianxiety), sedative, anticonvulsant, amnestic, and relaxant properties. Soon after their introduction, they became the most widely used class of psychotherapeutic drugs, and the term *anxiolytic* became synonymous with *benzodiazepine*. Diazepam (Valium) and chlordiazepoxide (Librium) are the classic benzodiazepines. Alprazolam (Xanax), clonazepam (Klonopin), lorazepam (Ativan), and triazoplam (Halcion) are other commonly prescribed benzodiazepines, and several others are also available.

What Is a Benzodiazepine?

A benzodiazepine is a drug of a specific chemical structure (Figure 6.1). The classification is therefore *structural*, not mechanistic. Back in 1960, before the concept of drug interaction with specific receptors on neuronal surfaces was understood, drugs were synthesized in the laboratory and their clinical effects were determined by testing them in both animals and humans. The chemical structure that provided the clinical effects was then named and all drugs of similar structure that produced similar clinical effects were given a group name based on the commonality in their chemical structure. In that era, drug manufacturers would make slight modifications to the structure to market competing and possibly better drugs. These modifications involved either changing side chain substituents (making a different compound of the same class) or slightly modifying the basic structure (creating a different chemical class but leaving the same biological action).

Today, with understanding of specific receptor-drug interactions, drugs are usually named by the receptors they affect or that underlie their major clinical action (for example, SSRIs: a serotonin 1_A agonist, a serotonin 3 antagonist, and so on). If discovered today, a benzodiazepine probably would be called a GABA receptor agonist. Because of what is now known of GABA receptors and because a specific binding site for benzodiazepines on the GABA receptor has been

General structure	Chlordiazepoxide (Librium)

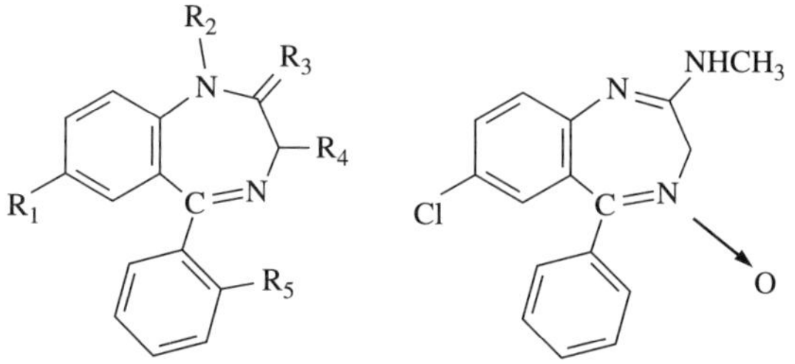

Drug	R$_1$	R$_2$		R$_3$	R$_4$	R$_5$
Diazepam	Cl	CH$_3$		= O	H$_2$	H
Nitrazepam	NO$_2$	H		= O	H$_2$	H
Flurazepam	Cl	(CH$_2$)$_2$N(C$_2$H$_5$)$_2$		= O	H$_2$	H
Flunitrazepam	NO$_2$	H		= O	H$_2$	F
Oxazepam	Cl	H		= O	OH	H
Temazepam	Cl	CH$_3$		= O	H$_2$	H
Clonazepam	NO$_2$	H		= O	H$_2$	Cl
Lorazepam	Cl	H		= O	OH	Cl
Clorazepate	Cl	H		= O	COOH	H
Nordiazepam	Cl	H		= O	H$_2$	H

FIGURE 6.1 Structures of some benzodiazepines. The basic "benzodiazepine" nucleus, which structurally defines this class of drugs, is shown on the left; chlordiazepoxide (the first marketed benzodiazepine) is shown on the right. Variations in the basic structure are located at the R$_1$–R$_5$ positions on the basic structure.

identified (see Figure 2.4), these and related drugs are called benzodiazepine receptor agonists (BZRAs). This term encompasses both benzodiazepines and several newer nonbenzodiazepines that are agonists at the same receptor and that are widely prescribed to improve the quality of sleep in the clinical management of insomnia (discussed later in this chapter).

Mechanism of Action: Benzodiazepine-GABA$_A$ Receptor

The benzodiazepines are agonists of the GABA-benzodiazepine-chloride receptor complex; they facilitate the binding of GABA (Figure 6.2). They do not directly stimulate the GABA receptor; rather, they bind to a site adjacent to the GABA receptor, producing a three-dimensional conformational change in the receptor structure that, in turn, increases the affinity of GABA for the receptor. That action, in turn, increases the inhibitory synaptic action of GABA, facilitating the influx of chloride ions, causing hyperpolarization of the postsynaptic neuron, depressing its excitability.

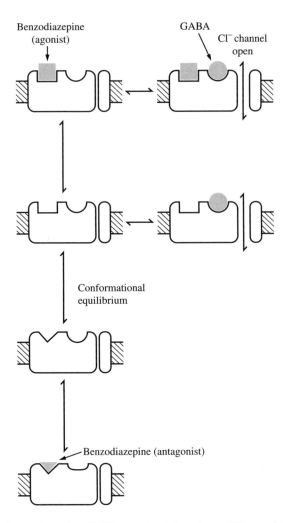

FIGURE 6.2 Benzodiazepine- GABA receptor interactions. BZD agonists (for example, diazepam) and antagonists (flumazenil) bind to a site on the GABA receptor that is distinct from the GABA-binding site. A conformational equilibrium exists between states in which the BZD receptor exists in its agonist-binding conformation *(top)* and its antagonist-binding conformation *(bottom)*. In the latter state, the GABA receptor has a much-reduced affinity for GABA, so the chloride channel remains closed. [Modified from Rang and Dale (1991), Figure 25.6.]

Benzodiazepines exert their anxiolytic properties by acting at limbic centers. Their actions at other regions (for example, cerebral cortex and brain stem) produce side effects such as sedation, increased seizure threshold, cognitive impairment, and muscle relaxation. Neuroanatomically, the *amygdala, orbitofrontal cortex,* and *insula* are associated with the production of behavioral responses to fearful stimuli and the central mediation of anxiety and panic. Electrical stimulation of these structures evokes behavioral and physiological responses that are associated with fear and anxiety. Electrical lesions of the amygdala in animals result in an anxiolytic effect. PET scanning of the brain demonstrates increased amygdala blood flow concomitant with anxiety responses; MRI scanning of the brain demonstrates amygdala abnormalities in panic disorder patients. Newly identified have been genetic variants in mice that associate altered genes for the production of a neurotrophic protein called BDNF (Chapter 7) that may predispose to anxiety and depressive disorders (Chen et al., 2006).

Artificially blocking GABAergic function can elicit anxiogenic-like effects, with both behavioral and physiologic alterations similar to symptoms of human anxiety states. As early as 1995, Saunders and colleagues "primed" or "kindled" the amygdala of rats by chronically blocking the function of the GABA$_A$ subtype of GABA receptors. Results indicated that increased activity of amygdala function (with lowered GABAergic inhibition of function) produced anxiogenic responses as measured both in animal models of anxiety and by increases in heart rate and blood pressure. Thus, hypofunctional GABA$_A$ receptor activity may sensitize the amygdala to anxiogenic responses to what might otherwise be considered nondistressing stimuli. This mechanism might develop pathological emotional responses, such as chronic, high levels of anxiety. The benzodiazepines may reset the threshold of the amygdala to a more normal level of responsiveness. Sigel (2002) details the molecular biology of the interaction between benzodiazepines and GABA$_A$ receptor function.

Pharmacokinetics

Fifteen benzodiazepine derivatives are currently available in the United States (Table 6.1), and still more are available in other countries. They differ from each other mainly in their pharmacokinetic parameters and by the routes through which they are administered. Pharmacokinetic differences include rates of metabolism to pharmacologically active intermediates and plasma half-lives of both the parent drug and any active metabolites. Of the benzodiazepines commercially available in the United States, 12 are available in dosage forms intended only for oral ingestion; 2 (diazepam and lorazepam) are available for both oral use and use by injection; and 1 (midazolam) is available only in injectable formulation.

Absorption and Distribution. Benzodiazepines are well absorbed when they are taken orally; peak plasma concentrations are achieved in about 1 hour. Some (for example, oxazepam and lorazepam) are

TABLE 6.1 Benzodiazepines

Drug name		Dosage form		Active metab-olite	Active compounds in blood	Mean elimination half-life in hours (range)
Generic	Trade	Oral	Paren-teral			
LONG-ACTING AGENTS						
Diazepam	Valium	X	X	Yes	Diazepam	24 (20–50)
					Nordiazepam	60 (50–100)
Chlordiazepoxide	Librium	X		Yes	Chlordiaze-poxide	10 (8–24)
					Nordiazepam	60 (50–100)
Flurazepam	Dalmane	X		Yes	Desalkylfluraz-epam	80 (70–160)
Halazepam	Paxipam	X		Yes	Halazepam	14 (10–20)
					Nordiazepam	60 (50–100)
Prazepam	Centrax	X		Yes	Nordiazepam	60 (50–100)
Chlorazepate	Tranxene	X		Yes	Nordiazepam	60 (50–100)
INTERMEDIATE-ACTING AGENTS						
Lorazepam	Ativan	X	X	No	Lorazepam	15 (10–24)
Clonazepam	Klonopin	X		No	Clonazepam	30 (18–50)
Quazepam	Dormalin	X		Yes	Quazepam	35 (25–50)
					Desalkylfluraz-epam	80 (70–160)
Estazolam	ProSom	X		Yes	Hydroxyestaz-olam	18 (13–35)
SHORT-ACTING AGENTS						
Midazolam	Versed		X	No	Midazolam	2.5 (1.5–4.5)
Oxazepam	Serax	X		No	Oxazepam	8 (5–15)
Temazepam	Restoril	X		No	Temazepam	12 (8–35)
Triazolam	Halcion	X		No	Triazolam	2.5 (1.5–5)
Alprazolam	Xanax	X		No	Alprazolam	12 (11–18)

absorbed more slowly, while others (for example, triazolam) are absorbed more rapidly. Clorazepate is metabolized in gastric juice to an active metabolite (nordiazepam), which is completely absorbed.

Metabolism and Excretion. Usually, psychoactive drugs are metabolized to pharmacologically inactive products, which are then excreted in urine (Chapter 1). Although some benzodiazepines behave this

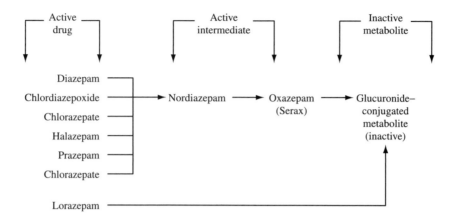

FIGURE 6.3 Metabolism of benzodiazepines. The intermediate metabolite nordiazepam is formed from many agents. Oxazepam (Serax) is commercially available and is also an active metabolite in the metabolism of nordiazepam to its inactive products.

way, several are first metabolized to intermediate, pharmacologically active products; these products, in turn, are detoxified by further metabolism before they are excreted (Figure 6.3). As can be seen from Table 6.1 and Figure 6.3, several benzodiazepines are metabolized into long-lasting, pharmacologically active metabolites; the primary one is nordiazepam, the half-life of which is about 60 hours, much longer (1 to 2 weeks) in the elderly. Thus, the long-acting benzodiazepines are so primarily because of the long half-life of a pharmacologically active metabolite. In contrast, the short-acting benzodiazepines are short acting because they are metabolized directly into inactive products.

Benzodiazepines in the Elderly.   The elderly have a reduced ability to metabolize long-acting benzodiazepines and their active metabolites. In this population, the elimination half-life for diazepam and its active metabolite is about 7 to 10 days. Since it takes about six half-lives to rid the body completely of a drug (Chapter 1), it may take an elderly patient 6 to 10 weeks to become drug-free after stopping the drug. With short-acting benzodiazepines, such as midazolam, pharmacokinetics are not so drastically altered, but the dose necessary to achieve effect is reduced by about 50 percent (Albrecht et al., 1999) (Figure 6.4).

Because all benzodiazepines can produce cognitive dysfunction, elderly patients can become clinically demented as a result. In general, benzodiazepines should be used only with great caution (if at all) for the elderly. Rang and Dale (1991) stated some years ago:

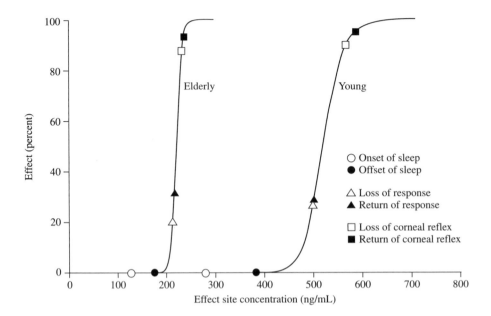

FIGURE 6.4 Concentration (effective dose-response) curve and clinical end points for young (24 to 28 years old) and elderly (67 to 81 years old) male volunteers receiving continuous infusion of midazolam (Versed) until the desired end points were attained. Plasma concentrations of drug were measured at the time of attainment of each clinical end point. In general, younger subjects required an effective site concentration about double that required in the elderly subjects. [From Albrecht et al. (1999), Figure 4.]

> At the age of 91, the grandmother of one of the authors was growing increasingly forgetful and mildly dotty, having been taking nitrazepam for insomnia regularly for years. To the author's lasting shame, it took a canny general practitioner to diagnose the problem. Cancellation of the nitrazepam prescription produced a dramatic improvement. (p. 637)

Paterniti and coworkers (2002) followed over 130 benzodiazepine-using elderly people for up to 4 years. Even periodic use was associated with prolonged decreases in cognitive performance, compared with non-drug-taking elderly.

Another significant problem with benzodiazepines in the elderly is a widely reported increase in the incidence of falls and bone fractures (Nurmi-Luthje et al, 2006; Allain et al., 2005), although one study has recently disputed this data (Wagner, 2007). Regardless, intensive physician education about the elderly, their families, and their caregivers is needed. Slowly, atypical antipsychotic drugs, such as quetiapine and risperidone (Chapter 9), are replacing the use of benzodiazepines for sedation and behavioral control in the elderly.

Pharmacological Effects

As stated, the clinical and behavioral effects of the benzodiazepines occur as a result of facilitation of GABA-induced neuronal inhibition at the various locations of $GABA_A$ receptors throughout the CNS. All benzodiazepines that exert actions similar to those exerted by diazepam are termed *pure agonists* because they faithfully facilitate GABA binding. Low doses moderate anxiety, agitation, and fear by their actions on receptors located in the amygdala, orbitofrontal cortex, and insula. Mental confusion and amnesia follow action on GABA neurons located in the cerebral cortex and the hippocampus. The mild muscle relaxant effects of the benzodiazepines are probably caused both by their anxiolytic actions and by effects on GABA receptors located in the spinal cord, cerebellum, and brain stem. The antiepileptic actions seem to follow from actions on GABA receptors located in the cerebellum and the hippocampus. The behavioral rewarding effects, drug abuse potential, and psychological dependency probably result from actions on GABA receptors that modulate the discharge of neurons located in the ventral tegmentum and the nucleus accumbens.

Clinical Uses and Limitations

From 1960 to the 1990s, the benzodiazepines were the drugs of choice for the short-term pharmacological treatment of stress-related anxiety and insomnia. They are easy to use, they have relatively low toxicity, and they are effective in producing a "tranquil" state with reductions in anxiety. The benzodiazepines, however, are not antidepressant; in fact they can intensify depression in much the same way that alcohol intensifies depression. As anxiolytics, however, their adverse effects and their potential for producing dependency are generally conceded to limit their therapeutic use to relatively short periods of time, perhaps a few days to as long as 3 to 4 weeks, and only for conditions where short-term therapy is beneficial. For longer-term treatment of such disorders as insomnia, generalized anxiety, phobias, panic disorder, and posttraumatic stress disorder, behavioral treatments and antidepressant drugs are now preferred over benzodiazepine therapy. In instances where a combination of cognitive-behavioral therapies and benzodiazepines are used together to treat anxiety, the benzodiazepines have the potential to interfere with the cognitive therapy, perhaps significantly reducing its efficacy (Figure 6.5). A cognitive inhibitor could certainly be predicted to block cognitive-based psychological therapies (Westra et al., 2002).

Benzodiazepines are generally not utilized for chronic anxiety or for treating depression. They should be avoided in situations requiring fine motor or cognitive skills or mental alertness, or in situations where alcohol or other central nervous system (CNS) depressants are used. They

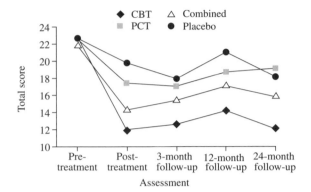

FIGURE 6.5 Effects of cognitive-behavioral therapy (CBT), pharmacotherapy (PCT), combination of CBT and PCT, and a placebo treatment on late-life insomnia (as measured by changes in total score for the patient version of the Sleep Impairment Index) in 78 adults ages 65 or older with chronic and primary insomnia. PCT consisted of a benzodiazepine—temazepam (Restoril)—administered in a dose of 7.5 to 30 milligrams 1 hour before bedtime. Pretreatment, posttreatment, and 3-, 12-, and 24-month follow-up assessments are illustrated. CBT was most effective, followed by combination treatment, PCT alone, and placebo. Benzodiazepine medication reduced the effectiveness of CBT. [Data from C. M. Morin et al., "Behavioural and Pharmacological Therapies for Late-Life Insomnia: A Randomized Controlled Trial," *Journal of the American Medical Association* 281 (1999), p. 997.]

should be used only with great caution in the elderly, in children or adolescents, and in anyone with a history of drug misuse or ongoing abuse.

One possible indication for benzodiazepine therapy is for the short-term treatment of anxiety that is so debilitating that the patient's life-style, work, and interpersonal relationships are severely hampered. A benzodiazepine may alleviate the symptoms of nervousness, dysphoria, and psychological distress without necessarily blocking the physiological correlates accompanying the state of anxiety. Usually, resolution of the psychological distress is accompanied by amelioration of the physiological symptoms. In cases of behavioral emergencies in mania, oral or intravenous benzodiazepines, alone or in combination with a mood stabilizer (Chapter 8) or an antipsychotic drug (Chapter 9), are recommended (Alderfer and Allen, 2003).

As sedatives, the benzodiazepines possess many of the characteristics of the barbiturates. Thus, they are used as hypnotics for the treatment of insomnia. Agents with rapid onset, a 2- to 3-hour half-life, and no active metabolites may be preferred to minimize daytime sedation. However, when daytime sedation or next-day anxiolysis is desired, the long-acting drugs with active metabolites might be preferred. Use in treating insomnia, however, is limited by the development of dependence as reflected by rebound increases in insomnia on discontinuation.

Because increased GABA activity inhibits neuronal function, the benzodiazepines have been used as muscle relaxants both to directly reduce states associated with increased muscle tension and to reduce the psychological distress that can predispose to muscle tension. However, they do not directly relax muscles. They relieve only the distress associated with muscle tension (much like alcohol).

Benzodiazepines are exceedingly effective in producing antero-grade amnesia (amnesia that starts at the time of drug administration and ends when the blood level of drug has decreased to a point where memory function is regained). For this use, either of two injectable benzodiazepines is reliable—lorazepam, when lasting amnesia is desirable, and midazolam, when shorter periods of amnesia are desirable. An example of a situation where amnesia might be a therapeutic goal and a benzodiazepine indicated is for performing surgery or invasive medical procedures (for example, a colonoscopy). Often, however, an amnestic effect is undesirable. For example, concern has been expressed about an illegally imported "date rape" drug, which turned out to be a benzodiazepine that is commercially marketed outside the United States. This drug, *flunitrazepam* (Rohypnol), is very similar to *triazolam* (Halcion; see Table 6.1); it produces anxiolysis, sedation, and amnesia, especially when taken with alcohol. When the drug and alcohol are ingested by an unknowing victim, the effect closely resembles the effect of a Mickey Finn (chloral hydrate in alcohol) or GHB (Chapter 5), and amnesia is achieved without the production of unconsciousness.[1]

Panic attacks and phobias can be treated with benzodiazepines such as *alprazolam* (Xanax), although the efficacy of benzodiazepines may be less than that of the serotonin-type antidepressants, which are actually more specific anxiolytics (Stocchi et al., 2003; Weisstaub et al., 2006). As discussed in Chapter 7, paroxetine (as well as other SSRIs) markedly reduces anxiety. Moreover, unlike with the benzodiazepines, cessation of use is not accompanied by rebound increases in anxiety, impaired psychomotor performance, impaired learning and cognition, reduced alertness, and the potential for dependence and abuse (Arkowitz and Lilienfeld, 2007).

Because benzodiazepines can substitute for alcohol, they are used both in treating acute alcohol withdrawal and in long-term therapy to reduce the rate of relapse to previous drinking habits. Today, however, certain of the antiepileptic mood stabilizers (Chapters 4 and 8) are viable

---

[1] Rohypnol intoxication (and the amnesia it causes) can begin within about 30 minutes, peak within 2 hours, and can persist for up to 8 hours. With a combination of Rohypnol and alcohol, the amnestic and intoxicating effects can last 8 to 18 hours. Disinhibition is another widely reported effect of Rohypnol, when ingested alone or in combination with alcohol.

alternatives. Finally, all benzodiazepines exert antiepileptic actions because they raise the threshold for generating seizures. In general, however, benzodiazepines are used as secondary drugs or as adjuvants to other, more specific anticonvulsants.

In summary, perhaps the only well-accepted situation in which benzodiazepines cannot readily be replaced by other drugs is the intentional production of anterograde amnesia, for example, in hospital situations where it is desirable to block the memory for certain unpleasant or painful procedures. The newer antidepressant/anxiolytic agents continue to reduce benzodiazepine use for the treatment of anxiety disorders.

Side Effects and Toxicity

Common acute side effects associated with benzodiazepine therapy are usually dose-related extensions of the intended actions, including sedation, drowsiness, ataxia, lethargy, mental confusion, motor and cognitive impairments, disorientation, slurred speech, amnesia, and induction or extension of the symptoms of dementia. At higher doses, mental and psychomotor dysfunction progress to hypnosis. Used for the treatment of insomnia, benzodiazepines are especially controversial; drugs can cause the expected sedation, or they can induce paradoxical agitation (anxiety, aggression, hostility, and behavioral disinhibition). The excitatory, or disinhibitory, effects resemble those produced by alcohol. In addition, cessation of use results in rebound increases in insomnia and anxiety.

Respiration is not seriously depressed, even at high doses. Attempted suicides by overdose are rarely successful unless the benzodiazepine is taken along with another CNS depressant, such as alcohol. This combination can cause a serious and potentially fatal drug interaction. Sleep patterns can be altered markedly. When short-acting agents are taken at bedtime, both early-morning wakening and rebound insomnia for the next night are common. When long-acting agents (or agents with active metabolites) are taken at bedtime, daytime sedation can be a problem.

Impairment of motor abilities—especially a person's ability to drive an automobile—is common. Verster and coworkers (2002a) demonstrated that low doses of alprazolam (Xanax), equivalent to a 0.15 gram% blood level of alcohol, markedly impaired driving ability. The ability to divide attention was especially impaired. This impairment is compounded by the drug-induced suppression of a person's ability to assess his or her own level of physical and mental impairment.

The cognitive deficits associated with benzodiazepine use are significant. In both children and adults, benzodiazepines can significantly interfere with learning behaviors, academic performance, and psychomotor functioning. Cognitive and generalized intellectual impairments can persist even long after the benzodiazepine is discontinued, although cognitive improvements after discontinuation are the norm.

> Patients who had evidence of impaired cognitive functions while on long-term benzodiazepine therapy did improve in these functions when therapy was discontinued. . . . Further, . . . patients who were able to discontinue their benzodiazepine intake after many years of use became more alert, more relaxed, and less anxious, and this change was accompanied by improved psychomotor functions. (Rickels et al., 1999, p. 107)

More recently, Stewart (2005) stated:

> Meta-analyses found that cognitive dysfunction did in fact occur in patients treated long-term with benzodiazepines, and although cognitive dysfunction improved after benzodiazepines were withdrawn, patients did not return to levels of functioning that matched benzodiazepine-free controls. (p. 9)

This statement is certainly cause for concern!

Tolerance and Dependence

When benzodiazepines are taken for prolonged periods of time, a pattern of dependence can develop. Early withdrawal signs include a return (and possible intensification) of the anxiety state for which the drug was originally given. Rebound increases in insomnia, restlessness, agitation, irritability, and unpleasant dreams gradually appear. In rare instances, hallucinations, psychoses, and seizures have been reported. Most of these withdrawal symptoms subside within 1 to 4 weeks. Morin and coworkers (2004) used cognitive-behavioral therapy to facilitate benzodiazepine withdrawal in elderly people with insomnia and benzodiazepine dependence.

Zitman and Couvee (2001) studied a large group of patients for whom benzodiazepines had been inappropriately prescribed for the treatment of depression. They were withdrawn from their benzodiazepine either with or without administration of concomitant paroxetine. Although two-thirds of the patients were successfully withdrawn, by 2 or 3 years after original discontinuation only 13 percent remained benzodiazepine-free. This illustration shows the attractiveness of the benzodiazepines and explains the inability of certain people to refrain from their use. Patients who have histories of drug or alcohol abuse are most apt to use these agents inappropriately, and abuse of benzodiazepines usually occurs as part of a pattern of abuse of more than one drug.

Effects in Pregnancy

During pregnancy, benzodiazepines and their metabolites freely cross the placenta and accumulate in the fetal circulation. Benzodiazepines administered during the first trimester of pregnancy have been reported to cause fetal abnormalities, although the risk is probably very small. Near the time of delivery, if a mother is on high doses of benzodiazepines, a fetus can develop benzodiazepine dependence or even a "floppy-infant syndrome," followed after delivery by signs of withdrawal. Because benzodiazepines are excreted in breast milk and because they can accumulate in nursing infants, taking benzodiazepines while breast-feeding is not recommended.

Flumazenil: A Benzodiazepine Receptor Antagonist

Flumazenil (Romazicon) is a benzodiazepine that binds with high affinity to benzodiazepine receptors on the $GABA_A$ complex (see Figure 6.2), but after binding, it exhibits no intrinsic activity. As a consequence, it competitively blocks the access of pharmacologically active benzodiazepines to the receptor, effectively reversing the antianxiety and sedative effects of any benzodiazepines administered before flumazenil.

Flumazenil is metabolized quite rapidly in the liver and has a short half-life (about 1 hour). Because this half-life is much shorter than that of most benzodiazepines, the benzodiazepine effects can reappear as flumazenil is lost, thus necessitating reinjection. Flumazenil is utilized as an antidote (administered by intravenous injection) when benzodiazepine overdosage is suspected.

Benzodiazepine Receptor Agonist Hypnotics

Any drug that activates the benzodiazepine receptor is termed a *benzodiazepine receptor agonist* (BZRA). The benzodiazepines obviously are in this category (all are BZRAs), and all can be used not only as anxiolytics but as sedatives for the treatment of insomnia. In addition to drugs that share the benzodiazepine structure, three drugs are currently available that are structurally not classified as benzodiazepines but nevertheless are agonists at the benzodiazepine receptor. These *nonbenzodiazepine BZRAs* are prescribed as hypnotic drugs intended for the treatment of insomnia. They are not prescribed as anxiolytics, primarily because of their short half-lives. These three drugs, as well as the benzodiazepines, have come under scrutiny because of their ability at hypnotic doses to induce amnesia; thus they are implicated in behavioral activities that occur while one is amnestic (for example, sleep driving, sleep eating, and so on).

Chronic insomnia, whether primary (idiopathic) in origin or associated with comorbid medical or psychiatric conditions, is a prevalent and disabling condition. It is simply characterized as lack of sleep or lack of good-quality sleep. It can manifest itself as difficulty falling asleep, difficulty staying asleep, waking up too early, or waking in the morning without feeling "refreshed." About 10 percent of people experience chronic insomnia. Roughly 50 percent of people with other medical or psychological conditions complain of insomnia. Consequences of insomnia include daytime fatigue, lack of energy, poor concentration and memory, moodiness and irritability, and difficulty completing tasks. Treatments can be either psychological or pharmacological. Of the psychological therapies, cognitive-behavioral therapies have been shown to be at least as effective as pharmacotherapies (Sivertsen et al., 2006; Morin et al., 2006). Practice parameters for the psychological and behavioral treatment of insomnia are available (Morgenthaler et al., 2006). These treatments are currently underutilized. Pharmacotherapies include two types of FDA-approved insomnia medications: agonists of the benzodiazepine receptor (BZRAs) and a melatonin receptor agonist (ramelteon).

Benzodiazepine BZRAs

As discussed earlier, all benzodiazepines exhibit hypnotic properties. Five of them (flurazepam, estazolam, quazepam, temazepam, and triazolam) are formally indicated for the treatment of insomnia (the manufacturers of these five have sought and obtained formal FDA approval to promote use for treating insomnia). Triazolam has the shortest half-life, 2 to 4 hours, and is associated with less daytime sedation. It may not provide adequate sedation through the night. Conversely, the others have longer half-lives and increase sleep maintenance, but they may take some time to induce sleep and have adverse cognitive consequences the next day (see Table 6.1). Dependence and tolerance are potentially harmful.

Nonbenzodiazepine BZRAS

Several drugs that are structurally not benzodiazepines nevertheless bind to the same receptors to which benzodiazepines bind. As agonists at these receptors, these drugs are referred to as nonbenzodiazepine BZRAs. To date, three such agents have been marketed. One is *zolpidem* (Ambien), marketed in the mid-1990s as a drug for the treatment of insomnia. Binding to a specific subgroup, the $GABA_{1A}$ receptor, it exhibits primarily a hypnotic rather than an anxiolytic effect. Other BZRAs under development exert weaker effects at the $GABA_{1A}$ receptor and are termed "partial BZRAs."

Zolpidem. Zolpidem (Ambien; Figure 6.6) is a nonbenzodiazepine that was marketed in 1993 for the short-term treatment of insomnia. Although structurally unrelated to the benzodiazepines, zolpidem acts

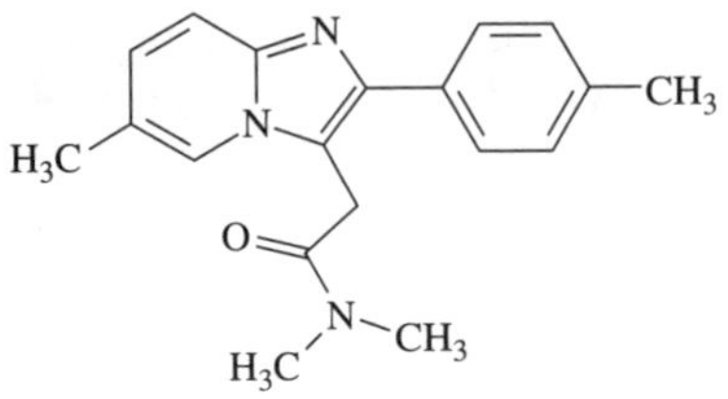

Zolpidem (Ambien)

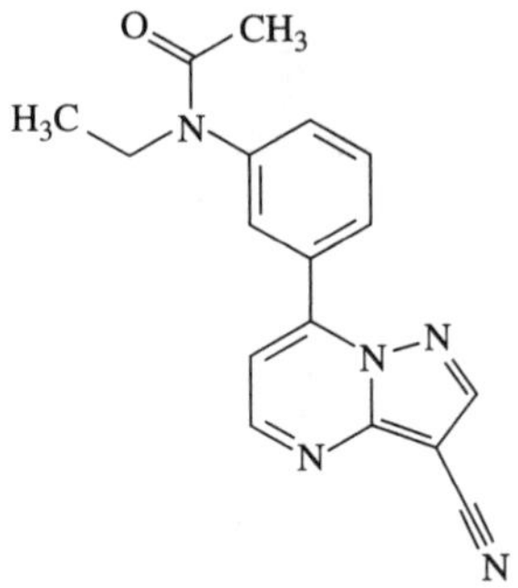

Zaleplon (Sonata)

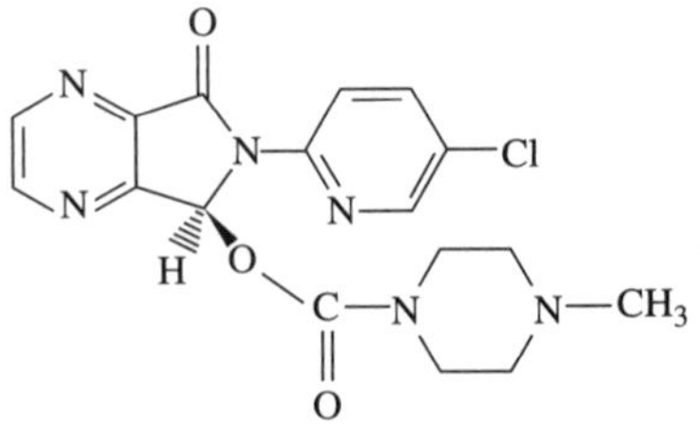

Eszopiclone (Lunesta)

FIGURE 6.6 Structural formulas of zolpidem (Ambien), zaleplon (Sonata), and eszopiclone (Lunesta). Note the close (but dissimilar) relationship of their basic three-ring structures to the benzodiazepine nucleus (see Figure 6.1). Thus, these three compounds are nonbenzodiazepines despite similar GABAergic actions and clinical effects.

similarly, binding to a specific subtype (type 1) of the GABA$_A$ receptor. It displays most of the actions of all the other benzodiazepine agonists: it is primarily a sedative rather than an anxiolytic, and its sedative actions overwhelm any anxiolytic effects. With a half-life of about 2 to 2.5 hours, zolpidem is often compared to triazolam (Halcion), a benzodiazepine with similar pharmacokinetics; at comparable doses, there appears to be little to differentiate the two drugs. A controlled-release formulation of zolpidem (Ambien CR) is available. Due to slower dissolution in the gastrointestinal tract, it is absorbed at a slower rate. Thus, its half-life is a bit longer, perhaps about 3 hours.

Zolpidem is rapidly absorbed from the gastrointestinal tract after oral administration, with about 75 percent of the administered drug reaching the plasma, the remainder being rapidly metabolized as it is being absorbed. Peak plasma levels are reached in about 1 hour. Following metabolism in the liver, the kidneys excrete the products. The calculated half-life is prolonged in the elderly.

At doses of 5 to 10 milligrams, zolpidem produces sedation and promotes a physiological pattern of sleep in the absence of anxiolytic, anticonvulsant, or muscle relaxant effects. Memory is adversely affected as it is by benzodiazepines.

Dose-related adverse effects of zolpidem include drowsiness, dizziness, and nausea. Zolpidem, in doses of 10 milligrams, exhibits minimal effects on memory or psychomotor performance in healthy volunteers participating in a driving-performance study; however, doses of 20 milligrams significantly impair performance and memory even 4 hours after taking the drug (Verster et al., 2002b). A high-dose incidence of nausea and vomiting tends to limit overdosage in suicide attempts. Overdoses to 400 milligrams (40 times the therapeutic dose) have not been fatal. In the elderly, confusion, falls, memory loss, and psychotic reactions have been reported.

Zaleplon. *Zaleplon* (Sonata; see Figure 6.6) is another nonbenzodiazepine agonist that binds to the $GABA_{1A}$ receptor. In general, it exerts actions similar to those of the benzodiazepines. It became commercially available in 1999 for clinical use as a hypnotic agent. Zaleplon is unique among hypnotic drugs because its half-life is very short (less than 1 hour) and only about 30 percent of the dose reaches the bloodstream; most undergoes first-pass metabolism in the liver. Because Zaleplon is so short-acting, it does not require that a person predict whether he or she will have insomnia on a particular night. Instead, if the person cannot fall asleep and stay asleep without pharmacological assistance, he or she has the option of taking this very short-acting agent without fear of detrimental effects the next morning.

Sleep is quite rapidly induced with zaleplon at doses of 5 to 10 milligrams, and sleep quality is improved without rebound insomnia. Zaleplon appears particularly noteworthy in its lack of deleterious effects on psychomotor function and driving ability the morning following use (Verster et al., 2002b). Allowing at least 4 hours from drug intake to driving results in no adverse effects (Patat et al., 2001). In fact, at 4 hours after oral administration, most of the drug is eliminated from the body. Dependence is unlikely to develop because of the short half-life: by morning the drug is metabolized. In essence, a person taking the drug withdraws daily, and drug does not persist in the body. At extremely high doses (25 to 75 milligrams), an abuse potential comparable to that seen for triazolam (Halcion) is seen.

Eszopiclone. *Eszopiclone* (Lunesta; see Figure 6.6) is also a nonbenzodiazepine approved for the treatment of insomnia. It is the active isomer of zopiclone (Immovane), which has been used outside the United States for many years. Eszopiclone shares all the actions of zolpidem and traditional benzodiazepines. Because of a half-life of 5 to 7 hours, eszopiclone has the most prolonged action of the nonbenzodiazepine BZRAs. Therefore, it might be preferable to the others for improving both sleep latency and sleep maintenance. However, this benefit is offset by increased risk of next-day sedation. It was the first of these agents to report data from long-term trials, and thus it has been approved by the FDA for longer-term use. At its highest dose level (3 mg), next-day memory impairments and poor performance on measures of psychomotor performance have been reported.

Partial Agonists at GABA$_A$ Receptors

"Full" BZRA agonists are effective anxiolytics and sedatives; however, their use is limited by rebound anxiety (on discontinuation), physical dependence (with extended use), abuse potential, and side effects that include ataxia, sedation, and memory and cognitive disturbances. Therefore, attempts have been made to identify "partial" agonists of GABA receptors (partial BZRAs) in the hope of providing anxiolytics that may be equally as effective without the side effects that limit the use of the benzodiazepines. To date, several have been examined, although none is currently available in the United States. The best studied of these agents are alpidem (marketed in Europe), etizolam, imidazenil, abecarnil, and bretazenil. Each of these partial agonists is in various stages of experimentation or trial for various clinical uses, including use as anticonvulsants.

Sleep Driving

In March 2007, the FDA released an advisory requesting that all manufacturers of sedative-hypnotic products that are used to induce and/or maintain sleep strengthen their product labeling to include risks of "sleep driving," which is defined as driving while not fully awake after ingestion of a sedative-hypnotic product and having no memory of the event—in other words, driving while still in a drug-induced amnestic state. Other behaviors reported to have occurred in such a state include making telephone calls and preparing and eating food and then having no later memory of having done so. In essence, the blood level of the drug is sufficient to block the formation of memory proteins in the absence of a state of unconsciousness or sleep. Thirteen products were listed on the FDA advisory. These included the three nonbenzodiazepine BZRAs (Ambien, Sonata, and Lunesta); the benzodiazepines Dalmane, Halcion, ProSom, and Restoril; the barbiturates Butisol, Carbrital, and Seconal; the melatonin-agonist Rozerem; and two miscellaneous agents (Doral and Placidyl). This advisory is probably not all-inclusive.

Ramelteon: A Selective Melatonin Receptor Agonist

Melatonin, available for many years as an over-the-counter drug for the treatment of insomnia, has repeatedly failed to demonstrate significant effects, except perhaps on people with disrupted sleep-wake cycles (for example, shift workers and people with jet lag). The sleep-wake cycle is controlled by homeostatic and circadian processes that regulate the drive for sleep that accumulates during waking. Neurons in the anterior hypothalamus coordinate the timing of this circadian system and maintain 24-hour periodicity, controlling the pineal gland in producing melatonin, with melatonin levels increasing as bedtime approaches, plateauing during the night, and decreasing as sleep ends in the morning. These anterior hypothalamic neurons contain a high concentration of melatonin receptors.

Ramelteon (Rozerem; Figure 6.7) is a melatonin receptor agonist, recently approved by the FDA for the treatment of insomnia characterized by difficulty with sleep onset. The drug is thought to be nonaddicting and therefore devoid of abuse potential (Johnson et al., 2006). Rebound insomnia following a period of nightly drug use has not been reported. In an available 8-milligram dose, it is taken 30 minutes before going to bed. A half-life of about 3 hours is thought to leave little morning drowsiness. In controlled trials, efficacy was quite modest, with sleep onset occurring only about 10 or 15 minutes earlier than after taking placebo and with total sleep time little affected (Borja and Daniel, 2006; Roth et al., 2006; Erman et al., 2006). Controlled trials against established anti-insomnia drugs, including the nonbenzodiazepine BZRAs, have not been reported. Therefore, its efficacy relative to other therapeutic options cannot be estimated at this time.

Serotonin Receptor Agonists as Anxiolytics

Anxiety may, at least in part, result from defects in serotonin neurotransmission, and drugs that augment serotonin activity are useful in the treatment of anxiety disorders. Perhaps the most widely used class

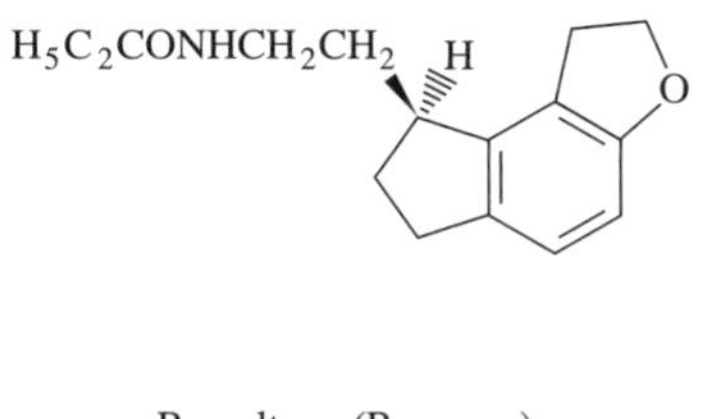

$H_5C_2CONHCH_2CH_2$

Ramelteon (Rozerem)

FIGURE 6.7 Structural formula of ramelteon (Rozerem).

of serotonin agonists are the SSRI-type antidepressants (Chapter 7). The six SSRI antidepressants that are clinically available are widely used in the treatment of all anxiety disorders and are, in fact, considered to be drugs of first choice for such use. We focus here on several other agents that act through direct stimulation of the postsynaptic serotonin 5-HT$_{1A}$ receptor.

Serotonin 5-HT$_{1A}$ receptors are found in high density in the hippocampus, the septum, parts of the amygdala, and the dorsal raphe nucleus, areas all presumed to be involved in fear and anxiety responses. Activity in the 5-HT$_{1A}$ receptor is thought to diminish neuronal activity. Mice selectively bred without 5-HT$_{1A}$ receptors display increased fear responses, suggesting that reductions in 5-HT$_{1A}$ receptor activity or density (presumably due to genetic deficits or environmental stressors) result in heightened anxiety (Rambos et al., 1998).

Buspirone

Clinical interest in serotonin anxiolytics began 20 years ago with demonstration of the anxiolytic action of *buspirone*, a selective serotonin 5-HT$_{1A}$ agonist. In 1986 the drug was approved for clinical use, and it is marketed under the trade name BuSpar. Thereafter, other related agents were identified, but they have not yet been marketed. Such drugs include gepirone, ipsapirone, and alnespirone. Buspirone (BuSpar) is a 5-HT$_{1A}$ agonist with demonstrable anxiolytic properties. It relieves anxiety in a unique fashion:

- Its anxiolysis occurs without significant sedation or hypnotic action, even in overdosage.

- Amnesia, mental confusion, and psychomotor impairment are minimal or absent.

- It does not potentiate the CNS depressant effects of alcohol, benzodiazepines, or other CNS sedatives (synergism does not occur).

- It does not substitute for benzodiazepines in treating anxiety or benzodiazepine withdrawal.

- It does not exhibit cross-tolerance or cross-dependence with benzodiazepines.

- It exhibits little potential for addiction or abuse.

- It exhibits an antidepressant effect in addition to its anxiolytic effect, making it potentially useful in depressive disorders with accompanying anxiety.

- Its effect has a gradual onset rather than the immediate onset of the action of the benzodiazepines.

- It is ineffective as a hypnotic in promoting the onset of sleep.

Buspirone is a weak agonist at 5-HT$_{1A}$ receptors. As a result, it exerts both an anxiolytic action and an antidepressant action (the antidepressant role of 5-HT$_{1A}$ receptors is discussed in Chapter 7). Buspirone is effective in the treatment of generalized anxiety disorder. It has also been recommended for patients who suffer from mixed symptoms of anxiety and depression, as well as for elderly people with agitated dementia.

Buspirone is most helpful in anxious patients who do not demand immediate gratification or the immediate response they associate with the benzodiazepine response. Slower and more gradual onset of anxiety relief is balanced by the increased safety and lack of dependency-producing aspects of buspirone. To see clinical effects takes several weeks of continuous treatment. Patients who have previously been taking benzodiazepines do poorly on buspirone. Chapter 1 presents a likely reason why the effects of buspirone are so subtle: most of the drug is detoxified by first-pass metabolism; only about 5 percent of orally administered drug reaches the bloodstream. Inhibition of metabolism (for example, by concurrent drinking of grapefruit juice) improves its efficacy by increasing its absorption.

Gepirone

Gepirone (Arisa, Variza) is another 5-HT$_{1A}$ agonist currently in clinical trial for use as both an antidepressant and an anxiolytic. In extended-release formulation, gepirone-ER (Figure 6.8) efficacy is comparable

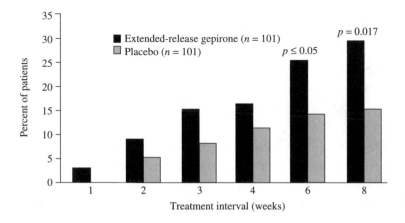

FIGURE 6.8 Percentage of patients achieving remission on a 17-item Hamilton Rating Scale for Depression. [Adapted from A. D. Feiger et al., "Gepirone Extended Release: New Evidence for Efficacy in the Treatment of Major Depressive Disorder," *Journal of Clinical Psychiatry* 4 (2003), p. 247, Figure 5.]

to standard agents, and side effects (for example, lightheadedness, nausea, dizziness) have been tolerable (Keller et al., 2005; Alpert et al., 2004; Robinson et al., 2003). The drug is currently under FDA review.

Repinotan

Repinotan is another 5-HT$_{1A}$ agonist being investigated for clinical use (Lutsep, 2002). Currently in clinical trials, it is showing efficacy not only as an anxiolytic but also as a brain-protective agent for ischemic stroke and traumatic brain injury (Berends et al, 2005).

Anticonvulsants as Anxiolytics

Pande et al. (2003, 2004) reported on the usefulness of the anticonvulsant *pregabalin* in the treatment of both generalized anxiety disorder and social anxiety disorder. The drug is a derivative of both GABA and the anticonvulsant *gabapentin* (Neurontin; Chapter 5). Pregabalin, in this study, was as effective as the benzodiazepine lorazepam (Ativan) and was of rapid onset, and patients taking this drug did not experience withdrawal symptoms on discontinuation (in sharp contrast to the withdrawal seen in patients taking lorazepam). Perhaps pregabalin will be another viable alternative to benzodiazepines. (Pregabalin is discussed further in Chapter 8.)

STUDY QUESTIONS

1. What are the advantages of benzodiazepines over barbiturates?
2. Describe the mechanism of action of benzodiazepines.
3. Describe evidence for and against a natural anxiolytic in the brain.
4. Describe the structure and function of the benzodiazepine receptor.
5. How might you describe anxiety or panic in terms of receptors or neurochemicals (at this point)?
6. List some of the clinical uses of benzodiazepines.
7. List three processes that might prolong the half-life of a benzodiazepine.
8. Why should the elderly avoid using long-acting benzodiazepines?
9. Describe the most clinically significant drug interaction that involves benzodiazepines.
10. Discuss benzodiazepine withdrawal and its treatment.

11. What is flumazenil and for what purpose can it be used?

12. Compare and contrast the mechanisms of action and clinical uses of benzodiazepines and buspirone.

13. To what benzodiazepine is zolpidem most often compared? Why?

14. Compare and contrast zolpidem, zaleplon, and eszopiclone.

15. Discuss the future treatment of anxiety disorders with either benzodiazepines or serotonin agonists.

REFERENCES

Albrecht, S., et al. (1999). "The Effects of Age on the Pharmacokinetics and Pharmacodynamics of Midazolam." *Clinical Pharmacology and Therapeutics* 65: 630–639.

Alderfer, B. S., and M. H. Allen (2003). "Treatment of Agitation in Bipolar Disorder Across the Life Cycle." *Journal of Clinical Psychiatry* 64, Supplement 4: 3–9.

Allain, H., et al. (2005). "Postural Instability and Consequent Falls and Hip Fractures Associated with Use of Hypnotics in the Elderly: A Comprehensive Review." *Drugs and Aging* 22: 749–765.

Alpert, J. E., et al. (2004). "Gepirone Extended-Release Treatment of Anxious Depression: Evidence from a Retrospective Subgroup Analysis in Patients with Major Depression." *Journal of Clinical Psychiatry* 65: 1069–1075.

Arkowitz, H., and S. O. Lilienfeld (2007). "A Pill to Fix Your Ills?" *Scientific American Mind* 18(1): 80–81.

Berends, A. C., et al. (2005). "A Review of the Neuroprotective Properties of the 5-HT1A Receptor Agonist Repinotan HCl (BAY x 3702) in Ischemic Stroke." *CNS Drug Reviews* 11: 379–402.

Borja, N. L., and K. L. Daniel (2006). "Ramelteon for the Treatment of Insomnia." *Clinical Therapeutics* 28: 1540–1555.

Chen, Z. Y., et al. (2006). "Genetic Variant BDNF (Val66met) Polymorphism Alters Anxiety-Related Behavior." *Science* 314 (5796): 140–143.

Erman, M., et al. (2006). "An Efficacy, Safety, and Dose-Response Study of Ramelteon in Patients with Chronic Primary Insomnia." *Sleep Medicine* 7: 17–24.

Katon, W., and P. Roy-Byrne (2007). "Anxiety Disorders: Efficient Screening Is the First Step in Improving Outcome." *Annals of Internal Medicine* 146: 390–391.

Keller, M. B., et al. (2005). "Relapse Prevention with Gepirone ER in Outpatients with Major Depression." *Journal of Clinical Psychopharmacology* 25: 79–84.

Kroenke, K., et al. (2007). "Anxiety Disorders in Primary Care: Prevalence, Impairment, Comorbidity, and Detection." *Annals of Internal Medicine* 146: 317–325.

Lutsep, H. L. (2002). "Repinotan, Bayer." *Current Opinions in Investigational Drugs* 3: 924–927.

Morgenthaler, T., et al. (2006). "Practice Parameters for the Psychological and Behavioral Treatment of Insomnia: An Update. An American Academy of Sleep Medicine Report." *Sleep* 29: 1415–1419.

Morin, C. M., et al. (2004). "Randomized Clinical Trial of Supervised Tapering and Cognitive Behavior Therapy to Facilitate Benzodiazepine Discontinuation in Older Adults with Chronic Insomnia." *American Journal of Psychiatry* 161: 332–342.

Morin, C. M., et al. (2006). "Psychological and Behavioral Treatment of Insomnia: Update of the Recent Evidence (1998–2004)." *Sleep* 29: 1398–1414.

Nurmi-Luthje, I., et al. (2006). "Use of Benzodiazepines and Benzodiazepine-Related Drugs Among 223 Patients with an Acute Hip Fracture in Finland: Comparison of Benzodiazepine Findings in Medical Records and Laboratory Assays." *Drugs and Aging* 23: 27–37.

Pande, A. C., et al. (2003). "Pregabalin in Generalized Anxiety Disorder: A Placebo-Controlled Trial." *American Journal of Psychiatry* 160: 533–540.

Pande, A. C., et al. (2004). "Efficacy of the Novel Anxiolytic Pregabalin on Social Anxiety Disorder: A Placebo-Controlled, Multicenter Trial." *Journal of Clinical Psychopharmacology* 24: 141–149.

Patat, A., et al. (2001). "Pharmacodynamic Profile of Zaleplon: A New Non-Benzodiazepine Hypnotic Agent." *Human Psychopharmacology* 16: 369–392.

Paterniti, S., et al. (2002). "Long-Term Benzodiazepine Use and Cognitive Decline in the Elderly: The Epidemiology of Vascular Aging Study." *Journal of Clinical Psychopharmacology* 22: 285–293.

Rambos, S., et al. (1998). "Serotonin Receptor 1_A Knockout: An Animal Model of Anxiety-Related Disorder." *Proceedings of the National Academy of Sciences* 95: 14476–14481.

Rang, H. P., and M. M. Dale (1991). *Pharmacology*, 2nd ed. Edinburgh: Churchill Livingstone.

Richards, J. G., and J. R. Martin (1998). "Binding Profiles and Physical Dependence Liabilities of Selected Benzodiazepine Receptor Ligands." *Brain Research Bulletin* 45: 381–387.

Rickels, K., et al. (1999). "Psychomotor Performance of Long-Term Benzodiazepine Users Before, During, and After Benzodiazepine Discontinuation." *Journal of Clinical Psychopharmacology* 19: 107–113.

Robinson, D. S., et al. (2003). "A Review of the Efficacy and Tolerability of Immediate-Release and Extended-Release Formulations of Gepirone." *Clinical Therapeutics* 25: 1618–1633.

Rollman, B., et al. (2005). "A Randomized Trial to Improve the Quality of Treatment for Panic and Generalized Anxiety Disorders in Primary Care." *Archives of General Psychiatry* 62: 1332–1341.

Roth, T., et al. (2006)."Effects of Ramelteon on Patient-Reported Sleep Latency in Older Adults with Chronic Insomnia." *Sleep Medicine* 7: 312–318.

Roy-Byrne, P. P., et al. (2005). "A Randomized Effectiveness Trial of Cognitive-Behavioral Therapy and Medication for Primary Care Panic Disorder." *Archives of General Psychiatry* 62: 290–298.

Saunders, S. K., et al. (1995). "Priming of Experimental Anxiety by Repeated Subthreshold GABA Blockade in the Rat Hippocampus." *Brain Research* 699: 250–259.

Sigel, E. (2002). "Mapping of the Benzodiazepine Recognition Site on GABA(A) Receptors." *Current Topics in Medicinal Chemistry* 2: 833–839.

Sivertsen, B., et al. (2006). "Cognitive Behavioral Therapy vs. Zopiclone for Treatment of Chronic Primary Insomnia in Older Adults: A Randomized Controlled Trial." *Journal of the American Medical Association* 295: 2851–2858.

Stewart, S. A. (2005). "The Effects of Benzodiazepines on Cognition." *Jounal of Clinical Psychiatry* 66 (Supplement 2): 9–13.

Stocchi, F., et al. (2003). "Efficacy and Tolerability of Paroxetine for the Long-Term Treatment of Generalized Anxiety Disorder." *Journal of Clinical Psychiatry* 64: 250–258.

Verster, J. C., et al. (2002a). "Effects of Alprazolam on Driving Ability, Memory Functioning, and Psychomotor Performance: A Randomized, Placebo-Controlled Study." *Neuropsychopharmacology* 27: 260–269.

Verster, J. C., et al. (2002b). "Residual Effects of Middle-of-the-Night Administration of Zaleplon and Zolpidem on Driving Ability, Memory Functions, and Psychomotor Performance." *Journal of Clinical Psychopharmacology* 22: 576–583.

Wagner, A. K., et al. (2007). "Effect of New York State Regulatory Action on Benzodiazepine Prescribing and Hip Fracture Rates." *Annals of Internal Medicine* 146: 96–103.

Weisstaub, N. V., et al. (2006). "Cortical 5-HT2A Receptor Signaling Modulates Anxiety-Like Behaviors in Mice." *Science* 313: 536–540.

Westra, H. A., et al. (2002). "Naturalistic Manner of Benzodiazepine Use and Cognitive Behavioral Therapy Outcome in Panic Disorder with Agoraphobia." *Journal of Anxiety Disorders* 16: 233–246.

Zitman F. G., and J. E. Couvee (2001). "Chronic Benzodiazepine Use in General Practice Patients with Depression: An Evaluation of Controlled Treatment and Taper-Off." *British Journal of Psychiatry* 178: 317–324.

Drugs That Are Used to Treat Psychological Disorders

The chapters in this part introduce drugs that are used to treat psychological disorders, including major depression (Chapter 7), bipolar disorder (Chapter 8), schizophrenia (Chapter 9), child and adolescent psychopharmacology (Chapter 10), and geriatric psychopharmacology (Chapter 11). Chapter 12 integrates psychopharmacology and psychological therapies into an overall treatment plan for psychological disorders.

Today, remarkable advances are being made in the pharmacological treatment of psychological disorders, allowing affected people to lead much more "normal" lives than they have ever been able to before in human history. The goals of these six chapters are to impart a sense of the historical development of therapeutics of each disorder, to cover the pharmacology of drugs currently being used to treat these disorders, to convey a sense of excitement about the promise of even better therapies, and to demonstrate that drug therapies are only a part (albeit a necessary part) of the overall management of the patient with psychological disorders.

The drugs are compartmentalized in these chapters under descriptive headings (antidepressants, mood stabilizers, antipsychotics, and so forth), but the headings do not adequately describe or define the drugs. For example, besides being used to relieve major depression, antidepressants are used as antianxiety drugs, as analgesics, and as antidysthymic agents. Many of the mood stabilizers, besides being used to treat bipolar disorder, are used to treat chronic pain syndromes, psychological disorders associated with agitation and aggression, and even substance abuse. Antipsychotic drugs, besides being used to treat schizophrenia, are now being used to treat bipolar disorder, explosive and aggressive disorders, autism, and other pervasive developmental disorders. Newer antipsychotic agents are even being used to treat depression and dysthymia. Nevertheless, the artificial distinctions are maintained to present the pharmacology of the drugs in a logical manner.

Chapter 7

Antidepressant Drugs

Depression

Depression, or major depressive disorder (MDD), is a chronic, recurring, and potentially life-threatening illness. MDD is currently the fourth most disabling disease worldwide, and by the year 2020, it will be the second leading cause of disability across the globe. According to a May 2007 report of the World Health Organization, depression accounts for 4.5 percent of the total worldwide burden of disease in terms of disability-adjusted life years. Depression also accounts for almost 12 percent of total years lived with disability worldwide. Depression worsens the health of people with other chronic illnesses, has a tendency to recur, and is associated with increasing disability over time. About 10 percent of men and up to 25 percent of women experience depression in their lifetime, and each year about 9 to 10 percent of the U.S. population, or approximately 30 million Americans, suffer with this illness. Depression is responsible for up to 70 percent of psychiatric hospitalizations and about 40 percent of suicides. People with depression fare more poorly at work, in social situations, and with their families than do people with a variety of general medical conditions. Unfortunately, it has been estimated that only about 21 percent of the yearly cases are adequately treated (Kessler et al., 2003), and the personal and societal costs are substantial (Stewart et al., 2003).

Depression is an *affective disorder*, characterized by (sometimes profound) alterations of emotion or mood. The diagnosis of a "major depressive episode" is based on the following criteria, of which at least five must be evident daily or almost every day for at least two weeks (American Psychiatric Association, 1994):

- Depressed or irritable mood
- Decreased interest in pleasurable activities and ability to experience pleasure (anhedonia)
- Significant weight gain or loss (> 5 percent change in a month)
- Insomnia or hypersomnia
- Psychomotor agitation or retardation
- Fatigue or loss of energy
- Feelings of worthlessness or excessive guilt
- Diminished ability to think or concentrate
- Recurrent thoughts of death or suicide (pp. 320–321)

Symptoms may be mild, moderate or severe, depending on the extent of impairment in daily social and occupational functioning. Severe depression may be associated with symptoms of psychosis or loss of touch with reality. People with relatively mild but prolonged symptoms that persist for at least 2 years are considered to have "dysthymia." Other subtypes include conditions of impaired function due to depressive symptoms that do not meet the specific diagnostic criteria and depressive symptoms that occur after a significant trauma (for example, death of a loved one), although posttraumatic symptoms can evolve into major depression (Berton and Nestler, 2006).

Symptoms of anxiety are also seen in many people with depression. Although many of the anxiety disorders have historically been treated with benzodiazepine anxiolytics (Chapter 6), today antidepressant treatment is also indicated for anxiety disorders. Not only are the antidepressant drugs efficacious for anxiety, they are less prone to be compulsively used, and they are less likely to impair learning, memory, and concentration than the benzodiazepines.[1] Stahl (1999a, 1999b) describes this historical evolution in the treatment of major depression and anxiety disorders (Figure 7.1).

Pathophysiology of Depression

Classically, depression was conceptualized as a problem, or deficiency, involving neurotransmitters, particularly the "monoamines" serotonin, norepinephrine, and dopamine. Restoring these neurotransmitters, usually by prolonging their presence in the synaptic cleft, was responsible for recovering a normal mood state. However, the neurotransmitter

---

[1]According to current diagnostic criteria, anxiety disorders include panic disorder (PD), obsessive compulsive disorder (OCD), posttraumatic stress disorder (PTSD), social phobia, and generalized anxiety disorder (GAD).

A. Treatment of Depression and Anxiety in the 1960s

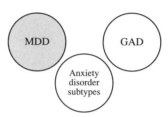

The earliest antidepressants were tricyclic antidepressants (TCAs) and monoamine oxidase inhibitors (MAOIs) and were conceptualized as targeting an entirely different syndrome (major depressive disorder [MDD]) than did the earliest anxiolytics, namely, benzodiazepines. At that time, benzodiazepines targeted anxiety disorders as a whole, including generalized anxiety disorder (GAD) or anxiety neurosis, which was much more broadly defined at that time, as well as anxiety disorder subtypes.

⬭ First-line treatments with antidepressants.
⬭ First-line treatments with anxiolytics.

B. Treatment of Depression and Anxiety in the 1970s and 1980s

As the TCA/MAOI era matured, mixtures of anxiety and depression were increasingly recognized and were treated both with these antidepressants and with buspirone as well as benzodiazepines. Benzodiazepines along with TCAs and MAOIs began to make inroads into treating anxiety disorder subtypes such as panic disorder, and in the case of the TCA clomipramine, obsessive-compulsive disorder (OCD).

⬭ First-line treatments with antidepressants.
⬭ First-line treatments with anxiolytics.
⬭ First-line treatments with either antidepressants or anxiolytics.

C. Treatment of Depression and Anxiety in the 1990s

Once the selective serotonin reuptake inhibitor (SRRI) era came into full swing, these agents eventually took over as first-line treatment choices not only of MDD but also of numerous anxiety disorder subtypes, from panic disorder and OCD to social phobia and posttraumatic stress disorder, but not GAD. Benzodiazepines became progressively second-line treatments of anxiety disorder, although buspirone continued as a first-line treatment of GAD.

⬭ First-line treatments with antidepressants.
⬭ First-line treatments with anxiolytics.

D. Treatment of Depression and Anxiety in the Twenty-First Century

When is an antidepressant an antidepressant, and when is an antidepressant an anxiolytic? Recently, the first antidepressant was approved for the treatment of GAD, namely, venlafaxine XR. Venlafaxine XR, as well as nefazodone and mirtazapine, has preliminary evidence of efficacy for some anxiety disorder subtypes, such as panic disorder, social phobia, and posttraumatic stress disorder. SSRIs, nefazodone, and mirtazapine have preliminary evidence of efficacy in generalized anxiety disorder. Virtually all forms of anxiety can now be treated by an antidepressant, with the documentation of efficacy of some antidepressants better than that of others. Perhaps the distinction between an antidepressant and an anxiolytic will cease to exist in the twenty-first century.

⬭ First-line treatments with antidepressants.

FIGURE 7.1 Progression in the treatment of major depressive disorder (MDD), generalized anxiety disorder (GAD), and anxiety disorder subtypes, from 1960 to 2000. [Adapted from Stahl (1999a), pp. 356–357.]

changes occur soon after drug administration—but the clinical antidepressant effect develops more slowly, often during several weeks of continuous treatment. This delay was hypothesized to be due to changes in receptor sensitivity caused by the chronic increase in synaptic levels of neurotransmitter. However, in the last few years, this view has broadened, and attention has shifted to the study of the long-term actions of antidepressant treatments on intracellular processes, such as second messengers, and their functions in the neuron.

Two of these second-messenger functions are (1) to protect neurons from damage due to injury or trauma and (2) to promote and maintain the health and stability of newly formed neurons. Research into these processes has led to a new way of thinking about depression (and the effect of antidepressant treatment) called the *neurogenic theory of depression*.

The neurogenic theory is a result of the relatively recent discovery that, contrary to what we once believed, (1) existing neurons are able to "repair" or "remodel" themselves and (2) the brain is capable of making new neurons. In particular, it is now known that new neurons are produced throughout life in the hippocampus (and the frontal cortex) of several species, including humans. The birth of new neurons is called *neurogenesis*. This finding is especially relevant to understanding depressive disorders because the hippocampus influences many functions that are impaired in a depressed person, such as attention, concentration and memory. At the same time, we know that the hippocampus is also very vulnerable to the effects of trauma, such as hypoglycemia, lack of oxygen, toxins, infections, and especially stress, and to the hormones that are activated by stressful situations (such as corticosterone). In fact, stressful situations are known both to reduce hippocampal and frontal cortical neurogenesis and to damage existing neurons. Both actions limit hippocampal and frontal cortical function.

Among the stressful conditions that can damage the hippocampus is a state of depression—not surprising, as stress is believed to be one of the most significant causes of depression; about 50 percent of depressed patients have some abnormality in their physiological responses to stress. Moreover, hippocampal nerve cells are among the most sensitive to stress-induced damage. In fact, it has been shown that the hippocampus physically shrinks in response to various stressors, including depression (Frodl et al., 2007) and that the longer an episode of depression goes untreated, the greater the amount of shrinkage (Figure 7.2). Consequently, depression is now viewed as a type of neurodegenerative disorder.

Just as a variety of stimuli can damage neurons and decrease neurogenesis, several factors are known to repair neurons and increase neurogenesis, among them, antidepressant drugs.[2] It has been proposed that the therapeutic delay in the clinical effect of antidepressants occurs

---

[2]Other stimuli include electroconvulsive therapy, exercise, light therapy, and so on.

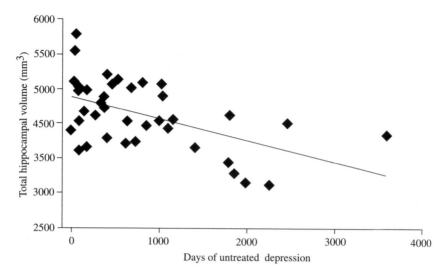

FIGURE 7.2 Reduction in total hippocampal volume correlated with days of untreated depression. The total time each patient had been in a depressive episode was divided into days during which the patient was receiving antidepressant medication versus days during which no antidepressant medication was given. The regression plot depicts the significant inverse relationship between total hippocampal volume and the length of time depression went untreated. [Adapted from Y. I. Sheline et al., "Untreated Depression and Hippocampal Volume Loss," *American Journal of Psychiatry* 160 (2003), Figure 1, p. 1517.]

because of the time required for new neurons to develop, mature, and become functional. This hypothesis is supported by the observation that the increase in neurogenesis requires chronic antidepressant administration, which is consistent with the time course for the therapeutic action of these medications (Duman, 2004; Thomas and Peterson, 2003).

A major focus of current research is to identify the cellular processes in the hippocampus and frontal cortex that are responsible for the protective effects of antidepressants. Most current studies are directed toward the second-messenger systems, which are activated by the synaptic action of neurotransmitters. This action in turn stimulates production of intracellular proteins that control the expression of certain genes. One of the intracellular targets of second-messenger systems is called *cAMP response-element binding protein* (CREB). The fact that the amount of CREB protein increases in the hippocampus during chronic antidepressant treatment provides additional evidence for the neurogenic hypothesis (Blendy, 2006 ; Malberg and Blendy, 2005).

In turn, it is known that CREB activates genes that control the production of a protein called *brain-derived neurotrophic factor* (BDNF). BDNF is one of a group of substances called *neurotrophins*, produced by many brain structures, which are important for the normal development and health of the nervous system. For example, when injected into the brain of rats, BDNF not only prevents the spontaneous death of some neurons but also helps to protect neurons that have been poisoned with various toxins. Conversely, in animals, chronic stress decreases the production and amount of BDNF (and other neurotrophic substances) in the brain and increases cell death. As predicted by the neurogenic hypothesis, levels of BDNF (and some other neurotrophic substances) increase in the hippocampus of rats chronically exposed to a wide range of antidepressants (Saarelainen et al., 2003). Of particular significance, several reports have shown that blood levels of BDNF are decreased in depressed patients, and some studies found that antidepressant treatment can reverse this effect (Angelucci et al., 2005; Duman and Monteggia, 2006; Jeanneteau and Chao, 2006; Kuipers and Bramham, 2006; Nair and Vaidya, 2006) (Figure 7.3).

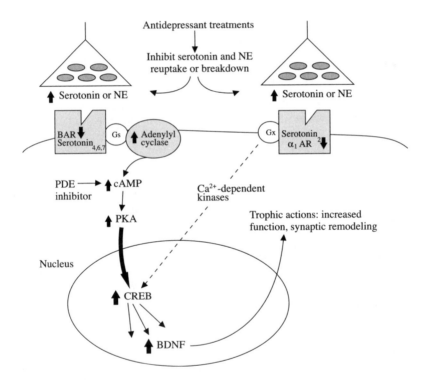

FIGURE 7.3 A model for the molecular mechanism of action of long-term antidepressant treatments. Antidepressants induce short-term increases in 5-HT and NE. Longer-term use decreases the function and expression of their receptors, but the cAMP signal transduction pathway is increased, including increased levels of adenyl cyclase and cAMP-dependent protein kinase (PKA), as well as translocation of PKA to the cell nucleus. Antidepressants increase expression and function of the transcription factor cAMP response element-binding protein (CREB), suggesting that CREB is a common postreceptor target for antidepressants. Brain-derived neurotrophic factor is also increased by antidepressant treatment; up regulation of CREB and BDNF could influence the function of hippocampal neurons or neurons innervating this brain region, increasing neuronal survival, function, and remodeling of synaptic or cellular architecture. [From Duman et al. (1997), p. 600.]

In summary, several lines of evidence suggest that depression is a consequence of stress that, like any injury, disease, or other type of physical trauma, damages the brain and weakens its ability to recover. Antidepressants relieve depressed mood by acting at the cellular level to promote neuronal survival and reverse stress-induced neuronal damage (Figure 7.4). Although the immediate effect of antidepressants is to modulate synaptic levels of neurotransmitters, their ultimate targets are the intracellular molecules responsible for maintaining neuronal health and plasticity. This reconceptualization of depressive disorder has broadened the search for new drug

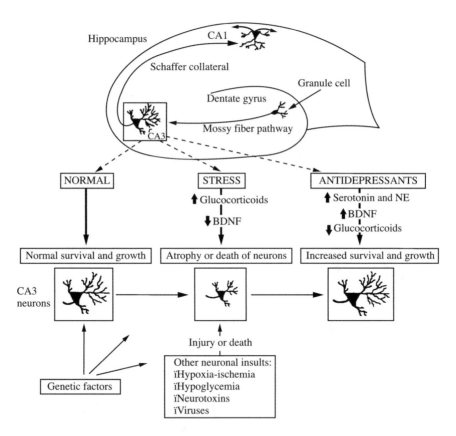

FIGURE 7.4 A molecular and cellular model for the action of antidepressants and the pathophysiology of stress-related disorders. Chronic stress decreases the expression of BDNF in the hippocampus, contributing to atrophy or death of neurons in the hippocampus. Elevated levels of glucocorticoids also decrease survival of these neurons, as do many other insults. Antidepressants increase the expression of BDNF and prevent the down regulation of BDNF elicited by stress, increasing neuronal survival or helping repair or protect neurons from further damage. See Figure 7.2. [From R. S. Duman, "A Molecular and Cellular Theory of Depression," *Archives of General Psychiatry* 54 (1997), p. 603.]

treatments, including agents that block the effect of stress hormones or that directly stimulate neurotrophic processes, as described later in this chapter.

Evolution of Antidepressant Drug Development

Over fifty years ago, the antidepressant properties of the drug *imipramine* were discovered accidentally. Since then, it has been learned that imipramine and similar drugs, called *tricyclic antidepressants* (TCAs; Table 7.1) block the presynaptic transporter protein receptors for the neurotransmitters norepinephrine and serotonin. Note that the term *tricyclic antidepressant* refers to a commonality in chemical *structure*, in contrast to newer antidepressants, which are defined by their mechanism of action. That is because, when the antidepressant effect of imipramine was discovered, its mechanism of action was unknown; thus, a structural classification had to suffice and persists today.

At about the same time the TCAs were discovered, another class of early antidepressant drugs called the *monoamine oxidase inhibitors* (MAOIs) was identified. The MAOIs bound to and blocked the enzyme monoamine oxidase. This enzyme normally metabolizes and regulates the amount of the biogenic amine transmitters in the presynaptic nerve terminal. Thus, the levels of these neurotransmitters increase and more transmitter is available for release when stimulated by an action potential reaching the nerve terminal. Both the TCAs and the MAOIs are effective in the treatment of major depression, but both possess adverse side effects, discussed later in this chapter. Together, we refer to these two classes of drugs as *first-generation antidepressants.*

Many problems with the first-generation agents prompted the search for new antidepressants that were equally effective and better tolerated, but less toxic. First was the development of several drugs that were slight modifications of the basic tricyclic structure but that still exhibited antidepressant efficacy. These drugs were termed *second-generation,* or *atypical, antidepressants* (see Table 7.1).

During the late 1980s and continuing through the 1990s, the *selective serotonin reuptake inhibitors* (SSRIs) were developed, the first of which was fluoxetine (Prozac; see Table 7.1). Five more were eventually marketed. Today, recognizing the limitations and side effects of the SSRIs, antidepressant drug research is progressing to identify compounds that act by different mechanisms. These drugs are not necessarily more clinically efficacious than the older TCAs, but they may have a more favorable profile of toxicity or side effects (Richelson, 2003). The availability of the newer drugs has not yet reduced the number of treatment-resistant patients with major depression: the new drugs have only altered the profile of side effects. Three main therapeutic improvements have still to be met: (1) superior efficacy, especially in the treatment of therapy-resistant depression, (2) faster onset of action, and (3) improved side effect profile. The following discussion of specific antidepressant drugs is subdivided into categories according to their chronology and the neurotransmitters on which each group is thought to act.

First-Generation Antidepressants

The first two classes of antidepressants (TCAs and MAOIs) were introduced into medicine in the late 1950s and early 1960s. Drugs of both classes increased the levels of norepinephrine and serotonin in the brain, leading to a concept that depression resulted from a relative deficiency of these neurotransmitters. Conversely, excesses in the amounts of these transmitters were thought to lead to a state of mania. This was called the *monoamine (receptor) hypothesis of mania and depression.* Although this interpretation is much too simplistic, until recently the concept has been extremely useful for guiding the development of new antidepressants.

Tricyclic Antidepressants

The term *tricyclic antidepressant* (TCA) describes a class of drugs that all have a characteristic three-ring molecular core (Figure 7.5). TCAs not only effectively relieve symptoms of depression; they also possess significant anxiolytic and analgesic actions. Historically, the

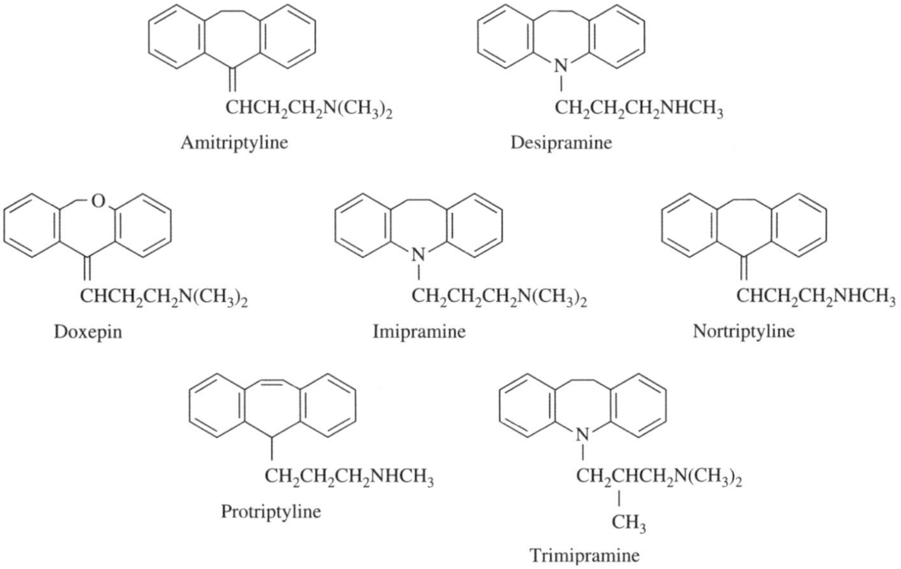

FIGURE 7.5 Chemical structures of seven tricyclic antidepressants.

TABLE 7.1 Drugs used to treat depression

Drug name: Generic (trade)	Sedative activity	Anticholinergic activity[a]	Elimination half-life (h)	Reuptake inhibition		
				Norepinephrine	Serotonin	Dopamine
TRICYCLIC COMPOUNDS						
Imipramine (Tofranil)	Moderate	Moderate	10–20	++	++	0
Desipramine (Norpramin)	Low	Low	12–75	+++	+	0
Trimipramine (Surmontil)	High	Moderate	8–20	+	+	0
Protriptyline (Vivactil)	Low	Moderate	55–125	+++	+	0
Nortriptyline (Pamelor, Aventil)	Low	Low	15–35	++	++	0
Amitriptyline (Elavil)	High	High	20–35	++	++	0
Doxepin (Adapin, Sinequan)	High	High	8–24	++	++	0
Clomipramine (Anafranil)	Low	Low	19–37	++	++++	0
SECOND-GENERATION (ATYPICAL) COMPOUNDS						
Amoxapine (Asendin)[b]	Moderate	Moderate	8–10	++	+	0
Maprotiline (Ludiomil)	Moderate	Moderate	27–58	+++	0	0
Trazodone (Desyrel)	High	Low	6–13	0	++	0
Bupropion (Wellbutrin)	Low	Low	8–14	0/+	0/+	++
Venlafaxine (Effexor)	Moderate	None	3–11	++	++++	0

[a]Anticholinergic side effects include dry mouth, blurred vision, tachycardia, urinary retention, and constipation.
[b]Also has antipsychotic effects due to blockage of dopamine receptors (Chapter 9).
0 = no effect; + = mild effect; ++ = moderate effect; +++ = strong effect; ++++ = maximal effect.

TABLE 7.1 Drugs used to treat depression (*continued*)

Drug name: Generic (trade)	Sedative activity	Anticholinergic activity[a]	Elimination half-life (h)	Reuptake inhibition		
				Norepinephrine	Serotonin	Dopamine
SELECTIVE SEROTONIN REUPTAKE INHIBITORS						
Fluoxetine (Prozac)	Moderate	None	24–96	0	++++	0
Sertraline (Zoloft)	Moderate	None	26	0	++++	0
Paroxetine (Paxil)	Moderate	None	24	+	++++	0
Citalopram (Celexa)	Moderate	None	33	0	++++	0
Fluvoxamine (Luvox)	Moderate	None	15	0	++++	0
Escitalopram (Lexapro)	Low	None	2–5	0	++++	0
DUAL-ACTION ANTIDEPRESSANTS						
Nefazodone (Serzone)	High	None	3–4	0	++++	0
Mirtazapine (Remeron)	High	Low	20–40	++	++++	0
Duloxetine (Cymbalta)	Moderate	Low	11–16	+++	+++	0
MAO INHIBITORS: IRREVERSIBLE						
Phenelzine (Nardil)	Moderate	None	2–4[c]	0	0	0
Isocarboxazid (Marplan)	Low	None	1–3[c]	0	0	0
Tranylcypromine (Parnate)	Moderate	None	1–3[c]	0	0	0
SELECTIVE NOREPINEPHRINE REUPTAKE INHIBITORS						
Reboxetine (Edronax)[d]	None	Low	13	++++	0	0
Atomoxetine (Strattera)	None	Low	5	++++	0	0

[c]Half-life does not correlate with clinical effect (see text).
[d]Not available in United States.
0 = no effect; + = mild effect; ++ = moderate effect; +++ = strong effect; ++++ = maximal effect.

TCAs were drugs of first choice for the treatment of major depression. The SSRIs, which today are widely prescribed, are no more effective and are considerably more expensive; they are, however, less toxic, and their use is associated with a higher rate of patient comfort and compliance. On the other hand, there may be some evidence that drugs that act on both serotonin and norepinephrine (serotonin-norepinephrine reuptake inhibitors—SNRIs—such as venlafaxine, discussed later in this chapter) may be more efficacious than drugs in either of the other two categories.

Imipramine (Tofranil) is the prototype TCA, but another clinically available TCA, *desipramine* (Norpramin), is the pharmacologically active intermediate metabolite of imipramine. Likewise, *amitriptyline* (Elavil) has an active intermediate metabolite, *nortriptyline* (Pamelor, Aventil). In fact, these two active intermediates may actually be responsible for much of the antidepressant effect of both imipramine and amitriptyline.

Mechanism of Action. TCAs exert five significant pharmacologic actions that account for both the therapeutic effects and side effects of these drugs:

1. They block the presynaptic norepinephrine reuptake transporter.
2. They block the presynaptic serotonin reuptake transporter.
3. They block postsynaptic histamine receptors.
4. They block postsynaptic acetylcholine receptors.
5. They block postsynaptic norepinephrine receptors.

The therapeutic effects of the TCAs result from blockade of presynaptic serotonin and norepinephrine reuptake transporters. Blockade of histamine receptors results in drowsiness and sedation, an effect similar to the sedation seen after administration of the classic antihistamine diphenhydramine (Benadryl). Blockade of acetylcholine receptors results in confusion, memory and cognitive impairments, dry mouth, blurred vision, increased heart rate, and urinary retention. Blockade of norepinephrine receptors affects blood pressure; one result may be a "dizzy" feeling when standing up too quickly from a sitting or reclining position. In general, nortriptyline and desipramine are reasonable choices for initial treatment of depression when therapy with a TCA is chosen. These two TCAs cause less sedation and cognitive impairment and exert fewer anticholinergic side effects than most other TCAs. Moreover, nortriptyline is known to have a therapeutic range, or window: the maximum response is most likely at blood levels of the drug between 0.05 and 0.15 micrograms per milliliter.

Pharmacokinetics.   The TCAs are well absorbed when administered orally. Because most of them have relatively long half-lives (see Table 7.1), taking them at bedtime can reduce the impact of unwanted side effects, especially persistent sedation. These drugs are metabolized in the liver, and, as discussed earlier, two TCAs are converted into pharmacologically active intermediates that are detoxified later (Figure 7.6). This combination of a pharmacologically active drug and active metabolite results in a

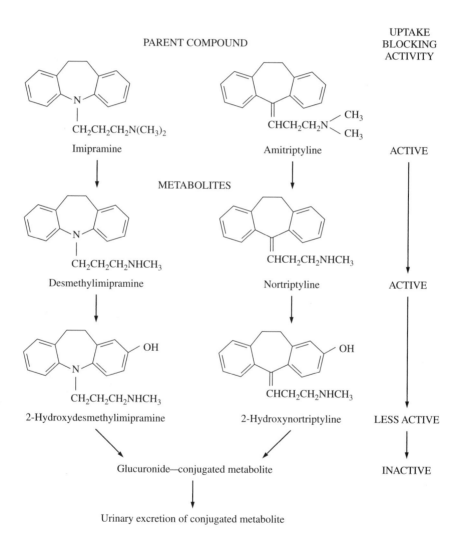

FIGURE 7.6 Metabolism of imipramine (Tofranil) and amitriptyline (Elavil). Note that the two active intermediates (desmethylimipramine and nortriptyline) are marketed commercially as Norpramin and Pamelor or Aventil, respectively.

clinical effect lasting up to 4 days, even longer in elderly patients (who can be adversely affected by the detrimental cognitive effects of these drugs; Chapter 11).

TCAs readily cross the placental barrier. However, in utero exposure does not affect global IQ, language development, or behavioral development in preschool children. No fetal abnormalities from these drugs have yet been reported.

Pharmacological Effects. All the TCAs attach to and inhibit (to varying degrees) the presynaptic transporter proteins for both norepinephrine and serotonin, which is thought to account for their therapeutic efficacy. The TCAs, however, have three clinical limitations. First, they are claimed to have a slow onset of action, although overall, TCAs seem to start acting as fast as any other antidepressant drug, provided that comparable dosage strategies can be tolerated. Second, the TCAs exert a wide variety of effects on the CNS, causing numerous bothersome side effects that the SSRIs do not cause. Third, in overdosage (as in suicide attempts), TCAs are cardiotoxic and potentially fatal because they can cause cardiac arrhythmias.

Because TCAs do not produce euphoria in normal people, they have no recreational or behavior-reinforcing value. Therefore, abuse and psychological dependence are not concerns. Similarly, in contrast to discontinuation of some SSRIs (discussed later), discontinuation of TCAs is not usually a cause for undue concern. The clinical choice of TCA is determined by effectiveness, tolerance of side effects, prior good response, family history of good response, and duration of action of the particular agent.

In depressed patients, TCAs elevate mood, increase physical activity, improve appetite and sleep patterns, and reduce morbid preoccupation. They are useful in treating acute episodes of major depression as well as in preventing relapses. Some patients resistant to other antidepressants respond favorably to a TCA. In addition, TCAs are clinically effective in the long-term therapy of dysthymia, and in treating bipolar depression (as an adjunct to a mood stabilizer), although the SSRIs are equally efficacious and better tolerated.

TCAs are effective analgesics in a variety of clinical pain syndromes; they are consistently superior to placebo in the treatment of chronic pain. Uses include diabetes-associated peripheral neuropathies, postherpetic neuralgia, migraine headache, fibromyalgia, chronic back pain, myofascial pain, and chronic fatigue. The antidepressant action may not only provide analgesic relief but promote well-being and improve affect as well as reduce physical discomfort. One recent review compared the analgesic effect of three types of antidepressants, and it concluded that the TCAs were slightly more efficacious than the selective norepinephrine reuptake inhibitors (SNRIs), which were more analgesic than the selective serotonin reuptake inhibitors (SSRIs) (Sindrup et al., 2005).

Side Effects. Side effects follow from the anticholinergic, antihistaminic, and antiadrenergic actions. In the patient on long-term TCA therapy, tolerance may develop to many of these side effects, but some will persist. Often, choosing a particular TCA with an awareness of its side effects can turn a disadvantage into a therapeutic advantage. For example, amitriptyline and doxepin are the most sedating of the TCAs, making them useful in treating people with comorbid agitation and insomnia. Administering one of these drugs at bedtime would provide both the antidepressant effect and the needed sedation.

The effects of TCAs on memory and cognitive function are significant. The direct adverse effects on cognition are related to their anticholinergic and antihistaminic properties, which may be partly compensated for by the improvement in mood. Relatively nonsedating compounds with minimal anticholinergic side effects cause less impairment of psychomotor or memory functions. Therefore, because the young and the elderly may be more susceptible to the anticholinergic-induced impairment of memory, patients at the extremes of age, if treated with TCAs, should probably receive a drug with low potency at blocking histaminic and cholinergic receptors.

As already noted, cardiac effects can be life-threatening when an overdose is taken, as in suicide attempts. The patient commonly exhibits excitement, delirium, and convulsions, followed by respiratory depression and coma, which can persist for several days. Cardiac arrhythmias can lead to ventricular fibrillation, cardiac arrest, and death. Thus, all TCAs can be lethal in doses that are commonly available to depressed patients. For this reason, it is unwise to dispense more than a week's supply of an antidepressant to an acutely depressed patient.

There have been reports of about 12 cases of sudden death in children receiving desipramine for the treatment of ADHD or depression. These deaths are certainly cause for concern when using TCAs to treat depression in children, and the therapeutic efficacy of TCAs in treating major depression in children is questionable anyway (Chapter 10). In cases where efficacy is more demonstrable—enuresis (bed-wetting), obsessive-compulsive disorder (OCD), and ADHD—use may be appropriate, but caution is warranted.

Monoamine Oxidase Inhibitors

Monoamine oxidase (MAO) is one of two enzymes that regulate the amount of monoamine neurotransmitters (as well as other substances) in the body, including norepinephrine, dopamine, and serotonin. There are two forms of the enzyme: MAO-A metabolizes dopamine, norepinephrine, and serotonin, as well as some other substances, such as tyramine; MAO-B also metabolizes dopamine, tyramine, and other substances. It is generally presumed that drug-induced inhibition of

MAO-A is responsible for the antidepressant activity. The blockade of metabolism causes transmitter molecules to build up in the terminal, which means that more transmitter than usual is released into the synaptic cleft when the neuron fires an action potential.

Three monoamine oxidase inhibitors (MAOIs) have been used since the late 1950s for treating major depressive illnesses.[3] Their use is limited by serious side effects involving potentially fatal interactions when taken with certain foods and medicines. The drugs include adrenalinelike drugs found in nasal sprays, antiasthma medications, and cold medicines. The foods include those that contain tyramine, a by-product of fermentation, such as many cheeses, wines, beers, liver, and some beans. Because MAO is also found in the gastrointestinal tract, inhibition of the enzyme blocks the metabolism of dietary tyramine. This substance increases blood pressure, and in the absence of MAO, the blood pressure increase may occasionally cause heart attacks or strokes. Nevertheless, although they are potentially dangerous, MAOIs can be used safely with strict dietary restrictions. Gardner and colleagues (1996) discuss the MAOI diet and its appropriate presentation to patients. A recent review of drug interactions supports the conclusion that caution is warranted when combining antidepressants with other CNS drugs, particularly MAOIs (Nieuwstraten et al., 2006).

Interest in MAOIs has remained strong because (1) they can be as safe as TCAs, (2) they can work in many patients who respond poorly to both TCAs and SSRIs, and (3) they are excellent drugs for the treatment of atypical depression (which presents primarily with anxiety and phobic symptoms), masked depression (such as hypochondriasis), anorexia nervosa, bulimia, bipolar depression, dysthymia, depression in the elderly, panic disorder, and phobias.

All three orally administered MAOIs are irreversible in their effect, since they form a chemical bond with the MAO enzyme, a bond that cannot be broken; enzyme function returns only as new enzyme is biosynthesized. For this reason, patients who need to switch from an MAOI to another type of antidepressant must still observe the dietary restrictions and other precautions for approximately 10 to 14 days, until new enzyme is produced. A few years ago, a specific MAO-A inhibitor (moclobemide) was developed that was reversible. That is, moclobemide did not bond as tightly to the enzyme as the classic MAOIs. Therefore, when levels of tyramine or similar substances increased sufficiently, moclobemide was eventually forced to detach from MAO. When detachment occurred, MAO was again able to metabolize the tyramine and the cardiotoxic risk was minimized. Unfortunately, although this was a logical approach for developing a better MAOI, moclobemide was not a very

---

[3]The three MAOIs are *phenelzine* (Nardil), *tranylcypromine* (Parnate), and *isocarboxazid* (Marplan).

efficacious antidepressant. The drug was marketed in Canada and European countries, but it was not released in the United States.

Interest in the MAOIs has recently undergone resurgence because of the availability of a new formulation. In 2006, the nonselective MAOI *selegiline* (Eldapril; Chapter 11) became commercially available as a transdermal patch that allows for slow, continuous absorption (in this form, it was marketed under the new trade name Emsam). At the low doses absorbed across the skin, food and drug interactions were not a concern because transdermal administration bypasses the gastrointestinal tract.[4] As initially reported by Amsterdam (2003), selegiline (as a 6-milligram patch applied daily) was robustly effective in reducing moderate to severe depression, with onset of effect in only a few days. Sexual functioning was not impaired, and compliance was excellent. Skin irritation was the only significant side effect. These initial positive results have recently been confirmed in a long-term study in which patients with MDD who responded to selegiline during acute treatment (10 weeks) were either maintained on the drug or switched to placebo. After 52 weeks, significantly fewer patients taking selegiline relapsed (16.8 percent) compared with the placebo group (30.7 percent), and they did so after a significantly longer time on the drug than those given the placebo (Amsterdam and Bodkin, 2006). This new formulation promises to be a very useful option for situations in which MAOIs are preferred (Goodnick, 2007).

Second-Generation Antidepressants

Efforts from the late 1970s to the mid-1980s to find structurally different agents that might overcome some of the disadvantages of the TCAs (slow onset of action, limited efficacy, and significant side effects) produced the so-called second-generation, or atypical, antidepressants (Figure 7.7). Their pharmacokinetic data and a comparison with standard TCAs are listed in Tables 7.1 and 7.2, respectively.

Maprotiline (Ludiomil) was one of the first clinically available antidepressants (other than the MAOIs) that modified the basic tricyclic structure (see Figure 7.7). It has a long half-life, blocks norepinephrine reuptake, and is as efficacious as imipramine (the gold standard of TCAs). However, it offers few, if any, therapeutic advantages. A major limitation of maprotiline is that it can cause seizures (although it rarely does), presumably because of the accumulation of active metabolites that excite the CNS. It is generally not an antidepressant of first choice.

---

[4]There is some evidence, however, that with the 9- and 12-milligram patches, the effect may be no different than with any other oral MAOI and dietary restrictions may again be needed.

TABLE 7.2 Advantages and disadvantages of second-generation antidepressants compared to tricyclic antidepressants

Drug	Advantages	Disadvantages
Maprotiline	Sedating and may be useful for agitation Does not antagonize antihypertensive effects of clonidine Minimal cognitive impairment	Increased incidence of seizures Increased lethality in overdose Has long half-life; therefore accumulates Increased incidence of rashes
Amoxapine	Low in sedative effects Low in anticholinergic effects Possibly effective for monotherapy for psychotic depression Has possible rapid onset Relieves anxiety and agitation	Can promote parkinsonian side effects and tardive dyskinesia Cannot separate antidepressant from "antipsychotic" effect Increased lethality in overdose
Trazodone	Relatively safe in overdose Sedating (may be useful in controlling agitation and hostility in geriatric patients) Useful as a hypnotic in conjunction with MAO inhibitors	Efficacy not clearly established May induce or exacerbate ventricular arrhythmia Can promote priapism Drowsiness is common
Bupropion	Low in sedative, hypotensive, and anticholinergic side effects Does not promote weight gain Lack of ECG changes May assist with weight loss May be "anticraving"	Tends to "overstimulate," with insomnia, terror Not effective for panic; unknown effectiveness for obsessive compulsive disorders Increased incidence of seizures in bulimia May induce perceptual abnormalities and psychosis Causes increase in prolactin
Venlafaxine	Low in anticholinergic and antihistaminic effects Improves psychomotor and cognitive function Few drug interactions	Can increase blood pressure May cause anxiety, nervousness, and insomnia
Clomipramine	Indicated in OCD Long half-life	Toxicity limits therapy Increased risk of seizures May increase risk of psychotic episodes May activate mania/hypomania Can promote weight gain Can decrease libido

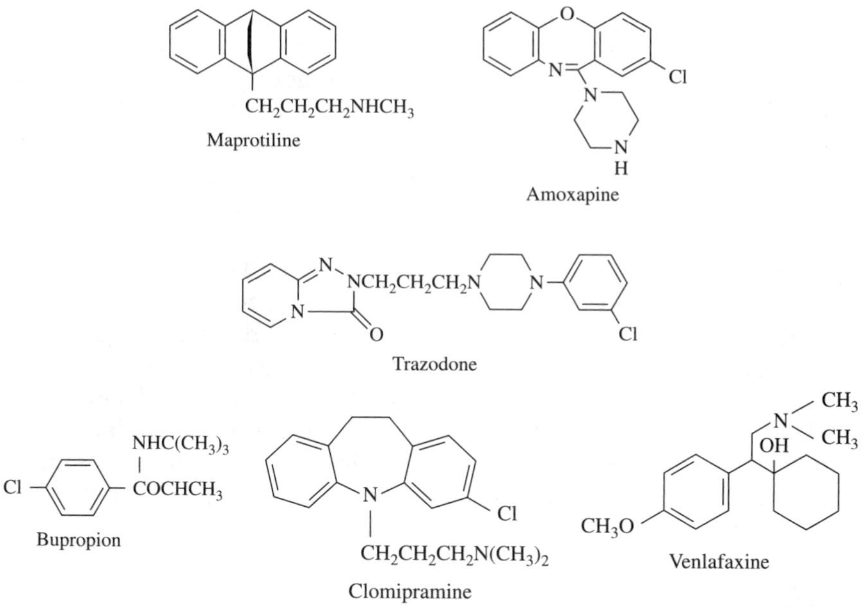

FIGURE 7.7 Chemical structures of six second-generation "atypical" antidepressants.

Amoxapine (Ascendin) (see Figure 7.7) is the second atypical anti-depressant, structurally different from the TCAs (see Figure 7.5). It is primarily a norepinephrine reuptake inhibitor, clinically as effective as imipramine, although it may be slightly better at relieving accompanying anxiety and agitation. Amoxapine may produce parkinsonianlike side effects as a result of postsynaptic dopamine receptor blockade. The drug is metabolized to an active intermediate, 8-hydroxy-amoxapine, which may be responsible for the dopamine receptor blockade. As with TCAs, overdosage can result in fatality. Amoxipine is not generally an antidepressant of first choice.

Trazodone (Desyrel) is the third atypical antidepressant (see Figure 7.7), therapeutically as efficacious as the TCAs. Its mechanism of antide-pressant action is unclear because it is not a potent reuptake blocker of either norepinephrine or serotonin. However, it blocks 5-HT$_2$ receptors, while its active metabolite, m-chlorophenylpiperazine, is a serotonin agonist. Drowsiness is the most common side effect, and the drug's main use is as an antidepressant sleeping pill. The drug is taken at bedtime to promote a good night's sleep. Its main side effect can be serious: in rare instances, priapism (prolonged and painful penile erection) occurs. This side effect requires prompt attention as it can lead to permanent impo-tence and infertility. The detrimental effects of trazodone on cognitive functioning appear modest when taken in overdose.

Clomipramine (Anafranil) (see Figure 7.7) is structurally a TCA (see Figure 7.5), but it has a greater effect on serotonin reuptake than the classic TCAs (Suhara et al., 2003). In addition, it and its active metabolite, desmethylclomipramine, also inhibit norepinephrine reuptake. Thus, it is classified as a *mixed serotonin-norepinephrine reuptake inhibitor* (SNRI), similar to venlafaxine. Clomipramine is approximately equal to the TCAs in both its efficacy and its profile of side effects.

Clomipramine has long been used to treat OCD; about 40 to 75 percent of patients with OCD respond favorably. The drug has also been used in the treatment of depression, panic disorder, and phobic disorders. Historically, it was the first antidepressant medication to be appreciated as having efficacy in the treatment of anxiety disorders, an observation later applied to the SSRI-type antidepressants. The remaining two second-generation atypical antidepressants will be discussed later in this chapter—venlafaxine on pages 227–228 and bupropion on pages 230–231.

Selective Serotonin Reuptake Inhibitors

Six SSRIs are currently available: fluoxetine (Prozac), paroxetine (Paxil), sertraline (Zoloft), fluvoxamine (Luvox), citalopram (Celexa), and escitalopram (Lexapro). All except the last are shown in Figure 7.8. These drugs are all potent blockers of the presynaptic transporter for serotonin reuptake. The degree to which they block reuptake of other neurotransmitters, primarily norepinephrine, varies greatly, with more than a twelvefold difference between citalopram (the most selective for serotonin) and fluoxetine (the least selective for serotonin). They do not block postsynaptic serotonin receptors of any subtype. Therefore, the primary acute neuronal effect of SSRIs is to make more serotonin available in the synaptic cleft, which activates all of the many postsynaptic receptors for serotonin. Such selectivity led to both the popularity and the side effects of SSRIs. Indeed, prior to adoption of the neurogenic hypothesis of depression, it was thought that increased synaptic serotonin levels were directly related to their therapeutic effect (a serotonin theory of depression).

The action of serotonin at all its postsynaptic receptors is believed to be responsible for all the actions of the six serotonin antidepressants—both their therapeutic actions and their side effects. The current view is that increased serotonin availability at 5-HT$_1$-type receptors is associated with antidepressant and anxiolytic effects, whereas increased serotonin availability at 5-HT$_2$-type and 5-HT$_3$-type receptors produces adverse effects. Increased 5-HT$_2$ receptor activity is associated with insomnia, anxiety, agitation, sexual dysfunction, and the production of a serotonin syndrome in higher doses. Increased 5-HT$_3$ receptor activity is

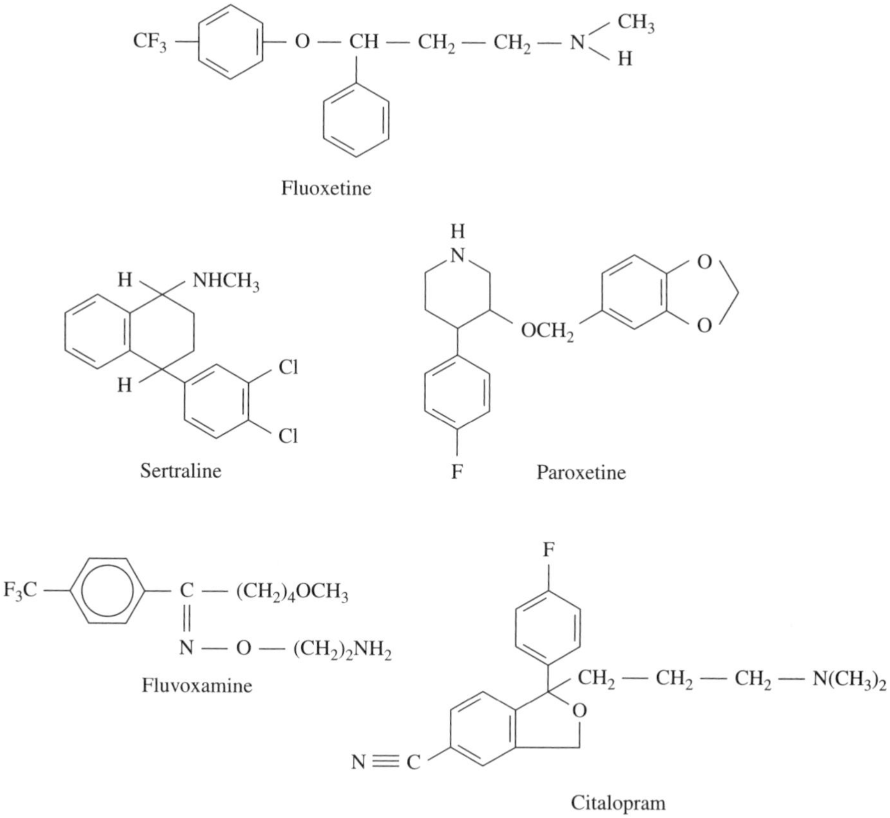

FIGURE 7.8 Chemical structures of five selective serotonin reuptake inhibitor (SSRI) antidepressants. The sixth SSRI, escitalopram, is the active isomer of citalopram and is therefore not shown.

responsible for the nausea that these drugs can cause (which has led to the development of 5-HT$_3$ antagonists as antiemetics). Because of their receptor selectivity, SSRIs demonstrate few anticholinergic or antihistaminic side effects. Nevertheless, some of them,, especially fluoxetine, are sedating. More recently, Wadsworth and coworkers (2005) demonstrated that long-term treatment with SSRIs may produce some cognitive impairment. Most important, these drugs are not fatal in overdosage because they are devoid of the cardiac toxicity produced by TCAs.

As a general statement, the clinical differences among individual SSRIs are minimal; all are equally effective (Kroenke et al., 2001). As noted in a recent review (Ruhé et al., 2006), after a first SSRI, any switch, either within or between all classes of antidepressants, appears legitimate. No unequivocal evidence is available to prove an advantage of a between-class switch (see Hansen et al., 2005, for a review that

TABLE 7.3 Ability of SSRIs to inhibit CYP liver enzymes of various subtypes

Drug	CYP-450 1A2	CYP-450 2C9	CYP-450 2C19	CYP-450 2D6	CYP-450 3A4
Citalopram (Celexa)	0	0	0	+	0
Escitalopram (Lexapro)	0	0	0	+	0
Fluoxetine (Prozac)	+	++	+/++	+++	+/++
Paroxetine (Paxil)	+	+	+	+++	+
Sertraline (Zoloft)	+	+	+	+/++	+
Fluvoxamine (Luvox)	+	++	++	+++	++

comes to the same conclusion, while noting the relationship between positive reports and drug company funding). However, they are not necessarily interchangeable: patients who discontinue one SSRI for lack of tolerability or response can sometimes be treated effectively with another. Differences lie in individual pharmacokinetics and in effects that inhibit cytochrome P (CYP) drug-metabolizing enzymes in the liver (Table 7.3), thus adversely and possibly dangerously interacting with other medicines that the patient may be taking. Genetic testing (Chapter 1) is commercially available to identify people with altered ability to metabolize SSRIs.

Approved therapeutic indications for SSRI therapy include major depression, dysthymia, and all the anxiety disorders (panic disorder, OCD, GAD, PTSD, phobias), although SSRIs also have benefit in other clinical situations. The conditions for which each of the newer drugs has, at present, been FDA approved are summarized in Table 7.4.

Before discussing individual SSRIs, we address four concerns associated with SSRI therapy: (1) the serotonin syndrome, (2) the serotonin discontinuation syndrome, (3) SSRI-induced sexual dysfunction, and (4) possible fetal effects if the mother takes the SSRI during pregnancy or periods of breast-feeding.

Serotonin Syndrome

High doses of an SSRI or the combination of an SSRI plus another serotoninergic drug can induce the disturbing reaction termed the *serotonin syndrome*. Accumulation of serotonin leads to a cluster of responses, characterized by cognitive disturbances (disorientation, confusion, hypomania), behavioral agitation and restlessness, autonomic nervous system dysfunctions (fever, shivering, chills, sweating, diarrhea, hypertension, tachycardia), and neuromuscular impairment (ataxia, increased reflexes, myoclonus) (Lane and Baldwin, 1997). Visual hallucinations have even been reported. Some

TABLE 7.4 FDA-approved indications for antidepressant medications

	ADHD	MDD	GAD	OCD	Panic	PTSD	Social anxiety	Bulimia	Premenstrual dysphoria	Smoking cessation	Diabetic neuropathy
SSRI											
Fluoxetine		✓		✓	✓			✓	✓		
Sertraline		✓		✓	✓	✓	✓		✓		
Fluvoxamine				✓			✓				
Paroxetine		✓	✓	✓	✓	✓	✓		✓(CR)		
Citalopram		✓									
Escitalopram		✓	✓								
SSNRI											
Duloxetine		✓	✓								✓
Venlafaxine		✓	✓(XR)		✓(XR)		✓(XR)				
Mirtazapine		✓									
SNRI											
Atomoxetine	✓										
NDRI											
Bupropion	✓	✓								✓	

SSRI = selective serotonin reuptake inhibitor
SSNRI = selective serotonin norepinephrine reuptake inhibitor
SNRI = selective norepinephrine reuptake inhibitor
NDRI = norepinephrine dopamine reuptake inhibitor
CR = controlled-release formulation of paroxetine
XR = extended-release formulation of venlafaxine

of these symptoms might result from excess serotonin at 5-HT$_2$ receptors, the site of action of the psychedelic drug LSD (Chapter 18). There is a positive relationship between the specificity of the SSRI for blocking the 5-HT transporter and the likelihood of producing the syndrome. For example, paroxetine (Paxil) is one of the most specific SSRIs, and it is perhaps the SSRI most implicated in causing the serotonin syndrome.

In theory, any drug that has a net effect of increasing serotonin function can produce the syndrome; usually, however, it results from the combination of an SSRI and other serotonergic drugs, especially since these drugs can inhibit each other's metabolic detoxification and potentiate each other's effects. The syndrome can even occur when SSRIs are combined with herbal substances such as St. John's wort or valerian (Chapter 19). Once the drugs are discontinued, the syndrome usually resolves within 24 to 48 hours; during this time, support is the primary treatment.

Serotonin Discontinuation Syndrome

A serotonin discontinuation syndrome occurs in perhaps 60 percent of SSRI-treated patients following abrupt cessation of drug intake. The syndrome was originally associated with discontinuation from paroxetine, but it can occur following discontinuation of any SSRI, although it is least likely with fluoxetine because of the drug's long half-life. Onset is usually within a few days and persists perhaps 3 to 4 weeks. Schatzberg and coworkers (1997) described five core somatic sets of symptoms:

- Disequilibria (dizziness, vertigo, ataxia)
- Gastrointestinal symptoms (nausea, vomiting, diarrhea)
- Flulike symptoms (fatigue, lethargy, myalgias, chills, headache)
- Sensory disturbances (paresthesia, sensation of electric shocks in the arms, legs, or head)
- Sleep disturbances (insomnia, vivid dreams)

Psychological symptoms include anxiety, agitation, uneasiness, restlessness, and irritability. Other, less frequently reported symptoms include hyperactivity, depersonalization, depressed mood, and memory problems (confusion, decreased concentration, and slowed thinking). All these somatic and psychological phenomena abate over time (and obviously disappear when the SSRI is restarted). It is felt that the syndrome results from a relative deficiency of serotonin when the SSRI is stopped; however, the exact mechanism may be more complex.

SSRI-Induced Sexual Dysfunction

Sexual dysfunction is often associated with major depressive disorder, and SSRI medications can further compound it. Up to 80 percent of depressed patients treated with SSRIs exhibit sexual dysfunction, including problems with orgasm, erection, sexual interest, desire, and psychological arousal (Stimmel and Gutierrez, 2006). In males, ejaculatory dysfunction seems most prominent. Loss of desire and sexual dysfunction can affect medication compliance and impair interpersonal relationships. Treatment of sexual dysfunction may involve discontinuation of the SSRI and switching to an antidepressant in another class (for example, bupropion). The use of sildenafil (Viagra) sometimes relieves males with erectile dysfunction (Nurnberg et al., 2001; Seidman et al., 2001).

Effects in Pregnancy and Breast-Feeding

SSRIs have been considered relatively safe for treating pregnant women who are depressed. Two recent studies (Alwan et al., 2007; Louik et al., 2007) agree that antidepressants are not a major cause of serious physical problems in newborns. But the studies considered the effect of the drugs only in the first trimester; they could not adequately assess the risks of many rare defects, and they did not include information on how long women had been taking antidepressants or at what doses.

In both studies, researchers interviewed mothers of more than 9500 infants with birth defects, including cleft palate and rare gastric, neural tube, and heart valve problems. Mothers who remembered being on SSRI antidepressants while pregnant were at no higher risk for most defects than a control group of women who said they had not taken antidepressants. However, the risk of some defects was higher for sertraline or paroxetine than for other SSRIs.

In July 2006, the FDA issued an alert that babies born to mothers who took SSRIs at 20 weeks or later in their pregnancies were six times more likely to have persistent pulmonary hypertension than babies born to mothers who did not take antidepressants during pregnancy (Chambers et al., 2006). Furthermore, recent reports have confirmed previous research demonstrating evidence of a *serotonergic discontinuation syndrome* in newborns exposed to SSRIs during pregnancy. Levinson-Castiel et al. (2006) reported an abstinence syndrome in 30 percent of newborns exposed to SSRIs in utero. Although they were criticized for using a rating scale originally devised for measuring neonatal opiate withdrawal, they found that newborns of mothers exposed to SSRIs during pregnancy had lower APGAR scores than did infants of nontreated mothers. Oberlander and colleagues (2006) reported that weight and gestational age of infants prenatally exposed to SSRIs were significantly less than for infants of depressed mothers not treated with medication, as was the proportion of infants born at less than 37 weeks. Furthermore, an increased proportion of SSRI-exposed infants had neonatal respiratory distress, jaundice, and feeding problems, which was not accounted for by the severity of the mothers' illness.

Nevertheless, despite having fluoxetine levels 65 percent of those of the mother, growth and development of newborns appear to be normal. A recent report by Ferreira and colleagues (2007) suggests that effects of prenatal SSRI exposure may be short-lived. They conducted a retrospective study of 76 mothers who were taking selective serotonin reuptake inhibitors or venlafaxine during the third trimester and 90 mothers who were not taking any antidepressants, psychotropic agents, or benzodiazepines at the time of delivery. They found that smoking, alcohol intake, and substance abuse were more frequent among treated mothers. In exposed infants, signs involving the central nervous system (63.2 percent) and the respiratory system (40.8 percent) were often observed. These signs appeared during the first day of life, with a median duration of 3 days for exposed newborns, and were resolved in 75 percent of cases within 3 to 5 days for term and premature newborns, respectively. All exposed premature newborns compared to 69.1 percent of term newborns presented behavioral manifestations, and the median length of stay was almost four times longer for exposed premature newborns than for those who were unexposed (14.5 versus 3.7 days).

Whether or not SSRIs taken during pregnancy might have subtle long-term effects on the newborn is unclear. However, in one recent study (Oberlander et al., 2007), measures of attention and activity levels of 4-year-old children with prolonged prenatal SSRI medication exposure and 4-year-olds without such exposure did not differ. Moreover, it is important to treat depression in women who happen to be pregnant. Cohen and coworkers (2006) found that 43 percent of women with a history of depression relapsed during pregnancy. Only 26 percent who stayed on their medication relapsed; 68 percent of those who discontinued medication relapsed. Although alternatives to the use of SSRIs may be preferred, continued treatment appears to be strongly indicated.

For treating postpartum depression in the mother, the SSRIs are preferred because of well-documented safety. Moreover, levels of drug in breast-feeding infants are extremely low—about 1 to 3 percent of the maternal concentration. Finding the most effective or most tolerable drug treatment for pregnant or breast-feeding patients may require some switching among the options; for an excellent table summarizing the procedure for switching from each antidepressant category to any of the others, see Bezchlibnyk-Butler and Jeffries (2005), pages 59–60.

Specific SSRIs

Fluoxetine. Fluoxetine (Prozac; see Figure 7.8) became clinically available in the United States in 1988 as the first SSRI-type antidepressant and the first non-TCA that could be considered a first-line antidepressant (not just for patients who have failed therapy with TCAs). Fluoxetine's efficacy is comparable to that of the TCAs, with few or no anticholinergic or antihistaminic side effects.

Besides major depression, fluoxetine has been used in the treatment of dysthymia, bulimia (an eating disorder), alcohol withdrawal, and virtually all the various subtypes of anxiety disorders. More recently, specific formulations of fluoxetine, sertraline, and paroxetine have been shown to be effective in relieving the symptoms of a controversial syndrome termed *premenstrual dysphoric disorder.* Pearlson and coworkers (2003) further demonstrated that symptoms of premenstrual dysphoric disorder recur when fluoxetine administration is stopped. For this use, the manufacturer of Prozac marketed fluoxetine under the trade name Sarafem.

Fluoxetine has a half-life of about 2 to 3 days, but its active metabolite *(norfluoxetine,* which is an even stronger reuptake inhibitor than fluoxetine) has a half-life of about 6 to 10 days. This prolonged action distinguishes fluoxetine from other SSRIs, which have half-lives of about 1 day and no active intermediates. Also because of its long half-life, fluoxetine need not be administered every day; it can be taken as infrequently as once a week (Schmidt et al., 2000). A once-weekly oral formulation of fluoxetine is commercially available under the trade name Prozac Weekly.

As with all SSRIs, fluoxetine's antidepressant action is of slow onset (about 4 to 6 weeks), and the drug and its metabolite thus tend to build with repeated doses over about 2 months, presumably because both compounds continue to accumulate. This action can explain not only the slow onset of peak therapeutic effect but the late onset of side effects and the prolonged duration of action following drug discontinuation. Therapeutic trials with fluoxetine should continue for at least 8 weeks before the drug is determined to be ineffective (Quitkin et al., 2003).

Significant and important side effects of fluoxetine include anxiety, agitation, and insomnia, which at the extreme can result in the serotonin syndrome. As discussed, sexual dysfunction is common, as is serotonin withdrawal syndrome, on discontinuation. However, the long half-life of fluoxetine limits the intensity of the syndrome and prolongs it over a period of several weeks.

Fluoxetine, sertraline, paroxetine, and fluvoxamine inhibit certain of the drug-metabolizing enzymes in the liver (see Table 7.3). Therefore, coadministration of any of these four drugs can increase the level of other drugs that the patient might be taking, even doubling the blood levels of caffeine after drinking usual doses of caffeine-containing beverages.

In 2004, the FDA approved a novel combination of fluoxetine and olanzapine (discussed in Chapter 9) for the treatment of depressive episodes associated with bipolar disorder (Chapter 8). The trade name of the combination product is Symbyax. The rationale for this use will become more apparent following discussion of bipolar disorder (Chapter 8) and the pharmacology of olanzapine (Chapter 9).

Sertraline. Sertraline (Zoloft; see Figure 7.8) was the second SSRI approved for clinical use in the United States. Clinically, like all SSRIs, it is as effective as TCAs in the treatment of major depression and dysthymia, and it has fewer side effects and improved patient compliance (Ravindran et al., 2000).

Sertraline is four to five times more potent than fluoxetine in blocking serotonin reuptake and it is more selective. Because of increased selectivity, serotonin-associated side effects (serotonin syndrome and serotonin discontinuation syndrome) may be more intense than with fluoxetine. Steady-state levels of the drug in plasma are achieved within 4 to 7 days, and its metabolites are less cumulative and less pharmacologically active. Like all SSRIs, sertraline has few anticholinergic, antihistaminic, and adverse cardiovascular effects, as well as a low risk of toxicity in overdose.

Paroxetine. Paroxetine (Paxil; see Figure 7.8) was the third SSRI available in the United States for clinical use in treating major depression, dysthymia, and the various anxiety disorders and premenstrual dysphoric disorder (Green, 2003). Paroxetine is also FDA-approved for treating generalized anxiety disorder (GAD), although this capability is probably shared by all SSRIs.

Like sertraline, paroxetine is more selective than fluoxetine in blocking serotonin reuptake. The drug's metabolic half-life is about 24 hours, and steady state is achieved in about 7 days; its metabolites are relatively inactive.

Paroxetine is perhaps the SSRI most associated with serotonin syndrome, serotonin discontinuation syndrome, new onset or precipitation of psychosis, paranoid ideations, temper dyscontrol, delusions, and even visual hallucinations. In 2006, it was reported that the use of paroxetine was associated with a small but statistically significant increase in the risk of cleft lip/palate deformities in newborns of women who took the drug during their pregnancy. In December 2006, the American College of Obstetricians and Gynecologists published a position statement that paroxetine probably should not be used during pregnancy.

Fluvoxamine. Fluvoxamine (Luvox), is a structural derivative of fluoxetine (see Figure 7.8). Like all SSRIs, fluvoxamine has well-described antidepressant properties, comparable in efficacy to the TCA imipramine, but fewer serious side effects and superior patient compliance. It has been shown effective in the treatment of all anxiety disorders.

Citalopram. Citalopram (Celexa; see Figure 7.8) is an SSRI available in Europe since 1989 and introduced into the United States in 1998 as the fifth SSRI. Citalopram is claimed to have a more rapid onset of action than fluoxetine, but this observation is probably related to differences in half-life and therefore to different times to peak plasma levels with continued dosing. Extremely large doses of citalopram have been associated with ECG irregularities, seizures, and rare fatalities. It has a lower incidence of inhibition of drug-metabolizing hepatic enzymes, so it might be better for patients who are taking multiple medications (Brosen and Naranjo, 2001).

Citalopram is well absorbed orally; peak plasma levels are reached in about 4 hours. Steady state is achieved in about 1 week, and maximal effects are seen in about 5 to 6 weeks. The elimination half-life is about 33 hours, enabling once-per-day dosing. The elderly have a reduced ability to metabolize citalopram; for older people, a 33 to 50 percent reduction in dose is necessary.

Citalopram has been reported to moderately reduce alcohol consumption in problem alcoholics. Citalopram might be expected to exert anxiolytic effects similar to those exerted by other SSRIs. Adverse effects of citalopram resemble those of other SSRIs.

Escitalopram. Escitalopram (Lexapro) was released in the United States in 2002 for the treatment of major depression. It is also approved for the treatment of GAD. The drug is the therapeutically active isomer (mirror-image molecule, Figure 7.9; see also Figure 7.8) of citalopram. As an active isomer, the only difference is potency: escitalopram is twice

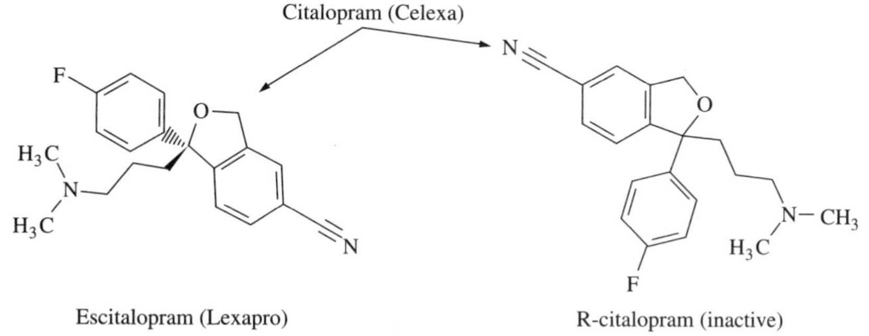

FIGURE 7.9 The SSRI citalopram (Celexa) is a racemic mixture of two enantiomers. The R-enantiomer is inactive; the S-enantiomer (Escitalopram) is active and is marketed as Lexapro. Citalopram is composed of both structures (one active and one inactive) present in equal amounts; escitalopram is the active half.

as potent as citalopram, so the prescribed dose is 50 percent of the dose of citalopram. In other words, 10 milligrams of escitalopram is equivalent to 20 milligrams of citalopram.

Dual-Action Antidepressants

Historically, the TCAs were the first dual-action antidepressants: they block the presynaptic reuptake of both norepinephrine and serotonin, but side effects due to their blockade of histamine and acetylcholine receptors limited their widespread use. The unitary action of the SSRIs, while associated with efficacy against a wide variety of anxiety and depressive disorders, is limited by side effects common to serotonin overactivity. Therefore, attempts have been made to expand on the concept that actions at two different synaptic sites may improve or maintain efficacy while limiting side effects. Most attempts to develop a dual-action antidepressant have resulted in medicines that inhibit the active presynaptic reuptake of both serotonin and norepinephrine. Kent (2000) and Tran and coworkers (2003) reviewed the pharmacology of several of these drugs.

Nefazodone

Nefazodone (Serzone; Figure 7.10) is a dual-action antidepressant chemically related to trazodone (see Figure 7.7) but with some important pharmacological distinctions. Nefazodone's strongest pharmacological action is 5-HT$_2$ receptor blockade, which distinguishes it from

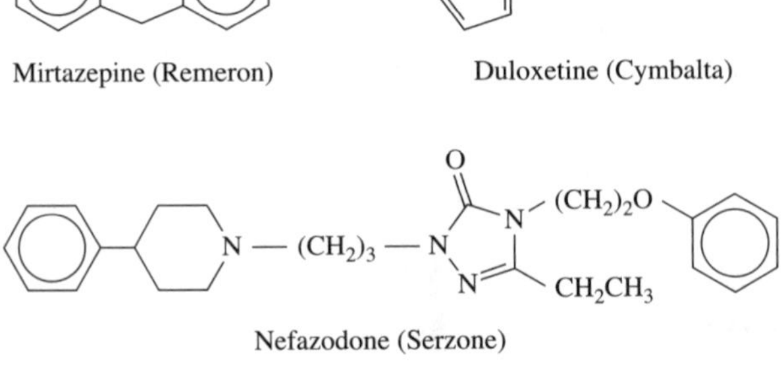

Mirtazepine (Remeron)

Duloxetine (Cymbalta)

Nefazodone (Serzone)

FIGURE 7.10 Chemical structures of three dual-action antidepressants.

the SSRIs; however, it also inhibits both serotonin and norepinephrine reuptake at its therapeutic dose. In 2003, a new warning was added to the information about this drug, stating that it produced liver failure at a rate about three to four times greater than that in the general population, resulting in death or necessitating liver transplantation. The drug was removed from the market in Canada in 2004, and although it is still available in the United States, it will no longer be marketed once present supplies are exhausted.

Milnacipran

Milnacipran (Ixel), another blocker of norepinephrine and serotonin reuptake (Tran et al., 2003), was shown in the treatment of major depression in hospitalized patients to be equivalent in efficacy to imipramine and superior to SSRIs. Although marketed in several countries around the world, as of this writing, it is not available in the United States, perhaps because the doses used in the clinical trials (around 50 up to 100 milligrams) were too low. This conclusion is supported by a recent study that found a 63.4 percent remission rate for milnacipran in outpatients with major depression, with a 150-milligram dose effective when a 100-milligram dose was insufficient (Okumura and Furukawa, 2006).

Recently, interest in milnacipran has centered on efficacy in the treatment of fibromyalgia, a disorder for the treatment of which pregabalin (Lyrica) has recently received FDA approval. Milnacipran reduces the chronic pain associated with fibromyalgia with concomitant improvements in global well-being, fatigue, and other domains of the disorder (Gendreau et al., 2005; Rooks, 2007).

Venlafaxine

Venlafaxine (Effexor) (see Figure 7.7) is classified as a mixed *serotonin-norepinephrine reuptake inhibitor*. The serotonin blockade occurs at lower doses than does the norepinephrine blockade, and at higher doses venlafaxine also inhibits the reuptake of dopamine. Venlafaxine lacks anticholinergic or antihistaminic effects, a distinct advantage. On the other hand, a recent study found that, while the response and remission rates to venlafaxine XR were the same as to bupropion XL, venlafaxine produced significantly more sexual side effects (Thase et al., 2006).

Concern has recently increased about venlafaxine's known association with blood pressure elevation in some 3 to 4 percent of patients using the sustained-release formulation and 2 to 13 percent of those taking the immediate-release preparation. Essentially, higher overdose fatality rates have been seen over the past 4 years, according to studies using population datasets. It's not clear if the increase in rates is because venlafaxine is being used in higher-risk groups (people with cardiac illnesses) instead of SSRIs or because patients prescribed venlafaxine were more likely than patients prescribed SSRIs to have been hospitalized, to have exhibited suicidal behavior, and to be taking other psychotropic medications. However, in December of 2006, the U.S. manufacturer issued a warning stating that prescriptions for Effexor should be written for the smallest quantity of capsules consistent with good patient management, in order to reduce the risk of overdose. Regardless of the causes, it is important to be aware of the possibility that venlafaxine is more toxic in overdose than SSRIs but less so than TCAs (Deshauer, 2007).

Venlafaxine improves psychomotor and cognitive function probably because of the relief of depression in combination with the lack of detrimental sedative and anticholinergic effects. It reportedly has comparable efficacy to clomipramine in treating OCD, with fewer adverse effects. In an extended-release formulation (Effexor EX), venlafaxine is FDA-approved for the treatment of generalized anxiety disorder (GAD) as well as panic and social anxiety.

Venlafaxine's primary metabolite is pharmacologically active; the half-lives of the parent compound and the primary metabolite are 5 hours and 11 hours, respectively. Venlafaxine appears to have only minimal effects on drug-metabolizing enzymes, and drug interactions are few.

Duloxetine

Duloxetine (Cymbalta; see Figure 7.10) is another dual-action antidepressant that binds to and blocks the reuptake transporters for norepinephrine and serotonin (Karpa et al., 2002). The blockade seems to be more complete than that of venlafaxine (Bymaster et al., 2005). The manufacturer that markets Prozac developed duloxetine, and now that fluoxetine is available in less expensive generic form, Cymbalta is being promoted as a replacement.

Studies have shown duloxetine to be clinically effective in the treatment of both depression (Goldstein et al., 2002) and anxiety (Dunner et al., 2003). In these studies, duloxetine was reported to significantly reduce physical symptoms of pain—such as backaches, headache, muscle and joint pain, and back and shoulder pain—to reduce interference with daily activities, and to reduce time in pain while awake. There is a close association between pain and the development of depressive symptoms (Bair et al., 2003), and this drug has been approved for the management of neuropathic pain associated with diabetic peripheral neuropathy. Duloxetine has been shown to be effective for the treatment of urinary stress incontinence (Norton et al., 2002). The mechanism underlying this action is unclear. In 2007, duloxetine was FDA-approved for the treatment of generalized anxiety disorder (Endicott et al., 2007; Rynn et al., 2007).

The half-life of duloxetine is about 12 hours, allowing once-daily dosing. Nausea is the most common side effect. Weight gain and sexual dysfunction have not yet been problems with the drug. Elevations in blood pressure (hypertension), thought to be possible with duloxetine, have not yet been a major problem in clinical studies.

Mirtazepine

Mirtazepine (Remeron; see Figure 7.10) was introduced into clinical use in the United States in 1997. Overall, mirtazepine is a dual-action antidepressant that increases the presynaptic release of both norepinephrine and serotonin through several actions:

1. It blocks central alpha$_2$ autoreceptors. By blocking adrenergic autoreceptors, it causes an increase in the release of norepinephrine.

2. It blocks adrenergic heteroceptors located on the terminals of serotonin-releasing neurons, where they normally inhibit the release of serotonin. When these adrenergic heteroceptors are blocked, 5-HT neurons release more serotonin.

3. The increased release of serotonin stimulates only 5-HT$_1$ receptors because 5-HT$_2$ and 5-HT$_3$ type receptors are specifically blocked by mirtazepine.

Although complicated, this mechanism explains how mirtazepine enhances both norepinephrine and serotonin neurotransmission. Because mirtazepine is a potent antagonist of postsynaptic 5-HT$_2$ and 5-HT$_3$ receptors, it does not produce the side effects of SSRIs (especially anxiety, insomnia, agitation, nausea, and sexual dysfunction). Mirtazepine is also a potent blocker of histamine receptors, and drowsiness is a prominent and often therapeutically limiting side effect. Sedation may be advantageous in depressed patients with symptoms of anxiety and insomnia, a common occurrence. Because of the drowsiness, the drug is best taken at bedtime and probably should not be combined with alcohol or other CNS depressants.

Other side effects of mirtazepine include increased appetite and weight gain. The drug may therefore be advantageous in certain situations, such as in the treatment of patients with anorexia, in patients with wasting diseases (for example, cancers and AIDS), and in the elderly where bedtime sedation and maintenance of body weight are a goal. Nelson and colleagues (2006) studied mirtazepine in elderly nursing home patients (average dose 20 milligrams at bedtime) and found it safe and effective; the depression scores of 50 percent of elderly patients were markedly reduced. An average weight gain of 1.3 pounds was considered to be beneficial in this population.

Mirtazepine is rapidly absorbed orally; peak blood levels occur 2 hours after administration. The elimination half-life is 20 to 40 hours, allowing once-a-day administration, usually at bedtime to maximize sleep and minimize daytime sedation.

Dopamine-Norepinephrine Reuptake Inhibitor: Bupropion

Bupropion (Wellbutrin, Zyban; see Figure 7.7) is a dopamine-norepinephrine reuptake inhibitor (DNRI). It is mechanistically unique as an antidepressant because it is the only available antidepressant that selectively inhibits the reuptake transporter for these two transmitters. It is without effect on serotonin neurons, and therefore it does not have the side effects associated with the use of SSRIs. Because of its potentiation of dopamine, it has been used to treat children with ADHD (Chapter 10), although efficacy is not very robust. Although bupropion is not commonly used as an anxiolytic, Zisook and coworkers (2001) reported that the drug was effective in treating grief following the death of a loved one. Bupropion is also useful as add-on, or augmenting, therapy in patients only partially responsive or nonresponsive to SSRIs (DeBattista et al., 2003) and in patients with difficult-to-treat bipolar depression (Erfurth et al., 2002). Unlike SSRIs, bupropion exhibits evidence of enhanced sexual functioning or minimal sexual dysfunction (Clayton et al., 2002; Fava and Rankin, 2002) and can be combined with SSRIs to counteract that side effect (Clayton et al., 2004). It may also reduce the fatigue associated with depression (Schonfeldt-Lecuona et al., 2006). Short-term treatment with long-acting bupropion (Wellbutrin SR) may result in weight loss, an advantage in patients in whom weight gain is a problem, although tolerance to this action appears to develop.

As an anticraving drug (Zyban), bupropion is widely used as part of nicotine replacement therapies for smoking cessation (Ferry and Johnston, 2003; West, 2003). Treatment of nicotine dependence is discussed further in Chapter 14.

Side effects of bupropion include anxiety, restlessness, tremor, and insomnia. More serious side effects include the induction of psychosis de novo and generalized seizures at higher doses. Bupropion is not effective in the treatment of panic disorder, and it may even exacerbate or precipitate panic in susceptible people. Higher-than-recommended doses of bupropion may cause a manic switch in patients with bipolar depression. For an update on bupropion, see Foley (2006).

Because bupropion and cocaine share similar mechanisms of action (blockade of dopamine reuptake), it's possible that bupropion exerts a reinforcing or dependency-inducing action. One study has shown that rats will self-administer bupropion; however, it does not seem to be abused by humans, perhaps because of the development of tolerance, but this conclusion remains unproven and the reason for the lack of abuse-liability is unclear (Tella et al., 1997).

Selective Norepinephrine Reuptake Inhibitors

Until recently, no antidepressant exhibited specific norepinephrine reuptake blockade in the absence of dopamine or serotonin reuptake blockade. Then two agents, *reboxetine* (Vestra, Edronax; Figure 7.11) and *atomoxetine* (Strattera; see Figure 7.11), were developed as selective norepinephrine reuptake inhibitors (SNRIs). Unfortunately, in two separate clinical trials, reboxetine was not found to have any more effect than placebo, and it has since been withdrawn from the market. Atomoxetine became commercially available in 2003 as the first nonstimulant drug to be approved by the FDA for the treatment of ADHD in children, adolescents, and adults. It is claimed to be as effective as methylphenidate, probably without abuse potential. The use of atomoxetine in children and adolescents is discussed in Chapter 10. Simpson and Plosker (2004) and Spencer and coworkers (2004) review the use of atomoxetine in adult ADHD.

Bymaster and coworkers (2002) reported that atomoxetine increases norepinephrine levels threefold in the prefrontal cortex without changing dopamine levels in the striatum or nucleus accumbens. By comparison, the ADHD stimulant medication methylphenidate increases striatal and nucleus accumbens dopamine and yet increases prefrontal cortical norepinephrine and dopamine levels only 1.5-fold. The absence of dopamine effects in the striatum and nucleus accumbens implies that atomoxetine is unlikely to have abuse potential and differentiates it from methylphenidate (Stahl, 2003).

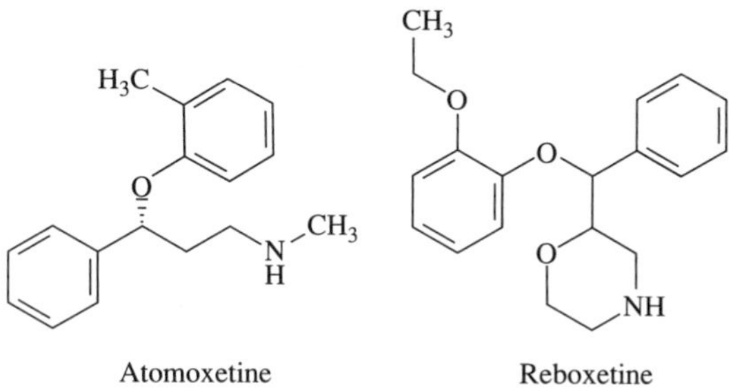

Atomoxetine   Reboxetine

FIGURE 7.11 Chemical structures of two adrenergic (primarily norepinephrine) reuptake inhibitor antidepressants.

Star*D Study

While basic research continues to improve our understanding of the pathophysiology of depressive disorders and the mechanisms of action of antidepressants, progress is also being made in the clinical management of depression. As with the other categories of psychotropic medications, discussed in subsequent chapters, a recent nationwide public health clinical trial, the Sequenced Treatment Alternatives to Relieve Depression (STAR*D) study, was conducted to determine the effectiveness of antidepressants as normally used in standard clinical practice, particularly for patients who had not responded to their initial antidepressant. The aim was to identify specific treatment strategies that would improve the long-term outcome of people with MDD.[5]

Procedure

There were four study levels; each tested different medications or medication combinations. At each step, those who did not become symptom-free or could not tolerate the treatment's side effects could enter the next level of treatment. The study was designed to mimic clinical practice by using psychiatrists and primary care physicians in both private practice and public clinics and by allowing participants, who were already seeking care at these facilities, to choose which of the available treatments were acceptable to them. This was the first study to provide solid scientific evidence regarding which next steps were best for treatment-resistant depression.

Over a 7-year period, a total of 4,041 outpatients, ages 18 to 75 years, were enrolled from 41 clinical sites around the country. Of these, 1,165 were excluded because they either did not meet the study requirements of having "at least moderate" depression (based on rating scales used in the study) or they chose not to participate. Thus, 2,876 "evaluable" people were included in Level 1 results. Level 2 results included 1,439 people who did not become symptom-free (did not achieve remission) in Level 1 and chose to continue. Level 3 results included 377 people, and Level 4 results included 142 people.

All Level 1 participants were treated with citalopram for 12 to 14 weeks. Citalopram was chosen for the first treatment because it usually does not induce troublesome withdrawal symptoms when it is stopped, it is easy to administer (once a day), it does not interact with other medications, and it is safe for older and medically fragile patients. Participants who became symptom-free moved on to a

---

[5]For a summary of the STAR*D clinical trial, provided by the National Institute of Mental Health, see http://www.nimh.nih.gov/healthinformation/stard/cfm.

12-month follow-up period during which citalopram was continued and patients were monitored.

In Level 2, patients had the option of switching to a different medication or adding to the existing citalopram. For those who wanted to switch, the choices were sertraline (Zoloft), bupropion-SR (Wellbutrin SR), or venlafaxine-XR (Effexor XR); "add-on" choices were either bupropion-SR or buspirone (Chapter 6). Participants who became symptom-free in Level 2 continued with the treatment in a follow-up period; participants who did not or who experienced intolerable side effects could continue on to Level 3. In Level 3, participants who chose to switch were randomly assigned to either mirtazepine (Remeron) or nortriptyline (Aventyl or Pamelor, a TCA) for up to 14 weeks. Both drugs work differently than the medications of Levels 1 and 2. In the Level 3 add-on group, participants were randomly prescribed either lithium (a mood stabilizer commonly used to treat bipolar disorder; Chapter 8) or triiodthyronine (T3) (a medication commonly used to treat thyroid conditions)

In Level 4, participants who had not become symptom-free in any of the preceding levels were taken off all other medications and randomly switched to one of two treatments, the monoamine oxidase inhibitor (MAOI) tranylcypromine (Parnate) or the combination of extended-release venlafaxine (Effexor XR) with mirtazepine.

Results

Only about 30 percent of the participants in the Level 1 portion reached "remission," and about 10 to 15 percent more were "responders," who did not achieve remission but whose symptoms decreased to at least half of what they were at the start of the trial. On average, it took nearly 6 weeks for a participant to respond and nearly 7 weeks to achieve remission. The average number of visits with the respective physician was between 5 and 6. Overall, about 9 percent of the participants in Level 1 stopped citalopram because of side effects. These results were very discouraging as they documented the poor efficacy of the chosen SSRI to achieve significant therapeutic benefits.

In Level 2, only 21 of the 1,439 participants said that all the choices were equally acceptable and allowed themselves to be randomized to a switch or an augmentation treatment. For all the other participants at least one option was unacceptable, and they chose to limit the range of treatments to which they would be randomized. Of those, 727 (51 percent) agreed to switch their medication and 565 (39 percent) agreed to receive "medication augmentation"; the rest received cognitive therapy. About 25 percent of the participants who switched became symptom-free. This result was the same for each of the three medication groups: no one drug was best, none worked more quickly than another, and there was no difference in side effects or serious problems. About one-third of the participants in the augmentation group achieved remission.

The most recent results describe comparisons between cognitive-behavioral therapy (CBT) and the various medications (Thase et al., 2007). Among patients who did not respond adequately to citalopram, CBT produced outcomes comparable to those of medications; antidepressant therapy was more rapidly effective than CBT while CBT was better tolerated than the antidepressants.

In the Level 3 switch group, 10 to 20 percent of participants achieved remission, with no significant overall difference between the two medications, although there were more troublesome side effects with lithium. In Level 4, 7 to 10 percent of participants became symptom-free. Although there were no significant differences between the two treatments, patients taking the venlafaxine-XR/mirtazapine combination reported more symptom reduction and were less likely to stop taking the medication because of side effects than the patients taking the MAOI tranylcypromine.

Conclusions

Over the course of all four treatment levels, about two-thirds of participants were able to achieve remission if they did not withdraw from the study. However, a substantial number of participants did withdraw: 21 percent after Level 1, 30 percent after Level 2, and 42 percent after Level 3. The data show that, overall, many patients with treatment-resistant depression can get better, but the odds of remission diminish with every additional treatment strategy needed. Furthermore, relapse rates were higher for those who entered the follow-up phase after more treatment steps. This was the case regardless of whether the participants had or had not reached remission. Interestingly, the time to relapse for those who did relapse was similar across all levels, ranging from 2.5 to 4.5 months. Nevertheless, relapse rates were much lower for those who achieved remission, confirming that remission is associated with a better prognosis even if it is achieved after several treatments.[6]

Antidepressants of the Future

The history of antidepressant drugs now encompasses almost 50 years. As is apparent in the descriptions of current drugs, we are still seeking the "perfect" antidepressant, one that is widely effective in bringing about the remission of acute episodes and preventing future

[6]For published reports on STAR*D, see Fava et al. (2006), McGrath et al. (2006), Nierenberg et al. (2006), Rush et al. (2006a, 2006b), and Trivedi et al. (2006a, 2006b).

relapses in the absence of significant side effects (Schechter et al., 2005). In this section, potential agents of the future are briefly examined. Because they come from numerous and diverse neurochemical categories, it is useful to organize these potential antidepressant medications into several groups.

Augmenting Agents

Modafinil (Provigil) is a nonstimulant wakefulness-promoting drug used to combat daytime fatigue in patients with narcolepsy. It does not produce typical psychostimulant-induced side effects, and, in narcoleptic patients, modafinil may also improve subjective well-being, fatigue, and concentration. A recent open-label study (Konuk et al., 2006) is consistent with previous reports demonstrating the efficacy and safety of modafinil as an augmenting agent for patients with only partial response to traditional antidepressant drugs.

Other drugs that may well serve as augmenting agents to supplement antidepressant medications in partially responsive patients include mood stabilizers such as *lamotrigine* (Ernst and Goldberg, 2003; Rocha and Hara, 2003) (Chapter 8); the newer atypical antipsychotic drugs (Papakostas et al., 2007), such as *quetiapine, aripiprazole*, and *amisulpride* (Chapter 9); and certain of the omega-3 fatty acids (discussed at the end of this chapter).

Serotonin 5-HT$_1$ Agonists and Antagonists

Chapter 6 introduced *buspirone* (BuSpar) as an anxiolytic agent and noted that it exerts its effects secondary to weak stimulation of serotonin 5-HT$_{1A}$ receptors. Its poor absorption could be modified but remains a clinical limitation. Antidepressive effects should be produced by either antagonizing presynaptic 5-HT$_{1A}$ autoreceptors (which would increase serotonin release) or by directly stimulating postsynaptic 5-HT$_{1A}$ receptors (which is believed to be responsible for the antidepressive/anxiolytic action). This agent might be most effective in combination with an SSRI (Adell et al., 2005). Feiger and coworkers (2003) reported efficacy of another serotonin 5-HT$_1$ partial agonist, *gepirone-ER*, as monotherapy for depression. This drug is not yet marketed. Several other drugs in this class are under development as either antidepressants or anxiolytic agents.

New Drugs Affecting Serotonin, Norepinephrine, and/or Dopamine

Because many side effects of the SSRIs are due to the stimulation of 5-HT$_2$ receptors, combinations of 5-HT$_2$ blocking drugs and SSRIs may be useful or at least more tolerable. Some new compounds with this action are under study, and there are a few older drugs with this property that are being reassessed. [In fact, the present drug mirtazepine (Remeron) has this characteristic.] A similar logic has led to additional combinations, such as a drug that stimulates postsynaptic 5-HT$_{1A}$ receptors and blocks alpha$_2$ receptors (for example, sunepitron). There are also some new approaches to reuptake blockers. One new class of compounds is much more potent at blocking both 5-HT/NE reuptake (Mahaney et al., 2006). Other experimental agents block the reuptake of both 5-HT and dopamine (minaprine, bazinaprine), and it has been argued that the benefits of antidepressant drugs with a "prodopaminergic" activity have not yet been sufficiently explored (Papakostas, 2006). Finally, a recent review summarizes preliminary positive results of an experimental compound, DOV 216,303 (azabicyclohexane), that inhibits the reuptake of all three monoamines, serotonin, norepinephrine, and dopamine. This drug has already been shown to be safe and equal to citalopram in reducing symptoms of depression as well as in side effects. As stated by the authors, "These findings provide preliminary evidence of a clinically meaningful antidepressant action with a molecule capable of inhibiting the three transmitters most closely linked to major depressive disorder" (Skolnick et al., 2006, p. 123).

Tianeptine is a novel antidepressant compound. In contrast to SSRIs, it *increases* the presynaptic neuronal uptake of serotonin in the brain and thus decreases serotonin neurotransmission. However, tianeptine appears to reduce stress-induced atrophy of neuronal dendrites, exerting a neuronal protective effect against stress (Czeh et al., 2001; Nickel et al., 2003) and restoring intracellular mechanisms adversely affected by stress and other insults (Dziedzicka-Wasylewska et al., 2002; Shakesby et al., 2002). Its efficacy against major depression is well documented (Dalery et al., 2001; Loo et al., 2001). Its use does not appear to be associated with adverse cognitive, psychomotor, sleep, cardiovascular, body weight, or sexual side effects. Tianeptine is also effective in bipolar depression, dysthymia, and anxiety. It appears quite useful in the elderly and in patients with chronic alcoholism. This fascinating new compound offers both an alternative medication to standard antidepressants and new insights into the pathophysiology of depression and anxiety.

Drugs Affecting Glutamate and GABA

There are several reasons for studying the possible role of excitatory (glutamate) and inhibitory transmitters (GABA) in depression. First, stressful stimulation increases levels of glutamate in the brain. Second, the receptors for glutamate and GABA are found in the brain structures associated with emotional regulation. Third, chronic antidepressant treatment (in laboratory animals) affects the major glutamate receptors. This approach benefits from the fact that we already have drugs that act on this neurotransmitter system, usually developed as anticonvulsants, as neuroprotective agents (to prevent neuronal death after stroke or brain damage), or to treat dementia. Because there are so many important therapeutic possibilities for such drugs, a great many are being developed and evaluated as treatments for a variety of disorders, including depression and anxiety. Pregabalin may be an example of such a drug.

Drugs Affecting Peptide Systems

All the antidepressant drugs discussed so far have therapeutic shortcomings such as limited efficacy and significant side effects. The neurogenic hypothesis of depression suggests that we might be able to develop novel therapeutic approaches involving neuroactive proteins (neuropeptides) that affect synaptic and intracellular metabolic processes. For example, drugs that act as antagonists at neurokinin (NK) receptors have the potential to provide therapeutic benefits for a number of conditions, including stress, anxiety, and depression.

Tachykinins.   The endogenous neurochemicals known as tachykinins were discovered 70 years ago, but compounds that antagonize their action are just now being developed. The tachykinins are products of two genes that produce substance P (SP) and the various neurokinins. The tachykinin peptides share a common chemical structure and act through three types of neurokinin receptors—termed Neurokinin$_1$ (NK$_1$), Neurokinin$_2$ (NK$_2$), and Neurokinin$_3$ NK$_3$)—to regulate a variety of physiological processes, especially processes related to inflammatory reactions, such as asthma, inflammatory bowel disorder, and migraine. SP is the most abundant tachykinin in the CNS and reacts with the NK$_1$ receptor. Neurons containing SP occur in many regions of the brain implicated in the pathogenesis of depression (midbrain, hypothalamus, amygdala, and hippocampus) and the protein is sometimes found with 5-HT and NE or their receptors. SP is released in response to stress and pain, and depressed patients have increased levels of SP in plasma and cerebrospinal fluid. Because chronic antidepressant treatment reduces SP, SP antagonists (also called NK$_1$ antagonists) might be expected to reduce stress, pain, and depression. One such agent, *aprepitant*, appeared to be effective in treating depression (Kramer et al., 2004) but failed in five clinical studies. However, recent studies demonstrate that two experimental NK$_2$ antagonists, saredutant and osanetant, have antidepressant effects in animals (Salome et al., 2006). The results of clinical trials are expected in 2008.

Hypothalamic Peptides.   During the past decade, there has been a dramatic increase in research involving peptides, located in the hypothalamus, that regulate feeding behavior. Recent observations have linked a couple of these "feeding peptides" to depression. One group of neurons in the hypothalamus produces melanin-concentrating hormone (MCH), which promotes appetite. Consequently, antagonists of the MCH$_1$ receptor are usually studied as possible diet drugs. In a battery of tests using laboratory animals, MCH$_1$ antagonists produced "antidepressant effects" (Borowsky et al., 2002), but no further information has been reported.

A second peptide, called alpha-melanocyte stimulating hormone (αMSH) produces the opposite effect—it acts to suppress appetite. The release of αMSH is controlled by two other hormones called melanocyte-stimulating hormone release-stimulating factor and melanocyte-stimulating hormone release-inhibiting factor (MIF). Older reports in the literature suggested that MIF had antidepressant-like effects in animals, which led to the development of an analog of this peptide hormone, called *nemifitide*, which also looked like an antidepressant in laboratory animal tests and was reported to have antidepressant effects in clinical trials. Nemifitide is unusual because it seems to work faster than classic antidepressants, improving depressive symptoms within 3 to 5 days. It interacts with several different types of receptors, including serotonin receptors and receptors for other peptides. It was reported to have minimal side effects and there were no dropouts due to adverse reactions (Montgomery et al.. 2006). If it retains an appetite-suppressing action, it could be an extremely successful drug. Unfortunately, nemifitide must be administered by subcutaneous injection, so further development may depend on the ability to produce an oral formulation or a transdermal patch.

Corticotropin-Releasing Factor and Glucocorticoid Peptides. We have discussed that stress is associated with depression. Hence it is not surprising that a great deal of effort has been directed toward understanding the physiological regulation of stress and its possible role in the etiology of major depressive disorder (Soares and Papakostas, 2007). Unfortunately, in spite of concerted efforts, progress has been modest.

A person's ability to cope with stress is primarily regulated by the physiological system known as the hypothalamic-pituitary-adrenal (HPA) axis. *Corticotropin-releasing factor* (CRF) is the driving force of this circuit. CRF is produced in the hypothalamus. Once synthesized, CRF is transported to the anterior lobe of the pituitary gland, where it stimulates the release of adrenocorticotropic hormone (ACTH). ACTH is then carried by the circulation to the adrenal cortex, where it promotes release of the glucocorticoid hormone cortisol. Cortisol is an essential response to stressful situations; it activates functions that are necessary for coping with stress, such as the release of glucose for energy, an increase in alertness and concentration, and a sharpening of cognitive processes. Cortisol levels are sensed by cells in the hypothalamus, reducing CRF release (a negative feedback inhibition). This feedback inhibition is important because too much cortisol is toxic to neurons in the hippocampus and inhibits neurogenesis.

In a depressed person, the HPA axis is hyperactive, and increased cortisol has been proposed as the reason the hippocampus of a depressed person may be smaller than normal. As discussed, hyperactivity of the HPA axis in a depressed patient may be normalized after successful antidepressant treatment. Accordingly, there has been intense effort to develop drugs that can intervene at some point in this system and restore balance to the HPA.

One glucocorticoid antagonist is already available. The drug mifepristone (which is a progesterone receptor antagonist and is used clinically to induce chemical abortion of early pregnancy) is currently in clinical trials for psychotic major depression. A recent review of this drug concluded that, although most studies are still preliminary, the results are "encouraging" (Gallagher and Young, 2006).

Drugs Affecting Second Messengers and Neurotropins

As discussed at the beginning of this chapter, attention has recently been directed to studying the intracellular effects of antidepressants, that is, the processes that take place after receptors have been activated. This has led to renewed interest in second-messenger systems, such as the cAMP pathway, and the beneficial effects of these biochemical events on neuronal health and survival. Many second-messenger pathways, whether activated by transmitters, hormones or neurotrophins, converge on the cAMP response element, or CREB, protein, and it has been shown that various antidepressants—SSRIs, TCAs, and MAOIs—activate CREB. Furthermore, there is some evidence for decreased CREB levels and less responsiveness to CREB activation in depressed people. These observations suggest that manipulations that increase second-messenger levels may have antidepressant potential.

One method of doing so is to block the degradation of cAMP by inhibiting the enzymes, called phosphodiesterases (PDEs), that break it down. Moreover, PDE4 inhibitors have been reported to induce the expression of the protein called brain-derived neurotrophic factor (BDNF) in the hippocampus. Unfortunately, although such inhibitors have been developed, their side effects so far have precluded clinical usefulness.

Substances with Miscellaneous Mechanisms of Action

In this section, we focus on a variety of substances that have been purported to exert antidepressant properties. Some of these substances are the hormone precursor dehydroepiandrosterone, a blocker of melatonin receptors (agomelatine), a compound manufactured in our body (S-adenosyl-methionine), and omega-3 fatty acids, found in certain fish. Evidence for and against their efficacy is presented.

Dehydroepiandrosterone. Dehydroepiandrosterone (DHEA) is a glucocorticoid hormone secreted by the adrenal glands, but its physiological role is unclear. It is a weakly active adrenal androgen that serves as a precursor to testosterone and estradiol, hormones that can have a positive effect on mood when administered exogenously. It may also increase the amount of available neurotrophins, which may also affect mood. Secretion of the hormone peaks at 20 to 25 years of age and declines by about 90 percent by age 70.

DHEA has been promoted to prevent a variety of disorders; perhaps the most enduring claims have been that DHEA may delay the aging process, improve mood, and delay the cognitive decline that occurs with age. Bloch and coworkers (1999) and Wolkowitz and coworkers (1999) conducted double-blind, randomized studies of DHEA on objective measurements of depression, dysthymia, and cognitive functioning. DHEA, but not placebo, improved depression ratings on all measurement scales, although it had no effect on cognitive function or sleep disturbance. Response rates (60 percent) were comparable to those seen with standard antidepressants. This result was supported by a recent randomized, double-blind, crossover trial of DHEA in two dosages (low dose for three weeks followed by high dose for three weeks), which showed antidepressive effects in middle-aged men and women during the 6 weeks of treatment, relative to baseline and to placebo treatment (Schmidt et al., 2005). DHEA treatment was also effective, relative to placebo, in reducing symptoms of mild depression or dysthymia in a group of HIV-positive adults. Response rates were 56 to 62 percent in the DHEA patients (depending on the outcome measure) and 31 to 33 percent in the placebo patients. There were few adverse effects and no worsening of their HIV status (Rabkin et al., 2006). In spite of these positive results, a recent review of the literature found "equivocal" support across all types of clinical reports for the long-term antidepressant benefits of DHEA in older men (Shamlian and Cole, 2006).

Because DHEA is usually classified as an androgen, it would not be surprising to see its use accompanied by the characteristic side effects of acne, male-pattern baldness, hirsutism, voice changes, and so on. In fact, the most common adverse effects in the 2005 study were acne and oily skin. More serious effects include the theoretical potential for causing breast or prostate cancer and liver damage.

Agomelatine. Abnormal circadian rhythms are common in depression and other mood disorders. For many patients with depression, symptoms are worse in the morning, with some improvement during the day. One major component in the regulation of diurnal rhythm is the hormone melatonin, which is derived from serotonin and has connections with serotonergic and noradrenergic structures. These considerations led to the development of a novel antidepressant, agomelatin (or agomelatine), which is an agonist at melatonin 1 and melatonin 2 receptors and an antagonist at 5-HT$_2$ receptors, with no detectable affinity for any other receptors.

In late-phase trials for the treatment of major depressive disorder, symptoms of depression significantly improved with agomelatine compared with placebo, and the drug appeared to be as efficacious as other SSRI/SNRI antidepressants but with fewer adverse effects. Analysis of data combined from three different trials suggested that the difference between agomelatine and placebo patients was greater in patients with more severe symptoms. As measured both subjectively and with polysomnographic recordings, agomelatine appeared to improve sleep quality and ease of falling asleep in depressed patients. Adverse events were generally mild to moderate with overall frequency and discontinuation rates close to those of placebo. Agomelatine is being developed as a once-daily treatment for MDD and its symptoms, particularly anxiety, and sleep and circadian disturbances. As of 2006, phase III trials have been completed and requests for approval have been submitted in western Europe (Bánki, 2006; Montgomery, 2006; Zupancic and Guilleminault, 2006).

S-Adenosyl-Methionine. S-adenosyl-methionine (SAM; SAMe) itself is not abundant in the diet but is normally produced in the liver from the amino acid methionine, which is plentiful in most diets. SAMe functions by donating its methyl group to any of a wide range of molecules that are subsequently transformed to homocysteine. The homocysteine is transformed to methionine and the process repeats. Folic acid and vitamin B$_{12}$ are necessary for its synthesis, and deficiencies of these vitamins result in low concentrations of SAMe in the central nervous system. Low blood or central nervous system levels of SAMe have been detected in people with cirrhosis of the liver, coronary heart disease, Alzheimer's disease, and depression.

Although SAMe is widely marketed for the treatment of depression, the evidence to indicate that it works remains inconclusive. Part of this difficulty may be due to the fact that oral absorption is poor, and less than 1 percent of the ingested drug reaches the bloodstream; oral doses have ranged from 200 to 1600 milligrams. Although several studies have found SAMe effective, most were small and poorly conducted. One of the best-designed studies, a double-blind, placebo-controlled study of 133 depressed people, actually failed to find intravenous SAMe more effective than placebo (Delle Chiaie and Pancheri, 1999).

No formulation of SAMe is regulated by the FDA; some formulations were found to contain no SAMe at all. As stated, oral absorption is almost nonexistent. Therefore, side effects are minimal and include mild insomnia, lack of appetite, constipation, nausea, dry mouth, sweating, dizziness, and nervousness; there is little information on the possible drug interaction effects of SAMe. Because SAMe is metabolized to homocysteine and because elevated homocysteine levels have been associated with early onset of atherosclerosis and coronary artery disease, there is concern that overuse of SAMe may predispose to these diseases. No reports of safety in pregnancy or breast-feeding are available.

Omega-3 Fatty Acids. Two types of omega-3 fatty acids are found in fatty fish like salmon, sardines, and mackerel: eicosapentaenoic acid, or EPA, and docosahexaenoic acid, or DHA. A third omega-3, alpha-linolenic acid, is found in plant foods such as flaxseed, soybean oil, walnuts, and canola oil. The American Heart Association recommends eating at least two servings of fatty fish each week, based on strong evidence that the omega-3 fats found in the fish help protect against cardiovascular disease.

Several lines of evidence also indicate an association between omega-3 polyunsaturated fatty acids and mood disorders. In his book *The Omega-3 Connection*, Andrew Stoll (2001) theorized a link between depression and heart disease: People with depression are more likely to develop heart problems than people without depression. When they do, they suffer more and are more likely to die than people who are not depressed. Low omega-3 fatty acid status is often present in heart disease and depression, and when people with heart disease or depression increase their intake of the long-chain omega-3 fatty acids EPA and DHA, their condition often improves.

Infrequent fish consumption is also associated with depression in epidemiological studies (Parker et al., 2006). In addition, some case reports and cohort studies show lower omega-3 concentrations in participants with unipolar and postpartum depression (Sontrop and Campbell, 2006). One recent report demonstrated that long-term low dietary intake of EPA is associated with an increased risk for depression in adolescents (Mamalakis et al., 2006). Data has been presented showing that, in 106 healthy people without major depression or any other diagnosed mood disorder, those with low blood levels of omega-3 fatty acids scored worse than those with high levels on tests designed to assess mood, personality, and impulsive behavior. People in the study with low blood levels of EPA and DHA were more likely than others to report experiencing symptoms of mild to moderate depression (Conklin et al., 2007).

However, in spite of the evidence linking low levels of omega-3 to mood disorders, there is less evidence that EPA or DHA are effective antidepressants. Peet and Horrobin (2002) and Nemets and coworkers

(2002) reported that EPA could be an effective augmenting agent in patients not fully responsive to standard antidepressant drugs. Zanarini and Frankenburg (2003) reported efficacy of EPA in treating aggressive and depressive symptoms in females with borderline personality disorder. But Marangell and coworkers (2003) failed to demonstrate a significant effect of DHA as monotherapy in patients with major depression. One review concluded that four of seven double-blind randomized controlled trials showed significant improvement of depression with treatment of at least 1 gram per day of an omega-3 fatty acid; that is, this treatment was effective only about half the time. And, although one recent study concluded that omega-3 fatty acids were effective in the treatment of postpartum depression, this interpretation is weakened because there was no placebo treatment (Freeman et al., 2006). It therefore remains unclear whether omega-3 supplementation is effective independent of antidepressant treatment for depressed patients in general or for only those with abnormally low concentrations of these substances (Sontrop and Campbell, 2006).

STUDY QUESTIONS

1. What is the relationship between depression and the biological amine transmitters in the brain?

2. Describe the probable mechanism of both acute and ultimate effects of antidepressant drugs. What might account for the delay in clinical effect?

3. List and differentiate the major classes of antidepressants.

4. Compare and contrast imipramine and fluoxetine.

5. Discuss what happens when a patient overdoses on a tricyclic antidepressant. Who is at risk?

6. Discuss the side effects of SSRIs. What is the serotonin syndrome? What is the serotonin discontinuation syndrome? Discuss the effects of these drugs on sexual function.

7. Which drug or class of drugs do you think is the "best" antidepressant? Defend your position.

8. Which antidepressants are used in the treatment of anxiety disorders? Why? How do these drugs differ from the benzodiazepine-type anxiolytics?

9. Discuss the strategies being used to discover the next generation of antidepressant drugs. Include drugs that act on the monoamines, on glutamate, and on peptides.

10. What is DHEA? What is its therapeutic potential? Its potential complications?

11. Discuss the possible role of omega-3 fatty acids in depression.

REFERENCES

Adell, A., et al. (2005). "Strategies for Producing Faster Acting Antidepressants." *Drug Discovery Today* 10: 578–585.

Alwan, S., et al. for the National Birth Defects Prevention Study (2007). "Use of Selective Serotonin-Reuptake Inhibitors in Pregnancy and the Risk of Birth Defects." *New England Journal of Medicine* 356: 2684–2692.

American College of Obstetricians and Gynecologists (2006). "Position Statement on Paroxetine." *Obstetrics and Gynecology* 108: 1601–1603.

American Psychological Association (1994). *Diagnostic and Statistical Manual of Mental Disorders, 4th Edition* (DSM-IV). Washington, DC: American Psychological Association.

Amsterdam, J. D. (2003). "A Double-Blind, Placebo-Controlled Trial of the Safety and Efficacy of Selegiline Transdermal System Without Dietary Restrictions in Patients with Major Depressive Disorder." *Journal of Clinical Psychiatry* 64: 208–214.

Amsterdam, J. D., and A. Bodkin (2006). "Selegiline Transdermal System in the Prevention of Relapse of Major Depressive Disorder: A 52-Week, Double-Blind, Placebo-Substitution, Parallel-Group C Clinical Trial." *Journal of Clinical Psychopharmacology* 26: 579–586.

Angelucci, F., et al. (2005). "BDNF in Schizophrenia, Depression and Corresponding Animal Models." *Molecular Psychiatry* 10: 345–352.

Bair, M. J., et al. (2003). "Depression and Pain Comorbidity." *Archives of Internal Medicine* 163: 2433–2445.

Bánki, M. C. (2006). "Agomelatin: the First 'Melatoninergic' Antidepressant." *Neuropsychopharmacology Hungary* 8: 105–112.

Berton, O., and E. J. Nestler (2006). "New Approaches to Antidepressant Drug Discovery: Beyond Monoamines." *Nature Reviews Neuroscience* 7: 137–151.

Bezchlibnyk-Butler, K. Z., and J. J. Jeffries, eds. (2005) *Clinical Handbook of Psychotropic Drugs*, 15th edition, pp. 59–60.

Blendy, J. A. (2006). "The Role of CREB in Depression and Antidepressant Treatment." *Biological Psychiatry* 59: 1144–1150.

Bloch, M., et al. (1999). "Dehydroepiandrosterone Treatment of Midlife Dysthymia." *Biological Psychiatry* 45: 1533–1541.

Borowsky, B., et al. (2002). "Antidepressant, Anxiolytic and Anorectic Effects of a Melanin-Concentrating Hormone-1 Receptor Antagonist." *Nature Medicine* 8: 825–830.

Brosen, K., and C. A. Naranjo (2001). "Review of Pharmacokinetic and Pharmacodynamic Interaction Studies with Citalopram." *European Neuropsychopharmacology* 11: 275–283.

Bymaster, F. P., et al. (2005). "The Dual Transporter Inhibitor Duloxetine: A Review of Its Preclinical Pharmacology, Pharmacokinetic Profile, and Clinical Results in Depression." *Current Pharmaceutical Design* 11: 1475–1493.

Chambers, C. D., et al. (2006). "Selective Serotonin-Reuptake Inhibitors and Risk of Persistent Pulmonary Hypertension of the Newborn." *New England Journal of Medicine* 354: 579–587.

Clayton, A. H., et al. (2002). "Prevalence of Sexual Dysfunction Among Newer Antidepressants." *Journal of Clinical Psychiatry* 63: 357–366.

Clayton, A. H., et al. (2004). "A Placebo-Controlled Trial of Bupropion SR as an Antidote for Selective Serotonin Reuptake Inhibitor-Induced Sexual Dysfunction." *Journal of Clinical Psychiatry* 65: 62–67.

Cohen, L. S., et al. (2006). "Relapse of Major Depression During Pregnancy in Women Who Maintain or Discontinue Antidepressant Treatment." *Journal of the American Medical Association* 295: 499–507.

Conklin, S. M., et al. (2007)."Serum Omega-3 Fatty Acids Are Associated with Variation in Mood, Personality and Behavior in Hypercholesterolemic Community Volunteers." *Psychiatry Research* 152: 1–10.

Czeh, B., et al. (2001). "Stress-Induced Changes in Cerebral Metabolites, Hippocampal Volume, and Cell Proliferation Are Prevented by Antidepressant Treatment with Tianeptine." *Proceedings of the National Academy of Sciences* 22: 12796–12801.

Dalery, J., et al. (2001). "Efficacy of Tianeptine vs Placebo in the Long-Term Treatment (16 Months) of Unipolar Major Recurrent Depression." *Human Psychopharmacology* 16: S39–S47.

DeBattista, C., et al. (2003). "A Prospective Trial of Bupropion-SR Augmentation of Partial and Non-Responders to Serotonergic Antidepressants." *Journal of Clinical Psychopharmacology* 23: 27–30.

Delle Chiaie, R., and P. Pancheri (1999). "Combined Analysis of Two Controlled, Multicentric, Double Blind Studies to Assess Efficacy and Safety of Sulfo-Adenosyl-Methionine (SAMe) vs. Placebo (MC1) and SAMe vs. Clomipramine (MC2) in the Treatment of Major Depression [in Italian; English Abstract]. *Giornale Italiano di Psicopatologia* 5: 1–16.

Deshauer, D. (2007). "Venlafaxine (Effexor): Concerns About Increased Risk of Fatal Outcomes in Overdose." *Canadian Medical Association Journal* 176: 39–40.

Duman, R. S. (2004). "Depression: A Case of Neuronal Life and Death?" *Biological Psychiatry* 56: 140–145.

Duman, R. S., and L. M. Monteggia (2006). "A Neurotrophic Model for Stress-Related Mood Disorders." *Biological Psychiatry* 59: 1116–1127.

Dunner, D., et al. (2003). "Duloxetine in Treatment of Anxiety Symptoms Associated with Depression." *Depression and Anxiety* 18: 53–61.

Dziedzicka-Wasylewska, M., et al. (2002). "Effect of Tianeptine and Fluoxetine on the Levels of Met-Enkephalin and mRNA Encoding Proenkephalin in the Rat." *Journal of Physiology and Pharmacology* 53: 117–125.

Endicott, J., et al. (2007). "Duloxetine Treatment for Role Functioning Improvement in Generalized Anxiety Disorder: Three Independent Studies." *Journal of Clinical Psychiatry* 68: 518–524.

Erfurth, A., et al. (2002). "Bupropion as Add-On Strategy in Difficult-to-Treat Bipolar Depressive Patients." *Neuropsychobiology* 45, Supplement 1: 33–36.

Ernst, C. L., and J. F. Goldberg (2003). "Antidepressant Properties of Anticonvulsant Drugs for Bipolar Disorder." *Journal of Clinical Psychopharmacology* 23: 182–192.

Fava, M., et al. (2006). "A Comparison of Mirtazepine and Nortryptyline Following Two Consecutive Failed Medication Treatments for Depressed Outpatients: A STAR*D Report." *American Journal of Psychiatry* 163: 1161–1172.

Fava, M., and M. Rankin (2002). "Sexual Functioning and SSRIs." *Journal of Clinical Psychiatry* 63, Supplement 5: 13–16.

Feiger, A. D., et al. (2003). "Gepirone Extended Release: New Evidence for Efficacy in the Treatment of Major Depressive Disorder." *Journal of Clinical Psychiatry* 64: 243–249.

Ferreira, E., et al. (2007). "Effects of Selective Serotonin Reuptake Inhibitors and Venlafaxine During Pregnancy in Term and Preterm Neonates." *Pediatrics* 119: 52–59.

Ferry, L., and J. A. Johnston (2003). "Efficacy and Safety of Bupropion SR for Smoking Cessation: Data from Clinical Trials and Five Years of Postmarketing Experience." *International Journal of Clinical Practice* 57: 224–230.

Foley, K. F., et al. (2006). "Bupropion: Pharmacology and Therapeutic Applications." *Expert Review Neurotherapy* 6: 1249–1265.

Freeman, M. P., et al. (2006). "Randomized Dose-Ranging Pilot Trial of Omega-3 Fatty Acids for Postpartum Depession." *Acta Psychiatrica Scandinavia* 113: 31–35.

Frodl, T., et al. (2007). "Association of the Brain-Derived Neurotrophic Factor Val66Met Polymorphism with Reduced Hippocampal Volumes in Major Depression." *Archives of General Psychiatry* 64: 410–416.

Gallagher, P., and A. H. Young (2006). "Mifepristone (RU-486) Treatment for Depression and Psychosis: A Review of the Therapeutic Implications." *Neuropsychiatric Disease and Treatment* 2: 33–42.

Gardner, D. M., et al. (1996). "The Making of a User-Friendly MAOI Diet." *Journal of Clinical Psychiatry* 57: 99–104.

Gendreau, R. M., et al. (2005). "Efficacy of Milnacipran in Patients with Fibromyalgia." *Journal of Rheumatology* 32: 1975–1985.

Goldstein, D. J., et al. (2002). "Duloxetine in the Treatment of Major Depressive Disorder: A Double-Blind Clinical Trial." *Journal of Clinical Psychiatry* 63: 225–231.

Goodnick, P. J. (2007). "Seligiline Transdermal System in Depression." *Expert Opinion in Pharmacotherapy* 8: 59–64.

Green, B. (2003). "Focus on Paroxetine." *Current Medical Research and Opinion* 19: 13–21.

Hansen, R. A., et al. (2005). "Efficacy and Safety of Second-Generation Antidepressants in the Treatment of Major Depressive Disorder." *Annals of Internal Medicine* 143: 415–426.

Jeanneteau, F., and M. V. Chao (2006). "Promoting Neurotrophic Effects by GCPR Ligands." *Novartis Foundation Symposium* 276: 181–189.

Karpa, K. D., et al. (2002). "Duloxetine Pharmacology: Profile of a Dual Mono-Amine Modulator." *CNS Drug Reviews* 8: 361–376.

Kent, J. M. (2000). "SNaRIs, NaSSAs, and NaRIs: New Agents for the Treatment of Depression." *Lancet* 355: 911–918.

Kessler, R. C., et al. (2003). "The Epidemiology of Major Depressive Disorder: Results from the National Comorbidity Survey Replication (NCS-R)." *Journal of the American Medical Association* 289: 3095–3105.

Konuk, N., et al. (2006). "Open-Label Study of Adjunct Modafinil for the Treatment of Patients with Fatigue, Sleepiness, and Major Depression Treated with Selective Serotonin Uptake Inhibitors." *Advances in Therapy* 23: 646–654.

Kramer, M. S., et al. (2004). "Demonstration of the Efficacy and Safety of a Novel Substance P (NK$_1$) Receptor Antagonist in Major Depression." *Neuropsychopharmacology* 29: 385–392.

Kroenke, K., et al. (2001). "Similar Effectiveness of Paroxetine, Fluoxetine, and Sertraline in Primary Care: A Randomized Trial." *Journal of the American Medical Association* 286: 2947–2955.

Kuipers, S. D., and C. R. Bramham (2006). "Brain-Derived Neurotrophic Factor Mechanisms and Function in Adult Synaptic Plasticity: New Insights and Implications for Therapy." *Current Opinion in Drug Discovery Development* 9: 580–586.

Lane, R., and D. Baldwin. (1997). "Selective Serotonin Reuptake Inhibitor-Induced Serotonin Syndrome: Review." *Journal of Clinical Psychopharmacology* 17: 208–221.

Levinson-Castiel, R., et al. (2006). "Neonatal Abstinence Syndrome After In Utero Exposure to Selective Serotonin Reuptake Inhibitors in Term Infants." *Archives of Pediatrics & Adolescent Medicine* 160: 173–176.

Loo, H., et al. (2001). "Efficacy and Safety of Tianeptine in the Treatment of Depressive Disorders in Comparison with Fluoxetine." *Human Psychopharmacology* 16: S31–S38.

Louik, C., et al. (2007). "First-Trimester Use of Selective Serotonin-Reuptake Inhibitors and the Risk of Birth Defects." *New England Journal of Medicine* 356: 2675–2683.

Mahaney, P. E., et al. (2006). "Synthesis and Activity of a New Class of Dual Acting Norepinephrine and Serotonin Reuptake Inhibitors: 3-(1H-Indol-1-yl)-3-Arylpropan-1-Amines." *Bioorganic and Medicinal Chemistry* 14: 8455–8466.

Malberg, J. E., and J. A. Blendy. (2005). "Antidepressant Action: To the Nucleus and Beyond." *Trends in Pharmacological Sciences* 26: 631–638.

Mamalakis, et al. (2006). "Depression and Serum Adiponectin and Adipose Omega-3 and Omega-6 Fatty Acids in Adolescents." *Pharmacology, Biochemistry and Behavior* 85: 474–479.

Marangell, L. B., et al. (2003). "A Double-Blind, Placebo-Controlled Study of the Omega-3 Fatty Acid Docosahexaenoic Acid in the Treatment of Major Depression." *American Journal of Psychiatry* 160: 996–998.

McGrath, P. J., et al., (2006). "Tranylcypromine Versus Venlafaxine Plus Mirtazepine Following Three Failed Antidepressant Medication Trials for Depression: A STAR*D Report." *American Journal of Psychiatry* 163: 1531–1541.

Montgomery, S. A. (2006). "Major Depressive Disorders: Clinical Efficacy and Tolerability of Agomelatine, a New Melatonergic Agonist." *European Neuropsychopharmacology* 16 Supplement 5: S633–S638.

Montgomery, S. A., et al. (2006). "Efficacy and Safety of 30 mg/d and 45 mg/d Nemifitide Compared to Placebo in Major Depressive Disorder." *International Journal of Neuropsychopharmacology* 9: 517–528.

Nair, A., and V. A. Vaidya (2006). "CyclicAMP Response Element Binding Protein and Brain-Derived Neurotrophic Factor: Molecules That Modulate Our Mood?" *Journal of Bioscience* 31: 423–434.

Nelson, J. C., et al. (2006). "Mirtazepine Orally Disintegrating Tablets in Depressed Nursing Home Residents 85 Years of Age and Older." *International Journal of Geriatric Psychiatry* 21: 898–901.

Nemets, B., et al. (2002). "Addition of Omega-3 Fatty Acid to Maintenance Medication Treatment for Recurrent Unipolar Depressive Disorder." *American Journal of Psychiatry* 159: 477–479.

Nickel, T., et al. (2003). "Clinical and Neurobiological Effects of Tianeptine and Paroxetine in Major Depression." *Journal of Clinical Psychopharmacology* 23: 155–168.

Nierenberg, A. A., et al. (2006). "A Comparison of Lithium and T_3 Augmentation Following Two Failed Medication Treatments for Depression: A STAR*D Report." *American Journal of Psychiatry* 163: 1519–1530.

Nieuwstraten, C., et al. (2006). "Systematic Overview of Drug Interactions with Antidepressant Medications." *Canadian Journal of Psychiatry* 51: 300–316.

Norton, P. A., et al. (2002). "Duloxetine Versus Placebo in the Treatment of Stress Urinary Incontinence." *American Journal of Obstetrics and Gynecology* 187: 40–48.

Nurnberg, H. G., et al. (2001). "Efficacy of Sildenafil Citrate for the Treatment of Erectile Dysfunction in Men Taking Serotonin Reuptake Inhibitors." *American Journal of Psychiatry* 158: 1926–1928.

Oberlander, T. F., et al. (2006). "Neonatal Outcomes After Prenatal Exposure to Selective Serotonin Reuptake Inhibitor Antidepressants and Maternal Depression Using Population-Based Linked Health Data." *Archives of General Psychiatry* 63: 898–906.

Oberlander, T. F., et al. (2007). "Externalizing and Attentional Behaviors in Children of Depressed Mothers Treated with a Selective Serotonin Reuptake Inhibitor Antidepressant During Pregnancy." *Archives of Pediatrics and Adolescent Medicine* 161: 22–29.

Okumura, K., and T. A. Furukawa (2006). "Remission Rates with Milnacipran 100 mg/day and 150 mg/day in the Long-Term Treatment of Major Depression." *Clinical Drug Investigation* 26: 135–142.

Papakostas, G. I., et al. (2007). "Augmentation of Antidepressants with Atypical Antipsychotic Medications for Treatment-Resistant Major Depressive Disorder: A Meta-Analysis." *Journal of Clinical Psychiatry.* In press.

Parker, G. P., et al. (2006). "Omega-3 Fatty Acids and Mood Disorders." *American Journal of Psychiatry* 163: 969–978.

Pearlson, T., et al. (2003). "Recurrence of Symptoms of Premenstrual Dysphoric Disorder After the Cessation of Luteal-Phase Fluoxetine Treatment." *Journal of Obstetrics and Gynecology* 188: 887–895.

Peet, M., and D. F. Horrobin (2002). "A Dose-Ranging Study of the Effects of Ethyl-Eicosapentaenoate in Patients with Ongoing Depression Despite Apparently Adequate Treatment with Standard Drugs." *Archives of General Psychiatry* 59: 913–919.

Quitkin, F. M., et al. (2003). "When Should a Trial of Fluoxetine for Major Depression Be Declared Failed?" *American Journal of Psychiatry* 160: 734–740.

Rabkin, J. G., et al. (2006). "Placebo-Controlled Trial of Dehydroepiandrosterone (DHEA) for Treatment of Nonmajor Depression in Patients With HIV/AIDS." *American Journal of Psychiatry* 163: 59–66.

Ravindran, A. V., et al. (2000). "Treatment of Dysthymia with Sertraline: A Double-Blind, Placebo-Controlled Trial in Dysthymic Patients Without Major Depression." *Journal of Clinical Psychiatry* 61: 821–827.

Richelson, E. (2003). "Interactions of Antidepressants with Neurotransmitter Transporters and Receptors and Their Clinical Relevance." *Journal of Clinical Psychiatry* 64, Supplement 13: 5–12.

Rocha, F., and C. Hara (2003). "Lamotrigine Augmentation in Unipolar Depression." *International Clinical Psychopharmacology* 18: 97–99.

Rooks, D. S. (2007). "Fibromyalgia Treatment Update." *Current Opinions in Rheumatology* 19: 111–117.

Ruhé, H. G., et al. (2006). "Switching Antidepressants After a First Selective Serotonin Reuptake Inhibitor in Major Depressive Disorder." *Journal of Clinical Psychiatry* 67: 1836–1855.

Rush, A. J., et al. (2006a). "Acute and Longer-Term Outcomes in Depressed Outpatients Requiring One or Several Treatment Steps: A STAR*D Report." *American Journal of Psychiatry* 163: 1905–1917.

Rush, A. J., et al. (2006b). "Bupropion-SR, Sertraline, or Venlafaxine-XR After Failure of SSRIs for Depression." *New England Journal of Medicine* 354: 1231–1242.

Rynn, M. et al. (2007). "Efficacy and Safety of Duloxetine in the Treatment of Generalized Anxiety Disorder: A Flexible-Dose, Progressive-Titration, Placebo-Controlled Trial." *Depression and Anxiety* 24: in press.

Saarelainen, T., et al. (2003). "Activation of the TrkB Neurotrophin Receptor Is Induced by Antidepressant Drugs and Is Required for Antidepressant-Induced Behavioral Effects." *Journal of Neuroscience* 23: 349–357.

Salome, N., et al. (2006). "Selective Blockade of NK2 or NK3 Receptors Produces Anxiolytic- and Antidepressant-like Effects in Gerbils." *Pharmacology, Biochemistry, and Behavior* 83: 533–539.

Schatzberg, A. F., et al. (1997). "Serotonin Reuptake Inhibitor Discontinuation Syndrome: A Hypothetical Definition." *Journal of Clinical Psychiatry* 58, Supplement 7: 5–10. (See also the other articles in Supplement 7.)

Schechter, L. E., et al. (2005). "Innovative Approaches for the Development of Antidepressant Drugs: Current and Future Strategies." *NeuroRx: Journal of the American Society for Experimental NeuroTherapeutics* 2: 590–611.

Schmidt, M. E., et al. (2000). "The Efficacy and Safety of a New Enteric-Coated Formulation of Fluoxetine Given Once Weekly During the Continuation Treatment of Major Depressive Disorder." *Journal of Clinical Psychiatry* 61: 851–857.

Schmidt, P. J., et al. (2005). "Dehydroepiandrosterone Monotherapy in Mid-Life Onset Major and Minor Depression." *Archives of General Psychiatry* 62: 154–162.

Schonfeldt-Lecuona, C., et al. (2006). "Bupropion Augmentation in the Treatment of Chronic Fatigue Syndrome with Coexistent Major Depression Episode." *Pharmacopsychiatry* 39: 152–154.

Seidman, S. N., et al. (2001). "Treatment of Erectile Dysfunction in Men with Depressive Symptoms: Results of a Placebo-Controlled Trial with Sildenafil Citrate." *American Journal of Psychiatry* 158: 1623–1630.

Shakesby, A. C., et al. (2002). "Overcoming the Effects of Stress on Synaptic Plasticity in the Rat Hippocampus: Rapid Actions of Serotoninergic and Antidepressant Agents." *Journal of Neuroscience* 22: 3638–3644.

Shamlian, N., and Cole, M. G. (2006). "Androgen Treatment of Depressive Symptoms in Older Men: A Systematic Review of Feasibility and Effectiveness." *Canadian Journal of Psychiatry* 51: 295–299.

Simpson, D., and Plosker, G. L. (2004). "Atomoxetine: A Review of Its Use in Adults with Attention Deficit Hyperactivity Disorder." *Drugs* 64: 205–222.

Sindrup, S. H., et al. (2005). "Antidepressants in the Treatment of Neuropathic Pain." *Basic and Clinical Pharmacology and Toxicology* 96: 399–409.

Skolnick, P., et al. (2006). "Preclinical and Clinical Pharmacology of DOV 216,303, a 'Triple' Reuptake Inhibitor." *CNS Drug Review* 12: 123–134.

Soares, C. N., and Papakostas, G. I. (2007) "Neuroendocrine-Based Treatments for Depression." *Essential Psychopharmacology*. In press.

Sontrop, J., and M. K. Campbell (2006). "Omega-3 Polyunsaturated Fatty Acids and Depression: A Review of the Evidence and a Methodological Critique." *Preventive Medicine* 42: 4–13.

Spencer, T., et al. (2004). "Nonstimulant Treatment of Adult Attention-Deficit/Hyperactivity Disorder." *Psychiatric Clinics of North America* 27: 373–383.

Stahl, S. M. (1999a). "Antidepressants: The Blue-Chip Psychotropic for the Modern Treatment of Anxiety Disorders." *Journal of Clinical Psychiatry* 60: 356–357.

Stahl, S. M. (1999b). "Mergers and Acquisitions Among Psychotropics: Antidepressant Takeover of Anxiety May Now Be Complete." *Journal of Clinical Psychiatry* 60: 282–283.

Stahl, S. M. (2003). "Mechanism of Action of Selective NRIs: Both Dopamine and Norepinephrine Increase in Prefrontal Cortex." *Journal of Clinical Psychiatry* 64: 230–231.

Stewart, W. F., et al. (2003). "Cost of Lost Productive Work Time Among U.S. Workers with Depression." *Journal of the American Medical Association* 289: 3135–3144.

Stimmel, G. L., and Gutierrez, M. A. (2006). "Sexual Dysfunction and Psychotropic Medications." *CNS Spectrum* 8, Supplement 9: 24–30.

Stoll, A. (2001). *The Omega-3 Connection*. New York: Simon & Schuster.

Suhara, T., et al. (2003). "High Levels of Serotonin Transporter Occupancy with Low-Dose Clomipramine in Comparative Occupancy Study with Fluvoxamine Using Positron Emission Tomography." *Archives of General Psychiatry* 60: 386–391.

Tella, S. R., et al. (1997). "Differential Regulation of Dopamine Transporter After Chronic Self-Admininstration of Bupropion and Nomifensine." *Journal of Pharmacology and Experimental Therapeutics* 281: 508–518.

Thase, M. E., et al. (2006). "A Double-Blind Comparison Between Bupropion XL and Venlafaxine XR: Sexual Functioning, Antidepressant Efficacy, and Tolerability." *Journal of Clinical Psychopharmacology* 26: 482–488.

Thase, M. E., et al. (2007). "Cognitive Therapy Versus Medication in Augmentation and Switch Strategies as Second-Step Treatments: A STAR*D Report." *American Journal of Psychiatry* 164: 739–752.

Thomas, R. M., and Peterson, D. A. (2003). "A Neurogenic Theory of Depression Gains Momentum." *Molecular Interventions* 3: 441–444.

Tran, P. V., et al. (2003). "Dual Monoamine Modulation for Improved Treatment of Major Depressive Disorder." *Journal of Clinical Psychopharmacology* 23: 78–86.

Trivedi, M. H., et al. (2006a). Evaluation of Outcomes with Citalopram for Depression Using Measurement-Based Care in STAR*D: Implications for Clinical Practice." *American Journal of Psychiatry* 163: 28–40.

Trivedi, M. H., et al. (2006b). "Medication Augmentation After the Failure of SSRIs for Depression." *New England Journal of Medicine* 354: 1243–1252.

Wadsworth, E. J., et al. (2005). "SSRIs and Cognitive Performance in a Working Sample." *Human Psychopharmacology* 8: 561–572.

West, R. (2003). "Bupropion SR for Smoking Cessation." *Expert Opinions in Pharmacotherapy* 4: 533–540.

Wolkowitz, O. M., et al. (1999). "Double-Blind Treatment of Major Depression with Dehydroepiandrosterone." *American Journal of Psychiatry* 156: 646–649.

World Health Organization (2007). *World Health Statistics 2007*, p. 16. Geneva: WHO Press.

Zanarini, M., and F. Frankenburg (2003). "Omega-3 Fatty Acid Treatment of Women with Borderline Personality Disorder: A Double-Blind, Placebo-Controlled Pilot Study." *American Journal of Psychiatry* 160: 167–169.

Zisook, S., et al. (2001). "Bupropion Sustained Release for Bereavement: Results of an Open Trial." *Journal of Clinical Psychiatry* 62: 227–230.

Zupancic, M., and C. Guilleminault (2006). "Agomelatine: A Preliminary Review of a New Antidepressant." *CNS Drugs* 20: 981–992.

Chapter 8

Drugs Used to Treat Bipolar Disorder

Bipolar Disorder

Bipolar disorder (manic-depressive disorder) is one of the 10 most disabling conditions in the world, with a prevalence of about 1 percent across all populations, regardless of nationality, race, or socioeconomic status. People who have the disorder lose many years of healthy functioning, in which their livelihood, marriage, social relationships, and even life, may be destroyed. The course of the illness is episodic, with alternating periods of mania and/or depression and intervening periods of at least some degree of remission. Although it may appear in childhood or adolescence, the diagnosis is difficult, and it is still being debated (Harris, 2005; Pavuluri et al., 2005; Schapiro, 2005; Chang et al., 2006). Generally, onset occurs in the third decade or later, and a significant delay often occurs between the appearance of symptoms and a correct diagnosis and treatment. Even among patients who are screened, only about 20 percent with bipolar disorder initially receive the correct diagnosis; 31 percent are diagnosed with unipolar depression and 49 percent receive no diagnosis. Most patients experience several episodes during the course of their lives and the risk of recurrence is always present.

A patient with bipolar disorder (BD) may be diagnosed with any of several subtypes of the disorder. The traditional subtype, bipolar I, includes at least one episode of full-blown mania with or without an episode of major depression. The disorder is classified as bipolar II if the manic episode is less severe, or "hypomanic," and episodes of major depression also occur. A patient is said to be a "rapid cycler" if at least four illness episodes occur in a 12-month period. Several other bipolar subtypes have been described, exhibiting varying degrees of severity in recurrent mood swings between depression and elation. Together, the variants bring the prevalence of all bipolar disorders to more than 3 percent of U.S. residents (Kupfer, 2005).

Despite intensive care and treatment, outpatients with bipolar disorder have a considerable degree of illness-related morbidity, including a threefold greater amount of time spent depressed than time spent manic (Post et al., 2003, 2005). Moreover, there is a high rate of mortality (Kupfer, 2005); one of every four or five untreated or inadequately treated patients commits suicide during the course of the illness, a rate ten times that of the general population (Osby et al., 2001). Other predictors of mortality in bipolar patients include male gender, history of alcoholism, and poor occupational status before the index episode, as well as a history of previous episodes, psychotic features, symptoms of depression during the index manic episode (termed "mixed mania"), and residual affective symptoms between episodes.

Diagnostic and Treatment Issues

Similar to unipolar depression, the symptoms of bipolar depression, as described by patients, include (in decreasing order of prevalence), sadness, insomnia, feelings of worthlessness, loss of energy and ability to concentrate, inability to enjoy everyday activities, thoughts of death and suicide, and an inability to function. Manic symptoms include various aspects of behavioral and physiological hyperactivity, such as erratic sleep, increased sexual interest, emotional elation and racing thoughts, increased physical activity, impulsiveness, poor judgment, and reckless and aggressive behavior. Comorbid substance abuse affects at least 60 percent of bipolar I and 50 percent of bipolar II patients, which may reflect attempts at self-medication and efforts at symptom relief.

Although a patient with bipolar disorder may present initially with either mania or depression, most patients seek treatment for depression. As a result, many are incorrectly diagnosed with unipolar depression and consequently receive inappropriate treatment with antidepressants alone. Unfortunately, while antidepressants can be effective against depressive symptomatology, they may induce or trigger a manic episode, referred to as a "switch," or "flip," resulting in serious adverse consequences for the patient. Recently, antidepressant-associated hypomania has been proposed as a third form of the disorder, bipolar III. Therefore, the administration or addition of a *mood stabilizer* is the best pharmacological treatment for bipolar depression (Bauer and Mitchner, 2004;

Mundo et al., 2006). Unfortunately, even combinations may still increase the risk of a manic flip, and the risk varies among the different antidepressants (Leverich et al., 2006).

Obviously, because of these significant differences in recommended pharmacological treatment, it is important to be able to differentiate between unipolar and bipolar depression. Unfortunately, the distinction is not always easy to make. Nevertheless, some clinical features have been proposed to help distinguish between major depressive disorder (unipolar depression) and bipolar depression (Perlis et al., 2006b). Unipolar depression usually develops after the age of 25 years, and may be preceded by an extended period of gradually worsening symptoms. Usually, unipolar patients have no history of mania or hypomania. In contrast, bipolar depression typically occurs before the age of 25 years, with a more abrupt onset of hours or days, and may be periodic or seasonal. Bipolar disorder is highly heritable and may run in families, which makes a thorough family history a crucial component of the diagnosis. Similarly, a personal history of disruptive behavioral patterns or evidence of mania, hypomania, increased energy, and decreased need for sleep may suggest a bipolar diagnosis, as would treatment-emergent mania or hypomania during antidepressant monotherapy.

Ideally, drugs identified as mood stabilizers should be able to do the following:

- Reduce acute symptoms of mania and depression, including symptoms presenting in mixed states
- Not cause a switch from depression to mania or mania to depression
- Prevent future relapses into mania or mixed or depressive episodes (Keck and Susman, 2003)

Medications are currently available to treat acute manic/mixed states and acute bipolar depression and for the prophylactic prevention of recurrent episodes. However, the quality of evidence for efficacy in each of these phases differs among the putative mood stabilizers. Table 8.1 summarizes the relative effectiveness of the available agents for each phase (see also Bauer, 2005). These drugs include the lithium ion, several anticonvulsant "neuromodulators," second-generation antipsychotics (SGAs), and a dietary supplement, the omega-3 fatty acids (Parker et al., 2006a). The use of these medications for treating bipolar disorder is discussed in this chapter; the antipsychotics are further discussed in Chapter 9.

The classic mood stabilizer is *lithium*. Although this ion may effectively control manic symptoms and reduce the recurrence of both manic and depressive episodes, its bothersome and serious side

TABLE 8.1 Quality of Evidence for the Use of Mood Stabilizers in Bipolar Disorder

A Double-blind placebo-controlled trials with adequate samples
B Double-blind comparator studies with adequate samples
C Open trials with adequate samples
D Uncontrolled observation or controlled study with ambiguous result
E No published evidence
F Available evidence negative

	Acute mania/Mixed	Mood stabilizer prophylaxis	Acute bipolar depression
Lithium	A+	A+	A
Valproic acid	A+	A−	D
Carbamazepine	A	B−	D
Lamotrigine	F	A+	A
Gabapentin	F	E	D
Topiramate	D	E	D
Aripiprazole	A	E	E
Haloperidol	A	E	E
Olanzapine	A+	E	A
Risperidone	A	E	D
Quetiapine	A	E	E
Ziprasidone	A	E	E
Omega-3	E	D	E

A+ is reserved for those instances when fewer than 40 studies have been reported and more than one double-blind placebo-controlled study supports the same finding. A− indicates positive outcomes on some but not all relevant measures. From G. S. Sachs, "Decision Tree for the Treatment of Bipolar Disorder," *Journal of Clinical Psychiatry* 64, Supplement 8 (2003), p. 37.

effects have necessitated a search for equally effective, safer, and more tolerable agents. Today, it is recognized that combination treatment with two or more medications is often required (Fawcett, 2003; Mondimore et al., 2003; Stahl 2004), preferably with adjunctive psychosocial interventions.

In 1996, the American Psychiatric Association published its first clinical practice guideline for the treatment of patients with bipolar disorder. A revision was published in 2002, emphasizing that the major objectives of intervention are to treat acute manic episodes and to reduce their frequency of recurrence. The most recent update was the result of a consensus conference in May of 2004, which reinforced the general treatment goals of (1) symptomatic remission, (2) full return of psychosocial functioning, and (3) prevention of relapses and recurrences (Suppes et al., 2005).

Drug therapy is the cornerstone of bipolar disorder treatment. For less severe acute manic episodes, first-line treatment is monotherapy with lithium, valproate (divalproex) or a second-generation antipsychotic (Suppes et al., 2005). The same guidelines apply for mixed episodes, except that lithium is less efficacious for that condition. For more severe situations, the combination of either lithium or valproate (or another neuromodulator anticonvulsant) and an antipsychotic is recommended.

First-line treatment of less severe acute bipolar depression is mono-therapy with the "third-generation" neuromodulator/anticonvulsant lamotrigine, with the addition of an antimanic agent if there is a history of severe mania. For maintenance treatment, regardless of whether the most recent episode was manic, depressed, or mixed, it is acceptable to stay on the acute-phase medication if it is well tolerated. However, if additional options are necessary, antipsychotics are recommended when the most recent episode is manic or mixed; if the most recent episode is depressed, either lithium or the combination of an antimanic and an antidepressant may be helpful. In 2004 a new combination product was approved for treating bipolar depression. It is trade-named Symbyax, and it contains the antipsychotic olanzapine (for mania; Chapter 9) and the antidepressant fluoxetine (for depression; Chapter 7). The treatment of bipolar disorder in children and adolescents is discussed in Chapter 10.

Pathophysiology and Mechanisms of Drug Action

Identifying the therapeutic action of mood stabilizers in the treatment of bipolar disorder has been particularly challenging, and as yet, there is no unifying hypothesis. It is difficult to understand how any single drug class can reduce symptoms of both mania and depression, and it has proven difficult to find a mechanism among the relevant drug classes that possesses this dual therapeutic efficacy. The mechanism would need to do the following:

- Occur at therapeutic drug concentrations
- Occur only after chronic exposure
- Involve pathways relevant to mood regulation

It might also need to be linked to common genes.

Mood stabilizers may have some neurobiological actions in common with antidepressants. This conclusion comes from growing evidence of similarities between the damaging effects of depression and bipolar disorder on the brain. As discussed in Chapter 7, severe depression is associated with an increase in neuronal vulnerability to injury or trauma, including stress, which may damage neural structures and produce functional impairment. Imaging and postmortem studies have shown similar types of structural changes in the brain of patients diagnosed with bipolar disorder. As in major depressive disorder, reductions in the volume of the prefrontal cortex and hippocampus are significant (Bertolino et al., 2003), the number of neurons and glial cells in the prefrontal cortex is decreased, and levels of the neurochemical N-acetyl-aspartate, which is considered a marker of neuronal "health," are lower (Coyle and Duman, 2003; Zarate et al., 2005).

Like antidepressants, mood stabilizers may reverse some of the impairments in brain structure and BDNF levels (Figure 8.1), reversals that could be relevant to the therapeutic benefit of mood stabilizers in bipolar disorder. In laboratory models, lithium was found to protect neurons against a variety of toxic agents and to promote the growth of neuronal processes; in the human brain, lithium increases levels of N-acetyl-aspartate and gray matter volume. However, in spite of their common neuroprotective effects, no universal mechanism has yet been identified to account for the therapeutic and neurobiological similarities between antidepressants and mood stabilizers. While antidepressants and antipsychotics have some common effects on neurotransmitter receptors in the brain (which could be relevant to their common antidepressant efficacy; Yatham et al., 2005), neither lithium nor the "neuromodulatory" anticonvulsants share these mechanisms of action. That is, unlike antidepressants and antipsychotics, lithium and many of the anticonvulsants do not exert their primary effect at neuronal

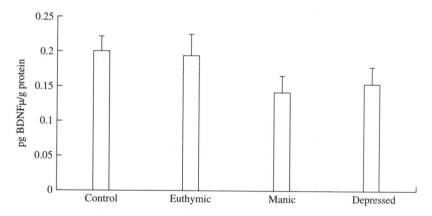

FIGURE 8.1 Serum BDNF levels in BD patients and healthy controls. Measurement is picograms of BDNF protein per microgram of total serum protein. [From A. B. M. Cunha et al., "Serum Brain-Derived Neurotrophic Factor Is Decreased in Bipolar Disorder During Depressive and Manic Episodes," *Neuroscience Letters* 398 (2006), p. 216.].

synapses. Rather, these drugs seem to act intracellularly to produce changes that "stabilize" neuronal membranes.

Currently, the most extensively studied putative mechanisms of mood stabilizers are the second- and third-messenger systems, that is, the intracellular biochemical processes produced by activation of G-protein-coupled receptors (see Figure 2.8). It has already been established that lithium, valproate, and carbamazepine interact with various enzymes involved in these intracellular signaling pathways. Although individual drugs may interact at different sites within the neurochemical systems, they may all ultimately produce some final common effect that is responsible for their clinical efficacy in bipolar disorder (Gould et al., 2004).[1] "Thus, the mood stabilizers may act to restore the balance among aberrant signaling pathways in specific areas of the brain and prevent degeneration" (Brunello, 2004).

STEP-BD Study

As with the antidepressants, progress is also being made in determining the best approach for clinical management of bipolar illness. To provide therapeutic guidelines for practitioners, a large-scale, federally funded trial, called the STEP-BD study, compared pharmacological treatments for bipolar disorder. The study was recently completed.

STEP-BD stands for Systematic Treatment Enhancement Program for Bipolar Disorder, and the study was one of the first of several NIMH-funded studies designed to determine the real-world effectiveness of the major psychiatric drug classes. Like the companion studies for depression (the STAR*D trial, discussed in Chapter 7) and schizophrenia (the CATIE trial, discussed in Chapter 9), this investigation involved large numbers of typical patients and used few exclusion criteria in an effort to make the results more generalizable for treatment in standard clinical practice.

To be enrolled at one of the 20 sites in the United States, patients had to meet the criteria for any type or subtype of bipolar disorder. After study entry, patients were assigned a "STEP-BD-certified" psychiatrist, who received 20 hours of training in standard care procedures

---

[1]One possibility is suggested by the fact that lithium and valproate, like antidepressants (as discussed in Chapter 7), increase the levels of proteins, such as cAMP response-element binding protein (CREB), which, in turn, activates genes that produce additional proteins (in particular, one called bcl-2) and a neurotrophic factor (brain-derived neurotrophic factor—BDNF) that are known to protect neurons from the toxic effects of injury or trauma. Because of this, the two drugs are sometimes referred to as "neuroprotective" agents. Such a broad, general effect on neuronal health may be the reason these drugs are also useful in the management of other clinical conditions, such as aggressive disorders, pain, and so on, discussed later in this chapter.

in the treatment of bipolar disorder. The guidelines for the procedures were written by a group of experts who identified nine separate decision points, corresponding to nine typical clinical situations. At each point there is a specified "menu of reasonable choices" that provides recommendations rather than rigid algorithms for appropriate, standard care. For the most part, participants were managed with an optimized mood stabilizer regimen (lithium, valproate, combined lithium and valproate, or carbamazepine) plus either one or two antidepressants. Additionally, patients were systematically monitored for suicidal symptoms. Patients were seen every three months for the first year, then every six months thereafter, and were encouraged to stay in the trial for five years.

The study began in 1998, and data collection from the final total of 4360 patients was completed on September 30, 2005. Results are gradually being analyzed and several major findings have already been published. One of the first papers (Perlis et al., 2006c) described the results in a subset of 1469 patients who had participated for at least two years (Figure 8.2). The researchers found that only 58.4 percent (858 patients) of this group achieved recovery (defined

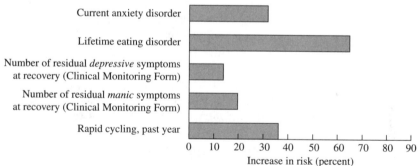

Depressive recurrence

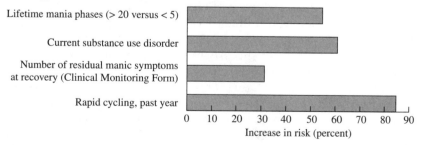

Manic/hypomanic/mixed recurrence

FIGURE 8.2 Factors associated with recurrence of bipolar disorder as determined from the STEP-BD study. [From R. H. Perlis et al. (2006c).].

as having only two symptoms of the disorder for at least 8 weeks). During the two-year follow-up period, almost half of this group, 48.5 percent or 416 patients, had a recurrence at some point, more commonly to a depressive episode (72 percent) than to a manic, hypomanic, or mixed episode (28 percent). Recurrence was most likely in those who had residual symptoms at recovery or had an additional psychiatric illness (for example, anxiety, an eating disorder, or substance abuse).

In March 2007, Sachs and coworkers published results of another STEP-BD trial. In this trial, patients received a mood stabilizer (lithium, valproate, carbamazepine or another FDA-approved agent) combined with either an antidepressant (bupropion or paroxetine) ($n = 179$) or placebo ($n = 187$). Subjects with bipolar I or bipolar II disorder were treated for up to 26 weeks to evaluate the effectiveness, safety, and tolerability of the adjunctive use of antidepressant medication. Unfortunately, the results showed no difference between the groups that received adjunct antidepressants and the groups that received placebo. At each criterion of response, the percent of patients in the respective groups was the same: only 23.5 percent of patients on the antidepressants and 27.3 percent of patients on placebo achieved recovery, which was defined as 8 consecutive weeks of euthymia (a normal mood). Only 17.9 percent on the antidepressant and 21.4 percent on the placebo experienced a transient remission (1 to 7 consecutive weeks of euthymia) while only 32.4 percent on antidepressant and 38 percent on placebo showed a 50 percent improvement in symptoms. The groups also did not differ in the percentage of patients who showed symptoms of switching into an episode of mood elevation (hypomania or mania): 10.1 percent on the antidepressant and 10.7 percent on placebo showed symptoms of switching. In summary, for the treatment of bipolar depression, mood-stabilizing monotherapy provided as much benefit and a comparable risk of switching as treatment with mood stabilizers combined with a standard antidepressant. Clearly, these results are disappointing and illustrate how much we have yet to achieve in the pharmacological treatment of bipolar disorder.

Patients who were treatment-resistant to the combination of a mood stabilizer and at least one antidepressant could choose to enter the next portion of the program. Each of the 66 participants who agreed was randomly assigned one of three additional agents, the anticonvulsant lamotrigine (Lamictal), the antipsychotic risperidone (Risperdal), or inositol (a sugar, which is an isomer of glucose and is normally a component of one of the second-messenger pathways). Recovery rates were 23.8 percent, 4.6 percent, and 17.4 percent, respectively, and were not statistically different from each other (perhaps because of the small number of subjects), although the relatively poor effect of the antipsychotic was unexpected (Nierenberg, et al., 2006).

One particularly important finding of the STEP-BD study was the confirmation of the notion that valproic acid may increase the risk of polycystic ovarian syndrome (PCOS). The large sample of 230 women (ages 18 to 44) made it possible to test this concern. They found PCOS symptoms (menstrual irregularities, acne, male-pattern hair loss, elevated testosterone, and excessive body hair) in 9 of 86 women (10.5 percent) on valproate compared to only 2 of 144 women on another agent (1.4 percent). These results show a clear increase in the risk of developing PCOS for women on valproic acid (Joffe, et al., 2006).

Lithium

Lithium has historically been the drug of first choice for treating bipolar disorder and reducing its rate of relapse.[2] Unfortunately, its clinical effectiveness is less than that predicted by clinical trials; relapse often occurs because of patient nonadherence to therapy. Therefore, the pharmacology of lithium and the reasons for patient noncompliance with this drug therapy must be clearly understood and alternative agents considered.

Lithium (Li+) is the lightest of the alkali metals (Figure 8.3) and shares some characteristics with sodium (Na+). In nature, lithium is abundant in some alkaline mineral spring waters. Devoid of psychotropic effects in normal people, lithium is effective in treating 60 to 80 percent of acute manic and hypomanic episodes, although in the last few years its use has declined because of limitations with regard to toxicities, side effects, compliance, and relapse.

[2]For a historical overview of lithium therapy and commentaries on lithium, see four related letters in *Archives of General Psychiatry* 54 (1997): 9–23.

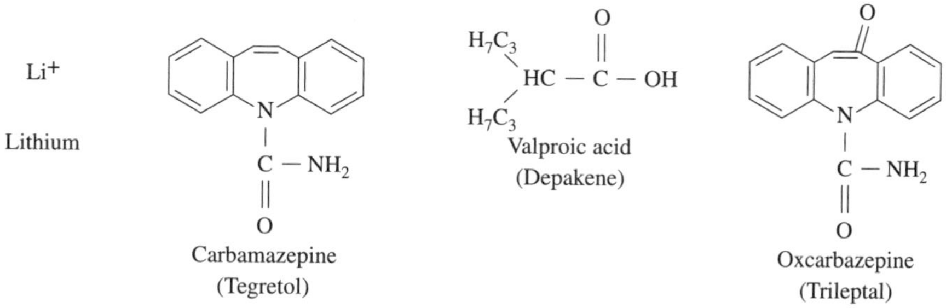

FIGURE 8.3 Drugs classically used in the treatment of bipolar disorder. Structures of newer anticonvulsants used in bipolar disorder are shown in Figure 5.4.

History

During the late 1940s, lithium chloride was recommended as a salt substitute for patients with heart disease. Wide use for this purpose resulted in cases of severe toxicity and death, causing it to be abandoned as a medicine. In 1949, however, an Australian physician, John Cade, noted that when lithium was administered to guinea pigs, the animals became lethargic. Taking an intuitive leap, Cade administered lithium to patients with acute mania and noted remarkable improvement. However, because of the earlier problems with lithium as a salt substitute, the medical community took more than 20 years to accept this agent as an effective treatment for mania. Fortunately, research in the 1970s found lithium to be clearly superior to placebo in the prophylaxis of bipolar disorder; less than a third of lithium-treated patients relapsed, compared with 80 percent of placebo-treated patients.

Many controlled studies demonstrate lithium's efficacy for acute mania, acute depressive episodes, and for maintenance treatment. Baldessarini and Tondo (2000) recommended lithium as a drug of first choice for both the treatment of acute manic attacks and the long-term management of bipolar disorder:

> We suggest that the growing American urge to abandon lithium maintenance therapy as ineffective, excessively toxic, or complicated is unwarranted. No other proposed mood-stabilizing treatment has such substantial research evidence of long-term efficacy in both type I and type II bipolar disorders, as well as yielding a substantial reduction of mortality risk. (p.190)

Lithium has therefore been referred to as the "gold standard" of bipolar treatment. Nevertheless, "real-world" evidence shows poorer outcomes than expected. One five-year study (Maj et al., 1998) reported that 28 percent of patients discontinued the drug, 38 percent experienced recurrence of the disorder even while they were taking the drug, and only 23 percent did not have recurrent episodes. Perhaps such results have led to the present situation, in which fewer clinicians are prescribing lithium in favor of neuromodulator anticonvulsants and second-generation antipsychotics.

Pharmacokinetics

Peak blood levels of lithium are reached within 3 hours of oral administration, complete absorption by 8 hours. The drug crosses the blood-brain barrier slowly and incompletely, and, although the clinical significance of the observation is unclear, there can be a twofold variation in the concentration of lithium in the brain compared with its concentration in plasma. However, the therapeutic efficacy of lithium is directly correlated with its blood level.

Lithium is not metabolized and is excreted unchanged by the kidneys, with only small amounts excreted through the skin. About half an oral dose is eliminated within 18 to 24 hours and the rest, which is taken up by the cells of the body, is excreted over the next 1 to 2 weeks. Thus, when therapy is initiated, lithium slowly accumulates over about 2 weeks until a steady state is reached, making once-daily dosing appropriate for many patients.

Lithium has a very narrow therapeutic range below which the drug is ineffective and above which side effects and toxicity are prevalent. Usually guidelines recommend about 0.8 to 1.2 milliequivalents per liter of blood (mEq/l) for acute treatment and 0.6 to 0.8 for maintenance. More adverse effects, increasing the likelihood of noncompliance, occur at levels above 1.5 mEq/l, and levels above 2.0 mEq/l are potentially lethal. Because lithium closely resembles table salt, when a patient lowers his or her salt intake or loses excessive amounts of salt, such as through sweating, lithium blood levels may rise, inadvertently producing intoxication. Consequently, patients taking lithium should avoid marked changes in sodium intake or excretion and replenish salts after excessive exercise or illness-induced dehydration.

Pharmacodynamics

The mechanism through which lithium exerts its mood-stabilizing effect is being studied in ongoing research. In therapeutic concentrations it has almost no discernible psychotropic effect in normal persons and, unlike many psychoactive drugs, does not produce sedation, depression, or euphoria. In general, a consensus is developing that the mood-stabilizing actions of lithium and other effective antibipolar agents (Li et al., 2002) may be due to effects on intracellular second-messenger signaling systems, particularly protein kinase enzyme pathways (Hashimoto et al., 2002; Kopnisky et al., 2003). Lithium, valproate, and lamotrigine are all known to inhibit the intracellular enzyme glycogen synthase kinase-3 (GSK-3). One consequence is an increase in the level of a protein, β-catenin, which promotes cell survival and stimulates axonal growth. GSK-3 is also involved in producing amyloid-β, which is a major component of the plaques that are found in Alzheimer's disease, suggesting that GSK-3 inhibitors might someday be treatments for that disorder.

As another example, Cui and coworkers (2007) recently found that lithium and valproate also protected neurons in the brains of rats (in culture) from damage due to oxidative stress. Oxidative stress occurs when intracellular enzymes cannot sufficiently reduce the levels of toxic substances produced by metabolic activity. In this environment, lithium and valproate increased the amount of the antioxidant enzyme glutathione, which plays an important role in reducing oxidative damage. Furthermore, chronic treatment with lamotrigine and carbamazepine had similar effects. Valproate also influences DNA to alter genetic processes that could protect cells from injury or toxic agents. These interactions are believed to increase levels of cellular protective proteins, such as CREB and *bcl-2* (Manji et al., 2001), and other neurotrophic substances such as BDNF (Einat and Manji, 2006; Zarate et al., 2006).

Recent evidence shows that the laboratory results may be relevant to the therapeutic effect of these drugs. It has been reported that levels of BDNF were significantly decreased in the blood serum of patients with bipolar disorder who were either manic or depressed compared to patients who were euthymic, or to healthy controls (see Figure 8.1). In July of 2007, neuroscientists reported the results of a study that compared the brains of bipolar patients on lithium with those of people without the disorder and those of bipolar patients not on lithium. They found that the volume of gray matter in the brains of the patients on lithium was as much as 15 percent more in areas that are critical for attention and controlling emotions (Bearden et al., 2007). The possibility that lithium may affect how genes are controlled means that it might also be helpful for treating genetic disorders. Evidence for this possibility was reported by researchers working with a mouse model of a lethal neurodegenerative disease called spinocerebellar ataxia type 1. Mice with this disease that were fed lithium showed improvement in coordination and memory, although lithium did not increase their life span (Watase et al., 2007).

Side Effects and Toxicity

Because of lithium's extremely narrow therapeutic range, lithium blood levels must be closely monitored. The occurrence and intensity of side effects and toxic reactions are usually related to plasma drug concentrations and involve the nervous system, the gastrointestinal (GI) tract, the kidneys, the thyroid, the cardiovascular system, and the skin.

At plasma levels of 1.5 to 2.0 mEq/l and sometimes lower, most reactions involve the GI tract, resulting in nausea, vomiting, diarrhea, and abdominal pain. Nevertheless, weight gain may be substantial during long-term therapy—up to 30 percent of patients become obese, a prevalence three times greater than in the general population (Elmslie et al., 2000; Chengappa et al., 2002)—which can profoundly affect compliance (Keck and McElroy, 2003).

Chronic lithium treatment may enlarge the thyroid, resulting in a goiter. Rashes and acne are common. As many as 60 percent of patients on lithium may experience increased thirst, water intake, and urine output (due to an impairment of renal concentrating ability). Although kidney function should be assessed periodically, permanent damage is rare.

Neurological side effects include a slight tremor, lethargy, impaired concentration, dizziness, slurred speech, ataxia, muscle weakness, and nystagmus (uncontrollable, jerky eye movements in any direction). Lithium-induced tremor is very common, and more than 30 percent of patients report this reaction even at therapeutic doses of 0.6 to 1.2 mEq/l. A hypothyroid condition may develop, and enlargement of the gland can occur at normal doses. Adverse effects on memory and cognition may be reported, and patients often complain of memory problems. Consistent with these effects, some researchers found improvements in motor performance, cognition, and creative ability after lithium withdrawal. Severe cognitive deficits are seen with lithium intoxication.

At plasma lithium levels above 2.0 mEq/l, more severe side effects include fatigue, muscle weakness, slurred speech, and worsening tremors. Thyroid gland function becomes more depressed and the gland may enlarge further, resulting in goiter. Muscle fasciculations, abnormal motor movements, psychosis, and stupor may occur. Above 2.5 mEq/l, toxic symptoms include muscle rigidity, coma, renal failure, cardiac arrhythmias, and death.

Treatment of poisoning or overdose is nonspecific; there is no antidote to lithium. Usually drug administration is stopped and sodium-containing fluids are infused immediately. If toxic signs are serious, hemodialysis, gastric lavage, diuretic therapy, antiepileptic medication, and other supports may be needed. Complete recovery may be prolonged, with full return of renal and neurological function taking weeks or months.

Substance Abuse

More than 55 percent of bipolar patients have a history of substance abuse, including alcohol (82 percent), cocaine (30 percent), marijuana (29 percent), sedatives or amphetamines (21 percent), and opioids (13 percent). In some patients the drug abuse preceded the first bipolar episode, and in others it developed afterward (Tohen et al., 1998). In either case, it may, at least initially, represent an attempt at self-medication for the symptoms accompanying the affective disorder. Regardless, comorbidity complicates treatment outcome and needs to be addressed during therapy.

Effects in Pregnancy

In general, lithium is not advised during pregnancy, particularly in the first trimester, as the risk of fetal malformation of the cardiovascular system is increased (Ernst and Goldberg, 2002). In particular, the tricuspid valve of the heart is at risk of a malformation. If mood stabilization is necessary during pregnancy, other agents (such as lamotrigine) are preferred, if possible. When a pregnant woman is on lithium therapy, the drug should be discontinued several days before delivery because (1) when the water breaks, acute dehydration will quickly increase lithium to toxic levels and (2) the newborn will have difficulty excreting the drug. On the other hand, it is important for the mother to restart her lithium within 24 hours of delivery to reduce the risk of relapse.

Viguera and coworkers (2000) addressed this issue in a study of 42 pregnant and 59 nonpregnant women with bipolar disorder and reported that discontinuation of lithium during pregnancy was followed by a recurrence rate similar to that of nonpregnant women. However, following delivery, there was a threefold increase in recurrence in postpartum women compared with nonpregnant women.

Breast-feeding is contraindicated during lithium therapy because lithium passes easily into breast milk, with levels approaching one-third to one-half of that in plasma, and infant levels are about equivalent to milk levels (Viguera et al., 2002). If mood-stabilizing therapy is necessary during breast-feeding, valproic acid is recommended because only about 1 to 3 percent of maternal levels reaches the infant (Piontek et al., 2000). Less information exists on the effects of infant exposure to lamotrigine (Lamictal) and topiramate (Topamax). Yonkers and coworkers (2004) review complications involved in medicating pregnant bipolar patients.

Noncompliance

Noncompliance is associated with significant morbidity, recurrent manic episodes, and greatly increased suicide risk. Nevertheless, up to 50 percent of patients on lithium stop taking the drug against medical advice. Some years ago it was felt that discontinuation of lithium treatment would result in treatment resistance when therapy was resumed, but this result does not appear to be the case.

Noncompliance seems to result primarily from intolerance of side effects, particularly memory impairment and cognitive slowing, weight gain, and the subjective feeling of reduced energy and productivity. Other reasons include missing the manic "highs," belief that the disorder has resolved and the drug is unnecessary, and feelings of stigmatism in having a psychiatric illness.

Baldessarini and coworkers (1999) reported that lithium therapy reduced suicidal behaviors in 77 percent of bipolar patients. Unfortunately, when patients stopped taking the drug, the rate of suicide attempts increased fourteenfold and the rate of completed suicides thirteenfold. The prophylactic effect of lithium was confirmed by Cipriani and coworkers (2005), who reported that lithium was effective in the prevention of suicide, deliberate self-harm, and death from all causes in patients with mood disorders. It should be appreciated that reduction of suicidal behavior occurs independently of lithium's effect on mood. There is growing evidence for the effectiveness of lithium as an antisuicide agent, even when used as an adjunct medication, in any situation in which suicide is a concern (Baldessarini et al., 2006).

Combination Therapy

Combination therapy—often lithium plus an antiepileptic or antipsychotic drug—can provide both greater therapeutic efficacy and better protection against relapse than lithium therapy alone. In fact, combination therapy has become the rule rather than the exception (Geddes et al., 2004), with lithium most effective for mania, for augmenting antidepressant efficacy in refractory patients (Bauer et al., 2000), and for maintenance; and an anticonvulsant such as lamotrigine often helpful against bipolar depression as well as mania (Goodwin et al., 2004).

"Neuromodulator" Anticonvulsant Mood Stabilizers

Only about 60 to 70 percent of patients with bipolar disorder can be adequately controlled by lithium alone, both for maintenance and for relapse prevention; and lithium is even less effective in controlling episodes of rapid-cycling mania. Therefore, there is a need for alternative agents effective in patients who are treatment-refractory, noncompliant with therapy, or intolerant of lithium's side effects. One alternative is anticonvulsants.

The basic pharmacology of the anticonvulsants was elucidated in Chapter 5. However, the variety of disorders for which these drugs are now used is much broader than their original indication for epilepsy. Their use in alcohol detoxification and relapse prevention is described in Chapter 4; Chapter 7 describes their use in the treatment of anxiety disorders (Stahl, 2004) and the control of emotional outbursts in such disorders as PTSD; Chapter 10 describes their use in treating aggressive and explosive behavioral disorders in children and adolescents. These applications, as well as their use in treating borderline personality disorder, are also summarized later in this chapter.

Such diversity of action and clinical utility obviously argues for more than an "anticonvulsant" action against epileptic seizures. Treating people afflicted with this variety of disorders with an antiepileptic drug may give the wrong impression that somehow they are "epileptic." To avoid this misconception, we introduce the broader term *neuromodulator* (to be used interchangeably with *anticonvulsant*), reflecting the diverse clinical applications of these agents.

First-generation anticonvulsants included phenobarbital, other barbiturates, and phenytoin and derivatives of phenytoin, none of which were useful in treating bipolar illness.[3] Second-generation anticonvulsants used included valproic acid (Divalproex, Depakote), and carbamazepine (Tegretol), which have significant side effects that limit their use.

In particular, many of the antiepileptic drugs (AEDs) produce birth defects. However, there is great variability among reports. This variability may be because the baseline rate of all major congenital anomalies in newborns in the U.S. population is between 2 and 4 percent (Montouris, 2005) and because epilepsy per se is associated with an increased risk of such anomalies (Perucca, 2005). Nevertheless, during the late 1990s the risk of malformations in infants exposed to valproate and carbamazapine was determined to be two to three times higher than in the general population. The North American Antiepileptic Drug (NAEED) Pregnancy Registry showed that malformations were four times more common in infants exposed to valproate than to all other anticonvulsant monotherapies combined (Ward and Wisner, 2007). There is also agreement that the magnitude of the risk increases in offspring exposed to polypharmacy (Perucca, 2005).

The most common congenital malformations from anticonvulsants are the same as the malformations in the general population, for example, heart defects, club foot, and cleft palate. The neural tube defect of spina bifida is the only malformation associated with specific agents. It is more common with valproate (1 to 5 percent of exposed infants) and carbamazepine (0.5 to 1 percent). Maternal folate supplementation has been postulated to reduce the risk of neural tube defects, but risk reduction has not been confirmed in pregnant women treated with anticonvulsants. Pernicious anemia can be masked by folate supplementation; therefore, a B12 level obtained before beginning folate treatment is a prudent recommendation. Carbamazepine has been associated with vitamin K deficiency. Because adequate levels of vitamin K are necessary for clotting, in utero carbamazepine exposure could increase the risk of neonatal bleeding (Ward and Wisner, 2007).

Carbamazepine

Studies conducted in the early 1990s indicated that carbamazepine (Tegretol; see Figure 8.3) might be as effective as lithium in preventing the recurrence of mania. However, in bipolar patients not previously treated with mood stabilizers, lithium is superior to carbamazepine in prophylactic efficacy (Hartong et al., 2003). Nevertheless, some patients who do not respond adequately to either agent alone are helped by the combination of the two drugs (Keck and McElroy, 2002). Because of the

---

[3]Phenytoin was never widely used as a mood stabilizer, although there are some positive reports from one group of investigators (Mishory et al., 2000; Bersudsky, 2005).

correlation between therapeutic effectiveness and plasma level, one reason patients may fail to respond to carbamazepine is inadequate blood levels. The therapeutic level for epilepsy and for bipolar disorder is estimated to be the same, between 8 to 12 μg/ml.

Several possible mechanisms have been proposed to explain carbamazepine's action in treating epilepsy and bipolar disorder. Its anticonvulsant effects may occur because it reduces neuronal excitation by blocking sodium channels and thus the ability of sodium to initiate action potentials. Its benefit for bipolar disorder may be related to the fact that carbamazepine, like lithium, inhibits enzyme activity in intracellular second-messenger systems, or to the observation that it may increase the density of receptors for an inhibitory neurotransmitter (Motohashi et al., 1989). In the treatment of bipolar disorder, carbamazepine is useful for prophylaxis, that is, reducing the frequency of episodes, and it may be the better choice for episodes of mixed mania and rapid cycling.

Adverse effects of carbamazepine include GI upset, sedation, ataxia, visual disturbances, and dermatological reactions, many of which may be caused by a metabolite, carbamazepine-epoxide. Although impairment of higher-order cognitive functioning is modest, some patients may be particularly sensitive to this side effect. More serious reactions involve the blood and range from a relatively benign reduction in white blood cell count (leucopenia) to, on rare occasions, a severe reduction, called agranulocytosis. For this reason it received a "black box" warning[4] and a recommendation for periodic blood analyses.

Drug interactions involving carbamazepine are common and result from drug-induced stimulation of drug-metabolizing enzymes, especially CYP-3A4 in the liver. As a result, acute blood levels may decrease, which may require increasing the dose by up to 100 percent to maintain a therapeutic blood level. This effect also extends to other drugs metabolized by the same enzyme family when combined with carbamazepine.

As stated, because carbamazepine is potentially teratogenic (Diav-Citrin, et al., 2001), it should not be administered during pregnancy if at all possible.

Oxcarbazepine

Oxcarbazepine (Trileptal) can be considered a new, safer carbamazepine, capable of replacing carbamazepine for all its uses with comparable efficacy and greatly improved safety. The difference is the result of a small structural variation between the two drugs (see Figure 8.3).

---

[4]A black box warning is an FDA-mandated list of adverse effects placed in a large black box just below the drug name on the package insert that accompanies every container of prescription medication received by a pharmacy.

Oxcarbazepine is essentially carbamazepine with an oxygen molecule attached to one of the rings. The liver can thus easily metabolize the drug by a process called hydroxylation. In fact, this process occurs within 5 minutes after drug absorption, and the monohydroxy derivative is the active form of the drug; oxcarbazepine is therefore an inactive "prodrug." Because of this easy metabolic process, there is no enzyme induction, no alteration in liver enzymes, no white blood cell problems, no required blood monitoring, and few drug interactions.

Oxcarbazepine is approved for use in epilepsy, and it is becoming widely used to treat bipolar disorder and other disorders treatable with carbamazepine (Centorrino et al., 2003; Ghaemi et al., 2003; Hellewell, 2002; Hummel et al., 2002). It has been shown to be superior to placebo in the treatment of acute mania in adults and comparable to lithium, valproate, and the antipsychotic haloperidol. However, Wagner and coworkers (2006) found no difference between oxcarbazepine and placebo in children and adolescents. There is less information about its use in pregnant women. Although it has caused birth detects in animals, outcomes of 94 pregnancies in women exposed to oxcarbazepine found no anomalies related to its use; however, these are too few cases to rule out adverse effects with confidence (Ward and Wisner, 2007). Moreover, oxcarbazepine does pass into breast milk.

Valproic Acid

Valproate (valproic acid, divalproex, Depakene, Depacon, Depakote; see Figure 8.3) is the second anticonvulsant that was systematically studied for treatment of bipolar illness, and it has been used for this disorder since its introduction in 1994. Several actions of valproic acid have been identified. First, it binds to and inhibits GABA transaminase, the enzyme that breaks down GABA. Therefore, the drug's anticonvulsant activity may be related to increased brain concentrations of GABA, as a result of its metabolic inhibition. Second, valproic acid may increase GABA by blocking its reuptake into glia and nerve endings. Third, valproic acid may also work by suppressing repetitive neuronal firing through inhibition of voltage-sensitive sodium channels. A fourth mechanism was proposed by Chen and coworkers (1999), who observed an effect of valproate on enzymes associated with the cellular organization of DNA. By influencing these enzymes and altering DNA function, valproate may be involved in gene transcription. As discussed on page 257, these genetic effects may be responsible for increasing the production of neuroprotective substances believed to be involved in mood stabilization.

Valproate is particularly effective in the treatment of acute mania, mixed states, schizoaffective disorder, and rapid-cycling bipolar disorder. It may be more effective than other agents in treating lithium-resistant patients, producing a positive response in up to 71 percent of patients.

The combination of valproate and lithium may be more efficacious than either agent alone. However, recently, it was reported that valproate was not more effective than lithium in a long-term, 20-month, maintenance trial for rapid-cycling BD (Calabrese et al., 2005a).

Valproic acid has traditionally been administered in divided doses through the day. A new extended-release preparation allows once-daily dosing, usually at bedtime, to improve compliance and help alleviate daytime sedation and memory impairment (Horne and Cunanan, 2003). There is no consistent evidence to show that giving this drug intravenously would speed the onset of action, which normally takes 3 to 10 days (Grunze et al., 1999; Phrolov et al., 2004). Depakene comes in capsules and as a syrup, while Depacon is the intravenous solution and Depakote is the formulation of tablets or delayed-release tablets.

Side effects associated with valproate include GI upset, sedation, lethargy, hand tremor, alopecia (hair loss), and some metabolic changes in the liver. In females starting valproate before the age of 20, the drug has been associated with an 8 percent prevalence of marked obesity, polycystic ovaries, and markedly increased levels of serum androgens (increased testosterone levels). Valproate may be slightly more detrimental to cognitive function than carbamazepine.

Like lithium and carbamazepine, valproate can be teratogenic, increasing the risk of spina bifida, neural tube defects, and developmental deficits in the infant. In fact, it has been suggested that this property may be related to its interaction with DNA. Withdrawal symptoms, including irritability, jitteriness, abnormal tone, feeding difficulties, and seizures have been described in infants whose mothers took valproate during pregnancy. The frequency of withdrawal symptoms was significantly related to the dose of valproate given to the mothers in the third trimester, and there was a tendency for both the frequency of the minor abnormalities and the major malformations to be related to the valproate dosage in the first trimester (Perucca, 2005; Vajda et al., 2006). There is also evidence that valproate during pregnancy carries particular risks for the neurodevelopment of children exposed in utero. A prospective study of children's intelligence quotients (IQs; mean age 7 years) found that children prenatally exposed to valproate had a mean IQ that was 11 points lower than children who were not exposed. The same study found no association between carbamazepine and cognitive dysfunction (Ward and Wisner, 2007). Consequently, caution must be exercised in using valproate in women who may become pregnant during drug therapy. Unlike lithium, little valproate is secreted in breast milk (Piontek et al., 2000), which makes it a preferred drug for use by nursing mothers who must take an antimanic drug.

Other serious side effects of valproate, which have resulted in black box warnings, include hepatotoxicity (liver damage) and pancreatitis (inflammation of the pancreas).

Lamotrigine

The third-generation anticonvulsant neuromodulator lamotrigine (Lamictal; Figure 8.4) has rapidly been accepted as an important monotherapeutic drug for treatment of acute bipolar depression, and rapid-cycling bipolar II disorder and the prevention of recurrent bipolar depressive episodes. That is, it was as effective as lithium in preventing relapse to any manic episode and better than lithium in preventing relapse to a depressive episode (Bowden et al., 2003). Conversely, it is not useful for acute mania. It is now a first-line therapy for patients with rapid-cycling bipolar II, as well as bipolar depression, and is less likely to cause a manic shift compared with the conventional antidepressants (Keck et al., 2003).

Although lamotrigine reportedly improved responsiveness in treatment-refractory patients with unipolar depression (Rocha and Hara, 2003), this observation has not been substantiated. To our knowledge, the possibility that lamotrigine in combination with antidepressants, such as SSRIs, would be helpful in treating bipolar depression in nonresponsive patients has not been investigated. In 2003 lamotrigine was approved for the long-term maintenance of adults with bipolar I disorder.

The major mechanism of action of lamotrigine is blocking voltage-dependent sodium-channel conductance. It has been found to inhibit depolarization of the glutaminergic presynaptic membrane, thus inhibiting release of glutamate, particularly in the cortex and hippocampus. This decrease in neuronal excitability may account for its antiepileptic, mood-stabilizing, and analgesic effects (Ketter et al., 2003), and it may also have some neuroprotective effects in people who suffer traumatic brain injuries (Pachet et al., 2003).

After oral administration, lamotrigine is rapidly and completely absorbed, and it reaches peak plasma concentrations in 1 to 5 hours. It is metabolized before excretion, with a half-life of 26 hours, which can decrease to about 7.4 hours when used with phenytoin or carbamazepine (requiring increased doses of lamotrigine) or increase to 60

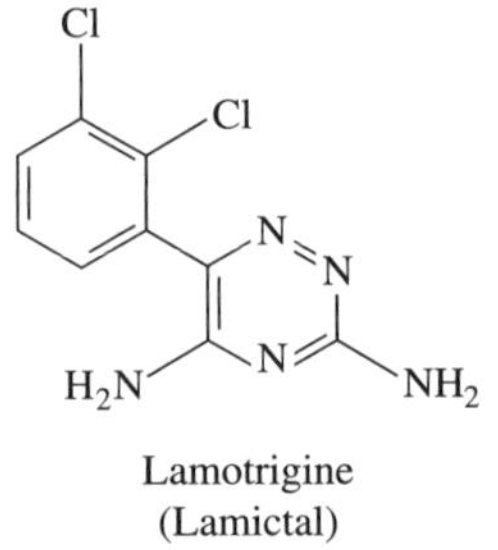

Lamotrigine
(Lamictal)

FIGURE 8.4 Chemical structure of lamotrigine (Lamictal).

hours when used with valproate (requiring decreased doses of lamotrigine) (Hurley, 2002). Therapeutic blood concentrations of lamotrigine used to treat epilepsy are in the range of about 1.5 to 5 µg/ml (mg/L), with adverse effects increasing with higher doses (Hirsch et al, 2004). It is presumed that the same concentration range applies to treatment of bipolar disorder.

Side effects associated with lamotrigine include dizziness, tremor, somnolence, headache, nausea, and rash. The most serious side effect is rash, which conceivably may be severe enough to require hospitalization and prove fatal. Adolescents are believed to be more prone to this reaction, so the drug is not indicated for patients younger than 16 years of age. The incidence of rash is currently about 1 in 500, which has not recently been a problem; a slow titration of dose over about 6 weeks is thought to reduce the incidence (Sokolenko and Kutcher, 2001; Calabrese et al., 2002).

In marked contrast to other antiepileptic agents, lamotrigine can improve cognitive functioning. In one study (Khan et al., 2004), after discontinuation of other drugs, separate groups of patients, diagnosed with either mania (349) or depression (966), were maintained for 8 to 16 weeks on lamotrigine monotherapy. Both groups showed cognitive improvements, manic patients more than depressed patients. Even after correcting for improvements in mood, there were significant improvements in cognition when switching from other medications.

The 12-year International Lamotrigine Pregnancy Registry Update (1992–2004) reported an incidence of major birth defects of 2.9 percent, which was the same as that of the general population of nonmedicated pregnant women (Cunnington et al., 2005). However, an 11.7 percent rate of malformations was reported when lamotrigine was used in combination with valproate in the first trimester (Ward and Wisner, 2007). In September 2006 the FDA issued an alert about the use of lamotrigine during the first trimester of pregnancy. Data from the North American Antiepileptic Drug Pregnancy Registry suggests a possible association between lamotrigine and cleft lip and/or oral palate. The total prevalence of these anomalies was 8.9 per 1000 births (representing 5 cases of oral cleft in 564 treated pregnant women), compared to the prevalence of oral clefts—0.5 to 2.16 per 1000 births—in nonepileptic mothers not taking lamotrigine. Since the number of cases of oral cleft in the treated women is so small and because other pregnancy registries have not replicated the finding, the validity of the association cannot be established and the clinical significance is uncertain (Holmes et al., 2006).

A single follow-up of 23 infants exposed to lamotrigine demonstrated no alterations or delays in development at 12 months of age. Data are still inadequate to determine the risks of developmental effects of fetal exposure to lamotrigine. No growth problems, postbirth occult malformations, neonatal seizures, or deviations in psychomotor development up to 1 year of age were observed in 62 infants exposed to lamotrigine in utero (Ward and Wisner, 2007). In 2004 the journal *Epilepsia* detailed the incidence in 322 mother/child pairs of serious adverse outcomes, which were defined as congenital abnormalities, gross developmental delay, or death. The percentages of children with these adverse outcomes by agent were valproate 25 percent, carbamazepine 14 percent, and lamotrigine 2 percent (Ward and Wisner, 2007). Today, lamotrigine appears to be the drug of choice for pregnant women with bipolar disorder (Cunnington et al., 2005; Ornoy, 2006; Vajda et al., 2006).

Gabapentin and Pregabalin

Introduced in the United States in 1993 as an anticonvulsant for the treatment of partial complex seizures, *gabapentin* (Neurontin; Figure 8.5) is also used for the treatment of anxiety, neuropathic pain, substance dependency, and behavioral dyscontrol, as well as bipolar disorder. Mechanistically, it is a GABA analogue, but it has little or no action on the GABA receptor. Although it increases GABA levels, perhaps by enhancing the synthesis or blocking the breakdown of GABA in the neuron, it is not clear how much the increase contributes to the efficacy of the drug. A derivative of gabapentin, *pregabalin* (Lyrica), was approved for use in the United States in 2005 for the treatment of pain states, such as diabetic peripheral neuropathy and postherpetic neuralgia, and as adjunctive therapy in the treatment of partial seizures in adults (Beydoun et al., 2005).

The most recent hypothesis for the mechanism of action of these two drugs is that they interact with a component of the calcium channels in presynaptic neuronal membranes to decrease the influx of calcium ions. As a result, less neurotransmitter is released, which translates into antiepileptic, analgesic, and anxiolytic effects (Chiu et al., 2005).

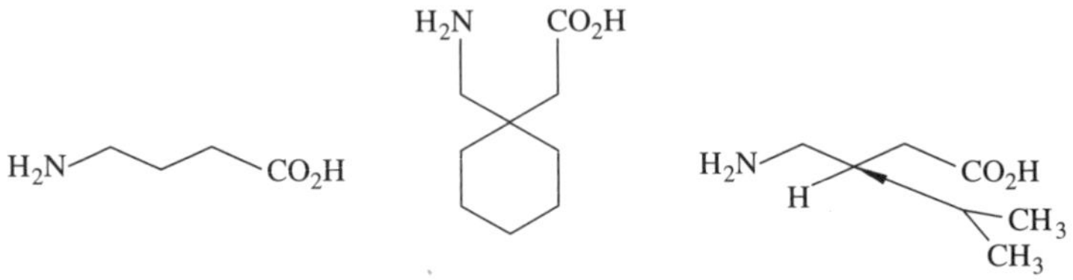

FIGURE 8.5 Chemical structures of GABA (gamma-aminobutyric acid, an inhibitory neurotransmitter), gabapentin (Neurontin); and pregabalin (Lyrica).

Gabapentin has an excellent pharmacokinetic profile: it is not bound to plasma proteins, it is not metabolized, it is excreted unchanged through the kidneys, with an elimination half-life of 5 to 7 hours, and it has few pharmacokinetic drug interactions. Gabapentin is absorbed by a saturable active transport mechanism from intestine to plasma, so doses up to 1500 mg can be given at any one time. Like gabapentin, pregabalin is excreted unchanged, and therefore it has no effect on the liver. It is two to three times as potent as gabapentin and has a slightly longer half-life of 6 to 8 hours.

It is clear that gabapentin (and presumably pregabalin) is not effective as monotherapy for bipolar disorder, and its most useful role is as adjunctive medication in patients resistant to one of the other mood stabilizers, such as lithium, valproate, or lamotrigine (Perugi et al., 2002). However, there is compelling evidence that these drugs may be very beneficial for neuropathic pain and at least some types of anxiety disorders, as described at the end of this section.

Topiramate

Topiramate (Topamax), discussed in Chapter 4 as an antiepileptic drug that is used to prevent relapse to detrimental drinking patterns in people with alcoholism, is a very potent anticonvulsant and is FDA-approved for the treatment of migraine headaches. Structurally different from other agents in this group, it is derived from the sugar D-fructose and was initially developed as an antidiabetic drug. Topiramate has multiple mechanisms of action. It exerts an inhibitory effect on sodium conductance, decreasing the duration of spontaneous bursts and the frequency of generated action potentials; it enhances GABA by unknown mechanisms; and it blocks the AMPA subtype glutamate receptor.

The initial positive results of open-label studies of the drug used to treat bipolar disorder were not supported by four recent clinical trials showing topiramate monotherapy to be ineffective in acute mania (Kushner et al., 2006). In addition, topiramate was no different than placebo when combined with either valproate or lithium for the treatment of bipolar I disorder (Chengappa et al., 2006). The main advantage of topiramate is that it is associated with weight loss rather than weight gain. This characteristic may make the drug useful as an adjunctive agent to offset the weight gain associated with other antimanic drugs. Preliminary evidence indicates positive effects in comorbid bipolar disorder and bulimia (Felstrom and Blackshaw, 2002) and bipolar disorder and binge eating (McElroy et al., 2004), and it may be preferred in obese patients with either unipolar or bipolar disorder who want to lose weight (Carpenter et al., 2002).

Unfortunately, the cognitive impairment (especially problems in word-finding) induced by topiramate is greater than that produced by other anticonvulsants, although impairment may occur more frequently at higher doses and with rapid dose increases. Other side effects include tingling in the extremities, irritability, anxiety, and depression. However, these effects may subside within a few weeks.

Topiramate is excreted unchanged and has a reduced likelihood of being involved in drug interactions mediated by the liver. However, this drug has the potential to increase plasma levels of other drugs excreted by the kidneys, such as lithium. It may also increase the incidence of kidney stones.

Zonisamide

Zonisamide (Zonegran) is an antiepileptic drug long available in Japan, which became available in the United States in mid-2000 for the treatment of epilepsy. Its major mechanism of action is reduction of neuronal repetitive firing by blocking sodium channels and preventing neurotransmitter release. It also acts on calcium channels, preventing the influx of calcium ions, and it may exert neuroprotective effects.

Preliminary studies showing positive effects in small numbers of patients with bipolar disorder were not supported by subsequent research. Overall, zonisamide has inconsistent effects against mania or bipolar depression and a high dropout rate, mostly due to side effects such as worsening of mood and sedation or lack of efficacy (Goodnick, 2007; McElroy et al., 2005; Wilson and Findling, 2007). Other side effects included reduced white blood cell counts, elevated liver enzymes, and several drug interactions. Like topiramate, this drug may be of use in treating binge eating.

Tiagabine

The mechanism of action of tiagabine as an anticonvulsant involves inhibition of the active reuptake of GABA by inhibiting the GABA transporter in the hippocampus and cerebral cortex. In spite of some initial positive reports, this drug has not been found efficacious in the treatment of bipolar disorder. Its use in the treatment of pain states is not known.

Retigabine

Retigabine is a newer antiepileptic drug, expected to become commercially available for the treatment of seizure disorders (Porter et al., 2007). Early evidence indicates that the drug may be effective in mania (Amann et al., 2006), as a neuroprotective agent (Boscia et al., 2006), and as an anxiolytic (Korsgaard et al., 2005). Undoubtedly, more will be written about this drug after its introduction.

Other Uses for Anticonvulsant Mood Stabilizers

In addition to their use in the treatment of bipolar disorder, the drugs in this category of mood stabilizers have been shown to have a variety of other therapeutic actions. There is increasing interest in the application of these agents in the treatment of neuropathic pain, anxiety disorders, borderline personality disorder, and other disorders that involve aggressive behaviors.

Neuropathic Pain

The overlap between the underlying pathophysiologic mechanisms of some epilepsy models and neuropathic pain models supports the rationale for using certain anticonvulsant drugs in the treatment of neuropathic pain. Patients with trigeminal neuralgia have been treated with carbamazepine for decades, and topiramate is the second antiepileptic drug, after valproate, to be approved for the prevention of migraine (in August of 2004). Because recommended doses are much lower than those for other indications, the cognitive side effects may not be as troublesome for migraine.

Gabapentin has proven effective against neuropathic pain induced by diabetic neuropathy, postherpetic neuralgia, and spinal cord injury. Data from clinical studies show that pregabalin (Lyrica) shares this analgesic effectiveness. Efficacy has been demonstrated in a number of clinical studies, including those in patients with diabetic neuropathy and fibromyalgia.[5] Treatment of neuropathic pain is seen as the drug's leading indication. McDonald and Portenoy (2006) provide an excellent review of the use of anticonvulsants in neuropathic pain states.

Anxiety Disorders

Pregabalin has shown early onset of action and short-term and long-term efficacy in patients with generalized anxiety disorder (Feltner et al., 2003; Pande et al., 2003). A 10-week, randomized, open-label trial

---

[5]In July 2004, Pfizer secured Europe-wide approval for Lyrica for use in the management of peripheral neuropathic pain as well as an adjunctive therapy in the treatment of partial epileptic seizures. Subsequently, in December 2004 the company gained FDA approval for use of Lyrica in neuropathic pain associated with diabetic peripheral neuropathy and postherpetic neuralgia, making it the first FDA-approved treatment for both of these neuropathic, pain states. Recently, the manufacturer of Lyrica has been promoting the drug for the treatment of fibromyalgia, a little-understood chronic pain condition that is thought to result from neurological changes in how patients perceive pain. At this time, formal FDA approval for this use is pending. In June 2007 the FDA approved Lyrica for the treatment of this disorder.

of tiagabine and paroxetine found that both agents significantly reduced anxiety and depressive symptoms and improved sleep quality and overall functioning (Rosenthal, 2003). In addition, topiramate has been found useful for the treatment of posttraumatic stress disorder (Berlant and VanKammen, 2002) in decreasing nightmares and flashbacks in the majority of patients. In social phobia, gabapentin was found to be superior to placebo (Pande et al., 1999), and one randomized placebo-controlled study found that gabapentin reduced panic symptoms in severe panic disorder (Pande et al., 2000).

Borderline Personality Disorder

Borderline personality disorder is characterized by affective instability, impulsivity, and aggression and is associated with considerable morbidity and mortality. It is a common comorbid condition with bipolar disorder. All the medications routinely used in treating bipolar disorder have been shown in published studies to have some value in treating borderline personality disorder: antidepressants, mood stabilizers, and antipsychotics ameliorate the irritability and anger and reduce the tempestuousness of the relationships and the impulsive aggressiveness of patients with borderline personality disorder.

At least two studies have been published showing that borderline personality disorder patients respond to valproic acid (Hollander et al., 2001; Frankenberg and Zanarini, 2002). Recently, topiramate was reported to reduce the subjective state of anger and the readiness to react with anger in a group of borderline male and female patients (Nickel et al., 2004, 2005, 2006), as well as having a beneficial effect on other symptoms related to borderline personality disorder (somatization, interpersonal sensitivity, and anxiety) (Loew et al., 2006). Preliminary (not placebo-controlled) evidence indicates that lamotrigine may have positive effects in borderline personality disorder (Pinto and Akiskal, 1998). Similarly, a research team looked back at borderline symptoms in the pair of large lamotrigine studies for bipolar patients and found that borderline symptoms appeared to improve along with the bipolar symptoms (Preston et al., 2004). Lithium has not been studied in a controlled trial in borderline personality disorder, but it is advocated for "targeting specific symptom domains" such as mood instability. The review by Soloff (1994) also includes a summary of the use of carbamazepine in borderline personality disorder.

Aggression and Behavioral Dyscontrol

Impulsive aggressive behavior is common in psychiatric disorders and accounts for significant morbidity and mortality. In a recent multicenter, randomized placebo-controlled study, Hollander and colleagues (2003) evaluated the effect of valproic acid in outpatients diagnosed with intermittent explosive disorder, posttraumatic stress disorder, or Cluster B personality disorders (borderline, antisocial, histrionic, and narcissistic disorders). They found statistically significant treatment effects only for the Cluster B group on measures such as verbal assault and assault against objects: valproate was superior to placebo in the treatment of impulsive aggression, irritability, and global severity. In a recent comparison study, carbamazepine and valproate were reported to produce a significant reduction in "impulsive aggression" compared with placebo (Stanford et al., 2005). As an adjunct medication, oxcarbazepine has reduced aggressive behavior in developmentally disabled adults (Jankowsky et al., 2003), and as monotherapy, topiramate was reported to reduce anger and depression in women with borderline personality disorder (Loew et al., 2006).

Atypical Antipsychotics

For decades, traditional antipsychotic drugs have been used to help control the symptoms and behaviors associated with acute mania. In fact, the use of traditional antipsychotic drugs predated the use of lithium by 20 years. However, the pharmacology of antipsychotic drugs, especially as these drugs are used to treat schizophrenia, is not presented until Chapter 9. Nevertheless, because traditional antipsychotics, especially the newer "atypical antipsychotics" (also called "second-generation antipsychotics" or "SGAs") are exceedingly effective and widely used to treat bipolar disorder, their use is presented here, before complete presentation of their pharmacology. All the SGAs have shown efficacy either as monotherapy or as adjunctive agents for acute mania, and they have all been approved for this indication. Recent comparisons show that there is no difference among them as agents for acute mania; aripiprazole, olanzapine, quetiapine, risperidone, and ziprasidone were found equally efficacious for acute episodes of mania, whether used as monotherapy or as adjunctive treatment, compared with placebo (Perlis et al., 2006a). Furthermore, the first-generation antipsychotic haloperidol was also shown to be as good as risperidone, olanzapine, carbamazepine, or valproate when used alone or as an add-on medication—although it was less efficacious than aripiprazole (Vieta et al., 2005). Not surprisingly, haloperidol also produced less weight gain but more movement disorders than the other agents (Cipriani et al., 2006).

Subsequent trials have examined the efficacy of the SGAs, mostly risperidone or olanzapine, for bipolar depression and maintenance of remission. Risperidone has been found effective in extension trials as monotherapy or adjunctive treatment in sustaining remission from mania while not inducing depression (Hirschfield et al., 2006; Rendell et al., 2006). Olanzapine (Tohen et al., 2006), quetiapine (Calabrese et al., 2005b), and aripiprazole (Keck et al., 2006) have all been found more effective than placebo for maintenance treatment, and olanzapine was reported comparable to lithium (Tohen et al., 2005). Olanzapine alone has also been reported to be as effective for bipolar depression as the antidepressant fluoxetine alone or in combination as the recently approved drug Symbyax (Amsterdam and Shults, 2005; Corya et al., 2006). Symbyax was also found to be as effective as lamotrigine for the treatment of bipolar depression (Brown et al., 2006).

Both Symbyax and lamotrigine had an equally low risk of inducing mania, which is a serious concern with antidepressant treatment for bipolar disorder. To determine whether there is a difference among the newer antidepressants in inducing mania, recent studies have examined the relative risk of three other antidepressants, sertraline, bupropion, and venlafaxine, producing a "switch" when used as adjuncts to mood stabilizers. Overall, the rate was higher for bipolar I (30.8 percent) than bipolar II (18.6 percent), although eventually only 23.3 percent of patients did not switch. However, venlafaxine was reported to be more likely than the other two antidepressants to produce a switch (Leverich et al., 2006; Post et al., 2006). These results suggest that people with bipolar II might be less vulnerable to an antidepressant-induced switch. This suggestion is supported by Altshuler and coworkers (2006), who found less switching with adjunctive selective serotonergic reuptake inhibitors in bipolar II than in bipolar I patients, and by Parker and coworkers (2006b), who successfully treated depressed bipolar II patients for 9 months with SSRIs, without any worsening of symptoms.

Although the newer antipsychotics may be less likely to elicit movement disorders than the older drugs, there is evidence that patients with bipolar disorder may be more susceptible to these side effects than patients diagnosed with schizophrenia. Ghaemi and coworkers (2006) reported that almost two-thirds of their bipolar I and bipolar II patients showed some evidence of extrapyramidal motor side effects in response to an SGA, including risperidone, olanzapine, quetiapine, ziprasidone, and aripiprazole. This rate is much higher than the rate reported in clinical trials, and if it is confirmed, it may require some refinement of SGA treatment in bipolar disorder.

Finally, in a recent meta-analysis addressing the use of second-generation atypical antipsychotics in the treatment of acute mania, Scherk and coworkers (2007) concluded:

> SGA agents as add-on medication to mood stabilizers are highly superior to mood stabilizers alone in improving acute manic symptoms, as indicated by greater reductions in mania scores, higher response rates, and fewer dropouts due to inefficacy. . . . Combination treatment with a second-generation atypical antipsychotic and a mood stabilizer should be the treatment of choice, in particular for severe manic episodes. (p. 442)

Omega-3 Fatty Acids

In countries where the diet is rich in fish oils, the incidence of bipolar disorder is quite low (Noaghiul and Hibbeln, 2003). Therefore, it is possible that fish oils may prevent BD, perhaps by protecting the brain from the neuronal injuries now being identified in this disorder. Omega-3 fatty acids, obtained from marine or plant sources, are known to damp these signal transduction pathways in a variety of cell systems (Parker et al., 2006a).

Stoll and coworkers (1999) found that augmentation of antimanic treatment with omega-3 fatty acids compared to placebo greatly increased the time before recurrence of a bipolar episode, even in patients who were not taking any other medication. Two recent reviews (Parker and coworkers, 2006a; Marengell and coworkers, 2006) have summarized the subsequent research regarding the association of omega-3 fatty acid consumption with rates of mood disorders, the relationship between physiological markers of omega-3 fatty acids and mood disorders, and results of omega-3 fatty acid treatment of mood disorders. But although there is some support for the role of omega-3 fatty acids in slowing the recurrence of episodes of bipolar and other mood disorders, the results of clinical trials have been inconsistent. In their review, Marengell and coworkers describe results of a pilot study of 10 women with bipolar disorder taking omega-3 fatty acids while attempting to conceive. They concluded that, although the agent was well tolerated, the current data could not support a recommendation for omega-3 fatty acid monotherapy as a substitute for standard pharmacologic treatment. Recent results of a small study of children with bipolar disorder are consistent with this conclusion. Over an 8-week period, only about 35 percent of the patients (6 to 17 years of age) had even a modest response of a 50 percent decrease in manic symptoms (Wozniak et al., 2007).

Miscellaneous Agents

Many patients are unresponsive to or intolerant of present antimanic medications, and alternative agents are much needed, especially those with unique mechanisms of action. Several different types of drugs have been tried.

The psychedelic drug *scopolamine*, which blocks the action of acetylcholine, produces some effects resembling manic symptoms, such as flight of ideas, talkativeness, and difficulties in concentration. Therefore, agents that potentiate the effect of acetylcholine might have some antimanic action. *Donepezil* inhibits the enzyme acetylcholinesterase and therefore might help patients with bipolar disorder. Although Burt and colleagues (1999) reported some improvement in 11 patients who were treatment-resistant to other medications, a recent double-blind placebo-controlled trial found no effect of adjunctive donepezil in patients with refractory mania (Evins et al., 2006).

Because lithium interferes with membrane ion function, *calcium channel blockers,* such as *verapamil,* have been tried, but their effectiveness remains questionable. *Clonidine,* an antihypertensive drug, has been tried in treatment-refractory patients with bipolar disorder. It was hypothesized that the action of clonidine in decreasing the release of norepinephrine might reduce manic episodes. Despite initial positive results, effectiveness remains unproved.

Recently, Kulkarni and colleagues (2006) reported that the hormonal agents *tamoxifen* and *medroxyprogesterone acetate* were more effective than placebo in improving the symptoms of mania in 13 women with acute bipolar affective disorder. Although most commonly used for its antiestrogenic property in the treatment of breast cancer, tamoxifen is a potent inhibitor of the enzyme protein kinase C, which is involved in intracellular signal transduction. It is this mechanism that may be the route by which it affects bipolar disorder.

Although not considered a mood stabilizer, the wakefulness promoting agent *modafinil* has been useful for alleviating fatigue accompanying many medical conditions, including depression.[6] A recent retrospective chart review study found modafinil effective in relieving fatigue and sleepiness in adults with unipolar or bipolar depression (Nasr et al., 2006). Because the effect of modafinil is believed to be mediated by an action of the drug on histamine receptors, rather than dopamine pathways, there is less risk of dependence. The authors report that no patient demonstrated a switch into mania or hypomania while on modafinil.

Psychotherapeutic and Psychosocial Treatments

Although not widely appreciated, a combination of drug therapy and psychotherapeutic interventions is the most effective treatment modality for bipolar illness:

> The increasing evidence of efficacy of the pharmacologic treatment of bipolar disorders has sometimes led clinicians to forget psychological interventions as an adjunctive treatment. (Colom et al., 2003, p. 402)

---

[6]Modafinil (as Provigil) is FDA-approved for helping persons with the disease *narcolepsy* stay awake during the day, maintaining daytime wakefulness and promoting more tiredness at bedtime.

Goals of psychotherapy and psychosocial treatments are to improve clinical outcomes, functional outcomes, and disease management skills (Bauer, 2001). Time to recovery and the likelihood of remaining well after an episode of bipolar depression are also significant (Miklowitz et al, 2007). Patients with bipolar disorder suffer from the psychosocial consequences of past episodes, the ongoing vulnerability to future episodes, and the burdens of adhering to a long-term treatment plan that may involve some unpleasant side effects. In addition, many patients have clinically significant mood instability between episodes. Successful treatment involves a social network primed to recognize the early symptoms of an episode, to seek help for patients who lack insight into their condition, and to assist with recognition of side effects and toxicities, thus aiding in compliance with therapy. Issues of importance include the following:

- Emotional consequences of periods of major mood disorder and diagnosis of a chronic mental illness
- Developmental deviations and delays caused by past episodes
- Problems associated with stigmatization
- Problems regulating self-esteem
- Fears of recurrence and consequent inhibition of normal psychosocial functioning
- Interpersonal difficulties
- Marriage, family, childbearing, and parenting issues
- Academic and occupational problems
- Other legal, social, and emotional problems that arise from reckless, violent, withdrawn, or bizarre behavior that may occur during episodes

It is also important to ensure that the manic state is not being caused by medications, such as antidepressants, caffeine, herbals containing ephedrine, behavioral stimulants (including illegal drugs, such as cocaine), corticosteroids (cortisone), anabolic steroids, antiparkinsonian drugs, over-the-counter cough and cold preparations, and diet aids. One must also rule out thyroid disease because mania secondary to thyroid hyperactivity is common.

Among the psychotherapy interventions used concomitantly with pharmacotherapy are group psychoeducation (Colom et al., 2003), cognitive-behavioral therapy (Lam et al., 2003; Otto et al., 2003), psychodynamically oriented therapy, family therapy, couples therapy, interpersonal psychotherapy, and self-help groups. As part of the STEP-BD study, Miklowitz and coworkers (2007) studied the efficacy of four disorder-specific psychotherapies in conjunction with pharmacotherapy in treating bipolar depression. Intensive psychotherapy given weekly or biweekly was superior to less intensive interventions in shortening the time to recovery and increasing the likelihood of remaining well.

For complete treatment, a practitioner well versed in the pharmacological management of poorly responsive bipolar patients is necessary. Other personnel are required to monitor the effectiveness of treatment, side effects, other causative factors, and compliance with therapy. Geller and Goldberg (2007) recently reviewed the efficacy of evidence-based psychotherapies for bipolar disorder.

STUDY QUESTIONS

1. Outline the pharmacological agents useful in the treatment of bipolar disorder. What are the major drugs in each category?

2. List the clinical uses of lithium.

3. Describe the correlations between plasma levels of lithium and the therapeutic and side effects of the drug.

4. How does lithium exert its antimanic effect?

5. List the major organ systems affected by lithium. What are the drug's major side effects on each system?

6. Discuss the effects of the various antimanic drugs on memory and cognitive behaviors.

7. Discuss the use of antimanic drugs in pregnancy and in the potentially pregnant female with bipolar disorder.

8. Discuss the comorbidity of bipolar disorder with other psychological disorders.

9. Which antiepileptic drugs are used in the treatment of bipolar disorder? List the advantages and disadvantages of each.

10. What intrudes on patient compliance with mood-stabilizing medication? What can be done to improve compliance?

11. What medications or diseases might precipitate or worsen bipolar illness?

12. How can a health care professional who is not the prescribing physician contribute to the well-being of the bipolar patient?

13. Describe the possible role of omega-3 fatty acids in bipolar illness.

REFERENCES

Altshuler, L. L., et al. (2006). "Lower Switch Rate in Depressed Patients with Bipolar II than Bipolar I Disorder Treated Adjunctively with Second-Generation Antidepressants." *American Journal of Psychiatry* 163: 313–315.

Amann, B., et al. (2006). "An Exploratory Open Trial on Safety and Efficacy of the Anticonvulsant Retigabine in Acute Manic Patients." *Journal of Clinical Psychopharmacology* 26: 534–536.

American Psychiatric Association (2002). "Practice Guideline for the Treatment of Patients with Bipolar Disorder (Revision)." *American Journal of Psychiatry* 159, Supplement (April).

Amsterdam, J. D., and J. Shults (2005). "Comparison of Fluoxetine, Olanzapine, and Combined Fluoxetine plus Olanzapine Initial Therapy of Bipolar Type I and Type II Major Depression—Lack of Manic Induction." *Journal of Affective Disorders* 87: 121–130.

Baldessarini, R. J., and L. Tondo (2000). "Does Lithium Treatment Still Work? Evidence of Stable Responses over Three Decades." *Archives of General Psychiatry* 57: 187–190.

Baldessarini, R. J., et al. (1999). "Effects of Lithium Treatment and Its Discontinuation on Suicidal Behavior in Bipolar Manic Depressive Disorders." *Journal of Clinical Psychiatry* 60, Supplement 2: 77–84.

Baldessarini, R. J., et al. (2006). "Decreased Risk of Suicides and Attempts During Long-Term Lithium Treatment: A Meta-Analytic Review." *Bipolar Disorders* 8: 625–639.

Bauer, M. S. (2001). "An Evidence-Based Review of Psychosocial Treatments for Bipolar Disorder." *Psychopharmacology Bulletin* 35: 109–134.

Bauer, M. S. (2005) "How Solid Is the Evidence for the Efficacy of Mood Stabilizers in Bipolar Disorder?" *Essential Psychopharmacology* 6: 301–318.

Bauer, M. S., and L. Mitchner (2004). "What Is a 'Mood Stabilizer'? An Evidence-Based Response." *American Journal of Psychiatry* 161: 3–18.

Bauer, M. S., et al. (2000). "Double-Blind, Placebo-Controlled Trial of the Use of Lithium to Augment Antidepressant Medication in Continuation Treatment of Unipolar Major Depression." *American Journal of Psychiatry* 157: 1429–1435.

Bearden, C. E., et al. (2007). "Greater Cortical Gray Matter Density in Lithium-Treated Patients with Bipolar Disorder." *Biological Psychiatry* 62: 7–16.

Berlant, J., and D. P. vanKammen (2002). "Open-Label Topiramate as Primary or Adjunctive Therapy in Chronic Civilian Posttraumatic Stress Disorder: A Preliminary Report." *Journal of Clinical Psychiatry* 63: 15–20.

Bersudsky, Y. (2005). "Phenytoin: An Anti-Bipolar Anticonvulsant?" *International Journal of Neuropsychopharmacology* 9(4): 479–484.

Bertolino, A., et al. (2003). "Neuronal Pathology in the Hippocampal Area of Patients with Bipolar Disorder: A Study with Proton Magnetic Resonance Spectroscopic Imaging." *Biological Psychiatry* 53: 906–913.

Beydoun, A., et al. (2005). "Safety and Efficacy of Two Pregabalin Regimens for Add-On Treatment of Partial Epilepsy." *Neurology* 64: 475–480.

Boscia, F., et al. (2006). "Retigabine and Fluptine Exert Neuroprotective Actions in Organotypic Hippocampal Cultures." *Neuropharmacology* 51: 283–294.

Bowden, C. L., et al. (2003). "A Placebo-Controlled 18-Month Trial of Lamotrigine and Lithium Maintenance Treatment in Recently Manic or Hypomanic Patients with Bipolar I Disorder." *Archives of General Psychiatry* 60: 392–400.

Brown, E. B., et al. (2006). "A 7-Week, Randomized Double-Blind Trial of Olanzapine/Fluoxetine Combination Versus Lamotrigine in the Treatment of Bipolar I Depression." *Journal of Clinical Psychiatry* 67: 1025–1033.

Brunello, N. (2004). "Mood Stabilizers: Protecting the Mood . . . Protecting the Brain." *Journal of Affective Disorders* 79: 15–20.

Burt, T., et al. (1999). "Donepezil in Treatment-Resistant Bipolar Disorder." *Biological Psychiatry* 45: 959–964.

Calabrese, J. R., et al. (2002). "Rash in Multicenter Trials of Lamotrigine in Mood Disorders: Clinical Relevance and Management." *Journal of Clinical Psychiatry* 63: 1012–1019.

Calabrese, J. R., et al. (2005a). "A 20-Month, Double-Blind, Maintenance Trial of Lithium Versus Divalproex in Rapid-Cycling Bipolar Disorder." *American Journal of Psychiatry* 162: 2152–2161.

Calabrese, J. R., et al. (2005b). "A Randomized, Double-Blind, Placebo-Controlled Trial of Quetiapine in the Treatment of Bipolar I or II Depression." *American Journal of Psychiatry* 162: 1351–1360.

Carpenter, L. L., et al. (2002). "Do Obese Depressed Patients Respond to Topiramate? A Retrospective Chart Review." *Journal of Affective Disorders* 69: 251–255.

Centorrino, F., et al. (2003). "Oxcarbazepine: Clinical Experience with Hospitalized Psychiatric Patients." *Bipolar Disorders* 5: 370–374.

Chang, K., et al. (2006). "An Open-Label Study of Lamotrigine Adjunct or Monotherapy for the Treatment of Adolescents with Bipolar Depression." *Journal of the American Academy of Child & Adolescent Psychiatry* 44: 298–304.

Chen, G., et al. (1999). "Valproate Robustly Enhances AP-1 Mediated Gene Expression." *Brain Research: Molecular Brain Research* 64: 52–58.

Chengappa, K. N., et al. (2002). "Changes in Body Weight and Body Mass Index Among Psychiatric Patients Receiving Lithium, Valproate, or Topiramate: An Open-Label, Nonrandomized Chart Review." *Clinical Therapeutics* 24: 1576–1584.

Chengappa, R., et al. (2006). "Adjunctive Topiramate Therapy in Patients Receiving a Mood Stabilizer for Bipolar I Disorder: A Randomized, Placebo-Controlled Trial." *Journal of Clinical Psychiatry* 67: 1698–1706.

Chiu, S. (2005). "GABApentin Treatment Response in Selective Serotonin Reuptake Inhibitor (SSRI)-Refractory Panic Disorder." *Psychiatry-Online*. http://www.priory.com/psych/gabapentin.htm.

Cipriani, A., et al. (2005). "Lithium in the Prevention of Suicidal Behavior and All-Cause Mortality in Patients with Mood Disorders: A Systematic Review of Randomized Trials." *American Journal of Psychiatry* 162: 1805–1819.

Cipriani, A., et al. (2006). "Haloperidol Alone or in Combination for Acute Mania." *Cochrane Database System Review* 3CD004362).

Colom, F., et al. (2003). "A Randomized Trial on the Efficacy of Group Psycho-education in the Prophylaxis of Recurrences in Bipolar Patients Whose Disease Is in Remission." *Archives of General Psychiatry* 60: 402–407.

Corya, S. A., et al. (2006). "A 24-Week Open-Label Extension Study of Olanzapine-Fluoxetine Combination and Olanzapine Monotherapy in the Treatment of Bipolar Depression." *Journal of Clinical Psychiatry* 67: 798–806.

Coyle, J. T., and R. S. Duman (2003). "Finding the Intracellular Signaling Pathways Affected by Mood Disorder Treatments." *Neuron* 38: 157–160.

Cui, J., et al. (2007). "Role of Glutathione in Neuroprotective Effects of Mood Stabilizing Drugs Lithium and Valproate." *Neuroscience* 144: 1447–1453.

Cunnington, M., et al. (2005). "Lamotrigine and the Risk of Malformations in Pregnancy." *Neurology* 64: 955–960.

Diav-Citrin, O., et al. (2001). "Is Carbamazepine Teratogenic? A Prospective Controlled Study of 210 Pregnancies." *Neurology* 57: 321–324.

Einat, H., and Manji, H. K. (2006). "Cellular Plasticity Cascades: Genes-to-Behavior Pathways in Animal Models of Bipolar Disorder." *Biological Psychiatry* 59: 1160–1171.

Elmslie, J. L., et al. (2000). "Prevalence of Overweight and Obesity in Bipolar Patients." *Journal of Clinical Psychiatry* 61: 179–184.

Ernst, C. L., and J. F. Goldberg (2002). "The Reproductive Safety Profile of Mood Stabilizers, Atypical Antipsychotics, and Broad-Spectrum Psychotropics." *Journal of Clinical Psychiatry* 63, Supplement 4: 42–55.

Evins, A. E., et al. (2006). "A Double-Blind, Placebo-Controlled Trial of Adjunctive Donepezil in Treatment-Resistant Mania." *Bipolar Disorder* 8: 75–80.

Fawcett, J. A. (2003). "Lithium Combinations in Acute and Maintenance Treatment of Unipolar and Bipolar Depression." *Journal of Clinical Psychiatry* 64, Supplement 5: 32–37.

Felstrom, A., and S. Blackshaw (2002). "Topiramate for Bulimia Nervosa with Bipolar II Disorder." *American Journal of Psychiatry* 159: 1246–1247.

Feltner, D. E., et al. (2003). "High Dose Pregabalin Is Effective for the Treatment of Generalized Anxiety Disorder." *Journal of Clinical Psychopharmacology* 23: 240–249.

Frankenburg, F. R., and M. C. Zanarini (2002). "Divalproex Sodium Treatment of Women with Borderline Personality Disorder and Bipolar II Disorder: A Double-Blind, Placebo-Controlled Pilot Study." *Journal of Clinical Psychiatry* 63: 442–446.

Geddes, J. R., et al. (2004). "Long-Term Lithium Therapy for Bipolar Disorder: Systematic Review and Meta-Analysis of Randomized Controlled Trials." *American Journal of Psychiatry* 161: 217–222.

Geller, R. E., and J. F. Goldberg (2007). "A Review of Evidence-Based Psychotherapies for Bipolar Disorder." *Primary Psychiatry* 14: 59–69. Available online at www.primarypsychiatry.com.

Ghaemi, S. N., et al. (2003). "Oxcarbazepine Treatment of Bipolar Disorder." *Journal of Clinical Psychiatry* 64: 943–945.

Ghaemi, S. N., et al. (2006). "Extrapyramidal Side Effects with Atypical Neuroleptics in Bipolar Disorder." *Progress in Neuro-Psychopharmacology & Biological Psychiatry* 30: 209–213.

Goodnick, P. J. (2007). "Bipolar Depression: A Review of Randomized Clinical Trials." *Expert Opinion in Pharmacotherapy* 8: 13–21.

Goodwin, G. M., et al. (2004). "A Pooled Analysis of Two Placebo-Controlled 18-Month Trials of Lamotrigine and Lithium Maintenance in Bipolar I Disorder." *Journal of Clinical Psychiatry* 64: 432–441.

Gould, T. D., et al. (2004). "Emerging Experimental Therapeutics for Bipolar Disorder: Insights from the Molecular and Cellular Actions of Current Mood Stabilizers." *Molecular Psychiatry* 9: 734–755.

Grunze, H., et al. (1999). "Intravenous Valproate Loading in Acutely Manic and Depressed Bipolar I Patients." *Journal of Clinical Psychopharmacology* 19: 303–309.

Harris, J. (2005). "Child and Adolescent Psychiatry: The Increased Diagnosis of 'Juvenile Bipolar Disorder': What Are We Treating?" *Psychiatric Services* 56: 529–531.

Hartong, E. G., et al. (2003). "Prophylactic Efficacy of Lithium Versus Carbamazepine in Treatment-Naïve Bipolar Patients." *Journal of Clinical Psychiatry* 64: 144–151.

Hashimoto, R., et al. (2002). "Lithium Induces Brain-Derived Neurotrophic Factor and Activates TrkB in Rodent Cortical Neurons: An Essential Step for Neuroprotection Against Glutamate Excitotoxicity." *Neuropharmacology* 43: 1173–1179.

Hellewell, J. S. (2002). "Oxcarbazepine (Trileptal) in the Treatment of Bipolar Disorders: Review of Efficacy and Tolerability." *Journal of Affective Disorders* 72, Supplement (December): S23–S34.

Hirsch, L. J., et al. (2004). "Correlating Lamotrigine Serum Concentrations with Tolerability in Patients with Epilepsy." *Neurology* 28: 1022–1026.

Hirschfield, R. M., et al. (2006). "An Open-Label Extension Trial of Risperidone Monotherapy in the Treatment of Bipolar I Disorder." *International Journal of Clinical Psychopharmacology* 21: 11–20.

Hollander, E., et al. (2001). "A Preliminary Double-Blind, Placebo-Controlled Trial of Divalproex Sodium in Borderline Personality Disorder." *Journal of Clinical Psychiatry* 62: 199–203.

Hollander, E., et al. (2003). "Divalproex in the Treatment of Impulsive Aggression: Efficacy in Cluster B Personality Disorders." *Neuropsychopharmacology* 28: 1186–1197.

Holmes, L. B., et al. (2006). "Increased Risk for Non-Syndromic Cleft Palate Among Infants Exposed to Lamotrigine During Pregnancy" (abstract). *Birth Defects Research Part A: Clinical and Molecular Teratology* 76: 318.

Horne, R. L., and C. Cunanan (2003). "Safety and Efficacy of Switching Psychiatric Patients from a Delayed-Release to an Extended-Release Formulation of Divalproex Sodium." *Journal of Clinical Psychopharmacology* 23: 176–181.

Hummel, B., et al. (2002). "Acute Antimanic Efficacy and Safety of Oxcarbazepine in an Open Trial with an On-Off-On Design." *Bipolar Disorders* 4: 412–417.

Hurley, S. C. (2002). "Lamotrigine Update and Its Use in Bipolar Disorders." *Annals of Pharmacotherapy* 36: 860–873.

Janowsky, D. S., et al. (2003). "Effects of Topiramate on Aggressive, Self-Injurious, and Disruptive/Destructive Behaviors in the Intellectually Disabled: An Open-Label Retrospective Study." *Journal of Clinical Psychopharmacology* 23: 500–504.

Joffe, H., et al. (2006). "Valproate Is Associated with New-Onset Oligoamenorrhea with Hyperandrogenism in Women with Bipolar Disorder." *Biological Psychiatry* 59: 1078–1086.

Keck, P. E., and S. L. McElroy (2002). "Carbamazepine and Valproate in the Maintenance Treatment of Bipolar Disorder." *Journal of Clinical Psychiatry* 63, Supplement 10: 13–17.

Keck, P. E., and S. L. McElroy (2003). "Bipolar Disorder, Obesity, and Pharmacotherapy-Associated Weight Gain." *Journal of Clinical Psychiatry* 64: 1426–1435.

Keck, P. E., and J. Susman (2003). "Introduction: Foundational Treatment for Bipolar Disorder." *Journal of Family Practice* Supplement (March): 4–5.

Keck, P. E., et al. (2003). "Advances in the Pharmacological Treatment of Bipolar Depression." *Biological Psychiatry* 53: 671–679.

Keck, P. E., et al. (2006). "A Randomized, Double-Blind, Placebo-Controlled 26-Week Trial of Aripiprazole in Recently Manic Patients with Bipolar I Disorder." *Journal of Clinical Psychiatry* 67: 626–637.

Ketter, T. A., et al. (2003). "Potential Mechanisms of Action of Lamotrigine in the Treatment of Bipolar Disorders." *Journal of Clinical Psychopharmacology* 23: 484–495.

Khan, A., et al. (2004). "Effect of Lamotrigine on Cognitive Complaints in Patients with Bipolar I Disorder." *Journal of Clinical Psychiatry* 65: 1483–1490.

Kopnisky, K. L., et al. (2003). "Chronic Lithium Treatment Antagonizes Glutamate-Induced Decrease of Phosphorylated CREB in Neurons via Reducing Protein Phosphorylase 1 and Increasing MEK Activities." *Neuroscience* 116: 425–435.

Korsgaard, M. P., et al. (2005). "Anxiolytic Effects of Maxipost (BMS-204352) and Retigabine via Activation of Neuronal Kv7 Channels." *Journal of Pharmacology & Experimental Therapeutics* 314: 282–292.

Kulkarni, J., et al. (2006). "A Pilot Study of Hormone Modulation as a New Treatment for Mania in Women with Bipolar Affective Disorder." *Psychoneuroendocrinology* 31: 543–547.

Kupfer, D. J. (2005). "The Increasing Medical Burden in Bipolar Disorder." *Journal of the American Medical Association* 293: 2528–2530.

Kushner, S. F., et al. (2006). "Topiramate Monotherapy in the Management of Acute Mania: Results of Four Double-Blind Placebo-Controlled Trials." *Bipolar Disorders* 8: 15–27.

Lam, D. H., et al. (2003). "A Randomized Controlled Study of Cognitive Therapy for Relapse Prevention for Bipolar Affective Disorder: Outcome of the First Year." *Archives of General Psychiatry* 60: 145–152.

Leverich, G. S., et al. (2006) "Risk of Switch in Mood Polarity to Hypomania or Mania in Patients with Bipolar Depression During Acute and Continuation Trials of Venlafaxine, Sertraline, and Bupropion as Adjuncts to Mood Stabilizers." *American Journal of Psychiatry* 163: 232–239.

Li, X., et al. (2002). "Synaptic, Intracellular, and Neuroprotective Mechanisms of Anticonvulsants: Are They Relevant for the Treatment and Course of Bipolar Disorders?" *Journal of Affective Disorders* 69: 1–14.

Loew, T., et al. (2006). Topiramate Treatment for Women with Borderline Personality Disorder: A Double-Blind, Placebo-Controlled Study" *Journal of Clinical Psychopharmacology* 26: 61–66.

Maj, M., et al. (1998). "Long-Term Outcome of Lithium Prophylaxis in Bipolar Disorder: A Five-Year Prospective Study of 402 Patients at a Lithium Clinic." *American Journal of Psychiatry* 155: 30–35.

Manji, H. K., et al. (2001). "Bipolar Disorder: Leads from the Molecular and Cellular Mechanisms of Action of Mood Stabilizers." *British Journal of Psychiatry* 178, Supplementum 41: S107–S119.

Marengell, L. B., et al. (2006). "Omega-3 Fatty Acids in Bipolar Disorder: Clinical and Research Considerations." *Prostaglandins Leuokot Essential Fatty Acids* 75: 315–321.

McDonald, A. A., and Portenoy, R. K. (2006). "How to Use Antidepressants and Anticonvulsants as Adjuvant Analgesics in the Treatment of Neuropathic Cancer Pain." *Journal of Supportive Oncology* 4: 43–52.

McElroy, S. L., et al. (2004). "Topiramate in the Long-term Treatment of Binge-Eating Disorder Associated with Obesity." *Journal of Clinical Psychiatry* 65: 1463–1469.

McElroy, S. L., et al. (2005). "Open-Label Adjunctive Zonisamide in the Treatment of Bipolar Disorders: A Prospective Trial." *Journal of Clinical Psychiatry* 66: 617–624.

Miklowskz, D. J., et al. (2007). "Psychosocial Treatments for Bipolar Depression." *Archives of General Psychiatry* 64: 419–426.

Mishory, A., et al. (2000). "Phenytoin as an Antimanic Anticonvulsant: A Controlled Study." *American Journal of Psychiatry* 157: 463–465.

Mondimore, F. M., et al. (2003). "Drug Combinations for Mania." *Journal of Clinical Psychiatry* 64, Supplement 5: 25–31.

Montouris, G. (2005). "Safety of the Newer Antiepileptic Drug Oxcarbazepine During Pregnancy." *Current Medical Research Opinion* 21: 693–701.

Motohashi, N., et al. (1989). "GABA$_B$ Receptors Are Up-Regulated by Chronic Treatment with Lithium or Carbamazepine: GABA Hypothesis of Affective Disorders." *European Journal of Pharmacology* 166: 95–99.

Mundo, E., et al. (2006). "Clinical Variables Related to Antidepressant-Induced Mania in Bipolar Disorder." *Journal of Affective Disorders* 92: 227–230.

Nasr, S., et al. (2006). "Absence of Mood Switch with and Tolerance to Modafinil: A Replication Study from a Large Private Practice." *Journal of Affective Disorders* 95: 111–114.

Nickel, M. K., et al. (2004). "Topiramate Treatment of Aggression in Female Borderline Personality Disorder Patients: A Double-Blind, Placebo-Controlled Study." *Journal of Clinical Psychiatry* 65: 1515–1519.

Nickel, M., et al. (2005). "Treatment of Aggression with Topiramate in Male Borderline Patients: A Double-Blind, Placebo-Controlled Study." *Biological Psychiatry* 57: 495–499.

Nickel, M., et al. (2006). "Topiramate Treatment for Women with Borderline Personality Disorder: A Double-Blind, Placebo-Controlled Study." *Journal of Clinical Psychopharmacology* 26: 61–66.

Nierenberg, A. A., et al. (2006). "Treatment-Resistant Bipolar Depression: A STEP-BD Equipoise Randomized Effectiveness Trial of Antidepressant Augmentation with Lamotrigine, Inositol, or Risperidone." *The American Journal of Psychiatry* 163: 210–216.

Noaghiul, S., and J. R. Hibbeln (2003). "Cross-National Comparisons of Seafood Consumption and Rates of Bipolar Disorder." *American Journal of Psychiatry* 160: 2222–2227.

Ornoy, A. (2006). "Neuroteratogens in Man: An Overview with Special Emphasis on the Teratogenicity of Antiepileptic Drugs in Pregnancy." *Reproductive Toxicology* 22: 214–226.

Osby, U., et al. (2001). "Excess Mortality in Bipolar and Unipolar Disorder in Sweden." *Archives of General Psychiatry* 58: 844–850.

Otto, M. W., et al. (2003). "Psychoeducational and Cognitive-Behavioral Strategies in the Management of Bipolar Disorder." *Journal of Affective Disorders* 73: 171–181.

Pachet, A., et al. (2003). "Beneficial Behavioural Effects of Lamotrigine in Traumatic Brain Injury." *Brain Injury* 17: 715–722.

Pande, A. C., et al. (1999). "Treatment of Social Phobia with Gabapentin: A Placebo-Controlled Study." *Journal of Clinical Psychopharmacology* 19: 341–348.

Pande, A., et al. (2000). " Placebo-Controlled Study of GABApentin Treatment of Panic Disorder." *Journal of Clinical Psychopharmacology* 20: 467–471.

Pande, A., et al. (2003). "Pregabalin in Generalized Anxiety Disorder: A Placebo-Controlled Trial." *American Journal of Psychiatry* 160: 533–540.

Parker, G., et al. (2006a). "Omega-3 Fatty Acids and Mood Disorders." *American Journal of Psychiatry* 163: 969–978.

Parker, G., et al. (2006b) "SSRIs as Mood Stabilizers for Bipolar II Disorder? A Proof of Concept Study." *Journal of Affective Disorders* 92: 205–214.

Pavuluri, M. N., et al. (2005). "Pediatric Bipolar Disorder: A Review of the Past 10 Years." *Journal of the American Academy of Child & Adolescent Psychiatry* 44: 846–871.

Perlis, R. H., et al. (2006a). "Atypical Antipsychotics in the Treatment of Mania: A Meta-Analysis of Randomized, Placebo-Controlled Trials." *Journal of Clinical Psychiatry* 67: 509–516.

Perlis, R. H., et al. (2006b). "Clinical Features of Bipolar Depression Versus Major Depressive Disorder in Large Multicenter Trials." *American Journal of Psychiatry* 163: 225–231.

Perlis, R. H., et al. (2006c). "Predictors of Recurrence in Bipolar Disorder: Primary Outcomes from the Systematic Treatment Enhancement Program for Bipolar Disorder (STEP-BD)." *American Journal of Psychiatry* 163: 217–224.

Perucca, E. (2005). "Birth Defects After Prenatal Exposure to Antiepileptic Drugs." *Lancet Neurology* 4: 781–786.

Perugi, G., et al. (2002). "Effectiveness of Adjunctive Gabapentin in Resistant Bipolar Disorders: Is It Due to Anxious–Alcohol Abuse Comorbidity?" *Journal of Clinical Psychopharmacology* 22: 584–591.

Phrolov, K., et al. (2004). "Single-Dose Intravenous Valproate in Acute Mania." *Journal of Clinical Psychiatry* 65: 68–70.

Pinto, O. C., and Akiskal, H. S. (1998). "Lamotrigine as a Promising Approach to Borderline Personality: An Open Case Series Without Concurrent DSM-IV Major Mood Disorder." *Journal of Affective Disorders* 51: 333–343.

Piontek, C. M., et al. (2000). "Serum Valproate Levels in 6 Breastfeeding Mother-Infant Pairs." *Journal of Clinical Psychiatry* 61: 170–172.

Porter, R. J., et al. (2007). "Randomized, Multicenter, Dose-Ranging Trial of Retigabine for Partial-Onset Seizures." *Neurology* 68: 1197–1204.

Post, R. M., et al. (2003). "Morbidity in 258 Bipolar Outpatients Followed for 1 Year with Daily Prospective Ratings on the NIMH Life Chart Method." *Journal of Clinical Psychiatry* 64: 680–690.

Post, R. M., et al. (2005). "The Impact of Bipolar Depression." *Journal of Clinical Psychiatry* 66: Supplement 5, 5–10.

Post, R. M., et al. (2006). "Mood Switch in Bipolar Depression: Comparison of Adjunctive Venlafaxine, Bupropion and Sertraline." *British Journal of Psychiatry* 189: 124–131.

Preston, G. A., et al. (2004). "Borderline Personality Disorder in Patients with Bipolar Disorder and Response to Lamotrigine." *Journal of Affective Disorders* 79: 297–303.

Rendell, J. M., et al. (2006) "Risperidone Alone or in Combination for Acute Mania." *Cochrane Database System Review* CD004043.

Rocha, F., and C. Hara (2003). "Lamotrigine Augmentation in Unipolar Depression." *International Clinical Psychopharmacology* 18: 97–99.

Rosenthal, M. (2003). "Tiagabine for the Treatment of Generalized Anxiety Disorder: A Randomized, Open-Label, Clinical Trial with Paroxetine as a Positive Control." *Journal of Clinical Psychiatry* 64: 1245–1249.

Sachs, G. S., et al. (2007). "Effectiveness of Adjunctive Antidepressant Treatment for Bipolar Depression." *New England Journal of Medicine* 356: 1711–1722.

Schapiro, N. A. (2005). "Bipolar Disorders in Children and Adolescents." *Journal of Pediatric Health Care* 19: 131–141.

Scherk, H., et al. (2007). "Second-Generation Antipsychotic Agents in the Treatment of Acute Mania." *Archives of General Psychiatry* 64: 442–455.

Sokolenko, M., and S. Kutcher (2001). "Lamotrigine." *Child and Adolescent Psychopharmacology News* 6 (August): 1–5.

Soloff, P. H. (1994). "Is There Any Drug Treatment of Choice for the Borderline Patient? *Acta Psychiatrica Scandinavica* 379, Supplement: 50–55.

Stahl, S. M. (2004). "Anticonvulsants as Anxiolytics, Part I: Tiagabine and Other Anticonvulsants with Actions on GABA." *Journal of Clinical Psychiatry* 65: 291–292.

Stanford, M. S., et al. (2005). "A Comparison of Anticonvulsants in the Treatment of Impulsive Aggression." *Experimental and Clinical Psychopharmacology* 13: 72–77.

Stoll, A. L., et al. (1999). "Omega-3 Fatty Acids in Bipolar Disorder: A Preliminary Double-Blind, Placebo-Controlled Trial." *Archives of General Psychiatry* 56: 407–412.

Suppes, T., et al. (2005). "The Texas Implementation of Medication Algorithms: Update to the Algorithms for Treatment of Bipolar I Disorder." *Journal of Clinical Psychiatry* 66: 870–886.

Tohen, M., et al. (1998). "The Effect of Comorbid Substance Abuse Disorders on the Course of Bipolar Disorder: A Review." *Harvard Review of Psychiatry* 6: 133–141.

Tohen, M., et al. (2005). "Olanzapine Versus Lithium in the Maintenance Treatment of Bipolar Disorder: A 12-Month, Randomized, Double-Blind, Controlled Clinical Trial." *American Journal of Psychiatry* 162: 1281–1290.

Tohen, M., et al. (2006). "Randomized, Placebo-Controlled Trial of Olanzapine as Maintenance Therapy in Patients With Bipolar I Disorder Responding to Acute Treatment With Olanzapine." *American Journal of Psychiatry* 163: 247–256.

Vajda, F. J., et al. (2006). "Foetal Malformations and Seizure Control: 52 Months Data of the Australian Pregnancy Registry." *European Journal of Neurology* 13: 645–654.

Vieta, E., et al. (2005). "Effectiveness of Aripiprazole v. Haloperidol in Acute Bipolar Mania: Double-Blind, Randomized, Comparative 12-Week Trial." *British Journal of Psychiatry* 187: 235–242.

Viguera, A. C., et al. (2000). "Risk of Recurrence of Bipolar Disorder in Pregnant and Nonpregnant Women After Discontinuing Lithium Maintenance." *American Journal of Psychiatry* 157: 179–184.

Viguera, A. C., et al. (2002). "Reproductive Decisions by Women with Bipolar Disorder After Pregnancy Psychiatric Consultation." *American Journal of Psychiatry* 159: 2102–2104.

Wagner, K. D., et al. (2006). "A Double-Blind, Randomized, Placebo-Controlled Trial of Oxcarbazepine in the Treatment of Bipolar Disorder in Children and Adolescents." *American Journal of Psychiatry* 163: 1179–1186.

Ward, S., and K. L. Wisner (2007). "Collaborative Management of Women with Bipolar Disorder During Pregnancy and Postpartum: Pharmacologic Considerations." *Journal of Midwifery & Womens Health* 52: 3–13.

Watase, K., et al. (2007) "Lithium Therapy Improves Neurological Function and Hippocampal Dendritic Arborization in a Spinocerebellar Ataxia Type 1 Mouse Model." *PLoS Med* 4(5): e182. doi:10.1371/journal.pmed.0040182.

Wilson, M. S., and R. L. Findling (2007). "Zonisamide for Bipolar Depression." *Expert Opinion in Pharmacotherapy* 8: 111–113.

Wozniak, J., et al. (2007). "Omega-3 Fatty Acid Monotherapy for Pediatric Bipolar Disorder: A Prospective Open-Label Trial." *European Neuropsychopharmacology* 17: 440–447.

Yatham, L. N., et al. (2005). "Atypical Antipsychotics in Bipolar Depression: Potential Mechanisms of Action." *Journal of Clinical Psychiatry* 66, Supplement 5: 40–48.

Yonkers, K. A., et al. (2004). "Management of Bipolar Disorder During Pregnancy and the Postpartum Period." *American Journal of Psychiatry* 161: 608–620.

Zarate, C. A., et al. (2005). "Molecular Mechanisms of Bipolar Disorder." *Drug Discovery Today: Disease Mechanisms* 2: 435–445.

Zarate, C. A., et al. (2006). "Cellular Plasticity Cascades: Targets for the Development of Novel Therapeutics for Bipolar Disorder." *Biological Psychiatry* 59: 1006–1020.

Chapter 9

Antipsychotic Drugs

Schizophrenia

Schizophrenia is a debilitating neuropsychiatric illness that typically strikes young people just when they are maturing into adulthood (Freedman, 2003). Affecting approximately 1 percent of the population, the disorder is associated with marked social and/or occupational dysfunction, and its course and outcome vary greatly. In the premorbid phase of the illness, subtle motor, cognitive, or social impairments are often observed but are not severe enough to place affected people outside the normal range of functioning (Miyamoto et al., 2003). In the prodromal phase, mood symptoms, cognitive symptoms, social withdrawal, or obsessive behaviors may develop. Onset of the full syndrome leads to substantial functional deterioration in self-care, work, and interpersonal relationships, especially during the first 5 to 10 years, after which clinical deterioration reaches a plateau and, in some situations, may actually improve. Nevertheless, schizophrenia is associated with an increased risk of suicide; approximately 10 to 15 percent of people with this disorder take their own lives, usually within the first 10 years of developing the illness (Sadock and Sadock, 2007; Keltner and Folks, 2005; Lieberman et al., 2001).

Schizophrenia is thought to be a neurodevelopmental disease, associated with significant abnormalities in brain structure and function. Because these abnormalities can be observed in patients who have never been treated with antipsychotic medications, they are considered to be inherent in the disease, not medication related (Torrey, 2002). The illness is presently viewed as a misconnection syndrome,

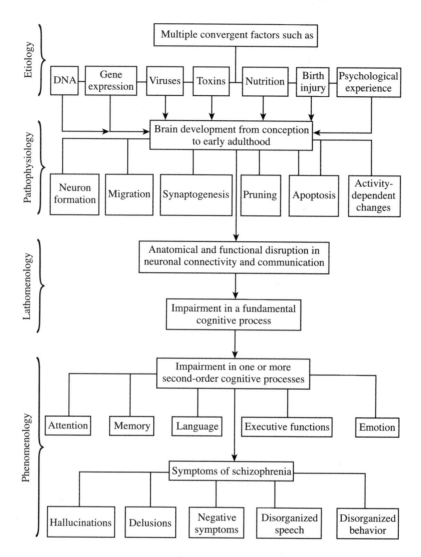

FIGURE 9.1 General model of the development of schizophrenia. [From Andreasen (1999), p. 783.]

reflecting a basic disorder in neural circuits, caused by many factors that affect brain development (Andreasen, 1999; Javitt and Coyle, 2004; Miyamoto et al., 2003) (Figure 9.1).

The symptoms of schizophrenia have classically been divided into positive and negative clusters. The positive symptoms are the symptoms typical of psychosis and include abnormalities in perception (hallucinations), inferential thinking (delusions), and disorganized, incoherent, and illogical speech (thought disorder). The negative symptoms reflect the absence of some normal human quality and include blunting of emotional expression (flattened affect), impoverishment of speech and mental creativity (alogia), loss of motivation and interest (avolition) and the ability to experience pleasure (anhedonia), and social withdrawal. This differentiation of symptomatology is important because the classic (first-generation) agents affect primarily the positive symptoms, while the newer, "atypical," or second-generation antipsychotic drugs may also reduce the negative symptoms, as well as depressive mood states that can accompany schizophrenia. Patients with schizophrenia also have impairments in many different cognitive systems, such as memory, attention, and executive function. Therefore, treatment is now aimed at more than reducing abnormal perceptions and thought processes; efforts are also being directed to improving cognitive functioning and quality of life so that patients with severe and persistent mental illness can successfully reintegrate into the community (American Psychiatric Association, 2004; Janicak et al., 2006; Sharma, 2002; Weickert et al., 2003).

Dopamine Involvement

Early scientific evidence supported a specific *dopamine theory* of schizophrenia, which proposed that the disorder developed from dysregulation of dopaminergic brain pathways, resulting in an overactivity of dopaminergic function (McGowan et al., 2004). This conclusion was derived first from the fact that abuse of stimulant drugs, such as amphetamine, which are known to increase synaptic dopamine concentration, produced a syndrome indistinguishable from the paranoid type of schizophrenia and second from the fact that antipsychotic drugs are *dopamine receptor antagonists* and block dopamine receptors in the brain. Dopamine receptors can be classified as either D_1 (of which there are two subtypes, D_1 and D_5) or D_2 (which has three subtypes, D_2, D_3, and D_4). It is now appreciated that not only do all antipsychotic drugs have an affinity for the D_2 receptor, this affinity remains the single best predictor of the effective clinical dose of an antipsychotic (Figure 9.2).

Unfortunately, dopamine, released by neurons in the basal ganglia of the brain, is crucial for maintaining normal coordination of movement. In fact, the loss of these neurons is responsible for the neurological disorder Parkinson's disease. Similarly, by blocking dopamine receptors, antipsychotic drugs produce the neurological side effect of parkinsonian symptoms (also known as extrapyramidal symptoms—EPS). Long-term, chronic antipsychotic administration may also elicit other syndromes of abnormal motor function such as tardive dyskinesia (TD), which may be irreversible.

Until recently, it was assumed that the risk of these neurological symptoms was an unavoidable consequence of antipsychotic drug

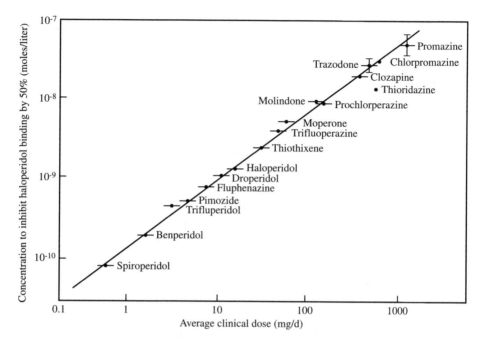

FIGURE 9.2 Correlation between the clinical potency and receptor-binding activities of neuroleptic drugs. Clinical potency is expressed as the daily dose used in treating schizophrenia, and binding activity is expressed as the concentration needed to produce 50 percent inhibition of haloperidol binding. Haloperidol binds to dopamine-2 receptors; other antipsychotic drugs compete for the same receptors. Thus, measuring the competitive inhibition of haloperidol binding correlates with potency of an antipsychotic drug.

therapy. However, the discovery of the second-generation antipsychotics (SGAs) has shown that this assumption is incorrect and that antipsychotic efficacy can be obtained with little or no EPS or TD (Correll et al., 2004; Janicak, et al., 2006). This is the primary advantage of the newer agents relative to the first-generation drugs.

Serotonin Involvement

As with dopamine, early investigations into the possible role of serotonin (5-HT) in schizophrenia followed from observations of the actions of psychoactive drugs. Because the psychedelic drug LSD produces hallucinations, it was initially proposed to be involved in the clinical syndrome seen in schizophrenia. LSD is one of a group of hallucinogenic drugs that are thought to exert their psychedelic effect as agonists at 5-HT$_{2A}$ receptors. For this reason, it was hypothesized that *5-HT$_2$ receptor antagonism* might be responsible for some of the beneficial actions of antipsychotics. Although it has since been concluded that serotonin does not play an important role in the etiology of schizophrenia, antagonism of this transmitter at 5-HT$_2$ receptors may be involved in the improved neurological side effect profile of the newer antipsychotic medications (see Meltzer, 2002, for the history of this concept).

Glutamate Involvement

In addition to amphetamine and LSD, the two psychedelic drugs *phencyclidine* (PCP) and *ketamine* (Chapter 18) have also provided insight into the neurochemistry of schizophrenia. These drugs also produce some schizophrenialike symptoms, such as hallucinations, out-of-body experiences, negative symptomatology, and cognitive deficits. The mechanism responsible for these effects is a potent blockade of NMDA-type glutamate receptors. This relationship suggests that there may be a glutamatergic dysfunction in the etiology of schizophrenia, which has prompted a glutamate-NMDA receptor hypofunction hypothesis of schizophrenia. This theory proposes that NMDA hypofunction results in excessive release of the excitatory neurotransmitters glutamate and acetylcholine in the frontal cortex, damaging cortical neurons and triggering the deterioration seen in patients with schizophrenia (Farber, 2003; Laruelle et al., 2003; Moghaddam, 2003; Rujescu et al., 2006).

Historical Background and Classification of Antipsychotic Drugs

Prior to 1950, there were no effective drugs for treating psychotic patients; these patients were usually permanently or chronically hospitalized. By 1955, more than half a million psychotic patients in the United States were residing in mental hospitals. A dramatic and steady reversal in this trend began in 1956, and by 1983 fewer than 220,000 patients were institutionalized despite a doubling in the number of admissions to state hospitals. By the early 1990s, people with schizophrenia were routinely stabilized on medication and rapidly discharged from institutions.[1] What accounted for this dramatic shift was a class of drugs called phenothiazines, the first category of antipsychotic agents.

Phenothiazines were initially developed as antihistamines and were first studied for their mildly sedating action. The sedative properties led

---

[1]Although the discharge rate of schizophrenics from institutions is high, there is concern about their ultimate functioning in society. Many patients who were discharged on phenothiazines failed to continue their medication, and they functioned poorly as a result. It has been estimated that about 50 percent of the adult homeless population in the United States may suffer from inadequately controlled schizophrenia.

the French anesthesiologist and surgeon H. Laborit to use *promethazine*, the first phenothiazine, to deepen anesthesia. This drug was administered in a "lytic cocktail" to patients the night before surgery to allay their fears and anxieties. Promethazine was soon followed by a second phenothiazine, *chlorpromazine* (Thorazine), which was found to reduce the amount of anesthetic drugs a patient needed without making the patient unconscious; rather, this treatment produced a state characterized by calmness, conscious sedation, and disinterest in and detachment from external stimuli. This condition was termed a *neuroleptic state* and chlorpromazine was the first neuroleptic drug.

Laborit persuaded many clinicians to try chlorpromazine, and later that year the French research psychiatrists Delay and Deniker studied its effect in schizophrenic patients. Although it did not provide a permanent cure, chlorpromazine was found to be remarkably effective in alleviating the clinical manifestations of psychosis (López-Muñoz et al., 2005). In conjunction with supportive therapy, its use allowed thousands of patients who otherwise would have been permanently hospitalized to return to their communities, albeit in a less than satisfactory state.

In the continuing search for more effective drugs with fewer side effects, alternatives to the phenothiazines have been developed. The second class of neuroleptics was the *butyrophenones*, developed in Belgium in the mid-1960s. Two butyrophenones are currently available, *haloperidol* (Haldol) and *droperidol* (Inapsine). Haloperidol is used in the treatment of schizophrenia, droperidol in the treatment of nausea and vomiting associated with surgery. Together, the phenothiazines and haloperidol are classified as "first-generation agents."

The first-generation antipsychotics (FGAs) are most effective against the positive symptoms of schizophrenia, and as noted, the doses required for clinical improvement were significantly correlated with their ability to block dopamine, D_2 receptors. Unfortunately, D_2 antagonism also produced undesirable neurological side effects, which included acute movement disorders, such as extrapyramidal symptoms similar to the symptoms of Parkinson's disease, and, in some cases, involuntary movement disorders resulting from chronic antipsychotic exposure, such as tardive dyskinesia.

Therefore, for the FGAs, binding to D_2 receptors resulted not only in clinical efficacy but in the likelihood of causing EPS as well. Indeed, the antipsychotic and EPS effects of neuroleptics are generally thought to be linked and inseparable. This idea led to a *neuroleptic threshold concept* of treatment, which held that the neuroleptic dose was gradually increased until EPS was produced. Thus, the "right" dose was the one that caused some degree of motor side effects.

Until recently, because of these and other numerous and serious side effects associated with their use, administration of these drugs was reserved for seriously ill patients. Symptom relief, especially from the delusions and hallucinations, was originally the most essential outcome measure. However, beginning in the late 1980s, breakthroughs occurred that were believed to offer patients a real chance of leading more normal lives. These developments began with the discovery of the first second-generation antipsychotic, clozapine (Clozaril). Clozapine was a major advance because it was effective for many patients (about 30 percent) who did not respond to standard treatment and because it produced little or no symptoms of movement disorders such as EPS or TD (and, in fact, may even reduce TD caused by other antipsychotics).

Unfortunately, clozapine itself had some serious side effects, which limited its use to patients who had not responded to conventional treatment. However, it prompted the development of other SGAs, collectively referred to as "atypical" antipsychotics. In addition to clozapine (Clozaril), they include risperidone (Risperdal), olanzapine (Zyprexa), quetiapine (Seroquel), and ziprasidone (Geodon). The latest atypical antipsychotic, aripiprazole (Abilify), may actually be the first of a new, third generation of antipsychotics (TGAs) because of a unique mechanism of action and prominent antidepressant effects. A second TGA (amisulpride) is expected to be marketed.

All the SGAs differ pharmacologically from the FGAs by having relatively less affinity for D_2 receptors (Grunder et al., 2003) and greater affinity for 5-HT (serotonergic) receptors. For some reason, this allows a separation between antipsychotic efficacy and induction of EPS or other movement disorders (with the exception of risperidone at higher doses) (Horacek et al., 2006; Kapur et al., 1999; Kapur and Remington, 2001; Kapur and Seeman, 2001; Stahl, 2003). Although none of the others share clozapine's superior efficacy for treatment of schizophrenic patients who are refractory to phenothiazine treatment, these drugs have shown that it is possible to separate therapeutic benefit from Parkinsonian side effects (Advokat, 2005).[2]

Initially, the SGAs also appeared to be more effective than FGAs against negative symptoms. However, that is still being debated because

---

[2]Several possible mechanisms might account for this property. First, 5-HT is known to inhibit dopamine release in the nigrostriatal but not the mesolimbic dopamine pathway. By blocking this action (either through 5-HT$_2$ receptor antagonism at the dopamine terminal or by 5-HT$_{1A}$ antagonism at the cell body), SGAs selectively enhance dopamine release in the striatum, which mitigates neuroleptic-induced EPS. Second, clozapine and quetiapine have a low affinity for the D_2 receptor and do not attach very tightly to these binding sites. Because the natural amount of dopamine in the nigrostriatal pathway is greater than that in the mesolimbic pathway, clozapine and quetiapine may be more easily displaced from the striatal dopamine receptors by the higher concentration of the endogenous transmitter. This occurrence would normalize dopaminergic activity in the nigrostriatal system and reduce pseudoparkinsonian side effects.

an apparent improvement in negative symptoms may be secondary to the absence of EPS or to other indirect causes, such as improvement in socialization and cognition, rather than a direct therapeutic effect (Rosenheck, 2003). In addition, the long-term benefits of SGAs on relapse, social and vocational functioning, and quality of life (Gardner et al., 2005; Jones et al., 2006) have not been as great as had been hoped. Finally, the therapeutic advantages of the SGAs in the treatment of schizophrenia have been mitigated by their own serious side effect profile, particularly weight gain and impairment of glucose and lipid metabolism.

Recently, criticisms about the comparative efficacy, safety, and cost-benefit ratio of the SGAs were raised and discussed in several meta-analyses and comparative studies of the first- and second-generation agents (Davis et al., 2003; Davis and Chen, 2004; Leucht et al., 2003). To address these issues, the National Institute of Mental Health (NIMH) conducted a large, double-blind, active control clinical trial, designed to directly compare the relative effectiveness of second-generation antipsychotics and the effectiveness of SGAs with that of a first-generation antipsychotic. As stated by the director of NIMH, "It is the largest, longest, and most comprehensive independent trial ever done to examine existing therapies for this disease."

CATIE and CUtLASS Studies

The Clinical Antipsychotic Trials of Intervention Effectiveness (CATIE) study was conducted in the United States between January 2001 and December 2004 at 57 clinical sites for up to 18 months or until treatment was discontinued for any reason. In the first of three phases, 1493 patients were randomly assigned to receive either one of three SGAs (olanzapine, risperidone, or quetiapine) or an FGA (perphenazine) under double-blind conditions. Ziprasidone was added later following its FDA approval. Results demonstrated that patients discontinued antipsychotic medications at a high rate, 64 to 82 percent across all the drugs, primarily because of lack of efficacy or intolerable side effects (EPS in the case of perphenazine and weight gain or metabolic changes from olanzapine). There was no overall difference in the rate of discontinuation between the SGAs and the FGA, perphenazine (Lieberman et al., 2005).

Of the 1493 patients who were enrolled in the study, 1052 were eligible for phase 2. This part of the study provided two treatment pathways. Patients who had not shown optimal improvement on one of the newer SGAs in the first phase or who had stopped treatment for any other reason were offered the option of random assignment to clozapine or to an SGA other than the one they had received in phase 1. A total of 99 patients entered this "efficacy" pathway. Patients who discontinued treatment for intolerability were offered the opportunity to receive treatment with an SGA other than the one they had previously received—excluding clozapine. A total of 444 patients entered this "tolerability" pathway. The remaining 509 patients (48 percent) did not enter phase 2.

In the "efficacy" pathway, clozapine treatment was found to be more effective than the other SGAs; patients receiving clozapine were less likely to discontinue therapy because of lack of therapeutic response than any of the other newer agents. In the "tolerability" pathway, the drugs olanzapine and risperidone were more effective than quetiapine or ziprasidone in time until discontinuation for any reason. Neither of the phase 2 pathways included either aripiprazole or any first-generation antipsychotic (McEvoy et al., 2006; Stroup et al., 2006).

A British comparison between SGAs and FGAs—Cost Utility of the Latest Antipsychotic Drugs in Schizophrenia (CUtLASS 1)—was reported in October 2006 (Jones et al., 2006). It evaluated 227 people with a diagnosis of schizophrenia who had an inadequate response or an adverse reaction to their previous medication. Prescriptions for either an FGA or an SGA (excluding clozapine) were monitored for 1 year, with blind assessments at 12, 26, and 56 weeks. The primary outcomes were a measure of quality of life, symptoms, adverse effects, participant satisfaction, and costs of care. Like the CATIE trial, the results of this study showed that patients with schizophrenia did just as well on antipsychotic drugs from either category, with patients taking FGA drugs actually showing a trend toward greater improvement on the quality of life scale and symptom scores. Participants expressed no clear preference, and the costs were similar.

Although antipsychotic drugs remain the "cornerstone of treatment for schizophrenia" (Lieberman et. al., 2005), the results of the CATIE and CUtLASS 1 trials have prompted a reassessment of the perceived advantages of the second-generation antipsychotics. The initial optimism generated by these new, "atypical" neuroleptics has been tempered by evidence that they do not improve clinical outcome as much as anticipated and are much more expensive than the older drugs.

At the same time, SGAs are much less likely to produce neurologic side effects relative to FGAs. These agents can therefore be used in clinical populations that are often more susceptible to adverse reactions to FGAs, such as the elderly and children, as well as to treat conditions such as bipolar disorder, depression, generalized anxiety, autism and other pervasive developmental disorders, PTSDs, and patients with borderline personality disorder. In all these situations, FGAs or "traditional" antipsychotic agents would normally be contraindicated. These nonschizophrenic uses are discussed at the end of this chapter. Finally, the absence of motor side effects allows for early, or "prodromal," use in young people with a family history of schizophrenia and early symptoms of the disease (Cannon et al., 2002).

First-Generation Antipsychotic Drugs: Phenothiazines

Historically, the phenothiazines (Figure 9.3; Table 9.1) were the most widely used drugs for treating schizophrenia. They were also used for other purposes, such as to treat nausea and vomiting, to sedate patients before anesthesia, to delay ejaculation, to relieve severe itching, to manage the psychotic component that may accompany acute manic attacks, to treat alcoholic hallucinosis, and to manage the hallucinations caused by psychedelic agents. Today, treatment of most of these conditions now involves the use of newer drugs.

Pharmacokinetics

The phenothiazines are absorbed erratically and unpredictably from the gastrointestinal tract. However, because patients usually take these drugs for long periods of time, the oral route of administration is effective and commonly used. Intramuscular injection of phenothiazines is even more effective: it increases the effectiveness of the drugs about four to ten times that achieved with oral administration. Once these drugs are in the bloodstream, they are rapidly distributed

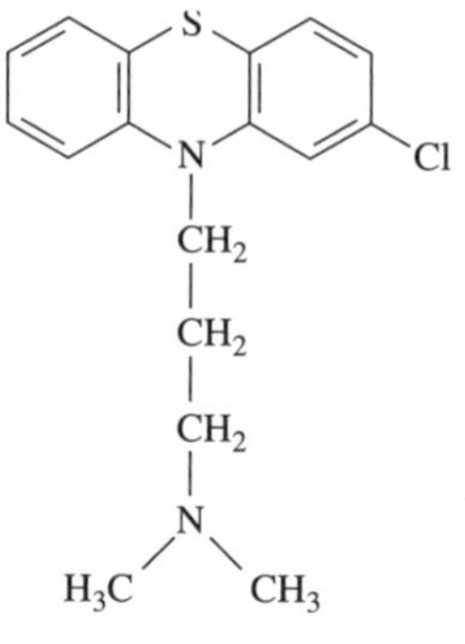

Chlorpromazine (Thorazine)

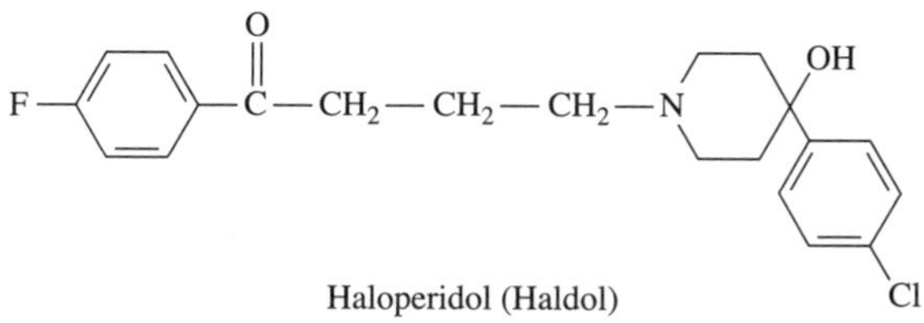

Haloperidol (Haldol)

Figure 9.3 Structural formulas of a phenothiazine (chlorpromazine) and a butyrophenone (haloperidol). Both are traditional antipsychotic drugs.

TABLE 9.1 Antipsychotic drugs

Chemical classification	Drug name: Generic (Trade)	Dose equivalent (mg)	Sedation	Autonomic side effects[a]	Involuntary movement
Phenothiazine	Chlorpromazine (Thorazine)	100	High	High	Moderate
	Prochlorperazine (Compazine)	15	Moderate	Low	High
	Fluphenazine (Prolixin)	2	Low	Low	High
	Trifluoperazine (Stelazine)	5	Moderate	Low	High
	Perphenazine (Trilafon)	8	Low	Low	High
	Acetophenazine (Tindal)	20	Moderate	Low	High
	Carphenazine (Proketazine)	25	Moderate	Low	High
	Triflupromazine (Vesprin)	25	High	Moderate	Moderate
	Mesoridazine (Serentil)	50	High	Moderate	Low
	Thioridazine (Mellaril)	100	High	Moderate	Low
Thioxanthene	Thiothixene (Navane)	4	Low	Low	High
	Chlorprothixene (Taractan)	100	High	High	Moderate
Butyrophenone	Haloperidol (Haldol)	2	Low	Low	Very high
Miscellaneous	Loxapine (Loxitane)	10	Moderate	Low	Moderate
	Molindone (Moban)	10	Moderate	Moderate	Moderate
	Pimozide (Orap)	2	Low	Low	Moderate
New generation	Clozapine (Clozaril)	50	Moderate	Moderate	Low
	Risperidone (Risperdal)	1	Low	Low	Low-Moderate
	Olanzapine (Zyprexa)	1.5	Moderate	Low	Low
	Quetiapine (Seroquel)	40	Low	Low	Low
	Ziprasidone (Geodon)	15	Low	Low	Low
	Aripiprazole (Abilify)	3	Low	Low	Low
	Amisulpride (Solian)	NA	Low	Low	Low

[a]Autonomic side effects include dry mouth, blurred vision, constipation, urinary retention, and reduced blood pressure.

throughout the body. The levels of phenothiazines that are found in the brain are low compared with the levels found in other body tissues; the highest concentrations are found in the lungs, liver, adrenal glands, and spleen.

The phenothiazines have half-lives of 24 to 48 hours, and they are slowly metabolized in the liver. The clinical effects of a single dose persist for at least 24 hours. Thus, taking the daily dose at bedtime often minimizes certain side effects (such as excessive sedation). The phenothiazines become extensively bound to body tissues, which partially accounts for their slow rate of elimination. Metabolites of some of the phenothiazines can be detected for several months after the drug has been discontinued. Slow elimination may also contribute to the slow rate of recurrence of psychotic episodes following cessation of drug therapy.

Pharmacological Effects

In addition to blocking D_2 receptors, the phenothiazines also block acetylcholine (muscarinic), histamine, and norepinephrine receptors. Cholinergic blockade results in dry mouth, dilated pupils, blurred vision, cognitive impairments, constipation, urinary retention, and tachycardia. Noradrenergic blockade can result in hypotension and sedation. Histaminergic blockade has sedating as well as antiemetic effects.

Brain Stem. Through actions on the brain stem, phenothiazines suppress the centers involved in behavioral arousal (the ascending reticular activating center) and vomiting (the chemoreceptor trigger zone). By suppressing activity in the reticular formation, the phenothiazines produce an indifference to external stimuli, reducing sensory input that would otherwise reach higher brain centers.

Hypothalamus-Pituitary. Dopaminergic pathways extend from the hypothalamus to the pituitary gland. Because the hypothalamus is intimately involved in vegetative and motivational processes, suppression of these functions by phenothiazines may produce changes in appetite and food intake, wide fluctuations in body temperature with changes in ambient temperature, and alterations in pituitary gland functions. The pituitary gland is responsible for regulating the secretion of sex hormones; therefore, dopaminergic blockade increases the release of the hormone prolactin, which can produce breast enlargement in males and lactation in females. Phenothiazines also reduce the release of other hormones. In men, ejaculation may be blocked; in women, libido may be decreased, ovulation may be blocked, and normal menstrual cycles may be suppressed, resulting in infertility.

Basal Ganglia. By blocking dopamine receptors in the basal ganglia, phenothiazines produce two main kinds of motor (neurologic) disturbances, which comprise the most bothersome and potentially serious side effects associated with the use of these agents. The two syndromes are (1) acute extrapyramidal reactions, which develop early in treatment in up to 90 percent of patients, and (2) tardive ("tardy," or late) dyskinesia, which occurs much later, during and even after cessation of chronic neuroleptic treatment. Acute extrapyramidal side effects include the following:

- Akathisia, a syndrome characterized by the subjective feeling of anxiety, manifested by restlessness, pacing, constant rocking back and forth, and other repetitive, purposeless, actions

- Dystonia, which presents as involuntary muscle contractions and sustained abnormal, bizarre postures of the limbs, trunk, head, and tongue

- Neuroleptic-induced (pseudo) parkinsonism, which resembles idiopathic (of unknown etiology) Parkinson's disease. (Drugs used to treat parkinsonism are discussed in Chapter 17.)

Neuroleptic-induced parkinsonism is characterized by tremor at rest, "cogwheel type" rigidity of the limbs, and slowing of movement, with a reduction in spontaneous activity. In idiopathic parkinsonism, these symptoms occur when the concentration of dopamine in the nuclei of the basal ganglia (caudate nucleus, putamen, and globus pallidus) decreases to about 20 percent of normal. The same symptoms are produced when neuroleptic drug-induced blockade of dopamine receptors reaches 80 or greater percent. If necessary, antiparkinsonian agents can be administered to control these symptoms, although tolerance may eventually develop to neuroleptic-induced parkinsonism.

Tardive dyskinesia (TD) is a much more puzzling and serious form of movement disorder. Victims exhibit involuntary hyperkinetic movements, often of the face and tongue but also of the trunk and limbs, which can be severely disabling. More characteristic are sucking and smacking of the lips, lateral jaw movements, and darting, pushing, or twisting of the tongue. Choreiform movements of the extremities are frequent. The syndrome appears a few months to several years after the beginning of neuroleptic treatment and is sometimes (~20 percent of the time) irreversible. The incidence of tardive dyskinesia has been estimated at about 20 percent of patients who are treated with phenothiazines, increasing about 4 percent for the first 5 years, but this side effect depends greatly on the particular drug, the dosage, and the age of the patient (it is most common in patients older than 50, with approximately 50 percent of the elderly affected after 5 years).

Unfortunately, there is no adequate treatment for this condition, except perhaps clozapine. Although dyskinesia may be controlled by restarting or increasing the dose of phenothiazine, in the short run parkinsonian side effects may be elicited, and eventually the intensity of the abnormal movements may increase.

Limbic System. Dopaminergic neurons of the central midbrain portion of the brain stem project to limbic structures that regulate emotional expression, as well as to limbic forebrain areas, where emotion and cognition are integrated. Increased sensitivity of dopamine receptors in these areas may be responsible for the positive symptoms of schizophrenia. Thus, a phenothiazine reduces the intensity of schizophrenic delusions and hallucinations, which are particularly sensitive to treatment. It decreases paranoia, fear, hostility, and agitation, and may dramatically relieve the restlessness and hyperactivity associated with an acute schizophrenic episode.

Side Effects and Toxicity

Much of the art of treating schizophrenic patients with antipsychotics lies in diagnosing and managing side effects. In general, the high-potency agents—agents that block dopamine receptors most strongly and require lower doses—produce more extrapyramidal side effects but less sedation, fewer anticholinergic actions, and less postural hypotension than the low-potency neuroleptics (Table 9.2). The choice of drug depends on the specific situation. When sedation is desired, a low-potency agent may be sufficient or a high-potency drug may be combined with a benzodiazepine. If anticholinergic side effects limit adherence, a high-potency drug may be more appropriate, and drug-induced movement disorders, if elicited, may be controlled with antiparkinsonian agents.

It has long been recognized that cognitive disturbances are evident in 40 to 60 percent of patients with schizophrenia. Neuropsychological tests show deficits in numerous "executive" functions, including attention, memory, problem solving, judgment, concept formation, planning, and language. These impairments impede psychosocial performance and eventual reintegration into society. Although it is generally agreed that antipsychotic drugs improve schizophrenic symptomatology, debate concerning their impact on cognitive function is ongoing (Bilder et al., 2002; Purdon et al., 2000; Sharma, 2002; Weiss et al., 2002). Anticholinergic and antihistaminergic actions of the antipsychotics produce memory impairment and sedation, respectively. If these effects are responsible for producing or worsening cognitive dysfunction, then agents without these side effects may appear to improve cognition (Carpenter and Gold, 2002). Ichikawa and colleagues (2002) suggest

---

TABLE 9.2 Possible therapeutic and adverse effects of receptor blockade by neuroleptics

---

Blockade of dopamine D_2 receptors
  Therapeutic effects
    Amelioration of the positive signs and symptoms of psychosis
  Adverse effects
    Extrapyramidal movement disorders: dystonia, parkinsonism, akathisia, tardive dyskinesia, rabbit syndrome
    Endocrine effects: prolactin elevation (galactorrhea, gynecomastia, menstrual changes, sexual dysfunction in males)
Blockade of muscarinic receptors
  Therapeutic effects
    Mitigation of extrapyramidal side effects
  Adverse effects
    Blurred vision
    Attack or exacerbation of narrow-angle glaucoma
    Dry mouth
    Sinus tachycardia
    Constipation
    Urinary retention
    Memory dysfunction
Blockade of serotonin $5\text{-}HT_{2A}$ receptors
  Therapeutic effects
    Amelioration of the negative signs and symptoms of psychosis
    Mitigation of extrapyramidal side effects
  Adverse effects
    Unknown
Blockade of histamine H_1 receptors
  Therapeutic effects
    Sedation
  Adverse effects
    Sedation
    Drowsiness
    Weight gain
    Potentiation of CNS depressant drugs
Blockade of α_1-adrenoceptors
  Therapeutic effects
    Unknown
  Adverse effects
    Potentiation of the antihypertensive effects of prazosin, terazosin, doxazosin, and labetalol
    Postural hypotension, dizziness
    Reflex tachycardia
Blockade of α_2-adrenoceptors
  Therapeutic effects
    Unknown
  Adverse effects
    Blockade of the antihypertensive effects of clonidine and methyldopa

that this may be the case with the newer drugs. They found that SGAs—but not FGAs—induced cortical acetylcholine release. It remains to be seen whether this neurochemical response is associated with improved cognitive performance.

Other potentially serious but less common side effects of phenothiazines include altered pigmentation of the skin, pigment deposits in the retina, permanently impaired vision, allergic (hypersensitivity) reactions, which include liver dysfunction and blood disorders, as well as the previously noted hormonal impairments. Although rare, one potentially lethal reaction to phenothiazines is the neuroleptic malignant syndrome (NMS). The NMS is an acute reaction that may occur to a variety of agents that increase dopaminergic tone. Its incidence in FGA-treated patients is 0.02 to 2.4 percent, and it has been reported to occur in response to the SGAs clozapine, risperidone, and olanzapine. The most common symptoms include fever, severe muscle rigidity of the "lead pipe" type, autonomic changes (such as fluctuating blood pressure), and altered consciousness that may progress to stupor or coma. The most important aspect of effective treatment is early recognition, immediate withdrawal of the responsible agent, and initiation of supportive measures. For additional information and references see Janicak and colleagues (2006) and Keltner and Folks (2005).

Tolerance and Dependence

One of the positive attributes of the phenothiazines is that they are not prone to compulsive abuse. They do not produce tolerance or physical or psychological dependence. Psychotic patients may take phenothiazines for years without increasing their dose because of tolerance; if a dose is increased, it is usually to increase control of psychotic episodes.

Alternative First-Generation Antipsychotics

Following the introduction of chlorpromazine and the other phenothiazines during the late 1950s and early 1960s, the limitations of these agents soon became apparent. Pharmaceutical manufacturers therefore attempted to find drugs with novel chemical structures that might exert antipsychotic efficacy without the accompanying side effects, especially the movement disorders. Although this goal was not realized until the mid-1990s, a few nonphenothiazine antipsychotic agents were developed in the 1960s and early 1970s.

Haloperidol

In 1967, haloperidol (Haldol; see Figure 9.3) was introduced as the first therapeutic alternative to the phenothiazines. A related compound, *droperidol* (Inapsine), was subsequently introduced into anesthesia for the treatment of postoperative nausea and vomiting. Although haloperidol is structurally different, its pharmacological efficacy and side effects are comparable to that of the phenothiazines. It produces sedation and an indifference to external stimuli, and it reduces initiative, anxiety, and activity. It is well absorbed orally and has a moderately slow rate of metabolism and excretion; stable blood levels can be seen for up to 3 days after the drug is discontinued. It takes approximately 5 days for 40 percent of a single dose to be excreted by the kidneys.

Haloperidol's mechanism of antipsychotic action is the same as that of the phenothiazines—it competitively blocks D_2 receptors. It does not produce some of the serious side effects occasionally seen in patients taking phenothiazines (such as jaundice and blood abnormalities). But because it is a high-potency D_2 antagonist, it causes parkinsonism and other motor disorders comparable to those induced by high-potency phenothiazines, and it may require adjunctive prophylactic antiparkinsonian medication. In general, however, haloperidol is effective for treating acutely psychotic patients, as it has a rapid onset, especially when given by injection.

Molindone

The two alternative medications molindone (Moban) and loxapine (Loxitane) were introduced in the early 1970s (Figure 9.4). Molindone is a structurally unique molecule resembling the neurotransmitter serotonin. Whether this similarity is relevant to its antipsychotic action is unknown. Molindone is comparable to the traditional antipsychotic drugs in dopamine receptor occupancy, therapeutic efficacy, and side effects, except that it has been shown to produce weight loss. It produces moderate sedation, although it has also been reported to increase motor activity and possibly induce a euphoric effect in rare cases. Both effects may be related to its reported block of the enzyme monoamine oxidase. Molindone may also produce parkinsonian movements similar to those seen in patients taking phenothiazines.

Loxapine

Loxapine (Loxitane) structurally resembles the atypical antipsychotic clozapine, and like the newer SGAs, it binds strongly to both dopaminergic and serotonergic receptors. Nevertheless, its actions differ little from the traditional antipsychotic drugs. Kapur and coworkers (1999) have proposed that although loxapine, unlike many traditional antipsychotics, has a high degree of 5-HT_2 receptor occupancy, it is not "atypical" because its 5-HT_2 occupancy is not greater than its D_2 occupancy. It has antipsychotic, antiemetic, and sedative properties and causes abnormal motor movements. It lowers convulsive thresholds somewhat more than the phenothiazines. Taken orally, loxapine is well absorbed, and it is metabolized and excreted within about 24 hours.

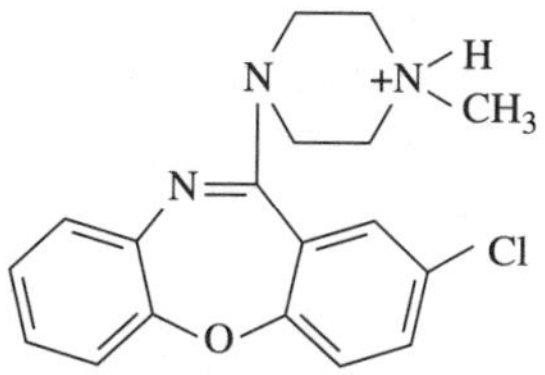

Loxapine (Loxitane)

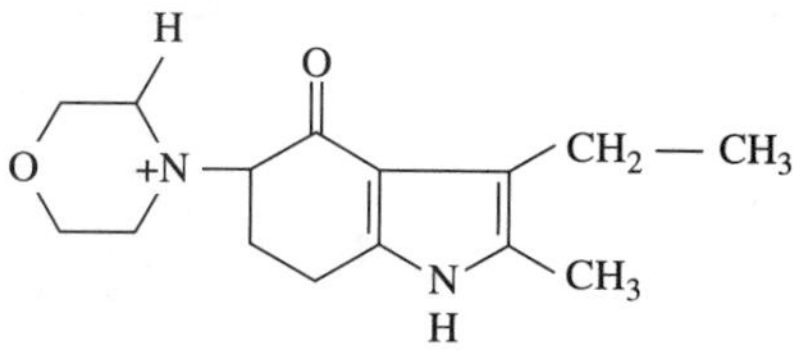

Molindone (Moban)

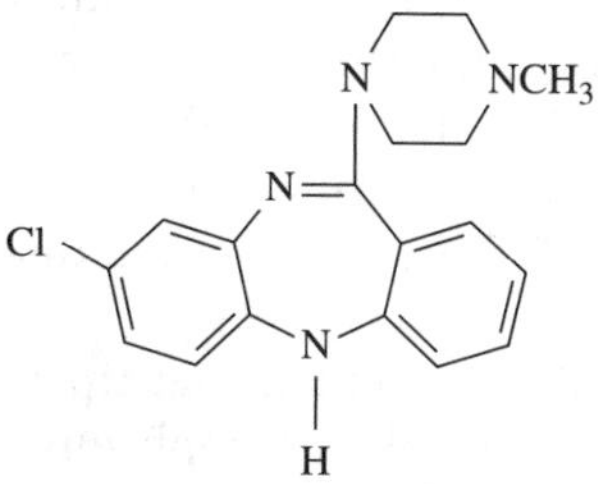

Clozapine (Clozaril)

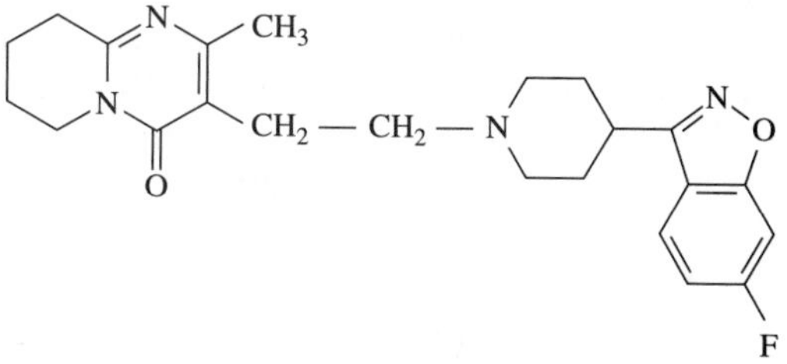

Risperidone (Risperdal)

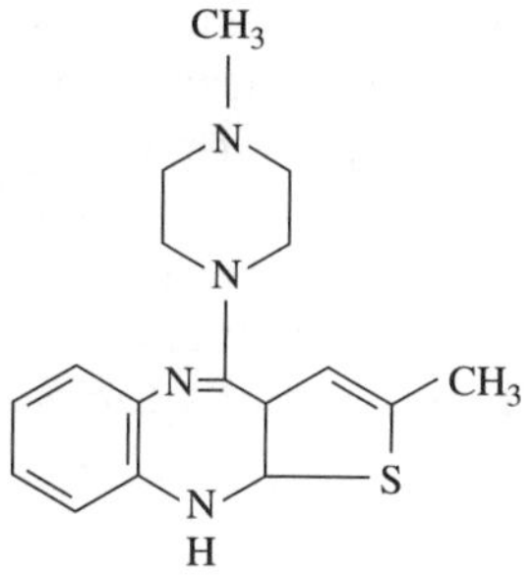

Olanzapine (Zyprexa)

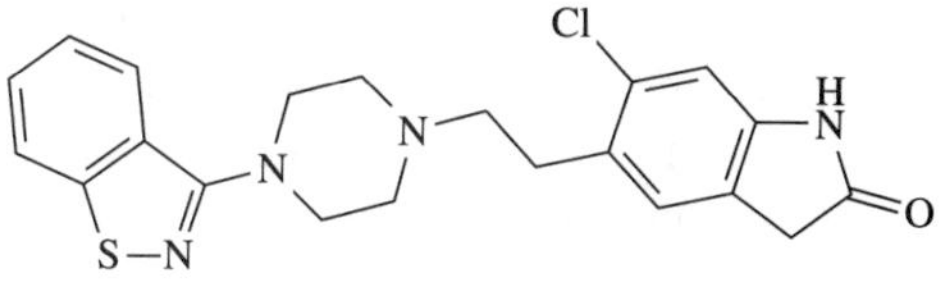

Ziprasidone (Geodon)

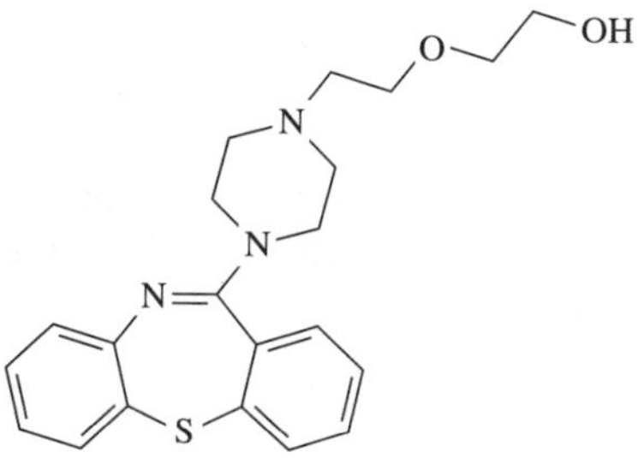

Quetiapine (Seroquel)

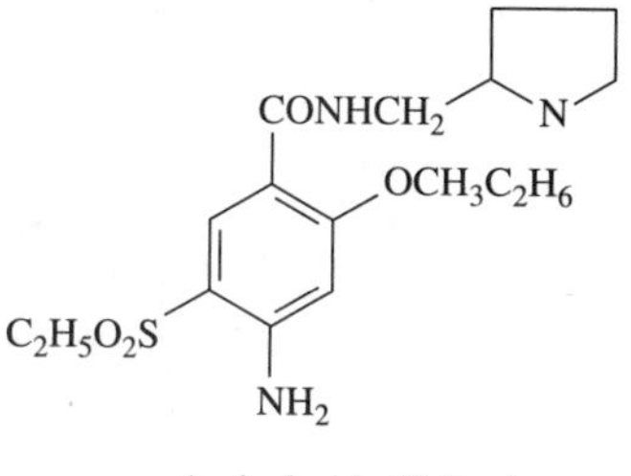

Amisulpride (Solian)

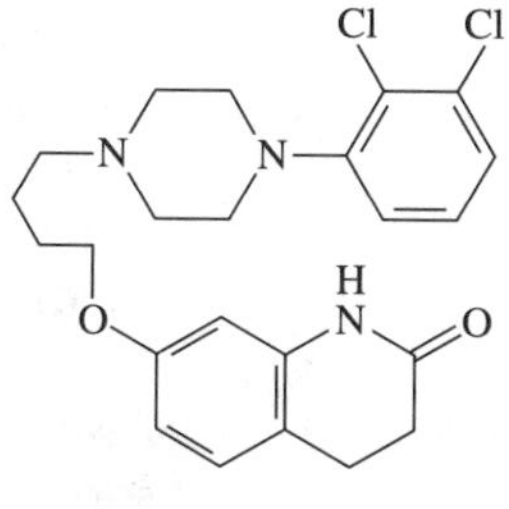

Aripiprazole (Abilify)

Figure 9.4 Structural formulas of some second-generation, atypical, antipsychotic drugs.

Pimozide

Although pimozide (Orap) is an antipsychotic drug, it is currently marketed in the United States for the treatment of motor and phonic tics in patients with Tourette's disorder who are unresponsive to other medications. In Europe and South America, it is more widely used as a neuroleptic antipsychotic drug. Besides the usual movement disorders of EPS and TD, the side effects that most limit the use of pimozide are electrocardiographic abnormalities (called QT prolongation) that are potentially dangerous. QT prolongation is discussed later in this chapter.

The discovery and development of the first-generation antipsychotics was a major advance in the treatment of schizophrenia. Nevertheless, it is recognized that there are three types of unsatisfactory outcomes for schizophrenic patients treated with phenothiazines and other FGAs. The first category includes patients who are treatment-resistant and refractory to medication, despite an adequate trial of an antipsychotic. The second consists of patients who have persistent negative symptoms, despite successful control of positive symptoms. The third consists of patients who are unable to tolerate the side effects of the antipsychotics. Present evidence suggests that, at the very least, SGAs may provide better options for patients in the third category.

Second-Generation (Atypical) Antipsychotic Agents

From 1975 to 1989, not a single new antipsychotic was marketed in the United States. Since then, clozapine (1989), risperidone (1994), olanzapine (1996), sertindole (1997), quetiapine (1997), ziprasidone (2001), and aripiprazole (2002) have been introduced. Amisulpride (Solian) is available in Europe and Australia but not yet in the United States. Each agent is unique in its pharmacology.

Clozapine

Clozapine (Clozaril; see Figure 9.4), the first atypical antipsychotic, has been demonstrated to be clinically superior to traditional antipsychotics, first, because it is effective in about one-third of patients who are resistant to conventional medications, and second, because it lacks the extrapyramidal side effects associated with the traditional neuroleptics (Volavka et al., 2002). In fact, for patients with primary parkinsonism who demonstrate psychotic symptoms (such as hallucinations and delusions), clozapine can effectively treat their psychosis without exacerbating the movement disorder (Comaty and Advokat, 2001; Parkinson Study Group, 1999).

Background. Synthesized in 1959, clozapine was introduced into clinical practice in Europe in the early 1970s. Its lack of extrapyramidal effects was immediately appreciated. However, in 1975 several schizophrenic patients in Finland died of severe infectious diseases after developing agranulocytosis (loss of white blood cells in the blood) while taking clozapine. As a result, clinical testing ceased and the drug was withdrawn from unrestricted use in Europe. Later, clozapine was reexamined for two major reasons: (1) the agranulocytosis was found to be reversible when the drug was discontinued, and (2) the drug was found to be therapeutically beneficial in patients who had failed to respond to the traditional antipsychotic medications.

In 1986 a large, multicenter trial of the drug in the United States found improvement in 30 percent of severely psychotic patients who were unresponsive to other drugs; only 1 to 2 percent developed agranulocytosis. More recent studies show that the rate of improvement may approach 60 percent with longer therapy. In some patients the improvements are striking; they are able to be discharged from hospitals or participate meaningfully in rehabilitation. Other clozapine responders do not improve substantially in their positive symptoms but report that their mood and sense of well-being are improved and their quality of life is better. Finally, a compelling amount of evidence suggested that clozapine reduced the risk of suicide in schizophrenia relative to other antipsychotics. This observation led to the International Suicide Prevention Trial (InterSePT) study that compared clozapine with another SGA, olanzapine, in patients with schizophrenia or schizoaffective disorder at risk for suicide (Meltzer et al, 2003). Clozapine was better than olanzapine at reducing suicidal behaviors and as a result is FDA-approved for reduction of suicide risk in patients with schizophrenia or schizoaffective disorder.

Pharmacokinetics. Clozapine is well absorbed orally and plasma levels of the drug peak in about 1 to 4 hours. The drug has two major metabolites, both of which are pharmacologically inactive. Its metabolic half-life varies from 9 to 30 hours. The optimal plasma level of clozapine is approximately 200 to 350 ng/ml, corresponding to a daily dose of 200 to 400 milligrams, although dosage must be individualized and may be as high as 900 milligrams per day, if clinically warranted. Monitoring plasma levels may be useful in optimizing treatment, for example, when psychotic symptoms recur, to determine whether noncompliance with therapy or abrupt discontinuation of the drug might be at fault (Tollefson et. al., 1999).

Pharmacodynamics. As noted, clozapine has a receptor profile that differs from the FGAs. It antagonizes D_2 receptors less strongly than D_1 receptors and substantially less than $5-HT_2$ receptors.

Other receptor types antagonized by clozapine include D_3 and D_4 receptors and 5-HT_{1A}, histaminergic, cholinergic (muscarinic), and adrenergic receptors.

Side Effects and Toxicity. Although clozapine's efficacy is well documented, its use is severely limited by its side effects and potential for serious toxicity. Common side effects include sedation, extreme weight gain, decrease in seizure threshold, sialorrhea (hypersalivation) and constipation, with rare instances of agranulocytosis.

Sedation occurs in about 40 percent of patients taking clozapine; it may be dose limiting and have a negative impact on compliance. It appears to be an antihistaminic effect. Taking the drug at bedtime may help improve compliance. Weight gain is a problem for up to 80 percent of patients; it can be severe, with gains of 20 pounds or more not unusual. Seizures occur at a greater rate with clozapine than with other antipsychotics, especially at high doses (600 to 900 milligrams per day), and it has a specific warning for this adverse event.

Sialorrhea (increased saliva production) occurs in one-third to one-half of patients, not only during the day but often much worse at night, with patients complaining of waking up with a wet pillow. The mechanism is believed to be due to an impaired ability to swallow, which causes saliva to accumulate. It may be severe and difficult to treat although it can disappear over time. Constipation occurs in about 30 percent of patients and can be quite bothersome. Education and stool softeners can help.

As discussed, the greatest concern with clozapine is the risk of developing severe, life-threatening (although reversible) agranulocytosis, with an incidence of about 1 to 2 percent (Tschen et al., 1999). White blood cell counts and absolute neutrophil counts must be monitored weekly for the first 6 months of therapy, then every 2 weeks for the next 6 months, then monthly thereafter, with more frequent monitoring if the white blood cell count decreases. Other drugs that can reduce white blood cell count (most notably carbamazepine; see Chapter 8) should not be taken concomitantly. The etiology of clozapine-induced agranulocytosis appears to involve an unusual cellular-toxic mechanism. Eutrecht (1992) demonstrated that clozapine could be metabolized not only in the liver but also by the white blood cells themselves (an extremely unusual situation). An intermediate compound in this metabolic process is reactive and is toxic to the cell, possibly destroying the white cells that produced the metabolite.

Risperidone

Risperidone (Risperdal; see Figure 9.4), the second atypical antipsychotic drug, was introduced in 1994. It is a potent antagonist at both D_2 and 5-HT_2 receptors, resulting in improved control of psychotic symptoms with a minimum of neuroleptic-induced EPS at low doses, less than 6 milligrams per day. However, the incidence of parkinsonian movement disorders and other effects of dopaminergic blockade (such as prolactin release) increases at higher doses.

Pharmacokinetics. Risperidone is well absorbed when taken orally, is highly bound to plasma proteins, and is metabolized to an active intermediate, 9-hydroxy-risperidone. A long-acting injectable form of risperidone (Risperdal Consta) has recently been approved. Using novel technology, the drug in this formulation is encapsulated in biodegradable polymer microspheres suspended in a water-based solution. A single intramuscular injection can last up to two weeks (Fleishhacker et al., 2003; Kane et al., 2003).

The metabolic half-life of risperidone is about 3 hours; that of the metabolite, which accounts for much of risperidone's action, is about 23 hours. In fact, recognition of this mechanism led to the approval on December 20, 2006, of the active metabolite 9-hydroxy-risperidone (paliperidone), under the trade name Invega. This metabolite is a once-daily oral medication, available in 3-, 6-, or 9-milligram doses, that delivers the drug through the OROS[3] extended-release formulation, with a recommended dose of 6 milligrams and a range of 3 to 12 milligrams. Because of a 23-hour half-life, once daily administration is satisfactory.

Pharmacodynamics. Risperidone is as effective as haloperidol in reducing the positive symptomatology of schizophrenia at doses that do not produce a high incidence of EPS. Although this drug might not be quite as effective as clozapine, its safety profile can make it a first-line agent for treating schizophrenia. In addition, it has been reported useful in the prodromal phases of schizophrenia (Cannon, et al., 2002) and in a variety of situations outside of schizophrenia.

Side Effects. Common side effects of risperidone include somnolence, agitation, anxiety, insomnia, headache, elevation of prolactin levels, EPS at high doses, and nausea. Weight gain is about 50 percent of that seen with either clozapine or olanzapine. Extrapyramidal symptoms are minimal at low doses (6 milligrams or less), although even low doses may elicit EPS in newly diagnosed patients with no previous exposure to antipsychotic drugs (Rosebush and Mazurek, 1999). Risperidone is considered to be safe in breast-fed infants; infant levels are only about 4 percent of the mother's (Ilett et al., 2004).

---

[3]OROS is a trademarked delivery system. It is a capsule-shaped tablet consisting of a multilayer core surrounded by a semipermeable membrane that allows slow release of the drug from the tablet. Adderall (Chapter 10) is also available in OROS formulation.

In 2004 the manufacturer reported an increased incidence of strokes and CNS ischemic attacks in elderly patients taking risperidone (see Chapter 11 for a more complete discussion).

Olanzapine

Introduced in 1996, olanzapine (Zyprexa; see Figure 9.4) structurally and pharmacologically resembles clozapine, without clozapine's toxicity on white blood cells.

Pharmacokinetics. Olanzapine is well absorbed orally. Peak plasma levels occur in about 5 to 8 hours. Metabolized in the liver, olanzapine has an elimination half-life in the range of 27 to 38 hours in both adults and children (Grothe et al., 2000). Gardiner and coworkers (2003) and Ambresin and coworkers (2004) studied olanzapine levels in infants of breast-feeding mothers who were taking the drug. They reported that infants received doses of only about 1 to 4 percent of that given to the mother, resulting in plasma levels of about 38 percent of those in the mother (Figure 9.5). No adverse effects were noted in the infants.

Pharmacodynamics. Olanzapine is at least comparable to haloperidol in efficacy (Rosenheck et al., 2003), with minimal EPS, although it is much more expensive and produces much more weight gain. Results from Kapur and coworkers (1999) showed complete block of 5-HT$_2$ receptors at low doses (5 milligrams per day) with increasing

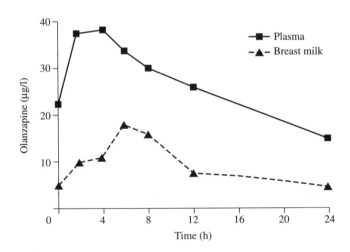

Figure 9.5 Plasma and breast milk olanzapine concentration following a dose of olanzapine to a mother who was taking olanzapine chronically. The dose was taken at time zero. [From Gardiner et al. (2003), p. 1430.]

D_2 blockade as doses increased from 5 to 20 milligrams per day. This relationship provides effective antipsychotic control at D_2 occupancy between 60 and 70 percent, while the greater serotonin blockade may contribute to a low incidence of EPS. Olanzapine has not been reported to cause agranulocytosis, which eliminates the need for white blood cell counts and may improve adherence.

As with risperidone, olanzapine is effective in adolescents (Findling et al., 2003). Zyprexa IntraMuscular was as effective or more effective than either lorazepam or haloperidol in treating aggressive and agitated behaviors, usually in an emergency room scenario. Other uses of olanzapine are discussed at the end of the chapter.

Sertindole

Sertindole (Serlect) was released in 1997 as the fourth atypical antipsychotic. It is primarily a 5-HT$_2$ receptor antagonist with lesser blockade of D_2 receptors. It therefore provides the requisite dual action of blocking 5-HT$_2$ and D_2 receptors thought to define SGAs. This dual action predicted therapeutic efficacy in treating schizophrenia, with a low incidence of EPS. Unlike risperidone and clozapine, sertindole has no affinity for histamine receptors and therefore is less sedative.

Although the drug compared favorably with other atypical antipsychotics, sertindole was found to have a major and potentially fatal side effect. The drug can adversely affect the heart, an action that can lead to severe cardiac arrhythmias. For this reason, sertindole was removed from the market in 1998. However, it is undergoing postmarketing review to determine whether there might be an acceptably safe way to use it (Lewis et al., 2005).

Quetiapine

Quetiapine (Seroquel; see Figure 9.4), the fifth SGA with combined 5-HT$_2$/D$_2$, receptor-blocking action, was introduced in 1997 (Arvanitis and Miller, 1997). It is effective, superior to placebo, and comparable to haloperidol in reducing positive symptoms of schizophrenia, with little EPS. It has been reported to reduce the expression of glutamate mRNA, an action consistent with a glutamatergic involvement in schizophrenia. Side effects include nausea, sedation, and dizziness, but weight gain did not differ between quetiapine- and placebo-treated patients. In addition to producing less weight gain, quetiapine has also been reported to exert beneficial effects on cognitive function. Despite a relatively short biological half-life (about 6 hours), a once-daily formulation was made available in June 2007.

There is evidence that Seroquel is useful for a number of other disorders (Adityanjee, 2002). It has been shown to be effective for people with obsessive-compulsive disorder who are resistant or unresponsive to SSRI therapy and in schizoaffective disorder, bipolar disorder, and severe agitation. In particular, Seroquel is used a great deal to treat adolescent mania (Chapter 8). It has also been found helpful in treating the nighttime awakenings and nightmares of posttraumatic stress disorder. Recent reports show benefit for borderline personality disorder, as well (discussed on pages 330–331).

Ziprasidone

Ziprasidone (Geodon; see Figure 9.4), approved in 2001, is the sixth atypical antipsychotic, and it shows efficacy for treating schizophrenia with low liability for causing EPS (Arato et al., 2002; Goodnik, 2001; Gunasekara et al., 2002). Ziprasidone is poorly absorbed orally, but once it is absorbed it is extensively metabolized to a variety of inactive by-products. Its half-life appears to be short, in the range of 6 hours. Perhaps its major clinical advantage is negligible weight gain.

Ziprasidone has some unique receptor actions. In addition to blocking 5-HT$_2$ and D$_2$ receptors, it is a partial agonist at 5-HT$_{1A}$ receptors (a buspironelike action) and it is a moderate inhibitor of serotonin and norepinephrine uptake. These receptor actions confer antidepressant and anxiolytic actions to the drug. Indeed, ziprasidone reduces both the depressive and the psychotic symptoms in people with schizoaffective disorder (Keck et al., 2001; Swainston and Scott, 2006). Ziprasidone was the first SGA to be approved for intramuscular use; an injectable formulation was approved in 2003 for rapid control of agitated behavior and psychotic symptoms. The limiting factor to the wide use of ziprasidone is its effect on the heart. The drug prolongs the QT interval, causing concern, but as yet no fatal reactions have occurred. However, QT prolongation may be a more serious problem in children and adolescents (Blair et al., 2005).

Aripiprazole

Aripiprazole (Abilify; see Figure 9.4) was approved in 2002 as perhaps the first of a new "third generation" (Potkin et al., 2003) because it has a different mechanism of action from those of the FGAs and SGAs. Aripiprazole is a partial agonist at D$_2$ and 5-HT$_{1A}$ receptors as well as an antagonist at 5-HT$_2$ receptors (Jordan et al., 2002). This "dopaminergic partial agonism" is meant to "stabilize" the system because, although it binds with high affinity to D$_2$ receptors, it has lower intrinsic activity (less efficacy). This means that under conditions of high dopamine levels, aripiprazole may replace dopamine at the receptor, but it will not produce as strong an effect as the natural transmitter. Conversely, when dopamine concentration is low, aripiprazole can produce a net increase in dopaminergic action (Lieberman, 2004; Stahl, 2002; Tamminga and Carlsson, 2002).

Partial agonism at 5-HT$_{1A}$ receptors confers some anxiolytic or anti-depressant actions, and this drug has been reported to augment the effect of SSRIs in patients with depression and anxiety disorders who were partial responders to the antidepressants (Schwartz, et al, 2007), and Abilify is currently (July 2007) under FDA review for this use.

To date, aripiprazole appears to be as effective as conventional and other second-generation agents. It does not cause QT prolongation or prolactin elevation, and it is not associated with weight gain or other glucose or lipid abnormalities. However, although rare, some cases of neuroleptic malignant syndrome were reported after treatment with this drug, and some evidence for the development of movement disorders, like akathisia, has been noted.

In June of 2007, the FDA accepted for priority review a supplemental new drug application (sNDA) of aripiprazole (Abilify) for the treatment of pediatric patients (13 to 17 years old) with schizophrenia. This sNDA is based on data from a 6-week, double-blind, randomized, placebo-controlled study of 302 children, conducted in 101 medical centers in 13 countries (Robb et al., 2007). The use of this antipsychotic for disorders besides schizophrenia is discussed at the end of this chapter.

Amisulpride

Amisulpride (Solian; see Figure 9.4) has a unique psychopharmacological profile. It selectively blocks D$_2$ and D$_3$ receptors in the limbic system but not in the basal ganglia, and it does not bind to D$_1$, D$_4$, or D$_5$ receptors, which may account for its lower incidence of EPS. Unlike all other SGAs, amisulpride does not block 5-HT$_2$ receptors, nor does it antagonize cholinergic, adrenergic, or histaminergic receptors. At low doses (50 to 300 milligrams per day) it preferentially blocks presynaptic dopamine receptors, which increases dopamine release. As a result, low doses increase dopaminergic activity in the mesolimbic system (Bressan et al., 2003). This may be the reason it has been reported to be effective in the treatment of dysthymia and depression as well as the negative symptoms of schizophrenia and to provide a better quality of life than does haloperidol. In addition to possible benefit for dysthymia and depression, this drug may be helpful in affective psychosis and chronic fatigue syndrome. In higher doses (up to 1200 milligrams per day), it was at least as effective as haloperidol, risperidone, and olanzapine in relieving psychosis, with EPS effects lower than those of haloperidol and comparable to those of risperidone and olanzapine. Although amisulpride has the benefit of producing less weight gain than risperidone and olanzapine and does not seem to be associated with diabetogenic effects, it may increase plasma prolactin levels. It has a half-life of about 12 hours—16 hours in the elderly (McKeage and Plosker, 2004)). At this time, amisulpride has not been FDA approved for use in the United States.

Prominent Side Effects of Second-Generation Antipsychotics

Although the use of SGAs is generally associated with fewer parkinso-nianlike symptoms than use of the FGAs, the SGAs are not without side effects, the most prominent of which are weight gain, a propensity to produce glucose intolerance (diabetes) along with elevation in blood lipids, and specific cardiac electrographic abnormalities that can be serious and even fatal.

Weight Gain

As a group, SGAs have a propensity to induce weight gain, with clozapine and olanzapine inducing the most, ziprasidone and aripiprazole the least (amisulpride probably also shares this advantage) (Allison and Casey, 2001; Figure 9.6). Weight gain occurs in 20 to 30 percent of people taking risperidone, olanzapine, and quetiapine, although the gain with risperidone is about half that brought on by the other two drugs. Weight gain in adolescents may be even greater than in adults (Ratzoni et al., 2002; Correll, 2007). This side effect may contribute to patient noncompliance with treatment and may adversely affect clinical outcome (Poyurovsky et al., 2003).

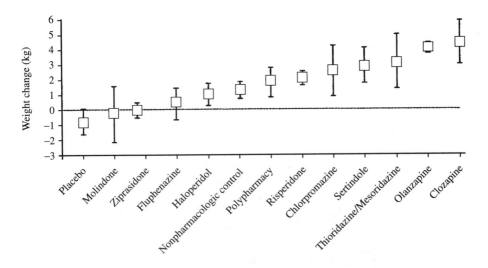

Figure 9.6 Estimated weight change after 10 weeks of treatment with standard drug doses. Shown are mean values and 95 percent confidence intervals. [From Allison and Casey (2001), p. 24.]

The mechanism responsible for this weight gain is still being elucidated (Newcomer, 2005); however, the most recent data suggest that this phenomenon is associated with the antihistaminergic aspects of the second-generation antipsychotics. Snyder and colleagues (discussed by Hampton, 2007) found a relationship between the SGAs that are most associated with this side effect and the stimulation of a hypothalamic AMP-activated protein kinase (AMPK). This enzyme, AMPK, is important for maintaining energy balance and has been linked to the regulation of food intake. The investigators found that histaminergic antagonism stimulated AMPK, and histamine decreased this stimulation. In mice given clozapine, AMPK activity quadrupled. This discovery may lead to the development of antipsychotics that retain their therapeutic benefit but do not produce weight gain and other metabolic problems.

Diabetes and Hyperglycemia

Patients who receive certain atypical antipsychotics are 9 to 14 percent more likely to develop adult-onset (Type II) diabetes than patients who receive traditional first generation antipsychotic drugs (Lindenmayer et al., 2003; Newcomer, 2005; Sernyak et al., 2002). Increases are seen in patients over 40 years of age who were taking clozapine, olanzapine, and quetiapine but not risperidone (Gianfrancesco et al., 2003). In patients under 40 years old, all agents increase the incidence of diabetes. These changes are independent of the weight gain induced by these drugs and seem to reflect a more rapid onset of diabetes. Newcomer and coworkers (2002) demonstrated that olanzapine and clozapine increased mean glucose levels as well as glucose and insulin levels after a glucose load. Both drugs induce a state of insulin resistance (Ebenbichler et al., 2003). Koller and Doraiswamy (2002) noted that this hyperglycemic effect could be quite severe, leading to diabetic ketoacidosis and even death. The American Diabetes Association and American Psychiatric Association have published suggested monitoring schedules for insulin resistance, recommending that blood levels be taken at 6 months and 1 year and then every 5 years thereafter. The long-term consequences of small elevations in blood glucose are unknown at this time but may include increased risk of cardiovascular disease (Wirshing et al., 2002).

Electrocardiographic Abnormalities

The "pacemaker" of the heart is the sinoatrial node, located in the right atrium of the heart. An electrical signal from the pacemaker flows over the atria and into the ventricles through the atrioventricular node. The ventricles then contract, propelling blood forward into the aorta and the arteries. Following depolarization and mechanical contraction, the ventricles repolarize to be ready for the next depolarization. Figure 9.7 illustrates the electrocardiogram (ECG) for one electrical cycle. The QT interval is the time from the start of spread of electricity to the

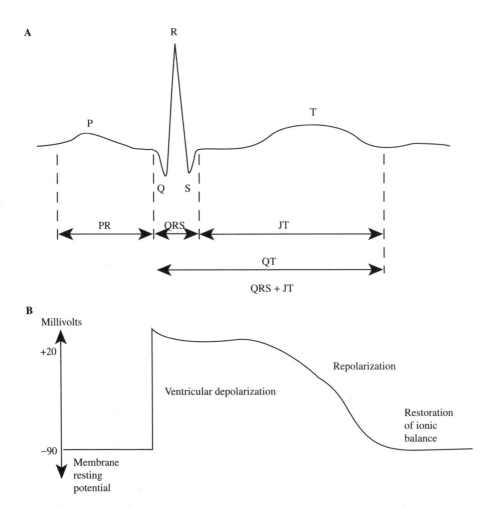

Figure 9.7 A. Normal electrocardiogram (ECG) in sinus rhythm. P wave = atrial electrical depolarization and leads to muscular contraction of the right and left ventricles. QRS complex = ventricular electrical depolarization and leads to muscular contraction of the right and left ventricles. JT = the time from the end of ventricular depolarization (QRS) to the end of ventricular repolarization. The QT interval includes both ventricular depolarization (QRS) and ventricular repolarization. **B.** Rapid ventricular depolarization and slower repolarization. Most of the QT interval represents ventricular repolarization.

ventricles to the end of ventricular repolarization. In essence, if this period is prolonged to about 500 milliseconds (0.5 second), the patient is at significant risk of developing the arrhythmia *torsades de pointes* (Figure 9.8), which can result in sudden death. The normal range for the QT interval for men below the age of 55 years is 350 to 430 milliseconds; for women, it is 350 to 450 milliseconds. Concern should arise when the QT interval is between 450 and 500 milliseconds; that is, the risk increases with a prolongation of 20 milliseconds or more. Besides drug-induced QT interval prolongation, *torsades de pointes* arrhythmias may at least partly be involved in sudden death in athletes and in infants (SIDS).

Many psychotropic medications, including neuroleptics, antidepressants, stimulants, and anxiolytics, may cause *torsades de pointes* (Al-Khatib et al., 2003; Witchel et al., 2003). Even nonpsychotropic drugs have caused it, and some drugs, such as the antihistamine Seldane and the gastric stimulant Propulsid, have been removed from the market for this reason. Among the FGAs, thioridazine is most associated with this side effect and is rarely prescribed. Among the SGAs, this was one reason sertindole was removed from the market and approval of ziprasidone was delayed until additional safety data could be examined: it prolongs the interval about 10 or 15 milliseconds. The current consensus is that, although ziprasidone modestly prolongs the QT interval (Figure 9.9), this event has not been associated with *torsades de pointes* or sudden death (Kelly and Love, 2001; Taylor, 2003). Even so, patients considered to be at risk (recent heart attack, heart disease, renal disease, and so on) should be medically evaluated, including obtaining a premedication ECG. Combining drugs that all prolong the QT interval probably should be avoided. Glassman and Bigger (2001) and Ray and coworkers

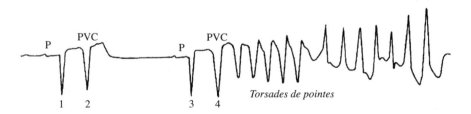

Figure 9.8 Characteristic development of *torsades de pointes* ventricular arrhythmia. Sinus beat with normal ventricular complex (1) followed by a premature ventricular contraction (PVC; 2) closely coupled to the sinus beat. After a long pause (2–3), this paired complex is repeated (3–4). The second PVC initiates a bizarre ventricular arrhythmia consistent with *torsades de pointes*. This ventricular arrhythmia is accompanied by poor contraction of ventricular muscle and therefore loss of contractility and output of blood from the heart, leading to a cardiac arrest.

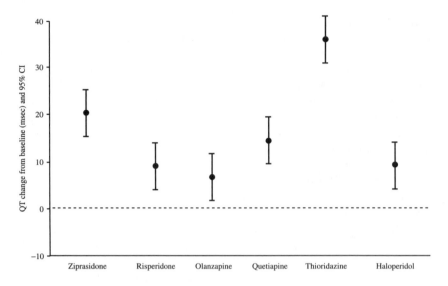

Figure 9.9. Results of studies showing QT interval changes associated with therapeutic doses of various antipsychotic drugs.

(2001) review this topic. Whether ziprasidone should be a first- or second-line drug, based on its potential to prolong the QT interval, is a clinical decision.

Additional Applications for Second-Generation Antipsychotics

The use of SGAs in nonpsychotic disorders has rapidly increased in the last few years (Tables 9. 3 and 9.4) (Trémeau and Citrome, 2006). With the exception of bipolar disorder, most of these applications have been "off-label," or non-FDA-approved. Although the FGAs were also known to be efficacious in these disorders, the improved neurological profile of the new agents and the inadequate response of many patients to their approved FGA medications for the respective illnesses have expanded the use of SGAs. Among the SGAs, most information has been obtained from studies of risperidone and olanzapine. However, there are numerous case reports and open-label studies describing benefits of all the SGAs in a variety of conditions. At present, it should be kept in mind that most of the available evidence comes from evaluations of SGAs as adjuncts to other psychotropics, that few direct comparisons between FGAs and SGAs have been published, and that there is not yet a great deal of information on the long-term safety of the new agents.

TABLE 9.3 Bipolar and other nonpsychotic indications FDA-approved for second-generation antipsychotic agents

SGA[a]	Bipolar mania	Bipolar depression	Bipolar maintenance	Other
Aripiprazole	Acute mania or mixed episodes	Bipolar I disorder, most recent episode manic or mixed		
Clozapine				Risk of recurrent suicidal behavior in schizophrenia or schizoaffective disorders
Olanzapine	Acute mania or mixed episodes; monotherapy or with lithium or valproate for manic episodes		Bipolar disorder maintenance monotherapy	
Olanzapine/fluoxetine combination		Bipolar depressive episodes		
Quetiapine	Acute manic episodes; monotherapy or with lithium or valproate	Bipolar depressive episodes		
Risperidone	Acute mania or mixed episodes; monotherapy or with lithium or valproate			Irritability in autism
Ziprasidone	Acute mania or mixed episodes			

[a]SGA = second-generation antipsychotic (oral form)
Safety issues. SGAs' safety profiles warrant caution. SGAs are less likely than first-generation antipsychotics (FGAs) to cause extrapyramidal symptoms (EPS) and tardive dyskinesia (TD) at therapeutic dosages, but they increase the risks of weight gain, diabetes, glucose intolerance, dyslipidemia, and hyperprolactinemia. Akathisia and hypotension also may occur.
Prescribing decisions. SGAs' potential adverse effects complicate clinical decision making. First it must be decided whether to use an SGA for the patient with a nonpsychotic disorder.
From Trémeau and Citrome (2006), p. 39.

TABLE 9.4 Second-generation antipsychotic uses in nonpsychotic disorders supported by evidence from published double-blind clinical trials[a]

SGA[b]	Unipolar depression	OCD[c]	Anxiety disorders	Dementia	Developmental disorders	Borderline personality disorder
Aripiprazole					Yes	
Clozapine						Yes
Olanzapine	Yes	Yes	Yes	Yes		
Quetiapine		Yes				
Risperidone		Yes	Yes	Yes	Yes	
Ziprasidone						

[a]Does not include studies of bipolar disorders, results from open trials, case reports, or studies not classified as double-blind with adequate numbers of subjects.
[b]SGA = second-generation antipsychotic
[c]OCD = obsessive-compulsive disorder
From Trémeau and Citrome (2006), p. 39.

Bipolar Disorder

Except for clozapine, all the newer antipsychotics are approved by the FDA for treatment of some aspect of bipolar disorder. Olanzapine (in 2000), risperidone (in 2004), quetiapine (in 2004), ziprasidone (in 2004; Keck et al., 2003b), and aripiprazole (in 2004; Keck et al., 2003a) are approved for monotherapy of acute bipolar mania and (with the exception of quetiapine) for mixed episodes. Olanzapine, risperidone and quetiapine are also approved as "add-ons" for treating bipolar mania in patients with a poor response to monotherapy. In April of 2004, a new product, Zyprexa IntraMuscular was marketed for acute treatment of severe agitation associated with schizophrenia. Side effects were modest and efficacy was reported to be superior to that of intramuscular haloperidol or lorazepam, with no drug-induced motor abnormalities.

A combination product containing olanzapine and fluoxetine (Symbyax) was approved (in 2003) for treating acute bipolar depression. Quetiapine is also approved for treating bipolar depressive episodes. For a series of articles that review the use of SGAs in bipolar disorder, see Volume 66, Supplement 3, of *the Journal of Clinical Psychiatry* (Hirschfeld, 2005).

Unipolar Depression

Although they were not double-blind clinical trials, several studies have provided evidence that SGAs may be helpful in augmenting the response of treatment-resistant depression. These SGAs include risperidone (Rapaport et al., 2006), olanzapine (Shelton et al., 2001; Shelton et al., 2005), quetiapine (Yargic et al., 2004), ziprasidone (Papakostas et al., 2004), and aripiprazole (Papakostas et al., 2005; Simon and Nemeroff, 2005). In most cases the antidepressant was an SSRI. SGAs are becoming widely used for this purpose.

Dementia

Although not approved for this indication by the FDA, antipsychotic drugs are widely used to treat delusions, aggression, and agitation in elderly patients (Carson et al., 2006; Jeste et al., 2005). Because FGAs may cause EPS, lower blood pressure, and increase the risk of falls, the use of SGAs for this population has become more common. The National Institute of Mental Health recently sponsored the CATIE-AD study to compare olanzapine, risperidone, and quetiapine with placebo in outpatients with symptoms of psychosis, agitation, and aggressiveness. Results showed no significant differences in effectiveness, measured as discontinuation for any cause, among the medications (Schneider et al., 2006). Other data suggest that olanzapine and quetiapine, perhaps because of their anticholinergic potency, may worsen cognition in older patients with dementia (Ballard et al., 2005).

However, in the past few years, an increased risk of stroke was noted in manufacturer-sponsored trials of risperidone and olanzapine (Wang et al., 2005), and in 2005 the FDA released a Public Health Advisory stating that treatment with SGA medications (olanzapine, aripiprazole, risperidone, or quetiapine) of behavioral disorders in elderly patients with dementia is associated with a slight increase in mortality. Most of the deaths were due to heart-related events or infections (primarily pneumonia). Although no individual trial showed an increase in mortality for the atypical agents as a group, the relative risk of death was 1.65 to 1.7 times higher than for placebo. Because the four SGAs that were studied belong to three different chemical classes, the FDA concluded that the effect was probably common across all atypical antipsychotics. The agency announced that it would require a black box warning describing this risk on the labels of the drugs and that it would also so designate the olanzapine-fluoxetine combination of Symbyax.[4]

In a recent Canadian study (Rochon et al., 2007; Figure 9.10), it was reported that 32.4 percent of the elderly residents in 485 nursing homes

[4]U.S. Food and Drug Administration, Center for Drug Evaluation and Research, "FDA Public Health Advisory: Deaths with Antipsychotics in Elderly Patients with Behavioral Disturbances," April 11, 2005. Available at http://www.fda.gov/Cder/drug/advisory/antipsychotics.htm.

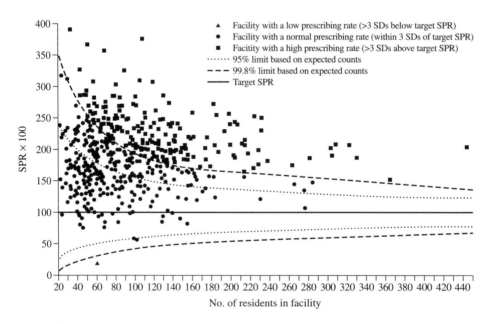

Figure 9.10 Plot of standardized prescribing rates (SPR) for antipsychotic drugs in 485 nursing homes in Ontario, Canada, based on an expected prescribing rate of 17 percent of patients (figured from Canadian guidelines for prescribing these drugs). Middle straight line is the expected rate; dotted lines above and below are 95 percent and 99.8 percent limits based on expected ranges of variance. The ordinate represents the size of the nursing home (as determined by number of residents). Thus, homes of all sizes routinely had prescription rates above guidelines. [From Rochon et al. (2007), Figure 2].

were dispensed an antipsychotic drug (mostly of the SGA-type), with wide variation among facilities (21 to 44 percent). The predicted rate, based on Canadian government recommendation for use, was 17 percent. The markedly increased rate of use was not based on unexpectedly high rates of psychosis or dementia; thus use was presumably for behavioral control.

Autism, Pervasive Developmental Disorder, Agitation, and Aggression

Antipsychotics represent one-third of all filled psychotropic prescriptions for patients with pervasive developmental disorders (PDD). Conventional antipsychotics are known to be effective in treating agitation, hyperactivity, aggression, stereotypic behaviors, tics, and affective lability in PDD (Lott et al., 2004) and autism spectrum disorders (McDougle et al., 1998, 2005; McCracken et al., 2002). Impairments of communication and social interaction are less affected. The undesirable neurologic side effects of FGAs, especially when used on a long-term basis, have shifted the focus toward SGAs. Most information to date has come from studies of risperidone, in which short-term (8 to 16 weeks) treatment with low doses (1 to 2 milligrams per day, up to 4.5 milligrams) was found to reduce aggression, tantrums, and self-injurious behavior. Recently, risperidone received FDA approval for the treatment of irritability associated with autistic behavior in children. Nevertheless, even in short-term studies, as many as 30 percent of children may fail to respond to risperidone, and after 6 months 33 percent of initial responders may fail to maintain their improvement. Concerns have also been raised about the long-term safety of this agent in children, particularly because of the increased release of prolactin. Chronic prolactin elevation may exert variable effects on puberty, may reduce bone mass, and is a risk factor in infertility, breast cancer, heart disease, and prostate abnormalities (Gagliano et al., 2004). Like other SGAs, risperidone, even in low doses, has been associated with weight gain and symptoms of the metabolic syndrome; in higher doses it has been associated with EPS, tardive dyskinesia, and the neuroleptic malignant syndrome.

As with risperidone, olanzapine has improved symptoms associated with pervasive developmental disorders in children and adults. Although significant improvement was seen in "irritability," "hyperactivity," and "excessive speech," only 3 out of 23 children in one study (aged 6 to 16 years) were considered overall responders. Increased appetite and weight gain were the major side effects (Potenza et al., 1999). A preliminary open-label study of ziprasidone in 12 patients (aged 8 to 20 years) reported a response rate of 50 percent after 6 weeks.

Double-blind studies have shown that treatment with antipsychotics has led to improvements not only in autism and PDD but in aggression and behavioral disruptions in children with conduct disorder and oppositional defiant disorder and in developmentally delayed adolescents and mentally retarded subjects of various ages (Buitelaar et al., 2001; Snyder et al., 2002; Vanden et al., 1993).

Walker and coworkers (2003) reported that quetiapine was effective against target symptoms of severe aggression and impulsivity in four criminal offenders with antisocial personality disorder. The use of antipsychotics in the management of agitation and aggression in youth has been reviewed and is covered in more detail in Chapter 10, where the use of antipsychotic drugs for aggression is compared with other agents.

Posttraumatic Stress Disorder

There is increasing evidence for the effectiveness of SGAs in treating psychotic symptoms of posttraumatic stress disorder (PTSD). Most of the data come from studies of combat-related PTSD in patients either unresponsive or partially responsive to antidepressants. Clinical case reports support the use of risperidone (Bartzokis et al., 2005), olanzapine (Stein et al., 2002), quetiapine (Adityanjee, 2002), ziprasidone (Siddiqui, et al, 2005), and aripiprazole (Lambert, 2006) in war veterans for reducing such symptoms as hyperarousal, reexperiencing, avoidance, nightmares, and flashbacks. Similarly, risperidone monotherapy was recently found useful for women with a current diagnosis of PTSD as a result of domestic violence or sexual abuse. A mean final risperidone dose of 2.6 milligrams per day significantly reduced avoidant and hyperarousal PTSD symptoms compared with the response of the placebo group, although there were no differences between the two groups on the Hamilton Rating Scales for Anxiety or Depression (Padala et al. 2006).

Obsessive-Compulsive Disorder

Risperidone (McDougle et al., 2000), olanzapine (Bystritsky et al., 2004), quetiapine (Atmaca et al., 2002; Denys et al., 2004; Mohr et al., 2002), and aripiprazole (Storch, et al, 2007) have been reported to be effective in augmenting the clinical response of patients with obsessive-compulsive disorder who were treatment-refractory to antidepressants. Other anxiety disorders that have been responsive to SGAs, as either monotherapy or add-on, include social anxiety (Barnett et al., 2002), generalized anxiety (Brawman-Mintzer et al., 2005), and panic disorder (Khaldi et al., 2003). Gao and coworkers (2006) recently reviewed the use of SGAs in the management of anxiety disorders.

Borderline Personality Disorder

Borderline personality disorder (BPD) affects about 2 percent of the population, and about 75 percent of patients with the diagnosis are female. The condition is characterized by brief, intense episodes of impulsiveness, hostility, and anger (including self-injurious behavior), as well as anxiety and depression.

Rocca and coworkers (2002) reported that risperidone could reduce aggression and depressive symptomatology and increase energy and global functioning in patients with borderline personality disorder.

Since then, a number of case reports and open-label studies and some clinical trials have reported similar results with clozapine (Grootens and Verkes, 2005; Zanarini and Frankenburg, 2001), quetiapine (Villeneuve and Lemelin, 2005), and olanzapine (Bogenschutz and Nurnberg, 2004). Recently, in an 8-week study, aripiprazole was found to be effective relative to placebo in improving a variety of symptoms in patients with BPD, including aggressiveness/hostility, paranoid thinking, anxiety, depression, and psychoticism. An advantage of this agent is the lack of weight gain compared with other SGAs (Nickel et al., 2006).

Other Applications

It has long been appreciated that clozapine can reduce psychotic reactions in patients with Parkinson's disease who are receiving dopaminergic agents. Because of clozapine's undesirable side effect profile, quetiapine has become the preferred treatment (Comaty and Advokat, 2001; Reddy et al., 2002). The efficacy of these drugs may be due to their low affinity for the dopamine receptor, which prevents interference with the treatment of Parkinson's disease. This is supported by a recent report that aripiprazole was not very effective for medication-induced psychosis in "probable" parkinsonian patients (Fernandez et al., 2004).

STUDY QUESTIONS

1. What are the positive and negative symptoms of schizophrenia? Why are these symptoms important in drug therapy and in rehabilitation?

2. Which neurotransmitters are most involved in the pathogenesis of schizophrenia?

3. What are the primary clinical differences between traditional and atypical antipsychotic drugs?

4. Discuss the mechanisms of action of traditional antipsychotics and atypical antipsychotics.

5. Discuss the side effects of phenothiazines.

6. Discuss the consequences of reducing the numbers of institutionalized schizophrenic patients.

7. Compare and contrast clozapine and chlorpromazine, clozapine and olanzapine.

8. Name the currently available atypical antipsychotic drugs. How are they alike? How do they differ?

9. What appears unique about ziprasidone, aripiprazole, and amisulpride?

10. What is the QT interval and how is it involved with psychotropic drugs?

11. Why might antipsychotic drugs induce weight gain and/or diabetes?

12. Compare and contrast the newer atypical antipsychotics in terms of their efficacy, diabetes potential, weight gain, QT effects, and other side effects.

REFERENCES

Adityanjee, S. C. (2002). "Clinical Use of Quetiapine in Disease States Other Than Schizophrenia." *Journal of Clinical Psychiatry* 63, Supplement 13: 32–38.

Advokat, C. (2005). "Differential Effects of Clozapine, Compared with Other Antipsychotics, on Clinical Outcome and Dopamine Release in the Brain." *Essential Psychopharmacology* 6: 73–90.

Al-Khatib, S. M., et al. (2003). "What Clinicians Should Know About the QT Interval." *Journal of the American Medical Association* 289: 2120–2127.

Allison, D. B., and D. E. Casey (2001). "Antipsychotic-Induced Weight Gain: A Review of the Literature." *Journal of Clinical Psychiatry* 62, Supplement 7: 22–31.

Ambresin, G., et al. (2004). "Olanzapine Excretion into Breast Milk: A Case Report." *Journal of Clinical Psychopharmacology* 24: 93–95.

American Psychiatric Association (2004). "Practice Guideline for the Treatment of Patients with Schizophrenia," 2nd ed. *American Journal of Psychiatry* 161 (February Supplement).

Andreasen, N. C. (1999). "A Unitary Model of Schizophrenia: Bleuler's 'Fragmented Phrene' as Schizencephaly." *Archives of General Psychiatry* 56: 781–787.

Arato, M., et al. (2002). "A 1-Year, Double-Blind, Placebo-Controlled Trial of Ziprasidone 40, 80 and 160 mg/day in Chronic Schizophrenia: The Ziprasidone Extended Use in Schizophrenia (ZEUS) Study." *International Clinical Psychopharmacology* 17: 207–215.

Arvanitis, L. A., and B. G. Miller (1997). "Multiple Fixed Doses of 'Seroquel' (Quetiapine) in Patients with Acute Exacerbation of Schizophrenia: A Comparison with Haloperidol and Placebo. The Seroquel Trial 13 Study Group." *Biological Psychiatry* 42: 233–246.

Atmaca, M., et al. (2002). "Quetiapine Augmentation in Patients with Treatment Resistant Obsessive-Compulsive Disorder: A Single-Blind, Placebo-Controlled Study." *International Clinical Psychopharmacology* 17: 115–119.

Ballard, C., et al. (2005). "Quetiapine and Rivastigmine and Cognitive Decline in Alzheimer's Disease: Randomised Double Blind Placebo Controlled Trial." *British Medical Journal* 330: 874.

Barnett, S. D., et al. (2002). "Efficacy of Olanzapine in Social Anxiety Disorder: A Pilot Study." *Journal of Psychopharmacology* 16: 365–368.

Bartzokis, G., et al. (2005). "Adjunctive Risperidone in the Treatment of Combat-Related Posttraumatic Stress Disorder." *Biological Psychiatry* 57: 474–479.

Bilder, R. M., et al. (2002). "Neurocognitive Effects of Clozapine, Olanzapine, Risperidone, and Haloperidol in Patients with Chronic Schizophrenia or Schizoaffective Disorder." *American Journal of Psychiatry* 159: 1018–1028.

Blair, J. et al. (2005). "Electrocardiographic Changes in Children and Adolescents Treated with Ziprasidone: A Prospective Study." *Journal of the American Academy of Child and Adolescent Psychiatry* 44: 73–79.

Bogenschutz, M. P., and G. Nurnberg (2004). "Olanzapine Versus Placebo in the Treatment of Borderline Personality Disorder." *Journal of Clinical Psychiatry* 65: 104–109.

Brawman-Mintzer, O., et al. (2005). "Adjunctive Risperidone in Generalized Anxiety Disorder: A Double-Blind, Placebo-Controlled Study." *Journal of Clinical Psychiatry* 66: 1321–1325.

Bressan, R. A., et al. (2003). "Is Regionally Selective D_2/D_3 Dopamine Occupancy Sufficient for Atypical Antipsychotic Effect? An In Vivo Quantitative [^{123}I]Epidepride SPET Study of Amisulpride-Treated Patients." *American Journal of Psychiatry* 160: 1413–1420.

Buitelaar, J. K., et al. (2001). "A Randomized Controlled Trial of Risperidone in the Treatment of Aggression in Hospitalized Adolescents with Subaverage Cognitive Abilities." *Journal of Clinical Psychiatry* 62: 239–248.

Bystritsky, A., et al. (2004). "Augmentation of Serotonin Reuptake Inhibitors in Refractory Obsessive-Compulsive Disorder Using Adjunctive Olanzapine: A Placebo-Controlled Trial." *Journal of Clinical Psychiatry* 65: 565–568.

Cannon, T. D., et al. (2002). "Antipsychotic Drug Treatment in the Prodromal Phase of Schizophrenia." *American Journal of Psychiatry* 159: 1230–1232.

Carpenter, W. T., Jr., and J. M. Gold (2002). "Another View of Therapy for Cognition in Schizophrenia." *Biological Psychiatry* 52: 969–971.

Carson, S., et al. (2006). "A Systematic Review of the Efficacy and Safety of Atypical Antipsychotics in Patients with Psychological and Behavioral Symptoms of Dementia." *Journal of the American Geriatric Society* 54: 354–361.

Comaty, J. E., and C. Advokat (2001). "Indications for the Use of Atypical Antipsychotics in the Elderly." *Journal of Clinical Geropsychology* 7: 285–309.

Correll, C. U. (2007). "Weight Gain and Metabolic Effects of Mood Stabilizers and Antipsychotics in Pediatric Bipolar Disorder: A Systematic Review and Pooled Analysis of Short-Term Trials." *Journal of the American Academy of Child and Adolescent Psychiatry* 46: 687–700.

Correll, C. U., et al. (2004). "Lower Risk for Tardive Dyskinesia Associated with Second-Generation Antipsychotics: A Systematic Review of 1-Year Studies." *American Journal of Psychiatry* 161: 414–425.

Davis, J. M., and N. Chen (2004). "Dose Response and Dose Equivalence of Antipsychotics." *Journal of Clinical Psychopharmacology* 24: 192–208.

Davis, J. M., et al. (2003). "A Meta-Analysis of the Efficacy of Second-Generation Antipsychotics." *Archives of General Psychiatry* 60: 553–564.

Denys, D., et al. (2004). "A Double-Blind, Randomized, Placebo-Controlled Trial of Quetiapine Addition in Patients with Obsessive-Compulsive Disorder

Refractory to Serotonin Reuptake Inhibitors." *Journal of Clinical Psychiatry* 65: 1040–1048.

Ebenbichler, C. F., et al. (2003). "Olanzapine Induces Insulin Resistance: Results from a Prospective Study." *Journal of Clinical Psychiatry* 64: 1436–1439.

Eutrecht, J. P. (1992). "Metabolism of Clozapine by Neutrophils: Possible Implications for Clozapine-Induced Agranulocytosis." *Drug Safety* 7, Supplement 1: 51–56.

Farber, N. B. (2003). "The NMDA Receptor Hypofunction Model of Psychosis." *Annals of the New York Academy of Sciences* 1003: 119–130.

Fernandez, H. H., et al. (2004). "Aripiprazole for Drug-Induced Psychosis in Parkinson Disease: Preliminary Experience." *Clinical Neuropharmacology* 27: 4–5.

Findling, R. L., et al. (2003). "A Prospective, Open-Label Trial of Olanzapine in Adolescents with Schizophrenia." *Journal of the American Academy of Child and Adolescent Psychiatry* 42: 170–175.

Fleishhacker, W. W., et al. (2003). "Treatment of Schizophrenia with Long-Acting Injectable Risperidone: A 12-Month Open-Label Trial of the First Long-Acting, Second-Generation Antipsychotic." *Journal of Clinical Psychiatry* 64: 1250–1257.

Freedman, R. (2003). "Schizophrenia." *New England Journal of Medicine* 349: 1738–1749.

Gagliano, A., et al. (2004). "Risperidone Treatment of Children with Autistic Disorder: Effectiveness, Tolerability, and Pharmacokinetic Implications." *Journal of Child and Adolescent Psychopharmacology* 14: 39–47.

Gao, K., et al. (2006). "Efficacy of Typical and Atypical Antipsychotics for Primary and Comorbid Anxiety Symptoms or Disorders: A Review." *Journal of Clinical Psychiatry* 67: 1327–1340.

Gardiner, S. J., et al. (2003). "Transfer of Olanzapine into Breast Milk, Calculation of Infant Drug Dose, and Effect on Breast-Fed Infants." *American Journal of Psychiatry* 160: 1428–1431.

Gardner, D. M., et al. (2005). "Modern Antipsychotic Drugs: A Critical Review." *Canadian Medical Association Journal* 172: 1703–1711.

Gianfrancesco, F., et al. (2003). "Antipsychotic-Induced Type 2 Diabetes: Evidence from a Large Health Plan Database." *Journal of Clinical Psychopharmacology* 23: 328–335.

Glassman, A. H., and J. T. Bigger (2001). "Antipsychotic Drugs: Prolonged QTc Interval, Torsade de Pointes, and Sudden Death." *American Journal of Psychiatry* 158: 1774–1782

Goodnik, P. J. (2001). "Ziprasidone: Profile on Safety." *Expert Opinions in Pharmacotherapy* 2: 1655–1662.

Grootens, K. P., and R. J. Verkes (2005). "Emerging Evidence for the Use of Atypical Antipsychotics in Borderline Personality Disorder." *Pharmacopsychiatry* 38: 20–23.

Grothe, D. R., et al. (2000). "Olanzapine Pharmacokinetics in Pediatric and Adolescent Inpatients with Schizophrenia." *Journal of Clinical Psychopharmacology* 20: 220–225.

Grunder, G., et al. (2003). "Mechanism of New Antipsychotic Medications: Occupancy Is Not Just Antagonism." *Archives of General Psychiatry* 60: 974–977.

Gunasekara, N. S., et al. (2002). "Ziprasidone: A Review of Its Use in Schizophrenia and Schizoaffective Disorder." *Drugs* 62: 1217–1251.

Hampton, T. (2007). "Antipsychotic's Link to Weight Gain Found." *Journal of the American Medical Association* 297: 1305–1306.

Hirschfeld, R. M. A. (2005). "Introduction: The Role of Atypical Antipsychotics in the Treatment of Bipolar Disorder." *Journal of Clinical Psychiatry* 66, Supplement 3: 3–4.

Horacek, J., et al. (2006). "Mechanism of Action of Atypical Antipsychotic Drugs and the Neurobiology of Schizophrenia." *CNS Drugs* 20: 389–409.

Ichikawa, J., et al. (2002). "Atypical, but Not Typical, Antipsychotic Drugs Increase Cortical Acetylcholine Release Without an Effect in the Nucleus Accumbens or Striatum." *Neuropsychopharmacology* 26: 325–339.

Ilett, K,. et al. (2004). "Transfer of Risperidone and 9-Hydroxyrisperidone into Human Milk." *Annals of Pharmacotherapy* 38: 273–276.

Janicak, P., et al. (2006). *Principles and Practice of Psychopharmacotherapy.* New York: Lippincott Williams & Wilkins.

Javitt, D. C., and J. T. Coyle (2004). "Decoding Schizophrenia: A Fuller Understanding for Signaling in the Brain of People with This Disorder Offers a New Hope for Improved Therapy." *Scientific American* 290: 48–56.

Jeste, D. V., et al. (2005). "Atypical Antipsychotics in Elderly Patients with Dementia or Schizophrenia: Review of Recent Literature." *Harvard Review of Psychiatry* 13: 340–351.

Jones, P. B., et al. (2006). "Randomized Controlled Trial of the Effect on Quality of Life of Second- vs First-Generation Antipsychotic Drugs in Schizophrenia: Cost Utility of the Latest Antipsychotic Drugs in Schizophrenia Study (CUtLASS 1)." *Archives of General Psychiatry* 63: 1079–1087.

Jordan, S., et al. (2002). "The Antipsychotic Aripiprazole Is a Potent, Partial Agonist at the Human 5-HT1A Receptor." *European Journal of Pharmacology* 441: 137–140.

Kane, J. M., et al. (2003). "Long-Acting Injectable Risperidone: Efficacy and Safety of the First Long-Acting Atypical Antipsychotic." *American Journal of Psychiatry* 160: 1125–1132.

Kapur, S., and G. Remington (2001). "Atypical Antipsychotics: New Directions and New Challenges in the Treatment of Schizophrenia." *Annual Reviews of Medicine* 52: 503–517.

Kapur, S., and P. Seeman (2001). "Does Fast Dissociation from the Dopamine D2 Receptor Explain the Action of Atypical Antipsychotics? A New Hypothesis." *American Journal of Psychiatry* 158: 360–369.

Kapur, S., et al (1999). "Clinical and Theoretical Implications of 5-HT2 and D2 Receptor Occupancy of Clozapine, Risperidone, and Olanzapine in Schizophrenia." *American Journal of Psychiatry* 156: 286–293.

Keck, P. E., et al. (2001). "Ziprasidone in the Short-Term Treatment of Patients with Schizoaffective Disorder: Results from Two Double-Blind, Placebo-Controlled, Multicenter Studies." *Journal of Clinical Psychopharmacology* 21: 27–35.

Keck, P. E., et al. (2003a). "A Placebo-Controlled, Double-Blind Study of the Efficacy and Safety of Aripiprazole in Patients with Acute Bipolar Disorder." *American Journal of Psychiatry* 160: 1651–1658.

Keck, P. E., et al. (2003b). "Ziprasidone in the Treatment of Acute Bipolar Mania: A Three-Week, Placebo-Controlled, Double-Blind, Randomized Trial." *American Journal of Psychiatry* 160: 741–748.

Kelly, D. L., and R. C. Love (2001). "Ziprasidone and the QTc Interval: Pharmacokinetic and Pharmacodynamic Considerations." *Psychopharmacology Bulletin* 35: 66–79.

Keltner, N. L., and D. G. Folks (2005). *Psychotropic Drugs*, 4th ed. Philadelphia: Mosby.

Khaldi, S., et al. (2003). "Usefulness of Olanzapine in Refractory Panic Attacks." *Journal of Clinical Psychopharmacology* 23: 100–101.

Koller, E. A., and P. M. Duraiswamy (2002). "Olanzapine-Associated Diabetes Mellitus." *Pharmacotherapy* 22: 841–852.

Lambert, M. T. (2006). "Aripiprazole in the Management of Post-Traumatic Stress Disorder Symptoms in Returning Global War on Terrorism Veterans." *International Clinical Psychopharmacology* 21: 185–187.

Laruelle, M., et al. (2003). "Glutamate, Dopamine and Schizophrenia from Pathophysiology to Treatment." *Annals of the New York Academy of Sciences* 1003: 138–158.

Leucht, S., et al. (2003). "New Generation Antipsychotics Versus Low-Potency Conventional Antipsychotics: A Systematic Review and Meta-Analysis." *Lancet* 361: 1581–1589.

Lewis, R., et al. (2005). "Sertindole for Schizophrenia." *Cochrane Database System Review* July 20 (3): CD001715

Lieberman, J. A. (2004) "Dopamine Partial Agonists: A New Class of Antipsychotic." *CNS Drugs* 18:251–267.

Lieberman, J. A., et al. (2001). "The Early Stages of Schizophrenia: Speculations on Pathogenesis, Pathophysiology, and Therapeutic Approaches." *Biological Psychiatry* 50: 884–897.

Lieberman, J. A., et. al. (2005). "Effectiveness of Antipsychotic Drugs in Patients with Chronic Schizophrenia." *New England Journal of Medicine* 353: 1209–1223.

Lindenmayer, J.-P., et al. (2003). "Changes in Glucose and Cholesterol in Patients with Schizophrenia Treated with Typical or Atypical Antipsychotics." *American Journal of Psychiatry* 160: 290–296.

López-Muñoz, F. et al. (2005). "History of the Discovery and Clinical Introduction of Chlorpromazine." *Annals of Clinical Psychiatry* 17: 113–135.

Lott, I. T., et al. (2004). "Longitudinal Prescribing Patterns for Psychoactive Medications in Community-Based Individuals with Developmental Disabilities: Utilization of Pharmacy Records." *Journal of Intellectual Disabilities Research* 48, Part 6: 563–571.

McCracken, J. T., et al. (2002). "Risperidone in Children with Autism and Serious Behavioral Problems." *New England Journal of Medicine* 347: 314–321.

McDougle, C. J. (1998). "A Double-Blind, Placebo-Controlled Study of Risperidone in Adults with Autistic Disorder and Other Pervasive Developmental Disorders." *Archives of General Psychiatry* 55: 633–641.

McDougle, C. J., et al. (2000). "A Double-Blind, Placebo-Controlled Study of Risperidone Addition in Serotonin Reuptake Inhibitor-Refractory Obsessive-Compulsive Disorder." *Archives of General Psychiatry* 57: 794–801.

McDougle, C. J., et al. (2005). "Risperidone for the Core Symptom Domains of Autism: Results from the Study by the Autism Network of the Research Units on Pediatric Psychopharmacology." *American Journal of Psychiatry* 162: 1142–1148.

McEvoy, J. P., et al. (2006). "Effectiveness of Clozapine Versus Olanzapine, Quetiapine and Risperidone in Patients with Chronic Schizophrenia Who Did Not Respond to Prior Atypical Antipsychotic Treatment." *American Journal of Psychiatry* 163: 600–610.

McGowan, S., et al. (2004). "Presynaptic Dopaminergic Dysfunction in Schizophrenia: A Positron Emission Tomographic [^{18}F] Fluorodopa Study." *Archives of General Psychiatry* 61: 134–142.

McKeage, K., and Plosker, G. L. (2004). "Amisulpride: A Review of Its Use in the Management of Schizophrenia." *CNS Drugs* 18: 933–956.

Meltzer, H. Y. (2002). "Commentary on 'Clinical Studies on the Mechanism of Action of Clozapine: The Dopamine–Serotonin Hypothesis of Schizophrenia.'" *Psychopharmacology* 163: 1–3.

Meltzer, H. Y., et al. (2003). "Clozapine Treatment for Suicidality in Schizophrenia: International Suicide Prevention Trial (InterSePT)." *Archives of General Psychiatry* 60: 82–91.

Miyamoto, S., et al. (2003). "Recent Advances in the Neurobiology of Schizophrenia." *Molecular Interventions* 3: 27–39.

Moghaddam, B. (2003). "Bringing Order to the Glutamate Chaos in Schizophrenia." *Neuron* 40: 881–884.

Mohr, N., et al. (2002). "Quetiapine Augmentation of Serotonin Reuptake Inhibitors in Obsessive-Compulsive Disorder." *International Clinical Psychopharmacology* 17: 37–40.

Newcomer, J. W. (2005). "Second-Generation (Atypical) Antipsychotics and Metabolic Effects: A Comprehensive Literature Review." *CNS Drugs* 19, Supplement 1: 1–93.

Newcomer, J. W., et al. (2002). "Abnormalities in Glucose Regulation During Antipsychotic Treatment of Schizophrenia." *Archives of General Psychiatry* 59: 337–345.

Nickel, M. K., et al. (2006). "Aripiprazole in the Treatment of Patients with Borderline Personality Disorder: A Double-Blind, Placebo-Controlled Study." *American Journal of Psychiatry* 163: 833–838.

Padala, P. R., et al. (2006). "Risperidone Monotherapy for Post-Traumatic Stress Disorder Related to Sexual Assault and Domestic Abuse in Women." *International Clinical Psychopharmacology* 21: 275–280.

Papakostas, G. I., et al. (2004). "Ziprasidone Augmentation of Selective Serotonin Reuptake Inhibitors (SSRIs) for SSRI-Resistant Major Depressive Disorder." *Journal of Clinical Psychiatry* 65: 217–221.

Papakostas, G. I., et al. (2005). "Aripiprazole Augmentation of Selective Serotonin Reuptake Inhibitors for Treatment-Resistant Major Depressive Disorder." *Journal of Clinical Psychiatry* 66: 1326–1330.

Parkinson Study Group (1999). "Low-Dose Clozapine for the Treatment of Drug-Induced Psychosis in Parkinson's Disease." *New England Journal of Medicine* 340: 757–763.

Potenza, M. N., et al. (1999). "Olanzapine Treatment of Children, Adolescents, and Adults with Pervasive Developmental Disorders: An Open-Label Pilot Study." *Journal of Clinical Psychopharmacology* 19: 37–44.

Potkin, S. G., et al. (2003). "Aripiprazole, an Antipsychotic with a Novel Mechanism of Action, and Risperidone vs. Placebo in Patients with Schizophrenia and Schizoaffective Disorder." *Archives of General Psychiatry* 60: 681–690.

Poyurovsky, M., et al. (2003). "Attenuation of Olanzapine-Induced Weight Gain with Reboxetine in Patients with Schizophrenia: A Double-Blind, Placebo-Controlled Study." *American Journal of Psychiatry* 160: 297–302.

Purdon, S. E., et al. (2000). "Neuropsychological Changes in Early-Phase Schizophrenia During 12 Months of Treatment with Olanzapine, Risperidone, or Haloperidol." *Archives of General Psychiatry* 57: 249–258.

Rapaport, M. H., et al. (2006). "Effects of Risperidone Augmentation in Patients with Treatment-Resistant Depression: Results of Open-Label Treatment Followed by Double-Blind Continuation." *Neuropsychopharmacology* 31: 2501–2513.

Ratzoni, G., et al. (2002). "Weight Gain Associated with Olanzapine and Risperidone in Adolescent Patients: A Comparative Prospective Study." *Journal of the American Academy of Child and Adolescent Psychiatry* 41: 337–343.

Ray, W. A., et al. (2001). "Antipsychotics and the Risk of Sudden Cardiac Death." *Archives of General Psychiatry* 58: 1161–1167.

Reddy, S., et al. (2002). "The Effect of Quetiapine on Psychosis and Motor Function in Parkinsonian Patients with and Without Dementia." *Movement Disorders* 17:676–681.

Robb, A. S., et al. (2007, May). "Efficacy of Aripiprazole in the Treatment of Adolescents with Schizophrenia." Presented at the Annual Meeting of the American Psychiatric Association, San Diego.

Rocca, P., et al. (2002). "Treatment of Borderline Personality Disorder with Risperidone." *Journal of Clinical Psychiatry* 63: 241–244.

Rochon, P. A., et al. (2007). "Variation in Nursing Home Antipsychotic Prescribing Rates." *Archives of Internal Medicine* 167: 676–683.

Rosebush, P. I., and M. F. Mazurek (1999). "Neurologic Side Effects in Neuroleptic-Naive Patients Treated with Haloperidol or Risperidone." *Neurology* 52: 782–785.

Rosenheck, R., et al. (2003). "Effectiveness and Cost of Olanzapine and Haloperidol in the Treatment of Schizophrenia: A Randomized Controlled Trial." *Journal of the American Medical Association* 290: 2693–2702.

Rujescu, D., et al. (2006). "A Pharmacological Model for Psychosis Based On N-Methyl-D-Aspartate Receptor Hypofunction: Molecular, Cellular, Functional and Behavioral Abnormalities." *Biological Psychiatry* 59: 721–729.

Sadock, B. J., and Sadock, V. A. (2007). *Kaplan and Sadock's Synopsis of Psychiatry.* New York: Lippincott Williams & Wilkins.

Schneider, L. S., et al. (2006). "Effectiveness of Atypical Antipsychotic Drugs in Patients with Alzheimer's Disease." *New England Journal of Medicine* 355: 1525–1538.

Schwartz, T. L., et al. (2007). "Aripiprazole Augmentation of Selective Serotonin or Serotonin Norepinephrine Reuptake Inhibitors in the Treatment of Major Depressive Disorder." *Primary Psychiatry* 14: 67–69.

Sernyak, M. J., et al. (2002). "Association of Diabetes Mellitus with Use of Atypical Neuroleptics in the Treatment of Schizophrenia." *American Journal of Psychiatry* 159: 561–566.

Sharma, T. (2002). "Impact on Cognition of the Use of Antipsychotics." *Current Medical Research and Opinions* 18, Supplement 3: S13–S17.

Shelton, R. C., et al. (2001). "A Novel Augmentation Strategy for Treating Resistant Major Depression." *American Journal of Psychiatry* 158: 131–154.

Shelton, R. C., et al. (2005). "Olanzapine/Fluoxetine Combination for Treatment-Resistant Depression: A Controlled Study of SSRI and Nortriptyline Resistance." *Journal of Clinical Psychiatry* 66: 1289–1297.

Siddiqui, Z., et al. (2005). "Ziprasidone Therapy for Post-Traumatic Stress Disorder." *Journal of Psychiatry & Neuroscience* 30: 430–431.

Simon, J. S., and C. B. Nemeroff (2005). "Aripiprazole Augmentation of Antidepressants for the Treatment of Partially Responding and Nonresponding Patients with Major Depressive Disorder." *Journal of Clinical Psychiatry* 66: 1216–1220.

Snyder, R., and the Risperidone Conduct Study Group (2002). "Effects of Risperidone on Conduct and Disruptive Behavior Disorders in Children with Subaverage IQs." *Journal of the American Academy of Child and Adolescent Psychiatry* 41: 1026–1036.

Stahl, S. M. (2002). "Dopamine System Stabilizers, Aripiprazole, and the Next Generation of Antipsychotics. Part 1: Goldilocks Actions at Dopamine Receptors; Part 2: Illustrating Their Mechanism of Action." *Journal of Clinical Psychiatry* 62: 841–842, 923–924.

Stahl, S. M. (2003). "Describing an Atypical Antipsychotic: Receptor Binding and Its Role in Pathophysiology." *Journal of Clinical Psychiatry* 5, Supplement 3: 9–13.

Stein, M. B., et al. (2002). "Adjunctive Olanzapine for SSRI-Resistant Combat-Related PTSD: A Double-Blind, Placebo-Controlled Study." *American Journal of Psychiatry* 159: 1777–1779.

Storch, E. A., et al. (2007). "Aripiprazole Augmentation of Incomplete Treatment Response in an Adolescent Male with Obsessive-Compulsive Disorder." *Depression and Anxiety*, in press.

Stroup, T. S., et al. (2006). "Effectiveness of Olanzapine, Quetiapine, Risperidone, and Ziprasidone in Patients with Chronic Schizophrenia Following Discontinuation of a Previous Atypical Antipsychotic." *American Journal of Psychiatry* 163: 611–622.

Swainston, H. T., and Scott, L. J. (2006). "Ziprasidone: A Review of Its Use in Schizophrenia and Schizoaffective Disorder." *CNS Drugs* 20: 1027–1052.

Tamminga, C. A., and A. Carlsson (2002). "Partial Dopamine Agonists and Dopaminergic Stabilizers, in the Treatment of Psychosis." *Current Drug Targets—CNS & Neurological Disorders* 1: 141–147.

Taylor, D. (2003). "Ziprasidone in the Management of Schizophrenia: The QT Interval Issue in Context." *CNS Drugs* 17: 423–430.

Tollefson, G. D., et al. (1999). "Controlled, Double-Blind Investigation of the Clozapine Discontinuation Symptoms with Conversion to Either Olanzapine or Placebo." *Journal of Clinical Psychopharmacology* 19: 435–443.

Torrey, E. F. (2002). "Studies of Individuals with Schizophrenia Never Treated with Antipsychotic Medications: A Review." *Schizophrenia Research* 58: 101–115.

Trémeau, F., and L. Citrome (2006). "Antipsychotics for Patients Without Psychoses?" *Current Psychiatry* 5: 33–44.

Tschen, A. C., et al. (1999). "The Cytotoxicity of Clozapine Metabolites: Implications for Predicting Clozapine-Induced Agranulocytosis." *Clinical Pharmacology and Therapeutics* 65: 526–532.

Vanden, B. R., et al. (1993). "Risperidone as Add On Therapy in Behavioural Disturbances in Mental Retardation: A Double-Blind Placebo-Controlled Cross-Over Study." *Acta Psychiatrica Scandinavia* 87: 167–171.

Villeneuve, E., and S. Lemelin (2005). "Open-Label Study of Atypical Neuroleptic Quetiapine for Treatment of Borderline Personality Disorder: Impulsivity as Main Target." *Journal of Clinical Psychiatry* 66: 1298–1303.

Volavka, J., et al. (2002). "Clozapine, Olanzapine, Risperidone, and Haloperidol in the Treatment of Patients with Chronic Schizophrenia and Schizoaffective Disorder." *American Journal of Psychiatry* 159: 255–262.

Walker, C. et al. (2003). "Treating Impulsivity, Irritability, and Aggression of Antisocial Personality Disorder with Quetiapine." *International Journal of Offender Therapy and Comparative Criminology* 47: 556–567.

Wang, P. S., et al. (2005). "Risk of Death in Elderly Users of Conventional vs. Atypical Antipsychotic Medications." *New England Journal of Medicine* 353: 2335–2341.

Weickert, T., et al. (2003). "Comparison of Cognitive Performance During a Placebo Period and an Atypical Antipsychotic Treatment Period in Schizophrenia: Critical Examination of Confounds." *Neuropsychopharmacology* 28: 1491–1500.

Weiss, E. M., et al. (2002). "The Effects of Second-Generation Atypical Antipsychotics on Cognitive Functioning and Psychosocial Outcomes in Schizophrenia." *Psychopharmacology* 162: 11–17.

Wirshing, D. A., et al. (2002). "The Effects of Novel Antipsychotics on Glucose and Lipid Levels." *Journal of Clinical Psychiatry* 63: 856–865.

Witchel, H. J., et al. (2003). "Psychotropic Drugs, Cardiac Arrhythmia, and Sudden Death." *Journal of Clinical Psychopharmacology* 23: 58–77.

Yargic, L. I., et al. (2004). "A Prospective Randomized Single-Blind, Multicenter Trial Comparing the Efficacy and Safety of Paroxetine with and Without Quetiapine Therapy in Depression Associated With Anxiety." *International Journal of Psychiatry in Clinical Practice* 8: 205–211.

Zanarini, M. C., and F. R. Frankenburg (2001). "Olanzapine Treatment of Female Borderline Personality Disorder Patients: A Double-Blind, Placebo-Controlled Pilot Study." *Journal of Clinical Psychiatry* 62: 849–854.

Chapter 10

Child and Adolescent Psychopharmacology

The United States is currently experiencing a silent epidemic of mental illness among youth and teenagers (Friedman, 2006). According to a recent National Comorbidity Survey (Kessler et al., 2005), half of all lifetime serious adult psychiatric illnesses (including depression, anxiety disorders, and substance abuse) start by 14 years of age, and three-fourths of them are present by 25 years of age. Lifetime prevalence estimates are as follows: anxiety disorders 29 percent, mood disorders 21 percent, impulse-control disorders 25 percent, substance abuse disorders 14 percent, any disorder 46 percent. Median age of onset is much earlier for anxiety (11 years of age) and impulse-control (11 years) disorders than for substance abuse (20 years) and mood disorders (30 years).

Delays between initial diagnosis and treatment are common. The median delay across disorders is nearly a decade; the longest delays are 20 to 23 years for anxiety disorders, 6 to 8 years for patients with mood disorders. However, the majority of mental illnesses in young people go unrecognized and untreated, leaving youth vulnerable to emotional, social, and academic impairments during a critical phase in their lives (Friedman, 2006). In total, about 14 to 25 percent of youths during their upbringing endure a mental disorder; the suicide rate rises rapidly over these years (Kutcher and Davidson, 2007); yet among youth and adolescents with mental health service needs, 67 percent receive no services, diagnosis, or treatment, at least until the disorder is deeply entrenched and much more difficult to treat

(Costello et al., 2007; McEwan et al., 2007). All this despite the fact that mental health disorders are the chronic disorders of young people!

If mental heath disorders in youth and adolescents are so prevalent, serious, and relatively unrecognized and untreated, what are the long-term consequences of nontreatment? Today, data are quite clear that youth with untreated childhood and adolescent mental health disorders function poorly as adults.

The term *conduct disorder* (CD) is used to encompass aggressive and antisocial behaviors, and it refers to actions that are sufficiently intense, frequent, or chronic to cause impairment and to warrant intervention (Kazdin, 2000), including fighting, lying, stealing, fire setting, property destruction, vandalism, truancy, and general rule breaking. Older literature associated conduct disorder in children with psychopathology in adulthood: 50 percent of conduct-disordered children progressed to antisocial personality disorder as adults. Certainly externalizing disruptive symptoms in childhood seems to be a marker for more pervasive psychopathology as adults. Lavigne and coworkers (2001) followed 510 preschool children with oppositional defiant disorder (ODD) for 5 years.[1] The presence of ODD in preschool was a strong predictor of later diagnosis of ODD (with or without comorbid ADHD) at ages 6 to 11 years. ODD exhibits a "developmental progression" to diverse outcomes (ODD or ADHD). Later depressive disorders or anxiety disorders occur comorbidly with ODD.

Cavell (2000) noted that children who show aggressive behavior and antisocial behaviors before age 12 are at greater risk of exhibiting adult criminality than are children who become aggressive at an older age. Childhood aggression is stable over time and is a factor in the emergence of school failure, peer rejection, and delinquency. The prognosis for aggressive children is poor: as time goes by, children become less responsive to treatment interventions; they do not "grow out of it."

Nansel and coworkers (2001) reported that 29 percent of 15,700 students in grades 6 through 10 reported moderate or frequent involvement in bullying: as a bully (13 percent), as an object of bullying (10.6 percent), or as both (13 percent). Bullies and their objects all demonstrate poorer social/emotional adjustments than students not involved in bullying and problem behaviors. Bullies have higher levels of conduct problems and dislike of school. Children bullied show higher levels of insecurity, anxiety, depression, loneliness, unhappiness, physical and mental symptoms, and low self-esteem. Students who both bullied and were themselves bullied exhibited the poorest psychosocial functioning

---

[1]The behavioral characteristics of ODD are similar to but less severe than those of CD, and include frequent arguments, anger and resentment, and refusal to comply with adult requests or rules.

overall. The long-term consequences of being a bully, being the object of bullying, or both are significant and persist into adulthood. Former bullies have a fourfold increase in criminal behavior by age 24 years; 60 percent of former bullies have at least one conviction, and 35 to 40 percent have three or more convictions. Bullying seems to limit the learning of socially acceptable ways of negotiating with others. Students bullied have higher levels of depression and poor self-esteem at the age of 23 years, even though harassment did not persist into adulthood.

Attention deficit/hyperactivity disorder (ADHD) is the most common psychological disorder of childhood, affecting 3 to 10 percent of school-age children. ADHD persists beyond childhood and into adulthood in about 40 to 60 percent of affected individuals. In adults, it is associated with a tenfold increase of antisocial personality disorder, up to a fivefold increased risk of drug abuse, a twenty-fivefold increase in risk for institutionalization for delinquency, and up to a nine-fold increased risk for incarceration.

About 3 million youths in the United States suffer from symptoms of *depression*, yet most fail to receive treatment. Without treatment, there is a high risk of school failure, social isolation, promiscuity, self-medication with drugs and alcohol, and suicide. Early onset of depression is associated with poor education, risk of adult depression, and bipolar and personality disorders. Not only does depression exist in adolescence, but adolescence is the period of greatest risk for the onset of depression. Lifetime rates range from 15 to 20 percent by late adolescence. Depressive episodes often have a protracted course and a high tendency for recurrence and onset of bipolar disorder. It is hoped that treatment of depressed youth with antidepressants may help prevent the onset of neuropsychological disorders that can eventually develop when depression remains untreated (Voelker, 2003).

Kasen and coworkers (2001) followed 700 depressed children into their twenties. They found that childhood depression was a strong predictor of personality disorders in adult life: antisocial, histrionic, dependent, and passive-aggressive personality disorders were increased tenfold, threefold, thirteenfold, and sevenfold, respectively. Similarly, Giaconia and coworkers (2001) followed 365 children from age 5 to age 21 years. They assessed major depression and drug disorders at age 18 and subsequent psychological functioning at age 21. Depressed adolescents later experienced multiple internalizing problems, interpersonal difficulties, poor psychological well-being, career dissatisfaction, and active depression. Drug-disordered adolescents were less likely to finish secondary education and more likely to be fired, and they experienced active drug disorders. Adolescents with both depression and drug disorder experienced lower global functioning, externalizing behavioral problems, and suicide. Adolescent depression persists into adulthood with ongoing disruption of interpersonal relationships, risk for substance abuse and early pregnancy, low educational attainment, poor occupational functioning, unemployment, and increased risk of suicide as adults.

Children and adolescents with untreated *anxiety disorders* are children and adolescents at risk. Woodward and Fergusson (2001) conducted a 21-year study of a birth cohort of 1265 New Zealand children in which they assessed the presence of any anxiety disorder in adolescence and the presence of psychological dysfunction as young adults. They found a linear association between the number of persistent anxiety disorders in adolescence and later persistent anxiety disorders, major depression, nicotine, alcohol, and illicit drug dependence, suicidal behavior, educational underachievement, and early parenthood. Similarly, Stein and coworkers (2001) noted that social anxiety disorder (SAD) during adolescence or young adulthood is an important predictor of subsequent depressive disorders. The presence of both SAD and depression in adolescence leads to "a more malignant course and character of subsequent depressive illness" (p. 251). For example, in youth with generalized anxiety disorder (GAD), 47 percent continue to have the disorder eight years later and many have the onset of a new anxiety disorder or depression. Adolescent GAD is associated with poor societal functioning as adults ("psychosocial adversity").

Pharmacological treatment of childhood and adolescent disorders is not new. In the late 1930s, amphetamines were used to treat ADHD. In the 1960s, tricyclic antidepressants were tried in young people but without demonstrated efficacy. In the 1970s, benzodiazepines were used to treat anxiety disorders in children. Significantly, in 1997, Emslie and colleagues demonstrated the efficacy of fluoxetine (Prozac) in reducing depression in adolescents (Figure 10.1). Although the effect was not robust and was only marginally greater than the effect achieved with psychological therapies, the demonstration led to the widespread prescription of fluoxetine for the treatment of childhood and adolescent depression. This use of fluoxetine and other antidepressants has come under much scrutiny.

Nationally, the number of prescriptions written for psychoactive medication for youth (ranging from preschooler through adolescence) has risen markedly over the last 15 years, nearly reaching adult utilization patterns. Initially, the increases reflected the increased use of medications to treat ADHD (stimulants), depression (mainly SSRI-type antidepressants), and bipolar and aggressive disorders (mood stabilizers). More recently, antipsychotic drugs (90 percent of which are of the "atypical" class) are increasingly used to treat children and adolescents (Olfson et al., 2006). Between 1993 and 2002, office visits that included prescriptions of atypical antipsychotic drugs increased from 201,000 per year to 1,224,000, a sixfold increase over a 10-year period. This cascade is expected to continue to escalate; in fact, in

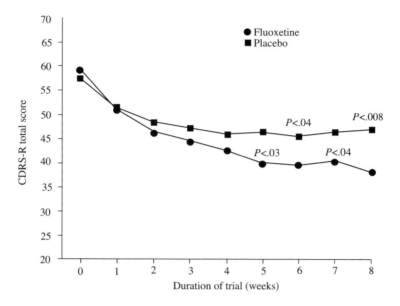

FIGURE 10.1 Weekly Children's Depression Rating Scale in 96 child and adolescent outpatients (aged 7 to 17 years) with nonpsychotic major depressive disorder treated with fluoxetine or placebo and evaluated weekly for 8 consecutive weeks. [From Emslie et al. (1997), p. 1035.]

2004, over 2 million prescriptions for antipsychotic drugs were written for children and adolescents (Aparasu and Bhatara, 2007). Most of the antipsychotic drugs were prescribed by psychiatrists and over 18 percent of visits to these specialists resulted in antipsychotic prescription. Antipsychotic drugs were prescribed for disruptive behavioral disorders (37.8 percent of prescriptions), mood disorders (31.8 percent), pervasive developmental disorders or mental retardation (17.3 percent), and psychotic disorders (only 14.2 percent). Much of this prescription for youth was "off-label": the drug prescribed was approved by the FDA either for another use or for adults. Multiple drug use is common; one 2006 estimate was that about 1.6 million youths were taking two or more psychiatric medicines (stimulants, antidepressants, antipsychotics, and anticonvulsant mood stabilizers), and about 280,000 of the patients were under the age of 10 years. Often these prescriptions are without demonstrated efficacy in youth, but the hope is that they will be effective because they were shown to be effective in adults and because the outlook for untreated disorders in youths is so dire.

Note that the absence of evidence of demonstrated efficacy is not evidence of lack of efficacy. Prescription is not always wrong, unhelpful, or harmful, but it is not always correct, helpful, or harmless. Careful and targeted use is vital. Equally vital is understanding that in many cases the medication probably corrects only behavioral manifestations, merely setting the stage for psychological interventions.

In sum, if we conclude that childhood and adolescent mental health disorders are common, undertreated, and lead to adverse outcomes as adults, then how might treatment be approached?

- We must agree that data argue for early and aggressive intervention in attempts both to control current symptoms and to prevent progression to persistent and prolonged mental health problems.

- Interventions should probably be multifaceted, involving psychological therapy, psychoeducation, interactive therapy with parents and teachers, and possibly medication. Combined therapy can reduce most mental health disorders about threefold, with positive effects persisting long after cessation of treatment.

- It must be decided whether planned interventions will be psychological, pharmacological, or both. The decision should be arrived at by all involved in therapy: prescriber, counselors, parents, patient, and perhaps educators. As much as possible, interventions should be based on available literature.

- It should be recognized that any medications prescribed serve only to control symptomatology; they seldom "cure" any mental health problem (with the possible exception of antidepressants that may reverse hippocampal pathology in depression) (MacQueen, 2006). Medications may only calm young people, making them (and their families) more receptive and more responsive to psychological interventions that might otherwise be ineffective.

- Many treatments for child and adolescent mental health disorders are in their infancy. Often therapies (especially pharmacological therapies) are incompletely documented in medical literature. However, the consequences of untreated adolescent mental health disorders are so dire that they argue for treatment even in the absence of definitive research conclusions.

- "Mental health professionals need to receive training and education in evidence-based pharmacological treatment because practitioners frequently encounter clients (children) on medication. . . . They need to understand the mechanisms and actions of the medication and how it affects behavior." (Meyers, 2006).

Behavioral and Aggressive Disorders

Although conduct and oppositional defiant disorders are highly prevalent in clinical practice, there are no medications specifically approved by the FDA for treating them. In addition, children and adolescents referred for treatment for behavioral and aggressive disorders are likely to show several other problems (for example, hyperactivity, pervasive developmental disorders, depression, and substance abuse) that raise their own separate challenges. Parents and siblings of children referred for therapies for conduct disorder often themselves show significant impairment (psychiatric disorder, marital discord, family stress, dysfunctional relationships, abusive parenting, and so on). All these problems need to be addressed as drug prescription is being considered (Shechtman and Birani-Nasaraladin, 2006).

Steiner and coworkers (2003) reviewed the state of pharmacological treatment of aggression in children as of the late 1990s. They stated that medication is a part of complete therapy of behavioral and aggressive disorders:

- *Psychostimulants* are useful for aggressive and conduct disorder, even in the absence of ADHD. Antisocial behaviors, such as stealing and lying, can also be reduced by psychostimulants.

- *Lithium* exhibits little consistency of efficacy, even though it has been reported to reduce pathological aggression and conduct disorder in children with explosive behaviors.

- *Traditional antipsychotic drugs* (haloperidol, for example) are effective but have significant and often severe side effects.

- The authors of this review called for study of newer, *second-generation atypical antipsychotic drugs* (Chapter 9), as these drugs were just being introduced in the late 1990s.

- *SSRIs* (for example, fluoxetine) can be effective in some adults, but there are too few studies in children to warrant conclusions.

- There is some evidence for efficacy of *clonidine* in pediatric hyperactivity and aggression and perhaps in pervasive developmental disorders, but the evidence for efficacy is weak.

- *Benzodiazepines*—for example, clonazepam (Klonopin) and alprazolam (Xanax)—can reduce agitation and irritability, but they can induce behavioral disinhibition. They must be used with great care in children with pathological aggression.

- Open trials suggested efficacy of the *anticonvulsant neuromodulators.* Valproic acid and carbamazepine (Tegretol) are effective for children with rage outbursts and pathologic aggression. The authors stated that controlled trials were needed.

Ipser and Stein (2007) performed a meta-analysis review of pharmacotherapy of disruptive behavioral disorders in children and adolescents. Results indicated that targeted pharmacotherapy is effective and well tolerated in children and adolescents with these disorders;

producing a twofold greater response rate than treatment with placebo (review of 14 studies and 823 patients). In this more recent review, lithium was most effective, followed by atypical antipsychotic agents. Stimulant therapy showed a positive but not significant effect, although efficacy was also seen with bupropion, methylphenidate, and reboxetine. Anticonvulsants exhibited marginal effects. In the only long-term study, young people who maintained risperidone therapy had fewer relapses than youth who discontinued the drug.

Several authors have reported efficacy of valproic acid (Depakone) in youth with conduct or oppositional defiant disorder as well as explosive temper and mood lability (Reeves et al., 2003; Hollander et al., 2003). Khanzode and coworkers (2006) reexamined the use of valproic acid in incarcerated youths diagnosed with severe conduct disorders. High doses (500 to 1500 milligrams per day) produced improvements in depression and impulse control but no improvement in other emotional states. The researchers suggested that an integrated approach combining pharmacotherapy with psychotherapy may be needed to achieve overall improvement. Psychotherapeutic interventions may be more beneficial in treating more complex emotional states involving self-esteem, consideration for others, and personal responsibility. Saxena and coworkers (2006) studied the use of valproic acid in youth (average age 11 years) who had parents with bipolar disorder and who displayed irritability, rapid mood shifts, and aggression. Valproate (dosed to a blood concentration of 50 to 120 micrograms per milliliter) improved both mood and aggressive symptoms, and over 75 percent of the young people studied were considered "responders."

Schur and coworkers (2003) reviewed the use of newer antipsychotic drugs for treatment of aggressive youth. They concluded that atypical antipsychotics (risperidone, olanzapine, quetiapine, ziprasidone, and aripiprazole) appear to be safe and effective. Pandina and colleagues (2006) came to the same conclusion when reviewing risperidone in the management of disruptive disorders. The first controlled clinical trial of risperidone in children and adolescents with disruptive behaviors was recently reported in 527 patients and results were very positive (Reyes et al., 2006).

Staller (2007) performed a useful chart review of a small number of highly aggressive preschool-aged children (ages 4 to 5 years) treated with medications. Here, clinicians were challenged by an increasing number of very young children showing extremes of behavior that include aggression, hyperactivity, impulsivity, and mood lability. Psychotropic medicines were used successfully in over three-quarters of these children; medicines included stimulants and atypical antipsychotics. The severity and uncertainty of diagnosis seemed to explain the use of these medications as a generic approach to treating severe behavioral dysregulation. Staller concluded that "research has yet to offer clear guidance" (p. 131).

In summary, as with adults, the results are inconsistent. But there is support for the use of lithium and, to a lesser extent, the antiepileptic drugs in controlling pathologically aggressive behavior in youth. The antipsychotic drugs may work more for the agitation than the underlying aggressive behavior. Stimulants and benzodiazepines are the least useful.

Autism Spectrum Disorders

The term *autism spectrum disorders* encompasses five pervasive developmental disorders, which include autism and its milder form, Asperger's syndrome. These are complex disorders whose core features include deficits in social interaction and speech/communication skills, repetitive behaviors, and restricted interests. Associated abnormalities may include seizures, electroencephalographic (EEG) abnormalities, affective instability, impulsivity, and aggression. A 2007 survey indicated an alarming increase in the incidence of autism spectrum disorders to a current estimate of 6.6 per 1000 for 8-year-old children (community range = 5.2 to 7.6 per 1000 8-year-old children)—equal to about 1 in 150 children (Centers for Disease Control and Prevention, 2007). Rates are three times higher in boys than in girls. The median age of earliest onset of diagnosis was about 5 years of age. For more than half the diagnosed children, developmental concerns had been expressed before 3 years of age. Cognitive impairment is seen in 68 percent of these children, and 8 percent have comorbid epilepsy. Wazana and coworkers (2007) discussed the possible reasons for the alarming increase in the reported diagnosis of autistic disorder.

McDougle and coworkers (2003) reviewed the use of drugs for amelioration of behavioral symptoms of autism (Figure 10.2) and other pervasive developmental disorders (PDDs):

- *Haloperidol and other traditional antipsychotic agents* were the most studied and the most effective drugs. Their use was limited by all the limitations common to this group of drugs (Chapter 9).

- *Risperidone, olanzapine, and newer atypical antipsychotic agents* are efficacious and are better tolerated than haloperidol. Of these drugs, risperidone has now received FDA-approval for this use. Ziprasidone exhibits efficacy without unwanted weight gain.

- *Selective serotonin reuptake inhibitor antidepressants* appear favorable in adult populations, but there have been no studies in children.

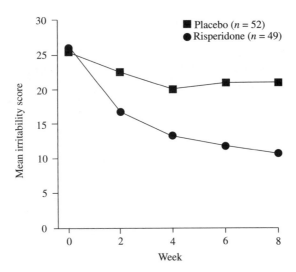

FIGURE 10.2 Mean score for irritability in risperidone- and placebo-treated children with autism. Total number of subjects studied = 101. Higher scores on the irritability subscale of the Aberrant Behavior Checklist indicate greater irritability. [Data from the Research Units on Pediatric Psychopharmacology Autism Network. From McDougle et al. (2003), p. 17.]

- *Naltrexone* (ReVia, Vivatrol), once thought to be effective, had minimal efficacy.
- *Clonidine*, although effective in clinical trials, was limited by a high rate of relapse.
- *Psychostimulants* reduced hyperactivity and irritability. However, they could also exacerbate irritability, produce insomnia, and precipitate aggression.
- *Buspirone* (BuSpar) and *neuromodulator mood stabilizers* are worthy of study.

Several reports addressed the use of risperidone for autism (Masi et al., 2003; Findling et al., 2004). All noted that risperidone improved mood disorders and reduced disruptive behaviors such as hyperactivity, fighting, anger, labile affect, negativity, and uncooperativeness. Risperidone today is generally considered as the medication of choice for treatment of autism spectrum disorders. In March 2007, the FDA approved Risperdal M-TAB orally disintegrating tablets for the symptomatic treatment of irritability in autistic children and adolescents. This FDA approval was the first for a drug to treat behaviors associated with autism in children: aggression, deliberate self-injury, and temper tantrums.

A similar atypical antipsychotic medication, olanzapine (Zyprexa), also reduced irritability, hyperactivity, and excessive speech patterns. However, improvement was less with olanzapine than with risperidone, and weight gain was greater with olanzapine. Reports of any usefulness of newer atypical antipsychotics such as aripiprazole (Abilify) are just beginning to appear. Shastri and colleagues (2006) reported successful use of aripiprazole in one person with autism. Valicenti-McDermott and Demb (2006) reported successful use of aripiprazole to control behavioral symptoms in 32 children with autism spectrum or mental retardation. Improvements were seen in 56 percent of children at a mean daily dose of 10 mg.[2] In one report, amisulpride was ineffective in a trial in children with severe autism and severe learning disabilities (Dinca et al., 2005). More reports should be forthcoming as newer agents that have lower propensity for producing diabetes and inducing weight gain are developed.

Hollander and colleagues (2001) reported positive results of an open trial of valproic acid (Depakote) in 10 children with autism spectrum disorders. About two-thirds of the children had a sustained response, most marked in affective instability and aggression. Interestingly, all children who had an abnormal EEG prior to initiation of drug therapy were responders. Although this was a pilot study, its results were consistent with the demonstrated efficacy of valproic acid for the treatment of target symptoms of impulsivity, aggression, and mood instability within a broad range of psychiatric disorders. It will be interesting to see whether a pretreatment EEG can be a predictor of responsiveness to valproate or risperidone.

There is now some evidence that fatty acid deficiencies or imbalances may contribute to childhood neurodevelopmental disorders, including autism spectrum disorders (Richardson, 2006; Sliwinski et al., 2006). Amminger and colleagues (2007) conducted a well-controlled 6-week pilot trial of 1.5 grams per day of omega-3 fatty acids (0.84 grams per day of eicosapentaenoic acid and 0.7 grams per day of docosahexaenoic acid) in 13 children (ages 5 to 17 years) with autistic disorders accompanied by severe tantrums, aggression, or self-injurious behavior. Results were positive and provided preliminary evidence that omega-3 fatty acids may be an effective adjunct therapy for children

---

[2]Aripiprazole is FDA-approved for use in adults to treat schizophrenia and bipolar disorder. It has been successfully used in children and adolescents to treat Asperger's syndrome, autistic behaviors, mood disorders, and conduct disorder. A conservative dosage regimen is 1 millgram per day for youth weighing less than 25 kilograms, 2 millgrams per day for youth weighing 25 to 50 kilograms, 5 milligrams per day for weights of 50 to 70 kilograms, and 10 milligrams per day for adolescents weighing more than 70 kilograms. The dose should be reduced by 50 percent in patients taking an SSRI and perhaps increased in patients taking carbamazepine (Citrome et al., 2007).

and adolescents with autism. Obviously, if the development of autism is associated with fatty acid deficiencies, it is interesting to speculate that early intervention with either a diet high in omega-3 fatty acids or else dietary supplementation may exert a preventive effect rather than merely the symptom control exerted by medications.

Attention Deficit/Hyperactivity Disorder

Nationally, 7.8 percent of youth aged 4 to 17 years had a reported attention deficit/hyperactivity disorder (ADHD) diagnosis, and 4.3 percent had both a disorder diagnosis and were currently taking medication for the disorder (Visser et al., 2007). ADHD is therefore the most commonly diagnosed and treated behavioral disorder of childhood and adolescence. The neurobiology of ADHD is poorly understood; imbalances in both dopaminergic and noradrenergic systems have been implicated in the origin and persistence of its core symptoms, which include inattention, hyperactivity, and impulsivity (Hunt, 2006). ADHD has important genetic, environmental, and biological etiologies that persist into adolescence and adulthood in a sizable majority of affected children (Spencer et al., 2007). Genetic polymorphisms (differences) of the dopamine neurotransmitter system have been identified in young people with ADHD. This is important since medications used to treat ADHD act through augmentation of the dopamine neurotransmitter system. This system has therefore been a focus of recent research. As reviewed by DeYoung and colleagues (2006):

> Dopaminergic neurotransmission is implicated in externalizing behavior problems, such as aggression and hyperactivity. Externalizing behavior is known to be negatively associated with cognitive ability. Activation of dopamine D_4 receptors appears to inhibit the functioning of the prefrontal cortex, a brain region implicated in cognitive ability. The 7-repeat allele of the dopamine D_4 receptor gene produces less efficient receptors, and this may alter the effects of dopamine on cognitive function.

Further,

> Allelic variations of the dopamine D_4 receptor gene appears to be a genetic factor moderating the association between externalizing behavior and cognitive ability.

Inefficiency of an altered D_4 receptor would explain not only externalizing behaviors and reduced cognitive ability but also the observation that children with ADHD who possess the 7-repeat allele of the dopamine D_4 receptor gene require about twice the dose of methylphenidate for symptom improvement and behavioral and cognitive normalization (Hamarman et al., 2004). The doses are illustrated in Table 10.1. McGough and coworkers (2006a) reported similar genetically related correlations with response to methylphenidate in preschoolers with ADHD. Besides the dopamine D_4 gene, several others have also been implicated but are less studied (Farone and Khan, 2006; Brookes et al., 2006).

In line with these genetic studies, Arnsten (2006) relates genetics to the mechanisms of action of medications useful in treating ADHD. Briefly, Arnsten states that the prefrontal cortex (PFC) is critical for the regulation of behavior, attention, and cognition. The PFC reduces the effect of distraction and divided attention. Lesions to the PFC produce a profile of distractibility, forgetfulness, impulsivity, poor planning, and locomotor hyperactivity (all prominent in ADHD). Optimal levels of norepinephrine and dopamine are essential for proper PFC control of behavior and attention. Genetic alterations in norepinephrine or dopamine receptors or systems contribute to dysregulation of PFC circuits in ADHD. Stimulant medications tend to augment deficient dopaminergic (or norepinephrine) systems, optimizing PFC regulation of behavior and attention.

Childhood ADHD is associated with high rates of maternal and paternal childhood ADHD. Children with ADHD frequently have mothers with mood disorders, anxiety disorders, and stimulant/cocaine dependence and fathers with a history of childhood disruptive behavioral disorder. Therefore, it is not surprising that

TABLE 10.1 Responsiveness to methylphenidate

	DRD$_4$ 7R +	DRD$_4$ 7R −	*p* value
Initial Improvement			
Mean dose MPH	30 mg	20 mg	$p = 0.0002$
Mean dose MPH adjusted for weight	1.00 mg/kg	0.49 mg/kg	$p = 0.0002$
Symptom normalization			
Mean dose MPH	47 mg	31 mg	$p = 0.0002$
Mean dose MPH adjusted for weight	1.70 mg/kg	0.79 mg/kg	$p = 0.0001$

$^+$ = gene present; − = gene absent
Adapted from Hamarman et al. (2004), p. 569.

a remarkable incidence of comorbid or concomitant disease occurs in children afflicted with ADHD. As many as two-thirds of elementary school-age children with ADHD who are referred for clinical evaluation have at least one other diagnosable psychiatric disorder. Concomitant diseases include conduct disorder, oppositional defiant disorder, learning disorders, anxiety disorders, mood disorders (especially depression), and substance abuse. Thus, comorbidity must be anticipated in planning treatment for ADHD.

Guidelines for Management of ADHD

In July 2007, a comprehensive practice parameter for the assessment and treatment of children and adolescents with ADHD was published (American Academy of Child & Adolescent Psychiatry, 2007). This guideline, the first in over a decade, outlines thirteen recommendations for best-treatment practices to cover areas of ADHD screening (one recommendation), evaluation (four recommendations), and treatment (eight recommendations). Each recommendation includes an indication of the strength of empirical evidence and clinical support. The guideline is both practical and based on evidence.[3] Diagnostic criteria, behavioral rating assessment scales, and medication options are discussed in detail. All clinicians involved in the treatment of patients with ADHD are encouraged to study this document.

Stimulant Treatment for ADHD

Stimulant drugs improve behavior and learning ability in 60 to 80 percent of children who are correctly diagnosed. The treatment of ADHD with psychostimulants has become one of the most broadly effective drug therapies of the twenty-first century. In December 1999, results of the Multimodal Treatment Study of Children with Attention-Deficit/Hyperactivity Disorder (MTA Cooperative Group, 1999) were published. In the study, a cohort of 579 children with ADHD was assigned to 14 months of medication management, intensive behavioral treatment, and the two combined, or standard community care. Carefully structured medication management resulted in a better outcome than did intensive behavioral treatment, and combined treatment yielded an outcome that was better than the out-

---

[3]A pocket card summary of the guidelines may be ordered at www.myguidelinescenter.com.

come of behavioral treatment but equivalent to the outcome of medication management. As stated:

> Thus, carefully crafted medication management was superior to behavioral treatment and to routine community care that included medication. Combined treatment did not yield significantly greater benefits than medication management for core ADHD symptoms, but it may have provided modest advantages for non-ADHD symptoms and positive functioning outcomes. (p. 1073)

Since this study covered a period of only 14 months, longer-term efficacy remained unknown. A 24-month follow-up of the MTA study (MTA Cooperative Group, 2004) revealed that cessation of drug therapy was associated with clinical deterioration, continued drug therapy was associated with only mild deterioration, and stimulant initiation (in the group not receiving stimulants in the early study) was associated with clinical improvements. The follow-up concluded: "Consistent use of stimulant medication was associated with maintenance of effectiveness but continued mild growth suppression" (p. 762). What is now clear is that stimulants improve behavioral symptoms of ADHD as well as cognitive functioning, academic performance, and social functioning, all consistent with normalization of a dysfunctional prefrontal cortex. Jensen and coworkers (2005) performed a cost-effectiveness analysis of implementing the results of the MTA study. Epstein and coworkers (2006) reported that improved behavioral end points were accompanied by positive neuropsychological outcomes.

Stimulants such as methylphenidate and the amphetamines are FDA-approved for use in treating ADHD in youth older than about 6 years of age. Today, however, we are recognizing the presence of ADHD in younger children, namely, in children of preschool age (Kratochvil et al., 2004). The National Institutes of Mental Health has funded a multicenter, randomized efficacy study designed to evaluate the short-term (5 weeks) and long-term (40 weeks) safety of methylphenidate in preschoolers with severe ADHD (the Preschool ADHD Treatment Study). Results to date indicate that immediate-release methylphenidate at doses of 2.5 to 7.5 milligrams three times daily produced significant reductions in scores on ADHD symptom scales, although effects were smaller than those cited for school-aged children on the same medication (Greenhill et al., 2006a). Swanson and coworkers (2006a) reported that preschoolers treated with methylphenidate lost both weight and height compared with nontreated children. The risks of reduced growth rates should be balanced against expected therapeutic benefits.

A persistent question involved whether or not there is any association between the use of stimulants during childhood and the later use of drugs of abuse. The answer is now quite clear: childhood and adolescent use of stimulant medication for ADHD is not associated with later substance abuse. Abuse is minimal among patients for whom stimulant medications are appropriately prescribed In fact, stimulant therapy for ADHD results in a nearly twofold *reduction* in the risk for later substance abuse (Wilens et al., 2003b).

In children who have ADHD comorbid with other psychological disorders, more than one medication may be needed. In ADHD comorbid with depression, treatment may involve a combination of a serotonin reuptake-blocking antidepressant (SSRI) as well as a stimulant. In cases of ADHD comorbid with bipolar illness, treatment may begin with a mood stabilizer, as the stimulant might precipitate a manic episode. ADHD with ODD/CD responds well to stimulant therapy. ADHD with a comorbid anxiety disorder appears to respond to a combination of stimulant medication and psychosocial therapies. ADHD with comorbid substance abuse requires treatment for both conditions, beginning with substance abuse therapy. Long-term treatment may involve use of stimulants and antidepressants.

The primary stimulants used in the treatment of ADHD are methylphenidate and various formulations of amphetamines. Secondary agents (nonstimulants) include buspirone (BuSpar) and bupropion (Wellbutrin), especially in refractory cases. Newer agents of interest as viable alternatives to psychostimulants include modafinil (Provigil) and atomoxetine (Strattera). Atomoxetine is the first of a new class of drugs known as selective norepinephrine reuptake inhibitors (Chapter 7).

Methylphenidate

Currently, methylphenidate preparations account for 90 percent of the prescribed medication for ADHD. Because it is so widely used and because no one dosage regimen is ideal, multiple different dosage forms and methods of delivering the drug to the bloodstream have been devised. Although clinically efficacious, methylphenidate has a short duration of action, as well as adverse effects especially on appetite (reduced appetite with growth suppression) and on sleep disturbances (drug-induced nighttime insomnia).

Methylphenidate (as Ritalin) is of rapid onset and short duration; thus, it must be administered two or three times daily. It is not administered in the evening to permit the blood level to drop, allowing normal sleep. The short half-life is a problem in some children who experience an end-of-dose rebound in dysfunctional behavior. Early sustained-release preparations of methylphenidate were disappointing. Recently, however, more dependable extended-release preparations have become available. The first of these was Concerta, a formulation consisting of a plastic shell coated with a layer of immediate-release methylphenidate and filled with methylphenidate in an osmotic medium that slowly releases the drug over a 10-hour period, providing gradually increasing plasma concentrations of the drug. The empty shell is then excreted in the feces. One daily dose of Concerta yields about the same plasma concentrations as three daily doses of immediate-release methylphenidate with essentially equal efficacy (Swanson et al., 2003; Wilens et al., 2003a). Steele and coworkers (2006a) reported that once-daily Concerta was statistically superior to three-times-daily administration of short-acting methylphenidate.

Other new formulations of methylphenidate for oral administration include Metadate CD, Methylin ER, Metadate ER, and Ritalin LA. In 2007, a transdermal methylphenidate delivery system (a "skin patch" sold under the trade name Daytrana) was introduced. The patch is applied daily and is worn for a maximum of 9 hours. Following removal, the effects of the methylphenidate continue for another 3 hours. Patches containing 10, 15, 20, and 30 milligrams are available. If removed before 9 hours, less drug is absorbed. While more effective than placebo patches in treating ADHD, the patch has not been directly compared with long-acting oral methylphenidate such as Concerta (Anderson and Scott, 2006; McGough et al., 2006b). Combining transdermal methylphenidate with behavioral therapies was more effective than the use of either alone (Pelham et al., 2005).

Also commercially available is dexmethylphenidate (Focalin), the active D-isomer of methylphenidate. This isomer has twice the potency of methylphenidate, so the dose of dexmethylphenidate is one-half the dose of methylphenidate. Focalin is available in an extended-release formulation (Focalin XR).

Volkow and coworkers addressed the question of why methylphenidate is not an "addicting" drug when taken orally, especially since its mechanism of action is essentially the same as that of cocaine, a highly "addicting" drug (Volkow et al., 2002a, 2002b). Both methylphenidate and cocaine block the presynaptic dopamine transporter and, as a result, increase the amount of dopamine in the synaptic cleft. Orally administered methylphenidate, however, slowly enters the brain, reaching maximal concentrations after 60 to 90 minutes

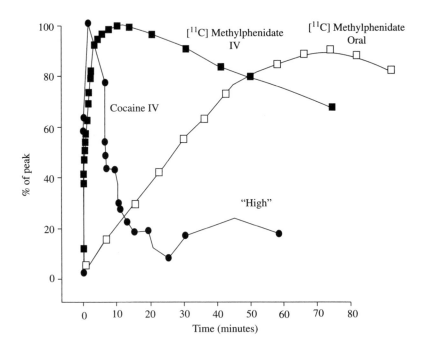

FIGURE 10.3 Peak concentrations of cocaine and methylphenidate in three situations. Cocaine was administered intravenously, reaching a peak within a few minutes. The "high" correlated with plasma levels of the drug. Methylphenidate was administered either intravenously or orally. A "high" was achieved only initially after the intravenous dose, paralleling the cocaine high. With oral administration, peak blood level was reached only after 70 minutes and no "high" was perceived. [Adapted from Volkow and coworkers (2002a, 2002b).]

(Figure 10.3). Once in the brain and attached to the dopamine transporter, it releases slowly, preventing further increase of dopamine. In contrast, inhaled or injected cocaine rapidly reaches peak concentrations in the brain; the concentrations are of short duration, allowing for repeated "highs." Therefore, the abuse potential (with oral administration) of methylphenidate is low and those to whom the drug is prescribed seldom abuse the drug.

Amphetamines

Since the late 1930s, amphetamines have been prescribed for the treatment of ADHD. Available amphetamines include *dextroamphetamine* (Dexedrine), *mixed amphetamine salts* (Adderall), and a new *extended-release formulation of Adderall* (Adderall XR). Pliszka and coworkers (2003) concluded that once-daily Adderall is similar to twice-daily methylphenidate. Rapport and coworkers (2002) conducted a meta-analysis of methylphenidate and Adderall. They concluded that Adderall is therapeutically equivalent or even superior to generic methylphenidate for improving a relatively wide range of behavior problems commonly displayed by children with ADHD. The issue of comparative equivalence remains unclear, as head-to-head comparisons of Concerta and Adderall in treating ADHD have not been reported. One interesting report studied driving-simulator performance by adolescent drivers with ADHD. Concerta improved driving performance while placebo and Adderall did not (Cox et al., 2006). Recently, Steele and coworkers (2006b) called for reevaluation of outcome measurements in ADHD treatment, advocating *remission* rather than *response* as the goal of therapy.

In 2005, concerns arose over the cardiac safety of amphetamines because of reports of rare heart attacks, strokes, and sudden deaths in patients taking amphetamines at recommended doses. Mild to moderate increases in blood pressure and in peripheral vascular resistance (increasing cardiac workload) can certainly be expected with the use of drugs that stimulate the autonomic nervous system. Stimulants should probably not be used in patients with hypertensive cardiovascular disease or in patients with cardiac disease. In most normal people, cardiac effects should be minor, and the benefits of medication therapy should be weighed against the risk of adverse effects. Nissen (2006) places this issue in perspective.

In March 2007, the FDA asked manufacturers of psychostimulants to prepare handout materials designed to advise patients and their families of possible heart-related problems, including sudden death in patients who have heart problems or heart defects, stroke and heart attacks in adults, and increases in blood pressure and heart rate. Warnings also include adverse psychiatric problems, including new or worsening behavioral and thought problems, new or worsening bipolar illness, new or worsening aggressive or hostility problems, and in children and teenagers, new psychiatric symptoms, including hearing voices, believing things that are not true, increased suspiciousness, or new manic symptoms. All these effects are predictable consequences seen in some people using any psychostimulant, whether for therapeutic purposes or for abuse purposes (Chapter 13).

Recently approved (2007) for treatment of ADHD is an "amphetamine pro-drug." *Lisdexamfetamine* (Vyvanse) is a new pharmacological product developed with the goal of demonstrating efficacy equal to that of the amphetamines with less abuse potential than amphetamines. In lisdexamfetamine a molecule of D-amphetamine is bonded to L-lysine, a naturally occurring amino acid, resulting in a molecule lacking biological activity (a pro-drug). When taken orally, the bond is broken by gastrointestinal enzymes, releasing the amphetamine, which is then absorbed. Doses of 10, 30, and 70 milligrams of lisdexamfetamine result in bioavailability of about 5 to 30 milligrams of dextroamphetamine. It is claimed that abuse potential is lower than that seen with dextroamphetamine, since Vyvanse is less effective if injected or "snorted" Because the lysine-amphetamine bond is less susceptible to breakdown and therefore is less of an agonist at the dopamine receptor, this claim remains to be proved. Since the manufacturer of Vyvanse also manufactures Adderall XR and since the latter drug loses patent protection in 2009, the significance and true motivation are unclear.

Alternative Medications for Treating ADHD

Although methylphenidate and amphetamines are the drugs of first choice in the treatment of ADHD, about 10 to 30 percent of ADHD patients do not respond adequately and are considered to be treatment-resistant. In addition, some children and their parents may desire that stimulants not be used. Therefore, there is a need for treatment alternatives.

Tricyclic antidepressants (especially *nortriptyline;* Chapter 7) have been studied and have occasionally been reported to be effective. However, cognitive impairments, limited efficacy, and rare cases of potentially fatal cardiac toxicities associated with tricyclic antidepressant use in children and adolescents pose considerable limitations.

Initial reports on other antidepressants indicate some usefulness of *fluoxetine* (Prozac) and *buspirone* (BuSpar), although the effects were not robust. Quintana and coworkers (2007), however, demonstrated a more robust effect of fluoxetine in ADHD with comorbid nonbipolar mood disorders in children and adolescents aged 6 to 18 years (open-label study with no placebo controls). Symptoms of inattention, overactivity, aggression, defiance, and depression were improved in 47 percent of participants. (The use of fluoxetine in ADHD is not addressed in the new practice parameters.) Of additional interest is the dopaminergic antidepressant *bupropion SR* (Wellbutrin); the drug has been reported effective in adults with ADHD and in both adults and adolescents with ADHD comborbid with other disorders such as depression or substance abuse (Solhkhah et al., 2005; Upadhyaya et al., 2004).

Two CNS-acting antihypertensive (blood pressure-lowering) dopaminergic agonists—*clonidine* (Catapres) and *guanfacine* (Tenex)—have been reported to have positive effects in the treatment of ADHD. These two drugs are generally considered to be second-line medications. To date, no homeopathic or herbal medications have been demonstrated to possess the necessary combination of safety and efficacy in treating ADHD.

Modafinil (Provigil) is a nonstimulant drug currently indicated to maintain daytime wakefulness in the treatment of narcolepsy, an inherited neurological disorder involving excess daytime sedation. Modafinil is distinct from methylphenidate and amphetamines because it is not classified as a stimulant and its abuse potential is minimal. Recent studies have documented the efficacy of modafinil in treating child and adolescent ADHD (Biederman et al., 2006; Greenhill et al., 2006b; Swanson et al., 2006b). The required dosage of about 300 to 400 milligrams once daily is significantly higher than that required to treat narcolepsy in adults. To date, the drug has not been FDA-approved for this use, probably because of the large dosage requirement, certain safety concerns, and concern over whether or not it offers significant clinical advantages over existing agents. If approved, it will undoubtedly be marketed for ADHD under a new trade name, presumably either Sparlon or Attenace.

Atomoxetine (Strattera), available since 2003, is the first of a series of selective norepinephrine reuptake inhibitor (SNRI) antidepressants approved by the FDA for use in treating ADHD in children 6 years of age and older as well as in adults. Therefore, like bupropion, atomoxetine exhibits a range of effectiveness that includes treatment of comorbid ADHD, depression, and anxiety (Kratochvil et al., 2005). Newcorn and coworkers (2006) and Biederman and coworkers (2007) reported on the efficacy of atomoxetine in treating children and adolescents with comorbid ADHD and oppositional defiant disorder (ODD). All three groups noted that ADHD youth without ODD responded to dose levels of 1.2 milligrams per kilogram per day, while ADHD youth with ODD required higher doses, usually 1.8 milligrams per kilogram per day. Jou and coworkers (2005) reported on the efficacy of atomoxetine in reducing ADHD symptoms in youth with pervasive developmental disorders. Here, atomoxetine did not exacerbate anxiety symptoms, which is a concern with stimulants in this patient population. Newcorn and coworkers (2006) reported that for youth who exhibit a robust response to atomoxetine, it may be possible to maintain effectiveness with reduced doses of the drug. A recent British study of 201 children with ADHD reported that atomoxetine was more effective in treatment-naive patients than in patients who had been previously treated with stimulant medication (Prasad et al., 2007).

Adverse effects of atomoxetine can include reduced appetite, weight loss, increased heart rate, and increased blood pressure. Blood pressure increases are minimal to modest. Atomoxetine has no adverse effects on QT interval on the ECG. As with other SNRI antidepressants (Chapter 7), not only are ADHD symptoms reduced, but social and family functioning sometimes improve.

Depression in Children and Adolescents

Perhaps the greatest controversy in child and adolescent psychopharmacology during the current decade is the controversy surrounding the use of antidepressant medication to treat major depressive disorders in children and adolescents. In essence, controversy surrounds the balance between expected benefits (effectiveness in relieving depression) versus potential risks (possibility of increasing the risk of suicide).

To understand this controversy, a bit of history is in order. First, research conducted in the 1990s demonstrated several important points:

- There was a high prevalence of suicidal ideation and completed suicides among children and adolescents with depressive disorders.

- Not only does depression exist in adolescence, but adolescence is the period of highest risk for onset of depression.

- Adolescent depression has a protracted, longitudinal course with persistence into adult life (adolescents do not "grow out of it"), which results in ongoing disruption of interpersonal relationships, risk for substance abuse, early pregnancy, low educational achievement, poor occupational functioning, unemployment, and continued risk of suicide.

- Childhood and adolescent depression is associated with later development of serious personality disorders in early adulthood; dependent, antisocial, passive-aggressive, and histrionic personality disorders increase threefold to thirteenfold over matched controls without depressive disorders (Kasen et al., 2001).

These data compelled clinicians to intervene aggressively to prevent teenagers from developing into troubled and dysfunctional adults, much less from taking their own lives. A partial answer was discovered in 1997 when Emslie and coworkers demonstrated that fluoxetine (Prozac) was superior to placebo treatment in lowering scores on the Children's Depression Rating Scale—Revised (Figure 10.4). Of note from this study, only one data point was significantly different from the score attained by placebo medication: the measurement of improvement taken at the end of 8 weeks of therapy—and the improvement over placebo, although statistically significant, was not robust. However, this one positive result led to widespread off-label use of fluoxetine for child and adolescent depression, culminating in the NIMH-funded TADS (Treatment for Adolescents with Depression Study) research, the first phase of which was published in 2004 [Treatment for Adolescents with Depression Study (TADS) Team, 2004]. In brief, the 12-week TADS study compared usual clinical management with fluoxetine (10 to 40 milligrams per day) alone, cognitive-behavioral therapy (CBT) alone, or the combination of CBT and fluoxetine (Figure 10.4A and B). Response to combination treatment (71 percent) was significantly greater than to fluoxetine alone (61 percent), CBT alone

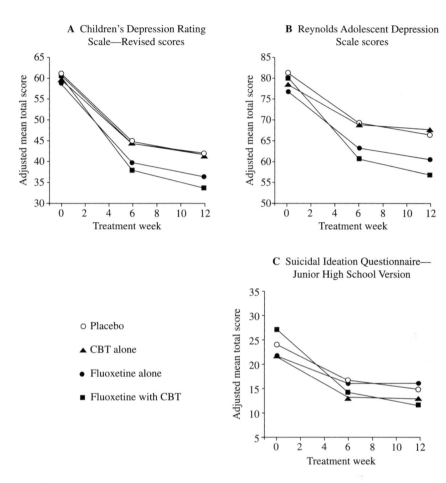

FIGURE 10.4 Mean scores for participants in the Treatment for Adolescents with Depression Study (TADS). CBT = cognitive behavioral therapy. [From Treatment for Adolescents with Depression Study (TADS) Team (2004).]

(43 percent), and placebo (usual clinical management, 35 percent). Fluoxetine monotherapy was superior to placebo and to CBT alone. Interestingly, suicidal ideation decreased in all conditions (Figure 10.4C). This study set the standard that the best treatment of child and adolescent depression is a combination of fluoxetine and CBT. Interestingly, studies with other SSRI-type antidepressants, including paroxetine (Paxil) and escitalopram (Lexapro), have reported generally negative results (Wagner et al., 2006). A new algorithm for the treatment of childhood depression was published by Hughes and colleagues in 2007.

The antidepressant *venlafaxine* (Effexor) has recently come under scrutiny, with new data indicating that any increased risk of suicidal attempts or ideation is much more common with this drug than with fluoxetine (Rubino et al., 2007). Venlafaxine extended release (Effexor-XR) was recently studied by Emslie and coworkers (2007), who note that, while clinically effective in reducing scores on the Children's Depression Rating Scale—Revised (CDRS-R), venlafaxine had significant adverse events including suicide attempts in two patients, onset of suicidal ideation in one patient, and self-injury in one patient. Hostility developed in four patients, two of whom required hospitalization. The researchers called venlafaxine a "third-line antidepressant in children and adolescents" (p. 223).

At about the same time the TADS study appeared, the FDA and corresponding agencies of the British and Canadian governments issued advisories regarding increased suicidal ideation in patients treated with SSRI antidepressants. This eventually led to the ban in Great Britain and Canada of the use of all antidepressants except fluoxetine in treating child and adolescent depression.[4]

Recently, a second phase of the TADS study was reported (Emslie et al., 2006; Vitiello et al., 2006). In brief, these two reports documented the efficacy and safety of combining CBT with fluoxetine therapy. Overall functioning and quality of life improved with therapy (Figure 10.5). Regarding suicide-related adverse events, at baseline, 29.2 percent of patients reported significant suicidal ideation, but the score improved during the course of treatment (Figure 10.6). Events still occurred, as expected, but their frequency decreased. The greatest improvements occurred in patients who received CBT, either alone or in combination with fluoxetine. An older British report documented the efficacy of CBT in mild to moderate depression in children and adolescents (Harrington et al., 1998), but a new report demonstrated that CBT was ineffective when added to fluoxetine therapy in moderately to severely depressed adolescents (Goodyer et al., 2007).

The issue of potential suicidal ideation and behaviors (but rarely completed suicides) has become so contentious that a PubMed search[5] by this author in mid-2007 using the two words "antidepressant" and "suicide" returned over 2,200 separate research article "hits" in the medical literature. Pertinent and relevant reports include those by Tiihonen and coworkers (2006), Rihmer and Akiskal (2006), and

---

[4]To date, fluoxetine has been the only antidepressant shown to be therapeutically effective in treating child and adolescent depression. As we will see later in this chapter, SSRIs are quite effective in treating child and adolescent anxiety disorders, including obsessive-compulsive disorder.

[5]The medical literature can be searched at www.ncbi.nlm.nih.gov/entrez or more simply by typing PubMed on a search engine such as Google.com.

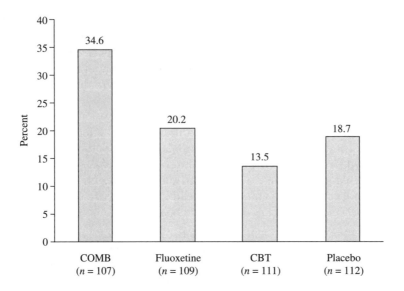

FIGURE 10.5 Proportion (percentage) of adolescents without functional impairment (Clinical Global Assessment Scale, CGAS, score >70 at the end of the 12-week study). CBT = cognitive-behavioral therapy; COMB = combination of fluoxetine and CBT. [From Vitiello et al. (2006).]

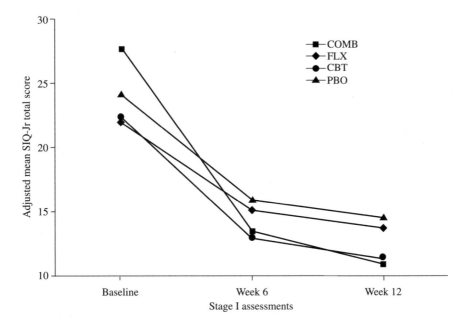

FIGURE 10.6 Self-reported suicidal ideation (SIQ-Jr) total score over 12 weeks of therapy. FLX = fluoxetine; CBT = cognitive-behavioral therapy; COMB = combination of fluoxetine and CBT; PBO = placebo therapy; SIQ-Jr = Suicidal Ideation Questionnaire, Grades 7–9.

Kratochvil and coworkers (2006). This entire mass of literature and debate cannot be adequately reviewed here, but perhaps one of the most reasonable perspectives in this area is presented by Gregory Simon in the Center for Health Studies at Group Health Cooperative in Seattle, Washington. In recent articles (Simon, 2006; Simon et al., 2006a, 2006b), he made the following points:

- Fluoxetine is the only drug whose antidepressant effect has been clearly established in a pediatric population and is the only drug approved in the United States for the treatment of depression in children and adolescents. If a health care provider chooses another drug, patients or their families should know that use of the drug is off-label and has not been proved to be effective.

- The FDA did not advise against the use of fluoxetine in children and adolescents; instead, they recommended more frequent follow-up care. Unfortunately, communicating information about risks had unintended effects, such as reducing prescriptions for child and adolescent depression by 25 percent.

- Unfortunately, reduction in prescriptions was accompanied by no improvement in rates of follow-up care. For example, in adults with depression, only 20 percent receive even minimal follow-up care (three or more visits to a practitioner over a three-month period). This is one of the poorest performances on the entire U.S. health care "report card."

- Suicide attempts (however their association) are unpredictable, especially among people at risk. All patients should be warned that suicidal ideation may arise suddenly and that agitation and restlessness may be early signs of danger.

- Regular follow-up is essential, and it will not happen by accident. Erratic follow-up care, the fatigue and hopelessness that accompany depression, high dropout rates from depression treatment, and a mistaken presumption that the "drug will work" are all barriers to follow-up. A treatment team of prescriber plus a mental health worker is a goal of care.

- Suicide is the most feared outcome of psychiatric illness. Among 10,000 children and adolescents who begin taking antidepressants for depression, approximately 6 will die by suicide during the next 6 months (probably with or without medication), and another 30 will be hospitalized after a serious suicide attempt. Of those 10,000 children and adolescents, 3000 will stop taking their medication within a few weeks, 4000 will never return for a follow-up visit, and 6000 will not recover from depression during the next 6 months.

- Of 2000 patients (of any age) who start antidepressants, one will make a serious suicide attempt while 800 will remain seriously depressed.[6] Treatment should be more closely monitored. Close monitoring is needed because treatment is so often unsuccessful, not because it is so risky.

- Although the rate of antidepressant use has increased dramatically during the past 20 years (and the rate of suicide has correspondingly decreased), the disappointing quality and outcomes of depression treatment have changed little. Our treatment of depression is growing wider, but it is often only inches deep. Unfortunately, the FDA advisories of possible increases in suicidality with antidepressant medication has led to decreases in the prescribing of antidepressants for children and adolescents, with the unintended consequence of greater risk of suicidality resulting from untreated depression (Bostic et al., 2006; Libby et al., 2007).

Simon suggests that the following statement be given to patients considering initiation of antidepressant treatment with medications:

> The FDA requires a warning that antidepressant medications can sometimes cause or increase thoughts of suicide. Studies in children and adolescents have shown that antidepressants can increase suicidal thoughts. However, other studies have shown that the overall risk of attempting suicide goes down after starting antidepressant medication. Even if antidepressants help most people who take them, some people may have very negative reactions. Thus, it is important that we have regular contact over the next few weeks. If you have thoughts about suicide or about harming yourself, please contact me right away.

Bridge and coworkers (2007) reported a meta-analysis evaluating both the beneficial effects and possible suicidal ideation and attempts in clinical trials of antidepressant medications in youth. Antidepressants have demonstrable efficacy for pediatric depression and anxiety disorders, with only nonsignificant increases in suicidal behaviors. No completed suicides have been reported in any clinical study. Therapy with fluoxetine is associated with a 21 percent increase in the rate of remission over placebo-treated young people, with other antidepressants being much less effective. Benefits of antidepressants to treat obsessive-compulsive disorder were similarly robust, and the greatest efficacy was observed in the treatment of non-OCD anxiety disorders. Overall, for all

---

[6]This finding is certainly in agreement with the results of the STAR*D study, Chapter 7.

indications, the benefits of therapy outweighed any perceived risks. Three new reports (Gibbons et al., 2007; Posner et al., 2007; Simon and Savarino, 2007) strongly support the use of antidepressants for patients with depression, with an accompanying editorial that concluded, "It is much more likely that suicidal behavior leads to treatment than that treatment leads to suicidal behavior" (Brent, 2007, p. 991).

Specific Antidepressants

Selective Serotonin Reuptake Inhibitors Fluoxetine has been widely used for the treatment of child and adolescent depression and has relieved depression in about 50 to 60 percent of takers (leaving 40 percent as nonresponders.). Even in responders, however, residual symptomatology and functional impairments can persist. Garland and Berg (2001) described five 14- to 17-year-old patients who developed a reversible, dose-dependent frontal lobe amotivational syndrome after taking fluoxetine (Prozac) and paroxetine (Paxil). The syndrome was characterized by masklike apathy, indifference, and loss of initiative and/or disinhibition. Each adolescent became indifferent to work performance and exhibited impulsive and disinhibited behaviors, poor concentration, and forgetfulness. The onset appeared to occur after a month of good functioning as a result of drug therapy. This state of apparent apathy and indifference may be one reason why fluoxetine and other SSRIs are excellent choices for treatment of obsessive-compulsive behaviors.

Chapter 7 discussed the pharmacology and side effects of the SSRIs at length. Common side effects include nausea, insomnia, behavioral activation, anxiety, restlessness, and reduced libido. The activating effects in children and adolescents are comparable to those seen in adults. Uncommon and potentially serious side effects include increased suicidal thoughts and behaviors as well as mania or hypomania (Connor and Meltzer, 2006). Of additional concern is the serotonin withdrawal syndrome that can be seen in anyone (including children and adolescents) who abruptly discontinues the SSRI. To minimize this reaction, a long-acting (long half-life) agent should be used, again indicating the use of fluoxetine over other SSRIs. If a dose of a short-acting antidepressant is missed (all but fluoxetine have half-lives of about 20 hours), a state of serotonin withdrawal can occur within 16 to 24 hours and can lead not only to serotonin withdrawal syndrome but to relapse to depression and thoughts of suicide. Regardless, today, fluoxetine combined with psychological therapies is the treatment of choice for child/adolescent depressive disorder.

Other Antidepressants. In brief, *tricyclic antidepressants* are no more effective than placebo in treating depression in children and adolescents. Significant side effects, higher patient attrition rates, and high toxicity (including fatalities) are limitations. The older *monoamine oxidase inhibitors* (MAOIs) are effective in treating adolescent depression, but their serious toxicities limit clinical use. The new transdermal preparation (skin patch) of an MAOI (selegiline, or Emsam) may necessitate reevaluation of this form of treatment (see Chapter 7), although no trials of transdermal selegiline have been reported for the treatment of depression in children or adolescents.

As discussed earlier, atomoxetine (Strattera) is the first commercially available drug in the new class of SNRI-type antidepressants (at least in the United States; reboxetine is available in Europe). *Atomoxetine* is approved for treatment of ADHD in children and adolescents, and it is expected to be effective in child and adolescent depression. Future research will undoubtedly explore this area of use. The drug should certainly be effective in situations of depression comorbid with ADHD or anxiety disorders, especially since, unlike fluoxetine, SNRIs may be better at increasing social functioning; they may improve patient motivation, energy, and self-perception.

Adjuvant Medications. Drugs of two additional classes of psychopharmacology are being evaluated to see whether they can be used as adjuvant medication to improve the efficacy of fluoxetine in child and adolescent depression. First, *lamotrigine* (Lamictal) is an antiepileptic mood stabilizer (Chapter 8) with potential use as an augmenting agent in the treatment of resistant unipolar depression (Gabriel, 2006; Schindler and Anghelescu, 2007). Guidelines for its use in treating adolescent treatment-resistant depression, along with suggested dosage schedules, have recently been published (Carandang, 2006). As adolescents may be more susceptible to severe lamotrigine-induced rash, a slow titration schedule to "ramp up" the dose over a 6-week period has been suggested (Table 10.2). Because fluoxetine (as well as several other SSRIs) and valproic acid (Depakote) may slow the rate of

---

TABLE 10.2 Recommended lamotrigine titration in adolescents

LAMOTRIGINE MONOTHERAPY

12.5 mg/d for weeks 1 and 2

25 mg/d for weeks 3 and 4

50 mg/d for week 5

100 mg/d for week 6

Target dose: Between 132 and 142 mg/d

LAMOTRIGINE ADDED TO SELECTED SSRI OR VALPROATE REGIMEN

12.5 mg every other day for weeks 1 and 2

12.5 mg/d for weeks 3 and 4

25 mg/d for week 5

50 mg/d for week 6

Target dose: Consider 75 mg/d

Adapted from Carandang (2006).

metabolism of lamotrigine, a dose reduction of about 50 percent will result in therapeutic concentrations (see Table 10.2).

Second, the atypical antipsychotic drug *aripiprazole* (Abilify) has antidepressant properties (Chapter 9) and has been used as an augmenting agent in adults with inadequate response to SSRI therapy (Berman et al., 2007; Papakostas et al., 2005). As aripiprazole is being widely used in the treatment of various behavioral disorders in children and adolescents, it is likely that it will be studied as an augmenting agent for child and adolescent depression only partially responsive or unresponsive to fluoxetine therapy.

The use of adjuvant medicines to treat child and adolescent depression has been poorly studied, but interest is growing. Given that mild to moderate depression is not generally considered to be an indication for use of SSRI therapy, and given that treatment with fluoxetine is often unsuccessful, there is a pressing need for adjuvant treatments (Jorm et al., 2006).

Results of preliminary studies with St. John's wort (Chapter 19) in child and adolescent depression have been unimpressive (Simeon et al., 2005), with only a suggestion that the herb "may be effective." More interesting is the recently reported result of the efficacy of *omega-3 fatty acids* in child and adolescent depression. Nemets and coworkers (2006) administered 1 gram per day of omega-3 fatty acids, containing both EPA and DHA (Chapter 8), to 28 children of an average age of 10 years. Results from 20 children who took the omega-3 fatty acids for 4 months were analyzed. Most had a greater than 50 percent reduction in Children's Depression Rating Scale scores compared with minimal improvement in a placebo group (Figure 10.7). No

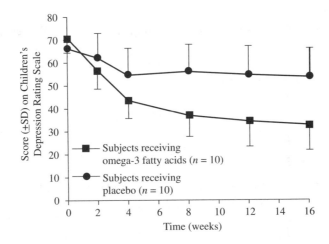

FIGURE 10.7 Children's Depression Rating Scale scores during 16 weeks of omega-3 fatty acid or placebo treatment. Differences between omega-3 and placebo were significant at weeks 8, 12, and 16.

side effects were reported. This quite impressive improvement with minimal side effects was considered to be "refreshing" in the pharmacology literature. Given its apparently benign nature, a trial of omega-3 fatty acids might be warranted in mild depression or where prescribed medication is of concern. If these preliminary results hold true to further study, one might then ask whether or not a deficiency of fatty acids might predispose a child or adolescent to depression and whether or not early dietary supplementation might avoid future development of a depressive disorder.

Depression and Psychiatric Comorbidity

Common psychiatric comorbidities with child and adolescent depression include anxiety disorders, ADHD, and behavioral disorders. In a study of 130 children and adolescents referred with depression, 46 percent had a comorbid anxiety disorder, 35 percent had ADHD, and 31 percent had oppositional defiant disorder or conduct disorder. Anxiety disorders commonly seen with depression include generalized anxiety disorder, panic disorder, and social phobias. For these disorders, psychological therapies are strongly indicated. Monotherapy with an SSRI is first-line treatment if drug therapy is chosen. If both depression and ADHD are thought to be present, first-line treatment is a stimulant with reassessment in two or three weeks. If both improve, continue the stimulant. If ADHD improves but depression continues, consider adding an SSRI. If neither improves, consider stopping the stimulant and treating the depression. Once depression improves, assess the ADHD and consider adding a stimulant. Atomoxetine (Strattera) is a viable option to stimulants because it is less anxiogenic.

Bipolar disorder often masks itself in children and adolescents as oppositional defiant disorder and conduct disorder. Thus, it is important to assess for symptoms of hypomania and mania to rule out ODD and CD. A practitioner in this situation often begins by treating the depression; first-line therapy is fluoxetine. If behavioral problems persist, an anticonvulsant neuromodulator such as valproic acid (Depakote) might be considered.

Anxiety Disorders in Children and Adolescents

The prevalence of any anxiety disorder in children and adolescents ranges in various studies from 5.7 percent to as high as 17.7 percent. A reasonable estimate is that about 10 percent of 15-year-olds meet diagnostic criteria for having an anxiety disorder. The rate of specific anxiety disorders varies from 6 percent having overanxious disorder (or generalized anxiety disorder) to between 1 and 2 percent having social phobia and separation anxiety disorder. Obsessive-compulsive disorder occurs in about 0.5 to 1.5 percent of children and adolescents. Bridge and coworkers (2007), in their meta-analysis of antidepressant efficacy, found considerable benefit when these drugs were used to treat both OCD and non-OCD anxiety disorders. This review is in agreement with the similar review by Reinblatt and Riddle (2007). A clinical practice parameter for the treatment of children and adolescents with anxiety disorders has recently been published (American Academy of Child & Adolescent Psychiatry, 2007). This practice parameter emphasizes treatment with a combination of pharmacotherapy and psychotherapy.

Generalized Anxiety Disorder

Generalized anxiety disorder (GAD) is characterized by excessive anxiety, worry, restlessness, fatigue, concentration difficulty, irritability, muscle tension, or sleep disturbances of 6 months duration or causing functional disturbances. The child may experience tension, apprehension, need for reassurance, and negative self-image, and, may have physical complaints. He or she may appear overly mature, perfectionistic, and sensitive to criticism. He or she may tend to seek reassurance for worries and self-doubt. Over 50 percent of children and adolescents with GAD have another anxiety disorder (social phobia, separation anxiety disorder, and/or panic disorder). Over 50 percent have a comorbid depressive disorder (the converse is also true). GAD has a high familial association; 40 percent of parents of children with GAD have had the disorder themselves during their childhood. There are currently no studies of possible association of GAD in children and adolescents with development of a substance abuse disorder.

The use of *benzodiazepines* (Chapter 6) may seem intuitively appropriate as a treatment for GAD in youth, but these drugs are clinically ineffective. Nonetheless, clonazepam (Klonopin) and alprazolam (Xanax) continue to be prescribed for this purpose. Behavioral activation (irritability, aggression, and tantrums), sleepiness, cognitive dysfunction, and addictive potential all must be considered as side effects of the use of benzodiazepines.

Tricyclic antidepressants have been tried, but there are no published reports of efficacy in children or adolescents. In addition, side effects are considerable (Chapter 7), and potentially fatal cardiovascular toxicities must be considered.

Buspirone (BuSpar; Chapter 6) has been effective in open trials. The drug is safe to use and more controlled trials are needed to further assess efficacy.

SSRIs are often very effective in reducing symptoms and improving functioning and are generally well tolerated in the treatment of child and adolescent GAD (Seidel and Walkup, 2006). Birmaher and coworkers (2003) reported that fluoxetine reduced GAD and other anxieties in 61 percent of 37 patients compared with a 35 percent

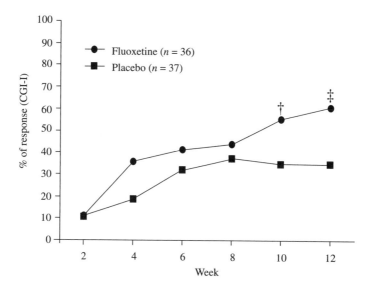

FIGURE 10.8 Effect of 12 weeks of treatment with fluoxetine compared with control in 37 patients with generalized anxiety disorder. Note the 8- to 10-week delay in onset of statistically significant response. CGI-I = clinical global impression—improvement; †p =.02; ‡p =.008. [From Birmaher et al. (2003), p. 420.]

reduction in 37 matched patients taking placebo (Figure 10.8). Despite this response, a substantial number of improved patients remained symptomatic. Rynn and coworkers (2001) reported on 22 children and adolescents (5 to 17 years) with GAD who were treated with sertraline (Zoloft) for 9 weeks. The drug was reported to be both safe and efficacious. Baumgartner and coworkers (2002) reported on a small number of adolescents with GAD who were medicated with citalopram (Celexa). Again the drug was reported to be effective with only minor and transient side effects. The Pediatric Psychopharmacology Anxiety Study Group (2001) reported on the efficacy of fluvoxamine (Luvox). Anxiety rating scales were significantly improved over the 8 weeks of the study. Cheer and Figgitt (2002) also reported on the efficacy of fluvoxamine in the management of anxiety disorders (including GAD) in children and adolescents. Therefore, efficacy of SSRIs in treating GAD was promising, regardless of agent studied.

Given the controversy concerning antidepressants and the small risk of precipitating suicidal ideation or suicide attempts, the question arises as to whether or not the use of SSRIs to treat GAD and other anxiety disorders incurs the same risk. Given that anxious children and adolescents are generally not as suicide-prone as are depressed children and given the much greater evidence for efficacy and the magnitude of benefit of SSRIs for pediatric anxiety disorders, the benefit/risk ratio for anxiety disorders is much more favorable than for depression (Seidel and Walkup, 2006).

Rynn and coworkers (2007) recently reported, in a large study of children and adolescents (ages 6 to 17 years) with GAD, that as an alternative medication, extended-release venlafaxine was modestly effective, with improvement rates averaging 69 percent versus a placebo response of 48 percent. The authors concluded that venlafaxine ER "may be an effective, well tolerated short-term treatment for pediatric GAD" (p. 290). On the other hand, as discussed, use of venlafaxine was associated with development of hostility in a few children and adolescents with depression. Whether this association carries over to children and adolescents with anxiety disorders is unknown.

Atypical neuroleptic agents have not been studied as a treatment for GAD in children or adolescents and probably are rarely indicated as therapy for GAD. There are as yet no reports on the usefulness of *nefazadone, bupropion,* or *mirtazapine* (see Chapter 7) for GAD in children or adolescents. Similarly, any usefulness of *atomoxetine* (Strattera) has been little studied, although anxiolytic effects of the drug have been noted in children with ADHD.

Social Anxiety Disorder

Within the past few years, social anxiety disorder (social phobia) has been separated from other anxiety disorders. It appears to be closely related to both GAD and avoidant personality disorder. It is a common anxiety disorder, with a 1-year prevalence estimated at 7 to 8 percent and a lifetime prevalence of 13 to 14 percent in patients aged between 15 and 54 years. It is certainly underrecognized and undertreated. Regardless, social anxiety disorder has a chronic course and is associated with significant morbidity. It is critical that patients receive an accurate diagnosis and appropriate treatment. Treatment of social anxiety disorder usually involves a combination of pharmacotherapy and psychotherapy (cognitive-behavioral therapy, social skills training, and exposure therapy) (Cottraux, 2005).

Many pharmacotherapies have been proposed for various subtypes of social anxiety disorder. Beta-adrenergic blockers (propranolol, for example) are useful in treating performance anxieties because they reduce the physical symptoms. SSRIs, MAOIs, and benzodiazepines all have been proposed. Lydiard and Bobes (2000) conducted a meta-analysis of three studies on the use of paroxetine (Paxil, an SSRI) for social anxiety disorder. In a total of 861 patients treated, paroxetine reduced symptomatology by 45 to 66 percent. Finally, Wagner and coworkers (2004) studied 322 children (8 to 11 years of age) in a well-controlled study of the efficacy of paroxetine in social anxiety disorder. About 48 percent were categorized as "very much" improved compared with 15 percent of children receiving placebo.

Obsessive-Compulsive Disorder

Obsessive-compulsive disorder (OCD) is a disorder of early onset characterized by recurrent obsessions or compulsions that are severe enough to be time-consuming or result in marked distress or significant impairment, especially of social life. In children, the incidence of OCD is thought to be rare, but in adolescents the reported prevalence is estimated at 2 to 3.6 percent. In fact, the majority of adults with OCD had an onset of the disorder during adolescence or earlier. OCD is now estimated as the fourth most common psychiatric disorder in children and adolescents.

Pharmacotherapy is an important component of the multimodal treatment of children and adolescents with OCD. However, treatment of children and adolescents with OCD should begin with the combination of cognitive-behavior therapy (CBT) and a single SSRI or CBT alone [Pediatric OCD Treatment Study (POTS) Team, 2004; O'Kearney, et al., 2006]. In the definitive POTS study, the rate for clinical remission was 53.6 percent for combined treatment, 39.3 percent for CBT alone, 21.4 percent for sertraline (Zoloft) alone, and 3.6 percent for placebo (Figure 10.9). Recently, March and coworkers (2007) reported that OCD with comorbid tic disorder responded less well to pharmacological treatment with sertraline. The authors suggest that

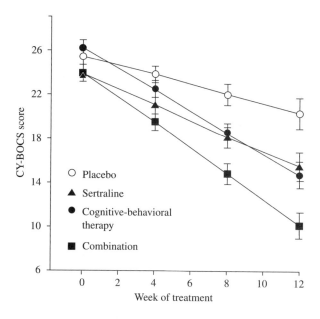

FIGURE 10.9 Weekly scores in the Children's Yale-Brown Obsessive-Compulsive Scale (CY-BOCS) for four treatment groups: placebo-treated, sertraline-treated, cognitive-behavioral therapy-treated, and combined treatment with sertraline plus cognitive-behavioral therapy. [From Pediatric OCD Treatment Study (POTS) Team (2004), Figure 2.]

with this comorbidity, therapy should begin with CBT alone or the combination of CBT and an SSRI of choice. Finally, in a brief case report, Storch and coworkers (2007) reported excellent response in a 13-year-old male to a 2.5 milligrams per day dose of aripiprazole, and that Yale-Brown OCS scores were reduced from 30 to 3 when combined with biweekly CBT.

Bipolar Disorder in Children and Adolescents

Pediatric bipolar disorder is a chronic and debilitating psychiatric illness associated with many short-term and long-term complications, including poor academic and social performance, legal problems, and increased risk of suicide. In addition, it is often complicated by other serious psychiatric disorders such as ADHD, ODD, CD, and substance abuse disorders. In 1997, the American Academy of Child and Adolescent Psychiatry published the first clinical practice parameters for the assessment and treatment of bipolar disorder in children and adolescents. This report was updated in 2005 (Kowatch et al., 2005) and again in 2007 (McClellan et al., 2007). In the 2007 edition, the authors state:

> The presentation of bipolar disorder in youth, especially children, is often considered atypical compared with that of the classic adult disorder, which is characterized by distinct phases of mania and depression. Children who receive a diagnosis of bipolar disorder in community settings typically present with rapid fluctuations in mood and behavior, often associated with comorbid ADHD and disruptive behavioral disorders. Thus, at this time it is not clear whether the atypical form of the disorder represents the same illness. The question of diagnostic continuity has important treatment and prognostic implications. Although more controlled trials are needed, mood stabilizers and atypical antipsychotic agents are generally considered the first line of treatment. Behavioral and psychosocial therapies are also generally indicated for juvenile mania to address disruptive behavior problems and the impact on family and community functioning. (p. 107)

Smarty and Findling (2007) reviewed the psychopharmacology literature published between 1995 and 2006 and concluded:

> [L]ithium, some anticonvulsants and second generation antipsychotics may be equally beneficial in the acute monotherapy for youth with mixed or manic states. However, because of limited response to monotherapy, there is increased justification for combination therapy. There is very limited data on the treatment of the

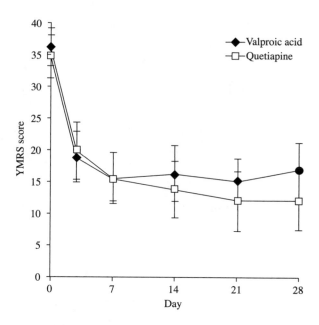

FIGURE 10.10 Young Mania Rating Scale (YMRS) scores over a 28-day treatment period in adolescents with a manic or mixed episode who received valproic acid (Depakote) or quetiapine (Seroquel). Scores decreased markedly with both treatments, differences between the drugs were not significant. [From DelBello, et al. (2006), Figure 2.]

depressed phase of bipolar illness in the youth. Also, very few studies have addressed the treatment of comorbidities and maintenance/relapse prevention. (p. 39)

DelBello and coworkers (2006) and Barzman and coworkers (2006) reported on controlled studies comparing valproic acid (Depakote, an anticonvulsant) and quetiapine (Seroquel, an atypical antipsychotic) in pediatric bipolar disorder (Figures 10.10 and 10.11). Quetiapine was at least as effective and it produced a quicker onset of response. Combinations of valproic acid and quetiapine are currently being considered, but one caution is in order: since valproic acid can reduce the rate of metabolism of drugs such as quetiapine,[7] Aichhorn and coworkers (2006) reported that this combination was associated with a 77 percent increase in quetiapine plasma levels.

Chang and colleagues (2006) report that lamotrigine (Lamictal), either as an adjunct therapy or as monotherapy, may be an effective

---

[7]Remember the interaction between valproic acid (or SSRIs) and lamotrigine discussed earlier.

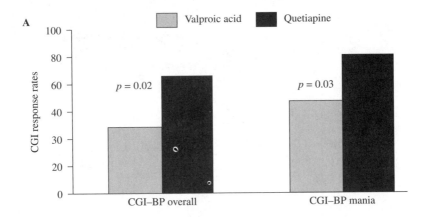

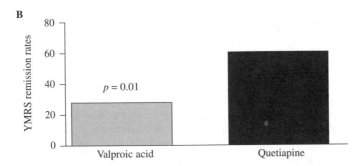

FIGURE 10.11 A. Clinical Global Improvement Scale score increases following treatment with valproic acid (Depakote) and quetiapine (Seroquel). Shown are improvements in overall bipolar illness (CGI-BP overall) and mania symptoms (CGI-BP mania). **B.** Improvements in the Young Mania Rating Scale (YMRS) score following treatment with valproic acid and quetiapine. [From DelBello et al. (2006), Figure 3.]

treatment for adolescents with bipolar disorder. In a study of 20 adolescents, 58 percent were considered to be in remission after 8 weeks of therapy. No controls were utilized. Precautions about the side effects of lamotrigine (rash and increased blood levels in the face of concomitant use of valproic acid or certain SSRIs) should be taken.

There are no reported clinical trials of antidepressant therapy in pediatric bipolar disorder. SSRIs can alleviate bipolar depression, although the risk of inducing mood destabilization (behavioral activation) is present if the drug is not used with a mood stabilizer.

A recent study (Wozniak et al., 2007) demonstrated that a high EPA omega-3 fatty acid supplement was effective for children with ADD, ADHD, bipolar disorder, and other educational and behavioral problems. The OmegaBrite D supplement of omega-3 fatty acids was evaluated for efficacy and safety over an 8-week period in 20 boys and girls (ages 6 to 17 years) with bipolar disorder. Half of the youths experienced a rapid 30 percent reduction in symptoms in the absence of side effects.

Recently, much interest has arisen over whether or not bipolar disorder can occur in youth of preschool age (3 to 6 years of age). This possibility is controversial (Scheffer and Niskala Apps, 2004) and presents diagnostic and validation problems. Luby and Belden (2006) suggest that children as young as 3 years can manifest diagnosable bipolar disorder and that they can be distinguished from disruptive-disordered preschoolers. These children are often referred with a diagnosis of ADHD and receive an eventual diagnosis of bipolar disorder (61 percent as bipolar disorder). Irritability and aggression are common presenting symptoms (Danielyan et al., 2007). Not surprisingly, diagnosis is often delayed: the mean number of years from the onset of mood symptoms to diagnosis of bipolar disease is 5 years, at most 12 years (Marchand et al., 2006). Scheffer and Niskala Apps (2004) describe several children diagnosed with bipolar disorder who had previously been treated with a stimulant (77 percent), an antipsychotic (64 percent), or an antidepressant (55 percent) and whose behaviors had worsened as a result. Adding a mood stabilizer such as valproic acid led to major reductions in symptomatology. They gave an example of a 4-year-old girl with rages, euphoria, irritability, and grandiosity made worse by stimulants and antidepressants. Valproic acid led to symptom control and improved behavioral and social functioning.

Endrass and coworkers (2007) asked whether childhood behavioral problems are associated with later development of bipolar disorder. They concluded that adolescents and children showing behaviors such as repeated running away from home and fighting are 2.6 to 3.5 times more likely to experience bipolar II disorder as adults than are youths with no history of conduct disorders.

Following mood stabilization, if the bipolar disorder is comorbid with ADHD, the addition of a psychostimulant may be necessary (Scheffer et al., 2005). Regardless, therapy for bipolar disorder in children and adolescents is challenging and expert assistance is essential. Adequate clinical response is difficult to achieve, relapses are frequent, side effects of drugs are considerable, and patient and family acceptance of this long-term disorder can be difficult.

Psychotic Disorders in Children and Adolescents

Schizophrenia and its related conditions are considered quite rare in children, and when it occurs it presents significant challenges to clinicians (Reimherr and McClellan, 2004). However, schizophrenia is relatively common in adolescents. About one in three patients with schizophrenia develops symptoms of psychosis between the ages of 10 and 20 years. Since childhood and adolescent schizophrenia is generally associated with a poor long-term outcome, effective treatments are needed for children and adolescents with psychotic disorders or, more hopefully, are in a prodromal phase that precedes first-episode psychosis (Flyckt et al., 2006; Marshall and Rathbone, 2006; Castro-Fornieles et al., 2007).

The current best psychopharmacological agents for the treatment of childhood- and adolescent-onset schizophrenia are the newer atypical antipsychotic drugs (see a review by Masi et al., 2006). While effective, haloperidol and the phenothiazines are best avoided because of their extrapyramidal side effects. Double-blind controlled studies have shown that clozapine (Clozaril), risperidone (Risperdal), olanzapine (Zyprexa), and quetiapine (Seroquel) are all effective for treating children and adolescents with this disorder. In children, no single agent has been shown to be any more or less effective than another (comparative studies have not been conducted in children). Clozaril, although effective, is probably a drug of second choice because of unique side effects (Gerbino-Rosen et al., 2005). Risperidone and olanzapine are quite effective, but weight gain has been a major problem. Quetiapine has been reported to be effective in limited trials (McConville et al., 2003; Kopala et al., 2006). Ziprasidone has been incompletely studied, but initial reports are encouraging (Meighen et al., 2004). However, its use in children and adolescents is limited by adverse electrocardiographic changes (QT interval prolongation) that may require close medical monitoring (Blair et al., 2005). Aripiprazole has been incompletely studied, but initial reports indicate limited effectiveness in treating psychosis in children and adolescents (Rugino and Janvier, 2005); in adults, however, it is comparable to other second-generation agents (Moeller et al., 2006). In June 2007 the FDA accepted for priority review (six-month review target) a supplemental new drug application (sNDA) of aripiprazole for the treatment of pediatric patients 13 to 17 years old with schizophrenia. This sNDA is based on data from a six-week, double-blind, randomized, placebo-controlled study in 302 children, conducted in 101 medical centers in 13 countries.

STUDY QUESTIONS

1. What is meant by an "off-label" use of a drug?

2. Why are psychotherapeutic drugs usually used "off-label" in children and adolescents?

3. Defend early therapeutic interventions in treating psychological disorders in children.

4. Which classes of psychotherapeutic drugs might be used to treat aggressive disorders in children and adolescents? Which might be of the most benefit?

5. Which classes of psychotherapeutic drugs might be useful in treating autism and other pervasive developmental disorders?

6. How might one of these classes be chosen over another?

7. Besides stimulant medications, what other classes of drugs might be considered for use in treating ADHD? Compare and contrast them with psychostimulants.

8. How does methylphenidate compare and contrast with cocaine?

9. Should depression in children be treated? Defend your answer.

10. Compare and contrast the tricyclic antidepressants and the SSRIs in childhood and adolescent depression.

11. What conditions might be comorbid with generalized anxiety disorder in children? How might this comorbidity affect therapy?

12. Compare and contrast the benzodiazepines and the SSRIs in the treatment of anxiety disorders in children and adolescents.

13. Compare and contrast the neuromodulator mood stabilizers and the atypical antipsychotics in the treatment of bipolar disorder in children and adolescents.

14. Discuss the relevant issues in the treatment of schizophrenia, schizoaffective disorder, and the prodromal phase of schizophrenia in children and adolescents.

REFERENCES

Aichhorn, W., et al. (2006). "Influence of Age, Gender, Body Weight, and Valproate Comedication on Quetiapine Plasma Concentrations." *International Clinical Psychopharmacology* 21: 81–85.

American Academy of Child & Adolescent Psychiatry (2007). "Practice Parameter for the Assessment and Treatment of Children and Adolescents with Anxiety Disorders." *Journal of the American Academy of Child & Adolescent Psychiatry* 46: 267–283.

American Academy of Child & Adolescent Psychiatry (2007). "Practice Parameter for the Assessment and Treatment of Children and Adolescents with Attention-Deficit-Hyperactivity Disorder." *Journal of the American Academy of Child & Adolescent Psychiatry* 46: 894–921.

Amminger, G. P., et al. (2007). "Omega-3 Fatty Acids Supplementation in Children with Autism: A Double-Blind Randomized, Placebo-Controlled Pilot Study." *Biological Psychiatry* 61: 551–553.

Anderson, V. R., and L. J. Scott (2006). "Methylphenidate Transdermal System: In Attention-Deficit/Hyperactivity Disorder in Children." *Drugs* 66: 1117–1126.

Aparasu, R. R., and V. Bhatara (2007). "Patterns and Determinants of Antipsychotic Prescribing in Children and Adolescents, 2003–2004." *Current Medical Research Opinions* 23: 49–56.

Arnsten, A. F. (2006). "Fundamentals of Attention-Deficit/Hyperactivity Disorder: Circuits and Pathways." *Journal of Clinical Psychiatry* 67 (Supplement 8): 7–12.

Barzman, D. H., et al. (2006). "The Efficacy and Tolerability of Quetiapine Versus Divalproex for the Treatment of Impulsivity and Reactive Aggression in

Adolescents with Co-occurring Bipolar Disorder and Disruptive Behavior Disorder(s)." *Journal of Child and Adolescent Psychopharmacology* 16: 665–670.

Baumgartner, J. L., et al. (2002). "Citalopram in Children and Adolescents with Depression or Anxiety." *Annals of Pharmacotherapy* 36: 1692–1697.

Berman, R. M., et al. (2007). "The Efficacy and Safety of Aripiprazole as Adjunctive Therapy in Major Depressive Disorder: A Multicenter, Randomized, Double-Blind, Placebo-Controlled Study." *Journal of Clinical Psychiatry* 68: 843–853.

Biederman, J., et al. (2006). "A Comparison of Once-Daily and Divided Doses of Modafinil in Children with Attention-Deficit/Hyperactivity Disorder: A Randomized, Double-Blind, and Placebo-Controlled Study." *Journal of Clinical Psychiatry* 67: 727–735.

Biederman, J., et al. (2007). "Effect of Comorbid Symptoms of Oppositional Defiant Disorder on Responses to Atomoxetine in Children with ADHD: A Meta-Analysis of Controlled Clinical Trial Data." *Psychopharmacology* 190: 31–41.

Birmaher, B., et al. (2003). "Fluoxetine for the Treatment of Childhood Anxiety Disorders." *Journal of the American Academy of Child & Adolescent Psychiatry* 42: 415–423.

Blair, J., et al. (2005). "Electrocardiographic Changes in Children and Adolescents Treated with Ziprasidone: A Prospective Study." *Journal of the American Academy of Child & Adolescent Psychiatry* 44: 73–79.

Bostic, J. Q., et al. (2006). "Elephants in the Room: Weighing the Benefits vs. the Risks of Antidepressant Treatment in Children." *Child & Adolescent Psychopharmacology News* 11 (4): 1–5.

Brent, D. (2007). "Antidepressants and Suicidal Behavior: Cause or Cure?" *American Journal of Psychiatry* 164: 989–991.

Bridge, J., et al. (2007). "Clinical Responses and Risk for Reported Suicidal Ideation and Suicide Attempts in Pediatric Antidepressant Treatment: A Meta-Analysis of Randomized Controlled Trials." *Journal of the American Medical Association* 297: 1683–1696.

Brookes, K., et al. (2006). "The Analysis of 51 Genes in DSM-IV Combined Type Attention Deficit Hyperactivity Disorder: Association Signals in DRD_4, DAT1, and 16 Other Genes." *Molecular Psychiatry* 11: 934–953.

Carandang, C. G. (2006). "Lamotrigine in Adolescent Treatment-Resistant Depression." *Child & Adolescent Psychopharmacology News* 11 (2): 1–10.

Castro-Fornieles, J., et al. (2007). "The Child and Adolescent First-Episode Psychosis Study (CAFEPS): Design and Baseline Results." *Schizophrenia Research* 91: 226–237.

Cavell, T. A. (2000). *Working with Parents of Aggressive Children: A Practitioner's Guide.* Washington, DC: American Psychological Association.

Centers for Disease Control and Prevention (2007). "Prevalence of the Autism Spectrum Disorders in Multiple Areas of the United States, Surveillance Years 2000 and 2002." Department of Health and Human Services, www.cdc.gov/autism.

Chang, K., et al. (2006). "An Open-Label Study of Lamotrigine Adjunct or Monotherapy for the Treatment of Adolescents with Bipolar Depression." *Journal of the American Academy of Child & Adolescent Psychiatry* 45: 298–304.

Cheer, S. M., and D. P. Figgitt (2002). "Spotlight on Fluvoxamine in Anxiety Disorders in Children and Adolescents." *CNS Drugs* 16: 139–144.

Citrome, L., et al. (2007). "Pharmacokinetics of Aripiprazole and Concomitant Carbamazepine." *Journal of Clinical Psychopharmacology* 27: 279–283.

Connor, D. F., and B. M. Meltzer (2006). *Pediatric Pharmacology: Fast Facts.* New York: Norton.

Costello, E. J., et al. (2007). "Service Costs of Caring for Adolescents with Mental Illness in a Rural Community, 1993–2000." *American Journal of Psychiatry* 164: 36–42.

Cottraux, J. (2005). "Recent Developments in Research and Treatment for Social Phobia (Social Anxiety Disorder)." *Current Opinions in Psychiatry* 18: 51–54.

Cox, D. J. et al. (2006). "Relative Benefits of Stimulant Therapy with OROS Methylphenidate Versus Mixed Amphetamine Salts Extended Release in Improving Driving Performance of Adolescents with Attention-Deficit/ Hyperactivity Disorder." *Pediatrics* 118: e704–e710.

Danielyan, A., et al. (2007). "Clinical Characteristics of Bipolar Disorder in Very Young Children." *Journal of Affective Disorders* 97: 51–59.

DelBello, M. P., et al. (2006). "A Double-Blind, Randomized Pilot Study Comparing Quetiapine and Divalproex for Adolescent Mania." *Journal of the American Academy of Child & Adolescent Psychiatry* 45: 305–313.

DeYoung, C. G., et al. (2006). "The Dopamine D_4 Receptor Gene and Moderation of the Association Between Externalizing Behavior and IQ." *Archives of General Psychiatry* 63: 1410–1416.

Dinca, O., et al. (2005). "Systematic Review of Randomized Controlled Trials of Atypical Antipsychotics and Selective Serotonin Reuptake Inhibitors for Behavioral Problems Associated with Pervasive Developmental Disorders." *Journal of Psychopharmacology* 19: 521–532.

Emslie, G. J., et al. (1997). "A Double-Blind, Randomized, Placebo-Controlled Trial of Fluoxetine in Children and Adolescents with Depression." *Archives of General Psychiatry* 54: 1031–1037.

Emslie, G. J., et al. (2006). "Treatment for Adolescents with Depression Study (TADS): Safety Results." *Journal of the American Academy of Child & Adolescent Psychiatry* 45: 1440–1455.

Emslie, G. J., et al. (2007). "Long-Term, Open-Label Venlafaxine Extended-Release Treatment in Children and Adolescents with Major Depressive Disorder." *CNS Spectrums* 12: 223–233.

Endrass, J., et al. (2007). "Are Behavioral Problems in Childhood and Adolescence Associated with Bipolar Disorder in Early Adulthood?" *European Archives of Psychiatry and Clinical Neuroscience* 257: 217–221.

Epstein, J. N., et al. (2006). "Assessing Medication Effects in the MTA Study Using Neuropsychological Outcomes." *Journal of Child Psychology and Psychiatry* 47: 446–456.

Farone, S. V., and S. A. Khan (2006). "Candidate Gene Studies of Attention-Deficit/Hyperactivity Disorder." *Journal of Clinical Psychiatry* 67 (Supplement 8): 13–20.

Findling, R. L., et al. (2004). "Long-Term, Open-Label Study of Risperidone in Children with Severe Disruptive Behaviors and Below-Average IQ." *American Journal of Psychiatry* 161: 677–684.

Flyckt, L., et al. (2006). "Predicting 5-Year Outcome in First-Episode Psychosis: Construction of a Prognostic Rating Scale." *Journal of Clinical Psychiatry* 67: 916–924.

Friedman, R. A. (2006). "Uncovering an Epidemic: Screening for Mental Illness in Teens." *New England Journal of Medicine* 26: 2717–2719.

Gabriel, A. (2006). "Lamotrigine Adjunctive Treatment in Resistant Unipolar Depression: An Open, Descriptive Study." *Depression and Anxiety* 23: 485–488.

Garland, E. J., and E. A. Baerg (2001). "Amotivational Syndrome Associated with Selective Serotonin Reuptake Inhibitors in Children and Adolescents." *Journal of Child and Adolescent Psychopharmacology* 11: 181–186.

Gerbino-Rosen, G., et al. (2005). "Hematological Adverse Events in Clozapine-Treated Children and Adolescents." *Journal of the American Academy of Child & Adolescent Psychiatry* 44: 1024–1031.

Giaconia, A., et al. (2001). "Major Depression and Drug Disorders in Adolescence: General and Specific Impairments in Early Adulthood." *Journal of the American Academy of Child & Adolescent Psychiatry* 40: 1426–1433.

Gibbons, R. D., et al. (2007). Relationship Between Antidepressants and Suicide Attempts: An Analysis of the Veterans Health Administration Data Sets." *American Journal of Psychiatry* 164: 1044–1049.

Goodyer, I., et al. (2007). "Selective Serotonin Reuptake Inhibitors (SSRIs) and Routine Specialist Care With and Without Cognitive Behaviour Therapy in Adolescents with Major Depresion: Randomised Controlled Trial." *British Medical Journal* 335: 142–147.

Greenhill, L. L., et al. (2006a). "Efficacy and Safety of Immediate-Release Methylphenidate Treatment for Preschoolers with ADHD." *Journal of the American Academy of Child & Adolescent Psychiatry* 45: 1284–1293.

Greenhill, L. L., et al (2006b). "A Randomized, Double-Blind, Placebo-Controlled Study of Modafinil Film-Coated Tablets in Children and Adolescents with Attention-Deficit/Hyperactivity Disorder." *Journal of the American Academy of Child & Adolescent Psychiatry* 45: 503–511.

Hamarman, S., et al. (2004). "Dopamine Receptor 4 (DRD4) 7-Repeat Allele Predicts Methylphenidate Dose Response in Children with Attention-Deficit/Hyperactivity Disorder: A Pharmacogenetic Study." *Journal of Child & Adolescent Psychopharmacology* 14: 564–574.

Harrington, R., et al. (1998). "Systematic Review of Efficacy of Cognitive Behaviour Therapies in Childhood and Adolescent Depressive Disorder." *British Medical Journal* 316: 1559–1563.

Hollander, E., et al. (2001). "An Open Trial of Divalproex Sodium in Autism Spectrum Disorders." *Journal of Clinical Psychiatry* 62: 530–534.

Hollander, E., et al. (2003). "Divalproex in the Treatment of Impulsive Aggression: Efficacy in Cluster B Personality Disorders." *Neuropsychopharmacology* 28: 1186–1197.

Hughes, C. W., et al. (2007). "Texas Children's Medication Algorithm Project: Update from Texas Consensus Conference Panel on Medication Treatment of Childhood Major Depressive Disorder." *Journal of the American Academy of Child & Adolescent Psychiatry* 46: 667–686.

Hunt, R. D. (2006). "The Neurobiology of ADHD." *Medscape Psychiatry & Mental Health* 11(2). www.medscape.com/viewarticle/541543.

Ipser, J., and D. Stein (2007). "Systematic Review of Pharmacotherapy of Disruptive Behavioral Disorders in Children and Adolescents." *Psychopharmacology* 191: 127–140.

Jensen, P. S., et al. (2005). "Cost-Effectiveness of ADHD Treatments: Findings from the Multimodal Treatment Study of Children with ADHD." *American Journal of Psychiatry* 162: 1628–1636.

Jorm, A. F. (2006). "Effectiveness of Complementary and Self-Help Treatments for Depression in Children and Adolescents." *Medical Journal of Australia* 185: 368–372.

Jou, R., et al. (2005). "Retrospective Assessment of Atomoxetine in Children and Adolescents with Pervasive Developmental Disorders." *Journal of Child and Adolescent Psychopharmacology* 15: 325-330.

Kasen, S., et al. (2001). "Childhood Depression and Adult Personality Disorder: Alternative Pathways of Continuity." *Archives of General Psychiatry* 58: 231–236.

Kazdin, A. E. (2000). "Treatments for Aggressive and Antisocial Children." *Child and Adolescent Psychiatric Clinics of North America* 9: 841–858.

Kessler, R. C., et al. (2005). "Lifetime Prevalence and Age-of-Onset Distributions of DSM-IV Disorders in the National Comorbidity Survey Replication." *Archives of General Psychiatry* 62: 593–602.

Khanzode, L. A., et al (2006). "Efficacy Profiles of Psychopharmacology: Divalproex Sodium in Conduct Disorder." *Child Psychiatry and Human Development* 37: 55–64.

Kopala, L. C., et al. (2006). "Treatment of a First Episode of Psychotic Illness with Quetiapine: An Analysis of 2-Year Outcomes." *Schizophrenia Research* 81: 29–39.

Kowatch, R. A., et al. (2005). "Treatment Guidelines for Children and Adolescents with Bipolar Disorder: Child Psychiatric Workgroup on Bipolar Disorder." *Journal of the American Academy of Child & Adolescent Psychiatry* 44: 213–235.

Kratochvil, C. J., et al (2004). "The Role of Stimulants in the Treatment of Preschool Children with Attention-Deficit Hyperactivity Disorder." *CNS Drugs* 18: 957–966.

Kratochvil, C. J., et al (2005). "Atomoxetine Alone or Combined with Fluoxetine for Treating ADHD with Comorbid Depressive or Anxiety Symptoms." *Journal of the American Academy of Child & Adolescent Psychiatry* 44: 915–924.

Kratochvil, C. J., et al. (2006). "Selective Serotonin Reuptake Inhibitors in Pediatric Depression: Is the Balance Between Benefits and Risks Favorable?" *Journal of Child and Adolescent Psychopharmacology* 16: 11–24.

Kutcher, S., and S. Davidson (2007). "Mentally-Ill Youth: Meeting Service Needs." *Canadian Medical Association Journal* 176: 417.

Lavigne, J. V., et al. (2001). "Oppositional Defiant Disorder with Onset in Preschool Years: Longitudinal Stability and Pathways to Other Disorders." *Journal of the American Academy of Child & Adolescent Psychiatry* 40: 1393–1400.

Libby, A. M., et al. (2007). "Decline in Treatment of Pediatric Depression After FDA Advisory on Risk of Suicidality with SSRIs." *American Journal of Psychiatry* 164: 884–891.

Luby, J., and A. Belden (2006). "Defining and Validating Bipolar Disorder in the Preschool Period." *Developmental Psychopathology* 18: 971–988.

Lydiard, R. B., and J. Bobes (2000). "Therapeutic Advances: Paroxetine for the Treatment of Social Anxiety Disorder." *Depression and Anxiety* 11: 99–104.

MacQueen, G. (2006). "An Update on the Pathophysiology of Major Depression: Neurophysiology for Clinicians." *Child & Adolescent Psychopharmacology News* 11 (6): 1–5.

March, J. S., et al. (2007). "Tics Moderate Treatment Outcome with Sertraline but Not Cognitive-Behavior Therapy in Pediatric Obsessive-Compulsive Disorder." *Biological Psychiatry* 61: 344–347.

Marchand, W. R., et al (2006). "Delayed Diagnosis of Pediatric Bipolar Disorder in a Community Mental Health Setting." *Journal of Psychiatric Practice* 12: 128–133.

Marshall, M., and J. Rathbone (2006). "Early Intervention for Psychosis." *Cochrane Database Systematic Reviews* 4: CD004718.

Masi, G., et al. (2003). "A 3-Year Naturalistic Study of 53 Preschool Children with Pervasive Developmental Disorders Treated with Risperidone." *Journal of Clinical Psychiatry* 64: 1039–1047.

Masi, G., et al. (2006). "Children with Schizophrenia: Clinical Picture and Pharmacological Treatment." *CNS Drugs* 20: 841–866.

McClellan, J., et al. (2007). "Practice Parameter for the Assessment and Treatment of Children and Adolescents with Bipolar Disorder." *Journal of the American Academy of Child & Adolescent Psychiatry* 46: 107–125.

McConville, B., et al. (2003). "Long-Term Safety, Tolerability, and Clinical Efficacy of Quetiapine in Adolescents: An Open-Label Extension Trial." *Journal of the American Academy of Child & Adolescent Psychopharmacology* 13: 75–82.

McDougle, C. J., et al. (2003). "Treatment of Aggression in Children and Adolescents with Autism and Conduct Disorder." *Journal of Clinical Psychiatry* 64, Supplement 4: 16–25.

McEwan, K., et al. (2007). "Bringing Children's Mental Health 'Out of the Shadows'." *Canadian Medical Association Journal* 176: 471–472.

McGough, J. J., et al. (2006a). "Pharmacogenetics of Methylphenidate Response in Preschoolers with ADHD." *Journal of the American Academy of Child & Adolescent Psychiatry* 45: 1314–1322.

McGough, J. J., et al. (2006b). "A Randomized, Double-Blind, Placebo-Controlled, Laboratory Classroom Assessment of Methylphenidate Transdermal System in Children with ADHD." *Journal of Attention Disorders* 9: 476–485.

Meighen, K. G., et al. (2004). "Ziprasidone Treatment of Two Adolescents with Psychosis." *Journal of the American Academy of Child & Adolescent Psychopharmacology* 14: 137–142.

Meyers, L. (2006). "Medicate or Not: An APA Working Group Reports on Use of Medications When Treating Children." *Monitor on Psychology* 37: 24–25.

Moeller, K. E., et al. (2006). "Relapse Rates in Patients with Schizophrenia Receiving Aripiprazole in Comparison with Other Atypical Antipsychotics." *Journal of Clinical Psychiatry* 67: 1942–1947.

MTA Cooperative Group (1999). "A 14-Month Randomized Clinical Trial of Treatment Strategies for Attention-Deficit/Hyperactivity Disorder." *Archives of General Psychiatry* 56: 1073–1086.

MTA Cooperative Group (2004). "National Institute of Mental Health Multimodal Treatment Study of ADHD Follow-Up: Changes in Effectiveness and Growth After the End of Treatment." *Pediatrics* 113: 762–769.

Nansel, T. R., et al. (2001). "Bullying Behaviors Among U.S. Youth: Prevalence and Association with Psychological Adjustment." *Journal of the American Medical Association* 285: 2094–2100.

Nemets, H., et al. (2006). "Omega-3 Treatment of Childhood Depression: A Controlled, Double-Blind Pilot Study." *American Journal of Psychiatry* 163: 1098–1100.

Newcorn, J. H., et al. (2006). "Low-Dose Atomoxetine for Maintenance Treatment of Attention-Deficit/Hyperactivity Disorder." *Pediatrics* 118: e1701–e1706.

Nissen, S. E. (2006). "ADHD Drugs and Cardiovascular Risk." *New England Journal of Medicine* 354: 1445–1448.

O'Kearney, R. T., et al. (2006). "Behavioral and Cognitive Behavioral Therapy for Obsessive Disorder in Children and Adolescents." *Cochrane Database Systematic* Reviews (October 18), CD004856.

Olfson, M., et al. (2006). "National Trends in the Outpatient Treatment of Children and Adolescents with Antipsychotic Drugs." *Archives of General Psychiatry* 63: 679–685.

Pandina, G. J., et al. (2006). "Risperidone in the Management of Disruptive Behavioral Disorders." *Journal of Child and Adolescent Psychopharmacology* 16: 379–392.

Papakostas, G. I., et al. (2005). "Aripiprazole Augmentation of Selective Serotonin Reuptake Inhibitors for Treatment-Resistant Major Depressive Disorder." *Journal of Clinical Psychiatry* 66: 1326–1330.

Pediatric OCD Treatment Study (POTS) Team (2004). "Cognitive-Behavior Therapy, Sertraline, and Their Combination for Children and Adolescents with Obsessive-Compulsive Disorder: The Pediatric OCD Treatment Study (POTS) Randomized Controlled Trial." *Journal of the American Medical Association* 292: 1969–1976.

Pediatric Psychopharmacology Anxiety Study Group (2001). "Fluvoxamine for the Treatment of Anxiety Disorders in Children and Adolescents." *New England Journal of Medicine* 344: 1279–1285.

Pelham, W. E., et al. (2005). "Transdermal Methylphenidate, Behavioral, and Combined Treatment for Children with ADHD." *Experimental and Clinical Psychopharmacology* 13: 111–126.

Posner, K., et al. (2007). "Columbia Classification Algorithm of Suicide Attempts (C-CASA): Classification of Suicidal Events in the FDA's Pediatric Suicidal Risk Analysis of Antidepressants." *American Journal of Psychiatry* 164: 1035–1043.

Prasad, S., et al. (2007). "A Multi-centre, Randomized, Open-Label Study of Atomoxetine Compared with Standard Current Therapy in UK Children and Adolescents with Attention-Deficit/Hyperactivity Disorder." *Current Medical Research and Opinion* 23: 379–394.

Quintana, H., et al. (2007). "Fluoxetine Monotherapy in Attention-Deficit/Hyperactivity Disorder and Comorbid Non-Bipolar Mood Disorders in Children and Adolescents." *Child Psychiatry and Human Development* 37: 241–253.

Rapport, M. D., et al. (2002). "Methylphenidate and Adderall Treatment for Children with ADHD: Has Therapeutic Equivalence Been Demonstrated?" *Child and Adolescent Psychopharmacology News* 7 (April): 4–12.

Reeves, R. R., et al. (2003). "EEG Does Not Predict Response to Valproate Treatment of Aggression in Patients with Borderline and Antisocial Personality Disorders." *Clinical Electroencephalography* 34: 84–86.

Reimherr, J. P., and J. M. McClellan (2004). "Diagnostic Challenges in Children and Adolescents with Psychotic Disorders." *Journal of Clinical Psychiatry* 65, Supplement 6: 5–11.

Reinblatt, S. P., and M. A. Riddle. (2007). "The Pharmacological Management of Childhood Anxiety Disorders: A Review." *Psychopharmacology* 191: 67–86.

Reyes, M., et al. (2006). "A Randomized, Double-Blind, Placebo-Controlled Study of Risperidone Maintenance Treatment in Children and Adolescents with Disruptive Behavior Disorders." *American Journal of Psychiatry* 163: 402–410.

Richardson, A. J. (2006). "Omega-3 Fatty Acids in ADHD and Related Neurodevelopmental Disorders." *International Review of Psychiatry* 18: 155–172.

Rihmer, Z., and H. Akiskal. (2006). "Do Antidepressants T(h)reat(en) Depressives: Toward a Clinically Judicious Formulation of the Antidepressant-Suicidality FDA Advisory in Light of Declining National Suicide Statistics from Many Countries." *Journal of Affective Disorders* 94: 3–13.

Rubino, A., et al. (2007). "Risk of Suicide During Treatment with Venlafaxine, Citalopram, Fluoxetine, and Dothiepin: A Retrospective Cohort Study." *British Medical Journal* 334 (February 3): 242.

Rugino, T. A., and Y. M. Janvier (2005). "Aripiprazole in Children and Adolescents: Clinical Experience." *Journal of Child Neurology* 20: 603–610.

Rynn, M. A., et al. (2001). "Placebo-Controlled Trial of Sertraline in the Treatment of Children with Generalized Anxiety Disorder." *American Journal of Psychiatry* 158: 2008–2014.

Rynn, M. A., et al. (2007). "Efficacy and Safety of Extended-Release Venlafaxine in the Treatment of Generalized Anxiety Disorder in Children and Adolescents: Two Placebo-Controlled Trials." *American Journal of Psychiatry* 164: 290–300.

Saxena, K., et al. (2006). "Divalproex Sodium Reduces Overall Aggression in Youth at High Risk for Bipolar Disorder." *Journal of Child and Adolescent Psychopharmacology* 16: 252–259.

Scheffer, R. E., and J. A. Niskala Apps (2004). "The Diagnosis of Preschool Bipolar Disorder Presenting with Mania: Open Pharmacological Treatment." *Journal of Affective Disorders* 82, Supplement 1: S25–S34.

Scheffer, R. E., et al. (2005). "Randomized, Placebo-Controlled Trial of Mixed Amphetamine Salts for Symptoms of Comorbid ADHD in Pediatric Bipolar Disorder After Mood Stabilization with Divalproex Sodium." *American Journal of Psychiatry* 162: 58–64.

Schindler, F., and I. G. Anghelescu. (2007). "Lithium Versus Lamotrigine Augmentation in Treatment-Resistant Unipolar Depression: A Randomized, Open-Label Study." *International Clinical Psychopharmacology* 22: 179–182.

Schur, S. B., et al. (2003). "Treatment Recommendations for the Use of Antipsychotics for Aggressive Youth (TRAAY). Part I: A Review." *Journal of the American Academy of Child & Adolescent Psychiatry* 42: 132–144.

Seidel, L., and J. T. Walkup (2006). "Selective Serotonin Reuptake Inhibitor Use in the Treatment of the Pediatric Non-Obsessive-Compulsive Disorder Anxiety Disorders." *Journal of Child and Adolescent Psychopharmacology* 16: 171–179.

Shastri, M., et al. (2006). "Aripiprazole Use in Individuals with Intellectual Disability and Psychotic or Behavioral Disorders: A Case Series." *Journal of Psychopharmacology* 20: 863–867.

Shechtman, Z., and D. Birani-Nasaraladin (2006). "Treating Mothers of Aggressive Children: A Research Study." *International Journal of Group Psychotherapy* 56: 93–112.

Simeon, J., et al. (2005). "Open-Label Study of St. John's Wort in Adolescent Depression," *Journal of Child and Adolescent Psychopharmacology* 15: 293–301.

Simon, G. E. (2006). "How Can We Know Whether Antidepressants Increase Suicide Risk?" *American Journal of Psychiatry* 163: 1861–1863.

Simon, G. E., and J. Savarino (2007). "Suicide Attempts Among Patients Starting Depression Treatment with Medications or Psychotherapy." *American Journal of Psychiatry* 164: 1029–1034.

Simon, G. E., et al. (2006a). "The Antidepressant Quandary—Considering Suicide Risk When Treating Adolescent Depression." *New England Journal of Medicine* 355: 2722–2723.

Simon, G. E., et al. (2006b). "Suicide Risk During Antidepressant Treatment." *American Journal of Psychiatry* 163: 41–47.

Sliwinski, S., et al. (2006). "Polyunsaturated Fatty Acids: Do They Have a Role in the Pathophysiology of Autism?" *Neuroendocrinology Letter* 27: 465–471.

Smarty, S., and R. L. Findling (2007). "Psychopharmacology of Pediatric Bipolar Disorder: A Review." *Psychopharmacology* 191: 39–54.

Solhkhah, R., et al. (2005). "Bupropion SR for the Treatment of Substance-Abusing Outpatient Adolescents with Attention-Deficit/Hyperactivity Disorder and Mood Disorders." *Journal of Child and Adolescent Psychopharmacology* 15: 777–786.

Spencer, T. J., et al (2007). "Attention-Deficit/Hyperactivity Disorder: Diagnosis, Lifespan, Comorbidities, and Neurobiology." *Ambulatory Pediatrics* 7, Supplement 1: 73–81.

Staller, J. A. (2007). "Psychopharmacologic Treatment of Aggressive Preschoolers: A Chart Review." *Progress in Neuro-Psychopharmacology & Biological Psychiatry* 13: 131–135.

Steele, M., et al. (2006a). "A Randomized, Controlled Effectiveness Trial of OROS-Methylphenidate Compared to Usual Care with Immediate-Release Methylphenidate in Attention-Deficit/Hyperactivity Disorder." *Canadian Journal of Clinical Pharmacology* 13: e50-e62.

Steele, M., et al. (2006b). "Remission Versus Response as the Goal of Therapy in ADHD: A New Standard for the Field." *Clinical Therapeutics* 28: 1892–1908.

Stein, M. B., et al. (2001). "Social Anxiety Disorder and the Risk of Depression: A Prospective Community Study of Adolescents and Young Adults." *Archives of General Psychiatry* 58: 251–256.

Steiner, H., et al. (2003). "Psychopharmacological Strategies for the Treatment of Aggression in Youth." *CNS Spectrums* 8: 298–308.

Storch, E., et al. (2007). "Aripiprazole Augmentation of Incomplete Treatment Response in an Adolescent Male with Obsessive-Compulsive Disorder." *Depression and Anxiety* 24, in press.

Swanson, J., et al. (2003). "Development of a New Once-a-Day Formulation of Methylphenidate for the Treatment of Attention-Deficit/Hyperactivity Disorder: Proof-of-Concept and Proof-of-Product Studies." *Archives of General Psychiatry* 60: 204–211.

Swanson, J., et al. (2006a). "Stimulant-Related Reductions of Growth Rates in the PATS." *Journal of the American Academy of Child & Adolescent Psychiatry* 45: 1304-1313.

Swanson, J., et al. (2006b). "Modafinil Film-Coated Tablets in Children and Adolescents with Attention-Deficit/Hyperactivity Disorder: Results of a Randomized, Double-Blind, Placebo-Controlled, Fixed-Dose Study Followed by Abrupt Discontinuation." *Journal of Clinical Psychiatry* 67: 137–147.

Tiihonen, J., et al (2006). "Antidepressants and the Risk of Suicide, Attempted Suicide, and Overall Mortality in a Nationwide Cohort." *Archives of General Psychiatry* 63: 1358–1367.

Treatment for Adolescents with Depression Study (TADS) Team (2004). "Fluoxetine, Cognitive-Behavioral Therapy, and Their Combination for Adolescents with Depression: Treatment for Adolescents with Depression Study (TADS) Randomized Controlled Trial." *Journal of the American Medical Association* 292: 807–820.

Upadhyaya, H., et al. (2004). "Bupropion SR in Adolescents with Comorbid ADHD and Nicotine Dependence: A Pilot Study." *Journal of the American Academy of Child & Adolescent Psychiatry* 43: 199–205.

Valicenti-McDermott, M. R., and H. Demb (2006). "Clinical Effects and Adverse Reactions of Off-Label Use of Aripiprazole in Children and Adolescents with Developmental Disabilities." *Journal of Child and Adolescent Psychopharmacology* 16: 549-560.

Visser, S. N., et al. (2007). "National Estimates and Factors Associated with Medication Treatment for Childhood Attention-Deficit/Hyperactivity Disorder." *Pediatrics* 119: S99–S106.

Vitiello, B., et al (2006). "Functioning and Quality of Life in the Treatment of Adolescents with Depression Study (TADS)." *Journal of the American Academy of Child & Adolescent Psychiatry* 45: 1419–1426.

Voelker, R. (2003). "Researchers Probe Depression in Children." *Journal of the American Medical Association* 289: 3078–3079.

Volkow, N. D., et al. (2002a). "Mechanism of Action of Methylphenidate: Insights from PET Imaging Studies." *Journal of Attention Disorders* 6, Supplement 1: S31–S43.

Volkow, N. D., et al. (2002b). "Relationship Between Blockade of Dopamine Transporters by Oral Methylphenidate and the Increases in Extracellular Dopamine: Therapeutic Implications." *Synapse* 43: 181–187.

Wagner, K. D., et al. (2004). "A Multicenter, Randomized, Double-Blind, Placebo-Controlled Trial of Paroxetine in Children and Adolescents with Social Anxiety Disorder." *Archives of General Psychiatry* 61: 1153–1162.

Wagner, K. D., et al. (2006). "A Double-Blind, Randomized, Placebo-Controlled Trial of Escitalopram in the Treatment of Pediatric Depression." *Journal of the American Academy of Child & Adolescent Psychiatry* 45: 280-288.

Wazana, A., et al. (2007). "The Autism Epidemic: Fact or Artifact?" *Journal of the American Academy of Child & Adolescent Psychiatry* 46: 721–730.

Wilens, T. E., et al. (2003a). "ADHD Treatment with Once-Daily OROS Methylphenidate: Interim 12-Month Results from a Long-Term Open-Label Study." *Journal of the American Academy of Child & Adolescent Psychiatry* 42: 424–433.

Wilens, T. E., et al. (2003b). "Does Stimulant Therapy of Attention-Deficit/Hyperactivity Disorder Beget Later Substance Abuse?" *Pediatrics* 111: 179–185.

Woodward, L. J., and D. M. Fergusson (2001). "Life-Course Outcomes of Young People with Anxiety Disorders in Adolescence." *Journal of the American Academy of Child & Adolescent Psychiatry* 40: 1086–1093.

Wozniak, J., et al. (2007). "Omega-3 Fatty Acid Monotherapy for Pediatric Bipolar Disorder: A Prospective Open-Label Trial." *European Neuropsychopharmacology* 17: 440–447.

Chapter 11

Geriatric Psychopharmacology

This chapter applies principles stated earlier in the book to several specific topics in geriatric psychopharmacology: drug treatment of depression, anxiety disorders, behavioral agitation and aggression, Alzheimer's disease, and Parkinson's disease. First, however, we present several general principles concerning the actions and effects of psychoactive drugs administered to elderly patients:

- Lower doses of medication are often as effective in the elderly as higher doses in younger people.
- When initiating drug therapy in the elderly, it is wise to "start low and go slow."
- Elimination half-lives are often prolonged in the elderly, sometimes to about twice as long as half-lives in younger people. This phenomenon can drastically reduce the total daily dose that may need to be administered.
- Sedative-hypnotic drugs, especially the long-half-life benzodiazepines, can be quite "dementing" in the elderly, causing marked and often prolonged loss of the ability to form memory.
- Sedative-hypnotic drugs can also induce psychomotor incoordination, resulting in an increased incidence of falls, altered driving behaviors, and so on.
- Depression and combined anxiety and depression are common in the elderly and need to be addressed and treated.

- Psychological therapies can be used effectively to treat anxiety disorders, sleep disorders, and other psychological disorders for which drugs are often prescribed.

- Inappropriate drug use in the elderly is a common problem with potentially tragic consequences.

- Underdiagnosis and undertreatment of psychological disorders occur frequently, perhaps most prominently in the treatment of anxious and depressive disorders.

Inappropriate Drug Use in the Elderly

The elderly are frequently prescribed medication that they do not need or that cause them significant problems either because of extensions of expected pharmacological effects or through adverse interactions with other medications. Inappropriate medication use in the elderly is a major functional and safety issue and may cause a substantial proportion of drug-related hospital or care-center admissions (Laroche et al., 2006, 2007). To help document inappropriate drug use in the elderly, M. H. Beers in 1997 developed specific criteria for inappropriate use, which included listing of drugs that were either ineffective or posed unnecessarily high risks for people over 65 years of age. In 2003, the list was updated to include 48 individual medicines or classes of medicines to avoid in older adults. Of these drugs, 66 were considered to have outcomes of high severity (Fick et al., 2003).

Since 2003, workers in different health care systems have developed modifications of the Beers criteria; examples are the Medication Appropriateness Index (Steinman et al., 2006), the 2006 Health Plan Employer Data and Information Set (HEDIS) (Pugh et al., 2006), the Zhan modification of the Beers criteria (Barnett et al., 2006), and the Improved Prescribing in the Elderly Tool (Barry et al., 2006). All attempt to identify medicines commonly considered of more risk than benefit to the elderly. All agree that the extent of inappropriate prescription use is common, with a rate between 20 percent and 40 percent. In elderly patients taking eight or more medications, the incidence of inappropriate drug use rises to well over 60 percent (Steinman et al., 2006). Among the psychoactive medicines, long-acting benzodiazepines are most commonly inappropriately prescribed, followed by drugs with anticholinergic side effects (for example, tricyclic antidepressants[1]), then antihistamines, skeletal muscle relaxants, and

---

[1]Other anticholinergic medications include such agents as gastrointestinal "antispasmotics."

opioid narcotics (Egger et al., 2006). Another problematic situation is concomitant use of two or more psychotropic medicines of the same therapeutic class. Inappropriate drug use can lead to suboptimal care that is considered to be not consistent with evidence-based clinical practice.

Considering the medications listed, it is obvious that all the lists of criteria for avoiding inappropriate drug use in the elderly recommend avoiding drugs that produce cognitive inhibition (with drug-induced dementia as the most severe manifestation), unwanted sedation (leading to falls and hip fractures), or bizarre behaviors and/or drug-induced delirium.[2] Long-acting benzodiazepines, tricyclic antidepressants (or other drugs with anticholinergic properties), and sedating antihistamines are prominent drugs of concern.

Control of Agitated and Aggressive Behaviors in the Elderly

Mention must be made here of the recent controversy regarding the use of atypical antipsychotic drugs to control agitated and aggressive behaviors in the elderly, especially residents of care centers. Examples of such drugs include olanzapine (Zyprexa), risperidone (Risperdal), and quetiapine (Seroquel).

In past years, use of pharmacological agents to control behavioral agitation and aggression in the elderly involved both benzodiazepines (which can intensify the dementias; Chapter 6) and first-generation antipsychotic drugs (phenothiazines and haloperidol; Chapter 9). Today, agitation and aggression are typically controlled through use of an atypical antipsychotic drug. Risperidone (Risperdal) has been perhaps most used, but quetiapine (Seroquel) has rapidly gained favor over risperidone, perhaps because quetiapine seems to cause less undesired weight gain and has less propensity to induce type 2 diabetes. In addition, cognitive improvements are often seen in patients switched from risperidone to quetiapine. Other studies report a more limited efficacy of quetiapine (Ballard et al., 2006; Kurlan et al., 2007).

In 2005, however, reports appeared linking the use of atypical antipsychotics for behavioral control in the elderly to a 1.7-fold increase in the rate of deaths associated with development of cardiac arrhythmias, cardiac arrests, and serious infections (Schneider et al., 2005; Jeste et al., 2005). The mechanisms responsible remain unknown. This result was, however, considered to be a "class" effect applicable to all

---

[2]Drugs that can cause delirium include drugs that cause anticholinergic effects.

atypical antipsychotics, and warnings were issued by the FDA advising prescribers of the problem. In reviewing the data, the *Medical Letter* (2005) published the following statement:

> Even though controlled clinical trials proving efficacy are lacking, Medical Letter consultants have found atypical antipsychotics such as risperidone and olanzapine beneficial in calming agitated or aggressive elderly patients. The FDA has found a slightly increased risk of mortality with such use, but there are no good alternatives. (p. 62)

Furthermore, Liperoti and coworkers (2005) analyzed 649 nursing home patients hospitalized for cardiac arrest or ventricular arrhythmias. Each patient was matched with a control patient from the same nursing home who was hospitalized for serious infections or gastrointestinal problems. Compared with no antipsychotic drug use (controls), use of traditional antipsychotic agents (phenothiazines or haloperidol) was associated with an 86 percent increase in the risk of adverse cardiac events. Use of atypical agents (risperidone in 70 percent of instances) was *not* associated with any degree of elevated risk. The authors concluded that the FDA warning was ill-advised because there was no association between atypical antipsychotic use and previously diagnosed cardiac disease. In our opinion, therefore, any FDA-perceived increase in risk is a relative "nonissue" and the benefits of controlling agitated and aggressive behaviors in institutionalized elderly outweigh any perceived increase in cardiac risk. Haupt and coworkers (2006) also reported no increase in mortality with the use of risperidone for behavioral control in the elderly. These authors concluded that the use of risperidone should be aimed at the treatment of patients in whom behavioral and psychological symptoms (such as psychosis, agitation, or aggression) are prominent and associated with significant distress, functional impairment, or potential danger to the patient.

Stracker and coworkers (2006) recently reported on the efficacy of aripiprazole (Abilify) on delirium in the elderly without adverse effects on the heart, weight, blood lipids, or glucose levels.

Undertreatment of the Elderly: Focus on Depression

In contrast to inappropriate or ill-advised drug use in the elderly, certain psychological illnesses in the elderly are poorly or inadequately treated. Perhaps foremost among them is depression. Undertreatment of depression in the elderly was even the focus of a United States Senate Special Committee on Aging in late 2006. At the hearings, it was noted that adults 65 years of age and older account for 20 percent of all suicides in the United States and have the highest suicide completion rate among any age group. In addition, only 8 percent of seniors with depression visit a mental health specialist in any given year.

On a positive note, it was also stated that a team approach to treating depression in the elderly was proving quite successful. This team approach program is called IMPACT (Improving Mood: Promoting Access to Collaborative Treatment). Research on IMPACT has been reported by Katon and coworkers (2005), Unutzer and coworkers (2006), and Hinton and coworkers (2006). IMPACT involved a team including a depression case manager (psychologist, social worker or a nurse), a primary care physician, and a consulting psychiatrist. Results stated:

> Tailored collaborative care actively engages older adults in treatment for depression and delivers substantial and persistent long term benefits. Benefits included less depression, better physical functioning, and an enhanced quality of life. The IMPACT model may show the way to less depression and healthier lives for older adults. (Hunkeler et al., 2006, p. 259)

In support of this collaborative care model, Reynolds and coworkers (2006) studied 116 patients over the age of 70 years who had been diagnosed with major depression. In a well-designed study of one year's duration, they compared the efficacy of placebo medication, medication alone, psychological therapy alone, and combined medication and psychological therapy. The medication chosen was paroxetine (Paxil); the psychological therapy chosen was weekly interpersonal psychotherapy. Combination therapy improved the percentage of patients achieving remission from 35 percent with either alone to 58 percent, a remarkable improvement. Results indicated that depression in the elderly can be treated and is best treated by a combination of antidepressant medication and psychological interventions. It is hoped that combined therapy will be more palatable for the elderly who suffer from major depression than is electroconvulsive treatment, currently a preferred treatment for severe depression in this population (Dombrovski and Mulsant, 2007). Paroxetine was effective in the Reynolds study; Kasper and coworkers (2006) demonstrated the efficacy of escitalopram (Lexapro) in the elderly (mean age 74 years; 82 percent female).

Nelson and coworkers (2006) reported results on the use of mirtazepine (Remeron) to treat major depression in 50 patients aged 85 years and older residing in nursing homes. In 45 percent of patients, mirtazepine (average dose 18 milligrams per day) was effective in decreasing the average Hamilton Rating Scale for Depression score from 17 at baseline to 7 at endpoint. Sedation and weight gain were prominent side effects. Administering the drug at bedtime made the sedation a positive effect. Weight gain was also seen as a positive effect in this age group, where maintaining adequate body weight is often a concern. Concern is always present when using sedative medication at bedtime in the elderly. In this study, the incidence of falls did not seem to increase; however, a control (placebo) group was not employed, so the incidence of falls could not be determined with certainty.

The presence of an anxiety disorder comorbid with a depressive disorder correlates with poorer outcome for depression treatment (Lenze et al., 2005). Similarly, a high pretreatment level of anxiety increases the risk of nonresponse to antidepressant treatment as well as the risk of recurrence in the first two years of maintenance treatment (Andreescu, et al, 2007). These results indicate that depressed elderly patients should be screened for anxiety disorders and treated for them, if they are present, as aggressively as for the depressive disorder.

In a small study of older patients with SSRI-resistant unipolar depression, Rutherford and coworkers (2007) reported that aripiprazole (Abilify) augmentation of citalopram therapy resulted in a 50 percent rate of remission (defined as a Hamilton Rating Scale for Depression score of less than 10). The results were encouraging for treatment of resistant depression in the elderly.

Parkinson's Disease

Chapter 9 discussed the first-generation, or traditional, antipsychotic agents (haloperidol and the phenothiazines) used to treat schizophrenia. The most prominent side effects of those drugs are movement disorders that resemble those seen in idiopathic Parkinson's disease (PD). Mechanistically, these side effects result from drug-induced blockade of dopamine-2 receptors, resulting in a hypodopaminergic state. PD is similarly associated with a hypodopaminergic state, characterized by a loss of dopamine neurons. The symptomatology of PD resembles the side effects of traditional neuroleptics; the goals of therapy are to replace the lost dopaminergic function and (hopefully) slow or reverse the loss of dopamine neurons.

PD is the second most common neurodegenerative disease after Alzheimer's disease. PD occurs in about 0.5 to 1 percent of people 65 to 69 years of age (about 1.5 million Americans and 6 million people worldwide), rising to 1 to 3 percent of people 80 years of age and older. More than 60,000 new cases are diagnosed in the United States each year. Although the cause of PD remains unknown, its symptoms are thought to follow from a deficiency in the number and function of dopamine-secreting neurons located primarily in the substantia nigra (a subthalamic area) of the brain. Progressive loss of these neurons is a feature of normal aging; however, most people do not lose the huge number of dopamine neurons required to cause the symptoms of PD (Standaert and Young, 2006).

Recently, Deuschl and coworkers (2006) reported that deep-brain electrical stimulation of the substantia nigra of patients with uncontrollable parkinsonism resulted in very positive clinical improvements. The technique involved permanent implantation of electrodes deep within the brain; it is obviously an experimental and very invasive form of treatment.

It has long been felt that genetic predisposition might play an important role in the etiology of PD and other disorders associated with faster-than-normal neuronal loss (loss of neurons in the substantia nigra in PD; loss of neurons in the hippocampus and cortex, leading to impairment in memory and cognitive ability in Alzheimer's disease). In the case of PD, the majority of cases are sporadic and of unknown origin, but mutations of at least six genes and the resulting abnormalities in protein formation can lead to genetically determined forms of the disease (Hardy et al., 2006; Lorincz, 2006; Wood-Kaczmar et al., 2006). Regardless of etiology, the clinical syndrome emerges when dopamine is depleted to about 20 percent of normal. In other words, the disease results when about 80 percent of dopamine neurons are lost. The clinical syndrome of PD has several cardinal features:

1. Bradykinesia (slowness and poverty of movement)

2. Muscle rigidity (especially a "cogwheel" rigidity)

3. Resting tremor, which usually abates during voluntary movement

4. Impairment of postural balance leading to disturbances of gait and falling

5. Without treatment, progression over 5 to 10 years to a state of severe rigidity and loss of movement in which patients cannot care for themselves

These characteristics and other frequently seen secondary manifestations of PD are listed in Table 11.1. The availability of effective treatments for the symptoms of PD has radically altered the prognosis of this disease. In most cases, good functional mobility can be maintained for many years and the life expectancy of an affected person has been greatly expanded. Replacement of the dopamine or the administration of either dopaminergic agonists or inhibitors of dopamine breakdown can restore function and ameliorate much of the symptomatology. These three approaches—dopamine replacement therapy, administration of a dopaminergic agonist, and administration of dopamine breakdown inhibitors—underlie today's treatment of the disease.

TABLE 11.1 Clinical features of Parkinson's disease

CARDINAL MANIFESTATIONS
  Resting tremor
  Bradykinesia (akinesia, hypokinesia)
  Cogwheel rigidity
  Postural reflex impairment

SECONDARY MANIFESTATIONS

Cognitive
  Dementia
  Bradyphrenia
  Visuospatial deficits, impaired
    attention and executive function

Psychiatric
  Depression
  Anxiety
  Sleep disturbances
  Sexual dysfunction

Craniofacial
  Masked facies
  Decreased eye blinking
  Blurred vision (impaired
    accommodation)
  Olfactory hypofunction
  Dysarthria (soft, palilalic speech)
  Sialorrhea

Autonomic
  Orthostatic hypotension
  Impaired gastrointestinal motility
    Constipation, dysphagia,
      sensation of fullness
  Urinary bladder dysfunction
    Urgency, frequency, loss of control
  Abnormal thermoregulation,
    increased sweating

Sensory
  Cramps
  Paresthesia
  Pain
  Numbness, tingling

Musculoskeletal
  Scoliosis
  Wrist and foot dystonia
  Peripheral edema

Skin
  Seborrhea

Other
  Micrographia
  Weight loss

From A. Colcher and T. Simuni, "Clinical Manifestations of Parkinson's Disease," *Medical Clinics of North America* 83 (1999), pp. 329–330.

Levodopa

Levodopa, a precursor drug to dopamine, continues to be the mainstay of therapy for Parkinson's disease, although today it is usually used in combination with other medications. Because a loss of dopamine is the primary problem in patients who have PD, replacement of the dopamine would be expected to ameliorate the symptoms of the disease. It does, but not by itself, because dopamine does not cross the blood-brain barrier from plasma into the CNS. However, the precursor compound in the biosynthesis of dopamine from the amino acid tyramine, a substance called *dihydroxyphenylalanine*, or *dopa* (Figure 11.1), crosses the blood-brain barrier and in the CNS is converted into dopamine, replacing the dopamine that is absent. Therefore, today, levodopa (the *levo* isomer being more active than the *dextro* isomer) is the most effective treatment for the motor disability, and many practitioners consider an initial beneficial response an important diagnostic criterion for the diagnosis of parkinsonism.

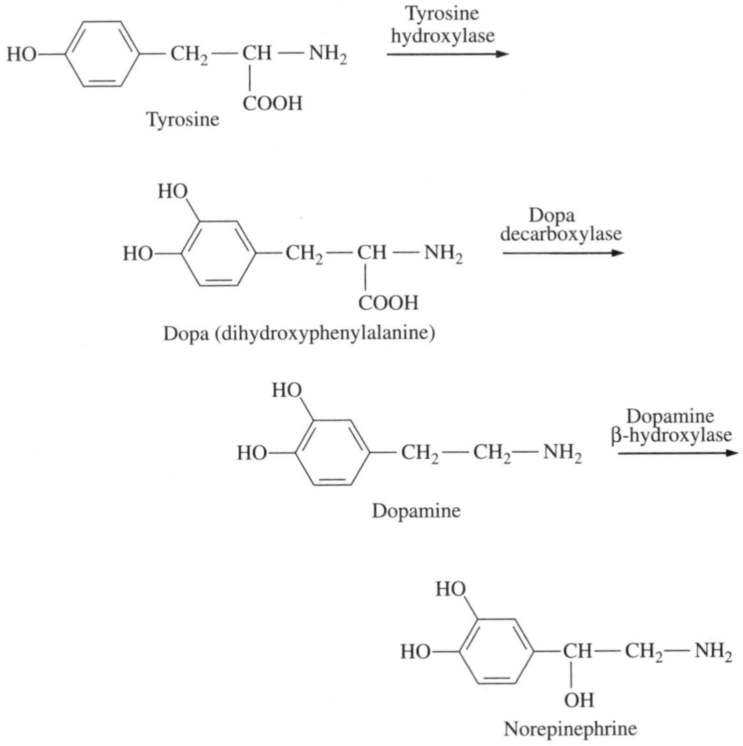

FIGURE 11.1 Synthesis of dopamine from tyrosine.

Mechanism of Action. Levodopa is itself largely inert; its therapeutic as well as its adverse effects result from its conversion to dopamine (Standaert and Young, 2006). Administered orally, levodopa is rapidly absorbed into the bloodstream, where most of it (about 95 percent) is converted to dopamine in the plasma. Although only a small amount (about 1 to 5 percent) of levodopa crosses the blood-brain barrier and is converted to dopamine in the brain, it is enough to alleviate the symptoms of PD. In the CNS, levodopa is converted to dopamine, primarily within the presynaptic terminals of dopaminergic neurons in the basal ganglia.

One problem with this therapy is that, when levodopa is administered by itself, large amounts are destroyed by enzymes located both in the intestine and in plasma, so little drug is available to cross the blood-brain barrier. In addition, the levodopa in the peripheral circulation is converted to dopamine in the body, resulting in undesirable side effects such as nausea. One approach to solving the problem is to reduce the high levels of dopamine in the systemic circulation while maintaining sufficient quantities in the brain. To do so, the biosynthetic pathway that leads to dopamine (see Figure 11.1) must be examined. Since the enzyme *dopa decarboxylase* is responsible for converting dopa to dopamine by inhibiting this enzyme in the systemic circulation but not in the brain, systemic biotransformation of the drug should be reduced, with a concomitant reduction in blood levels of dopamine and therefore in side effects. The drug would need a unique characteristic: it would have to be active in the body but not cross the blood-brain barrier into the brain. Thus, the metabolic conversion would occur in the CNS but not in the periphery.

An example of such a drug is *carbidopa*, which is available in combination with levodopa (the combination is marketed as Sinemet). By combining carbidopa with levodopa, the effective dose of levodopa is reduced by 75 percent, with a concomitant reduction in side effects and no loss of CNS therapeutic effect. The current treatment of PD relies heavily on the use of Sinemet. The combination of levodopa and carbidopa provides near maximal therapeutic benefit with the fewest side effects.

Limitations of Levodopa Therapy. As discussed, as time goes on, each dose of levodopa becomes less effective and the patient's symptoms fluctuate dramatically between doses, eventually developing into the wearing-off phenomenon. Part of the phenomenon is due to the short half-life of levodopa and can be minimized by increasing the dose and by decreasing the interval between doses. This adjustment, however, risks the development of levodopa-induced movement disorders (for example, dyskinesias), which can be as uncomfortable and disabling as the rigidity and akinesia of parkinsonism.

An unanswered question with levodopa therapy is whether or not this drug adversely accelerates the course of PD. One theory of the disease is that the metabolism of dopamine produces free radicals that contribute to the death of the dopamine-releasing neurons. Oxidative stress may therefore be an important precipitating mechanism, and neuroprotective drugs might eventually be of more use in prevention of the disease (Standaert and Young, 2006, pp. 528–529). For the present, however, there is continuing concern that ameliorating symptoms may be aggravating the disease. Thus, levodopa therapy is often delayed until the symptoms of PD cause an unacceptable degree of functional impairment.

COMT Inhibitors

A relatively new advance in the PD therapeutic regimen involves an enzyme called *catechol-o-methyltransferase* (COMT). Even with the Sinemet combination, much of an oral dose of levodopa is wasted. COMT in the vasculature of the gastrointestinal tract and liver converts levodopa to an inactive metabolite with no clinical benefit. The half-life and clinical effects of Sinemet can be increased with the addition of a COMT-inhibitory drug. In 1998, the first of these drugs—*tolcapone* (Tasmar)—was introduced; it blocks the COMT enzyme, increasing the half-life of levodopa and prolonging its effect. Unfortunately, tolcapone has caused a few cases of serious liver toxicity, so in late 1998 it was withdrawn from the market in Canada and in Europe. In the United States, its use is restricted to cases where all other adjunctive therapies have failed and close monitoring of liver function is required.

A second COMT inhibitor, *entacapone,* became available in 2001 under the trade name Comtan; entacapone has not yet been associated with liver toxicity. Like tolcapone, entacapone inhibits peripheral COMT; it does not alter central COMT. Inhibition of peripheral degradation of levodopa increases central levodopa and, therefore, central dopamine concentrations. Coadministration of entacapone with levodopa plus carbidopa potentiates the effects of levodopa in patients with PD and reduces the so-called wearing-off phenomenon (within a year or two of taking Sinemet—the beneficial effects of therapy last for progressively shorter and shorter periods of time after each dose). In 15 to 20 percent of patients, the result may be extreme and disabling: doses that originally were effective for 8 hours last for only 1 or 2 hours.

In 2004, the FDA approved a fixed combination product containing levodopa, carbidopa, and entacapone (available under the trade name Stalevo). As noted, the carbidopa increases the amount of dopamine in the brain while the entacapone inhibits the degradation of dopamine through inhibition of its degradative enzyme COMT. The combination provides more dopamine to the brain for a longer period of time, providing more "on" time and less "wearing off" associated with each dose of the drug (Hauser, 2004).

Dopamine Receptor Agonists

Between one and five years after the start of levodopa therapy, most patients gradually become less responsive. One hypothesis for this effect is that the progression of PD may be associated with an increasing inability of dopamine neurons to synthesize and store dopamine. To relieve this problem, attempts have been made to identify drugs that directly stimulate postsynaptic dopamine receptors in the basal ganglia. These drugs do not depend on the ability of existing dopaminergic neurons to synthesize dopamine. In addition, if the free radical theory described in the previous subsection is accepted, these drugs would avoid the biotransformation of dopamine into potentially neurotoxic metabolites. As a result, they are increasingly being advocated for use in early stages of PD, especially in patients younger than about 65 years. These drugs might also be effective in the later stages of PD, when dopamine neurons are largely absent or nonfunctional.

Several dopamine receptor agonists are available in the United States for the treatment of PD (Figure 11.2): *bromocriptine* (Parlodel), *pergolide* (Permax), *pramipexole* (Mirapex), and *ropinirole* (Requip). Bromocriptine has been available since 1978, pergolide since 1989, and both have structures that closely resemble that of dopamine. They are considered to be only marginally effective, and they have a number of bothersome and potentially serious side effects. For example, pergolide has come under much criticism because its use has been associated with damage to the valves of the heart, involving perhaps 20 percent or more of the patients who have taken the drug (Zanettini et al., 2007; Schade et al., 2007). In March 2007 the manufacturers of pergolide voluntarily removed the drug from sale in the United States.

Pramipexole and ropinirole were marketed in 1997. Unlike the older two drugs, pramipexole and ropinirole are indicated for use in early-onset PD; their efficacy and safety profile is much better than that of the two older drugs. Both can increase quality of life in the early stages of the disease by improving motor problems and decreasing fluctuations in response to levodopa. Their long half-lives may at least partially explain the reduction in the wearing-off phenomenon of levodopa therapy. Side effects of dopamine agonists include somnolence, dizziness, nausea, hallucinations, insomnia, and (rarely) sleep attacks (Ferreira et al., 2006). In reviewing the topic of dopamine agonists, Factor (1999) concluded:

> There is much talk about what properties are essential to an ideal antiparkinson drug. Such a drug has a central site of action, mimics dopamine, activates postsynaptic receptors, lacks potency for

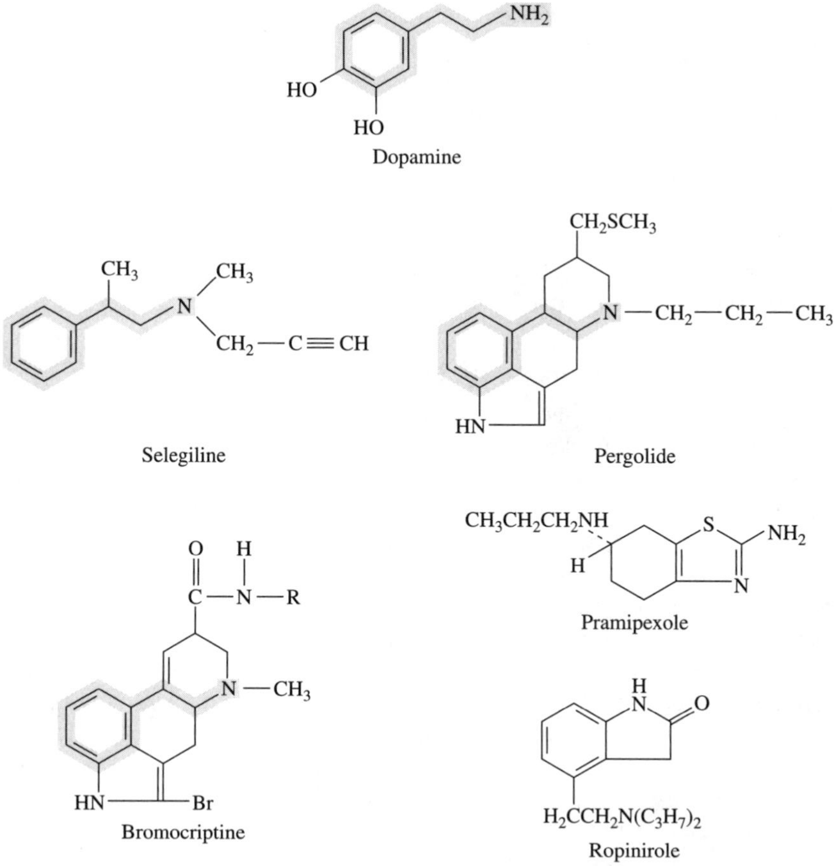

FIGURE 11.2 Structures of dopamine, selegiline, and four dopamine receptor agonists that are used to treat parkinsonism. The shaded portions, which are shared by selegiline, bromocriptine, and pergolide, resemble dopamine. The two newer dopamine receptor agonists are structurally unique and have greater affinity for dopamine-3 receptors than do older dopamine receptor agonists (which stimulate dopamine-2 receptors).

presynaptic receptors on dying cell terminals, and has no requirements for metabolic conversion. Dopamine agonists fulfill many of these requirements but still lack the potency of L-dopa, which for all its faults is still the best antiparkinson drug available today. Therefore, there is no ideal drug, but there is an acceptable standard of treatment, which currently is a combination of L-dopa and the dopamine agonists. As dopamine agonists are refined and improved, the medical community will move closer to providing patients with a still higher standard of care and an enhanced quality of life. (p. 439)

In April 2006, a new dopamine agonist in the form of transdermal patches was released in several European countries for the treatment of early PD as well as adjuvant therapy to levodopa in treating advanced PD. *Rotigotine* (Neupro) is formulated in a once-daily transdermal patch that releases drug over a 24-hour period. The patches are started with daily dosing of 2 mg/24 h to a final dose of 6 mg/24 h. Side effects include nausea, dizziness, and somnolence. Rotigotine was recently reviewed by Spliner (2007), Watts and coworkers (2007), and Babic and coworkers (2006). In June 2007, the drug was formally approved by the FDA for use in the United States.

Selective Monoamine Oxidase-B Inhibitors

Selegiline (Eldepryl) (see Figure 11.2) reduces the symptoms of PD through a unique mechanism. The enzyme monoamine oxidase (MAO) exists in two forms (isoenzymes): MAO-A and MAO-B. Both are present in the brain; MAO-A is more closely involved with norepinephrine and serotonin nerve terminals, while MAO-B has preferential affinity for dopamine neurons located in the substantia nigra. Selegiline selectively and irreversibly inhibits MAO-B.[3] As a result, selegiline inhibits the local breakdown of dopamine, thus preserving the small amounts of dopamine that are present. Both actions enhance the therapeutic effect of levodopa. Unlike the older nonselective MAO inhibitors used as clinical antidepressants (Chapter 7), selegiline does not inhibit peripheral metabolism of levodopa; thus it can safely be taken with levodopa. Selegiline also seems to interfere less with tyramine-containing foods, at least at doses less than 9 mg daily. Unfortunately, in PD, selegiline's usefulness is limited.

Approved by the FDA in May 2006, *rasagiline* (Azilect) is the second selective MAO-B inhibitor for PD. However, rasagiline may also possess a potential neuroprotective effect (Guay, 2006). A neuroprotective action against the progression of PD represents an interesting new approach to treating this devastating disease.

Muscarinic Receptor Antagonists

Although widely used before the introduction of levodopa, certain anticholinergic agents (muscarinic antagonists) are now used much less and are considered second-tier agents for the treatment of symptoms of PD. Their use was originally postulated on the basis of an unopposed cholinergic system after death of the dopaminergic neurons.

Occasionally, anticholinergic drugs are used as an adjunct to levodopa in patients with difficult-to-control tremors. Anticholinergic

---

[3]In Chapter 7, selegiline was discussed as the new antidepressant transdermal skin patch, marketed under the trade name Emsam.

drugs relieve tremor in about 50 percent of patients, but they do not reduce rigidity or motor slowing. Cognitive dysfunction limits their use, especially in the elderly, who may have an underlying cognitive disorder (Lu and Tune, 2003). Representative agents include *trihexyphenidyl* (Artane), *procyclidine* (Kemadrin), *biperiden* (Akineton), *ethopropazine* (Parsidol), and *benztropine* (Cogentin). Occasionally, the antihistaminic drug *diphenhydramine* (Benadryl) is also used (Benadryl has significant anticholinergic properties).

Amantadine and Memantine

Amantadine (Symmetrel) is an antiviral agent (used to treat viral influenza) with modest antiparkinsonian actions. Its mechanism of action in PD is unclear; it may alter dopamine release or reuptake, or it may have anticholinergic properties. Amantadine and a related drug, *memantine*, are active at NMDA-type glutaminergic receptors; this action perhaps offers a degree of "brain protection" that may contribute to its effects. Side effects are usually mild and reversible. A possible cognitive-enhancing effect might benefit the cognitive decline that may accompany PD in the elderly.

Bonuccelli and Del Dotto (2006) and Singh and coworkers (2007) discuss new pharmacological horizons for the future treatment of PD.

Alzheimer's Disease

Alzeimer's disease (AD) is the most common neurodegenerative disease and it accounts for about two-thirds of all cases of dementia, with vascular causes and other rarer, neurodegenerative diseases making up the majority of the remaining cases (Nussbaum and Ellis, 2003). AD is a progressive neurodegenerative disease that results in the irreversible loss of neurons, particularly in the cerebral cortex and hippocampus. Onset occurs generally after 60 years of age but is being increasingly reported in people younger than 65 years. Its prevalence is about 1 percent among people 65 to 69 years of age and increases with age to 40 or 50 percent among people 95 years of age and older (Figure 11.3). In essence, prevalence doubles every 5 years after age 65, projecting an increase of the disease from 2.32 million cases in the late 1990s to 8.64 million by the year 2047 (Figure 11.4). Currently, slightly more than 5 million Americans are living with AD. About 500,000 Americans younger than 65 years have either early-onset AD or another form of dementia.

Time between symptom onset and death may span 8 to 10 years. The gradual and continuous decline caused by AD is characterized by cognitive deterioration, changes in behavior, loss of functional independence, and increasing requirements for care. Hallmarks of AD include

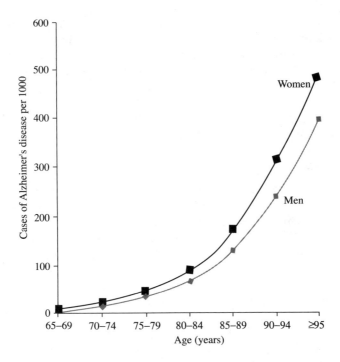

FIGURE 11.3 Prevalence of Alzheimer's disease as a function of age in men and women. [From Nussbaum and Ellis (2003), p. 1357.]

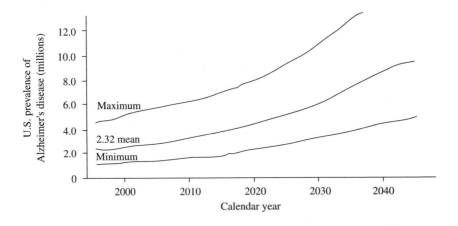

FIGURE 11.4 Projected prevalence of Alzheimer's disease from 1997 to 2047; 1997 prevalence 2.32 million. [From R. Brookmeyer et al., "Projections of Alzheimer's Disease in the United States and the Public Health Impact of Delaying Disease Onset," *American Journal of Public Health* 88 (1998), p. 1340.]

progressive impairment in memory, judgment, decision making, orientation to physical surroundings, and language. Dementia (defined as cognitive impairment with the inability to form recent memory) is the critical feature of AD. Diagnosis is based on neurological examination and the exclusion of other causes of dementia. A definitive diagnosis can be made only at autopsy.

The neuropathological changes seen in AD include beta-amyloid-rich senile plaques, neurofibrillary tangles, and neuronal degeneration (Samanta et al., 2006). Drugs approved for treating AD include acetylcholinesterase inhibitors (AChE-I) and an N-methyl-D-aspartate (NMDA) glutamate receptor antagonist. New therapeutic efforts are being directed at the development of products that may reduce the formation of the amyloid plaques (Archer et al., 2006) or the formation of other proteinaceous products such as presenilins (Shen and Kelleher, 2007).

The economic impact of the medications is important. It is currently estimated that the costs of informal and formal care for one patient with mild (early-onset) AD is about $1500 monthly, a patient with moderate AD $2100, and a patient with severe (advanced) AD $3100 or higher (these costs escalate markedly when nursing home care is needed). Use of a cholinesterase inhibitor can be associated with savings of over $9000 (or 7.5 percent of total expenditure) from diagnosis to death (Grossberg, 2003). Savings are attributable to reduced nursing home care because patients may remain more functional for a longer period of time before nursing home care is needed. Reducing nursing home entrance by only one year equates to enormous savings. AChE-I medications, however, only delay onset of AD; they do not cure or prevent AD. Current therapy is therefore discouraging.

AD is associated not only with cognitive impairments but with a myriad of bothersome mood alterations and behavioral symptoms that pose further challenges to treatment:

- Depression with AD is common and is usually treated with anti-depressant medications that lack anticholinergic side effects. Thus, SSRIs are used rather than the tricyclic agents (Chapter 7). An example: Lyketsos and coworkers (2003) demonstrated the beneficial effects of sertraline (Zoloft).

- Treatment for apathy may be considered. Drugs employed include psychostimulants, the antidepressant bupropion, the dopamine receptor agonist bromocriptine, and the antiparkinsonian agent amantadine. Memantine, an agent similar to amantadine, has been approved for AD.

- Psychosis, agitation, and other behavioral disturbances may require treatment with a newer atypical antipsychotic agent, although such treatment is controversial. Benzodiazepines and other sedatives are associated with worsening cognition and falls and should be avoided.

- Of possible benefit in treating behavioral symptoms are the anti-epileptic mood stabilizers, the sedating antidepressants trazodone and mirtazepine, and the SSRIs.

Currently, no treatment can prevent or cure AD, although there is hope for the future. Cholinesterase inhibitors (of which four are approved for the treatment of AD) can delay the onset of symptoms. Estrogen replacement (for women), antioxidants (for example, vitamin E), and nonsteroidal anti-inflammatory drugs (NSAIDs) all may have some usefulness. Of these treatments, estrogen has been found to be of little value, although vitamin E, either alone or in combination with an AChE-I, may prevent further cognitive decline among patients with moderate AD (Sano, 2003). Ginkgo biloba (Chapter 19) has been shown to be without effect in improving cognitive function in patients with AD (Mintzer, 2003). Selegiline can be as effective as vitamin E, but selegiline is associated with more side effects.

On a more positive note, Schaefer and coworkers (2006) with an accompanying editorial by Morris (2006) demonstrated that a diet rich in fish oils, primarily the omega-3 fatty acid decosahexaenoic acid (DHA), resulted in a 47 percent reduction in the incidence of AD in a large population of British elderly. Indeed, there may be a correlation between low levels of DHA and increased risk of AD. Freund-Levi and coworkers (2006) reported that omega-3 fatty acids may improve cognition in elderly people with mild symptoms of AD. Currently, multiple studies are underway to determine the association between omega-3 fatty acids and dementia risk.

In addition, new drugs that may block the formation of amyloid plaques are being investigated. Among these drugs are *tramiprosate* (Alzhemed) and NF-kB. Tramiprosate is thought to reduce the number of amyloid plaques in the brain (Greenberg et al., 2006; Gervais et al., 2007); NF-kB may reduce the production of amyloid plaques (Paris et al., 2007). Presuming that reduction of amyloid plaques may improve the outcome of AD, drugs like these would be very significant advances in therapy.

Other experimental drugs being investigated for possible efficacy in treating AD include MEM-3454, a selective alpha7 nicotinic acetylcholine receptor agonist (Mazurov et al., 2006), and MEM-1003, a novel calcium channel blocker that is thought to reduce age-related cognitive impairments (Rose et al., 2007).

Farlow and Cummings (2007) recently published consensus guidelines and medication strategies for persons in different stages of Alzheimer's disease.

Acetylcholinesterase Inhibitors (AChE-I)

There is now considerable evidence that deficits in the functioning of acetylcholine-secreting neurons (cholinergic deficits) are strongly correlated with the cognitive impairments of AD. Originally this idea stemmed from the observation that drugs that block the actions of acetylcholine (for example, scopolamine) are intense cognitive inhibitors. Therefore, drugs that increase acetylcholine (for example, that prevent its metabolic breakdown) might be cognitive enhancers and slow the rate of progression of cognitive decline seen in AD. Consistent with this idea is the observation that patients with severe AD show AChE levels that are 60 to 85 percent lower than normal, which implies very little residual AChE in the cortex—a condition that is still compatible with life but no longer optimal for brain function (Giacobini, 2003). Today, a cholinergic dysfunction hypothesis of AD suggests that the disease results from a selective loss in cholinergic neurons, accounting for the decrease in AChE levels (Jones, 2003).

The most successful effort to increase cholinergic functioning has targeted the AChE enzyme, inhibition of which increases levels of acetylcholine in the brain. Trinh and coworkers (2003) suggest a trial of an AChE-I in patients with mild to moderate AD who exhibit neuropsychiatric and/or functional impairments.

Four AChE-I medications have been approved by the FDA for the treatment of AD: *tacrine* (Cognex), *donepezil* (Aricept), *rivastigmine* (Excelon), and *galantamine* (Razadyne). Each improves cholinergic neurotransmission by preventing the synaptic breakdown of acetylcholine in the brain. These drugs can produce modest improvements in cognition, but their side effects include nausea, diarrhea, abdominal cramping, and anorexia. The side effects result from inhibition of AChE in the periphery (in the body), not from the elevations of acetylcholine in the brain. In small numbers of patients receiving AChE-I medication, drug-induced, reversible increases in aggressive behaviors may be seen; these behaviors are reversible with drug discontinuation (or dosage reductions), and treatment with antipsychotic drugs (without stopping the AChE-I) is inappropriate. The modest efficacy combined with these side effects tends to limit therapeutic usefulness of these agents.

Tacrine was the first of these agents to be approved; it is now the least used of the four, primarily because it needs frequent administration and can cause a reversible toxicity in the liver. Liver toxicity is not associated with donepezil, rivastigmine, and galantamine (Standaert and Young, 2006).

Donepezil appears to be selective for AChE in the brain more than in the periphery. It has a long half-life and produces fewer gastrointestinal side effects. It is much more tolerable than tacrine. Wilkinson and coworkers (2003) reported very modest efficacy of donepezil in 616 patients with vascular dementia; the results were of dubious clinical significance. Petersen and coworkers (2005) reported that donepezil may slow the progression of cognitive decline in early AD but that the protective effect was lost after 18 months of treatment. Winblad and coworkers (2006) reported that donepezil improved cognitive ability and helped preserve patient functioning. Side effects included diarrhea and hallucinations.

Rivastigmine is clinically effective, producing modest improvements in cognitive functioning. It is better tolerated than tacrine but somewhat less so than donepezil. In contrast to the other three agents, rivastigmine causes a very slowly reversible inhibition of AChE, prolonging its therapeutic action (Darreh-Shori et al., 2002). Under development is a rivastigmine transdermal patch. This product produces beneficial effects; a 10-cm^2 patch produces an effect comparable to that achieved with a 12-mg/day capsule (Winblad et al., 2007a). Caregivers prefer the patch to the capsule (Winblad et al., 2007b).

Galantamine appears to have a safety and efficacy profile similar to that of rivastigmine in measures of both cognitive functioning and functional ability. Doody (2003) concludes:

> Cholinesterase inhibitors have positive effects compared with placebo in the treatment of AD—affecting cognition, function and behavioral outcomes. They are effective in mild to moderate disease, and preliminary data suggest that this effect is mirrored in severe disease as well. . . .
>
> There are limitations to these medications, however, because although stabilization occurs, there is typically only a modest improvement from baseline. Additionally, the effects are not sustained indefinitely, and the disease continues to progress even while patients are receiving treatment with cholinesterase inhibitors. Adverse effects are manageable, and with careful titration, patients can tolerate increases quite well; however, side effects can include diarrhea, nausea, vomiting, dyspepsia, asthenia, dizziness, headache, weight loss, and even anorexia—sometimes to such an extreme that patients must discontinue treatment. Additional therapies for AD need to be developed that include highly tolerable agents with alternative mechanisms of action and broader efficacy to delay disease onset, arrest the disease, and even reverse the progression of the disease entirely. Until these new therapies are developed, the cholinesterase inhibitors will remain important treatments for AD. (p. 17)

Recently interest has been expressed in a naturally occurring AChE-I called huperzine A. This substance, derived from the plant *Huperzia serrata,* has been used for centuries as a Chinese folk medicine. It has AChE-I activity, and it also seems to possess a neuroprotective action that may make it something more than a "mere palliative" (Haviv et al., 2007). Its short duration of action in the body has been a therapeutic problem, but Wang and coworkers (2007) successfully prolonged its action by encapsulating the substance in "microspheres," which when injected subcutaneously extended the action of the drug for up to two weeks.

Memantine

As discussed in Chapter 3, *glutamate* is the principal excitatory neurotransmitter in the brain. Glutaminergic overactivity may result in neuronal damage, a phenomenon termed *excitotoxicity*. Excitotoxicity ultimately leads to neuronal calcium overload and has been implicated in neurodegenerative disorders (Standaert and Young, 2006, pp. 528–529). In addition, glutaminergic NMDA receptor activity appears to be important in memory processes, dementia, and the pathogenesis of AD. Glutaminergic overstimulation at NMDA receptors is thought to be toxic to neurons, and prevention of this neurotoxicity affords a degree of brain protection to limit further deterioration.

Memantine (Namenda) is a new moderate-affinity noncompetitive NMDA receptor antagonist that has been shown to reduce clinical deterioration in patients with moderate to severe AD, a phase associated with significant distress for patients and caregivers alike and for which no other treatments are available (Koch et al., 2005; McShane et al., 2006). It appears to have therapeutic potential without the undesirable side effects associated with high-affinity NMDA antagonists such as ketamine (Chapter 18). Available in Germany since 1982, it became available for use in the United States in 2004.

Van Dyck and coworkers (2006), Tariot (2006), and Cummings and coworkers (2006) all reported improved cognition, patient functioning, and behaviors, while agitation and other negative behaviors were ameliorated, in AD patients treated with a combination of an AChE-I and memantine. It is felt that the combination may delay nursing home placement, a step that can be exceedingly distressing to patients with AD and their caregivers.

As with other NMDA antagonists, high brain concentrations of memantine can inhibit glutaminergic mechanisms of synaptic plasticity that are believed to underlie learning and memory. In other words, at high doses, memantine can produce the same amnestic effects as does ketamine. However, at lower, clinically relevant doses, memantine seems to promote cellular plasticity, can preserve or enhance memory, and can protect against the excitotoxic destruction of cholinergic neurons. As a "weak" NMDA antagonist, memantine may reduce overactive NMDA receptor activity that would be neurotoxic while sparing synaptic responsiveness required for normal behavioral functioning, cognition, and memory.

Atypical Antipsychotics

Earlier in this chapter we discussed the use of atypical antipsychotics for the elderly. New studies have examined their effects on people with AD. Schneider and coworkers (2006) in a 42-site, double-blind, placebo-controlled study of 421 outpatients with AD, psychosis, aggression, or agitation reported that the adverse effects of atypical antipsychotics offset any advantages in their efficacy for behavioral calming.[4] Livingston and coworkers (2007) reported that AD patients taking atypical antipsychotics (primarily risperidone) were no more likely to experience cognitive decline than matched AD patients not taking one of these drugs.

Principles of Care for Patients with Alzheimer's Disease

Recently, the American Association for Geriatric Psychiatry has outlined minimal care standards and principles for patients with AD and their caregivers. Consequently, the association issued a position statement calling on clinicians to treat AD as part of their typical practice (Lyketsos et al., 2006). The statement focuses on the following five important areas of therapy:

1. Disease therapies for AD, targeting aspects of the current pathophysiological understanding of the disease

2. Symptomatic therapies for cognitive symptoms

3. Symptomatic therapies for other neuropsychiatric symptoms

4. Interventions targeted at and the provision of supportive care for patients

5. Interventions targeted at and the provision of supportive care for caregivers[5]

Disease therapies (item 1) include therapies aimed at preventing deposits of amyloid plaques and preventing excitotoxic neuronal damage. Therapies for cognitive symptoms include the AChE-I drugs and memantine. Therapies for other symptoms might include treatments for depression, agitation, aggression, and delusions, among

---

[4]This study was called the Clinical Antipsychotic Trials of Interventional Effectiveness-Alzheimer's Disease, or CATIE-AD.

[5]For this intervention, see B. G. Vickrey et al., "The Effect of a Disease Management Intervention on Quality and Outcome of Dementia Care: A Randomized, Controlled Trial." *Annals of Internal Medicine* 145 (2006): 713–726, and S. H. Belle et al., "Enhancing the Quality of Life of Dementia Caregivers from Different Ethnic Groups: A Randomized Controlled Trial," *Annals of Internal Medicine* 145 (2006): 727–738.

other symptoms; therapies can be both nonpharmacological and pharmacological. Supportive care for patients and caregivers should be tailored to the condition, circumstances, and progression of functional and cognitive decline. Caregivers need to be educated about AD and how their services are essential. They especially need to be given emotional support and respite.

STUDY QUESTIONS

1. What is Parkinson's disease?

2. What does Parkinson's disease have in common with traditional neuroleptic drugs? Why?

3. List the various ways that dopaminergic action in the brain might be augmented or potentiated.

4. Explain how carbidopa potentiates the action of levodopa.

5. Explain how a COMT inhibitor potentiates the action of levodopa.

6. Differentiate the newer from the older dopamine receptor agonists.

7. How does selegiline work in the treatment of Parkinson's disease?

8. Besides treatment with drugs, how might parkinsonism be managed? List the nonpharmacological options.

9. What is the currently accepted hypothesis for the genesis of Alzheimer's disease?

10. What are the currently available medications used to treat Alzheimer's disease?

11. Differentiate cholinesterase inhibitors from each other and from memantine.

12. How is glutamate involved in the action of memantine and how does this involvement relate to neuroprotection?

REFERENCES

Andreescu, C., et al. (2007). "Effect of Comorbid Anxiety on Treatment Response and Relapse Risk in Late-Life Depression: Controlled Study." *British Journal of Psychiatry* 190: 344–349.

Archer, H. A., et al. (2006). "Amyloid Load and Cerebral Atrophy in Alzheimer's Disease: An 11-C-PIB Positron Emission Tomography Study." *Annals of Neurology* 60: 145–147.

Babic, T., et al. (2006). "Rotigotine Transdermal Patch Enables Rapid Titration to Effective Doses in Advanced-Stage Ideopathic Parkinson Disease: Subanalysis of a Parallel Group, Open-Label, Dose-Escalation Study." *Clinical Neuropharmacology* 29: 238–242.

Ballard, C., et al. (2006). "Atypical Antipsychotics for Aggression and Psychosis in Alzheimer's Disease." *Cochrane Database of Systematic Disease* 1: Article CD003476.

Barnett, M. J., et al. (2006). "Comparison of Rates of Potentially Inappropriate Medications Use According to the Zhan Criteria for VA Versus Private Sector Medicare HMOs." *Journal of Managed Care Pharmacy* 12: 362–370.

Barry, P. J., et al. (2006). "Inappropriate Prescribing in the Elderly: A Comparison of the Beers Criteria and the Improved Prescribing in the Elderly Tool (IPET) in Acutely Ill Elderly Hospitalized Patients." *Journal of Clinical Pharmacology and Therapeutics* 31: 617–626.

Bonuccelli, U., and P. Del Dotto (2006). "New Pharmacologic Horizons in the Treatment of Parkinson's Disease." *Neurology* 67, Supplement 2: S30–S38.

Cummings, J. L., et al. (2006). "Behavioral Effects of Memantine in Alzheimer's Disease Patients Receiving Donepezil Treatment." *Neurology* 67: 57–63.

Darreh-Shori, T., et al. (2002). "Sustained Cholinesterase Inhibition in AD Patients Receiving Rivastigmine for 12 Months." *Neurology* 59: 563–572.

Deuschl, G., et al. (2006). "Randomized Trial of Deep-Brain Stimulation for Parkinson's Disease." *New England Journal of Medicine* 355: 896–908.

Dombrovski, A. Y., and B. H. Mulsant (2007). "ECT: The Preferred Treatment for Severe Depression in Late Life." *International Psychogeriatrics* 19: 10–14.

Doody, R. S. (2003). "Current Treatments for Alzheimer's Disease: Cholinesterase Inhibitors." *Journal of Clinical Psychiatry* 64, Supplement 9: 11–17.

Egger, S. S., et al. (2006). "Prevalence of Potentially Inappropriate Medication Use in Elderly Patients: Comparison Between General Medical and Geriatric Wards." *Drugs and Aging* 23: 823–837.

Factor, S. A. (1999). "Dopamine Agonists." *Medical Clinics of North America* 83: 415–443.

Farlow, M. R., and J. Cummings (2007). "Effective Pharmacologic Management of Alzheimer's Disease." *American Journal of Medicine* 120: 388–397.

Ferreira, J. J., et al. (2006). "Sleep Disruption, Daytime Somnolence, and 'Sleep Attacks' in Parkinson's Disease: A Clinical Survey in PD Patients and Age-Matched Healthy Volunteers." *European Journal of Neurology* 13: 209–214.

Fick, D. M., et al. (2003). "Updating the Beers Criteria for Potentially Inappropriate Medication Use in Older Adults: Results of a U.S. Consensus Panel of Experts." *Archives of Internal Medicine* 163: 2716–2724.

Freund-Levi, Y., et al. (2006). "Omega-3 Fatty Acid Treatment of 174 Patients with Mild to Moderate Alzheimer's Disease: OmegAD Study." *Archives of Neurology* 63: 1402–1408.

Gervais, F., et al. (2007). "Targeting Soluble Abeta Peptide with Tramiprosate for the Treatment of Brain Amyloidosis." *Neurobiology of Aging* 28: 537–547.

Giacobini, E. (2003). "Cholinergic Function and Alzheimer's Disease." *International Journal of Geriatric Psychiatry* 18: S1–S5.

Greenberg, S. M., et al. (2006). "A Phase 2 Study of Tramiprosate for Cerebral Amyloid Angiopathy." *Alzheimer's Disease and Associated Disorders* 20: 269–274.

Grossberg, G. T. (2003). "Diagnosis and Treatment of Alzheimer's Disease." *Journal of Clinical Psychiatry* 64, Supplement 9: 3–6.

Guay, D. R. (2006). "Rasagiline (TVP-1012): A New Selective Monoamine Oxidase Inhibitor for Parkinson's Disease." *American Journal of Geriatric Pharmacotherapy* 4: 330–346.

Hardy, J., et al. (2006). "Genetics of Parkinson's Disease and Parkinsonism." *Annals of Neurology* 60: 389–398.

Haupt, M., et al. (2006). "Mortality in Elderly Dementia Patients with Risperidone." *Journal of Clinical Psychopharmacology* 26: 566–570.

Hauser, R. A. (2004). "Levodopa/Carbidopa/Entacapone (Stalevo)." *Neurology* 62, Supplement 1: 564–574.

Haviv, H., et al. (2007). "Bivalent Ligands Derived from Huperzine A as Acetylcholinesterase Inhibitors." *Current Topics in Medicinal Chemistry* 7: 375–387.

Hinton, L., et al. (2006). "Gender Disparities in the Treatment of Late-Life Depression: Qualitative and Quantitative Findings from the IMPACT Trial." *American Journal of Geriatric Psychiatry* 14: 884–892.

Hunkeler, E. M., et al. (2006). "Long-Term Outcomes from the IMPACT Randomized Trial for Depressed Elderly Patients in Primary Care." *British Medical Journal* 332: 259–263.

Jeste, D. V., et al. (2005). "Atypical Antipsychotics in Elderly Patients with Dementia or Schizophrenia: Review of Recent Literature." *Harvard Review of Psychiatry* 13: 340–351.

Jones, R. W. (2003). "Have Cholinergic Therapies Reached Their Clinical Boundary in Alzheimer's Disease?" *International Journal of Geriatric Psychiatry* 18: S7–S13.

Kasper, S., et al. (2006). "Escitalopram in the Long-Term Treatment of Major Depressive Disorder in Elderly Patients." *Neuropsychobiology* 54: 152–159.

Katon, W. J., et al. (2005). "Cost-Effectiveness of Improving Primary Care Treatment of Late-Life Depression." *Archives of General Psychiatry* 62: 1313–1320.

Koch, H., et al. (2005). "Memantine: A Therapeutic Approach in Treating Alzheimer's and Vascular Dementia." *Current Drug Targets* 4: 499–506.

Kurlan, P., et al. (2007). "Quetiapine for Agitation or Psychosis in Patients with Dementia and Parkinsonism." *Neurology* 68: 1356–1363.

Laroche, M. L., et al. (2006). "Impact of Hospitalization in an Acute Medical Geriatric Unit on Potentially Inappropriate Medication Use." *Drugs and Aging* 23: 49–59.

Laroche, M. L., et al. (2007). "Is Inappropriate Medication Use a Major Cause of Adverse Drug Reactions in the Elderly?" *British Journal of Clinical Pharmacology* 63: 177–186.

Lenze, E. J., et al. (2005). "Efficacy and Tolerability of Citalopram in the Treatment of Late-Life Anxiety Disorders: Results from an 8-Week, Randomized, Placebo-Controlled Trial." *American Journal of Psychiatry* 162: 145–150.

Liperoti, R., et al. (2005). "Conventional and Atypical Antipsychotics and the Risk of Hospitalization for Ventricular Arrhythmias or Cardiac Arrest." *Archives of Internal Medicine* 165: 696–701.

Livingston, G., et al. (2007). "Antipsychotics and Cognitive Decline in Alzheimer's Disease: The LASAS-Alzheimer's Disease Longitudinal Study." *Journal of Neurology, Neurosurgery, and Psychiatry* 78: 25–29.

Lorincz, M. T. (2006). "Clinical Implications of Parkinson's Disease Genetics." *Seminars in Neurology* 26: 492–498.

Lu, C., and L. Tune (2003). "Chronic Exposure to Anticholinergic Medications Adversely Affects the Course of Alzheimer's Disease." *American Journal of Geriatric Psychiatry* 11: 458–461.

Lyketsos, C., et al. (2003). "Treating Depression in Alzheimer's Disease. Efficacy and Safety of Sertraline Therapy and the Benefits of Depression Reduction: The DIADS." *Archives of General Psychiatry* 60: 737–746.

Lyketsos, C. G., et al. (2006). "Position Statement of the American Association for Geriatric Psychiatry Regarding Principles for Care of Patients with Dementia Resulting from Alzheimer's Disease." *American Journal of Geriatric Psychiatry* 14: 561–572.

Mazurov, A., et al. (2006). "Selective Alpha7 Nicotinic Acetylcholine Receptor Ligands." *Current Medicinal Chemistry* 13: 1567–1584.

McShane, R., et al. (2006). "Memantine for Dementia." *Cochrane Database for Systematic Reviews,* Article CD003154.

Medical Letter (2005). "Atypical Antipsychotics in the Elderly." *Medical Letter on Drugs and Therapeutics* 47 (August 1): 61–62.

Mintzer, J. E. (2003). "The Search for Better Noncholinergic Treatment Options for Alzheimer's Disease." *Journal of Clinical Psychiatry* 64, Supplement 9: 18–22.

Morris, M.C. (2006). "Docosahexaenoic Acid and Alzheimer's Disease." *Archives of Neurology* 63: 1527–1528.

Nelson, J. C., et al. (2006). "Mirtazepine Orally Disintegrating Tablets in Depressed Nursing Home Residents 85 Years of Age and Older." *International Journal of Geriatric Psychiatry* 21: 898–901.

Nussbaum, R. L., and C. E. Ellis (2003). "Alzheimer's Disease and Parkinson's Disease." *New England Journal of Medicine* 348: 1356–1364.

Paris, D., et al. (2007). "Inhibitors of AB Production by NF-KB Inhibitors." *Neuroscience Letters,* 415: 11–16.

Petersen, R., et al. (2005). "Vitamin E and Donepezil for the Treatment of Mild Cognitive Impairment." *New England Journal of Medicine* 352: 2379–2388.

Pugh, M. J., et al. (2006). "Assessing Potentially Inappropriate Prescribing in the Elderly Veterans Affairs Population Using the HEDIS 2006 Quality Measure." *Journal of Managed Care Pharmacy* 12: 537–545.

Reynolds, C. F., et al. (2006). Maintenance Treatment of Major Depression in Old Age." *New England Journal of Medicine* 354: 1130–1138.

Rose, G. M., et al. (2007). "Efficacy of MEM 1003, a Novel Calcium Channel Blocker, in Delay and Trace Eyeblink Conditioning in Older Rabbits." *Neurobiology of Aging* 28: 766–773.

Rutherford, B., et al. (2007). "An Open Trial of Aripiprazole Augmentation for SSR Non-Remitters with Late-Life Depression." *International Journal of Geriatric Psychiatry*: in press.

Samanta, M. K., et al. (2006). "Alzheimer Disease and Its Management: A Review." *American Journal of Therapeutics* 13: 516–526.

Sano, M. (2003). "Noncholinergic Treatment Options for Alzheimer's Disease." *Journal of Clinical Psychiatry* 64, Supplement 9: 23–28.

Schade, R., et al. (2007). "Dopamine Agonists and the Risk of Cardiac-Valve Regurgitation." *New England Journal of Medicine* 356: 29–38.

Schaefer, E. J., et al. (2006). "Plasma Phosphatidylcholine Docosahexaenoic Acid Content and Risk of Dementia and Alzheimer's Disease." *Archives of Neurology* 63: 1545–1550.

Schneider, L. S., et al. (2005). "Risk of Death with Atypical Antipsychotic Drug Treatment for Dementia: Meta-Analysis of Randomized Placebo-Controlled Trials." *Journal of the American Medical Association* 294: 1934–1943.

Schneider, L. S., et al. (2006). "Effectiveness of Atypical Antipsychotic Drugs in Patients with Alzheimer's Disease." *New England Journal of Medicine* 355: 1525–1538.

Shen, J., and R. J. Kelleher III (2007). "The Presenilin Hypothesis of Alzheimer's Disease: Evidence for a Loss-of-Function Pathogenic Mechanism." *Proceedings of the National Academy of Science of the USA* 104: 403–409.

Singh, N., et al. (2007). "Advances in the Treatment of Parkinson's Disease." *Progress in Neurobiology* 81: 29–44.

Splinter, M. Y. (2007). "Rotigotine: Transdermal Dopamine Agonist Treatment of Parkinson's Disease and Restless Legs Syndrome." *Annals of Pharmacotherapy* 41: 285–295.

Standaert, D. G., and A. B. Young (2006). "Treatment of Central Nervous System Degenerative Disorders." In L. L. Brunton, J. S. Lazo, and K. L. Parker, eds., *Goodman and Gilman's The Pharmacological Basis of Therapeutics,* 11th ed. (pp. 527–545). New York: McGraw-Hill.

Steinman, M. A., et al. (2006). "Polypharmacy and Prescribing Quality in Older People." *Journal of the American Geriatric Society* 54: 1516–1523.

Stracker, D. A., et al. (2006). "Aripiprazole in the Treatment of Delirium." *Psychosomatics* 47: 385–391.

Tariot, P. N. (2006). "Contemporary Issues in the Treatment of Alzheimer's Disease: Tangible Benefits of Current Therapies." *Journal of Clinical Psychiatry* 67, Supplement 3: 15–22.

Trinh, N., et al. (2003). "Efficacy of Cholinesterase Inhibitors in the Treatment of Neuropsychiatric Symptoms and Functional Impairment in Alzheimer's Disease: A Meta-Analysis." *Journal of the American Medical Association* 289: 210–216.

Unutzer, J., et al. (2006). "Reducing Suicidal Ideation in Depressed Older Primary Care Patients." *Journal of the American Geriatric Society* 54: 1550–1556.

Van Dyck, C. H., et al. (2006). "A Responder Analysis of Memantine Treatment in Patients with Alzheimer Disease Maintained on Donepezil." *American Journal of Geriatric Psychiatry* 14: 428–437.

Wang, C., et al. (2007). "Prolonged Effects of Poly(lactic-co-glycolic acid) Microsphere-Containing Huperzine A on Mouse Memory Dysfunction Induced by Scopolamine." *Basic Clinical Pharmacology and Toxicology* 100: 190–195.

Watts, R. L., et al. (2007). "Randomized, Blind, Controlled Trial of Transdermal Rotigotine in Early Parkinson Disease." *Neurology* 68: 272–276.

Wilkinson, D., et al. (2003). "Donepezil in Vascular Dementia: A Randomized, Placebo-Controlled Study." *Neurology* 61: 479–486.

Winblad, B., et al. (2006). "Donepezil in Patients with Severe Alzheimer's Disease: Double-Blind, Parallel-Group, Placebo-Controlled Study." *Lancet* 367: 1057–1065.

Winblad, B., et al. (2007a). "A Six-Month Double-Blind, Randomized, Placebo-Controlled Study of a Transdermal Patch in Alzheimer's Disease—Rivastigmine Patch Versus Capsule." *International Journal of Geriatric Psychiatry* 22: 456–467.

Winblad, B., et al. (2007b). "Caregiver Preference for Rivastigmine Patch Relative to Capsules for Treatment of Probable Alzheimer's Disease." *International Journal of Geriatric Psychiatry* 22: 485–491.

Wood-Kaczmar, A., et al. (2006). "Understanding the Molecular Causes of Parkinson's Disease." *Trends in Molecular Medicine* 12: 521–528.

Zanettini, R., et al. (2007). "Valvular Heart Disease and the Use of Dopamine Agonists for Parkinson's Disease." *New England Journal of Medicine* 356: 39–46.

Integrating Psychopharmacology and Psychological Therapies in Patient Care

In December 1999 the Surgeon General of the United States released a report that criticized the state of mental health treatment (U.S. Department of Health and Human Services, 1999). A few facts the Surgeon General's report put forth follow.

- The mental health field is plagued by disparities in the availability of and access to its services.

- A key disparity often hinges on a person's financial status: formidable financial barriers block off needed mental health care from too many people, from those who have health insurance with inadequate mental health benefits to the 44 million Americans who have no insurance at all.

- About one in five Americans experiences a mental disorder over the course of a year.

- Mental illness represents more than 15 percent of the overall burden of disease from all causes and slightly more than the burden associated with all forms of cancer.

- Mental illness, including suicide, ranks second in the burden of disease, second only to cardiovascular disease.

- Depression ranks second only to ischemic coronary artery (heart) disease in the magnitude of disease burden. Schizophrenia, bipolar disorder, obsessive-compulsive disorder, panic disorder, and post-traumatic stress disorder also contribute significantly to the burden represented by mental illness.

- Stigmatization is the most formidable obstacle to future progress in the arena of mental illness and health.

- Nearly two-thirds of all people with diagnosable mental conditions do not seek treatment, although mental disorders can be effectively treated in about 75 percent of cases.

A U.S. Presidential Commission on Mental Health report (U.S. Department of Health and Human Services, 2003) noted that care for the mentally ill must go beyond prescribing medication and crisis management of symptoms. The report called for counselors to help patients lead a fuller life, including—but moving beyond—administering drugs. The report was, in fact, a call for complete integration of mental health care. The commission issued a vision statement as well as six goals for treatment, along with recommendations for achieving these goals.

Vision statement of the Commission

We are committed to a future where recovery is the expected outcome and when mental illness can be prevented or cured. We envision a nation where everyone with mental illness will have access to early detection and the effective treatment and supports essential to live, work, learn, and participate fully in their community.

Goals of the Commission report

1. *Mental health is essential to health.* Every individual, family, and community will understand that mental health is an essential part of overall health.

2. *Early mental health screening and treatment in multiple settings.* Every individual will have the opportunity for early and appropriate mental health screening, assessment, and referral to treatment.

3. *Consumer/family-centered care.* Consumers and families will have the necessary information and the opportunity to exercise choice over the care decisions that affect them. Continuous healing relationships will be a key feature of care.

4. *Best care science can offer.* Adults with serious mental illness and children with serious emotional disturbance will have ready access to the best treatments, services, and supports leading to

recovery and cure. Research will be accelerated to enhance the prevention of, recovery from, and ultimate discovery of cures for mental illnesses.

The commission stated:

> These goals provide a set of ideals toward which to work. Symptom reduction via pharmacological means is only part of the plan: all mental health care should be delivered in an integrated fashion. All mental health personnel should understand their clients' medications well enough to allow them to interact meaningfully with other professionals. These goals require collaborative efforts, mutual respect, and a true heath care team approach.

The commission was calling for a mental health care treatment team, including both a prescriber (usually a physician) and one or more mental health care professionals. Nonprescribing members of the team should be familiar with the pharmacology, uses, limitations, and side effects of the drugs being used by their clients. They should also know about alternative medications and therapies that may provide equal or superior effectiveness with a more appropriate spectrum of side effects for the particular client. Clinicians must be able to professionally communicate with each other, monitor drug therapy, and institute psychological therapies appropriate to the condition under treatment. They should monitor for both positive and negative effects and be sensitive to the meaning medications have for their clients, as effective psychotherapy depends on the ability of patients to comply with treatment requirements.

Many prescribers (with the exception of psychiatrists) are not experts at diagnostic testing for mental health disorders. They may write prescriptions only for concerns expressed by the patient or for medications requested by the patient (Keitz et al., 2007). Ideally, they may utilize an algorithm for management of chronic mental health disorders such as depression (Dunn and Tierney, 2006). Algorithms, however, rarely include psychological or behavioral interventions. They usually fail to acknowledge that psychological or behavioral therapies are effective and certainly exert augmenting effects when combined with medication therapy.

Witko and coworkers (2005) discuss a collaborative care model for treating psychological problems in primary care medicine. They begin by stating that physicians do not have enough time to treat psychological issues, that they are inadequately trained to deliver such care, and that 20 percent (minimum) of their patients have serious psychological problems. Often, primary care physicians may treat patients by themselves, usually by prescription for psychotherapeutic medications. Many barriers exist that perpetuate this situation, which only serves to limit effective care of patients with mental health issues. Physicians and psychologists have different training, work styles, language, and theoretical paradigms, and they have different expectations and views of each other's work. Patient resistance to referral (being labeled as having a mental health problem), lack of mutual feedback, lack of collaboration, and lack of respect are additional barriers to collaboration. Cost is considered to be a major factor limiting collaboration (two practitioners are more expensive than one), but Witko and coworkers state:

> Having physicians and psychologists providing services in their area of expertise would improve the quality of patient care and allow physicians to use the time they would have spent counseling to care for other patients. Physicians and psychologists must both take responsibility for successful collaboration. Collaborative efforts will succeed when relationships are based on mutual respect, recognition of each other's areas of expertise and limitations, and enough knowledge of the other's profession to be able to communicate effectively. (p. 801)

Gilbody and coworkers (2006) performed a meta-analysis evaluating the efficacy of collaborative care on both the short-term and long-term treatment of depression. Collaborative care involved a role for three distinct professionals working together within the primary care setting: a case manager, a primary care practitioner, and a mental health professional. Meta-analysis involved 37 studies including 12,355 patients with depression who were randomized to receive either collaborative care or usual primary care. Results confirmed the effectiveness of collaborative care in improving short-term outcomes in depression as well as significant long-term benefits (for up to five years). A recent editorial on the role of collaborative care concluded that "the evidence base is now sufficient for the emphasis to shift from research to dissemination and implementation" (Simon, 2006, p. 250).

Primary care physicians need from psychologists complete and accurate diagnoses of mental health problems being experienced by their patients. They may need feedback on side effects of medications that interfere either with medication compliance or with the client's quality of life. They may appreciate recommendations for therapies that the therapist has observed to work on other clients. They are likely to accept medication recommendations that will serve to improve patient's lives.

Regardless of their individual roles, the most important goal of all therapies is to work toward the maximum benefit to the client. Communication is of utmost importance as it allows all professionals to work toward this common goal.

Limitations to Pharmacological Therapy

There is a general perception among physicians and their patients that medications alone can alleviate illness, be it physical or psychological. In other words, it is expected that, if taken, the medicine will "work."

To be sure, in most cases of bacterial infections, an antibiotic can be prescribed, and if the antibiotic is taken in compliance with directions, the bacterium will be eliminated from the body and the patient's infection will resolve. With chronic physical diseases, however, such as hypertension, diabetes, and elevated cholesterol, the medication will usually not work if life-style changes are not made. The same holds true for the treatment of psychological illnesses.

- In the STAR*D study (Chapter 7), medication efficacy in treating depression in adults was only 30 percent with the first drug. With multiple medication switches or augmentation, the remission rate increased to about 60 percent. Of course, this leaves about 40 percent without remission, despite intensive medication trials. Recently, Thase and coworkers (2007) demonstrated that in depressed persons who failed to respond to citalopram therapy, an augmentation strategy adding cognitive therapy resulted in the same likelihood of remission and similar symptomatic improvement as did switching from citalopram to either sustained-release bupropion or buspirone.

- In the TADS study (Chapter 10), efficacy in treating depression in children and adolescents was only about 35 percent with medication alone. Adding cognitive-behavioral therapies markedly improved results.

- In the STEP-BD study (Chapter 8), although remission of bipolar symptoms could be achieved in about 60 percent of people with the disorder, 50 percent of responders relapsed frequently.

- In the CATIE and CUtLASS studies (Chapter 9), patients with schizophrenia were relatively noncompliant with medication prescription, regardless of which antipsychotic was prescribed.

- Recently, Swartz and coworkers (2007) concluded that medications alone are not sufficient to offer rehabilitative outcomes and that adjunctive psychosocial therapies are needed to make meaningful gains such as being able to work, attend school, or maintain a home.

In these studies, therapy with medication was less effective than was anticipated by the prescriber, the client, the client's family, and even by mental health practitioners. Therefore, it is important to recognize the limitations to pharmacological therapy.

Developing a Plan to Integrate Pharmacological and Psychological Therapies

Medication alterations can often result in clinical improvement. Currently, many mental health practitioners may not be familiar with methods to integrate pharmacology information into their daily practice. To do so, they must first take a medication history and keep a running record of a client's medications, emphasizing potential side effects. They should follow up with the development of an effective means of communication with the client's prescriber.

Client Medication List

Figure 12.1 is a one-page medication record suggested for use by mental health clinicians for each client seen for therapy.

- In column 2, list all medications the client is taking, whether the medicine is psychoactive or administered for another reason (for example, hypertension, diabetes, elevated blood lipids, gastric reflux, and so on). List the names by which you easily recognize the drugs (for example, Abilify for aripiprazole).

- In column 4, list the classification of the drug (antipsychotic, benzodiazepine, antidepressant, blood pressure, diabetes, and so on).

- In column 6, list the side effects for which you might want to be on the alert (for example, benzodiazepines = cognitive impairment; olanzapine = weight gain; SSRI = agitation, insomnia, sexual dysfunction; bupropion = worsening anxiety).

Medication history for: _____

Date	Drug (generic/ trade)	Currently taking (Y/N)	Class of drug	Indication	Side effects/ Discontinued

FIGURE 12.1 Medication history form. See the text for details.

With a medication list, the clinician can observe for side effects that might otherwise be missed, perhaps further improving patient care.

Suggested Communication Letter

Communication with a client's prescriber is vital to developing and maintaining a treatment team approach to care. Figure 12.2 is a sample client communication letter. This letter acknowledges the

---

Date: _____

To: _____   From: _____

My client _____ is your patient.
I saw him/her on _____ (date).

My diagnoses are _____
_____

I have planned the following treatment(s): _____
_____

My client says that he/she is taking the following medications:
  1. _____   4. _____   7. _____
  2. _____   5. _____   8. _____
  3. _____   6. _____   9. _____

I have the following concerns:
  1. _____
    _____
  2. _____
    _____
  3. _____
    _____
  4. _____
    _____

If you would like to discuss your patient with me, I can be reached at
_____.

                      Sincerely,

                      _____

FIGURE 12.2 Patient communication form.

prescriber's referral and lists diagnoses and treatments. As clients frequently receive medications from more than one prescriber, it lists medications the client claims to be taking. It communicates in one place all diagnoses, services, medications, and concerns for a client. For reference, the appendix to this chapter on pages 432–438 lists the major psychotherapeutic drugs, their range of usual daily doses, and other data.

Clinical Examples

The following examples provide food for thought about how knowledge of medication side effects and alternatives can benefit a client. These examples are from a clinical psychologist who evaluated patients, made clinical diagnoses, determined that problems may have arisen as a result of prescribed medications, and made clinical recommendations that resulted in improvements in the quality of life of the patient. As will become clear, knowledge of psychopharmacology was essential.

Client A is a 45-year-old male who was prescribed lithium for a diagnosis of bipolar II disorder. He presented with complaints of an 80-pound weight gain and an inability to remember names. The psychologist recognized these problems as side effects of lithium therapy. Searching the medical literature,[1] the psychologist identified a study on the efficacy of valproic acid for bipolar II. With this recommendation, the prescribing physician made the medication switch. Thereafter, Client A lost about 40 pounds and his memory function improved, allowing him to continue working.

Five years later, Client A presented with complaints of listlessness, lack of energy, and sexual dysfunction. The psychologist learned that a physician had diagnosed the client with depression and had prescribed escitalopram (Lexapro) in addition to the client's valproic acid. The psychologist suggested discontinuation of escitalopram and valproate and initiation of aripiprazole (Abilify) and/or lamotrigine (Lamictal). The prescriber followed the recommendation and replaced the valproate and escitalopram with aripiprazole. About two weeks later, the client reported that the new drug was "intolerable" and complained of aches, myalgias, flulike symptoms, and electric shocks in his head. The psychologist determined that the client had serotonin withdrawal syndrome (rather than side effects of aripiprazole) and counseled the client about serotonin withdrawal syndrome. Three weeks later, the symptoms had ceased, the client was

---

[1]Visit www.ncbi.nlm.nih.gov/entrez/query.fcgi or go to the PubMed search site and add it to your "favorites" list.

more energized, sexual function was improving, and no bipolar symptoms were reported. Continual progress was made over the next few months.

Clients B and C were two men, both in their late twenties, referred by a physician for evaluation of cognitive difficulties. Testing was performed and diagnosis was made of notable cognitive dysfunction, with greatest difficulty with word finding. Medication review revealed that both clients had recently been prescribed topiramate (Topamax). Replacement of the Topamax (prescribed for anxiety and PTSD) with pregabalin (Lyrica) led to rapid resolution of the cognitive difficulties.

Client D was a 48-year-old woman diagnosed with depression and anxiety. She was prescribed sertraline (Zoloft) and showed some improvement. However, she gradually developed a panic disorder and was referred to a psychologist. Further history-taking revealed that she had recently undergone breast surgery for breast lesions that were diagnosed as benign breast cysts. It turned out that Client D was a heavy coffee drinker. Sertraline interferes with the metabolism of caffeine, in essence doubling her blood level of caffeine. Caffeinism is associated with increasing anxiety (the panic disorder) and the development of benign breast cysts. Cessation of caffeine drinking (small amounts of caffeinated coffee and the remainder decaffeinated) led to resolution of the panic disorder.

Client E was a 28-year-old Gulf-War veteran with severe PTSD exhibiting as nighttime terror with threatening actions toward his wife. Moreover, he was amnestic for these episodes. Medication review revealed a prescription for zolpidem (Ambien) for sleep. It was determined that the Ambien might be causing the amnesia. Replacement of Ambien with gabapentin at bedtime improved PTSD symptoms and the amnestic episodes were resolved.

Client F was an 88-year-old female care center resident, whose family took her to therapy for increasing dementia. Medication review revealed that she had been receiving imipramine (Tofranil) for depression and diazepam (Valium) for anxiety and sleep difficulties. As tricyclic antidepressants have anticholinergic difficulties, they can cause cognitive impairments. Benzodiazepines are well known to worsen dementias. Cessation of these medicines and replacement with quetiapine (Seroquel) and mirtazepine (Remeron) at bedtime led to cognitive improvements, reductions in anxiety, better sleep patterns, and improvements in appetite.

Client G was a 5-year-old girl presenting with rages and aggressive behaviors made worse by psychostimulants and antidepressants. She was prescribed valproic acid (Depakote) and showed marked improvement in behavior. Referred to a psychologist, it was decided that with behavioral improvement, family therapy could be instituted to address problems underlying the client's behaviors. It was explained that the medication did not solve the problem but only made it possible to calm the child and allow the family to address underlying problems. With family therapy, the valproic acid may eventually be stopped.

Client H was a 42-year-old woman with severe depression unresponsive to SSRI therapy. She was also socially withdrawn from family, friends, and coworkers. Replacement of the SSRI with a 6-mg/day selegiline (Emsam) patch (Chapter 7) led to marked clinical improvement.

Client I was a 28-year-old woman with bipolar I illness. She had experienced multiple bouts of mania and was treated with lithium. However, weight gain and cognitive impairments led to noncompliance, which led to additional manic episodes. These bouts cycled on and off for months. Recommendation was made to her prescriber to consider a switch from lithium to either lamotrigine (Lamictal) or aripiprazole (Abilify). She was stabilized on a modest dose of aripiprazole with excellent results.

What do these cases have in common? First, all clients had been prescribed reasonable medications as therapy. Second, while efficacious, all the medications had significant side effects that limited optimal life functioning. Third, suggestions were made for reasonable modifications in therapy that often resulted in improved compliance, life functioning, or amenability to the institution of psychological therapies. Keitz and coworkers (2007) demonstrated that physicians usually comply with reasonable requests and are quite amenable to meeting expectations.

Limitations to Current Practice

In some areas of the country, specially trained psychologists can be licensed to prescribe psychotherapeutic medications, thus adding prescribing privileges to the armamentarium of treatment modalities for DSM-IV diagnoses. With the ability to discuss, recommend, and prescribe psychotropic medications, a unique specialty is emerging. At the time of writing, the legislatures in two states (New Mexico and Louisiana) have passed legislation to allow prescribing psychologists to prescribe medications. At least nine other states are considering similar legislation. In addition, specially trained psychologists who are on active military duty have been authorized to prescribe psychotherapeutic drugs to active military personnel. All this reflects the need for prescribers capable of prescribing psychotropic medications as part of an overall plan of treatment.

To make specific suggestions for a client, it is important to be aware of three important factors that may affect patient compliance. Also, by addressing these three points, long lists of medicines can be drastically narrowed to reasonable therapeutic recommendations that serve to benefit the client:

- *Can the client afford the prescribed medication?* Patients and physicians alike are susceptible to ads for heavily promoted brand name (expensive!) medications. New medicines often do have significant advantages over older medicines, but they also have their own constellation of side effects. One might reasonably suggest pregabalin (Lyrica), for example, for treatment of symptoms of PTSD or bipolar disorder, but it would hardly make sense to prescribe pregabalin for a client who cannot afford the medication and probably would not fill a prescription once any free sample was exhausted. Generic gabapentin, at much lower cost, would be a reasonable alternative. Thankfully, in the last couple of years, numerous psychotherapeutic drugs have become available in less expensive generic forms.

- *Can the client tolerate any degree of weight gain?* As has become apparent in this text, some medications are associated with weight gain while others are not. Similarly, some clients can tolerate a degree of weight gain while undesirable weight gain might lead to noncompliance in others. In choosing an antidepressant, for example, mirtazepine (Remeron) might be appropriate for a client who can tolerate weight gain, while duloxetine (Cymbalta) or atomoxetine (Strattera) might be appropriate for a client who desires to lose weight. The same considerations apply in the treatment of bipolar disorder and behavioral disorders associated with anger, agitation, and aggressive behaviors.

- *Can the client tolerate any degree of cognitive dysfunction?* Many psychotherapeutic drugs are associated with drug-induced cognitive dysfunction; among them are benzodiazepines, tricyclic antidepressants, lithium, some anticonvulsant mood stabilizers, and some antipsychotic drugs. Other psychotherapeutic agents are associated with cognitive improvement, including lamotrigine, some antidepressants, and some newer atypical antipsychotic drugs. The young, the elderly, and people suffering from traumatic brain injury (for example) might not tolerate agents that can be detrimental to cognitive functioning. Others, however, might be able to tolerate some degree of cognitive slowing, if therapeutic benefit seems to outweigh the side effect. If these agents are prescribed, professionals need to know that dysfunction may interfere not only with the efficacy of cognitive therapies but also with overall life functioning.

Examples of Areas of Needed Involvement

The treatment of chronic pain in this country could use improvement. Too often, patient complaints of pain result in the prescription of opioid narcotics (Chapter 16), commonly a combination of OxyContin and Vicodin for "breakthrough" pain. The classic model of pain management advocated by John Bonica seems to have been forgotten (Loeser, 2001). This model seeks to minimize opioid use through a "layering" of medications. Nonsteroidal anti-inflammatory drugs (Chapter 15) form a base for therapy. Norepinephrine-acting antidepressants (Chapter 7) contribute analgesic, anxiolytic, and antidepressant actions. Anticonvulsants such as gabapentin (Neurontin) and pregabalin (Lyrica) (Chapter 8) provide additional analgesic and anxiolytic actions. Only after these three drugs are optimized should opioids be considered. Bonica advocates a collaborative approach to the management of chronic pain, with a pain management team of a prescribing physician, a physical therapist, and a psychologist caring for the patient., Other specialists can be consulted as needed.

The possible introduction of rimonabant (Acomplia), a cannabinoid receptor antagonist (Chapter 17), may require collaborative care of persons who take this medication. Rimonabant may be considered as an anhedonic, removing the pleasurable effects of sweet and fattening foods, alcohol, cigarettes, marijuana, and perhaps other drugs of abuse. Reported side effects include anxiety and depression, as might be expected from an anhedonic drug. In July 2007 the manufacturer removed rimonabant from FDA consideration because of the concerns raised by the findings of depression and increased suicidal ideation. It is unknown whether rimonabant will come to market in the United States in the near future. If rimonabant or similar drugs should become clinically available, mental health workers should be prepared to offer assistance.

A final example involves withdrawal effects on the newborn when a mother takes serotonin-acting antidepressants during pregnancy. As SSRIs are considered to be relatively safe for a mother to take during her pregnancy and since these medications markedly reduce episodes of major depression during pregnancy, a newborn may have to withdraw from the medication following delivery. Decisions need to be made about whether or not to prescribe an antidepressant during pregnancy, whether or not to offer alternative treatments, whether to taper the medication prior to labor and delivery, and how to handle neonatal withdrawal syndrome should it occur. A collaborative care treatment team of the obstetrician and a mental health professional is important in deciding on an appropriate course of management.

REFERENCES

Barlow, D. H., et al. (2000). "Cognitive-Behavioral Therapy, Imipramine, or Their Combination for Panic Disorder: A Randomized Controlled Trial." *Journal of the American Medical Association* 283: 2529–2536.

Dunn, J. D., and J. G. Tierney (2006). "A Step Algorithm for the Treatment and Management of Chronic Depression." *American Journal of Managed Care* 12: S335–S343.

Gilbody, S., et al. (2006). "Collaborative Care for Depression: A Cumulative Meta-Analysis and Review of Longer-Term Outcomes." *Archives of Internal Medicine* 166: 2314–2321.

Keitz, S. A., et al. (2007). "Behind Closed Doors: Management of Patient Expectations in Primary Care Practices." *Archives of Internal Medicine* 167: 445–452.

Loeser, J. D., et al. (2001). *Bonica's Management of Pain*, 3rd ed. Philadelphia: Lippincott Williams & Wilkins.

Simon, G. (2006). "Collaborative Care for Depression." *British Medical Journal* 332: 249–250.

Swartz, M. S., et al. (2007). "Effects of Antipsychotic Medications on Psychosocial Functioning in Patients with Chronic Schizophrenia: Findings from the NIMH CATIE Study." *American Journal of Psychiatry* 164: 428–436.

Thase, M. E., et al. (2007). "Cognitive Therapy Versus Medication in Augmentation and Switch Strategies as Second-Step Treatments: A STAR*D Report." *American Journal of Psychiatry* 164: 739–752.

U.S. Department of Health and Human Services (1999). *Mental Health: A Report of the Surgeon General.* Rockville, MD: U.S. Department of Health and Human Services, Substance Abuse and Mental Health Services Administration, Center for Mental Health Services, National Institutes of Health, National Institute of Mental Health.

U.S. Department of Health and Human Services (2003). *President's New Freedom Commission on Mental Health, Final Report.* Publication SMA 03-3832, National Institute of Mental Health.

Witko, K. D., et al. (2005). "Care for Psychological Problems." *Canadian Family Physician* 51: 799–801.

REFERENCE CHART FOR PSYCHOTHERAPEUTIC DRUGS

The appendix to this chapter that follows is a quick-reference medication chart prepared by John Preston. It is reproduced here with his permission. The chart presents a list of recommended doses for psychotherapeutic drugs. The recommended doses are intended for general reference only, not as a guideline for prescribing for individual patients. It supplements the discussion of the pharmacology of these medicines presented in Chapters 7–11. The chart is designed to answer questions about the average doses of psychotherapeutic medicines encountered in clinical practice.

CHAPTER 12 APPENDIX

Quick Reference to Psychotropic Medication

developed by John Preston, Psy.D., ABPP; modified by Robert M. Julien, M.D., Ph.D.

To the best of our knowledge recommended doses and side effects listed below are accurate. However, this is meant as a general reference only, and should not serve as a guideline for prescribing of medications. Please check the manufacturer's product information sheet or the PDR for any changes in dosage schedule or contraindications. (Brand names are registered trademarks.)

Antidepressants

Names		Usual daily dosage range	Sedation	Weight gain	Cognitive impairment	Generic available
Generic	**Brand**					
imipramine	Tofranil	150–300 mg	mid	0–low	mid	yes
desipramine	Norpramin	150–300 mg	low	0–low	mid	yes
amitriptyline	Elavil	150–300 mg	high	0–low	mid	yes
nortriptyline	Aventyl, Pamelor	75–125 mg	mid	0–low	low	yes
protriptyline	Vivactil	15–40 mg	mid	0–low	mid	yes
trimipramine	Surmontil	100–300 mg	high	0–low	mid	yes
doxepin	Sinequan, Adapin	150–300 mg	high	0–low	mid	yes
clomipramine	Anafranil	150–250 mg	high	0–low	mid	yes
maprotiline	Ludiomil	150–225 mg	high	0–low	low	yes
amoxapine	Asendin	150–400 mg	mid	0–low	low	yes
trazodone	Desyrel	150–400 mg	mid	0–low	low–mid	yes

Antidepressants (continued)

Names		Usual daily dosage range	Sedation	Weight gain	Cognitive impairment	Generic available
Generic	**Brand**					
fluoxetine	Prozac, Sarafem	20–80 mg	low	low	0–low	yes
bupropion-XL[1]	Wellbutrin-XL	150–400 mg	low	0	0	yes
sertraline	Zoloft	50–200 mg	low	low	0	yes
paroxetine	Paxil	20–50 mg	low	low	0	yes
venlafaxine-XR[1]	Effexor-XR	75–350 mg	low	low	0	yes
fluvoxamine	Luvox	50–300 mg	low	low	0	yes
mirtazapine	Remeron	15–45 mg	mid	low–mid	low	yes
citalopram	Celexa	10–60 mg	low	low	0	yes
escitalopram	Lexapro	5–20 mg	low	low	0	yes
duloxetine	Cymbalta	20–80 mg	low	low	0	no
atomoxetine	Strattera	60–120 mg	low	0	0	no
MAO INHIBITORS						
phenelzine	Nardil	30–90 mg	low	0	0	yes
tranylcypromine	Parnate	20–60 mg	low	0	0	yes
selegiline	Emsam (patch)	6–12 mg	low	0	0	no

[1]Available in standard formulation and time release (XR or XL). Prozac available in 90-mg time-release/weekly formulation.

Bipolar Disorder Medications

Names		Serum level[1]	Weight gain	Cognitive impairment	Generic available
Generic	Brand				
lithium carbonate	Eskalith, Lithonate	0.6–1.5	high	high	yes
olanzapine/ fluoxetine	Symbyax	—[2]	high	high	no
carbamazepine	Tegretol, Equetro	4–10+	low	low	yes
oxcarbazepine	Trileptal	—[2]	low	low	yes
valproic acid	Depakote	50–100	mid	mid	yes
gabapentin	Neurontin	—[2]	low	low	yes
lamotrigine	Lamictal	1–5	0	0	yes
topiramate	Topamax	—[3]	0	mid–high	no
tiagabine	Gabitril	—[3]	0	low–mid	no

[1]Lithium levels are expressed in mEq/l, carbamazepine, valproic acid, and lamotrigine levels in mcg/ml.
[2]Serum monitoring may not be necessary.
[3]Not yet established.

Psychostimulants

| Names | | Daily |
Generic	Brand	dosage range[1]
methylphenidate[2]	Ritalin	5–50 mg
methylphenidate	Concerta[3]	18–54 mg
methylphenidate	Metadate	5–40 mg
methylphenidate[2]	Methylin	10–60 mg
methylphenidate	Daytrana (patch)	15–30 mg
dexmethylphenidate	Focalin	5–40 mg
dextroamphetamine[2]	Dexedrine	5–40 mg
pemoline	Cylert	37.5–112.5 mg
D- and L-amphetamine	Adderall	5–40 mg
modafinil	Provigil, Sparlon	100–400 mg

[1]Adult doses. [2]Available in generic formulation. [3]Sustained release.

Antiobsessional

| Names | | Daily |
Generic	Brand	dosage range[1]
clomipramine	Anafranil	150–250 mg
fluoxetine	Prozac	20–80 mg
sertraline	Zoloft	50–200 mg
paroxetine	Paxil	20–60 mg
fluvoxamine	Luvox	50–300 mg
citalopram	Celexa	10–60 mg
escitalopram	Lexapro	5–20 mg

[1]Often higher doses are required to control obsessive-compulsive symptoms than the doses generally used to treat depression.

Antipsychotics

| Names | | Daily | Weight | Cognitive | Generic |
Generic	Brand	dosage range[1]	gain	impairment	available
LOW POTENCY					
chlorpromazine	Thorazine	50–800 mg	low	mid	yes
thioridazine	Mellaril	150–800 mg	low	mid	yes
clozapine	Clozaril	300–900 mg	high	low	yes
mesoridazine	Serentil	50–500 mg	low	mid	no
quetiapine	Seroquel	150–400 mg	low	0	no
HIGH POTENCY					
molindone	Moban	20–225 mg	low	low	no
perphenazine	Trilafon	8–60 mg	low	low	yes
loxapine	Loxitane	50–250 mg	low	low	yes
trifluoperazine	Stelazine	2–40 mg	low	mid	yes
fluphenazine	Prolixin[2]	3–45 mg	low	low	yes
thiothixene	Navane	10–60 mg	low	low	yes
haloperidol	Haldol[2]	2–40 mg	low	low	yes
pimozide	Orap	1–10 mg	low	low	no
risperidone	Risperdal[3]	4–16 mg	mid	low	no
paliperidone	Invega	3–12 mg	mid	low	no
olanzapine	Zyprexa	5–20 mg	high	low	no
ziprasidone	Geodon	60–160 mg	0	0	no
aripiprazole	Abilify	15–30 mg	0	0	no

[1]Usual daily oral dosage.
[2]Dose required to achieve efficacy of 100 mg chlorpromazine.
[3]Available in time-release IM format.

Antianxiety

| Names | | Single-dose |
Generic	Brand	dosage range
BENZODIAZEPINES[1]		
diazepam	Valium	2–10 mg
chlordiazepoxide	Librium	10–50 mg
prazepam	Centrax	5–30 mg
clorazepate	Tranxene	3.75–15 m
clonazepam	Klonopin	0.5–2.0 m
lorazepam	Ativan	0.5–2.0 m
alprazolam	Xanax, XR	0.25–2.0 mg
oxazepam	Serax	10–30 mg
OTHER ANTIANXIETY AGENTS[2]		
buspirone	BuSpar	5–20 mg
gabapentin	Neurontin	200–600 mg
hydroxyzine	Atarax, Vistaril	10–50 mg
propranolol	Inderal	10–80 mg
atenolol	Tenormin	25–100 mg
guanfacine	Tenex	0.5–3 mg
clonidine	Catapres	0.1–0.3 mg

[1]All benzodiazepines produce cognitive impairment and are available in generic formulation.
[2]All agents listed are available in generic formulation.

Hypnotics[1]

| Names | | Single-dose |
Generic	Brand	dosage range
flurazepam[2]	Dalmane	15–30 mg
temazepam[2]	Restoril	15–30 mg
triazolam[2]	Halcion	0.25–0.5 mg
estazolam[2]	ProSom	1.0–2.0 mg
quazepam[2]	Doral	7.5–15 mg
zolpidem	Ambien	5–10 mg
zaleplon	Sonata	5–10 mg
eszopiclone	Lunesta	1–3 mg
ramelteon	Rozerem	4–16 mg
diphenhydramine[2]	Benadryl	25–100 mg

[1]All hypnotics produce cognitive impairment.
[2]Available in generic formulation.

Over-the-Counter

Name	Daily dose
St. John's Wort[1, 2]	600–1800 mg
SAMe[3]	400–1600 mg
Omega-3[4]	1–9 g

[1]Treats depression and anxiety.
[2]May cause significant drug-drug interactions.
[3]Treats depression.
[4]Treats depression and bipolar disorder.

Common Side Effects

**Anticholinergic effects
(block acetylcholine)**

- Dry mouth
- Constipation
- Urinary retention
- Blurred vision
- Memory impairment
- Confusional states

**EXTRAPYRAMIDAL EFFECTS
(dopamine blockade in basal ganglia)**

- Parkinsonlike effects: rigidity, shuffling gait, tremor, flat affect, lethargy
- Dystonias: Spasms in neck and other muscle groups
- Akathisia: Intense, uncomfortable sense of inner restlessness
- Tardive dyskinesia: Often a persistent movement disorder (lip smacking, writhing movements, jerky movements)

Note: These are common side effects. All medications can produce specific or unique side effects.

Drugs That Stimulate Brain Function: Psychostimulants

Classically, psychostimulant drugs were defined by their behavioral effects in animals; they increased the behavioral activity of animals. In human beings, psychostimulants elevate mood, increase motor activity, increase alertness, allay sleep, and increase the brain's metabolic activity. As a behavioral description, the term *psychostimulant* does not specify neurotransmitter or receptor processes. The term says little about therapeutic usefulness, just as it says little about abuse and dependency liabilities. Each psychostimulant must be described individually—its pharmacology, its mechanism of action, any therapeutic properties or potential, and its abuse and dependency issues.

The psychostimulants are discussed in two chapters. Chapter 13 describes the psychostimulants classically thought to act through potentiation of dopaminergic neurotransmission, thus directly activating the reward system involving the nucleus accumbens and the limbic and frontal cortex. These drugs include cocaine, amphetamine, methamphetamine, and several amphetamine-related psychostimulants. These drugs have historical and continuing uses in medicine and significant abuse issues as well. Chapter 14 details the pharmacology of caffeine and nicotine, the most widely used recreational drugs. Neither drug has much therapeutic value, but both are attractive to users because of their psychostimulant properties. Their overuse can result in moderate to extreme degrees of habituation or dependence. The toxicities associated with smoking cigarettes and the treatment of nicotine dependence are discussed as well.

Chapter 13

Cocaine, the Amphetamines, and Nonamphetamine Behavioral Stimulants

Cocaine and the amphetamines are powerful psychostimulants that markedly affect mental functioning and behavior. To exert their acute behavioral stimulant effects, these drugs act to augment the action of several neurotransmitters, the most important of which is dopamine. Cocaine and the amphetamines, in addition to other actions, increase dopaminergic activity on the nucleus accumbens, other limbic structures, and the limbic cortex associated with behavioral reinforcement, compulsive abuse, drug dependency, and cue-induced drug craving.[1] Cocaine and the amphetamines are therefore widely recognized as

---

[1]Through a dopaminergic augmentation, cocaine and the amphetamines activate a complicated circuit involving the prefrontal cortex and its modulation of the ventral tegmentum (VT) and the nucleus accumbens (NA). As frontal cortical projections to the VT and the NA involve cellular mechanisms that underlie normal learning and memory, reductions in synaptic plasticity with repeated exposure to drugs may underlie cue-induced behaviors that trigger relapse to drug use following a drug-free period (Kalivas et al., 2006; Kalivas and Volkow, 2005; Steketee, 2005; Rebec and Sun, 2005). Relapse may even involve alterations in specific protein neuromodulators such as extracellular signal-related kinase (ERK; Lu et al., 2006) or cocaine- and amphetamine-regulated transcript (CART) peptides (Stein et al., 2006; Stanek, 2006; Moffett et al., 2006).

important drugs of compulsive abuse. Paradoxically, these drugs also have a variety of therapeutic uses, although today, reasonable alternatives are available for most of them. All psychostimulants have significant side effects, toxicities, and patterns of abuse.

In low doses, cocaine and other psychostimulants evoke an alerting, arousing, or behavior-activating response that is not unlike a normal reaction to an emergency or stress. Physiologically, blood pressure and heart rate increase, pupils dilate, blood flow shifts from skin and internal organs to muscle, and oxygen levels rise, as does the level of glucose in the blood. In the CNS, psychostimulants produce positive and attractive effects that include an elevation of mood, induction of euphoria, increased alertness, reduced fatigue, a sense of increased energy, decreased appetite, improved task performance, and relief from boredom.

These positive effects, however, are offset by many negatives. Anxiety, insomnia, and irritability are common side effects. As doses increase, irritability and anxiety become more intense, and a pattern of psychotic behavior may appear. Eventually, intense dependence develops, a dependence that so far has resisted treatment and rehabilitation.

COCAINE

The leaves of *Erythroxylon coca* have been used since ancient times in their native South America for religious, mystical, social, euphoriant, and medicinal purposes—most notably to increase endurance, promote a sense of well-being, reduce fatigue, increase stamina, induce euphoria, and alleviate hunger (Calatayud and Gonzalez, 2003). Chewing the leaves as an endurant produced a usual total daily dose of cocaine of up to about 200 milligrams, a point that will become more important later in this discussion. Today, the relevant clinical issues related to cocaine's history have to do largely with the changes over time in dosage, route of administration, patterns of use, and technology of production.

The active alkaloid in *E. coca* was isolated in 1855 and purified and named cocaine in 1860. At the same time, the introduction of the syringe and hypodermic needle led to many attempts to use cocaine to produce local anesthesia for surgery. Perhaps the first medical report of cocaine's local anesthetic action was made in 1880.[2] Further identification of cocaine's local anesthetic properties were made by several surgeons, and cocaine became widely used for topical anesthesia, spinal anesthesia, and nerve blocks from about 1884 until about 1918, when procaine

---

[2]At that time, no other anesthetics (general or local) had been discovered. Surgery was limited to brief procedures conducted without anesthetic or with the patient under alcohol intoxication.

(Novocaine) was developed as the first synthetic local anesthetic. Procaine is devoid of psychological and dependence-producing effects.

In 1884, Sigmund Freud obtained cocaine, studied its psychological effects, used it himself, and prescribed it for his patients. Freud advocated the use of cocaine to treat depression and to alleviate chronic fatigue. He described cocaine as a magical and marvelous drug with the ability even to cure opioid (morphine and heroin) addiction. While using cocaine to relieve his own depression, Freud described the drug as inducing exhilaration and lasting euphoria, which in no way differs from the normal euphoria of the healthy person. However, he did not immediately perceive its side effects—tolerance, dependence, a state of psychosis, and withdrawal depression. In his later writings, Freud called cocaine the "third scourge" of humanity, after alcohol and heroin, perhaps an appropriate description.

In the United States, around the end of the nineteenth century, there were no restrictions regarding the sale or consumption of cocaine. Thus, the drug was incorporated in numerous patent medicines and the beverage Coca-Cola, which contained approximately 60 milligrams of cocaine per 8-ounce serving. In the late 1800s, however, concern about cocaine's toxicities increased, with several hundred reports of cocaine intoxication and several reported deaths. About 1910, President Taft proclaimed cocaine as Public Enemy Number 1, and in 1914 the Harrison Narcotic Act banned the incorporation of cocaine in patent medicines and beverages. With enforcement of the Narcotic Act, cocaine use decreased during the 1930s and cocaine was largely replaced by the newly available amphetamines, which were cheaper and produced longer-lasting yet similar effects. Cocaine all but disappeared until the late 1960s, when tight federal restrictions on amphetamine distribution raised the cost of amphetamines, once again making cocaine attractive.[3]

In the late 1970s and early 1980s, a new epidemic of cocaine use began with the widespread availability of "crack" cocaine intended for use by inhalation (smoking) rather than by injection. This cocaine epidemic continues today, although relatively inexpensive and widely available methamphetamine is currently more widely encountered. Cocaine users today are characterized by three patterns of use:

- Occasional users usually nasally "snort" (inhale) "lines" of powder containing cocaine hydrochloride; each line usually contains about 25 milligrams of the drug.

- Frequent, heavy users either snort the drug or smoke the free-base form for a recreational high.

---

[3]Because their net effects are nearly indistinguishable, cocaine and the amphetamines can be used almost interchangeably as euphoriants. Availability, price, and sociocultural considerations now largely determine their comparative popularity.

- Regular users have developed tolerance to cocaine and either inject water-soluble solutions of cocaine hydrochloride in doses of 100 milligrams to 1 gram or more or smoke the "free-base" form of cocaine in similar doses. These users usually continue a drug use "run" until their money runs out.

The use of high doses of either cocaine hydrochloride or the base form of cocaine is characterized by high-dose, rapid-onset effects and the rapid development of both toxicity and dependency. One of the most addictive and reinforcing of the abused drugs, cocaine has been used at some time by about 25 million people in the United States. With the increased availability of methamphetamine, the numbers of users of cocaine has rapidly declined. In 2002, an estimated 2 million people were current cocaine users, 567,000 of whom used crack cocaine during the same time period. The percentage of young adults (ages 18 to 25 years) who had ever used cocaine rose steadily from below 1 percent in the 1960s to 17.9 percent in 1984. By 1996, the rate had dropped to 10.1 percent, but it climbed to 15.4 percent in 2002.

Cocaine use is associated with a range of violent premature deaths, including homicides, suicides, and accidents. Although cocaine dependence occurs more commonly in males than in females, smoked cocaine abuse is particularly common in women of childbearing years, certainly a risk factor for harm to both the mother and the fetus should the smoker become pregnant.

Forms of Cocaine

The leaf of *E. coca* contains about 1 percent cocaine. When the leaves are soaked and mashed, cocaine is extracted in the form of coca paste (60 to 80 percent cocaine). Coca paste is usually treated with hydrochloric acid to form the less potent, water-soluble salt *cocaine hydrochloride* before it is exported. The powdered hydrochloride salt can be absorbed through the nasal mucosa (snorted) and, because this salt form is water soluble, it can be injected intravenously. However, in the hydrochloride form, cocaine decomposes when it is heated and is destroyed at the temperature of smoke, making it unsuitable for use by inhalation. In contrast, cocaine base, also known as *freebase* or *crack cocaine*, is insoluble in water but is soluble in alcohol, acetone, or ether. Heating the freebase converts cocaine to a stable vapor that can be inhaled. The name *crack* is derived from the sound of cocaine crystals popping when smoked.

Cocaine hydrochloride ("crystal" or "snow"), when snorted as a line of drug, provides a dose of about 25 milligrams; a user might sniff about 50 to 100 milligrams of drug at a time. The smoking of crack cocaine yields average doses in the range of 250 milligrams to 1 gram (Table 13.1). The consequences of these higher doses are severe and are discussed later in this chapter.

TABLE 13.1 Effects of cocaine administration

Administration		Initial onset of action(s)	Duration of "high" (min)	Average acute dose (mg)	Peak plasma levels (ng/ml)	Purity (%)	Bioavailability (% absorbed)
Route	Mode						
Oral	Coca leaf chewing	300–600	45–90	20–50	150	0.5–1	25
Oral	Cocaine HCl	600–1800		100–200	150–200	20–80	20–30
Intranasal	Snorting cocaine HCl	120–180	30–45	5–30	150	20–80	20–30
Intravenous	Cocaine HCl	30–45	10–20	25–50	300–400	10–100	100
				>200	1000–1500		
Smoking	Coca paste	8–10	5–10	60–250	300–800	40–85	6–32
	Free base	8–10	5–10	250–1000	800–900	90–100	6–32
	Crack	8–10	5–10	250–1000	?	50–95	6–32

From M. S. Gold, "Cocaine (and Crack): Clinical Aspects," in J. H. Lowinson, P. Ruiz, R. B. Millman, and J. G. Langrod, eds., *Substance Abuse: A Comprehensive Textbook*, 3rd ed. (Baltimore: Williams & Wilkins, 1997), p. 185.

Pharmacokinetics

Absorption

Cocaine is absorbed from all sites of application, including mucous membranes, the stomach, and the lungs. Thus, cocaine can be snorted, smoked, taken orally, or injected intravenously. Table 13.1 presents some pharmacokinetic data for common methods of administration. Snorted intranasally, cocaine hydrochloride poorly crosses the mucosal membranes since the drug is a potent vasoconstrictor (one of its defining pharmacological actions), constricting blood vessels and limiting its own absorption. As a consequence, only about 20 to 30 percent of the snorted drug is absorbed through the nasal mucosa into blood, with plasma levels not peaking for 30 to 60 minutes. The time course of the pharmacological effects (the subjective "high") parallels the plasma levels as well as the amount of drug actually in brain tissue. With nasal inhalation, the euphoric effect is prolonged (because the drug is absorbed slowly) and the drug may persist in plasma for up to 6 hours.

When cocaine base is vaporized and smoked, drug molecules pass through the pharynx into the trachea and onto lung surfaces, from which absorption is rapid and quite complete. Onset of effects is within seconds, peaks at 5 minutes, and persists for about 30 minutes. Only about 6 to 32 percent of the initial amount vaporized ever reaches plasma.

Intravenous injection of cocaine hydrochloride bypasses all the barriers to absorption, placing the total dose of drug immediately into the bloodstream. The 30- to 60-second delay in onset of action simply reflects the time it takes the drug to travel from the site of injection through the pulmonary circulation and into the brain.

Distribution

Cocaine penetrates the brain rapidly; initial brain concentrations far exceed the concentrations in plasma. After it penetrates the brain, cocaine is rapidly redistributed to other tissues. Cocaine freely crosses the placental barrier, achieving levels in the unborn equal to those in the mother.

Metabolism and Excretion

Cocaine has a biological half-life in plasma of only about 50 minutes; it is rapidly and almost completely metabolized by enzymes located both in plasma and in the liver. Although it is rapidly removed from plasma, it is more slowly removed from the brain, in which it can be detected for 8 or more hours after initial use. Urine can test positive for cocaine for up to 12 hours. The major metabolite of cocaine is the inactive compound *benzoylecgonine* (Figure 13.1), which can be detected in the urine for about 48 hours and much longer (up to 2 weeks) in chronic users. Urine detection of benzoylecgonine forms the basis of drug testing for cocaine use. The persistence of the metabolite in urine implies that high-dose, long-term users might accumulate drug in their body tissues.

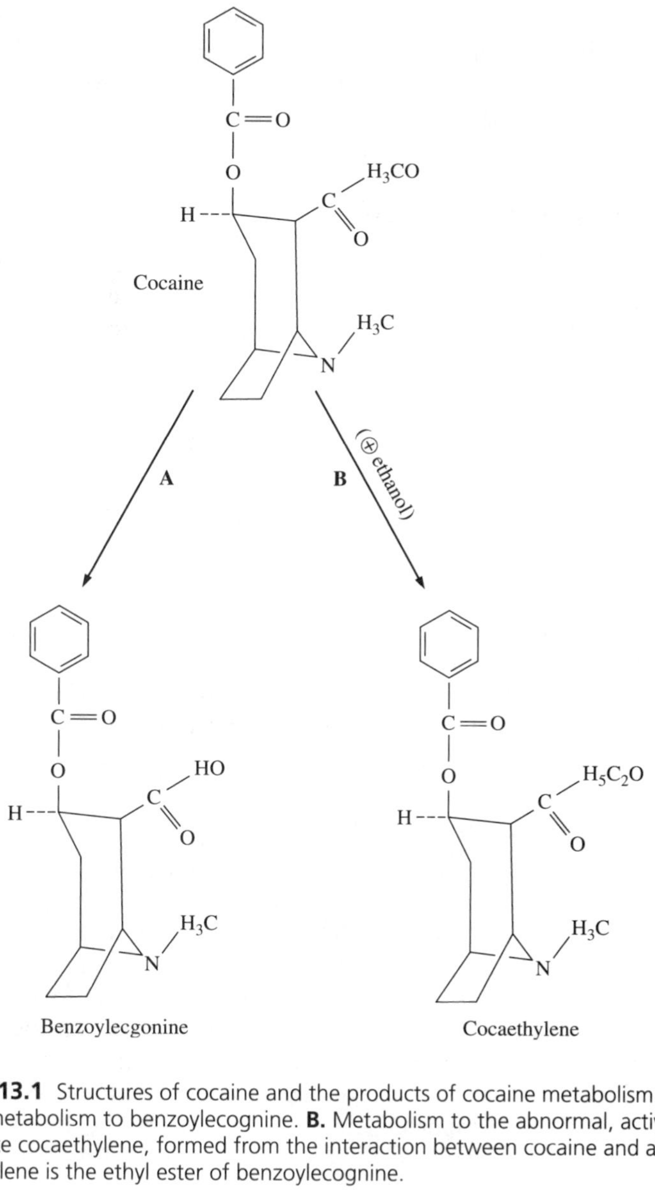

FIGURE 13.1 Structures of cocaine and the products of cocaine metabolism. **A.** Normal metabolism to benzoylecognine. **B.** Metabolism to the abnormal, active metabolite cocaethylene, formed from the interaction between cocaine and alcohol. Cocaethylene is the ethyl ester of benzoylecognine.

The metabolic interaction between cocaine and ethanol is interesting and important. In people who use cocaine and concurrently drink alcohol, a unique ethyl ester of benzoylecgonine is produced by the liver enzymes that metabolize the two drugs. This metabolite (called *cocaethylene;* see Figure 13.1) is pharmacologically as active as cocaine in blocking the presynaptic dopamine reuptake transporter, potentiating the euphoric effect of cocaine, increasing the risk of dual dependency, and increasing the severity of withdrawal with chronic patterns of use (Bunney et al., 2001). The cocaethylene metabolite is actually more toxic than cocaine and exacerbates cocaine's toxicity (Wilson et al., 2001). The half-life of cocaethylene is about 150 minutes, outlasting cocaine in the body.

Mechanism of Action

Pharmacologically, cocaine has three prominent actions that account for virtually all its physiological and psychological effects; cocaine is the only drug that possesses these three characteristics.

1. It is a potent *local anesthetic.*
2. It is a *vasoconstrictor,* strongly constricting blood vessels and raising blood pressure.
3. It is a powerful *psychostimulant* with strong behavioral reinforcing qualities.

The psychostimulant property leads to compulsive abuse of and dependence upon the drug. Therefore, this section focuses on the actions that lead to its psychostimulation and its behavior-reinforcing properties. Its vasoconstrictive and local anesthetic actions contribute to severe cardiovascular and cerebrovascular toxicities.

Dopaminergic Actions

For 25 years, cocaine has been known to potentiate the synaptic actions of dopamine, norepinephrine, and serotonin. The potentiation occurs as a result of cocaine's ability to block the active reuptake of these three transmitters into the presynaptic nerve terminals from which they were released (Figure 13.2). Currently, most focus is on cocaine's blockade of the presynaptic transporter for dopamine as being crucial to its behavior-reinforcing and psychostimulant properties, although blockade of serotonin reuptake is being reexamined. Blockade of the dopamine transporter markedly increases the levels of dopamine within the synaptic cleft, an observation well documented in

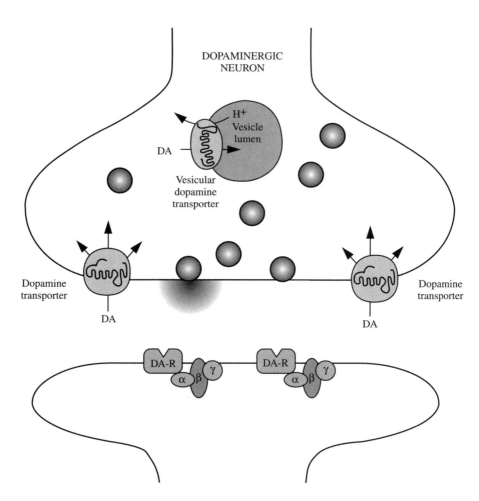

FIGURE 13.2 Dopamine nerve terminal and transporter proteins involved in the active uptake of dopamine (DA). Two transporters are shown. The first is a vesicular DA transporter located in the cytoplasm of the presynaptic neuron, bound to DA-containing storage vesicles. This transporter carries DA from the cytoplasm into storage. The second type of DA transporter is found on the synaptic membrane of the presynaptic neuron and functions to transport DA from the synaptic cleft into the presynaptic nerve terminal, recycling the transmitter and ending the process of synaptic transmission. It is the second transporter that is blocked by cocaine, prolonging the action of DA in the synaptic cleft. Amphetamines function to induce the release of increased amounts of DA from the storage vesicles into the synaptic cleft. The result is the same: increased amounts of DA at the postsynaptic receptor (DA-R). [From S. G. Amara and M. S. Sonders, "Neurotransmitter Transporters as Molecular Targets for Addictive Drugs," *Drug and Alcohol Dependence* 51 (1998), Figure 1.]

animal and human studies. Increased dopamine levels in the nucleus accumbens (NA) and other components of the dopaminergic reward system seem to be responsible for the euphoric/psychostimulant effects of the drug.

Dopamine, cocaine, and cocaethylene all decrease the discharge rate of neurons located in both the ventral tegmental area (VTA) and the NA, indicating that dopamine exerts inhibitory effects on the postsynaptic receptors, probably reducing inhibitory modulation of excitatory transmission from the prefrontal cortex to the VTA and the NA (Steketee, 2005). Cocaine markedly potentiates the dopamine-induced decrease in discharge rate: the potentiation occurs secondary to blockade of dopamine reuptake, potentiating its inhibitory action on postsynaptic receptors.

In 1991, the presynaptic transporter protein for dopamine, which is blocked by cocaine, was cloned and characterized. This transporter protein is a 619-amino-acid protein with 12 putative membrane-spanning regions; both termini of the protein are located in the intracellular cytoplasm of the presynaptic neuron (refer to Figure 2.7). Cocaine competes with dopamine for this receptor; the cocaine blocks the binding of dopamine and prolongs its presence in the synaptic cleft.

Serotoninergic Actions

Augmentation of dopaminergic neurotransmission as a basis for euphoria/reward/dependency had gone nearly unchallenged for many years. Rocha and coworkers (1998) studied cocaine effects in mice that genetically lacked either the presynaptic dopamine transporter or the postsynaptic serotonin 5-HT_{1B} receptor. In mice lacking the dopamine transporter, dopamine would not be expected to serve as a positive reinforcer, but contrary to expectations, the drug was indeed a reinforcer. Thus, other pathways must be involved, pathways that involve the binding of cocaine to the serotonin transporter, supporting the reinforcing effects of cocaine. The researchers concluded:

> The serotonin system may provide an additional component of reinforcement, which in the case of dopamine-transporter-deficient mice seems to be sufficient to initiate the self-administration behavior. (p. 175)

Also, in mice genetically bred to lack the serotonin 5-HT_{1B} receptor, cocaine's effects were greater than those in normal control mice. In addition, the genetically altered mice were even more motivated to self-administer cocaine. Thus, serotonin 5-HT_{1B} receptors may put the brake on or antagonize the reinforcing effects of cocaine.

Perhaps people with altered serotonin receptor function have increased susceptibility to cocaine dependence. B. B. Little and co-workers (1998) tested the hypothesis that alterations in brain serotonin transporter exist in chronic users of cocaine and alcohol. Their results lent support to the hypothesis of genetically defective transporter function in drug dependence. Sora and coworkers (2001) studied mice without either dopamine or serotonin transporter and concluded that (1) cocaine may normally work to provide rewarding actions at both transporters and/or (2) either dopamine or serotonin transporters can modulate cocaine reward in the lifelong absence of the other transporter. Filip and coworkers (2005) recently reviewed the status of knowledge about a possible role of the serotonergic sytem in cocaine addiction.

Pharmacological Effects in Human Beings

Effects of Short-Term, Low-Dose Use

Low-dose (25 to 75 milligrams) nontoxic *physiological responses* to cocaine include increased alertness, motor hyperactivity, tachycardia, vasoconstriction, hypertension, bronchodilation, increased body temperature, pupillary dilation, increased glucose availability, and shifts in blood flow from the internal organs to the muscles. *Psychological effects* of low doses include an immediate euphoria, giddiness, enhanced self-consciousness, and forceful boastfulness that last only about 30 minutes. This period is followed by one of milder euphoria mixed with anxiety, which can last for 60 to 90 minutes, followed by a more protracted anxious state that spans hours.

During acute and subacute intoxication, thoughts typically race, and speech becomes talkative and rapid, often pressured, even garrulous, and sometimes tangential and incoherent. Appetite is markedly suppressed but later rebounds. Sleep is delayed; fatigue is postponed but later rebounds. Conscious awareness and mental acuity are increased but are followed by depression. Motor activity is increased, with agitation, restlessness, and a feeling of constant motion. Perhaps most important, cocaine promotes one's desire to take more cocaine, even instead of such important reinforcers as food.

Low-dose acute effects of cocaine are difficult to maintain because either (1) the perceived effects promote increased use or (2) tolerance develops and higher doses must be taken to perceive continued effects or avoid withdrawal. Thus, a person "graduates" rapidly to the use of higher doses and the onset of increased risks and toxicities.

Cocaine has long been known to function as a discriminative stimulus in several species of animals, a fundamental mechanism by which a drug can control behavior. Also, cocaine use can be followed by an increase in cocaine craving, an effect that may, like its positive reinforcing effect, increase the likelihood of additional cocaine consumption. Extinction training (a form of behavioral conditioning that removes the reward associated with a learned behavior) can reduce the tendency toward relapse. Sutton and coworkers (2003) demonstrated that extinction training during cocaine withdrawal induces increases of subunits of AMPA-type glutamate receptors in the NA. The authors conclude that "extinction-induced plasticity in AMPA receptors may facilitate control over cocaine seeking by restoring glutaminergic tone in the NA, and may reduce the propensity for relapse under stressful situations in prolonged abstinence" (p. 70). Kalivas and coworkers (2006) state that cognitive enhancement, either through pharmacological agents or cognitive behavioral training, can be an effective treatment for cocaine dependence as they increase cognitive regulation of striatal habit circuitry and fortify cognitive regulation of behavior.

Effects of Moderate-Dose Use

As the dose or duration of use of cocaine increases, all the effects are intensified, and a rebound depression follows. There is a progressive loss of coordination, followed by tremors and eventually seizures. CNS activation is followed by depression, dysphoria, anxiety, somnolence, and drug craving. Although sexual interest may be heightened by using cocaine, and high doses (injected or smoked) are sometimes described as orgasmic, cocaine is not an aphrodisiac. Sexual dysfunction is common in heavy users, as they lose interest in interpersonal and sexual interactions. Further, when dysfunction is combined with the isolation that a cocaine-dependent person experiences, normal interpersonal, sensual, and sexual interactions are markedly compromised.

Organ-specific medical and physiological risks and complications of cocaine use are listed in Table 13.2. In the CNS, acute use of cocaine may cause local depletions of oxygen (cerebral ischemia), vascular thrombosis, intracranial hemorrhage and hemorrhagic strokes, cerebral atrophy, seizures, and movement disorders.

Cardiac complications associated with moderate use include hypertensive crises, cardiac ischemia (lack of oxygen), heart attacks, cardiac arrhythmias, sudden death, heart failure, infected heart tissue or valves, and rupture of the aorta. Complications can occur during prolonged use or with single use.

Nasal and pulmonary complications include nasal-septal perforation, pulmonary lesions, hemorrhage, edema, and infections. Gastrointestinal and renal complications can also be seen (see Table 13.2).

TABLE 13.2 Organ-specific medical and physiological risks and complications of cocaine use

Central nervous system
  Ischemic or hemorrhagic strokes
  Seizures
  Movement disorders
  Intracranial hemorrhage

Cardiac complications
  Acute myocardial infarction (heart attack)
  Cardiac arrhythmias
  Sudden cardiac arrest and death
  Heart failure
  Myocarditis (infections of the heart)
  Ruptured aorta

Pulmonary complications
  Nasal-septal perforations
  Inhalation injuries
  Immunity-related diseases
  Pulmonary edema, hemorrhage
  Bronchiolitis (inflamation of the bronchial tree)

Gastrointestinal complications
  Ulcers, perforations of the stomach and upper intestine
  Bowel ischemia (lack of oxygen)
  Intestinal infarction

Renal complications
  Renal failure
  Renal ischemia

Maternal, fetal, and neonatal complications
  Maternal
    Spontaneous abortion, abruptio placentae
    Placenta previa, stillbirth
  Fetal
    Growth retardation, premature delivery
    Congenital anomalies
    Cerebral infarction and/or hemorrhage
  Neonatal
    Drug withdrawal, seizure disorders
    Cardiovascular system complications

Modified from M. S. Boghdadi and R. J. Henning, "Cocaine: Pathophysiology and Clinical Toxicology," *Heart and Lung* 26 (1997): 466–483.

With or without alcohol, cocaine plays a role in fatal automobile crashes. The mechanisms are unclear but probably involve visual deficits, alterations in judgment, incoordination, and feeling of power.

Effects of Long-Term, High-Dose Use

Although low doses of cocaine can cause CNS stimulation that is pleasurable and euphoric, higher doses produce toxic symptoms, including anxiety, sleep deprivation, hypervigilance, suspiciousness, paranoia, and persecutory fears. A person taking cocaine may become hyperreactive, paranoid, and impulsive and may display a repetitive, compulsive pattern of behavior. The person can have a markedly altered perception of reality and become aggressive or homicidal in response to imagined persecution. These behaviors make up what is called a *toxic paranoid psychosis.*

Other high-dose, long-term effects of cocaine use include interpersonal conflicts (resulting from the sense of isolation and paranoia), depression, dysphoria, and bizarre and violent psychotic disorders that can last days or weeks after a person stops using the drug. In its most extreme form, a cocaine psychosis is characterized by paranoia, impaired reality testing, anxiety, a stereotyped compulsive repetitive pattern of behavior, and vivid visual, auditory, and tactile hallucinations. More subtle changes in behavior may include irritability, hypervigilance, extreme psychomotor activation, paranoid thinking, impaired interpersonal relations, and disturbances of eating and sleeping. An acutely toxic dose of cocaine has been estimated to be about 2 milligrams per kilogram of body weight. Thus, 150 milligrams of cocaine is a toxic one-time dose for a 150-pound (70-kilogram) person. Serious physiological toxicity follows higher doses.

Comorbidity

Cocaine-dependent people are typically young (12 to 39 years of age), dependent on at least three drugs, and male (75 percent). They tend to have coexisting psychopathology (30 percent have anxiety disorders, 67 percent suffer from clinical depression, and 25 percent exhibit paranoia). About 85 to 90 percent are alcohol dependent.

Chronic cocaine use produces virtually every psychiatric syndrome: affective disorders (mania and depression), schizophrenialike syndromes, personality disorders, and so on. Over 50 percent (and perhaps even 70 percent) of cocaine abusers meet criteria for the presence of a neuropsychological disorder (major depression, anxiety disorder, bipolar affective disorder, antisocial personality disorder, posttraumatic stress disorder, or attention deficit/hyperactivity disorder). Thus, toxicities or withdrawal complications may indicate either high-dose drug toxicities or the onset of symptoms of a coexisting neuropsychological disorder (or both).

Most cocaine-dependent people also have problems with other drugs of abuse. Like alcoholics and heroin addicts, cocaine addicts often show a certain profile on personality tests—they are reckless, rebellious, and have a low tolerance for frustration and a craving for excitement. In fact, most of them have been or will be alcoholics or heroin addicts as well. They use opiates and alcohol either to enhance the effects of cocaine or to medicate themselves for unwanted side effects—calming jitters, dulling perceptions, and reducing paranoia to indifference. Intravenous drug users often take cocaine and heroin together in a mixture known as a speedball. Probably more than half of people treated for cocaine abuse are also alcoholic, and the rate of alcoholism in the families of cocaine addicts is high. Comorbidity of cocaine dependence with other psychological or drug-dependency disorders is discussed further in the section on treatment of cocaine dependence.

Cocaine and Pregnancy

One of the tragedies of the late twentieth century was the birth of thousands of infants who were thought to have been injured in utero by cocaine taken by their mothers while pregnant. Figure 13.3 outlines the effects of cocaine on the fetus. Indirect effects result from cocaine's vasoconstrictive action on the mother's blood vessels, decreasing blood flow to the uterus and placenta and reducing oxygen delivery to the fetus. In humans, the most common consequences to the infant of cocaine abuse during pregnancy include premature birth, respiratory distress, bowel infarctions, cerebral infarctions, reduced head circumference, and increased risk of seizures (Keller and Snyder-Keller, 2000). Obviously, cocaine use during pregnancy should be considered to be fetotoxic. The exact mechanism of cocaine-induced fetal injury may be related to placental vasoconstriction and fetal hypoxia produced by the drug, with the resulting intermittent vascular disruptions and ischemia in the embryo and fetus actually causing injury.

In Figure 13.3, note that cocaine also exerts adverse direct effects on the fetus. Cocaine easily crosses the placental barrier, and fetal concentrations can equal those in the mother. Direct organ toxicity can involve the heart, the CNS, the urinary system, and the GI tract. Vasoconstriction in either the mother or the fetus can increase blood pressure in the fetus, leading to intracerebral hemorrhage, thickening of heart muscle, and various vascular and structural abnormalities. As the brain develops, exposure of the fetus to cocaine may promote serious destructive lesions, leading to a neonatal neurological syndrome typified by abnormal sleep patterns, tremors, poor feeding, irritability,

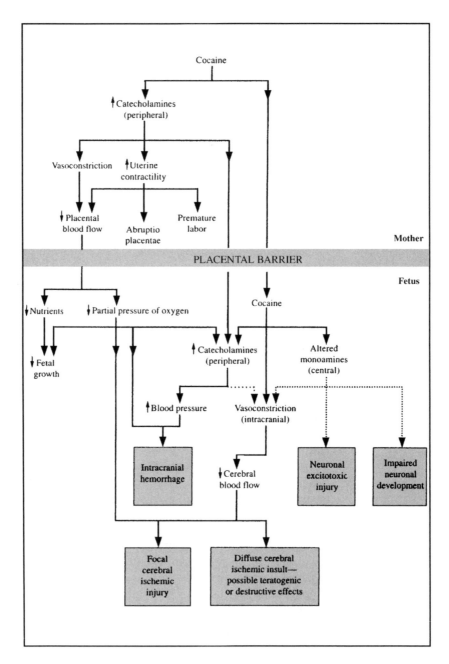

FIGURE 13.3 Deleterious effects of maternal cocaine use on the fetus. Effects that appear plausible on the basis of current information but whose confirmation requires more supporting evidence are indicated by dotted lines. ↑ denotes increase and ↓ denotes decrease. [From J. J. Volpe, "Effects of Cocaine Use on the Fetus," *New England Journal of Medicine* 327 (1992), p. 401.]

occasional seizures, and an increased risk or incidence of sudden infant death syndrome (SIDS).

Some have tried to define a fetal cocaine syndrome. However, because of the wide spectrum of indirect and direct effects on the fetus, any such syndrome is not as clearly defined as the fetal alcohol syndrome, and cocaine use by the mother is usually only one of many undesirable influences in the children's lives. Babies born into a drug-using environment and possibly into poverty experience little physical or emotional nurturing, so bonding is incomplete or absent. Cocaine's effects on the unborn and newborn may also be related to poor nutrition, poor hygiene, and neglect. Cocaine compromises the mother or any caregiver's ability to respond to the baby through talking, eye contact, and tactile stimulation. The specific interactional behavior of cocaine-using mothers is still under investigation.

Does use of cocaine during pregnancy result in a "crack baby"? The answer is far from clear. On the one hand, Singer and coworkers (2002) reported that cocaine-exposed children had significant cognitive deficits and a doubling of the rate of developmental delay during their first two years of life. The authors proposed that cocaine-exposed children will continue to have learning difficulties at school age. On the other hand, Frank and coworkers (2001) performed a meta-analysis of studies assessing possible links between cocaine use by a pregnant mother and childhood difficulties in the offspring. The authors concluded that crack/cocaine exposure in utero has not been demonstrated to affect physical growth, developmental scores, or motor development. Difficulties in offspring in these areas seemed to be more related to prenatal exposure to tobacco, marijuana, or alcohol and to the quality of the child's environment.

Singer and colleagues (2004) assessed the effects of maternal cocaine use on cognitive functioning in offspring at the age of 4 years. Verbal and performance IQ scales were not affected; but prenatal exposure to cocaine was associated with an increased risk for specific cognitive impairments and IQs below the normative mean at age 4 years. The researchers also concluded that environmental intervention through foster or adoptive care was associated with a lower likelihood of mental retardation among cocaine-exposed children, despite heavier drug exposure. Therefore, considering the role of environment and time to recover (from 2 to 4 years of age), the effects of prenatal cocaine exposure may diminish over time, especially in the context of environmental interventions (Williams and Ross, 2007).

Neurotoxicity of Cocaine

The possible neurotoxic effects of cocaine are difficult to measure by the persistence of neurological abnormalities for a period following cessation of drug use. Cocaine is a short-acting drug and is not present in the body if the drug is not repeatedly ingested, smoked, or injected. Toomey and coworkers (2003) conducted a twin study (all males) in which only one member had had heavy stimulant abuse (cocaine and/or methamphetamine) that ended at least one year before the evaluation. Subjects underwent a comprehensive battery of neuropsychological tests. Timed tests demonstrated evidence of long-term residual neuropsychological impairments in the abusers consistent with persistent psychomotor slowing and slowed reactions associated with cocaine abuse. In contrast, abusers (abstinent for at least one year) exhibited improved performance on attentional tests, suggesting that the positive effects of stimulants on attentional measures (such as ADHD) may persist after drug discontinuation.

Drug-abstinent users may show persistent detrimental changes in their brains with associated alterations in memory function. Bartzokis and colleagues (1999) demonstrated that in men who were cocaine dependent, doses of cocaine usually caused a "subclinical" form of brain damage of the kind usually caused by vascular insufficiency. It is possible that this kind of injury could predispose to early-onset dementia and other neurological syndromes as subtle brain damage accumulates and adds to normal aging. K. Y. Little and coworkers (2003) demonstrated that cocaine users lose a specific protein in the brain, which might reflect damage to dopaminergic neurons. Thus, they speculate that this loss could play a role in causing disordered mood and motivational processes in more severely dependent patients.

Pharmacological Treatment of Cocaine Dependency

At the outset, it should be stated that there are no proven pharmacotherapies for cocaine addiction (Sofuoglu and Kosten, 2006). Cognitive behavioral therapy has proved somewhat useful in preventing relapse and pharmacotherapy can fortify cognitive regulation of behavior (Kalivas et al., 2006; Vocci and Elkashef, 2005). Pharmacological strategies include blocking euphoria, reducing withdrawal and negative mood symptoms (for example, depression), ameliorating craving, and enhancing the prefrontal cortical projections that seem to be impaired in cocaine-dependent patients (Dackis, 2004). Since frontal cortical projections to the ventral tegmentum and nucleus accumbens are glutaminergic, compounds regulating glutaminergic transmission are in early clinical trial. Agents include such drugs as topiramate and tiagepine (Sofuoglu et al., 2005; Gonzalez et al., 2007) and are discussed in Chapter 10.

Since cocaine as a euphoriant drug acts indirectly by blocking the presynaptic reuptake of dopamine, agents that can substitute for cocaine as either direct or indirect dopaminergic agonists might be thought to ameliorate not only withdrawal symptoms but also craving and relapse. Disulfiram (Antabuse), used as an aversion agent in the treatment of alcoholism, has dopaminergic effects and has been shown to be effective in clinical trials (K. M. Carroll et al., 2004). Other dopaminergic agents include bupropion (Wellbutrin) and amantadine (Symmetrel). L-dopa (Chapter 11) was shown to be without beneficial effect (Mooney et al., 2007).

In common with other classes of abused drugs, cocaine dependence has been shown to be strongly associated with depression (Rounsaville, 2004). Therefore, antidepressant drugs appear indicated. Of these, serotonin reuptake inhibitors are relatively ineffective, but agents such as desipramine (a tricyclic antidepressant) and bupropion (Wellbutrin, discussed earlier) are effective. Other comorbid psychiatric disorders are anxiety disorders, bipolar disorder, borderline personality disorder, and/or antisocial personality disorder. Each requires treatment for cocaine abuse treatment to be effective.

Anticraving or antirelapse agents are an area of intense study. Studies are currently focusing on two areas: antiepileptic neuromodulators and cannabinoid antagonists. Gabapentin (Neurontin; Chapter 8), a neuromodulator, has been reported to be effective in the treatment of cocaine dependence, although Gonzalez and coworkers (2007) found it to be without effect.

Gamma-vinyl-GABA (Vigabatrin, an antiepileptic drug available in Europe and in clinical trial in the United States) exhibits anticraving effects against abused drugs, including cocaine (Brodie et al., 2005). Vigabatrin is an irreversible inhibitor of the enzyme *GABA transaminase;* it increases GABA activity and attenuates drug-induced increases in extracellular nucleus accumbens dopamine as well as the behaviors associated with this dopamine increase. Vigabatrin is being studied for use in treating cocaine dependence; its use is limited by a drug-induced loss of some portion of visual field (peripheral vision) in about 10 to 30 percent of people taking the drug (McDonagh et al., 2003). A more recent study demonstrated that short-term use of vigabatrin is less damaging to visual fields (Fechtner et al., 2006).

Cannabinoid antagonists can be demonstrated to be remarkably effective anticraving agents (Fattore et al., 2007). Early reports document the reduction in cocaine reinforcement behaviors in mice lacking cannabinoid receptors (Soria et al., 2005); in rats, a cannabinoid antagonist (rimonabant) reduced cocaine-seeking behaviors (Xi et al., 2006). Human studies of rimonabant as an anticocaine agent have not yet been reported.

Many cocaine abusers seeking treatment have a history of childhood attention deficit/hyperactivity disorder (ADHD), and approximately 15 percent of cocaine abusers seeking treatment may have adult ADHD. Early studies of the efficacy of long-acting *methylphenidate* (Ritalin SR) on people with comorbid cocaine dependence abuse and adult ADHD reported that the combined intervention of the drug plus relapse prevention therapy reduced both the ADHD and the cocaine dependency. Levin and coworkers (2007) in a placebo-controlled study of 106 people with comorbid ADHD and cocaine dependency reported that methylphenidate-induced reductions in ADHD symptoms were accompanied by reductions in cocaine use.

Novel Approaches to the Treatment of Cocaine Addiction

Several different approaches are being investigated for development of new treatments for cocaine dependence. In one, new dopamine reuptake inhibitors, which may substitute for cocaine and reduce craving and relapse, are being investigated (F. I. Carroll et al., 2006).

In another approach, a cocaine vaccine, termed TA-CD, is in clinical trial. This vaccine may slow the entry of cocaine into the brain, thereby inhibiting its euphoriant effect (Martell et al., 2005). The vaccine is created by attaching molecules of cocaine to a large protein molecule, which is then used to stimulate the body's immune system to produce antibodies that recognize and bind any cocaine taken. The vaccine is given intramuscularly in a series of inoculations. The cocaine-specific antibodies persist for at least 6 months. Even if successful, unless comorbid psychological issues are addressed, a cocaine-dependent person who has these antibodies in the blood may move to another drug. The vaccine must stimulate a very strong immune response so that every single cocaine molecule is mopped up if someone uses again. Otherwise, a small number could reach the brain and act like a teaser, causing the user to take even more to satisfy the craving completely. Other forms of therapy would also be necessary as it is more than just the physiological addiction that causes people to use again (relapse). Craving is a very complex issue that won't necessarily be solved with a pharmacological intervention. There are also ethical issues around when and how this vaccine might be used.

A very unusual approach to treating cocaine dependency involves intranasal administration of a bioengineered "filamentous bacteriophage displaying cocaine-sequestering antibodies on its surface" that can bind cocaine that is in the blood and thereby block its effects, at least in rats (Dickerson and Janda, 2005).

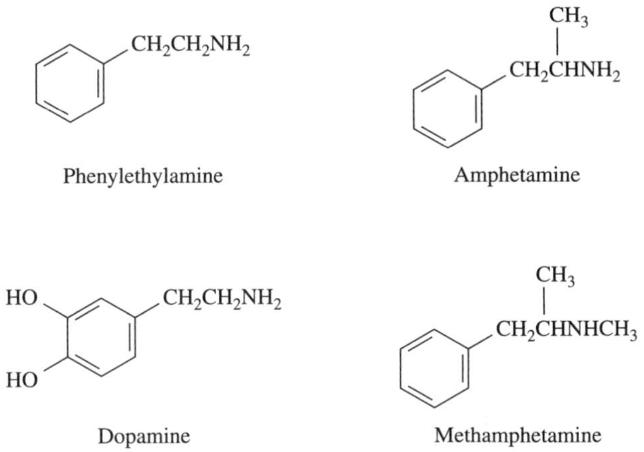

FIGURE 13.4 The basic sympathomimetic amine nucleus (phenylethylamine), the neurotransmitter dopamine (dihydroxyphenylethylamine), and the structures of amphetamine and methamphetamine.

AMPHETAMINES

The amphetamines (Figure 13.4) are a structurally defined group of drugs that produce a variety of effects on both the CNS and the autonomic nervous system.[4] Amphetamines are also called *sympathomimetic agents* because they mimic the actions of adrenaline (epinephrine, one of the transmitters of our "sympathetic" nervous system). Amphetamines produce vasoconstriction, hypertension, tachycardia, and other signs and symptoms of our normal alerting response. These drugs also stimulate the CNS, producing tremor, restlessness, increased motor activity, agitation, insomnia, and loss of appetite. These actions result from an indirect action involving the presynaptic release of dopamine and norepinephrine and, to a lesser extent, direct stimulation of postsynaptic catecholamine receptors. Amphetamines have limited yet appropriate

---

[4]The *autonomic nervous system* (ANS) is frequently called the visceral nervous system because it regulates and maintains the homeostasis of the body's internal organs. It controls the function of the heart, the flow of blood, and the functioning of the digestive tract, and it regulates other internal functions that are essential for maintaining the balance necessary for life. The ANS comprises two subdivisions—the *sympathetic* and the *parasympathetic*. The function of the parasympathetic nervous system can be viewed as maintaining our "vegetative" functions, while the sympathetic nervous system handles the body's reaction to stress, fright, fear, and other responses that demand an immediate alerting response. Neurotransmitters in the sympathetic division of the ANS include epinephrine (adrenaline), norepinephrine, and dopamine.

clinical use; they are widely abused, with significant personal and public health consequences. Representative amphetamines for clinical use in treating ADHD (Chapter 10) include *amphetamine* (Adderall), *dextroamphetamine* (Dexedrine, DextroStat), and *methamphetamine* (Methadrine). Because of its notorious reputation as an illicit drug, methamphetamine is rarely if ever used clinically.

Amphetamines have long been used to treat a variety of disorders. Between 1935 and 1946, a list of 39 conditions for which amphetamines could be used in treatment was developed. The list included schizophrenia, morphine addiction, tobacco smoking, head injury, radiation sickness, hypotension, seasickness, severe hiccups, and caffeine dependence. During World War II, amphetamines were used to fight fatigue and enhance the performance of people in the armed services. In the 1960s, amphetamines were used as diet pills. Today, use is largely restricted to the clinical treatment of childhood, adolescent, and adult ADHD (Chapter 10). Spencer and coworkers (2004) discuss psychostimulants in adult ADHD.

Large-scale abuse (usually oral ingestion of amphetamine tablets) began in the late 1940s, primarily by students and truck drivers in efforts to maintain wakefulness, temporarily increase alertness, and delay sleep. Amphetamines continued to be used (and abused) as appetite suppressants, despite the fact that the anorectic effect persists only over the first two weeks of treatment, after which time it diminishes. In the late 1960s, the abuse pattern of amphetamines changed with the advent of injectable forms of amphetamine. These injectable products (by legitimate manufacturers) have been discontinued, so injection of methamphetamine today is illicit. Interest in the amphetamines today involves two areas:

• Therapeutic use in the treatment of narcolepsy and ADHD

• Compulsive misuse and drug dependency, especially with methamphetamine

Mechanism of Action

The amphetamines exert virtually all their physical and psychological effects by causing the release of norepinephrine and dopamine from presynaptic storage sites in nerve terminals (Chapter 2). Other minor actions augment this releasing action, and all actions add up so that amphetamines act as highly potent releasers of dopamine (Barr et al., 2006). The behavioral stimulation and increased psychomotor activity appear to follow from the resulting stimulation of the dopamine receptors in the mesolimbic system, including the nucleus accumbens. The high-dose stereotypical behavior (including constant repetition of meaningless acts) appears to involve dopamine neurons in the basal ganglia. At a deeper level, Jaworski and Jones (2006) discuss CART peptides (cocaine- and amphetamine-related transcript proteins) in the reward and reinforcement actions of amphetamines.

The actions leading to an increase in aggressive behavior are complex. Clinically, this behavioral stimulant action is seen primarily in adults suffering from psychostimulant toxicity and consists of increases in stereotypical, repetitive behaviors. In children, low doses of amphetamines are used therapeutically to reduce aggressive behavior and activities characteristic of ADHD; in adults with a history of ADHD, behavioral calming can also occur.

Pharmacological Effects

As stated, amphetamines exert their peripheral and central actions largely by causing the release of norepinephrine and dopamine from presynaptic nerve terminals (see Figure 13.2). All the physical and behavioral effects of the amphetamines appear to follow from this action. Note that the release of dopamine increases the amount of dopamine available to the postsynaptic receptor, much as does cocaine. Both drugs have the net effect of increasing the amount of dopamine available (although through two different mechanisms), so cocaine abusers have difficulty distinguishing between the subjective effects of 8 to 10 milligrams of cocaine and 10 milligrams of dextroamphetamine when the doses are administered intravenously.

The pharmacological responses to amphetamines vary with the specific drug, the dose, and the route of administration. In general, with amphetamine itself, effects may be categorized as those observed at low to moderate doses (5 to 50 milligrams), usually administered orally, and those observed at high doses (more than approximately 100 milligrams), often administered intravenously. These dose ranges are not the same for all amphetamines. For example, dextroamphetamine is three to four times more potent than amphetamine. Low to moderate doses of dextroamphetamine range from 2.5 to 20 milligrams, while high doses are 50 milligrams or more. Because methamphetamine is even more potent, dose ranges must be lowered even more, although massive doses are taken by methamphetamine-dependent people who have developed a tolerance to the drug.

At low doses, all amphetamines increase blood pressure, slow heart rate, relax bronchial muscle, and produce a variety of other responses that follow from the body's alerting response. In the CNS, amphetamine is a potent psychomotor stimulant, producing increased alertness, euphoria, excitement, wakefulness, a reduced sense of fatigue, loss of appetite, mood elevation, increased motor and speech activity, and a feeling of power. Although task performance is improved, dexterity may deteriorate. When short-duration, high-intensity energy output is desired, such as during an athletic competition, a user's performance may be enhanced, despite the fact that his or her dexterity and fine motor skills may be impaired. Amphetamine metabolites are excreted in the urine and are detectable for up to 48 hours.

At moderate doses (20 to 50 milligrams), additional effects of amphetamine include stimulation of respiration, slight tremors, restlessness, a greater increase in motor activity, insomnia, and agitation. In addition, amphetamines prevent fatigue, suppress appetite, promote wakefulness, and cause sleep deprivation.

A person who chronically uses high doses of amphetamine suffers from a different set of drug effects. Stereotypical behaviors include continual, purposeless, repetitive acts, sudden outbursts of aggression and violence, paranoid delusions, and severe anorexia. The harmful effects that are seen in the high-dose user include psychosis and abnormal mental conditions, weight loss, skin sores, infections resulting from neglected health care, and a variety of other consequences that occur both because of the actions of the drug itself and because of poor eating habits, lack of sleep, or the use of unsterile equipment for intravenous injections. Most high-dose users show a progressive deterioration in their social, personal, and occupational affairs. Also seen is amphetamine psychosis with paranoid ideation; many addicts must be hospitalized intermittently for treatment of episodes of psychosis. Today, psychosis is especially seen in people who abuse methamphetamine.

Cognitive Effects

Numerous studies have shown that one-time or even daily therapeutic doses of amphetamines can improve cognitive processing speed, attention, concentration, and psychomotor performance. This property underlies the use of amphetamine (Adderall, for example) and amphetaminelike drugs (for example, methylphenidate) as therapeutic treatments for child and adult ADHD. However, high-dose amphetamine abuse, especially with methamphetamine, is associated with cognitive impairments and profound neuropsychological deficits (Nordahl et al., 2003).

The toxic dose of amphetamine varies widely. Severe reactions can occur from low doses (20 to 30 milligrams). On the other hand, people who have not developed tolerance have survived doses of 400 to 500 milligrams. Even larger doses are tolerated by chronic users. The slogan "Speed kills" refers not only to a direct fatal effect of single doses of amphetamine but also to the deteriorating mental and physical condition that occurs in the addicted user.

Effects in Pregnancy

The possibility of adverse effects of amphetamines taken either licitly or illicitly during pregnancy are incompletely studied. There is no clear-cut pattern of congenital anomalies, although there is some consensus that infants born of amphetamine-using mothers have a degree of growth retardation and lower birth weights. An increased rate of intracerebral hemorrhage can be observed, probably brought on by drug-induced increases in blood pressure in both the mother and the fetus. In the long term, there is some evidence of psychometric deficits, poor academic performance, behavioral problems, cognitive slowing, and general maladjustment. Smith and colleagues (2006), in perhaps the largest study of methamphetamine-abusing pregnant women, reported that offspring of these mothers were 3.5 times more likely to be small for gestational age than offspring of nonexposed mothers.

Dependence and Tolerance

As potent psychomotor stimulants and behavior-reinforcing agents, the amphetamines are prone to compulsive abuse. Physical dependence is readily induced in both humans and laboratory animals and follows a classical positive conditioning model (the positive reward leads to further drug use). Once drug use is stopped, a person experiences a withdrawal syndrome, although it is less dramatic than the withdrawal associated with either opioids (Chapter 16) or barbiturates (Chapter 5). Withdrawal symptoms associated with the amphetamines include increased appetite, weight gain, decreased energy, and increased need for sleep. Patients may develop a voracious appetite and sleep for several days after amphetamines are discontinued. Paranoid symptoms may persist during drug withdrawal but generally do not develop as a result of withdrawal. The patient suddenly discontinuing amphetamine use may develop severe depression and become suicidal. Management of amphetamine withdrawal does not require detoxification, but it does require appropriate and cautious clinical observation of the patient, recognition of depression, and treatment with an appropriate antidepressant drug if clinically necessary. Antipsychotic drugs, such as risperidone, quetiapine, or aripiprazole (Chapter 9), may be necessary to treat paranoid or psychotic reactions or behaviors.

Tolerance rapidly develops and can necessitate higher and higher doses, which starts a vicious circle of drug use and withdrawal. At this point, tolerance to the euphoriant effects develops, and periods of prolonged binge drug use begin. This tolerance, combined with the memory of drug-induced highs, leads to further drug intake, social withdrawal, and a focus on procuring drugs. Comer and coworkers (2001) studied the effects of 5 and 10 milligrams of methamphetamine twice daily on nonusers in a controlled setting. Positive feelings toward the drug were experienced only on day 1; on subsequent days the subjects felt a loss of positive effects and increases in negative feelings (dizziness, nausea, depression, and so on). This rapid development of tolerance to the positive effects may lead to the psychotic consequences in long-term use. There has been concern about the long-term outcomes of amphetamine and methylphenidate use for treatment of ADHD. Poulton (2006) reviews this topic and concludes:

> It would appear that the medical complications associated with amphetamine addiction are not relevant to the therapeutic use of stimulant medication in the treatment of ADHD, although there is limited information on extended periods of treatment lasting 10 years or more. (p. 551)

Methamphetamine

Methamphetamine is a more potent drug than dextroamphetamine. Generally considered to be an illicit drug, manufactured in clandestine laboratories, methamphetamine was actually a licit drug, effective in the treatment of ADHD. Today, however, after so much negative publicity, it is rarely used legitimately and illicit use dominates. Methamphetamine is easily synthesized from readily obtainable chemicals, including pseudoephedrine. In animals, methamphetamine has been implicated as a neurotoxic agent, and toxicity has now been demonstrated in humans.

Like cocaine hydrochloride, methamphetamine (the hydrochloride salt) is broken down at the temperatures that must be achieved for it to be vaporized for smoking. However, when converted to its crystalline form, methamphetamine can be effectively vaporized and inhaled in smoke. As a drug of abuse, crystalline methamphetamine is also known as ice, speed, crystal, crank, and go, with considerable overlap in nomenclature with other amphetamines except for "ice," which refers to the smokable form of methamphetamine. The speed of crystalline methamphetamine's absorption through the lungs and mucous membranes is as rapid as or even more rapid than intravenous injection. Thus, ice is to methamphetamine as crack is to cocaine: the crystalline, smokable form of the parent compound. However, unlike cocaine, methamphetamine has an extremely long half-life (about 12 hours), resulting in an intense, persistent drug action. As a form of methamphetamine, crystalline methamphetamine varies in purity (Qi et al., 2006).

Pharmacokinetics

Smoking ice results in its near-immediate absorption into plasma, with additional absorption continuing over the next 4 hours. The blood level then progressively declines. The biological half-life of methamphetamine is more than 11 hours. After distribution to the brain, about 60 percent of the methamphetamine is slowly metabolized in the liver, and the end products are excreted through the kidneys, along with unmetabolized methamphetamine (about 40 percent is excreted unchanged) and small amounts of its pharmacologically active metabolite, amphetamine.

Pharmacological Effects

The effects of methamphetamine closely resemble the effects produced by cocaine. Both drugs are potent psychomotor stimulants and positive reinforcers; self-administration is extremely difficult to control and modify, especially in abusers who use the drug either by injection or by smoking. Repeated high doses of methamphetamine are associated with violent behavior and paranoid psychosis. Such doses cause long-lasting decreases in dopamine and serotonin in the brain. These changes appear to be persistent, at best. Just as prolonged cocaine use can result in psychoses resembling paranoid schizophrenia, smoking crystalline methamphetamine produces a pattern of acute delusional and psychotic behavior. However, unlike that of cocaine, ice-induced psychosis can persist for days or weeks. Fatalities have resulted from cardiac toxicity (Wijetunga et al., 2004).

Neurotoxicity

As noted, prolonged use of methamphetamine is associated with a variety of toxicities, including psychosis. The etiology of these persistent, if not irreversible, toxicities is unclear; oxidative stress, excitotoxicity, and mitochondrial dysfunction may be involved (Quinton and Yamamoto, 2006; Yamamoto and Bankson, 2006). Anatomical toxicities have been reported in various areas of the limbic cortex as smaller hippocampal size, as white matter replacing grey matter, as corpus callosal changes, as metabolic and blood flow changes, as decreases in the levels of presynaptic dopamine transporters in several brain regions, and as reduced levels of serotonin transporters (see Barr, et al., 2006, for a review). Bowyer and coworkers (2007) stated that the neurotoxicity was related to altered "synaptic plasticity-related genes, with disruption specifically in the parietal cortex" (p. 66). This characteristic, together with dopamine transporter abnormalities in the nucleus accumbens, may underlie neurotoxicity and persistent psychotic effects. In rhesus monkeys, neurotoxic abnormalities persist for as long as four years after the last drug exposure. Iyo and coworkers (2004) describe this in humans for as long as three years following cessation of high-dose use.

While these anatomical changes were being described, persistent mental alterations following cessation of methamphetamine use were also being reported. The anatomical changes correlate well with susceptibility to or persistence of behavioral and mental abnormalities, such as persistent psychosis. Sato first noted in 1992 that behavioral and mental changes appear to persist long after drug use. Laboratory studies in the 1990s noted evidence of neuronal death (loss of both dopaminergic and serotonergic neurons) in rodents treated with large doses of methamphetamine.

Ernst and coworkers (2000) studied 26 abstinent methamphetamine abusers with a history of methamphetamine dependence. The abusers were "clean," had no history of alcohol abuse or dependence, and had used methamphetamine for at least 12 months at least 5 days per week and took at least 0.5 gram per day. The subjects displayed metabolic abnormalities in frontal cortex, frontal white matter, and basal ganglia. Neuronal reductions averaged about 6 percent and indicated reduced neuronal density or neuronal content, primarily in frontal lobes. The researchers concluded that the abnormalities "may be related to persistent abnormal behaviors, such as violence, psychosis, and personality changes, which are observed in some individuals months or even years after their last drug use" (p. 1348). This conclusion can explain the alterations seen in frontal lobe "executive functioning" observed in longtime methamphetamine users, even during periods of abstinence.

Volkow and coworkers (2001a, 2001b) demonstrated in detoxified methamphetamine abusers that dopamine transporter function was reduced in the basal ganglia for at least 11 months after drug cessation and that the reductions were associated with persistent motor slowing and memory impairments. Glucose metabolism was also reduced in the basal ganglia, indicating reduced neuronal activity even long after cessation of drug use. Sekine and coworkers (2001, 2006) extended this work and demonstrated a reduction dependent on dose and on duration of use in dopamine transporter density and function in the basal ganglia and (even more) in the frontal cortex and the nucleus accumbens (executive and reward centers). The alterations persisted long after cessation of drug use. The reductions were associated with persistent neuropsychiatric symptoms. Volkow and coworkers (2001c) correlated the reduction in transporter density with reductions in dopamine-2 receptors and with reductions in brain metabolism in dopamine-innervated areas of the brain. Therefore, methamphetamine selectively injures dopamine neurons, generally without inducing cell death.

Larsen and coworkers (2002) examined the mechanism leading to methamphetamine-caused neurotoxicity. They started with the hypothesis that methamphetamine induces redistribution of dopamine from the intracellular nerve terminal vesicular storage pool into the cytoplasm, where the dopamine can be oxidized to produce reactive oxygen species that, in turn, cause the neurotoxic damage. In their studies in rodents, methamphetamine promoted the synthesis of dopamine via "up regulation" of the activity of the enzyme *tyrosine hydroxylase*. This activity elevated the dopamine levels in the cytoplasm and promoted the formation of "autophagic granules," particularly in neuronal terminals and ultimately in the cell bodies of dopamine neurons. Larsen and coworkers proposed that "methamphetamine neurotoxicity results from the induction of a specific cellular pathway that is activated when DA cannot be effectively sequestered in synaptic vesicles, thereby producing neuronal stress and degeneration" (p. 8951).

Wang and coworkers (2004) compared brain glucose metabolism, motor tests, and verbal memory tests in three groups of patients: a control group of people who were not drug dependent, methamphetamine abusers evaluated after a short period (less than 6 months) of abstinence, and methamphetamine abusers evaluated after a long period (12 to 17 months) of abstinence. After both short-term and long-term abstinence, abusers exhibited persistent decreases in glucose metabolism both in the basal ganglia and in the nucleus accumbens, implying long-lasting changes in dopamine cell activity as well as the "persistence of amotivation and anhedonia observed in detoxified methamphetamine abusers" (p. 242). As noted, severe and persistent deficits can be seen in working memory, attention, and executive functioning. The cognitive defects can occur concomitant with the persistent psychiatric behaviors and drug-related psychosis (Barr et al., 2006). Salo and coworkers (2007) correlated reduced viability of dopaminergic neurons with persistent impairments in attention. They postulated that this dopaminergic damage may account for methamphetamine-induced inability to weigh long-term risks against the immediate reward.

These data indicate that long-term methamphetamine abuse leads to persistent reductions in striatal, frontal cortical, and nucleus accumbens dopamine function, activity, and numbers. The reductions are associated with persistent positive psychotic symptom ratings. Thus, methamphetamine abuse leads both to neurotoxic injury in humans (actual structural damage) and to a chronic psychotic state that may be difficult to treat. These permanent or at least persistent neurobehavioral alterations may be expressed as alterations in sleep or sexual function, depression, movement disorders, frontal lobe "executive" functioning, or schizophrenia.

Treatments of methamphetamine psychosis have been disappointing and are primarily "supportive." Akiyama (2006) studied 32 incarcerated females suffering from methamphetamine-induced psychosis. Psychotic relapses following discontinuation were common, sometimes persisting for over 30 months. Auditory and visual hallucinations, delusions of persecution, thought broadcasting, depression, and suicidal ideation were all common. Antidepressant drugs (Chapter 7) and both "traditional" and "atypical" antipsychotic drugs (Chapter 9) may be useful.

NONAMPHETAMINE BEHAVIORAL STIMULANTS

An amphetamine is any drug with the basic amphetamine nucleus (see Figure 13.4). A *nonamphetamine behavioral stimulant* does not have this basic nucleus (Figure 13.5), but it shares the same action of potentiating the sympathomimetic actions of the neurotransmitter dopamine. Nonamphetamine stimulants include ephedrine (found in nature in the

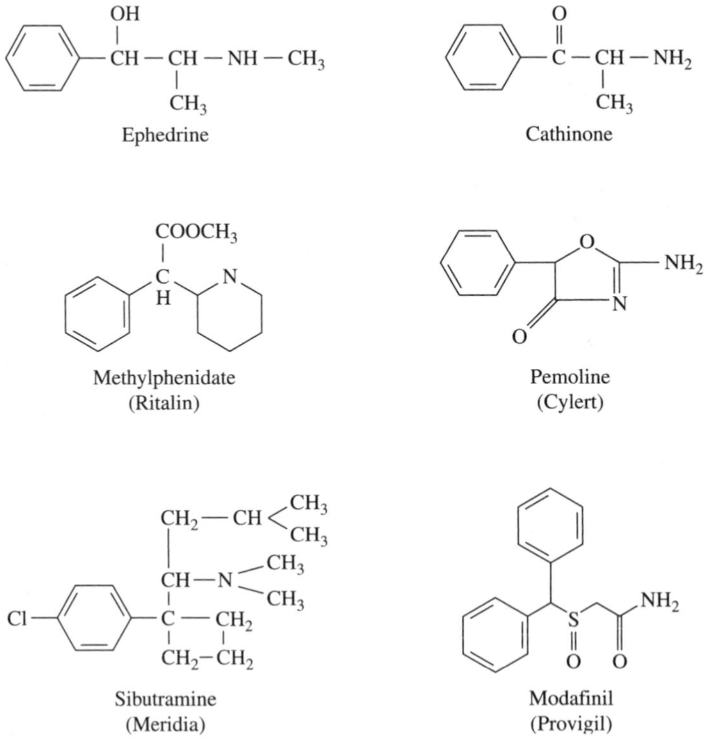

FIGURE 13.5 Structures of two naturally occurring catecholamine psychostimulants—ephedrine (from *Ephedra*, or ma-huang) and cathinone (from *Catha edulis*, or khat)]—and four synthetic noncatecholamine psychostimulants used in medicine—methylphenidate (Ritalin), pemoline (Cylert), sibutramine (Meridia), and modafinil (Provigil).

Chinese herb ma-huang), pseudoephedrine, methylphenidate, pemoline, sibutramine and the herbal substance khat.

Ephedrine today has little use in medicine other than IV use in anesthesiology to transiently increase blood pressure. Most use of ephedrine has been in herbal medicine (Chapter 19). Ephedrine acts by transiently releasing body epinephrine, a normal adrenal hormone that causes elevations in blood pressure and heart rate. Ephedrine also transiently reduces appetite. Historically, it has been incorporated into numerous herbal and dietary supplements for both energy and weight loss. Unfortunately, the drug can be toxic or even fatal when combined with other stimulant drugs such as caffeine. Pseudoephedrine is used in cough and cold medicines to relieve nasal congestion. However, as a compound used in the illicit manufacture of methamphetamine, its use has been placed under prescription-only restriction.

Methylphenidate (Ritalin) is a nonamphetamine behavioral stimulant in which the regular-release formulation has a half-life of 2 to 4 hours. Its primary medical use is in the treatment of ADHD (Chapter 10). Mechanistically, methylphenidate increases the synaptic concentration of dopamine by blocking the presynaptic dopamine transporter (a cocainelike action) and also perhaps by slightly increasing the release of dopamine (an amphetaminelike or ephedrinelike action). When methylphenidate is injected intravenously, experienced cocaine users can perceive a cocainelike or amphetaminelike rush, an action not usually experienced with oral dosage. Volkow and coworkers (1998) demonstrated that at clinically relevant doses, methylphenidate blocked more than 50 percent of the dopamine transporters 60 minutes after oral administration (Figure 13.6). They postulated

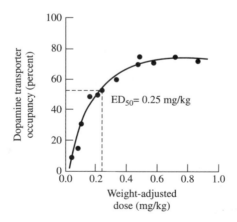

FIGURE 13.6 Levels of dopamine transporter occupancy for weight-adjusted doses of methylphenidate. Also shown is the dose required to occupy 50 percent of the dopamine transporters (ED_{50}). [From Volkow et al. (1998), p. 1327.]

that the slow uptake of methylphenidate into the brain after oral administration accounts for the low rate of positive reinforcement effects seen with use of the drug.

Although this clinical action of methylphenidate is thought to be exerted through dopaminergic increases, Gainetdinov and coworkers (1999) demonstrated in mice that lacked the gene for the dopamine transporter that methylphenidate still calmed hyperactivity in a novel environment, presumably by raising serotonin levels to balance the animal's high level of dopamine in the brain. In these animals, fluoxetine (Prozac; Chapter 7) exerted a methylphenidatelike action, presumably by also blocking the presynaptic serotonin transporter. Thus, at least in some people, ADHD may represent an imbalance between dopamine and serotonin systems.

Pemoline (Cylert) is a CNS stimulant structurally dissimilar to either methylphenidate or amphetamine (see Figure 13.5). Pemoline is presumed to reduce ADHD symptoms by potentiating CNS dopaminergic transmission. It is thought to have a lower abuse potential than does either methylphenidate or amphetamine. Its use is limited by reports of rare instances of hepatitis, necessitating close monitoring of liver function. Indeed, the risks of pemoline outweigh its usefulness in treating ADHD and the drug has been removed from the market.

Sibutramine (Meridia) is a serotonin, norepinephrine, and (to a lesser extent) dopamine reuptake inhibitor (it blocks their presynaptic transporter proteins). Sibutramine, formerly marketed as an antiobesity agent, is structurally related to amphetamine (see Figure 13.5), but it is not literally an amphetamine. Sibutramine is rapidly metabolized in the liver to active metabolites that are responsible for the drug's pharmacological actions. These metabolites reach a peak concentration in plasma in 3 to 4 hours; their half-life is 14 to 16 hours. Modest weight losses for up to a year have been reported, and the drug does not appear to have a potential for compulsive misuse. Significant increases in heart rate and blood pressure have been reported and may limit the use of the drug. Appolinario and coworkers (2002) reported that sibutramine produced complete resolution of binge eating in obese patients. Since the drug is a serotonin and norepinephrine reuptake inhibitor, it is probably an antidepressant drug, although it is not marketed for this purpose. However, in combination with other serotonin-type antidepressants, it may predispose to development of serotonin syndrome (Chapter 7).

Modafinil (Provigil; see Figure 13.5) is a nonamphetamine psychostimulant whose exact mechanism of psychostimulant action remains unclear but is thought to be unique. Modifinil may potentiate excitatory glutamate neurotransmission and inhibit the activity of GABA neurons in the cerebral cortex and the nucleus accumbens, altering the balance between glutamate and GABA transmission. It may not be associated with dependence or compulsive abuse. Modafinil is used clinically to maintain daytime wakefulness in the treatment of narcolepsy, an inherited disorder of sleep. Chapter 5 discussed the use of gamma hydroxybuyrate (GHB) to improve sleep patterns in people with narcolepsy. Note that modafinil and GHB act through vastly different mechanisms and therapeutic approaches.

Potential uses of modafinil include cognitive improvement in patients with Alzheimer's disease, use in the treatment of ADHD (Chapter 10), and potentiation of the action of antidepressant drugs (Chapter 7). The drug appears to have only minimal peripheral side effects, such as drug-induced hypertension. Modafinil is an important addition to the pharmacological treatment of narcolepsy as well as an interesting stimulant for evaluation for use in the treatment of other CNS disorders amenable to treatment with a psychostimulant. Recently, the manufacturer of modafinil has requested FDA approval for use of the active isomer of the drug, with the generic name nuvigil, in treating ADHD, under a new trade name, Sparlon. The status of approval of the isomer form is still pending.

Catha edulis is a flowering shrub in East Africa. The leaves and fresh shoots are commonly known as *khat*. Khat can be chewed (like loose tobacco) or brewed as a tea at a daily dose of up to several hundred grams. Khat has stimulant properties similar to those of amphetamine or cocaine. The active components of khat are cathinone (see Figure 13.5) and cathine (closely related in structure). Khat must be used fresh as the pharmacologically more active substance cathinone deteriorates within about 48 hours after harvest. Cathinone increases the levels of dopamine in the CNS and therefore is considered to be the primary psychostimulant in khat (Patel, 2000; Al-Hebshi and Skaug, 2005). The cathine appears to be a mild psychostimulant, comparable to caffeine in potency. Khat is being increasingly encountered as a substance of abuse in the United States and elsewhere.

STUDY QUESTIONS

1. Compare and contrast cocaine and amphetamine.

2. What is crack? What is ice?

3. Describe the three major actions of cocaine.

4. Discuss the effects of cocaine on the fetus.

5. What are some of the issues in and therapeutic approaches to treating cocaine dependence?

6. Describe the behavioral states that are observed in high-dose amphetamine users.

7. Describe the effects of amphetamine on neurotransmission, neurotransmitters, and the CNS reward system.

8. Discuss the evidence for and against methamphetamine neurotoxicity.

9. Compare and contrast psychostimulants with clinical antidepressants.

10. What is meant by the phrase "Speed kills"?

11. What is modafinil? How does it differ from amphetamine? What are its potential uses?

REFERENCES

Akiyama, K. (2006). "Longitudinal Clinical Course Following Pharmacological Treatment of Methamphetamine Psychosis Which Persists After Long-Term Abstinence." *Annals of the New York Academy of Sciences* 1074: 125–134.

Al-Hebshi, N. N., and Skaug, N. (2005). "Khat (*Catha edulis*): An Updated Review." *Addiction Biology* 10: 299–307.

Appolinario, J. C., et al. (2002). "An Open-Label Trial of Sibutramine in Obese Patients with Binge-Eating Disorder." *Journal of Clinical Psychiatry* 63: 28–30.

Barr, A. A., et al. (2006). "The Need for Speed: An Update on Methamphetamine Addiction." *Journal of Psychiatry and Neuroscience* 31: 301–313.

Bartzokis, G., et al. (1999). "Magnetic Resonance Imaging Evidence of 'Silent' Cerebrovascular Toxicity in Cocaine Dependence." *Biological Psychiatry* 45: 1203–1211.

Bowyer, J. F., et al. (2007). "A Threshold Neurotoxic Amphetamine Exposure Inhibits Parietal Cortex Expression of Synaptic-Plasticity-Related Genes." *Neuroscience* 144: 66–76.

Brodie, J. D., et al. (2003). "Treating Cocaine Addiction: From Preclinical to Clinical Trial Experience with Gamma-Vinyl GABA." *Synapse* 50: 261–265.

Bunney, E. B., et al. (2001). "Electrophysiological Effects of Cocaethylene, Cocaine, and Ethanol on Dopaminergic Neurons of the Ventral Tegmental Area." *Journal of Pharmacology and Experimental Therapeutics* 297: 696–703.

Calatayud, J., and A. Gonzalez (2003). "History of the Development and Evolution of Local Anesthesia Since the Coca Leaf." *Anesthesiology* 98: 1503–1508.

Carroll, F. I., et al. (2006). "Development of the Dopamine Transporter Selective RTI-336 as a Pharmacotherapy for Cocaine Abuse." *AAPS Journal* 8: 196–203.

Carroll, K. M., et al. (2004). "Efficacy of Disulfiram and Cognitive Behavioral Therapy in Cocaine-Dependent Outpatients: A Randomized, Placebo-Controlled Trial." *Archives of General Psychiatry* 61: 264–272.

Comer, S. D., et al. (2001). "Effects of Repeated Oral Methamphetamine Administration in Humans." *Psychopharmacology* 155: 397–404.

Dackis, C. (2004). "Recent Advances in the Pharmacotherapy of Cocaine Dependence." *Current Psychiatry Reports* 6: 323–331.

Dickerson, T. J., and Janda, K. D. (2005). "Recent Advances for the Treatment of Cocaine Abuse: Central Nervous System Immunopharmacotherapy." *AAPS Journal* 7: E579–E586.

Ernst, T., et al. (2000). "Evidence for Long-Term Neurotoxicity Associated with Methamphetamine Abuse: A ^{1}H MRS Study." *Neurology* 54: 1344–1349.

Fattore, L., et al (2007). "An Endocannabinoid Mechanism in Relapse to Drug Seeking: A Review of Animal Studies and Clinical Perspectives." *Brain Research— Brain Research Reviews* 53: 1–16.

Fechtner, R. D. et al. (2006). "Short-Term Treatment of Cocaine and/or Methamphetamine Abuse with Vigabatrin: Ocular Safety Pilot Results." *Archives of Ophthalmology* 124: 1257–1262.

Filip, M., et al. (2005). "The Serotonergic System and Its Role in Cocaine Addiction." *Pharmacological Reviews* 57: 685–700.

Frank, D. A., et al. (2001). "Growth, Development, and Behavior in Early Childhood Following Prenatal Cocaine Exposure: A Systematic Review." *Journal of the American Medical Association* 285: 1613–1625.

Gainetdinov, R. R., et al. (1999). "Role of Serotonin in the Paradoxical Calming Effect of Psychostimulants on Hyperactivity." *Science* 283: 397–401.

Gonzalez, G., et al. (2007). "Clinical Efficacy of Gabapentin Versus Tiagabine for Reducing Cocaine Use Among Cocaine Dependent Methadone-Treated Patients." *Drug and Alcohol Dependence* 87: 1–9.

Iyo, M., et al. (2004). "Neuromechanism of Developing Methamphetamine Psychosis: A Neuroimaging Study." *Annals of the New York Academy of Sciences* 1025: 288–295.

Jaworski, J. N., and D. C. Jones (2006). "The Role of CART in the Reward/ Reinforcing Properties of Psychostimulants." *Peptides* 27: 1993–2004.

Kalivas, P. W., and N. D. Volkow (2005). "The Neural Basis of Addiction: A Pathology of Motivation and Choice." *American Journal of Psychiatry* 162: 1403–1413.

Kalivas, P. W., et al. (2006). "Animal Models and Brain Circuits in Drug Addiction." *Molecular Interventions* 6: 339–344.

Keller, R. W., and A. Snyder-Keller (2000). "Prenatal Cocaine Exposure." *Annals of the New York Academy of Sciences* 909: 217–232.

Larsen, K. E., et al. (2002). "Methamphetamine-Induced Degeneration of Dopaminergic Neurons Involves Autophagy and Upregulation of Dopamine Synthesis." *Journal of Neuroscience* 22: 8951–8960.

Levin, F. R., et al. (2007). "Treatment of Cocaine Dependent Treatment Seekers with Adult ADHD: Double-Blind Comparison of Methylphenidate and Placebo." *Drug and Alcohol Dependence* 87: 20–29.

Little, B. B., et al. (1998). "Cocaine Abuse During Pregnancy." In L. C. Gilstrap and B. B. Little, eds., *Drugs and Pregnancy*, 2nd ed. (pp. 419–444). New York: Chapman & Hall.

Little, K. Y., et al. (2003). "Loss of Striatal Vesicular Monoamine Transporter Protein (VMAT2) in Human Cocaine Users." *American Journal of Psychiatry* 160: 47–55.

Lu, L., et al. (2006). "Role of ERK in Cocaine Addiction." *Trends in Neuroscience* 29: 695–703.

Martell, B. A., et al. (2005). "Vaccine Pharmacotherapy for the Treatment of Cocaine Dependence." *Biological Psychiatry* 58: 158–164.

McDonagh, J., et al. (2003). "Peripheral Retinal Dysfunction in Patients Taking Vigabatrin." *Neurology* 61: 1690–1694.

Moffett, M., et al. (2006). "Studies of Cocaine- and Amphetamine-Regulated Transcript (CART) Knockout Mice." *Peptides* 27: 2037–2045.

Mooney, M. E., et al. (2007). "Safety, Tolerability, and Efficacy of Levodopa-Carbidopa Treatment for Cocaine Dependence: Two Double-Blind, Randomized, Clinical Trials." *Drug and Alcohol Dependence* 88: 214–223.

Nordahl, T. E., et al. (2003). "Neuropsychological Effects of Chronic Methamphetamine Use on Neurotransmitters and Cognition: A Review." *Journal of Neuropsychiatry and Clinical Neurosciences* 15: 317–325.

Patel, N. B. (2000). "Mechanism of Action of Cathinone: The Active Ingredient of Khat (*Catha edulis*)." *East African Medical Journal* 77: 329–332.

Poulton, A. (2006). "Long-Term Outcomes of Stimulant Medication in Attention-Deficit Hyperactivity Disorder." *Expert Review of Neurotherapy* 6: 551–561.

Qi, Y., et al. (2006). "Australian Federal Police Seizures of Illicit Crystalline Methamphetamine (Ice) 1998–2002: Impurity Analysis." *Forensic Science International* 164: 201–210.

Quinton, M. S., and B. K. Yamamoto (2006). "Causes and Consequences of Methamphetamine and MDMA Toxicity." *AAPS Journal* 8: E337–E347.

Rebec, G. V., and W. Sun (2005). "Neuronal Substrates of Relapse to Cocaine-Seeking Behavior: Role of Prefrontal Cortex." *Journal of Experimental and Analytical Behavior* 84: 653–666.

Rocha, B. A., et al. (1998). "Increased Vulnerability to Cocaine in Mice Lacking the Serotonin-1B Receptor." *Nature* 393: 175–178.

Rounsaville, B. J. (2004). "Treatment of Cocaine Dependence and Depression." *Biological Psychiatry* 56: 803–809.

Salo, R., et al. (2007). "Attentional Control and Brain Metabolites in Methamphetamine Abusers." *Biological Psychiatry* 61: 1272–1280.

Sato, M. (1992). "A Lasting Vulnerability to Psychosis in Patients with Previous Methamphetamine Psychosis." *Annals of the New York Academy of Sciences* 654: 160–170.

Sekine, Y., et al. (2001). "Methamphetamine-Related Psychiatric Symptoms and Reduced Brain Dopamine Transporters Studied with PET." *American Journal of Psychiatry* 158: 1206–1214.

Sekine, Y., et al. (2006). "Brain Serotonin Transporter Density and Aggression in Abstinent Methamphetamine Abusers." *Archives of General Psychiatry* 63: 90–100.

Singer, L. T., et al. (2002). "Cognitive and Motor Outcomes of Cocaine-Exposed Infants." *Journal of the American Medical Association* 287: 1952–1960.

Singer, L. T., et al. (2004). "Cognitive Outcomes of Preschool Children with Prenatal Cocaine Exposure." *Journal of the American Medical Association* 291: 2448–2456.

Smith, L. M. et al. (2006). "The Infant Development, Environment, and Lifestyle Study: Effects of Prenatal Methamphetamine Exposure, Polydrug Exposure, and Poverty on Intrauterine Growth." *Pediatrics* 118: 1149–1156.

Sofuoglu, M., and T. R. Kosten (2006). "Emerging Pharmacological Strategies in the Fight Against Cocaine Addiction." *Expert Opinion on Emerging Drugs* 11: 91–98.

Sofuoglu, M., et al. (2005). "Tiagabine Affects the Subjective Responses to Cocaine in Humans." *Pharmacology, Biochemistry, and Behavior* 82: 569–573.

Sora, I., et al. (2001). "Molecular Mechanisms of Cocaine Reward: Combined Dopamine and Serotonin Transporter Knockouts Eliminate Cocaine Place Preference." *Proceedings of the National Academy of Sciences* 98: 5300–5305.

Soria, G., et al. (2005). "Lack of CB1 Cannabinoid Receptor Impairs Cocaine Self-Administration." *Neuropsychopharmacology* 30: 1670–1680.

Spencer, T., et al. (2004). "Stimulant Treatment of Adult Attention-Deficit/ Hyperactivity Disorder." *Psychiatric Clinics of North America* 27: 361–372.

Stanek, L. M. (2006). "Cocaine- and Amphetamine-Related Transcript (CART) and Anxiety." *Peptides* 27: 2005–2011.

Stein, J., et al. (2006). "Processing of Cocaine- and Amphetamine-Regulated Transcript (CART) Precursor Proteins by Prohormone Convertases (PCs) and Its Implications." *Peptides* 27: 1919–1925.

Steketee, J. D. (2005). "Cortical Mechanisms of Cocaine Sensitization." *Critical Reviews of Neurobiology* 17: 69–86.

Sutton, M. A., et al. (2003). "Extinction-Induced Upregulation in AMPA Receptors Reduces Cocaine-Seeking Behaviour." *Nature* 421: 70–75.

Toomey, R., et al. (2003). "A Twin Study of the Neuropsychological Consequences of Stimulant Abuse." *Archives of General Psychiatry* 60: 303–310.

Vocci, F. J., and Elkashef, A. (2005). "Pharmacotherapy and Other Treatments for Cocaine Abuse and Dependence." *Current Opinions in Psychiatry* 18: 265–270.

Volkow, N. D., et al. (1998). "Dopamine Transporter Occupancies in the Human Brain Induced by Therapeutic Doses of Oral Methylphenidate." *American Journal of Psychiatry* 155: 1325–1331.

Volkow, N. D., et al. (2001a). "Association of Dopamine Transporter Reduction with Psychomotor Impairment in Methamphetamine Abusers." *American Journal of Psychiatry* 158: 377–382.

Volkow, N. D., et al. (2001b). "Higher Cortical and Lower Subcortical Metabolism in Detoxified Methamphetamine Abusers." *American Journal of Psychiatry* 158: 383–389.

Volkow, N. D., et al. (2001c). "Low Level of Brain Dopamine D_2 Receptors in Methamphetamine Abusers: Association with Metabolism in the Orbitofrontal Cortex." *American Journal of Psychiatry* 158: 2015–2021.

Wang, G.-J., et al. (2004). "Partial Recovery of Brain Metabolism in Methamphetamine Abusers After Protracted Abstinence." *American Journal of Psychiatry* 161: 242–248.

Wijetunga, M., et al. (2004). "Acute Coronary Syndrome and Crystal Methamphetamine Use: A Case Series." *Hawaii Medical Journal* 63: 8–13.

Williams, J. H., and L. Ross (2007). "Consequences of Prenatal Toxin Exposure for Mental Health in Children and Adolescents: A Systematic Review." *European Child & Adolescent Psychiatry* 16: 243-253.

Wilson, L. D., et al. (2001). "Cocaine, Ethanol, and Cocaethylene Cardiotoxicity in an Animal Model of Cocaine and Ethanol Abuse." *Academic Emergency Medicine* 8: 211–222.

Xi, Z. X., et al (2006). "Cannabinoid CB1 Receptor Antagonist AM251 Inhibits Cocaine-Primed Relapse in Rats: Role of Glutamate in the Nucleus Accumbens." *Journal of Neuroscience* 26: 8531–8536.

Yamamoto, B. J., and M. G. Bankson (2006). "Amphetamine Neurotoxicity: Cause and Consequences of Oxidative Stress." *Critical Reviews in Neurobiology* 17: 87–118.

Chapter 14

Caffeine and Nicotine

CAFFEINE

Caffeine is the most commonly consumed psychoactive drug in the world; in the United States it is consumed daily by up to 80 percent of the adult population. Caffeine is found in significant concentrations in coffee, tea, cola drinks, chocolate candies and ice creams, fortified waters, and cocoa (Table 14.1). Caffeine is probably one of the most widely used stimulants in sports, with documented efficacy and safety (Magkos and Kavouras, 2005).

The average cup of coffee contains about 100 milligrams of caffeine.[1] A 12-ounce bottle of cola contains about 40 milligrams. The caffeine content of chocolate may be as high as 25 milligrams per

---

[1]The caffeine content of coffee varies widely. One hundred milligrams is often used as an average. However, among locally popular "gourmet" coffees, one company's coffee averages 200 milligrams per 8 fluid ounces. Thus, a 12-ounce cup of black coffee has 300 milligrams; the 16-ounce "grande" has 400 milligrams. Mixed coffee drinks have less caffeine because of added milk or flavorings. Another company's coffee averages 80 to 90 milligrams; the coffee of a third company has 100 to 125 milligrams of caffeine per 8 ounces. McCusker and coworkers (2003) found wide variances in caffeine content (260 to 564 milligrams) in the same 16-ounce beverage at the same outlet on 6 consecutive days.

TABLE 14.1 Caffeine content in beverages, foods, and medicines

Item	Caffeine content Average (mg)	Range
Coffee (5-ounce cup)	100	50–150
Tea (5-ounce cup)	50	25–90
Cocoa (5-ounce cup)	5	2–20
Chocolate (semisweet, baking) (1 ounce)	25	15–30
Chocolate milk (1 ounce)	5	1–10
Cola drink (12 ounces)	40	35–55
OTC stimulants (NoDoz, Vivarin)[a]	100+	
OTC analgesics (Excedrin)	65	
(Anacin, Midol, Vanquish)	33	
OTC cold remedies (Coryban-D, Triaminic)	30	
OTC diuretics (Aqua-ban)	100	

[a]OTC = over the counter.

ounce. Over-the-counter (OTC) wakefulness-promoting drugs (for example, NoDoz, Vivarin) contain as much as 200 milligrams of caffeine per tablet. Excedrin contains 75 milligrams of caffeine per tablet, Anacin about half that amount, and NoDoz 100 milligrams (the same as a cup of brewed coffee). Many herbal-based OTC products contain fairly large amounts of caffeine. Among regular caffeine users, daily intake averages between 200 and 500 milligrams, correlating with two to five cups of coffee daily. Regulatory agencies impose no restrictions on the sale or use of caffeine, nor is the human consumption of caffeine-containing beverages commonly considered to be drug abuse.

"Energy drinks" are being fortified with extra-large amounts of caffeine and may put imbibers at risk. Aimed primarily at younger people, these "ergogenic aids" are intended to enhance athletic performance and aid cognitive functioning, although high doses can result in tremors, insomnia, gastrointestinal upset, agitation, panic, and tachycardia. One of these products, Rocketst*r Zero Carb, purports to be "bigger, faster, and stronger" and to enable the imbiber to "party like a rock star." One 24-ounce can is fortified with 320 milligrams of caffeine, equivalent to four cups of coffee. Adverse reactions to such large amounts of caffeine include insomnia, agitation, and anxiety.

Pharmacokinetics

Taken orally, caffeine is rapidly and completely absorbed. Significant blood levels of caffeine are reached in 30 to 45 minutes; complete absorption occurs over the next 90 minutes. Levels in plasma peak at about 2 hours and decrease thereafter.

Caffeine is freely and equally distributed throughout the total water in the body. Thus, caffeine is found in almost equal concentrations in all parts of the body and the brain. Like all psychoactive drugs, caffeine freely crosses the placenta to the fetus.

The liver metabolizes most caffeine before the kidneys excrete it. Only about 10 percent of the drug is excreted unchanged. Caffeine's half-life of elimination varies from about 2.5 hours to 10 hours (Magkos and Kavouras, 2005). In predisposed people, a long half-life can account for nighttime wakefulness. Caffeine's half-life is extended in infants, in pregnant women, and in the elderly. During the latter part of pregnancy, the half-life of caffeine increases from 3 to 10 hours. In cigarette smokers, caffeine's half-life is shortened; however, when smoking is terminated, caffeine's half-life increases. The reduced metabolism of caffeine can result in an increase in plasma caffeine levels and may contribute to cigarette withdrawal symptoms in heavy coffee drinkers, particularly since caffeine can induce or intensify anxiety disorders, such as panic disorder (Lambert et al., 2006).

It now appears that some coffee drinkers are "slow metabolizers" and some are more rapid metabolizers. Cornelius and coworkers (2006) studied these two populations in a group of Costa Rican caffeine users and found a genetic basis for the differences in metabolism; they also found isoenzyme differences in their CYP-1A2 drug-metabolizing enzymes. In addition, slow metabolizers under the age of 50 years who were moderate- to high-level coffee drinkers were several times more likely to suffer nonfatal heart attacks than were matched controls who drank little coffee.

The structure and metabolism of caffeine are shown in Figure 14.1. The two major metabolites of caffeine, theophylline and paraxanthine, behave similarly to caffeine; a third metabolite, theobromine, does not. Caffeine is metabolized by the CYP-1A2 subgroup of hepatic drug-metabolizing enzymes. Certain SSRI-type antidepressants such as fluoxetine and fluvoxamine (Chapter 7) are potent inhibitors of CYP-1A2, and people taking these antidepressants can exhibit unexpected toxicity or intolerance to caffeine as plasma levels of caffeine rise, including de novo production of "caffeinism" (defined in the next section) with severe anxiety reactions.

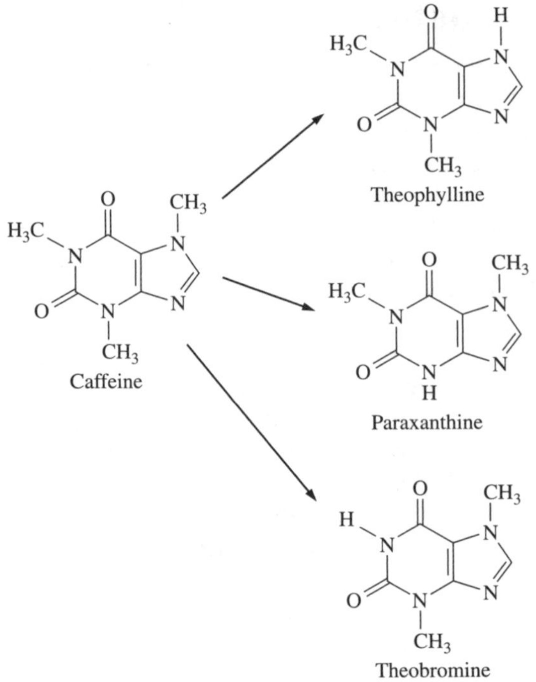

FIGURE 14.1 Metabolism of caffeine to three end products.

Pharmacological Effects

The CNS-stimulant, cardiac, respiratory, and diuretic effects of caffeine have been known for many years. Therapeutically, these effects have been used to treat a variety of disorders including asthma, narcolepsy, and migraine and as an adjunct to aspirin or other analgesics in treating headache and other pain syndromes.

Caffeine is an effective psychostimulant, ingested to obtain a rewarding effect, usually described as feeling more alert and competent. Behavioral effects seen at the lower doses of caffeine include increased mental alertness, a faster and clearer flow of thought, and wakefulness. Fatigue is reduced and the need for sleep is delayed. This increased mental awareness results in sustained intellectual effort for prolonged periods of time without significant disruption of coordinated intellectual or motor activity. Tasks that involve delicate muscular coordination and accurate timing or arithmetic skills may be adversely affected. These effects occur after oral doses as small as 100 or 200 milligrams (1 to 2 cups of coffee). Most people adjust, or titrate, their intake of caffeine to achieve these beneficial effects while minimizing undesirable effects. Heavy consumption of coffee (12 or more cups per day, or 1.5 grams of caffeine) can cause agitation, anxiety, tremors, rapid breathing, and insomnia. The lethal dose of caffeine is about 10 grams, equivalent to 100 cups of coffee.

People with anxiety disorders tend to be sensitive to the anxiogenic properties of caffeine, especially if they usually avoid caffeinated products and do not develop a tolerance to caffeine's effect. In general, people with anxiety disorders are wise to totally avoid caffeinated products.

Caffeinism is a clinical syndrome, characterized by both CNS and peripheral symptoms, produced by the overuse or overdoses of caffeine. CNS symptoms include increases in anxiety, agitation, insomnia, and mood changes. Peripheral symptoms include tachycardia, hypertension, cardiac arrhythmias, and gastrointestinal disturbances. Caffeinism is usually dose related, with doses higher than about 500 to 1000 milligrams (1 gram, or 5 to 10 cups of coffee) causing the most unpleasant effects. Cessation of caffeine ingestion resolves these symptoms. Much lower doses of caffeine produce this syndrome in sensitive people, such as people who have an underlying anxiety disorder. The usually ingested doses of caffeine do not induce panic attacks in normal people, but in people predisposed to panic disorders, the peripheral and the CNS effects of caffeine are exaggerated.

Outside the CNS, caffeine exerts significant effects, some beneficial and some adverse. Caffeine has a slight stimulant action on the heart. It increases both cardiac contractility (increases the workload of the heart) and cardiac output. Although this effect might predispose a person to hypertension (caffeine does raise blood pressure in adults prone to hypertension), caffeine also dilates the coronary arteries, providing more oxygen to the harder-working heart. As stated, slow metabolizers of caffeine who are moderate to heavy caffeine users have an increased risk of nonfatal heart attacks. Whether others can suffer cardiac problems as a result of caffeine ingestion is unclear (Rodrigues and Klein, 2006). Boiled or unfiltered coffee is associated with increased blood cholesterol levels and may increase the risk of coronary artery disease (Cornelis and El-Sohemy, 2007), although moderate levels of coffee brewed otherwise may be beneficial, perhaps due to antioxidants found in coffee. Thus, it remains controversial whether or not caffeine increases the incidence of heart disease and deaths due to cardiac disease. Certainly, people with hypertension or heart disease might do well to minimize exposure to caffeinated products, especially boiled, "French press," or unfiltered coffee. Currently, there is no evidence that coffee consumption may increase the rates or risks of cancers (Higdon and Frei, 2006).

It should be noted that caffeine exerts an opposite effect on cerebral blood vessels; it constricts these vessels, thus decreasing blood flow to the brain by about 30 percent and reducing pressure within the brain. This action can effect striking relief from headaches, especially migraines. Other physical actions of caffeine include bronchial relaxation (an antiasthmatic effect), increased secretion of gastric acid, and increased urine output.

Caffeine consumption has been associated with improved glucose tolerance and a lower risk of type 2 diabetes. The same effect has been found for decaffeinated coffee, indicating that some substance in coffee other than caffeine may be responsible. Even caffeine-induced weight loss may be responsible (Van Dam, 2006; Greenberg et al., 2006).

Mechanism of Action

Caffeine exerts a variety of effects on the CNS. In Figure 14.2, note the close structural resemblance of caffeine and a naturally occurring substance in the brain called adenosine. It should therefore not be surprising that caffeine might bind to any receptors to which adenosine binds. Caffeine does have a strong affinity for adenosine receptors, but binding is not accompanied by adenosinelike action; caffeine blocks access of adenosine to its receptors, and thus caffeine is classified as an adenosine antagonist at physiological concentrations comparable to one or more cups of coffee (Figure 14.3). In mice lacking a specific subtype of adenosine receptor, caffeine has only depressant (not stimulant) effects on behavioral activity (Ledent et al., 1997).

Since caffeine is an adenosine antagonist, a pharmacological effect of caffeine would not be expected unless adenosine receptors were tonically active under stimulation by adenosine (Magkos and Kavouras, 2005). Adenosine is a *neuromodulator* that influences the release of several neurotransmitters in the CNS. There do not appear to be discrete adenosinergic pathways in the CNS; rather, adenosinergic neurons form a diffuse system that appears to exert sedative, depressant, and anticonvulsant actions; blockade of adenosine receptors produces

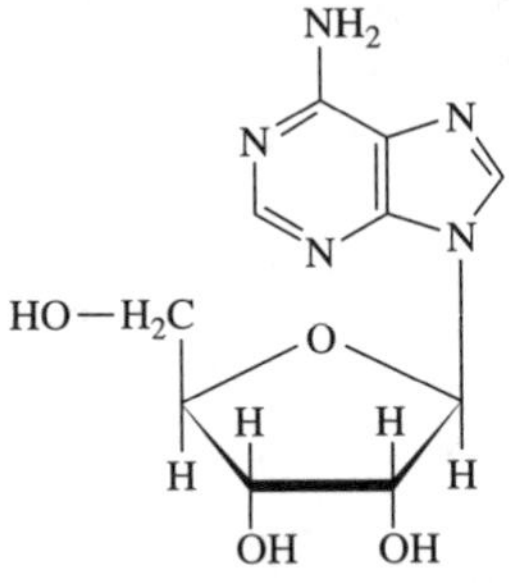

FIGURE 14.2 Structure of adenosine. Note the similarity of adenosine to caffeine (shown in Figure 14.1).

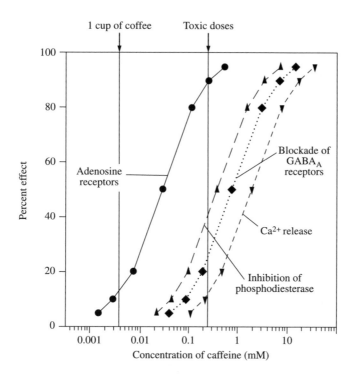

FIGURE 14.3 Adenosine receptors as site of action of caffeine. Concentration-dependent effects of caffeine to block adenosine receptors, to block GABA receptors, to inhibit calcium ion release (Ca^{2+}), and to inhibit the activity of the enzyme phosphodiesterase. At concentrations approximating 1 cup of coffee and continuing through to a toxic dose, only the adenosine receptors are affected. [From J. W. Daly and B. B. Fredholm, "Caffeine—An Atypical Drug of Dependence," *Drug and Alcohol Dependence* 51 (1998), p. 201.]

actions considered to be stimulating or anxiogenic. Adenosine receptors decrease the discharge rate of many central neurons, increasing the activity of dopaminergic, cholinergic, glutaminergic, and noradrenergic neurons. Blockade of these receptors accounts for the modest reward and the increased vigilance and mental acuity actions of caffeine. Adenosine also limits the release of acetylcholine, inhibition of which by caffeine accounts for the arousal effects of caffeine.

The positive stimulatory effects of caffeine appear in large measure to be due to blockade of the adenosine receptors that stimulate GABAergic neurons of inhibitory pathways to the dopaminergic reward system of the striatum. Therefore, caffeine may produce its behavioral effects by removing the negative modulatory effects of adenosine from dopamine receptors, thus indirectly stimulating dopaminergic activity. Caffeine does not induce a release of dopamine in the nucleus accumbens; it leads to a release of dopamine in the prefrontal cortex, which is consistent with caffeine's alerting effects with only mild behavioral reinforcing properties. In fact, caffeine appears to fulfill some of the criteria for drug dependency and shares with amphetamines and cocaine a certain specificity of action on the cerebral dopaminergic system. However, it does not act on the dopaminergic structures related to reward, motivation, and addiction. Satel (2006) recently reviewed the addictive potential of caffeine and concluded that it does not fit the common perception of drug dependency.

Reproductive Effects

Is caffeine safe during pregnancy? Caffeine, the most widely used psychotropic drug, is consumed by at least 75 percent of pregnant women via caffeinated beverages, but the safety of this habit during pregnancy is unresolved. As early as 1980, the U.S. Food and Drug Administration cautioned pregnant women to minimize their intake of caffeine. On the other hand, D'Ambrosio (1994) concluded that it is difficult to implicate caffeine, even at the highest levels of daily consumption, as a genotoxin to humans. A 1999 study by Klebanoff and coworkers concluded that the consumption of large amounts of caffeine (perhaps more than 6 to 10 cups of coffee per day) is associated with an increased risk of spontaneous abortion but that moderate consumption does not increase the risk. Wisborg and coworkers (2003) reported a study of over 18,000 pregnancies in Denmark that attempted to determine whether there was an association between coffee consumption during pregnancy and the risks of either stillbirth or infant death in the first year of life. Pregnant women who drank 8 or more cups of coffee per day during pregnancy had an increased risk of having a stillbirth compared with women who did not consume caffeine. Adjusting for smoking habits and alcohol consumption modestly reduced the risk. There was no association between caffeine consumption and infant deaths during the first year of life. The overall risk of stillbirth increased from 4 per 1000 births in nonusers of caffeine to 12 per 1000 in drinkers of 8 or more cups of coffee per day. At 4 to 7 cups per day, the risk was 7 per 1000 births.

It does not appear that caffeine itself is a human teratogen, and caffeine does not appear to affect the course of normal labor and delivery. Browne (2006) recently reviewed literature on possible adverse fetal effects and concluded that "there is no evidence to support a teratogenic effect of caffeine in humans" (p. 324). Higdon and Frei (2006) stated: "Currently available evidence suggests that it may be prudent for pregnant women to limit coffee consumption to 3 cups per day, ingesting no more than 300 milligrams per day of caffeine to exclude any increased probability of spontaneous abortion or impaired fetal growth" (p. 101). This limit certainly seems reasonable.

Tolerance and Dependence

Chronic use of caffeine, even in regular daily doses as low as 100 milligrams, is associated with habituation and tolerance, and discontinuation may produce low-grade withdrawal symptoms. People who drink a great deal of coffee complain of headache (the most common symptom), drowsiness, fatigue, and a generally negative mood state on withdrawal from caffeine. Withdrawal symptoms typically begin slowly, maximize after 1 or 2 days, and cease within a few days; readministering caffeine rapidly relieves withdrawal symptoms. Other reported withdrawal signs include impaired intellectual and motor performance, difficulty with concentration, drug (caffeine) craving, and other psychological complaints. Greden and Walters (1997) wrote:

> Caffeine . . . will continue to be the norm in most people. However, caffeinism and caffeine withdrawal also continue to be common and clinically important but unrecognized, underdiagnosed even when recognized, and untreated in many treatment settings. . . . Clinicians who actively consider the diagnosis of caffeinism in their patients will be surprised at how many afflicted subjects are identified, impressed at how many are helped by removal of the offending agent, and pleased to know that almost all are grateful. (p. 305)

NICOTINE

Nicotine is one of the three most widely used psychoactive drugs in our society; the others are caffeine and ethyl alcohol. Despite the fact that nicotine has no therapeutic applications in medicine, its widespread use and its well-defined toxicity give it immense importance. Nicotine and the other ingredients in tobacco are responsible for a wide variety of health problems, including the deaths of more than 1100 Americans every day. Every year, 440,000 Americans and 4.3 million people worldwide die prematurely as a result of cigarette smoking. Approximately 900,000 people in the United States become addicted to smoking each year. Smoking is now the leading cause of preventable death in the United States and the single most important cause of morbidity and premature mortality worldwide. Interestingly, nicotine-dependent people who are psychiatrically ill consume about 70 percent of all cigarettes smoked, at least in the United States (Grant et al., 2004). Cigarette smoking is also common in people of low socioeconomic classes: smoking prevalence among Medicaid recipients is about 40 percent greater than the prevalence in the overall U.S. adult population. Therefore, Medicaid recipients are disproportionately affected by tobacco-related disabilities and diseases (Centers for Disease Control and Prevention, 2006).

Prior to about the mid-1960s, cigarette smoking was considered chic. Today, after more than 45 years of U.S. government reports on the adverse health consequences of cigarettes, cigarette smoking is being increasingly shunned as unhealthy and unwise. Nevertheless, each day 6000 American teenagers try their first cigarette and 3000 children become regular smokers; almost 1000 of them will eventually die from diseases related to smoking. Also, 9 in 10 smokers become addicted before age 21. Today, in the United States, 3 million adolescents are smokers. Advertisements for cigarettes still appeal to children, and, in subtle ways, the depiction of smoking as okay continues.

On the positive side, half of all people who have ever smoked cigarettes have quit, and the proportion of American adults who smoke fell from 50 percent in 1965 to 25 percent in 1998. About 1 million potential deaths have been averted or postponed by people who have quit smoking. Millions more deaths will be avoided or postponed in the twenty-first century. More than 30 years ago, the Surgeon General of the United States identified smoking as the major preventable cause of death and disability, and this finding will probably continue to be the case. In this discussion, it is important to note the following:

- Nicotine is the primary active ingredient in tobacco.
- Nicotine is only one of about 4000 compounds released by the burning of cigarette tobacco.
- Nicotine accounts only for the acute pharmacological effects of smoking and for the dependence on cigarettes. The adverse, long-term cardiovascular, pulmonary, and carcinogenic effects of cigarettes are related to other compounds contained in the product.
- Although nicotine itself may have some adverse effects, its delivery device (the tobacco cigarette) is responsible for much of its toxicity.

Pharmacokinetics

Nicotine is readily absorbed from every site on or in the body, including the lungs, buccal and nasal mucosa, skin, and gastrointestinal tract. Easy and complete absorption forms the basis for the recreational abuse of smoked or chewed tobacco, as well as the medical use of nicotine (in treating nicotine dependency) in chewing gums, nasal sprays, transdermal skin patches, and smokeless inhalers.

Nicotine is suspended in cigarette smoke in the form of minute particles (tars), and it is quickly absorbed into the bloodstream from the lungs when the smoke is inhaled, although absorption is much slower than once thought and arterial concentrations of nicotine rise rather slowly. It is likely that blood rapidly saturates with nicotine, and blood leaving the lungs (to the left side of the heart) can carry only a modest amount of drug. Thus, the arterial concentration rises slowly, even though blood carried to the brain at the initiation of smoking is nearly saturated with nicotine, accounting for the early "rush" perceived with the first cigarette.

Most cigarettes contain between 0.5 and 2.0 milligrams of nicotine, depending on the brand. Only about 20 percent (between 0.1 and 0.4 milligram) of the nicotine in a cigarette is actually inhaled and absorbed into the smoker's bloodstream; the hepatic enzyme CYP-2A6 rapidly metabolizes the remainder. People in whom the CYP-2A6 enzyme is absent (or inhibited by certain drugs) have higher blood levels of nicotine and lower levels of its metabolite. A recent study reports that because of improved cigarette design, "smoke nicotine yield" has increased by about 11 percent over the past 7 years, increasing the addictive potential of cigarettes (Harvard School of Public Health, 2007).

A smoker can readily avoid acute toxicity because inhalation as a route of administration offers exceptional controllability of the dose. The user-controlled frequency of breaths, the depth of inhalation, the time the smoke is held in the lungs, and the total numbers of cigarettes smoked all allow the smoker to regulate the rate of drug intake and thus control the blood level of nicotine. The pharmacokinetic goals of nicotine administration were summarized by Sellers (1998):

> Tobacco smoking is a complex but highly regulated behavior that has as its goal the maintenance of steady-state brain levels of the highly addictive psychoactive agent nicotine. Smokers "self-regulate" the level of nicotine in their system to produce desired effects (e.g., relaxation, increased concentration) and to avoid unpleasant adverse effects associated with too high (e.g., dizziness) or too low concentrations (e.g., desire to smoke or withdrawal). (p. 179)

Smokers wake in the morning in a state of nicotine deficiency. Characteristically, they will smoke one or more cigarettes fairly rapidly to achieve a blood level of about 15 milligrams per liter and continue smoking through the day to maintain this level. The smoker does not behave this way consciously, but the behavior occurs nevertheless. The elimination half-life of nicotine in a chronic smoker is about 2 hours, necessitating frequent administration of the drug to avoid withdrawal symptoms or drug craving. When nicotine is administered orally in the form of snuff, chewing tobacco, or gum, blood levels of nicotine are comparable to the levels achieved by smoking.

Nicotine is quickly and thoroughly distributed throughout the body, rapidly penetrating the brain, crossing the placental barrier, and appearing in all bodily fluids, including breast milk. There are no barriers in the body to the distribution of nicotine.

The liver metabolizes approximately 80 to 90 percent of the nicotine administered to a person either orally or by smoking before the

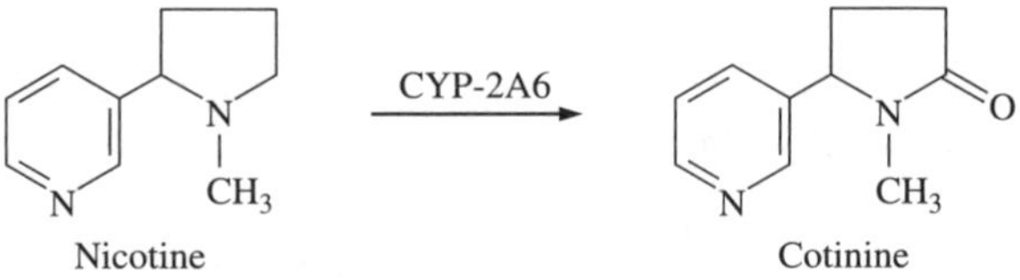

FIGURE 14.4 Structures of nicotine and its metabolite cotinine.

kidneys excrete it. The primary metabolite of nicotine is *cotinine* (Figure 14.4), and this substance serves as a marker of both tobacco use and exposure to environmental smoke.

Pharmacological Effects

Nicotine is the only pharmacologically active drug in tobacco smoke apart from carcinogenic tars. It exerts powerful effects on the brain, the spinal cord, the peripheral nervous system, the heart, and various other body structures.

Effects on the Brain

In the early stages of smoking, nicotine causes nausea and vomiting by stimulating both the vomiting center in the brain stem and the sensory receptors in the stomach. Tolerance to this effect develops rapidly. Nicotine stimulates the hypothalamus to release a hormone, antidiuretic hormone, which causes fluid retention. Nicotine reduces the activity of afferent nerve fibers coming from the muscles, leading to a reduction in muscle tone. This action may be involved (at least partially) in the relaxation a person may experience as a result of smoking. Nicotine also reduces weight gain, probably by reducing appetite.

Nicotine produces multiple actions in the CNS, resulting in increases in psychomotor activity, cognitive functioning, sensorimotor performance, attention, and memory consolidation. Rose and coworkers (2003) reported that nicotine increases blood flow to the CNS structures that mediate arousal and reward, suggesting a link between activation of these structures and the positive motivational effects of nicotine. Brody and coworkers (2002) reported that exposure to cues related to cigarette smoking increased brain activity in areas associated with arousal, compulsive behaviors, sensory integration, and episodic memory. Areas included the orbitofrontal cortex, prefrontal cortex, and anterior insula (a region of brain implicated in conscious urges). Naqvi and coworkers (2007) recently demonstrated that smokers with brain damage involving the insula were more likely than smokers with brain injury not involving the insula to undergo a disruption of smoking addiction. Damage involving the insula was characterized by the "ability to quit smoking easily, immediately, without relapse, and without persistence of the urge to smoke," suggesting that "the insula is a critical neural substrate in the addiction to smoking" (p. 531).

Nicotine improves performance in a variety of cognitive tasks, such as vigilance and rapid information processing, probably a reflection of activation of frontal cortical executive functioning (Rose et al., 2003). The beneficial effects of nicotine seem to be greatest for tasks requiring working memory rather than long-term memory. Smokers often state that they will smoke a cigarette before doing a complex task that requires attention and arousal, perhaps combining the drug's anxiolytic action with its stimulant action. The brain regions activated by nicotine include areas involved in cognition, working memory, attention, motivation, mood and emotion (frontal lobes and cingulate cortex), and behavioral arousal and vigilance (locus coeruleus).

Several reports note an antidepressant effect of nicotine as well as the comorbidity of depression and cigarette use. Salin-Pascual and coworkers (1996), who first noted a high frequency of cigarette smoking among people with major depression, found that, in nonsmokers, transdermal nicotine patches produced remarkable improvements in depression (Figure 14.5). They postulated that the high rate of smoking among depressed people might, in part, represent an attempt at self-medication to assist in dealing with some of their depressive

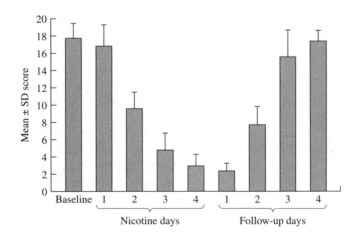

FIGURE 14.5 Hamilton Rating Scale for Depression ratings of 10 depressed patients before, during, and after administration of nicotine patches. A significant reduction was observed on the second day of nicotine patches and continued until the second follow-up day. [From Salin-Pascual et al. (1996), p. 388.]

symptoms. In agreement with this concept, Fergusson and colleagues (1996), in a study of 16-year-olds, reported:

> There was evidence of clear comorbidity between depressive disorders and nicotine dependence in this cohort of 16-year-olds; subjects with depression had odds of nicotine dependence that were more than 4.5 times the odds for those without depression. This relationship was similar for male and female subjects. These results suggest that comorbidities between nicotine dependence and depression are well established by the age of 16 years. (p. 1047)

Riggs and coworkers (1999) noted that most of the risk for adolescent smoking, as well as the subsequent development of non-tobacco substance involvement, is mediated through the presence of conduct disorder. Additional comorbidity, such as ADHD and depression, adds to the already high risk of smoking imparted by conduct disorder. This study highlights the contribution of comorbidity to smoking initiation and the need for coordinated assessment and treatment of smoking cessation along with concurrent treatment of other drug use and psychiatric comorbidity such as ADHD and major depression in adolescents.

Anda and coworkers (1999), in a retrospective survey of over 9000 adults, found a strong relationship between smoking behaviors and adverse childhood experiences, including emotional, physical, and sexual abuse; spouse abuse; parental separation or divorce; and growing up with a substance-abusing, mentally ill, or incarcerated household member. At least one of these experiences was listed by 63 percent of respondents. As the number of adverse experiences increased, the likelihood of being an early and a current smoker increased, as did the likelihood of being currently depressed. The authors speculated that for these people cigarette smoking may provide a mood-elevating effect and that "unconscious selection of cigarette use could occur in situations of chronic distress, such as depression" (p. 1657). How conduct disorder and adult ADHD fit into this pattern was not addressed.

Since depression and a propensity to smoke nicotine-containing cigarettes may be closely linked, does cessation of smoking in patients with a history of depression lead to relapse to depressive episodes? Tsoh and coworkers (2000) and Glassman and coworkers (2001) addressed this issue and noted that cessation of smoking placed depressed patients at risk of relapse, at least over a one-year period post cessation (Figure 14.6). This risk needs to be kept in mind during treatment for smoking cessation in patients with a history of depression or dysthymia.

Nicotine exerts a potent behavior-reinforcing action, especially in the early phases of drug use. The reinforcing action of nicotine

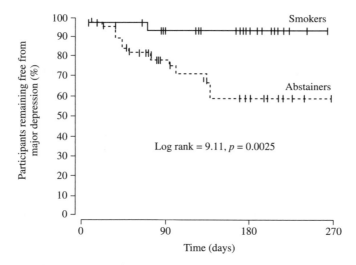

FIGURE 14.6 Time (in days) for people who were smokers and had a history of major depression to relapse to an episode of depression. Two groups of depressed patients were studied. One group (solid line) of 34 smokers continued to smoke and few relapsed. The second group of 42 patients (dashed line) abstained from smoking, and almost 50 percent experienced a depressive episode within 4 months of smoking cessation. [From Glassman et al. (2001), p. 1931.]

involves indirect activation of midbrain dopamine neurons. In the veteran smoker, this reinforcing action diminishes, and the user smokes primarily to relieve or avoid withdrawal symptoms. Spring and coworkers (2003) studied the rewarding effects of cigarette smoking in schizophrenic patients, depressed patients, and patients with no psychiatric history. While all three groups of patients recognized the drawbacks associated with smoking, schizophrenic and depressed smokers perceived more benefits than did nonpatients and found cigarettes more appealing than alternative rewards. Thus, these two groups of patients found that smoking offered ongoing rewards while patients without a mental health history did not. This may be important for the tailoring of smoking withdrawal programs to different patient populations.

Some of the acute effects and motivational responses elicited by nicotine can be modulated by the endogenous cannabinoid system (Chapter 17), which argues for the existence of a physiological interaction between the nicotine and the cannabinoid systems (Gonzalez et al., 2002). Similarly, there is close association between the nicotine and the opioid narcotic receptor systems, particularly in the context of nicotine addiction (McGehee, 2006). Much remains to be learned about these interactions.

Effects on the Body

In addition to its effects on the CNS, normal doses of nicotine can increase heart rate, blood pressure, and cardiac contractility. In nonatherosclerotic coronary arteries, nicotine initiates vasodilation, increasing blood flow to meet the increased oxygen demand of the heart muscle. In atherosclerotic coronary arteries (which cannot dilate), however, cardiac ischemia can result when the oxygen supply fails to meet the oxygen demand created by the drug's cardiac stimulation. This occurrence can precipitate angina or myocardial infarction (heart attack). Importantly, cessation of smoking reduces long-term cardiac mortality.

> A substantial progressive decrease in the mortality rates among nonsmokers over the past half century (due to prevention and improved treatment of disease) has been wholly outweighed among cigarette smokers by a progressive increase in the smoker vs. nonsmoker death rate ratio due to earlier and more intensive use of cigarettes. Among the men born around 1920, prolonged cigarette smoking from early adult life tripled age-specific mortality rates, but cessation at age 50 halved the hazard, and cessation at age 30 avoided almost all of it. (Doll et al., 2004, p. 1519)

Mechanism of Action

Nicotine exerts virtually all its CNS and peripheral effects by activating certain specific acetylcholine receptors (nicotinic receptors). In the peripheral nervous system, activation of these receptors causes an increase in blood pressure and heart rate, causes release of epinephrine (adrenaline) from the adrenal glands, and increases the tone, secretions, and activity of the gastrointestinal tract.

In the CNS, the nicotine-sensitive acetylcholine receptors are widely distributed and may be located on the presynaptic nerve terminals of dopamine-, acetylcholine-, and glutamine-secreting neurons. Activation of nicotinic receptors by nicotine facilitates the release of these transmitters and increases their actions in the brain.

Nicotine increases dopamine levels in the mesocorticolimbic system involving the ventral tegmentum, nucleus accumbens, and forebrain. This increase accounts for the behavioral reinforcement, stimulant, antidepressant, and addictive properties of the drug.

The increased acetylcholine resulting from nicotine administration contributes to the cognitive potentiation and memory facilitation properties of the drug. It may also be responsible for the arousal effects commonly seen with smoking. It is at least theoretically possible that nicotine (if administered other than by cigarette smoking) might have some use in delaying the onset of some of the cognitive deficits seen in Alzheimer's disease. Finally, the facilitation of glutaminergic neurotransmission might contribute to the improvement in memory functioning seen in nicotine users.

Tolerance and Dependence

Nicotine does not appear to induce any pronounced degree of biological tolerance. On the other hand, nicotine clearly induces both physiological and psychological dependence in a majority of smokers (Breslau et al., 2001; Hughes, 2001). Only a minority appears capable of abrupt cessation of smoking without abstinence symptoms, and even they are prone to craving and relapse. As early as 1988, the Surgeon General of the United States (U.S. Department of Health and Human Services, 1988) came to the following conclusions:

- Cigarettes and other forms of tobacco are addicting.
- Nicotine is the drug in tobacco that causes addiction.
- The pharmacological and behavioral processes that determine tobacco addiction are similar to those that determine addiction to drugs such as heroin and cocaine.
- More than 300,000 cigarette-addicted Americans die yearly as a consequence of their addiction. [Today this number approaches 440,000 per year.]

Despite all the verbal exchanges between public, regulatory, medical, political, and industry sources, the scientific case that nicotine is addictive is overwhelming:

> Patterns of use by smokers and the remarkable intractability of the smoking habit point to compulsive use as the norm. Studies in both animal and human subjects have shown that nicotine can function as a reinforcer, albeit under a more limited range of conditions than with some other drugs of abuse. In drug discrimination paradigms, there is some cross-generalization between nicotine on the one hand, and amphetamine and cocaine on the other. A well-defined withdrawal syndrome has been delineated which is alleviated by nicotine replacement. Nicotine replacement also enhances outcomes in smoking cessation, roughly doubling success rates. In total, the evidence clearly identifies nicotine as a powerful drug of addiction, comparable to heroin, cocaine, and alcohol. (Stolerman and Jarvis, 1995, p. 2)

Withdrawal from cigarettes is characterized by an abstinence syndrome that is usually not life-threatening. Abstinence symptoms include a severe craving for nicotine, irritability, anxiety, anger, difficulty in concentrating, restlessness, impatience, increased appetite, weight gain, and insomnia. The period of withdrawal may be intense and persistent, often lasting for many months. The difficulty in handling cigarette dependence is illustrated by the fact that cigarette smokers who seek treatment for other drug and alcohol problems often find it harder to quit cigarette smoking than to give up the other drugs. Even Sigmund Freud continued his cigar habit (20 per day) until death, in spite of an endless series of operations for mouth and jaw cancer (the jaw was eventually totally removed), persistent heart problems that were exacerbated by smoking, and numerous attempts at quitting.

Abstinent smokers displaying signs of withdrawal often tend to increase their caffeine (coffee) consumption; blood caffeine levels increase and remain elevated for as long as 6 months. The symptoms of nicotine withdrawal, caffeine withdrawal, and caffeine toxicity are similar enough to be confused; symptoms of nicotine withdrawal may be a mixture of nicotine withdrawal and caffeine toxicity.

A recent report from the Harvard School of Public Health (2007) clearly documents that cigarette manufacturers have increased the nicotine content in all types and brands of cigarettes by about 11 percent over a recent 7-year period. The increased amount of drug in the delivery product (cigarettes) must create an increased addictive potential of continued smoking.

Toxicity

As discussed, both the acute pharmacological effects and the withdrawal signs seen on cessation of smoking result from the nicotine in tobacco. The tar in tobacco is mainly responsible for the diseases associated with long-term tobacco use. Of the 440,000 deaths of people in the United States who die prematurely each year from tobacco use, 82,000 are caused by noncancerous lung diseases, 115,000 are caused by lung cancer, 30,000 are caused by cancers of other body organs, and more than 200,000 result from heart and vascular diseases. A person's life is shortened 14 minutes for every cigarette smoked. In other words, a person who smokes two packs of cigarettes a day for 20 years loses about 13 or 14 years of his or her life.

More than 50 million people (one out of every five Americans) alive today will die prematurely from the effects of smoking cigarettes. Cigarette smoking, the nation's greatest public health hazard, is the nation's most preventable cause of premature death, illness, and disability. For each of the approximately 22 billion packs of cigarettes sold yearly in the United States, $3.45 was spent on medical care attributable to smoking, and $3.73 in productivity losses were incurred, for a total cost of $7.18 for each and every pack smoked. The total economic toll exceeds $157 billion each year in the United States—$75 billion in direct medical costs and $82 billion in lost productivity (Centers for Disease Control and Prevention, 2004).

Cardiovascular Disease

The carbon monoxide in smoke decreases the amount of oxygen delivered to the heart muscle, while nicotine increases the amount of work the heart must do (by increasing the heart rate and blood pressure). Both carbon monoxide and nicotine increase the incidence of atherosclerosis (narrowing) and thrombosis (clotting) in the coronary arteries. These three actions (and others as well) seem to underlie the dramatic increase in the risk of death from coronary heart disease in smokers compared to nonsmokers (Teo et al.,2006). Cigarette smokers manifest a 50 percent increase in the progression of atherosclerosis when compared with people who have never smoked (Figure 14.7).

Besides occurring in the coronary arteries, atherosclerosis occurs in other arteries as well, most notably the aorta (in the abdomen), the carotid arteries (in the neck), and the femoral and other arteries of the

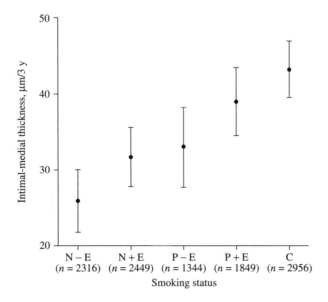

FIGURE 14.7 Mean and 95 percent confidence intervals of three-year progression in the wall thickness of the carotid artery, shown by smoking status category, after adjustment for demographic characteristics, cardiovascular risk factors, and life-style variables. N = nonsmoker. P = past smoker. C = current smoker. +E = with exposure to environmental tobacco smoke. –E = without exposure to environmental tobacco smoke. [From G. Howard et al., "Cigarette Smoking and Progression of Atherosclerosis: The Atherosclerosis Risk in Communities (ARIC) Study," *Journal of the American Medical Association* 279 (1998), p. 122.]

legs. Cigarette-induced occlusion of these vessels blocks the blood flow to important body organs and results in ischemic damage, strokes, and other disorders, causing great discomfort and disability and necessitating continuing and often futile surgical interventions.

Pulmonary Disease

In the lungs, chronic smoking results in a smoker's syndrome, characterized by difficulty in breathing, wheezing, chest pain, lung congestion, and increased susceptibility to infections of the respiratory tract. Cigarette smoking impairs ventilation and greatly increases the risk of emphysema (a form of irreversible lung damage). Smoke exposure also reduces the efficacy of the immune defense mechanisms in the lungs. About 9 million Americans suffer from cigarette-induced chronic bronchitis and emphysema. In fact, 70 percent of pulmonary diseases and deaths are tobacco related; 57,000 deaths per year result from emphysema alone.

Cancer

Although nicotine itself is not carcinogenic, the relationship between smoking and cancer is now beyond question. Cigarette smoking is the major cause of lung cancer in both men and women, causing approximately 112,000 deaths in the United States every year. More women today die from cigarette-induced lung cancer than die from breast cancer, a remarkable testament to the carcinogenicity of cigarettes. Harris and coworkers (2004) followed 940,000 male and female smokers and nonsmokers for 6 years and concluded that the risk of dying from lung cancer was the same for smokers of very low-tar, low-tar, and medium-tar cigarettes. Risk increased only in smokers of very high-tar, non-filtered cigarettes. Only smokers who quit smoking and people who never smoked had a significantly lower risk of lung cancer. Interestingly, smokers who switch from cigarettes to spit (chewing) tobacco continue to have higher risks of dying from major tobacco-related diseases than do former smokers who quit using tobacco entirely (Henley et al., 2007).

Smoking is also a major cause of cancers of the mouth, voice box, and throat. Concomitant alcohol ingestion greatly increases the incidence of these problems. In addition, cigarette smoking is a primary cause of more than 50 percent of the nearly 10,000 deaths every year that result from bladder cancer; it is a primary cause of pancreatic cancer, and it increases the risk of cancer of the uterine cervix twofold. Of all cancer deaths in the United States, 30 percent (154,000 annually) would be prevented if no one smoked.

There has been thought that early screening for lung cancer [using computerized tomography (CT) scans] might identify cigarette-induced lung cancers at an early stage, allowing for early diagnosis and surgical treatment. Bach and coworkers (2007) recently demonstrated that while this may be true, such early detection and lung removal surgery did not result in any meaningful reduction in the risk of death from the cancer.

Effects of Passive Smoke

In 1986, the Surgeon General of the United States (C. Everett Koop, M.D.) released the first Surgeon General's report on the health consequences of being exposed to the smoke of cigarettes smoked by other people (U.S. Department of Health and Human Services, 1986). Twenty years later, a second report was released (U.S. Department of Health and Human Services, 2006). It documents that in 2005, exposure to secondhand smoke killed more than 3000 adult nonsmokers from lung cancer, 46,000 from coronary heart disease, and 430 newborns from sudden infant death syndrome. Secondhand smoke also causes nonfatal health concerns such as coughing, phlegm, and reduced lung function. Most nonsmokers feel that secondhand smoke is harmful and that nonsmokers should be protected in the workplace.

Policies prohibiting workplace smoking have many benefits; they protect nonsmokers from environmental exposure, they reduce tobacco use by smokers, and they change public attitudes about tobacco use from acceptable to unacceptable.

Effects During Pregnancy

About 1 million babies in the United States are born each year after prenatal cigarette smoke exposure from maternal smoking; this number does not include involuntary maternal exposure to passive smoke (Ng and Zelikoff, 2007). Cigarette smoking adversely affects the developing fetus, leading to increases in the rates of spontaneous abortion, stillbirth, early postpartum death, and preterm deliveries. The risk of intrauterine growth retardation is increased 40 percent, and low birth weights are common, although the weight of a smoker's low-birth-weight offspring usually rises to normal at about 18 months of age. Even women exposed to passive smoke inhalation have low-birth-weight children. More than 2000 infant deaths per year are attributed to maternal smoking. Respiratory diseases, such as asthma, are commonly observed in offspring. Sudden infant death syndrome (SIDS), various immunological diseases, and other medical problems have all been implicated, with various levels of confirmatory data (U.S. Department of Health and Human Services, 2006, Chapter 5).

Cigarette smoking reduces oxygen delivery to the developing fetus, causing a variable degree of fetal hypoxia, which can result in long-term intellectual and physical deficiencies. Milberger and co-workers (1996) presented evidence suggesting that school-age children born of mothers who smoked during pregnancy have lower intelligence quotients (IQs) and an increased prevalence of ADHD when compared with children born of nonsmoking mothers. Thus, maternal smoking may well cause persistent neurobehavioral deficits. Indeed, maternal smoking results in offspring at increased risk of developing later childhood externalizing problems, including ADHD, oppositional defiant behavior, and conduct disorder.

Therapy for Nicotine Dependence

The mid-1990s saw dramatic advances in the recognition of nicotine dependence as a biological reality and in its treatment. Perhaps the first and most important advance at that time was the development and clinical application of *nicotine replacement therapies,* specifically nicotine-containing gum, transdermal nicotine-containing patches, and nicotine-containing nasal sprays and inhalers. Later in the 1990s came the identification of the antidepressant drug bupropion (Wellbutrin, Zyban) as a substance that could reduce cigarette cravings and relieve the distress of comorbid depression. The most recent advance has been the introduction of a new *partial nicotine receptor agonist,* varenicline (trade name Chantix).

In 1996, the first clinical practice guidelines for the treatment of nicotine-dependent people was published. This was followed by a year 2000 guideline titled "A Clinical Practice Guideline for Treating Tobacco Use and Dependence, A U.S. Public Health Service Report" (Tobacco Use and Dependence Clinical Practice Guideline Panel, 2000). This report concluded:

- Tobacco dependence is a chronic condition that warrants repeated treatment until long-term or permanent abstinence is achieved.

- Effective treatments for tobacco dependence exist and all tobacco users should be offered those treatments.

- Clinicians and health care delivery systems must institutionalize the consistent identification, documentation, and treatment of every tobacco user at every visit.

- Brief tobacco dependence treatment is effective and every tobacco user should be offered at least brief treatments.

- There is a strong dose-response relationship between the intensity of tobacco dependence counseling and its effectiveness.

- Three types of counseling were found to be especially effective: practical counseling, social support as part of treatment, and social support arranged outside treatment.

- Tobacco dependence treatments are cost effective relative to other medical and disease prevention interventions; as such, all health insurance plans should include as a reimbursed benefit the counseling and pharmacotherapeutic treatments identified as being effective.

- Six first-line pharmacotherapies for tobacco dependence are effective: nicotine gum, nicotine inhaler, nicotine nasal spray, nicotine patch, sustained-release bupropion, and varenicline. The first four are replacement therapy and the last two are drugs to reduce craving and relapse. At least one of these six medications should be prescribed in the absence of contraindications.

Rigotti (2002) reviewed the efficacy of both nicotine replacement therapies and bupropion. She first noted that combining any pharmacotherapy and counseling was more effective than either alone. The efficacy of behavioral interventions combined with pharmacotherapy has been verified by other researchers, including Ranney and colleagues (2007) and Stead and coworkers (2006). Unfortunately, interventional therapies have had only modest effects for young people who smoke (Grimshaw and Stanton, 2006; Thomas and Perera, 2006). Coleman (2004) and Fiore and coworkers (2004) discuss the effectiveness of even very brief interventions and advice.

The objective of nicotine replacement therapy is to replace smoking cigarettes as a source of the nicotine and replace the cigarette with a patch, gum, inhaler, or nasal spray. Once the cigarette is replaced, the dose of nicotine in the replacement product can be slowly reduced and then eliminated. Each product has demonstrable efficacy in randomized, controlled trials. Nicotine-containing patches double the long-term smoking cessation rate, while nicotine gum increases cessation rates by 50 to 70 percent. For heavy smokers, gum containing 4 milligrams of nicotine per piece is more effective than gum containing 2 milligrams. All forms of replacement therapy indicate similar efficacy at 12 weeks; compliance is highest for the patch, intermediate for the gum, and lowest for the vapor inhaler and nasal spray. Figure 14.8 illustrates the plasma nicotine levels achieved after a smoker has smoked a cigarette, received nicotine nasal spray, begun chewing nicotine gum, or applied a nicotine patch.

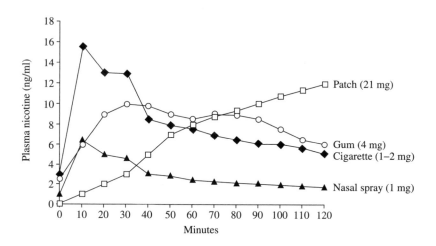

FIGURE 14.8 Plasma nicotine levels after a smoker has smoked a cigarette, received nicotine nasal spray, begun chewing nicotine gum, or applied a nicotine patch. The amount of nicotine in each product is shown in parentheses. The pattern produced by use of a nicotine inhaler (not shown) is similar to that for nicotine gum. [From Rigotti (2002), p. 510.]

Although nicotine-containing medications are known to help people stop smoking, not everyone is helped by them or wants to use them. This prompted the evaluation of antidepressant drugs as smoking cessation agents. A recent review (Hughes et al., 2007) concluded that the antidepressants bupropion (Wellbutrin, Zyban) and nortriptyline (Pamelor) double a person's chances of giving up smoking and have an acceptable rate of side effects. Unfortunately, selective serotonin reuptake inhibitor antidepressants (SSRIs) such as fluoxetine (Prozac) are not effective. Of the two shown to be effective, bupropion is the most studied and most widely used. Bupropion delays smoking relapse and also results in less weight gain. Interestingly, bupropion and nortriptyline appear to work equally well in both depressed and nondepressed smokers; this suggests that these drugs help smokers quit in some way other than as antidepressants. It is not known whether or not norepinephrine reuptake inhibitors such as atomoxetine (Strattera) are efficacious. Figure 14.9 offers a smoking cessation strategy that may be used by health care workers in compliance with the recommendations of the U.S. Public Health Service.

In late 2006, a new approach to treating nicotine dependence was introduced (Cahill et al., 2007). Varenicline (Chantix; Figure 14.10) is pharmacologically classified as a *partial nicotine receptor agonist*. The drug binds weakly to the receptor, which normally binds nicotine strongly. It is therefore weaker than nicotine, partially stimulating the receptor: it reduces withdrawal symptoms but blocks the access of nicotine to the receptor, making nicotine less of a stimulant. Since nicotine indirectly induces the release of dopamine (from whence follows its stimulant and behaviorally reinforcing action), varenicline enables a low-level release of dopamine, offering some agonist effect at dopamine receptors. However, by blocking nicotine's access to its receptors, continued smoking is less satisfying, which reduces a person's need to smoke and may help the person to quit completely and maintain abstinence (Tonstad et al., 2006; Onchen et al., 2006; Keating and Siddiqui, 2006; Zierler-Brown and Kyle, 2007).

Compared with bupropion, varenicline was significantly more effective at maintaining abstinence (Jorenby et al., 2006; Gonzales et al., 2006; Nides et al., 2006). In one study of over 1000 smokers, Jorenby and colleagues (2006) compared varenicline titrated to a dose of 1 milligram twice daily with bupropion (Wellbutrin, Zyban) titrated to a dose of 150 milligrams twice daily. The results are summarized in Figures 14.11 and 14.12 (pages 504 and 505). As shown, varenicline was significantly more effective than bupropion in achieving initial abstinence

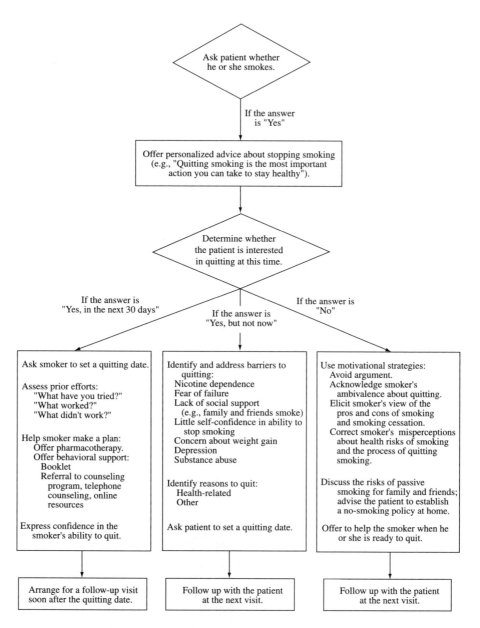

FIGURE 14.9 Smoking cessation strategy for health care workers. The strategy uses the steps recommended in Public Health Service guidelines: ask, advise, assess, assist, and arrange follow-up. [From Rigotti (2002), p. 508.]

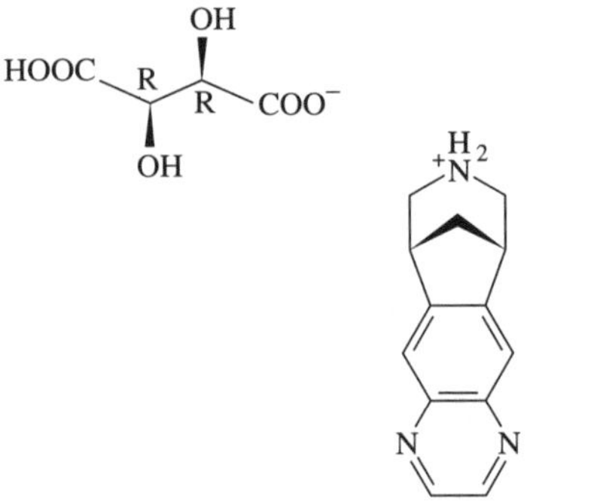

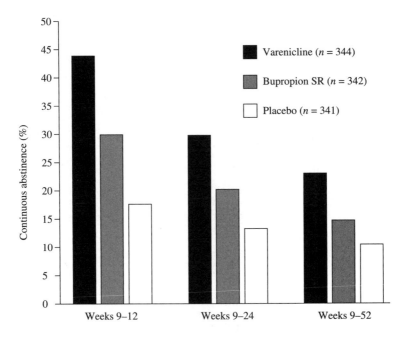

Varenicline (Chantix)

FIGURE 14.10 Structure of varenicline, illustrated as the commercially available tartrate salt Chantix.

FIGURE 14.11 Percentage of smokers maintaining continuous smoking abstinence at periods 9–12 weeks, 9–24 weeks, and 9–52 weeks during treatment with varenicline (1 milligram twice daily), bupropion-SR (150 milligrams twice daily), or placebo. [From Jorenby et al. (2006), Figure 2.]

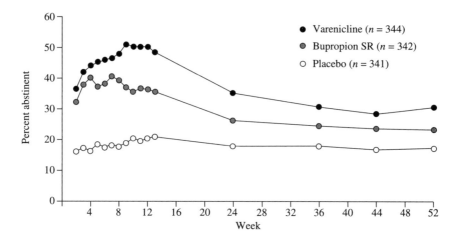

FIGURE 14.12 Percentage of smokers maintaining abstinence over a 52-week period of treatment with varenicline (1 milligram twice daily), bupropion-SR (150 milligrams twice daily), or placebo. [From Jorenby et al. (2006), Figure 3.]

from smoking at 12 weeks and maintaining this superiority through 52 weeks of treatment. Pooling available data indicates that varenicline increases the odds of quitting and maintaining abstinence for 12 months or longer about threefold compared with placebo, and one and a half times compared with patients treated with bupropion (Figure 14.13). Nausea is the primary side effect of varenicline at usual doses of 1 to 2 millgrams per day. Note that unlike with bupropion, nicotine replacement therapy is not indicated with varenicline, as varenicline is a partial blocker of nicotine's receptors; excess nicotine might overcome the partial block caused by varenicline.

Therapy with varenicline is indicated for 12 weeks; positive responders undergo a second 12 weeks of therapy to support continued abstinence. Patients taking the drug are offered a behavioral modification program called GETQUIT.[2] This program uses cognitive-behavioral principles to help educate smokers about managing cravings and behavioral triggers. A "habit changer" identifies and addresses personal triggers to smoke, and daily communications help patients track their progress.

An interesting investigational therapy in development is a nicotine vaccine (similar to a cocaine vaccine; Chapter 13), administered by intramuscular injection. A vaccine against nicotine addiction induces

[2]Visit www.get-quit.com for information.

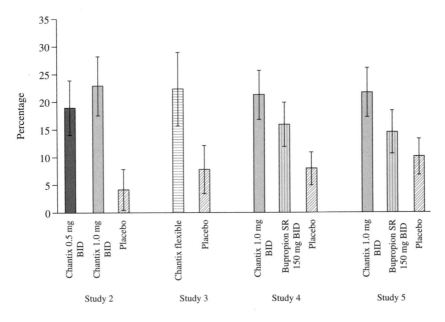

FIGURE 14.13 Manufacturer-supplied pooled data from five studies comparing rates of continuous smoking abstinence in weeks 9 through 52 with treatment with varenicline (0.5 or 1.0 milligram twice daily), bupropion (150 milligrams twice daily), or placebo. [From Pfizer Laboratories monograph LAB-0327-2.0, May, 2006.]

sufficient nicotine-specific antibodies that sequester nicotine in the blood and prevent it from entering the brain (Maurer and Bachmann, 2006; Heading, 2007). In this way, the addictive properties of cigarettes are eliminated and smokers attempting to quit may be able to smoke one or two cigarettes without effect, as the nicotine is sequestered. Essentially, like a cocaine vaccine, a nicotine vaccine targets the progression from lapses to full relapse rather than withdrawal symptoms. Agents being studied include NicQb (also known as nicotine-Qbeta) and NicVAX. These vaccines are currently in clinical trial. The vaccines and other investigational therapies are reviewed by Siu and Tyndale (2007).

STUDY QUESTIONS

1. Differentiate the CNS stimulant actions of caffeine from those of amphetamine and cocaine.

2. Describe the mechanism of action of caffeine. How does this mechanism explain the clinical effects of the drug?

3. What is the relationship between panic attacks and caffeine?

4. Discuss the effects of caffeine in the cardiovascular system.

5. What evidence is there for and against the use of caffeine by women who are pregnant or breast-feeding?

6. Discuss the political, health, and economic issues related to tobacco. Should the FDA regulate nicotine as a drug?

7. List some of the statistics about the health effects of cigarettes.

8. Discuss the antidepressant property of nicotine. Might this property contribute to cigarette dependence? Why?

9. Are cigarettes addicting or are they merely habit forming? Defend your position.

10. Discuss the clinical uses and limitations of nicotine replacement devices. How might their efficacy be boosted?

11. If nicotine exerts an antidepressant action, what drugs or therapies might assist in withdrawal and relapse prevention?

12. Should tobacco products be banned in our society? Defend your views.

13. Compare and contrast varenicline with bupropion for smoking cessation.

REFERENCES

Anda, R. F., et al. (1999). "Adverse Childhood Experiences and Smoking During Adolescence and Adulthood." *Journal of the American Medical Association* 282: 1652–1658.

Bach, P. B., et al. (2007). "Computed Tomography Screening and Lung Cancer Outcomes." *Journal of the American Medical Association* 297: 953–961.

Blum, A., et al. (2004). "The Surgeon General's Report on Smoking and Health 40 Years Later: Still Wandering in the Desert." *Lancet* 363: 97–98.

Breslau, N., et al. (2001). "Nicotine Dependence in the United States: Prevalence, Trends, and Smoking Persistence." *Archives of General Psychiatry* 58: 810–816.

Brody, A. L., et al. (2007). "Brain Metabolic Changes During Cigarette Craving." *Archives of General Psychiatry* 59: 1162–1172.

Browne, M. L. (2006). "Maternal Exposure to Caffeine and Risk of Congenital Abnormalities: A Systematic Review." *Epidemiology* 17: 324–331.

Cahill, K., et al. (2007). "Nicotine Receptor Partial Agonists for Smoking Cessation." *Cochrane Database of Systematic Reviews*, Issue 1, Article CD006103.

Centers for Disease Control and Prevention (2004). "The Health Consequences of Smoking: A Report of the Surgeon General." Office of Smoking and Health, United States Department of Health and Human Services, Washington, DC. www.cdc.gov/tobacco or www.surgeongeneral.gov

Centers for Disease Control and Prevention (2006). "State Medicaid Coverage for Tobacco-Dependence Treatments, United States, 2005." *MMWR Weekly* 55: 1194–1197.

Coleman, T. (2004). "Use of Simple Advice and Behavioural Support." *British Medical Journal* 328: 397–399.

Cornelis, M. C., and El-Sohemy, A. (2007). "Coffee, Caffeine, and Coronary Heart Disease." *Current Opinions in Lipidology* 18: 13–19.

Cornelius, M. D., et al., (2006). "Coffee, CYP1A2 Genotype, and Risk of Myocardial Infarction." *Journal of the American Medical Association* 295: 1135–1141.

D'Ambrosio, S. M. (1994). "Evaluation of the Genotoxicity Data on Caffeine." *Regulatory Toxicology and Pharmacology* 19: 243–281.

Doll, R., et al. (2004). "Mortality in Relation to Smoking: 50 Years' Observations on Male British Doctors." *British Medical Journal* 328: 1519–1528.

Fergusson, D. M., et al. (1996). "Comorbidity Between Depressive Disorders and Nicotine Dependence in a Cohort of 16-Year-Olds." *Archives of General Psychiatry* 53: 1043–1047.

Fiore, M. C., et al. (2004). "Preventing 3 Million Premature Deaths and Helping 5 Million Smokers Quit: A National Action Plan for Tobacco Cessation." *American Journal of Public Health* 94: 205–210. The entire February 2004 issue is devoted to tobacco.

Glassman, A. H., et al. (2001). "Smoking Cessation and the Course of Major Depression: A Follow-up Study." *Lancet* 357: 1929–1932.

Gonzales, D., et al. (2006). "Varenicline, an α4β2 Nicotinic Acetylcholine Receptor Partial Agonist, vs. Sustained-Release Bupropion and Placebo for Smoking Cessation: A Randomized Controlled Trial." *Journal of the American Medical Association* 296: 47–55.

Gonzalez, S., et al. (2002). "Changes in Endocannabinoid Contents in the Brain of Rats Chronically Exposed to Nicotine." *Brain Research* 954: 73–81.

Grant, B. F., et al. (2004). "Nicotine Dependence and Psychiatric Disorders in the United States." *Archives of General Psychiatry* 61: 1107–1115.

Greden, J. F., and A. Walters (1997). "Caffeine." In J. H. Lowinson, P. Ruiz, R. B. Millman, and J. G. Langrod, eds., *Substance Abuse: A Comprehensive Textbook*, 3rd ed. (pp. 294–307). Baltimore: Williams & Wilkins.

Greenberg, J. A., et al. (2006). "Coffee, Diabetes, and Weight Control." *American Journal of Clinical Nutrition* 84: 682–693.

Grimshaw, G. M., and Stanton, A. (2006). "Tobacco Cessation Interventions for Young People." *Cochrane Database of Systematic Reviews*, Issue 4, Article CD003289.

Harris, J. E., et al. (2004). "Cigarette Tar Yields in Relation to Mortality from Lung Cancer in the Cancer Prevention Study II Prospective Cohort, 1982–8." *British Medical Journal* 328: 72–76.

Harvard School of Public Health (2007). "Trends in Smoke Nicotine Yield and Relationship to Design Characteristics Among Popular U.S. Cigarette Brands, 1997–2005." A Report of the Tobacco Research Program, Division of Public Health Practice, Harvard School of Public Health.

Heading, C. E. (2007). "Drug Evaluation: CYT-002-NicQb, A Therapeutic Vaccine for the Treatment of Nicotine Addiction." *Current Opinions on Investigational Drugs* 8: 71–77.

Henley, S. J., et al. (2007). "Tobacco-Related Disease Mortality Among Men Who Switched from Cigarettes to Spit Tobacco." *Tobacco Control* 16: 22–28.

Higdon, J. V., and B. Frei (2006). "Coffee and Health: A Review of Recent Human Research." *Critical Reviews in Food Science and Nutrition* 46: 101–123.

Hughes, J. R. (2001). "Distinguishing Nicotine Dependence from Smoking: Why It Matters to Tobacco Control and Psychiatry." *Archives of General Psychiatry* 58: 817–818.

Hughes, J. R., et al. (2007). "Antidepressants for Smoking Cessation." *Cochrane Database of Systematic Reviews*, Issue 1, Article CD000031.

Jorenby, D. E., et al. (2006). "Efficacy of Varenicline, an α4β2 Nicotinic Acetylcholine Receptor Partial Agonist, vs Placebo or Sustained-Release Bupropion for Smoking Cessation: A Randomized Controlled Trial." *Journal of the American Medical Association* 296: 56–63.

Keating, G. M., and M. A. A. Siddiqui (2006). "Varenicline: A Review of Its Use as an Aid to Smoking Cessation Therapy." *CNS Drugs* 20: 945–960.

Klebanoff, M. A., et al. (1999). "Maternal Serum Paraxanthine, a Caffeine Metabolite, and the Risk of Spontaneous Abortion." *New England Journal of Medicine* 341: 1639–1644.

Lambert, R.A., et al. (2006). "A Pragmatic, Unblinded, Randomized, Controlled Trial Comparing an Occupational Therapy-Led Lifestyle Approach and Routine GP Care for Panic Disorder Treatment in Primary Care." *Journal of Affective Disorders* 99: 63–71.

Ledent, C., et al. (1997). "Aggressiveness, Hypoalgesia, and High Blood Pressure in Mice Lacking the Adenosine A2a Receptor." *Nature* 388: 674–678.

Magkos, F., and S. A. Kavouras (2005). "Caffeine Use in Sports, Pharmacokinetics in Man, and Cellular Mechanisms of Action." *Critical Reviews in Food Science and Nutrition* 45: 535–562.

Maurer, P., and M. F. Bachmann (2006). "Therapeutic Vaccines for Nicotine Dependence." *Current Opinions on Molecular Therapy* 8: 11–16.

McCusker, R. R., et al. (2003). "Caffeine Content of Specialty Coffees." *Journal of Analytical Toxicology* 27: 520–522.

McGehee, D. S. (2006). "Nicotinic and Opioid Receptor Interactions in Nicotine Addiction." *Molecular Interventions* 6: 311–314.

Milberger, S., et al. (1996). "Is Maternal Smoking During Pregnancy a Risk Factor for Attention Deficit Hyperactivity Disorder in Children?" *American Journal of Psychiatry* 153: 1138–1142.

Naqvi, N. H., et al. (2007). "Damage to the Insula Disrupts Addiction to Cigarette Smoking." *Science* 315: 531–534.

Ng, S. P., and J. T. Zelikoff (2007). "Smoking During Pregnancy: Subsequent Effects on Offspring Immune Competence and Disease Vulnerability in Later Life." *Reproductive Toxicology* 23: 428–437.

Nides, M., et al. (2006). "Smoking Cessation with Varenicline, a Selective α4β2 Nicotinic Receptor Partial Agonist: Results from a 7-Week, Randomized, Placebo- and Bupropion-Controlled Trial with 1-Year Follow-up." *Archives of Internal Medicine* 166: 1561–1568.

Onchen, C., et al. (2006). "Efficacy and Safety of the Novel Selective Nicotinic Acetylcholine Receptor Partial Agonist, Varenicline, for Smoking Cessation." *Archives of Internal Medicine* 166: 1571–1577.

Ranney, L., et al. (2006). "Systematic Review: Smoking Cessation Intervention Strategies for Adults and Adults in Special Populations." *Archives of Internal Medicine* 145: 845–856.

Riggs, P. D., et al. (1999). "Relationship of ADHD, Depression, and Non-Tobacco Substance Use Disorders to Nicotine Dependence in Substance-Dependent Delinquents." *Drug and Alcohol Dependence* 54: 195–205.

Rigotti, N. A. (2002). "Treatment of Tobacco Use and Dependence." *New England Journal of Medicine* 346: 506–512.

Rodrigues, I. M., and Klein, L. C. (2006). "Boiled or Filtered Coffee? Effects of Coffee and Caffeine on Cholesterol, Fibrinogen, and C-Reactive Protein." *Toxicology Reviews* 25: 55–69.

Rose, J. E., et al. (2003). "PET Studies of the Influence of Nicotine on Neural Systems in Cigarette Smokers." *American Journal of Psychiatry* 160: 323–333.

Salin-Pascual, R. J., et al. (1996). "Antidepressant Effect of Transdermal Nicotine Patches in Nonsmoking Patients with Major Depression." *Journal of Clinical Psychiatry* 57: 387–389.

Satel, S. (2006). "Is Caffeine Addictive? A Review of the Literature." *American Journal of Drug and Alcohol Abuse* 32: 493–502.

Sellers, E. M. (1998). "Pharmacogenetics and Ethnoracial Differences in Smoking." *Journal of the American Medical Association* 280: 179–180.

Siu, E. C., and R. F. Tyndale (2007). "Non-Nicotinic Therapies for Smoking Cessation." *Annual Review of Pharmacology and Toxicology* 47: 541–564.

Spring, B., et al. (2003). "Reward Value of Cigarette Smoking for Comparably Heavy Smoking Schizophrenic, Depressed, and Nonpatient Smokers." *American Journal of Psychiatry* 160: 316–322.

Stead, L. F., et al. (2006). "Telephone Counseling for Smoking Cessation." *Cochrane Database of Systematic Reviews,* Issue 13, Article CD002850.

Steensland, P., et al. (2007) "Varenicline, an $\alpha 4\beta 2$ Nicotinic Acetylcholine Receptor Partial Agonist, Selectively Decreases Ethanol Consumption and Seeking." *Proceedings of the National Academy of Sciences* 104: 12518–12523.

Stolerman, I. P., and M. J. Jarvis (1995). "The Scientific Case That Nicotine Is Addictive." *Psychopharmacology* 117: 2–10.

Teo, K. K., et al. (2006). "Tobacco Use and Risk of Myocardial Infarction in 52 Countries in the INTERHEART Study: A Case-Controlled Study." *Lancet* 368: 642–658.

Thomas, R., and R. Perera (2006). "School-Based Programmes for Preventing Smoking." *Cochrane Database of Systematic Reviews,* Issue 3, Article CD001293.

Tobacco Use and Dependence Clinical Practice Guideline Panel, Staff, and Consortium Representatives (2000). "A Clinical Practice Guideline for Treating Tobacco Use and Dependence, A U.S. Public Health Service Report." *Journal of the American Medical Association* 283: 3244–3254.

Tonstad, S., et al. (2006). "Effect of Maintenance Therapy with Varenicline on Smoking Cessation: A Randomized Controlled Trial." *Journal of the American Medical Association* 296: 64–71.

Tsoh, J. Y., et al. (2000). "Development of Major Depression After Treatment for Smoking Cessation." *American Journal of Psychiatry* 157: 368–374.

U.S. Department of Health and Human Services (1986). "The Health Consequences of Involuntary Smoking: A Report of the Surgeon General." Centers for Disease Control and Prevention, Office of Smoking and Health. U.S. Government Printing Office. www.cdc.gov/tobacco.

U.S. Department of Health and Human Services (1988). "The Health Consequences of Smoking—Nicotine Addiction: A Report of the Surgeon General." Centers for Disease Control and Prevention, Office of Smoking and Health. U.S. Government Printing Office. www.cdc.gov/tobacco.

U.S. Department of Health and Human Services (2006). "The Health Consequences of Involuntary Exposure to Tobacco Smoke: A Report of the Surgeon General." Centers for Disease Control and Prevention, Office of Smoking and Health. U.S. Government Printing Office. www.cdc.gov/tobacco

Van Dam, R. M. (2006). "Coffee and Type 2 Diabetes: From Beans to Beta Cells." *Nutrition, Metabolism and Cardiovascular Disease* 16: 69–77.

Wisborg, K., et al. (2003). "Maternal Consumption of Coffee During Pregnancy and Stillbirth and Infant Death in the First Year of Life: Prospective Study." *British Medical Journal* 326: 420–422.

Zierler-Brown, S. L., and J. A. Kyle (2007). "Oral Varenicline for Smoking Cessation." *Annals of Pharmacotherapy* 41: 95–99.

Analgesic Drugs and Psychedelics

Part 5 focuses on two specialized topics in psychopharmacology. First are two chapters dealing with the pharmacology of drugs used to treat pain: Chapter 15 covers the nonnarcotic or nonopioid analgesics (such as aspirin), and Chapter 16 concentrates on the pharmacology of opioid (narcotic) analgesics, the treatment of opioid dependency, and the uses of opioid receptor antagonists. The importance of the nonopioid analgesics is their capability of reducing the dose of coadministered opioid while contributing their own pain relief and anti-inflammatory effects.

Chapters 17 and 18 present the pharmacology of drugs characterized by their ability to produce altered states of consciousness. Chapter 17 discusses the pharmacology of tetrahydrocannabinol (the active ingredient in marijuana) and drugs that function as blockers of the receptors through which tetrahydrocannabinol exerts its actions (cannabinoid antagonists). Chapter 18 presents the pharmacology of psychedelic drugs, including those found in nature as well as those synthetically produced. Included in this chapter are drugs considered as "club drugs" because of their ability to increase energy (an amphetaminelike action) and produce altered states of consciousness.

Chapter 15

Nonnarcotic Anti-Inflammatory Analgesics

Previous chapters have described the pharmacology of drugs used to treat psychological disorders such as anxiety, insomnia, depression, mania, and psychosis. In this chapter we begin a two-chapter discussion of the treatment of pain and the pharmacology of analgesic drugs. We have already addressed the issue of pain in Chapters 7 and 8: many of the antidepressants and the anticonvulsant neuromodulators possess prominent analgesic actions, reducing the amounts of morphine (or other opioids) necessary to achieve relief of extreme pain.

Pain, anxiety, and depression are often inseparable, and all three need to be addressed during treatment of the patient with chronic pain syndromes (for example, fibromyalgia, chronic fatigue syndrome, chronic back pain, and so on). Although opioid narcotics (Chapter 16) are effective in the treatment of severe acute pain (for example, surgery- or injury-caused pain), they are much less effective in the treatment of chronic pain (for example, chronic lower-back pain) (Martell et al., 2007). In the treatment of chronic pain, therefore, efforts must be made to apply and optimize three kinds of medications before opioid narcotics are utilized (Wasan, 2005):

1. Analgesic/anti-inflammatory drugs discussed in this chapter

2. Antidepressant/anxiolytic medications having a norepinephrine-potentiating action (Chapter 7)

3. Mood stabilizer anticonvulsants with analgesic action (Chapter 8)

Only then is an opioid added, and then only when pain cannot be controlled by the first three types of drugs.

The value of antidepressants and mood stabilizers lies in their capacity to modulate the pain experience and to treat symptoms that trigger, exacerbate, or compound the effects of pain, notably depression, anxiety, sleep disturbances, anger, and other states of neural excitation (Shanti et al., 2006). As discussed by Durie and McCarson (2006), antidepressants and nonopioid analgesic/anti-inflammatory drugs work synergistically to reduce nociceptive (pain-producing) sensory activation and to block both pain- and stress-evoked emotional responses that involve alterations in hippocampal and spinal cord gene expression.

The nonnarcotic analgesics are commonly called *nonsteroidal analgesic anti-inflammatory drugs* (NSAIDs). These drugs act at the local (peripheral) site of tissue injury to reduce the inflammatory response associated with tissue injury and to reduce the transmission of pain impulses to the CNS. The NSAIDs do not produce euphoria, and they are not considered to be drugs of abuse. NSAIDs do not bind to opioid receptors, but they exert a prominent morphine-sparing effect in improving pain relief in a variety of clinical situations (Gilron et al., 2003). The historical development of NSAIDs and the future of anti-inflammarory drug therapy was recently reviewed by Rainsford (2007).

The NSAIDs are a group of chemically unrelated drugs (Figure 15.1) that block the generation of peripheral pain impulses by inhibiting the synthesis and release of chemical mediators called *prostaglandin*. Prostaglandins are body hormones that perform a variety of functions, including the production of local inflammatory responses. NSAIDs act by inhibiting the enzyme cyclooxygenase. *Cyclooxygenase* (also called *prostaglandin synthetase*) functions to convert a precursor substance (arachidonic acid) to prostaglandins. NSAIDs are therefore also called *cyclooxygenase inhibitors*.

There are two closely related forms of cyclooxygenase enzyme: COX-1 and COX-2. COX-1 primarily functions to mediate the production of prostaglandins that protect and regulate cell function in the gastrointestinal (GI) tract and in blood platelets during normal physiological conditions. Among other things, this action permits platelets to function normally as initiators of blood clotting. COX-2 has fewer roles under normal conditions; however, in response to stressors such as inflammation, COX-2 is markedly induced by chemical mediators associated with inflammation. Such induction by immune or inflammatory stimuli leads to the production of prostaglandins that mediate

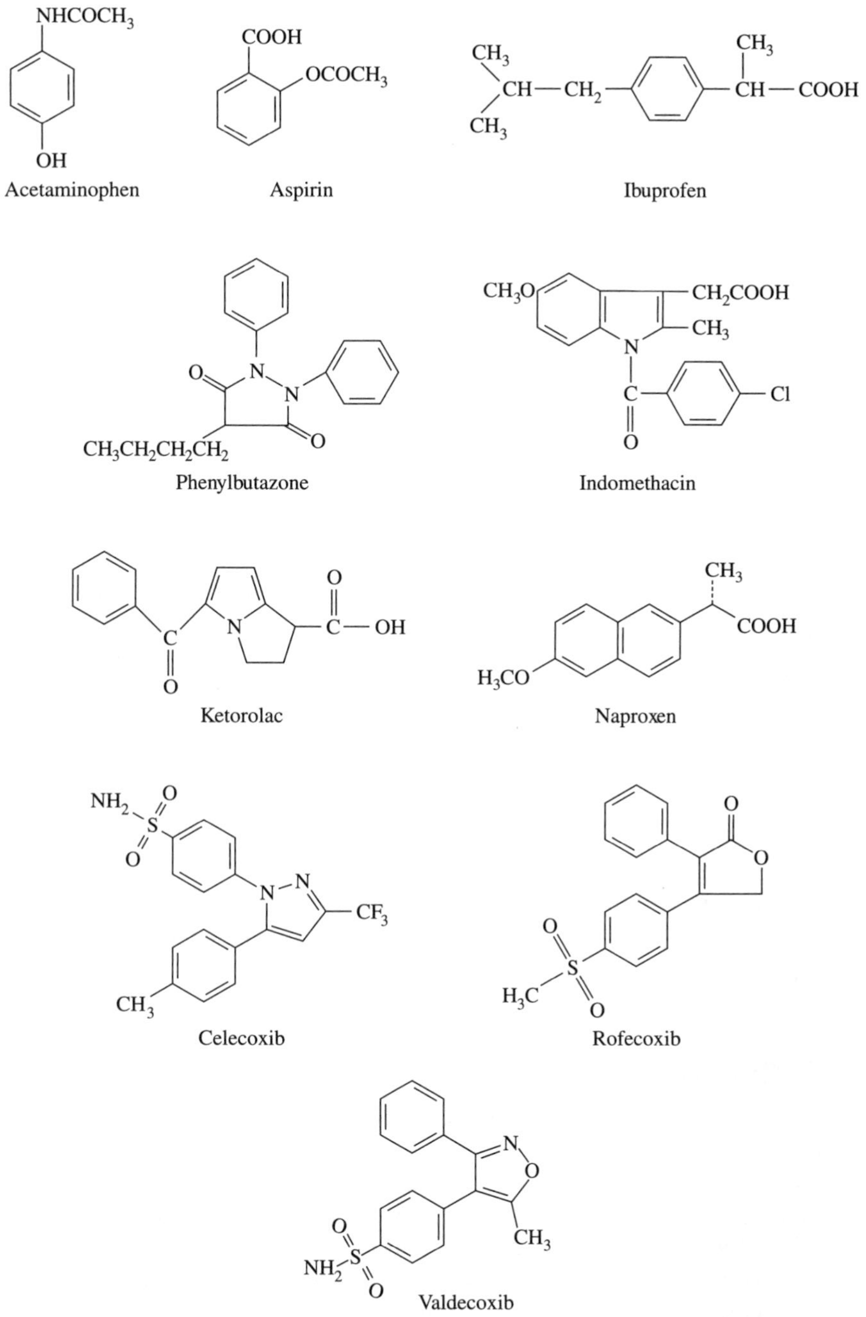

FIGURE 15.1 Structural formulas of representative anti-inflammatory analgesics.

inflammation and pain. COX-2 (in contrast to COX-1) is therefore considered as an *inducible enzyme*. It is induced in peripheral tissues and in the spinal cord in response to such immune instigators as autoimmune diseases (for example, osteoarthritis and rheumatoid arthritis), for which anti-inflammatory drugs are so effective therapeutically.

Classical NSAIDs, such as aspirin, nonselectively inhibit the cyclooxygenase enzyme (both COX-1 and COX-2). Therefore, they would be expected to adversely affect both the GI tract and platelet function, as well as reducing pain and inflammation. By 2004, three prescription-only selective inhibitors of the COX-2 enzyme were marketed. Because of drug-induced complications, two were removed from the market and only one (celecoxib, trade name Celebrex) remains. New (and presumably safer) COX-2 selective agents are in various stages of development. These include etoricoxib (Arcoxia), lumiracoxib (Prexige), and licofelone. In April 2007, an FDA panel recommended against approving etoricoxib because studies found the drug no more effective than naproxen (a nonselective COX inhibitor) while being associated with three times as many cases of stroke, heart attack, or death. The drug, however, currently remains available in 63 countries, although the new results may reduce the number. The status of lumiracoxib and licofelone is pending.

The effects of anti-inflammatory analgesic drugs (selective or nonselective) include the following:

- Reduction of inflammation (an anti-inflammatory effect)
- Reduction in body temperature when the patient has a fever (an antipyretic effect)
- Reduction of pain without sedation (an analgesic effect)
- Inhibition of platelet aggregation (an anticoagulant effect)—nonselective drugs only

Nonselective Cyclooxygenase Inhibitors

Nonselective cyclooxygenase (COX) inhibitors are drugs that inhibit both COX-1 and COX-2 variants of the COX enzyme. The prototype nonselective NSAID is aspirin; hence, all nonselective NSAIDs can be referred to as aspirinlike drugs. Other nonselective NSAIDs include acetaminophen, ibuprofen, mefenamic acid (Ponstel), meclofenamate sodium (Meclomen), tolmetin (Tolectin), diclofenac (Voltaren), piroxicam (Feldene), and nabumetone (Relafen). These drugs are used as analgesics and for the long-term treatment of the pain and inflammation associated with arthritis. Nonselective COX inhibitors exert clinically significant effects on pain, inflammation, blood platelets, and the GI tract. These effects differentiate these drugs from the opioid analgesics, such as morphine, and from the selective COX-2 inhibitors. Opioid analgesics, although powerfully analgesic, do not exert anti-inflammatory effects, and they do not affect blood platelet function. The selective COX-2 inhibitors have the same analgesic and anti-inflammatory actions as the nonselective agents discussed here, but they do not affect platelet function.

Aspirin

In the United States, between 10,000 and 20,000 tons of aspirin are consumed each year. *Aspirin* is the most popular and most effective analgesic, antipyretic, and anti-inflammatory drug. As an analgesic, aspirin is most effective for low-intensity pain, as increased doses rapidly reach a ceiling beyond which additional drug provides little more analgesia than do lower doses (all NSAIDs demonstrate this ceiling effect against pain). The ceiling is reached with doses of between about 650 milligrams and 1300 milligrams (a single, full-strength, regular aspirin contains 325 milligrams of drug).

Aspirin's antipyretic (fever-lowering) effect follows the inhibition of prostaglandin synthesis in the hypothalamus, a structure in the brain that modulates body temperature. However, one caution is necessary regarding the use of aspirin to reduce fever in children. An association exists between the use of aspirin for the fever that accompanies varicella (chicken pox) or influenza and the subsequent development of Reye's syndrome, including severe liver and brain damage and even death. Therefore, in children, aspirin use is precluded for the treatment of virus-induced febrile illness.

Aspirin exerts important effects on blood coagulation. For blood to coagulate, platelets must first be able to aggregate, an action requiring the presence of prostaglandins.[1] Aspirin binds to blood platelets, irreversibly inhibiting their function for the 8- to 10-day lifetime of the platelet. Homeostasis is inhibited, reducing the tendency for blood to clot. In daily low doses (usually requiring only 80 to 160 milligrams per day), aspirin is used to prevent blood from clotting in diseased coronary arteries, markedly reducing the incidence of occlusive strokes and heart attacks secondary to the development of atherosclerotic plaques in the cerebral and coronary blood vessels.

Sohn and Krotz (2006) state, "Inhibition of platelet aggregation by aspirin . . . is a cheap, safe, and effective strategy to prevent myocardial infarction (heart attacks) or stroke and is thus the most established strategy of secondary prevention of atherothrombotic disease" (p. 1275). Karlikaya

---

[1]Platelets are small components of the blood that adhere to vascular membranes after injury to a vessel. They form an initial plug, over which a blood clot eventually forms to limit bleeding from a lacerated blood vessel.

and coworkers (2006) state, "Daily low-dose aspirin has a protective effect in reducing the risk of early death in stroke" (p. 263). This protective effect exerted by reducing the ability of the blood to clot increases the risk of gastrointestinal bleeding, but the benefits in the prevention of heart attacks and thrombotic (occlusive) strokes outweigh the risks of serious bleeding in adults with coronary heart disease (Colwell, 2006).

Because of the anticoagulant effect, it has been postulated that aspirin or other NSAIDs might be useful in reducing cognitive decline in the elderly, perhaps even in reducing the incidence of late-life dementias. Recent studies, however, have reported that these drugs are ineffective in reducing cognitive decline or delaying the onset of Alzheimer's disease (Kang et al., 2007; ADAPT Research Group, 2007).

Side effects of aspirin are common. Gastric upset occurs frequently and can range from mild upset and heartburn to severe, destructive ulcerations and bleeding of the stomach or upper intestine. Poisoning due to aspirin overdosage is not infrequent and can be fatal. Mild intoxication can produce ringing in the ears, auditory and visual difficulties, mental confusion, thirst, and hyperventilation. In aspirin-sensitive people, a single dose of aspirin can precipitate an asthma attack. And aspirin increases oxygen consumption by the body, which increases the production of carbon dioxide, an effect that stimulates respiration. Therefore, an overdose of aspirin is often characterized by a marked increase in respiratory rate, which causes the overdosed person to appear to pant. This overdose effect results in other severe metabolic consequences that are beyond this discussion.

Acetaminophen

Acetaminophen (Tylenol) is an effective alternative to aspirin both as an analgesic and as an antipyretic agent. However, acetaminophen has only minor actions as an anti-inflammatory agent. Therefore, it is less useful than aspirin in the treatment of acute inflammation or chronic arthritis. However, as a pain-relieving agent, acetaminophen is as effective as aspirin. The usual oral dose of acetaminophen is 325 to 1000 milligrams, with daily doses averaging 1000 milligrams. Total daily doses should not exceed 4000 milligrams (2000 milligrams for people with alcoholism).

Acetaminophen has three advantages over aspirin. First, acetaminophen does not inhibit platelet function, so bruising easily is not a problem. (On the other hand, acetaminophen is not useful for preventing vascular clotting or for prophylaxis against heart attacks or stroke.) Second, no reports have associated acetaminophen with Reye's syndrome; therefore, it has an improved margin of safety in children. Third, acetaminophen generally produces less gastric distress and less ringing in the ears than does aspirin.

On the negative side, an acute overdose (either accidental or intentional) might produce severe or even fatal liver damage. Alcoholics appear to be especially susceptible to the hepatotoxic effects of even moderate doses of acetaminophen and should avoid acetaminophen while they persist in heavy consumption of alcohol. Finally, there has recently been association between the use of acetaminophen (and other NSAIDs except aspirin) and the development of hypertension (high blood pressure) in a small minority of women who consume these drugs nearly daily (Armstrong and Malone, 2003). Women who are hypertensive would be wise to discuss the use of acetaminophen with their physician before taking it.

In summary, acetaminophen has proved to be a reasonable substitute for aspirin when analgesic or antipyretic effectiveness is desired, especially in children and in patients who cannot tolerate aspirin.

Ibuprofen

Ibuprofen (Advil) and related drugs (Table 15.1) such as fenoprofen (Nalfon) and ketoprofen (Orudis) exert aspirinlike analgesic, antipyretic, and anti-inflammatory effects and are often better tolerated than

TABLE I5.1 Ibuprofen and related drugs: Available formulations and recommendations for anti-inflammatory therapy

Nonproprietary name	Trade name	Formulation	Usual anti-inflammatory dose
Ibuprofen	Motrin, Advil, Nuprin, Medipren	Tablets	400 mg, three to four times a day
Naproxen	Naprosyn, Aleve, Anaprox	Tablets, suspension	250–500 mg, twice a day
Fenoprofen	Nalfon	Tablets, capsules	300–600 mg, three to four times a day
Ketoprofen	Orudis, Oravail	Capsules	150–300 mg, two to four times a day
Flurbiprofen	Ansaid, others	Tablets	50–75 mg, two to four times a day
Oxaprozin	Daypro	Tablets	600–1200 mg, once a day
Mefenamic acid	Ponstel	Tablets	250 mg, three to four times a day
Celecoxib	Celebrex	Capsules	100 mg, twice a day

aspirin. Their analgesic effectiveness is comparable to that of acetaminophen, aspirin, codeine, aspirin with codeine, and propoxyphene. Like other NSAIDs, ibuprofen's actions result from drug-induced inhibition of prostaglandin synthesis. The incidence and severity of side effects produced by ibuprofen are somewhat lower than those of aspirin, but gastric distress and the formation of peptic ulcers have occasionally been reported. Like aspirin (but unlike acetaminophen), ibuprofen and related drugs inhibit platelet aggregation and therefore interfere with the clotting process. These drugs should be used with caution in patients who suffer from peptic ulcer disease or bleeding abnormalities. Ibuprofen, unlike most other NSAIDs, is not secreted in breast milk, but in general, NSAIDs are not recommended for breast-feeding mothers or pregnant women.

FDA-approved indications for ibuprofen include use as an analgesic and use for the symptomatic treatment of various forms of arthritis, tendonitis, bursitis, and dysmenorrhea (painful menstrual cramps). The anti-inflammatory effect is comparable to that of aspirin. The generally lower level of gastrointestinal side effects (in comparison with aspirin) must be measured against its generally greater cost.

Recently, Clark and coworkers (2007) studied 300 children (ages 6 to 17 years old) who presented for emergency room treatment with musculoskeletal pain. They were administered acetaminophen, ibuprofen, or codeine. At 60 minutes post administration, patients in the ibuprofen group had significantly better pain relief.

Indomethacin and Sulindac

Indomethacin (Indocin), available for over 40 years, is an effective anti-inflammatory drug that is used primarily for treating rheumatoid arthritis and similar disorders. However, its use is limited by its toxicity. Indomethacin is an analgesic, antipyretic, and anti-inflammatory agent. Its clinical effects closely resemble those of aspirin. Side effects occur in about 50 percent of the patients who take indomethacin; gastric dysfunction is the most prominent. Paradoxically, drug-induced headache limits its use in about 50 percent of patients. Other side effects are rare but potentially serious.

Sulindac (Clinoril) is an NSAID that is structurally and pharmacologically related to indomethacin. Sulindac is itself inactive, but its metabolite (sulindac sulfide) is very active. Its efficacy is comparable to that of indomethacin but perhaps with a lower level of gastrointestinal toxicities (less than indomethacin but greater than many other NSAIDs).

Ketorolac

Ketorolac (Toradol) is an analgesic and anti-inflammatory agent available in both oral and intravenous formulations. Ketorolac is the only NSAID available for injection. Administered either intramuscularly or intravenously, ketorolac is effective in the short-term treatment of moderate to severe pain. Like the other NSAIDs, ketorolac inhibits prostaglandin synthesis. Its analgesic potency is comparable to that of low doses of morphine, and it offers an anti-inflammatory action not offered by morphine. Its concomitant use with morphine offers synergistic action, reducing the required analgesic dose of morphine by about 50 percent. Ketorolac is not recommended for use in obstetrics because it and other NSAIDs can adversely affect uterine contraction and fetal circulation.

Side effects of ketorolac include excessive bleeding (due to platelet inhibition) and renal failure; the latter is minimized by limiting the use of the drug to a few days after surgery. Used orally, analgesic efficacy differs little from other orally administered NSAIDs.

Diclofenac

Diclofenac (Voltaren) is another nonspecific NSAID, available since 1988 and indicated for treatment of acute and chronic pain of arthritis and for the mitigation of painful menstrual periods. The half-life of diclofenac is short (about two hours), so delayed-release preparations are commonly used when a more prolonged analgesic action is desired. The precautions applicable to other nonspecific NSAIDs apply to diclofenac.

Nabumetone

Nabumetone (Relafen) is a nonspecific NSAID available since 1991 for the treatment of arthritis and other conditions treatable with similar drugs. Nabumetone itself is inactive; it is rapidly converted in the body to a pharmacologically active metabolite that is a potent inhibitor of prostaglandin synthetase. Its gastrointestinal toxicity appears to be somewhat lower than that of aspirin or indomethacin. The drug is primarily indicated for the long-term treatment of the pain and inflammation associated with arthritis.

Miscellaneous Nonspecific NSAIDs

Several other nonspecific cyclooxygenase inhibitors are available for use in treating various forms of arthritis or painful menstrual periods. These agents include *meloxicam* (Mobic), *naproxen* (Aleve, Anaprox), *oxaprozin* (Daypro), *piroxicam* (Feldene), and *tolmetin* (Tolectin). These drugs, as well as several of the drugs discussed earlier, were introduced in medicine in the late 1980s to early 1990s as alternatives to aspirin. Since the patent protection of most of these drugs has expired, they are available in generic form, and few manufacturers promote their use today. As we will see, however, naproxen in particular may exert a cardioprotective effect not shared by most other NSAIDs. Naproxen, however, offers less protection against heart attacks than does aspirin.

Selective COX-2 Inhibitors

Only since the late 1990s have the roles of cyclooxygenase enzymes in health and disease been extensively explored, in particular, the role of "inducible" COX-2[2] in inflammation (O'Banion, 1999) and in the prevention of various cancers (Agency for Healthcare Research and Quality, 2006). COX-2 enzyme is expressed in certain malignant cells of epithelial tissues such as colon, breast, prostate, bladder, lung, and pancreas, and it plays a role in tumor proliferation and growth. It is best demonstrated in cancers of the colon. COX-2 inhibitors reduce the risk of these cancers and therefore have a role in cancer chemoprotection, probably as an adjunct to more traditional anticancer medications (Marnett and DuBois, 2002; Ricchi et al., 2003). Whether COX-2 inhibitors will play a beneficial role in the treatment of noncarcinogenic inflammatory diseases of the colon is as yet unclear. It is interesting that the nonselective COX inhibitor aspirin is similarly effective in reducing the long-term risk of colorectal cancers. A dose of 300 milligrams or more daily for 5 years is effective in the primary prevention of colon cancers after a latent period of about 10 years (Flossmann and Rothwell, 2007).

Selective COX-2 inhibitors are as effective as aspirin and other nonselective NSAIDs for the relief of pain and the reduction of inflammation while halving the rate of associated gastric ulcerations (Figure 15.2). Consequently, prior to September 2004 the selective COX-2 inhibitors became wildly popular as modern NSAIDs that were clinically effective while reducing the incidence of gastric ulcerations. Unfortunately, two of the three selective COX-2 inhibitors that were clinically available were withdrawn from the market because of adverse cardiac complications.

Celecoxib

Celecoxib (Celebrex) was the first selective COX-2 inhibitor; it was released in 1998. The drug is as effective as aspirin in reducing the pain and inflammation of rheumatoid arthritis and osteoarthritis without the gastrointestinal toxicity and platelet blockade produced by aspirin. Celecoxib is associated with a 50 percent reduction in the occurrence of drug-induced gastric ulcerations and hemorrhages (see Figure 15.2). However, although the incidence of skin bruising is less frequent, the lack of effect on blood platelets causes loss of the protective effect of aspirin in reducing the incidence of heart attacks and strokes, although

---

[2]"Inducible" means that the enzyme level of COX-2 in the body, normally low, increases markedly in response to inflammation.

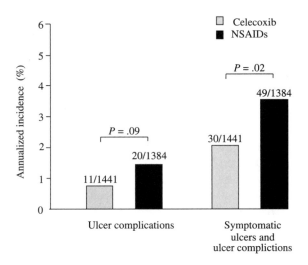

FIGURE 15.2 Annualized incidences of upper gastrointestinal tract ulcer complications alone and with symptomatic gastrointestinal ulcers. Left two bars represent ulcer complications for 1441 patient-years of celecoxib and 1384 patient-years of nonselective NSAIDs. The right two bars represent ulcer complications plus the presence of symptomatic ulcers in the same populations of patients. The numbers above the bars indicate events per patient-years of exposure. The annualized incidence of ulcer complications in celecoxib-treated patients was 0.76 percent (11 events per 1441 patient-years) versus an incidence of 1.45 percent (20 events per 1384 patient-years) in patients taking NSAIDs. When symptomatic ulcers were added, the percentage of complications in each group increased, but celecoxib patients still exhibited a 40 percent reduction in total complications. [From F. E. Silverstein et al., "Gastrointestinal Toxicity with Celecoxib vs. Nonsteroidal Anti-Inflammatory Drugs for Osteoarthritis and Rheumatoid Arthritis: The CLASS Study: A Randomized Controlled Study," *Journal of the American Medical Association* 284 (2000), p. 1251.]

whether it increases the rate over that of placebo is unclear (Agency for Healthcare Research and Quality, 2006). Currently, celecoxib remains commercially available. Because it lacks antithrombotic action (it lacks a blocking action on platelet function), it might possibly slightly increase the incidence of heart attacks over the use of aspirin (while reducing the likelihood of gastrointestinal bleeding).

Rofecoxib

Rofecoxib (Vioxx), the second COX-2 inhibitor, was introduced into medicine in 2000. It was approved for the treatment of osteoarthritis, acute pain, and menstrual pain, with some superiority over naproxen in reducing the incidence of gastric ulcerations. Unfortunately, its use was associated with an increased risk of heart attacks, so the drug was removed from the market in September 2004.

Valdecoxib

The third selective COX-2 inhibitor, *valdecoxib* (Bextra), was introduced into medicine in 2002. Like refecoxib, valdecoxib was associated with an increased rate of cardiovascular side effects and it was voluntarily withdrawn from the market in April 2005.

Lumiracoxib

Lumiracoxib (Prexige) is another orally administered selective COX-2 inhibitor. It is intended for the short-term treatment of postsurgical pain. It differs from the other orally administered agents in that it is more rapidly absorbed after oral administration and has a relatively short half-life. It is about half as potent as celecoxib (therefore the dose is twice as high). The drug has been approved for use in the United Kingdom and may become available in the United States.

Nonopioid Analgesics of the Future: Nitric Oxide-Donating Analgesics

Advances beyond COX-2 inhibition are being explored and are needed since the nonselective NSAIDs do not protect against gastrointestinal bleeding and ulcerations and since the COX-2 inhibitors do not block platelet action and therefore do not offer cardiac protection against atherothrombotic catastrophes. An interesting example of possible agents of the future is a class of drugs called nitroaspirins, or nitric oxide-donating aspirins. Some are in various stages of clinical trial. Agents include naproxcinod (for treating osteoarthritis), NCX-4016 (as an insulin-sensitizing agent for treating type 2 diabetes), and NCX-6560 for cardiovascular disease. Other potential uses are for the treatment of asthma, ocular diseases, and allergic rhinitis (among others). These drugs are new chemical entities that are obtained by adding a nitric oxide-releasing moiety to aspirin, other analgesics, or even cholesterol-lowering agents. Each drug consists of a parent molecule (for example, aspirin) linked to a "spacer" via an ester linkage, which is in turn connected to the nitric oxide-releasing moiety.

Nitric oxide is normally found in the body and contributes to protecting the lining of the walls of blood vessels and endothelial tissues such as those lining the gastrointestinal tract. Therefore, the aspirin moiety contributes the analgesic, anti-inflammatory, and antiplatelet actions while the nitric oxide protects both the GI tract and coronary blood vessels (Brzozowski et al., 2003). These drugs also protect against carcinomas of the GI tract (Konturek et al., 2006; Rigas, 2007). Nitric oxide-donating analgesics have a potential for a wide range of therapeutic applications because of analgesic, anti-inflammatory, cardioprotective, and chemopreventive actions (Turnbull et al., 2006). They exhibit antiatherosclerotic and antioxidant effects in the walls of blood vessels, for example, in mice with genetic increases in cholesterol (Napoli et al., 2002), and they also reduce vascular injury in blood vessels, promoting vascular remodeling after injury (Yu et al., 2002).

STUDY QUESTIONS

1. What is an NSAID? What does this term mean?
2. List the various actions of aspirin. How might each action be used therapeutically? Which ones might present clinical problems?
3. What is meant by the term *COX inhibitor*?
4. Differentiate between COX-1 and COX-2.
5. How is the anticoagulant action of aspirin "good"? How is it "bad"?
6. Describe the theoretical advantages of COX-2 inhibitors over NSAIDs (nonselective COX inhibitors).
7. What is the correlation between COX enzyme and tumor genesis? How might COX inhibitors be of benefit?
8. What is a nitric oxide-releasing aspirin? What are its advantages? What might be its clinical uses?

REFERENCES

ADAPT Research Group (2007). "Naproxen and Celecoxib Do Not Prevent AD in Early Results from a Randomized Controlled Trial." *Neurology* 68: 1800–1808.

Agency for Healthcare Research and Quality (2006). "Comparative Effectiveness and Safety of Analgesics for Osteoarthritis: Executive Summary from AHRQ." *Medscape Internal Medicine* 8: 1–14. Available at www.effectivehealthcare.ahrq.gov/reports/final.cmf.

Armstrong, E. P., and D. C. Malone (2003). "The Impact of Nonsteroidal Anti-Inflammatory Drugs on Blood Pressure, with an Emphasis on Newer Agents." *Clinical Therapeutics* 25: 1–18.

Brzozowski, T., et al. (2003). "Implications of Reactive Oxygen Species and Cytokines in Gastroprotection Against Stress-Induced Gastric Damage by Nitric Oxide-Releasing Aspirin." *International Journal of Colorectal Diseases* 18: 320–329.

Clark, E., et al. (2007). "A Randomized, Controlled Trial of Acetaminophen, Ibuprofen, and Codeine for Acute Pain relief in Children with Musculoskeletal Trauma." *Pediatrics* 119: 460–467.

Colwell, J. A. (2006). "Aspirin for the Primary Prevention of Cardiovascular Events." *Drugs Today* 42: 467–479.

Durie, V., and K. E. McCarson (2006). "Effects of Analgesic or Antidepressant Drugs on Pain- or Stress-Evoked Hippocampal and Spinal Neurokinin-1 Receptor and Brain-Derived Neurotrophic Factor Gene Expression in the Rat." *Journal of Pharmacology and Experimental Therapeutics* 319: 1235–1243.

Flossmann, E., and P. Rothwell (2007). "Effect of Aspirin on Long-Term Risk of Colorectal Cancer: Consistent Evidence from Randomized and Observational Studies." *Lancet* 369: 1603–1613.

Gilron, I., et al. (2003). "Cycooxygenase-2 Inhibitors in Postoperative Pain Management: Current Evidence and Future Directions." *Anesthesiology* 99: 1198–1208.

Kang, J. H., et al. (2007). "Low Dose Aspirin and Cognitive Function in the Women's Health Study Cognitive Cohort." *British Medical Journal* 334: 987–997.

Karlikaya, G., et al. (2006). "Does Prior Aspirin Use Reduce Stroke Mortality?" *Neurologist* 12: 263–267.

Konturek, P. C., et al. (2006). "NO-Releasing Aspirin Exerts Stronger Inhibitory Effect on Barrett's Adenocarcinoma Cells than Traditional Aspirin." *Journal of Physiology and Pharmacology* 57, Supplement 12: S15–S24.

Marnett, L. J., and R. N. DuBois (2002). "COX-2: A Target for Colon Cancer Prevention." *Annual Review of Pharmacology and Toxicology* 42: 55–80.

Martell, B. A., et al. (2007). "Systematic Review: Opioid Treatment for Chronic Back Pain: Prevalence, Efficacy, and Association with Addiction." *Annals of Internal Medicine* 146: 116–127.

Napoli, C., et al. (2002). "Chronic Treatment with Nitric Oxide-Releasing Aspirin Reduces Plasma Low-Density Lipoprotein Oxidation and Oxidative Stress, Arterial Oxidation-Specific Epitopes, and Artherogenesis in Hypercholesterolemic Mice." *Proceedings of the National Academy of Sciences* 99: 12467–12470.

O'Banion, M. K. (1999). "Cyclooxygenase-2: Molecular Biology, Pharmacology, and Neurobiology." *Critical Reviews in Neurobiology* 13: 45–82.

Rainsford, K. D. (2007). "Anti-Inflammatory Drugs in the 21st Century." *Subcellular Biochemistry* 42: 3–27.

Ricchi, P., et al. (2003). "Nonsteroidal Anti-Inflammatory Drugs in Colorectal Cancer: From Prevention to Therapy." *British Journal of Cancer* 88: 803–807.

Rigas, B. (2007). "The Use of Nitric Oxide-Donating Nonsteroidal Anti-Inflammatory Drugs in the Chemoprotection of Colorectal Neoplasia." *Current Opinions in Gastroenterology* 23: 55–59.

Shanti, B. F., et al. (2006, April). "Adjuvant Analgesia for Management of Chronic Pain." *Practical Pain Management,* 18–27.

Sohn, H. Y., and F. Krotz (2006). "Cyclooxygenase Inhibition and Atherothrombosis." *Current Drug Targets* 7: 1275–1284.

Turnbull, C. M., et al. (2006). "Therapeutic Effects of Nitric Oxide-Aspirin Hybrids." *Expert Opinion on Therapeutic Targets* 10: 911–922.

Wasan, A. D. (2005). "Treating Depression and Anxiety in Chronic Pain Patients." *Pain Management Rounds* 2 (2): 1–6. May be obtained online at www.painmanagementrounds.org. Click on "archives" and choose volumes 2–4.

Yu, J., et al. (2002). "Nitric Oxide-Releasing Aspirin Decreases Vascular Injury by Reducing Inflammation and Promoting Apoptosis." *Laboratory Investigation* 82: 825–832.

Chapter 16

Opioid Analgesics

Pain is one of the most common of human experiences and one of the most common reasons people seek medical care. Pain is a major cause of disability and has enormous economic consequences. It exacts a tremendous physical, psychological, social, and vocational toll on the sufferer, family, friends, and health care workers.

Pain can be defined as a highly undesirable and unpleasant sensory and emotional experience often associated with actual or potential tissue damage. Acute pain is biologically desirable as it functions as a warning system against real or potential damage to the body. Chronic pain, however, serves no useful purpose, causes suffering, limits activities of daily living, and increases the costs of health care and disability. Pain also often occurs comorbid with anxiety and depression, and all may need to be addressed during treatment.

Pain is modulated, enhanced, or diminished by both cerebral and peripheral mechanisms. Cerebral factors include the placebo response, psychological phenomena, and conscious cognitive activation (Price, 2003). These factors are powerfully affected by the opioid analgesics, whereas the NSAIDs (Chapter 15) mostly affect the peripheral inflammatory responses. In addition to invoking endogenous opioids (endorphins), central mechanisms activate antinociceptive pathways beginning in the limbic forebrain and relayed through the brain stem to primary afferent nociceptive sites in the dorsal horn of the spinal cord, modulating the intensity of the pain response as these afferent impulses enter the spinal cord.

When body tissues are damaged, tissue injury is accompanied by the activation of *nociceptive* (pain-sensing) neurons (Figure 16.1)

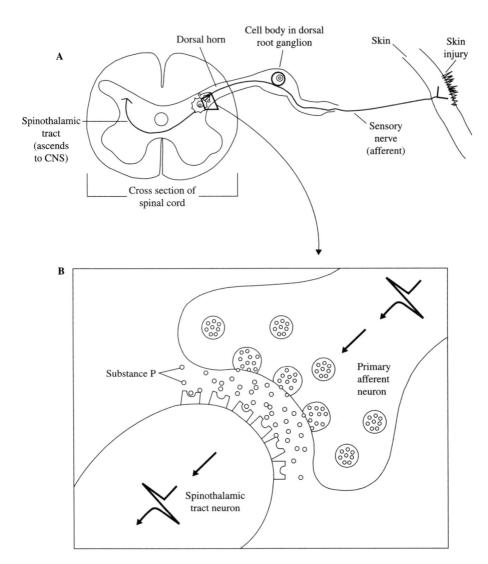

FIGURE 16.1 A. Activation of peripheral nociceptive (pain) fibers results in the release of substance P and other pain-signaling neurotransmitters from nerve terminals in the dorsal horn of the spinal cord. The cell body for the nerve is located in the dorsal root ganglion. **B.** Enlargement of synapse between afferent nociceptive neuron and a spinothalamic tract neuron. Substance P is thought to be a major nociceptive neurotransmitter.

in response to mechanical, thermal, or chemical injuries. With tissue injury or during inflammation, nociceptors become sensitized, discharge spontaneously, and produce ongoing pain. The cell bodies of the axons from these neurons are located in the dorsal root ganglia, and their bidirectional axon relays pain impulses to a synapse in the dorsal horn of the spinal cord and from there to the brain (Figure 16.2). In the brain, the mechanisms associated with the modulation and transfer of pain impulses are very complex: a host of different processes involve multiple neurotransmitters and neuromodulators (DeLeo and Winkelstein, 2002).

Among other events, prolonged discharge of the neurons causes release of glutamate from nerve terminals located in the dorsal horn of the spinal cord. The glutamate then activates a specific type of glutamate receptor in the spinal cord (N-methyl-D-aspartate, or NMDA, receptors; Chapter 3). Activation of NMDA receptors causes the spinal cord neurons to become more responsive to all its inputs, resulting in increased sensitization of the neurons to painful input. When this happens, not only does the spinal cord become sensitized to pain, but the neurons also become less sensitive to the analgesic action of opioid drugs, such as morphine. One major goal of drug therapy is therefore to reduce spinal cord sensitization to pain through modulation of glutamate release. Morphine (Ostermeier et al., 2000) and cannabinoids

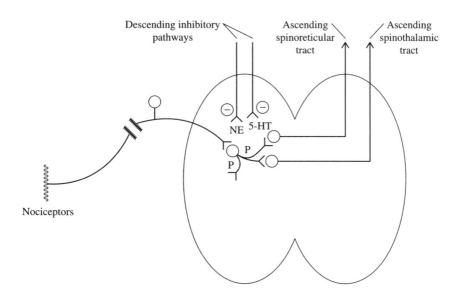

FIGURE 16.2 Release of substance P in the dorsal horn of the spinal cord with transmission of secondary relay pathways to higher centers. Descending inhibitory pathways (–) are also shown. NE = norepinephrine; 5-HT = serotonin.

(Rice et al., 2002) appear to act by altering the release of glutamine, although by slightly different mechanisms. Analgesic drugs therefore can modulate pain processes by the following actions:

- Reducing the peripheral inflammatory response to tissue injury (NSAIDs)

- Blocking NMDA receptors in the spinal cord (dextromethorphan and ketamine; Chapter 18)

- Reducing repetivive activity in injured neurons (anticonvulsant "neuromodulators")

- Modulating neuronal responsiveness in the dorsal horn of the spinal cord through activation of inhibitory endorphin-secreting neurons or inhibitory GABA-secreting neurons (opioid analgesics, neuromodulators)

- Activating descending inhibitory neurons projecting from the brain stem to the dorsal horn of the spinal cord (for example, opioids or antidepressants)

- Modulating the central processing of pain stimuli, reducing the sensory and affective components of pain (opioids)

Drugs that we call *opioids* mimic the actions of our intrinsic, or endogenous, *endorphins* (the normal biological neurotransmitter at opioid or endorphin receptors). Drugs that so act are called *opioid agonists,* since they mimic the analgesic actions both of our endogenous endorphins (acting on the same set of receptors) and of morphine, the major analgesic in the opium poppy. Endorphins and opioids exert much of their analgesic action by acting presynaptically on nociceptive afferent sensory neurons to inhibit the release of pain-inducing transmitters (such as substance P) in the dorsal horn of the spinal cord (Figure 16.3).

Chronic pain, such as that produced by nerve injury, sets up ongoing spinal processes of neuroadaptation with associated physiological changes in spinal circuitry and glutamate receptor adaptive changes. Chronic pain is thought to be poorly responsive to opioids but quite responsive to anticonvulsant neuromodulators (Chapter 8). For this reason, treatment of chronic pain with only opioid therapy is usually ill-advised, as efficacy is limited and the risk of developing drug dependence is high.

Besides the physical component of pain, there are affective components (notably anxiety and depression) that determine a person's emotional response to real or perceived distress. Indeed, the affective component may be the underlying factor in the mechanism of chronic pain for which no objective cause can be identified. If depression or anxiety is present, opioids are ill-advised in favor of antidepressant/

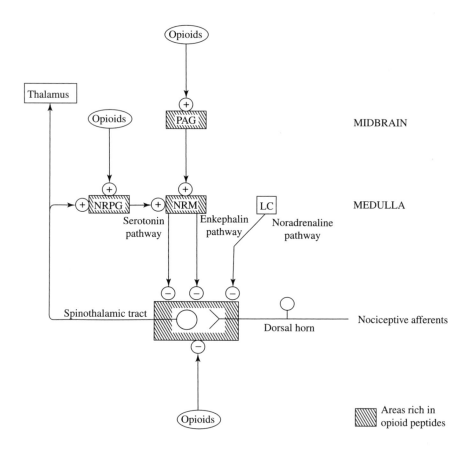

FIGURE 16.3 Sites of action of opioids on pain transmission. Opioids excite neurons in the periaqueductal gray matter (PAG) and in the midbrain and medulla. From there, serotoninergic and enkephalinergic neurons run to the dorsal horn and exert an inhibitory influence on transmission. Opioids also act directly on the dorsal horn. The locus coeruleus (LC) sends noradrenergic neurons to the dorsal horn, which also inhibits transmission. The pathways shown in this diagram represent a considerable oversimplification, but they depict the general organization of the supraspinal control mechanisms.

anxiolytic therapies, both pharmacological and behavioral. For people with chronic pain, treatment focuses on behavior modification, hypnosis, cognitive-behavioral therapy, or self-management approaches that include biopsychosocial models of therapy (Cianfrini and Doleys, 2006).

History

Opium is extracted from poppy seeds and has been used for thousands of years to produce euphoria, analgesia, sleep, and relief from diarrhea and cough (Bernstein et al., 2007). In ancient times, opium was used primarily for its constipating effect and later for its sleep-inducing properties (noted by writers such as Homer, Hippocrates, Dioscorides, Virgil, and Ovid). Even in those times, recreational abuse and addiction were common. From the early Greek and Roman days through the sixteenth and seventeenth centuries, the medicinal and recreational uses of opium were well established. Combined with alcohol, the mixture was called *laudanum* (named by Paracelsus in 1520), meaning "something to be praised," and it was referred to as the "stone of immortality." Thereafter, opium and laudanum were used for practically every known disease.

In the early 1800s, morphine was isolated from opium as its active ingredient. Since then, morphine has been used throughout the world as the premier agent for treating severe pain. Recognition of the addictive properties of opium, morphine, and other opioids has led to restrictions of their use to the treatment of conditions for which they are known to be effective. After the invention of the hypodermic needle in 1856 and especially after the Civil War (when opioid addiction was referred to as "soldier's disease"), a new type of drug user appeared in the United States—one who self-administered opioids by injection. By about 1910, concern began to mount about the dangers of opioids and the dependence they could induce. In 1914 the Harrison Narcotic Act was passed, and the use of most opioid products was strictly controlled. Nonmedical uses of opioids were banned, although today nonmedical use continues, despite intense efforts to eradicate it.

The use of opioids is deeply entrenched in society; it is widespread and impossible to stop. Opioids exert pleasurable effects, produce tolerance and physiological dependence, and have a potential for compulsive misuse—all liabilities that are likely to resist any efforts at legal control. Also, the opioids will continue to be used in medicine because they are irreplaceable as pain-relieving agents. Opioids dramatically relieve emotional as well as physical pain. This property contributes to making them extremely seductive for self-administration. Savage (2005) stated:

> Therapeutic opioid use is increasing and greater volumes of prescriptions for opioid medications are being distributed through legitimate channels, from manufacturer to pharmacy to patient, creating greater opportunities for the diversion of opioids for non-therapeutic use. . . . [From] 1997 through 2001 . . . there has been a 1.5- to a 4.3-fold increase in therapeutic opioid demand. (p. 1)

Savage illustrates his point in a figure reproduced here as Figure 16.4

Furthermore, regarding the seeking of opioids for nontherapeutic purposes, the rates of involvement of prescription opioids in patients presenting to emergency rooms more than doubled between 1996 and 2001 (Figure 16.5). These numbers are continuing to increase: after marijuana, prescription pain pills (opioids) are currently

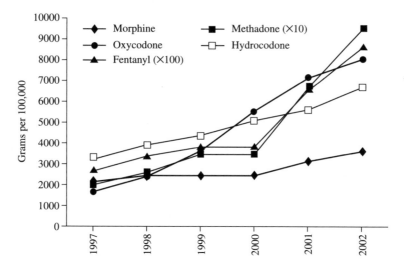

FIGURE 16.4 Increase in therapeutic opioid use in the United States between 1997 and 2002. [From Savage, (2005), Figure 1.]

the drugs most often illicitly abused by people in the United States, far surpassing the numbers of people who abuse psychedelic drugs, cocaine, methamphetamine, inhalants, and even heroin. Figure 16.6 illustrates the increase through 2004 in the abuse of opioids, with

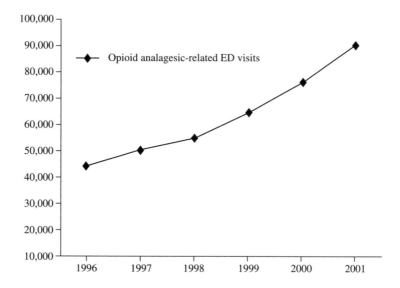

FIGURE 16.5 Rates of opioid misuse between 1996 and 2001. [From Savage, (2005), Figure 2.]

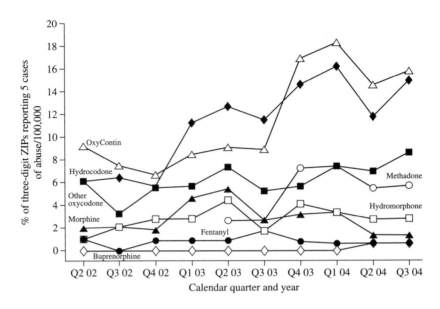

FIGURE 16.6 Percentage of zip codes in the United States in which at least five cases of abuse per 100,000 people were detected for each opioid by calendar quarter of each year 2002–2004. [From T. J. Cicero et al., "Trends in Abuse of OxyContin and Other Opioid Analgesics in the United States: 2002–2004," *Journal of Pain* 6 (2005), Figure 3, p. 667.]

short-acting preparations of hydrocodone (Vicodin and generic equivalents) and long-acting oxycodone (OxyContin) far exceeding abuse of other opioids.

Terminology

Before proceeding, some terms need definition. *Opium* comes from a Greek word (*opion*) that means "juice"; more specifically, it refers to the juice or exudate from the poppy *Papaver somniferum*. An *opiate*, strictly defined, is a drug extracted from the exudate of the poppy. Therefore the term is restricted to two drugs that are naturally found in the exudates: *morphine* and *codeine*. An *opioid* is any exogenous drug (natural, semisynthetic, or synthetic) that binds to an opiate receptor and produces agonistic, or morphinelike, effects.

Endorphin is an all-inclusive term that applies to an endogenous substance (a substance naturally formed in the body) that exhibits pharmacological properties of morphine. There are three families of endogenous opioid peptides—*enkephalins, dynorphins,* and *beta endorphins*. The topic of endogenous opioids is large and complex. The interested reader is referred to the review by Akil and coworkers (1998).

Opioids occur in nature in two places: in the juice of the opium poppy (morphine and codeine) and within our own bodies as any of the endorphins. All other opioids either are prepared from morphine (*semisynthetic opioids*, such as heroin) or are synthesized from other precursor compounds (*synthetic opioids*, such as fentanyl).

The term *narcotic* is derived from the Greek word *narke*, meaning "numbness," "sleep," or "stupor." Originally referring to any drug that induced sleep, the term later became associated with opioids, such as morphine and heroin. Today, it is an imprecise and pejorative term, sometimes used in a legal context to refer to a wide variety of abused substances that includes nonopioids, such as cocaine and marijuana. The term is not useful in a pharmacological context, and its use in referring to opioids is discouraged. It is not used in this chapter.

Opioid Receptors

Opioids are agonists at highly specific receptor sites, and the analgesic potency of the agonist correlates with the affinity of the agonist for the opioid receptor. There is general agreement on the existence of at least three types of opioid receptors: *mu, kappa,* and *delta.* The genes encoding these three families, as well as the receptors themselves, have been cloned, sequenced, and well studied (Kieffer, 1999).

Receptors on which endorphins and exogenous opioids act are widely distributed throughout the central nervous system, and each type of opioid receptor is differentially distributed. Some regions of the CNS (for example, the spinal cord) have all three types of receptors; other regions have predominantly one type (the thalamus, for example, has primarily mu receptors). The clinical significance of this distribution is still unclear. However, overall, it seems that mu receptor agonists display not only the strongest analgesic actions but also the highest abuse liability (Kieffer, 1999).

Mu receptors are located in the brain, in the spinal cord, and in the periphery. Morphine is the classic example of a mu agonist. Morphine exerts powerful effects on the brain (especially in the thalamus and striatum), the brain stem (where it slows respiration), and the spinal cord (where it exerts a strong analgesic action). In contrast, the delta receptor agonists exhibit little addictive potential and are also poor analgesics. Delta receptors are thought to modulate the activity of mu receptors. Kappa agonists exert modest analgesic effects, little or no respiratory depression, miosis (pinpoint pupils), and little or no dependence effects. In fact, activation of kappa receptors may serve to antagonize mu receptor-mediated actions in the brain (Pan, 1998). The use of kappa agonists is limited by strong and unpleasant dysphoric responses that can accompany their use (Kieffer, 1999).

In the mid-1990s the opioid receptors were first isolated, purified, cloned, and sequenced, and their three-dimensional structures were modeled. All opioid receptors belong to a superfamily of G-protein-coupled receptors, all of which possess seven membrane-spanning regions (Figure 16.7) similar to the receptors discussed earlier. Each receptor type (mu, kappa, delta) arises from its own gene and is expressed through a specific messenger RNA (mRNA). Each receptor is a chain of approximately 450 amino acids, and the amino acid sequences are about 60 percent identical to one another and 40 percent different (see Figure 16.7). The diversity is responsible for

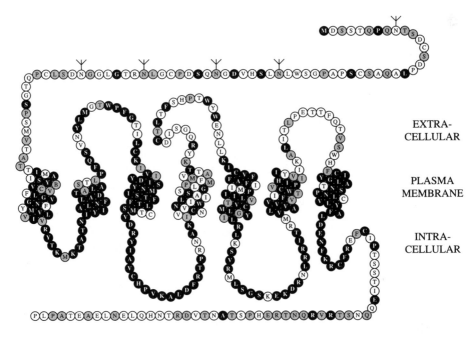

FIGURE 16.7 Two-dimensional model of the rat mu opioid receptor. The receptor is a chain of about 390 amino acids (the letter in each circle is the first letter of the individual amino acid), with seven transmembrane coils and a terminal chain both intracellular (linked to a G protein, not illustrated) and extracellular (binds the transmitter). Amino acids conserved in mu, delta, and kappa receptors are shown in black; amino acids conserved in mu and either delta or kappa receptors are shown in gray; amino acids preset only in the mu receptor (not in delta or kappa receptors) are shown in white. [From M. Satoh and M. Minami, "Molecular Pharmacology of the Opioid Receptors," *Pharmacology and Therapeutics* 68 (1995), Figure 1.]

the specific fit of an endogenous endorphin or an exogenous opioid to a specific receptor. A fit for a fentanyl derivative for a mu receptor is illustrated in Figure 16.8. In this figure, note that the flat, two-dimensional drawing of the receptor shown in Figure 16.7 is now depicted more realistically as a three-dimensional receptor with seven helical coils embedded in the membrane and three amino acid loops and a terminal chain (located in the extracellular, synaptic space) forming a fit with the opioid.

What is the consequence of the binding of an opioid agonist to a mu receptor? As discussed, the primary action of opioid receptor activation (by either an endorphin or an opioid) is reduction in or inhibition of neurotransmission, which occurs largely through opioid-induced presynaptic inhibition of neurotransmitter release (Figure 16.9). Changes are different for each receptor type and may explain the differences in receptor function (for example, mu receptor action induces euphoria and is a positive reinforcer, while kappa

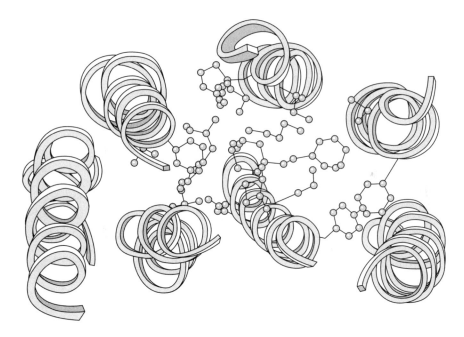

FIGURE 16.8 Speculative three-dimensional depiction of interaction of the mu opioid receptor with the potent pure mu agonist lofentanyl. Transmembrane helices are depicted by coils. The cell membrane within which the coils reside is not illustrated. Lofentanyl structure is shown by the connected small balls, which represent carbon molecules of the drug. Specific side chains of amino acids on the receptor helices bind with specific portions of the lofentanyl molecule. [Original details by H. Moereels, L. M. Kaymans, J. Leysen, and P. Janssen, Janssen Research Foundation, Beerse, Belgium.]

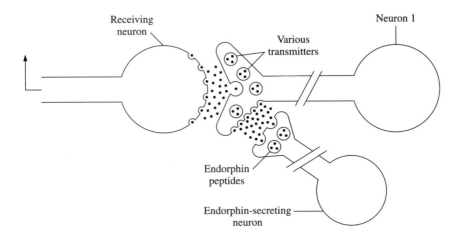

FIGURE 16.9 Simplified illustration demonstrating the presynaptic inhibition (exerted by an endorphin-secreting neuron) on neuron 1, inhibiting its release of transmitter. In the spinal cord, neuron 1 would be a primary afferent (sensory pain neuron), with enkephalin-inhibiting substance P release. In the ventral tegmentum, neuron 1 might be a GABA-secreting neuron, with an endorphin-inhibiting GABA release, disinhibiting a dopaminergic neuron, a mechanism of opioid-induced reward.

receptor activation causes dydphoria and is not reinforcing). Snyder and Pasternak (2003) present a historical review of the development of our knowledge about opioid receptors.

Mu Receptors

Mu opioid receptors are present in all structures in the brain and spinal cord involved in morphine-induced analgesia. The structures include the periaquadctal gray matter, spinal trigeminal nucleus, caudate and geniculate nuclei, thalamus, and spinal cord (dorsal horn). Mu receptors are also present in brain-stem nuclei involved in control of respiration (and in morphine's depression of respiration), in brainstem structures involved in initiation of nausea and vomiting, and in the nucleus accumbens, an area involved in the compulsive abuse of opioids and other drugs subject to compulsive abuse. Few or no mu receptors are found in the cerebral cortex or cerebellum.

Kappa Receptors

Kappa receptors are found in the basal ganglia, nucleus accumbens, ventral tegmentum, deep layers of the cerebral cortex, hypothalamus, periaquaductal gray matter, dorsal horn of the spinal cord, and in the periphery. Binder and coworkers (2001) studied two experimental kappa agonists that do not cross the blood-brain barrier but act only in the periphery. They were both analgesic and anti-inflammatory. The researchers concluded that the agonists might potentiate centrally acting opioids or standard anti-inflammatory NSAIDs (Chapter 15).

As stated, kappa receptors in the CNS may actually antagonize mu receptor activity. Kappa receptors produce modest amounts of analgesia, dysphoria (as opposed to mu receptor-induced euphoria), disorientation, rare feelings of depersonalization, and only mild respiratory depression. The mixed agonist-antagonist drugs, such as pentazocine (Talwin), are agonists at the kappa receptors. Dynorphin is the endorphin with the greatest affinity for the kappa receptor. Salvinocin A is discussed further in Chapter 18.

The hallucinogenic agent salvinorin A (from the psychedelic mint plant *Salvia divinorum*) is a potent agonist (stimulant) of the kappa opioid receptor (Chavkin et al., 2004). Therefore, kappa receptor activation may be related to the modulation of human perception. For example, bremazocine, a potent kappa-opioid receptor agonist, is more analgesic than is morphine, without displaying euphoria, dependence, or respiratory depression. Unfortunately, the perceptual side effects (space and time distortions, visual distortions, body image distortions, depersonalization, derealization, and loss of self-control) limit its use as a clinical analgesic (Dortch-Carnes and Potter, 2005).

Delta Receptors

The enkephalins are the endogenous endorphins for the delta receptors. These receptors have limited analgesic effects, but they do display a prominent effect on emotional states: they exert robust antidepressant and anxiolytic effects, suggesting potential as clinical antidepressants and anxiolytics (Jutkiewicz, 2006). In agreement with the discussion of the involvement of brain-derived neurotrophic factor in depression, delta opioid agonists increase the levels of this substance (Narita et al., 2006; Torregrossa et al., 2006).

Classification of Opioid Analgesics

Classification of opioids is usually according to the receptors to which they bind and the consequences of the binding. Thus, an individual opioid is called an *agonist*, a *partial agonist*, a *mixed agonist-antagonist*, or a *pure antagonist* at the given receptor (Table 16.1). All the strong opioids, such as morphine, primarily act as agonists at mu receptors, and their pharmacological effects, including analgesia, respiratory depression, miosis, euphoria, reward, and constipation, all follow from this action.

TABLE 16.1 Classification of opioid analgesics by analgesic properties

Pure agonists	Mixed agonist-antagonists	Pure antagonists	Partial agonists
Morphine	Nalbuphine (Nubain)	Naloxone (Narcan)	Buprenorphene (in Suboxone)
Codeine	Butorphanol (Stadol)	Naltrexone (Trexan,	Tramadol (Ultram)[a]
Heroin	Pentazocine (Talwin)	ReVia, Vivitrol)	
Meperidine (Demerol)	Dezocine (Dalgan)	Nalmefene (Revex)	
Methadone (Dolophine)			
Oymorphone (Numorphan)			
Hydromorphone (Dilaudid)			
Fentanyl (Sublimaze)			

[a] Tramadol also blocks reuptake of norepinephrine and serotonin.

Pure Agonists

An agonist is a drug that has an affinity for (binds to) cell receptors to induce changes in the cell characteristic of the natural neurotransmitter chemical (for example, an endorphin) for the receptor (Chapter 1). Morphine is the prototype opioid analgesic, and there are many others, including methadone, an orally active, long-acting opioid used to treat heroin dependency. All these strong opioids bind to mu receptors (Table 16.2). Therefore, a mu agonist produces analgesia, respiratory depression, and euphoria and has a propensity to cause dependence. So far, all attempts to separate analgesia from euphoria, dependence, and respiratory depression have been unsuccessful, and attempts in the foreseeable future are likely to be so as well.

Pure Antagonists

Pure antagonists have *affinity* for a receptor (here, the mu receptor), but after attaching they elicit no change in cellular functioning (they lack intrinsic activity). What they do is compete with the mu agonist for the receptor, precipitating withdrawal in an opioid-dependent person and reversing any analgesia caused by the agonist. One example is the clinical use of the opioid antagonist naltrexone in treatment programs for heroin addicts, where heroin taken after the antagonist elicits no analgesic or euphoric effects.

TABLE 16.2 Classification of opioid analgesics by actions at opioid receptors

Compound	Receptor types[a]		
	Mu	**Kappa**	**Delta**
Morphine	+++	+	+
Naloxone	−	−	−
Pentazocine	+/0	+	NA
Butorphanol	+/0	+	NA
Nalbuphine	−	+	NA
Buprenorphine	++	+	+
Fentanyl	+++	+	+
Dezocine	+	+	+

[a] The mu receptor is thought to mediate supraspinal analgesia, respiratory depression, euphoria, and physical dependence; the kappa receptor, spinal analgesia, miosis, and sedation. Categorizations are based on best inferences about actions in humans. See text for further explanation. Agonists are indicated by one or more plus signs, antagonists by a minus sign, and agents that have no significant action at the receptor by zero. NA = data not available.

Mixed Agonist-Antagonists

A mixed agonist-antagonist drug produces an agonistic effect at one receptor and an antagonistic effect at another. Clinically useful mixed drugs are kappa agonists and weak mu antagonists (they bind to both kappa and mu receptors, but only the kappa receptor is activated). In contrast to a pure agonist, a mixed agonist-antagonist usually displays a ceiling effect for analgesia; in other words, it has decreased efficacy compared to a pure agonist and usually is not so effective in treating severe pain. Also, when a mixed agonist-antagonist is administered to an opioid-dependent person, the antagonist effect at a mu receptor precipitates an acute withdrawal syndrome. *Pentazocine* (Talwin) is the prototype mixed agonist-antagonist.

Partial Agonists

A partial agonist binds to opioid receptors but has a low intrinsic activity (low efficacy). It therefore exerts an analgesic effect, but the effect has a ceiling at less than the maximal effect produced by a pure agonist. *Buprenorphine* (in Suboxone) is the prototype partial opioid agonist. When administered to a person who is not opioid dependent, analgesia is observed; when administered to an opioid-dependent person, however, blockade of the pure agonist can occur and withdrawal can be precipitated. Compared to a mixed agonist-antagonist, the partial agonist buprenorphine binds to all three types of opioid receptors with higher efficacy at mu receptors than do the mixed agonist-antagonist agents. Its potential for producing respiratory depression is lower than that of morphine.

Morphine: A Pure Opioid Agonist

Of the two analgesics found in the opium poppy, morphine and codeine, morphine (Figure 16.10) is the more potent and represents about 10 percent of the crude exudate. Codeine is much less potent and constitutes only 0.5 percent of the crude exudate. Despite decades of research, no other drug has been found that exceeds morphine's effectiveness as an analgesic, and no other drug is clinically superior for treating severe pain.

Pharmacokinetics

Morphine is usually administered by injection, but it may also be given orally or rectally. Under development is an intranasal delivery system for morphine (Rylomine). This product would have a rapid onset of action in situations where parenteral use is not desired. Orally, morphine is available in immediate-release formulation and as a long-acting,

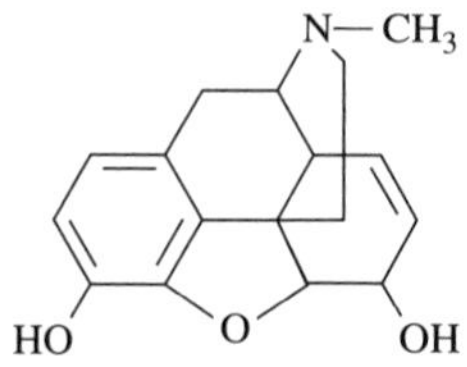

Morphine

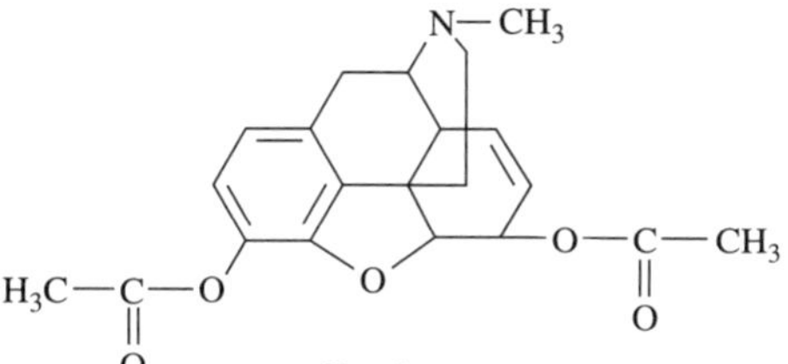

Heroin

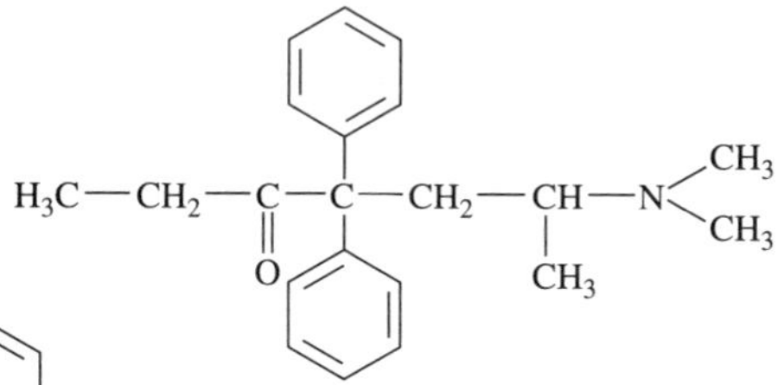

Methadone (Dolophine)

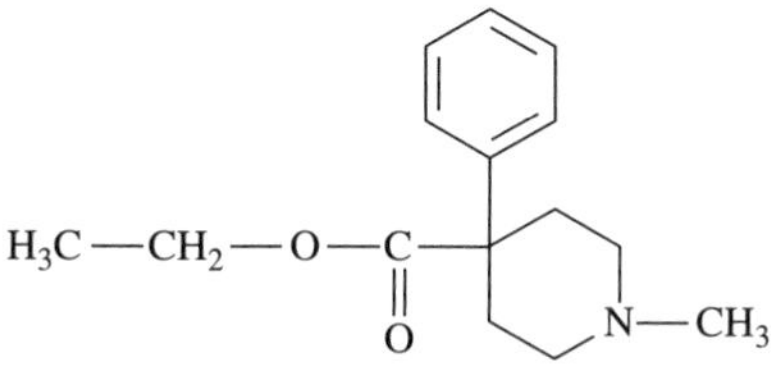

Meperidine (Demerol)

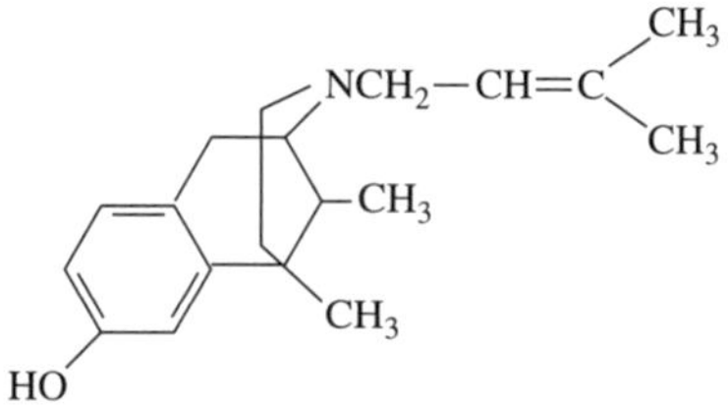

Pentazocine (Talwin)

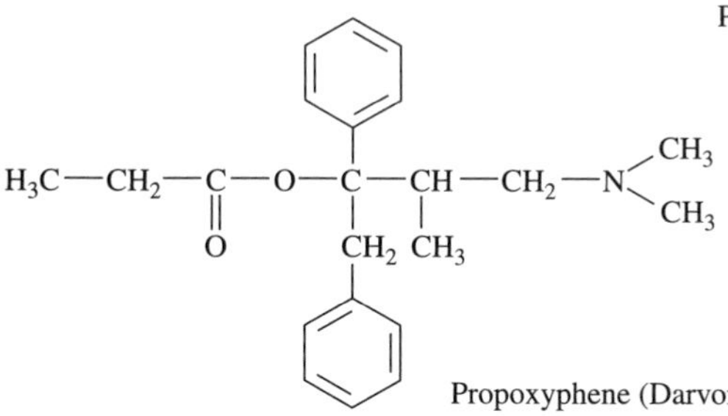

Propoxyphene (Darvon)

FIGURE 16.10 Structures of morphine, heroin, and four synthetic analgesics.

time-release product (MS-Contin). In general, absorption of morphine from the gastrointestinal tract is slow and incomplete compared to absorption following injection or inhalation. Absorption through the rectum is adequate, and several opioids (morphine, hydromorphone, and oxymorphone) are available in suppository form.[1]

The action of opioids in the spinal cord has led to the administration of morphine directly into the spinal canal (through small catheters), placing the drug right at its site of action and avoiding its effects both on higher CNS centers (maintaining wakefulness and avoiding respiratory depression) and in the periphery (avoiding drug-induced constipation). In medicine, this technique is used to control the pain of obstetric labor and delivery, to treat postoperative pain, and (for long-term use) to relieve otherwise intractable pain associated with terminal cancer and chronic pain. Morphine administered by injection must be given with great care to avoid potentially fatal respiratory depression.

For millennia, crude opium has been smoked for recreational purposes; the rapidity of onset of drug action rivals that following intravenous injection. Morphine itself is rarely abused in this manner; heroin is the preparation of choice. However, for therapeutic use, a nebulized form of morphine has been found to be effective, for example, in patients with terminal illnesses who cannot tolerate injections (Thipphawong et al., 2003). Nebulizer preparations have not yet been marketed.

Morphine crosses the blood-brain barrier fairly slowly, as it is more water soluble than lipid soluble. Other opioids (such as heroin and fentanyl) cross the blood-brain barrier much more rapidly. Only about 20 percent of administered morphine reaches the CNS. This may explain why the "flash" or "rush" following intravenous injection of heroin is much more intense than that perceived after injecting morphine.

Opioids reach all body tissues, including the fetus; infants born of addicted mothers are physically dependent on opioids and exhibit withdrawal symptoms that require intensive therapy. The habitual use of morphine or other opioids during pregnancy does not seem to increase the risk of congenital anomalies; thus these drugs are not considered to be teratogenic. However, there are increased risks of birth-related problems and fetal growth retardation. Other delays and impairments observed in the development of opioid-exposed children may relate more to environmental and social-developmental problems.

The liver metabolizes morphine, and one of its metabolites (morphine-6-glucuronide) is actually 10 to 20 times more potent as an analgesic than morphine. Much of the analgesic action of morphine

---

[1]This kind of preparation might be indicated for patients suffering from muscle-wasting diseases who cannot tolerate other routes of administration.

is mediated by this active metabolite. The half-lives of morphine and morphine-6-glucuronide are both 3 to 5 hours. Patients with impaired kidney function tend to accumulate the metabolite and thus may be more sensitive to morphine administration.

Urine-screening tests can be used to detect codeine and morphine as well as their metabolites. Because heroin is metabolized to monoacetylmorphine and then to morphine, and because street heroin also contains acetylcodeine (which is metabolized to codeine), heroin use is suspected when monoacetylmorphine, morphine, and codeine are present in urine. Frequently, urinalysis cannot accurately determine which specific drug (heroin, codeine, or morphine) has been used. Furthermore, codeine is widely available in cough syrups and analgesic preparations, and even poppy seeds contain small amounts of morphine. Depending on the drug that was taken, morphine and codeine metabolites may be detected in a patient's urine for 2 to 4 days.

Pharmacological Effects

Morphine produces a syndrome characterized by analgesia, relaxed euphoria, sedation, a sense of tranquility, reduced apprehension and concern, respiratory depression, suppression of the cough reflex, and pupillary constriction.

Analgesia. Morphine produces intense analgesia and indifference to pain, reducing the intensity of pain and thus reducing the associated distress by altering the central processing of pain. Morphine analgesia occurs without loss of consciousness and without affecting other sensory modalities. The pain may actually persist as a sensation, but patients feel more comfortable and are able to tolerate the pain. In other words, the perception of the pain is significantly altered.

Euphoria. Morphine produces a pleasant euphoric state, which includes a strong feeling of contentment, well-being, and lack of concern. This effect is part of the affective, or reinforcing, response to the drug. Use of exogenous opioids gives a person access to the reinforcement system, especially in the nucleus accumbens. Once opioids reach this positive reward system, normally reserved to reward the performance of species-specific survival behaviors, the user has a profoundly rewarding experience.

Opioid use becomes an acquired drive state that permeates all aspects of human life. With acute use, all painful feelings, emotions, and physical discomforts become tolerable. Even the knowledge that withdrawal will follow, that life and livelihood are imperiled, that only more drug will avail withdrawal, that legal apprehension or even death may follow—becomes tolerable as long as drug is present. Separate neural pathways that cause withdrawal events to be perceived as life-threatening and the subsequent physiological reactions often lead to renewed opioid consumption. As discussed in the section on the treatment of chronic alcoholism in Chapter 4, the drive to resume ingestion of drug now appears to involve the endogenous cannabinoid system, as cannabinoid receptor antagonists can block the compulsion to return to drug use (Chapter 17). The same cannabinoid system that can propel a return to alcohol drinking probably is involved in a compulsion to return to opioid use.

Regular users of morphine describe the effects of intravenous injection in ecstatic and often sexual terms, but the euphoric effect becomes progressively less intense after repeated use. At this point, users inject the drug for one or more of several possible reasons: to try to reexperience the euphoria felt after the first few injections, to maintain a state of pleasure and well-being, to prevent mental discomfort that may be associated with reality, or to prevent withdrawal symptoms.

The mechanism of morphine's positive reinforcing and euphoria-producing action probably involves dopaminergic as well as mu receptors. Opioids activate mu receptors within the mesolimbic dopamine reward system by means of the dopaminergic ventral tegmental–nucleus accumbens pathway that is involved in the rewarding effects of cocaine and alcohol. As stated by Narita and coworkers (2001):

> Various studies provide arguments to support substantial roles for mu-opioid receptors and the possible involvement of delta-opioid receptors in the development of physical and psychological dependence on morphine. Noradrenergic transmission originating in the locus coeruleus is most likely to play the primary causal role in the expression of physical dependence on morphine. In contrast, many studies have pointed to the mesolimbic dopaminergic pathway projecting from the ventral tegmental area to the nucleus accumbens as a critical site for the initiation of psychological dependence on opioids. (p. 1)

In the ventral tegmental area, morphine inhibits GABA neurons via mu opioid receptors, thus disinhibiting dopaminergic neurons and increasing dopamine input in the nucleus accumbens and in other areas; this phenomenon may be involved in the mechanism of reward, that is, the positive reinforcement of opioid addiction.

Sedation and Anxiolysis. Morphine produces anxiolysis, sedation, and drowsiness, but the level of sedation is not so deep as that produced by the CNS depressants. Although people who are taking morphine doze, they can usually be awakened readily. During this state, cognitive slowing is prominent, accompanied by a lack of concentration, apathy, complacency, lethargy, reduced mentation, and a sense of tranquility. Obviously, in such a state, cognitive impairment results.

Depression of Respiration. Morphine causes a profound depression of respiration by decreasing the respiratory center's sensitivity to higher levels of carbon dioxide in the blood. Respiratory rate is reduced even at therapeutic doses; at higher doses, the rate slows even further, respiratory volume decreases, breathing patterns become shallow and irregular, and, at sufficiently high levels, breathing ceases. Respiratory depression is the single most important acute side effect of morphine and is the cause of death from acute opioid overdosage. The combination of morphine (or other opioid) with alcohol or other sedatives is especially dangerous.

Suppression of Cough. Opioids suppress the cough center, which is located in the brain stem. Opioids have historically been used as cough suppressants; codeine is particularly popular for this purpose. Today, however, less addicting drugs are used as cough suppressants, and opioids have become inappropriate choices for treating persistent cough.

Pupillary Constriction. Morphine (as well as other mu and kappa agonists) causes pupillary constriction (miosis). Indeed, pupillary constriction in the presence of analgesia is characteristic of opioid ingestion.

Nausea and Vomiting. Morphine stimulates receptors in an area of the medulla that is called the chemoreceptor trigger zone. Stimulation of this area produces nausea and vomiting, which are the most characteristic and unpleasant side effects of morphine and other opioids, but they are not life-threatening.

Gastrointestinal Symptoms. Morphine and the other opioids relieve diarrhea as a result of their direct actions on the intestine, the most important action of opioids outside the CNS. Opioids cause intestinal tone to increase, motility to decrease, feces to dehydrate, and intestinal spasm (and cramping) to occur. This combination of decreased propulsion, increased intestinal tone, decreased rate of movement of food, and dehydration hardens the stool and further retards the advance of fecal material.. Nothing more effective than the opioids has yet been developed for treating severe diarrhea. Two opioids have been developed that only very minimally cross the blood-brain barrier into the CNS. One is *diphenoxylate* (the primary active ingredient in Lomotil), and the other is *loperamide* (Imodium). These two drugs are exceedingly effective opioid antidiarrheals but are not analgesics, nor are they prone to compulsive abuse because they do not reach the CNS.

Endocrine Effects. Morphine and other opioids exert subtle but important effects on the functioning of the endocrine system (Katz, 2005). Effects include reduced libido in men and menstrual irregularities and infertility in women. These effects occur secondary to drug-induced reductions in sex hormone releasing agents from the hypothalamus. As a result, testosterone levels in males fall, as do the levels of luteinizing and follicle-stimulating hormones in females. If a person is taking an opioid for chronic pain, both the reduction in sex hormones and the chronic pain may result in loss of sexual desire and performance, alterations in gender role, fatigue, mood alterations, loss of muscle mass and strength, abnormal menses, infertility, and osteoporosis and fractures (Katz, 2005). Therefore, it may be unclear whether opioid-induced hypogonadism or the chronic pain was responsible.

Other Effects. Morphine can release histamine from its storage sites in mast cells in the blood, which can result in localized itching or more severe allergic reactions, including bronchoconstriction (an asthmalike constriction of the bronchi of the lungs). Opioids also affect white blood cell function, perhaps producing complex alterations in the immune system. It is advisable, perhaps, to avoid the use of morphine in patients with compromised immune function.

Tolerance and Dependence

The development of tolerance and dependence with repeated use is a characteristic feature of all opioid drugs, including morphine. The use of all mu agonist opioids is severely limited because of the development of tolerance, the presence of uncomfortable side effects, and the potential for compulsive abuse.

The molecular basis of tolerance is now thought to involve glutaminergic mechanisms (Celerier et al., 2000). It appears that glutaminergic NMDA receptors may regulate mu receptor mRNA, accounting for the development of tolerance to the continuous presence of opioid. Akil and coworkers (1998) review the intracellular alterations induced by morphine and their relation to the development of tolerance after prolonged exposure to opioids. Christensen and coworkers (2000) review the complex interaction among glutamate, NMDA receptor blockade, analgesia, and the development of tolerance and dependence.

The rate at which tolerance develops varies widely. When morphine or other opioids are used only intermittently, little, if any, tolerance develops, and the opioids retain their initial efficacy. When administration is repeated, tolerance may become so marked that massive doses have to be administered to either maintain a degree of euphoria or prevent withdrawal discomfort (avoidance of discomfort is more common). The degree of tolerance is illustrated by the fact that the dose of morphine can be increased from clinical doses (50 to 60 milligrams per day) to 500 milligrams per day over as short a period as 10 days.

Tolerance to one opioid leads to cross-tolerance to all other natural and synthetic opioids, even if they are chemically dissimilar.

Cross-tolerance, however, does not develop between the opioids and the sedative hypnotics. In other words, a person who has developed a tolerance for morphine will also have a tolerance for heroin but not for alcohol or benzodiazepines.

Physical dependence was described in Chapter 1 as an altered state of biology induced by a drug whereby withdrawal of a drug is followed by a complex set of biological events typical for that class of drugs. Acute withdrawal from opioids has been well studied since it can be easily precipitated in a drug-dependent person by injecting the opioid antagonist naloxone (Narcan). Withdrawal results in a profound reduction in the release of dopamine in the nucleus accumbens and a threefold increase in the release of norepinephrine in various structures, including the hippocampus, nucleus accumbens, and locus coeruleus. The firing rate of neurons located in the locus coeruleus is actively inhibited by morphine, returns to baseline levels with tolerance, and rises dramatically during withdrawal; these phenomena may be involved in the mechanism of dependence.

Symptoms of withdrawal are, in general, the opposite of pharmacological effects (Table 16.3) and include restlessness, dysphoria, drug craving, sweating, extreme anxiety, depression, irritability, fever, chills,

TABLE 16.3 Acute effects of opioids and rebound withdrawal symptoms

Acute action	Withdrawal sign
Analgesia	Pain and irritability
Respiratory depression	Hyperventilation
Euphoria	Dysphoria and depression
Relaxation and sleep	Restlessness and insomnia
Tranquilization	Fearfulness and hostility
Decreased blood pressure	Increased blood pressure
Constipation	Diarrhea
Pupillary constriction	Pupillary dilation
Hypothermia	Hyperthermia
Drying of secretions	Lacrimation, runny nose
Reduced sex drive	Spontaneous ejaculation
Peripheral vasodilation; flushed and warm skin	Chilliness and "gooseflesh"

From R. S. Feldman, J. S. Meyer, and L. F. Quenzer, *Principles of Neuropsychopharmacology* (Sunderland, MA: Sinauer, 1997), Table 12.8, p. 533.

retching and vomiting, increased respiratory rate (panting), cramping, insomnia, explosive diarrhea, and intense aches and pains. The magnitude of these acute withdrawal symptoms depends on the dose of opioid that had been used, the frequency of previous drug administration, and the duration of drug dependence. Acute opioid withdrawal is not considered to be life threatening, although it can seem unbearable to the person experiencing it.

To help alleviate the symptoms of acute withdrawal, several approaches have been tried, none with great success (O'Connor, 2005). These approaches include clonidine-assisted detoxification, buprenorphine-assisted detoxification, and rapid anesthesia-aided detoxification (RAAD). Clonidine is a drug that acts on the sympathetic nervous system to reduce some of the physical manifestations of withdrawal. Buprenorphine will be discussed later in this chapter.

In *rapid anesthesia-aided detoxification* (RAAD), a pure opioid antagonist, such as naloxone or naltrexone, and the sympathetic blocker clonidine are administered intravenously to the opioid-dependent person while he or she is asleep under general anesthesia. The procedure goes on for about 72 hours, during which time the withdrawal signs are blunted. The objective is to enable the patient to tolerate high doses of an opioid antagonist and thus undergo complete detoxification while unconscious. After awakening, the patient is maintained on orally administered naltrexone to reduce opioid craving and undergoes supportive psychotherapy and group therapies for relapse prevention and to address the underlying causes of addiction. The RAAD technique is controversial, in part because it is expensive, it involves the risks of anesthesia, and it focuses only on short-term dependence rather than on long-term cravings and social adjustments. One study compared the three techniques of detoxification and concluded that RAAD was no less safe or effective than other techniques (Collins et al., 2005).

No matter the method of opioid withdrawal, following acute withdrawal focus is directed toward a protracted *abstinence syndrome*, beginning when the acute phase of opioid withdrawal ends and persisting for up to six months. Symptoms of this syndrome include depression, abnormal responses to stressful situations, drug hunger, decreased self-esteem, anxiety, and other psychological disturbances. Complicating the diagnosis of prolonged abstinence syndrome is the high prevalence of other psychiatric disorders (for example, affective and personality disorders) in opioid-dependent patients; antisocial personality disorder and major depression are the most common comorbidities. Antidepressants such as imipramine or desipramine (Chapter 7) can be robustly effective.

Several behavioral theories have been posited to account for continued opioid use:

- Continued use avoids the distress and dysphoria associated with withdrawal (a negative reinforcing effect).

- The euphoria produced by the opioids leads to their continued use (a positive reinforcing effect).

- Preexisting dysphoric or painful affective states are alleviated (presuming that the opioids were initially used as a type of self-medication to treat these symptoms, and dependence gradually developed).

- Preexisting psychopathology may be the basis for initial experimentation and euphoria, but repeated use is prompted by the desire to avoid withdrawal.

- Some people have deficient endorphin systems that are corrected by the use of opioids.

- Because repeated use of opioids leads to permanent dysfunction in the endorphin system, normal function eventually requires the continued use of exogenous opioids.

- Drug effects and drug withdrawal can become linked through environmental cues and internal mood states. Emotions and external cues recall the distress of withdrawal or the memory of opioid euphoria or opioid reduction of dysphoria or painful affective states.

To varying degrees, all these theories are probably involved in a given person's use of opioids. Opioid tolerance and dependence lie not merely in a few predisposed people; they can develop in anyone who uses the drugs repeatedly, not necessarily people who are abusing them. A patient in the chronic pain of terminal illness should not be denied opioids, despite the inevitable development of tolerance and dependence.

Other Pure Opioid Agonists

As stated earlier, another naturally occurring opioid found in the opium poppy is codeine. Several synthetic and semisynthetic opioids are also agonists of the mu opioid receptor.

Codeine

Codeine is one of the most commonly prescribed opioids; it is usually combined with aspirin or acetaminophen for the relief of mild to moderate pain. These combination products are frequently sought drugs of abuse. About 40 percent of people who use them meet the criteria for codeine dependence (Sproule et al., 1999), and the use of codeine-containing products is strongly associated with endogenous depression—a dual-diagnosis problem (Romach et al., 1999). The plasma half-life and duration of action is about 3 to 4 hours.

Pharmacokinetically, codeine is metabolized by the hepatic drug-metabolizing enzyme CYP-2D6 to morphine, and many of the clinical effects attributed to codeine (for example, pain relief and euphoria) may, in fact, result from the actions of morphine. Four of the six SSRI-type antidepressants (fluoxetine, fluvoxamine, sertraline, and paroxetine; Chapter 7) can block the pain relief of codeine because they block the conversion of codeine to morphine. For patients taking one of these drugs, an analgesic drug other than codeine may be necessary.

Heroin

Heroin (diacetylmorphine) is three times more potent than morphine and is produced from morphine by a slight modification of chemical structure (see Figure 16.10). The increased lipid solubility of heroin leads to faster penetration of the blood-brain barrier, producing an intense rush when the drug is either smoked or injected intravenously. Heroin is metabolized to monoacetylmorphine and morphine; morpine is eventually metabolized and excreted. Heroin is legally available in Great Britain and Canada, where it can be used clinically. The drug is not legal in the United States, but it is widely used illicitly. When heroin is smoked together with crack cocaine, euphoria is intensified, the anxiety and paranoia associated with cocaine are tempered, and the depression that follows after the effects of cocaine wear off seems to be reduced. Unfortunately, this combination creates a multidrug addiction that is extremely difficult to treat.

Hydromorphone and Oxymorphone

Hydromorphone (Dilaudid) and oxymorphone (Numorphan; available only for use by injection) are both structurally related to morphine. Both drugs are as effective as morphine, and they are six to ten times more potent than morphine. Somewhat less sedation but equal respiratory depression is observed.

Palladone is a new, long-acting formulation of hydromorphone that is taken once daily for treatment of chronic pain in patients who have developed a tolerance to opioids and thus can tolerate the high dose of 12 to 32 milligrams per day (the dose of short-acting hydromorphone is about 1 to 2 mg). The half-life of Palladone is about 18 hours. The reason for its half-life length is that it is taken as an immediate-dissolving capsule containing controlled-release pellets, not that any alteration occurs in the rate of elimination of drug molecules from the body.

Meperidine

Meperidine (Demerol) is a synthetic opioid whose structure differs from that of morphine (see Figure 16.10). Because of this structural difference, meperidine was originally thought to be free of many of the undesirable properties of the opioids. However, meperidine is addictive; it can be substituted for morphine or heroin in addicts and is widely prescribed medically. It is one-tenth as potent as morphine, produces a similar type of euphoria, and is equally likely to cause dependence. Meperidine's side effects differ from morphine's and include more excitatory effects, such as tremors, delirium, hyperreflexia, and convulsions. These effects are produced by a metabolite of meperidine (normeperidine) that appears to be responsible for the CNS excitation. Meperidine and normeperidine can accumulate in people who have kidney dysfunction or who use only meperidine for their opioid addiction. Following discontinuation, withdrawal symptoms develop more rapidly than with morphine because of the shorter duration of action of meperidine.

Methadone

Methadone (Dolophine) is a synthetic mu agonist opioid (see Figure 16.10), the pharmacological activity of which is very similar to that of morphine. Methadone was first shown to cover for and block the effects of heroin withdrawal in 1948. In 1965 it was introduced as a substitute treatment for opioid dependency, and since then it has become the principal pharmacological agent for prevention of abstinence symptoms and signs. The outstanding properties of methadone are its effective analgesic activity, its efficacy by the oral route, its extended duration of action in suppressing withdrawal symptoms in physically dependent people, and its tendency to show persistent effects with repeated administration.

Today, methadone has two primary legitimate uses: (1) as an orally administered substitute for heroin in methadone maintenance treatment programs and (2) as a long-acting analgesic for the treatment of chronic pain syndromes. Federal prescription regulations clearly separate these two uses. Physicians who do not practice in federally licensed methadone treatment programs may not prescribe the drug for the maintenance of opioid dependency; the drug may be prescribed only through licensed methadone maintenance treatment program centers. However, office-based physicians may prescribe methadone for the treatment of either acute pain or chronic pain.

The main objectives of methadone maintenance treatment programs are rehabilitation of the dependent person and reduction of needle-associated diseases, illicit drug use, and crime. Randomized controlled trials of methadone maintenance programs have shown that they generally fulfill these aims. Although there are a number of predictors of the success of a program, the most important is the magnitude of the daily methadone dose. Programs that prescribe average daily doses exceeding 100 milligrams have higher retention rates and lower illicit drug use rates than those in which the average dose is less.

Even where liberal doses are used (sometimes up to 160 milligrams per day or higher), about one-third of the clients regularly experience withdrawal (they are called *nonholders*) and two-thirds (called *holders*) do not on a once-daily dosing schedule. Thus, to maintain compliance, prescribers must be free to regulate doses to meet individual requirements. (The generally accepted half-life of methadone is 24 hours.) Dyer and coworkers (1999) determined that this variability was a pharmacokinetic (not a receptor or pharmacodynamic) consequence, as some clients appear to metabolize methadone more quickly; small changes in plasma concentration can lead to relatively large changes in clinical effect (for example, withdrawal). Dyer and his colleagues concluded that (1) once-daily dosage is not suitable for at least one-third of clients; (2) dividing the daily dose may be more appropriate for nonholders; (3) use of a longer-acting opioid might be considered.

As well as some methadone maintenance programs may work, they reach only 170,000 of the estimated 810,000 opioid-dependent people in the United States. Fiellin and coworkers (2001a) studied stable methadone maintenance program clients and offered data showing that they can be well cared for by community physicians; the researchers suggest steps to take in order to do so.

In recent years, diversion of methadone (from methadone clinic programs and from physicians' prescriptions for analgesic effects) has become a major problem (see Figure 16.6). When the large doses prescribed for an opioid-dependent person (40 to 100 milligrams) are taken by a nonopioid-dependent person, severe respiratory depression and death frequently result.

LAAM

Levo-alpha acetylmethadol (LAAM) is related to methadone. It is an oral opioid analgesic that was approved in mid-1993 for the clinical management of opioid dependence in heroin addicts. LAAM is well absorbed from the gastrointestinal tract. It has a slow onset and a long duration of action (about 72 hours). It is metabolized to compounds that are also active as opioid agonists. Its primary advantage over methadone is its long duration of action; in maintenance therapy it is administered by mouth three times a week.

With LAAM, a major controversy relates both to dose-related efficacy and to comparative efficacy with methadone. Eissenberg and coworkers (1997) studied the problem of dose efficacy. They noted that heroin use decreased as the LAAM dose was increased (presumably fewer people were experiencing withdrawal symptoms as the dose increased) to 100/100/140 milligrams Monday, Wednesday, and Friday. At this dosage, opioid use, opioid craving, and withdrawal symptoms were all reduced. Johnson and coworkers (2000) compared LAAM with methadone and with a new drug, buprenorphine, for opioid maintenance. LAAM and buprenorphine were administered three times a week, methadone daily. Low doses of methadone (20 milligrams per day) were ineffective. Higher doses of methadone (60 to 100 milligrams), 75- to 115-milligram doses of LAAM, and 16- to 32-milligram doses of buprenorphine all substantially reduced the use of illicit opioids (heroin). The use of LAAM has not been widespread.

Oxycodone

Oxycodone (Percodan, OxyContin) is another semisynthetic opioid similar in action to morphine. The short-acting preparation (Percodan) is primarily prescribed for the treatment of acute pain. Usual doses are about 5 milligrams every 4 to 6 hours. Percodan has been associated with widespread abuse, dependence, and deaths from overdosage. OxyContin is a long-acting product intended for the treatment of chronic or long-lasting pain, such as the pain that often accompanies cancer and persistent musculoskeletal problems. Drug tolerance usually develops and doses are high (tablets of OxyContin contain from 10 to 80 milligrams).

OxyContin goes by many street names: poor man's heroin, hillbilly heroin, oxy, OC, killer, and oxycotton, among others. Street prices are ten times the prescription price, usually about $1 per milligram of drug. Abusers crush the pills, destroying the time-release mechanisms, and either snort the powder, smoke the drug, or dilute it in water and inject it. Thus, while chronic pain patients are certainly physically dependent on the drug, high-dose abusers are true addicts. Today there is immense abuse of OxyContin, much of it through diversion (see Figure 16.6), which has been responsible for untold numbers of deaths. Drastically needed are immediate efforts to add the opioid antagonist naloxone to OxyContin so that use by smoking or injection would precipitate withdrawal.[2] To date, the manufacturer has been slow to respond to the problem of widespread abuse, possibly because yearly sales of OxyContin easily exceed $1 billion!

Propoxyphene

Propoxyphene (Darvon) is an analgesic compound that is structurally similar to methadone (see Figure 16.10). As an analgesic for treating mild to moderate pain, it is less potent than codeine but more potent than aspirin. When propoxyphene is taken in large doses, opioidlike effects are seen; when it is used intravenously, addicts recognize it as an opioid. Taken orally, propoxyphene does not have much potential for abuse. Some cases of drug dependence have been reported, but to date they have not been of major concern. Because commercial intravenous

---

[2]If the oxycodone/naloxone product were taken as intended (orally), the naloxone would not be absorbed and the oxycodone would be an effective analgesic. However, if injected, the naloxone would precipitate withdrawal.

preparations of propoxyphene are not available, intravenous abuse is encountered only when someone attempts to inject solutions of the powder that is contained in capsules that are intended for oral use.

Fentanyl and Its Derivatives

Fentanyl (Sublimaze) and three related compounds, *sufentanil* (Sufenta), *alfentanil* (Alfenta), and *remifentanyl* (Ultiva), are short-acting, intravenously administered opioid agonists that are structurally related to meperidine. These four compounds are intended to be used during and after surgery to relieve surgical pain. In addition, fentanyl is also available both in a transdermal skin patch (Durapatch) (Viscusi et al., 2004) and as an oral lozenge on a stick (a "lollipop," marketed under the trade name Actiq). The transdermal route of drug delivery offers prolonged, rather steady levels of drug in blood; the lollipop is used for the short-term treatment of surgical pain in children and for unrelieved pain in chronic pain patients who are intolerant of injections.

Some advances in pain management involve new and developing delivery routes for fentanyl. *AerolLEF* is an investigational fentanyl product that is delivered via an inhaled nebulizer mist. The fentanyl is inhaled as encapsulated liposomes that provide rapid analgesia and an extended duration of action; the lung serves as a reservoir for the prolonged effect. An *E-trans fentanyl* delivery system is an on-demand mechanism in which patients deliver the drug through the skin by means of a low-intensity electrical current. *Fentora* is an investigational fentanyl buccal tablet that is partially absorbed through the mouth and partially absorbed through the stomach. It is intended for unrelieved pain in cancer patients and is similar to the fentanyl lollipop.

Fentanyl and its three derivatives are 80 to 500 times as potent as morphine as analgesics and profoundly depress respiration. Death from these agents is invariably caused by respiratory failure. In illicit use, fentanyl is known by several nicknames including "china white." Numerous derivatives (such as *methylfentanyl*) have been manufactured illegally; they emerge periodically and have been responsible for many fatalities.

Partial Opioid Agonists

Pure agonists (such as morphine) have strong activity at mu opioid receptors. In contrast to morphine, two drugs, buprenorphine and tramadol, have a lower level of activity at these same receptors. Since they retain some of the analgesic activity of morphine, they have been referred to as partial opioid agonists.

Buprenorphine

Buprenorphine (Subutex) is a newer, semisynthetic partial opioid agonist whose action is characterized by a limited stimulation of mu receptors, which is responsible for its analgesic properties. As a partial agonist, however, there is a ceiling to its analgesic effectiveness as well as to its potential for inducing euphoria and respiratory depression. Buprenorphine has a prolonged duration of action (about 24 hours) because it binds very strongly to mu receptors; this characteristic also limits its reversibility by naloxone should reversal be considered necessary. The most common side effects are flulike symptoms, headache, sweating, sleeping difficulties, nausea, and mood swings.

Johnson and coworkers (2000) found buprenorphine comparable to methadone and LAAM for treatment of opioid-dependent people. Kakko and coworkers (2003) reported that buprenorphine was safe and effective as a maintenance medication in treating heroin addiction. Petry and coworkers (1999) found that, because of its ceiling effect, doses four times the daily maintenance dose could be given twice weekly without the occurrence of either agonist effects or withdrawal symptoms. However, the use of buprenorphine has been associated with considerable abuse throughout the world, as the drug is a partial agonist at mu receptors and exerts morphinelike effects.

The abuse problem can be largely solved through the addition of the opioid antagonist naloxone to the buprenorphine (Alho et al., 2007). The combination is trade named Suboxone and is marketed and approved for the office-based maintenance treatment of heroin or other opioid dependence. Suboxone is FDA classified as a Schedule III agent, intended for office-based opioid dependency treatment under the Federal Drug Addiction Treatment Act of 2000. Therefore, unlike methadone and LAAM, a physician in his or her office can prescribe Suboxone for the treatment of opioid dependence. Also, patients can take the drug home instead of appearing at a clinic every day. Resnick (2003) discusses this legislation. Fiellin and coworkers (2001b, 2002) discuss the role of Suboxone as an office-based treatment option. Fudala and coworkers (2003) and Amass and coworkers (2004) further discuss this new treatment option, encouraging physicians to undergo training to use these agents and administer them comfortably as part of their medical practice. Allen (2006) discusses physician requirements for prescribing Suboxone for opioid dependence.

In Suboxone treatment programs, the preparation can be used to maintain opioid dependency or as part of an opioid withdrawal program. Umbricht and coworkers (1999) used buprenorphine as a tapering medication for rapid opioid detoxification; they followed buprenorphine with successful naltrexone therapy. The researchers concluded that the combination was an acceptable and safe treatment for shortened opioid detoxification and induction of naltrexone maintenance. Kakko and coworkers (2007) compared the efficacy of methadone maintenance with Suboxone maintenance for heroin dependence. Overall, the two treatments were equally efficacious: urine samples free of illicit opioids reach approximately 80 percent with either treatment. The authors concluded that "broad implementation of strategies using buprenorphine as first-line treatment should be considered" (p. 797). An accompanying editorial by Brady (2007) expands on the success of this treatment.

Marsch and coworkers (2005) reported that, in adolescents 13 to 18 years old with opioid dependency, combining Suboxone with behavioral interventions was quite effective in preventing relapse to opioid use. Suboxone has as yet not been associated with significant diversionary problems and illicit use.

Tramadol

Tramadol (Ultram), available in Europe for many years, became available for use as an analgesic in the United States in 1995. The drug exhibits a unique dual analgesic action: (1) it is a partial agonist at mu receptors, and (2) it blocks the presynaptic reuptake of norepinephrine and serotonin, both contributing to its analgesic action. In the United States, tramadol is available only for oral use. Well absorbed orally, the drug undergoes a two-step metabolism, and the first metabolite (monodemethyl tramadol) is as active or more active than the parent compound. As a partial agonist, the drug exhibits a ceiling effect on analgesia (it is not as analgesic as morphine), which limits respiratory depression and abuse potential. Side effects are considerable and include drowsiness and vertigo, nausea, vomiting, constipation, and headache. Additive sedation with CNS depressants is observed. Reports of the use of tramadol in treating opioid dependency are not available.

There has been concern about the combination of tramadol and serotonin-type antidepressant drugs: the combination may increase the toxicity of the antidepressants (causing a serotonin syndrome; Chapter 7). This drug combination should probably be avoided, if possible.

Mixed Agonist-Antagonist Opioids

Four commercially available drugs are classified as mixed agonist-antagonist opioids: pentazocine, butorphanol, nalbuphine, and dezocine (Figure 16.11). Each of these drugs binds with varying affinity to the mu and kappa receptors. The drugs are weak mu agonists; most of their analgesic effectiveness (which is limited) results from their stimulation of kappa receptors (see Table 16.2). Low doses cause

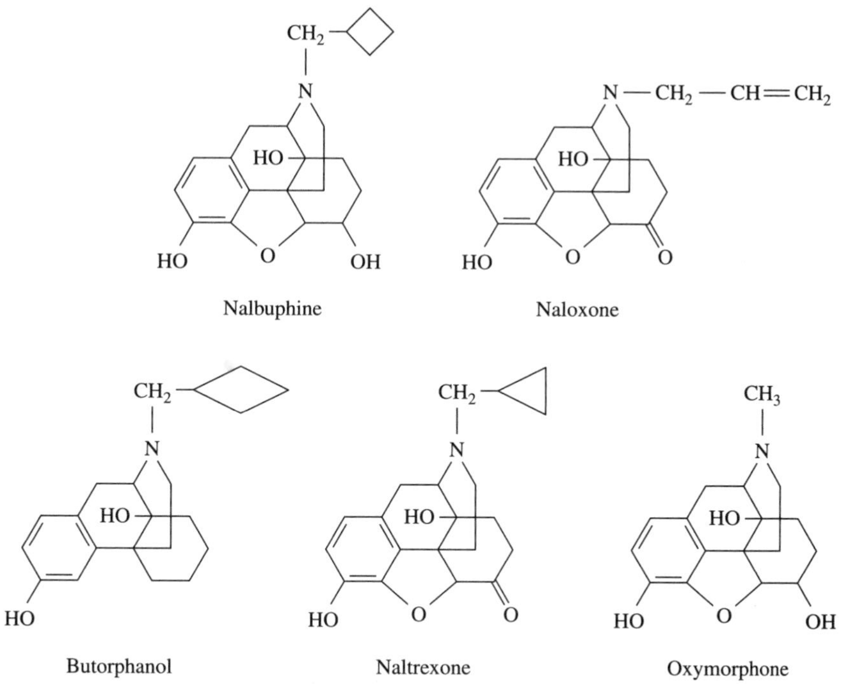

FIGURE 16.11 Structural formulas of oxymorphone and four analogues. Oxymorphone is a pure mu agonist. Nalbuphine and butorphanol have mixed agonistic and antagonistic properties. Naloxone and naltrexone are pure antagonists.

moderate analgesia; higher doses produce little additional analgesia. In opioid-dependent people, these drugs precipitate withdrawal. A high incidence of adverse psychotomimetic side effects (dysphoria, anxiety reactions, hallucinations, and so on) is associated with the use of these agents, limiting their therapeutic use but increasing their attraction for illicit use.

Pentazocine (Talwin) and *butorphanol* (Stadol) are prototypical mixed agonist-antagonists. Neither has much potential for producing respiratory depression or physical dependence. In 1993 butorphanol, previously available for use by injection, became available as a nasal spray, the first analgesic so formulated. After spraying into the nostrils, peak plasma levels (and maximal effect) are achieved in 1 hour, with a duration of 4 to 5 hours. Use of the nasal spray can be euphoric and abuse of butorphanol spray appears to be increasing.

The abuse of pentazocine has also been increasing, particularly in combination with tripelennamine, an antihistamine. This combination of drugs, called "Ts and blues," has caused serious medical complications, including seizures, psychotic episodes, skin ulcerations, abscesses, and muscle wasting. (The latter three effects are caused by the repeated injections rather than by the drugs themselves.)

Nalbuphine (Nubain) is primarily a kappa agonist of limited analgesic effectiveness. Because it is also a mu antagonist, it is not likely to produce either respiratory depression or patterns of abuse.

Dezocine (Dalgan) was introduced in 1990 as the newest of the agonist-antagonist drugs. As a moderate mu agonist and a weak delta and kappa agonist, dezocine can substitute for morphine. Its clinical efficacy and potential for abuse appear limited.

Pure Opioid Antagonists

Three pure opioid antagonists are clinically available: naloxone, naltrexone, and nalmefene. Each is a structural derivative of oxymorphone, a pure opioid agonist (see Figure 16.11). All three have an affinity for opioid receptors (especially mu receptors), but after binding they exert no agonistic effects of their own. Therefore, they antagonize the effects of opioid agonists.

Naloxone (Narcan) is the prototype pure opioid antagonist: it has no effect when injected into nonopioid-dependent people, but it rapidly precipitates withdrawal when injected into opioid-dependent people. Naloxone is neither analgesic nor subject to abuse. Because naloxone is neither absorbed from the gastrointestinal tract nor absorbed across the oral mucosa, it must be given by injection. Its duration of action is very brief, in the range of 15 to 30 minutes. Thus, for continued opioid antagonism, it must be reinjected at short intervals to avoid return of the depressant effects caused by the longer-acting agonist opioid. Naloxone is used to reverse the respiratory depression that follows acute opioid intoxication (overdoses) and to reverse opioid-induced respiratory depression in newborns born of opioid-dependent mothers. The limitations of naloxone include its short duration of action and its parenteral route of administration.

Naltrexone (Trexan, ReVia) became clinically available in 1985 as the first orally absorbed, pure opioid antagonist approved for the treatment of heroin dependence. The actions of naltrexone resemble those of naloxone, but naltrexone is well absorbed orally and has a long duration of action, necessitating only a single oral daily dose of about 40 to 100 milligrams. Naltrexone is used clinically in treatment programs when it is desirable to maintain a person on chronic therapy with an opioid antagonist rather than with an agonist such as methadone. In people who take naltrexone daily, any injection of an opioid agonist such as heroin is ineffective. Naltrexone can cause nausea (which can be quite severe in some people) and dose-dependent liver toxicity, which can be a problem in patients with preexisting liver disease.

One problem with naltrexone is that the drug must be taken in order to be effective. Trite as that sounds, the opioid-dependent person must choose between taking naltrexone or returning to heroin use. Therefore, treatment compliance is poor and only highly motivated addicts take the drug. Comer and coworkers (2002), in 12 recently detoxified heroin-dependent people, injected a long-acting intramuscular injectable preparation of naltrexone (the drug was suspended in an oil preparation that, when injected intramuscularly, slowly released the drug over a period of weeks or months). The injection completely antagonized heroin-induced subjective effects for a period of five weeks. Side effects were limited to discomfort at the injection site. In 2006, the FDA approved a new long-acting preparation of injectable naltrexone (Vivitrol) for the maintence of sobriety in withdrawn alcoholics. The success of this preparation is still open to question. However, this kind of product might be useful in opioid-dependent people who are motivated to maintain abstinence from opioids—for example, professional people who have more to gain by being off opioids (maintaining their occupational employment) than by remaining on opioids.

As discussed in Chapter 4, both oral and long-acting injectable formulations of naltrexone are approved by the FDA for use in the treatment of alcoholism to reduce the craving for alcohol during the maintenance period of treatment. It is thought that such action follows from the antagonism of endorphin action rather than from an as yet unidentified action outside the opioid system. Whether therapy is useful or not is unclear. Ceasing to take naltroxone would certainly be expected to result in loss of any positive effects. Carroll and coworkers (2001) reported that contingency management (mainly voucher rewards) significantly improved the response to naltrexone.

Naltrexone may have a specific preventive role in reducing self-injurious behaviors (White and Schultz, 2000). It is thought that self-injurious behavior can be used to maintain a high level of endogenous opioids, either to prevent decreases in endorphins or to experience the euphoric effect of opioid stimulation following injury. Roth and coworkers (1996) reported that the self-injurious behaviors of six out of seven female patients ceased entirely during naltrexone therapy, with resumption of injurious behavior when the drug was withdrawn.

Nalmefene (Revex), introduced in 1996, is an injectable pure opioid antagonist with a half-life of about 8 to 10 hours, in contrast to the short half-life of injected naloxone. The drug is useful by injection for the treatment of acute opioid-induced respiratory depression caused by overdosage. With its long half-life, the incidence of it wearing off and the depressant action of the agonist opioid returning is greatly reduced. If administered to an addict, however, the precipitation of withdrawal can be prolonged and require additional medical treatment. Mason and coworkers (1999) studied the effects of orally administered nalmefene as an alternative to naltrexone in alcoholic patients.[3] Treatment for 12 weeks was effective in preventing relapse. The oral preparation is not available commercially.

There has been discussion about whether or not nalmefine therapy might be a treatment for gambling addiction (pathological gambling) either alone or as part of therapy involving Gamblers Anonymous. Grant and coworkers (2006), in a multicentered trial, demonstrated the effectiveness of the drug in 207 men and women diagnosed with pathological gambling. A total of 50 percent of subjects receiving the lowest doses of nalmefine (25 milligrams per day) were much or very much improved compared with 34 percent of placebo-receiving subjects. Unfortunately, results from a study later in 2006 (unpublished) failed to find a statistical superiority of nalmefine (20 and 40 milligrams per day) compared to placebo. This finding has tempered enthusiasm for this therapy.

Opioid Combinations

Opioids are irreplaceable as strong and effective pain-relieving agents. However, their dependency potential is enormous, as is the problem of diversion of the drug to illicit users. The major problems, therefore, are twofold: (1) how to maintain efficacy while reducing dependence potential and (2) how to reduce diversion, or use of the drug by others than those for whom the drug was intended.

The first problem has been addressed for years, first by developing analgesics thought to have less dependency potential. Unfortunately, most attempts have failed. For example, heroin was initially developed as a semisynthetic alternative to morphine, which occurs naturally from opium. Meperidine and numerous other drugs were similarly developed. As yet, it has been impossible to separate analgesia, dependence, and respiratory depression, and abuse continues to be a huge problem.

Another approach was to combine the opioid with an analgesic that did not induce dependency. The second analgesic is used to potentiate opioid-induced analgesia using less opioid. For example, for decades, codeine has been combined with aspirin or acetaminophen as a less addicting analgesic product. Currently, a combination of morphine and dextromethorphan is being evaluated for the treatment of moderate to severe pain. This product is not yet commercially available.

Other morphine-sparing analgesic regimens combine morphine (or another opioid) with an anticonvulsant neuromodulator (Chapter 8)

---

[3]Nalmefene is currently available only in injectable form. For this study, experimental tablets of nalmefene were supplied by the manufacturer.

such as lamotrigine (Arguelles et al., 2002) or gabapentin (Matthews and Dickenson, 2002).

As discussed, diversion and abuse of opioids persists, as shown by the wide abuse of oxycodone, fentanyl, morphine, and other opioids. *Suboxone* (the combination of buprenorphine and naltrexone) is one attempt at combining an opioid with an antagonist in an effort to reduce abuse. When buprenorphine was first developed as a partial opioid agonist in the late 1990s, abuse of the drug was encountered. However, combining the drug with naloxone in 2003 (as Suboxone) maintained analgesic efficacy while reducing diversion. The reason is as follows. Buprenorphine is effective given orally, sublingually, or by injection. Naloxone is not absorbed orally or sublingually and is effective as an antagonist only when it is injected. Therefore, when Suboxone is taken sublingually, the buprenorphine is absorbed (and is effective) while the naloxone is not absorbed and is ineffective. However, when this product is crushed, dissolved, and injected, the naloxone is placed in the bloodstream and precipitates withdrawal. Therefore, it is not attractive as a product of abuse.

Several years ago, the same idea was applied to the mixed agonist-antagonist *pentazocine* (Talwin). Pentazocine was widely abused soon after its introduction. A combination pentazocine/naloxone preparation (Talwin Nx) was marketed, essentially ending abuse of pentazocine.

Today one of the major forms of opioid abuse (besides heroin) is the diversionary use of OxyContin, a long-acting formulation of oxycodone. Adding naloxone to OxyContin would end most of the widespread intravenous abuse of oxycodone. The manufacturer has so far not done so, undoubtedly because it would have a severe economic impact on company profits.

Pharmacotherapy of Opioid Dependence

Opioid dependence is a brain-related medical disorder (characterized by predictable signs and symptoms) that can be effectively treated with significant benefits for the patient and for society. However, society must make a commitment to offer effective treatment for opioid dependence to all who need it. Everyone dependent on opioids should have access to methadone, LAAM, or Suboxone (buprenorphine/naloxone) maintenance therapy. Not only must government policies ensure availability of the programs, but insurance coverage for the programs should be a required benefit in public and private insurance. In any treatment of opioid dependence, pharmacotherapy is the foundation. Medicines are used for the following functions:

- Maintain dependence on orally administered medications (methadone, LAAM, or Suboxone), thus reducing the use of heroin or other injected agonists

- Maintain detoxification in predisposed people (oral naltrexone), combined with random urine checks and vouchers to ensure compliance

- Maintain detoxification in less compliant people (intramuscular injections of Vivitrol) and eliminate the positive reinforcement effects of heroin should that drug be smoked or injected

- Treat comorbid disorders, especially affective disorders such as depression, that complicate recovery

In addition to appropriate pharmacotherapy, nonpharmacological support services are pivotal to successful therapy, whether the therapy is agonist maintenance or detoxification. How much nonpharmacological support is optimal? Can there be too little? Can there be too much? Kraft and coworkers (1997) determined that large amounts of support for methadone-maintained clients are not cost-effective, but moderate amounts of support are better than minimal amounts. They concluded that there is a floor below which supplementary support should not fall. Similarly, Avants and coworkers (1999) reported that intensive day treatment programs for unemployed, inner-city methadone patients cost twice as much and were no more effective than a program of enhanced methadone maintenance services, which consisted of standard methadone maintenance plus a weekly skills training group and referral to on-site and off-site services.

Should the goal of methadone or buprenorphine maintenance be eventual withdrawal from agonist therapy? Although data are poor, it is felt that total abstinence from all opioids need not be an objective for all addicts. Goals, however, must include prevention of major relapse to the use of illicitly obtained, injectable opioids (such as heroin). Continuing medically managed supportive opioid therapy may be necessary for many addicts, an approach that follows models of medical illness.

Until recently, the objective has been medically managed withdrawal to an opioid-free state. This goal can be reached successfully in patients who are highly motivated to remain opioid-free. Examples include addicted medical personnel whose continued licensure to practice their profession is contingent on complete abstention from opioids. The continued ingestion of naltrexone implies that an opioid agonist will be ineffective. In many addicts, however, naltrexone therapy is unacceptable, and continued opioid therapy is needed. For these patients, the benefits of maintenance therapy, including significant reductions in illicit opioid use, are increases in treatment retention and improved psychosocial functioning, which have been clearly demonstrated within the methadone maintenance model.

Goldstein (1994) reviewed more than 20 years of administering methadone maintenance therapy to 1000 heroin addicts in New Mexico. More than half the patients were traced and analyzed. Of these

500, more than one-third are now dead; causes include violence, overdosage, and alcoholism. About one-quarter are still enmeshed in the criminal justice system. Another one-quarter go on and off methadone maintenance, indicating that opioid dependence, whether on heroin or on methadone, is a lifelong condition for a considerable fraction of the addict population. With half of the treated population of 1000 addicts unaccounted for, the data are obviously incomplete. It is likely that many of these unaccounted-for former addicts are either drug-free or are stabilized on an opioid and are functional in their communities. The successful graduates of therapy are the most difficult to track because they usually prefer to remain anonymous in their communities.

Hser and coworkers (2001) reported a remarkable 33-year followup of 581 male heroin addicts who were first identified in the early 1960s. At follow-up in 1996–1997, 284 were dead and 242 were interviewed; the mean age at interview was 57 years. Of the 242, 20 percent tested positive for heroin (an additional 9.5 percent refused to provide a urine sample, and 14 percent were incarcerated, for whom urinalysis was unavailable); 22 percent were daily alcohol drinkers; 67 percent smoked; many reported illicit drug use (heroin, cocaine, marijuana, amphetamines). The group also reported high rates of physical health, mental health, and criminal justice problems. Long-term heroin abstinence was associated with less criminality, morbidity, and psychological distress and with higher employment.

It therefore appears that setting a goal of total abstinence is seldom accompanied by a positive outcome and leads to a productive life-style in only a minority of opioid dependency cases. If detoxification to a drug-free state is chosen, as soon as opioid-withdrawn people relapse, they must be readmitted to agonist maintenance programs immediately and receive both adequate doses and the necessary supportive therapies. The most interesting data now support prolonged opioid maintenance (with methadone or buprenorphine/naloxone) as a treatment goal. Unfortunately, many people still see physical dependence on an opioid as "bad" in and of itself. This attitude must be changed before widespread attempts at long-term opioid maintenance can be fully evaluated.

STUDY QUESTIONS

1. Describe the location of opioid receptors in the brain and in the spinal cord.

2. How are pain impulses modulated as they enter the spinal cord?

3. What is substance P and how is it influenced by opioid analgesics?

4. What might be the effects of the endorphins?

5. What is an opioid agonist? What is an opioid antagonist? What is a mixed agonist-antagonist? A partial agonist? Give an example of each.

6. What might lead a person to misuse or abuse opioids? What are the signs of opioid misuse/abuse?

7. Differentiate between naloxone and naltrexone. How might each one be used?

8. Describe the various ways that opioid dependence might be handled or treated.

9. Why are tricyclic antidepressants analgesic?

10. Differentiate between the opioid modulation of afferent pain impulses and the affective component of pain.

11. Give your thoughts for and against the existence of endogenous opioid peptides (endorphins) that serve as natural opioids.

12. If a patient suffers from chronic pain, what two classes of drugs should be optimized before starting opioid therapy? If opioid therapy is started, how should the opioids be administered?

13. Differentiate the use of opioids for people with chronic, nonmalignant pain and the use of opioids for people with pain due to a terminal malignancy.

14. What is buprenorphine? What are its potential uses? Why combine it with naloxone?

15. What allows this drug to be used in medical clinics located in the community and outside licensed methadone clinics?

16. Discuss the various options in the pharmacological management of opioid withdrawal and in the prevention of relapse.

REFERENCES

Akil, H., et al. (1998). "Endogenous Opioids: Overview and Current Issues." *Drug and Alcohol Dependence* 51: 127–140.

Alho, H., et al. (2007). "Abuse Liability of Buprenorphine-Naloxone Tablets in Untreated IV Drug Users." *Drug and Alcohol Dependence* 88: 75–78.

Allen, J. (2006). "Office-Based Treatment of Opioid Dependence: New Hope for Patients with Concomitant Pain and Addiction Issues." *Practical Pain Management* 6: 52–55.

Amass, L., et al. (2004). "Bringing Buprenorphine-Naloxone Detoxification to Community Treatment Providers: The NIDA Clinical Trials Network Field Experience." *American Journal of Addictions* 13, Supplement 1: S42–S66.

Arguelles, C. F., et al. (2002). "Peripheral Antinociceptive Action of Morphine and the Synergistic Interaction with Lamotrigine." *Anesthesiology* 96: 921–925.

Avants, S. K., et al. (1999). "Day Treatment Versus Enhanced Standard Methaone Services for Opioid-Dependent Patients: A Comparison of Clinical Efficacy and Cost." *American Journal of Psychiatry* 156: 27–33.

Bernstein, D., et al. (2007). "Complex Interplay of Participants in Opioid Therapy: A Historical and Contemporary View of Societal, Medical, Manufacturer, Payer, and Legal Interactions Affecting the Prescription and Use of Opioids for Pain Management." *Practical Pain Management* 7: 10–36.

Binder, W., et al. (2001). "Analgesic Antiinflammatory Effects of Two Novel Kappa-Opioid Peptides." *Anesthesiology* 94: 1034–1044.

Brady, K. T. (2007). "Medical Treatment of Opiate Dependence: Expanding Treatment Options." *American Journal of Psychiatry* 164: 702–704.

Carroll, K. M., et al. (2001). "Targeting Behavioral Therapies to Enhance Naltrexone Treatment of Opioid Dependence: Effects of Contingency Management and Significant Other Involvement." *Archives of General Psychiatry* 58: 755–761.

Celerier, E., et al. (2000). "Long-Lasting Hyperalgesia Induced by Fentanyl in Rats: Preventive Effect of Ketamine." *Anesthesiology* 92: 465–472.

Chavkin, C., et al. (2004). "Salvinorin A, an Active Component of the Hallucinogenic Sage *Salvia divinorum*, Is a Highly Efficacious Kappa-Opioid Receptor Agonist: Structural and Functional Considerations." *Journal of Pharmacology and Experimental Therapeutics* 308: 1197–1203.

Christensen, D., et al. (2000). "Complete Prevention but Stimulus-Dependent Reversion of Morphine Tolerance by the Glycine/NMDA Receptor Antagonist (+)-HA966 in Neuropathic Rats." *Anesthesiology* 92: 786–794

Cianfrini, L. R., and D. M. Doleys (2006). "The Role of Psychology in Pain Management." *Practical Pain Management* 6: 18–28.

Collins, E. D., et al. (2005). "Anesthesia-Assisted vs Buprenorphine- or Clonidine-Assisted Heroin Detoxification and Naltrexone Induction: A Randomized Trial." *Journal of the American Medical Association* 294: 903–913.

Comer, S. D., et al. (2002). "Depot Naltrexone: Long-Lasting Antagonism of the Effects of Heroin in Humans." *Psychopharmacology* 159: 351–360.

DeLeo, J. A., and B. A. Winkelstein (2002). "Physiology of Chronic Spinal Pain Syndromes: From Animal Models to Biomechanics." *Spine* 27: 2526–2537.

Dortch-Carnes, J., and D. E. Potter (2005). "Bremazocine: A Kappa-Opioid Agonist with Potent Analgesic and Other Pharmacologic Properties." *CNS Drug Reviews* 11: 195–212.

Dyer, K. R., et al. (1999). "Steady-State Pharmacokinetics and Pharmacodynamics in Methadone Maintenance Patients: Comparison of Those Who Do and Do Not Experience Withdrawal and Concentration-Effect Relationships." *Clinical Pharmacology and Therapeutics* 65: 685–694.

Eissenberg, T., et al. (1997). "Dose-Related Efficacy of Levomethadyl Acetate for Treatment of Opioid Dependency." *Journal of the American Medical Association* 277: 1945–1951.

Fiellin, D. A., et al. (2001a). "Methadone Maintenance in Primary Care: A Randomized Controlled Trial." *Journal of the American Medical Association* 286: 1724–1731.

Fiellin, D. A., et al. (2001b). "Office-Based Treatment for Opioid Dependence: Reaching New Patient Populations." *American Journal of Psychiatry* 158: 1200–1204.

Fiellin, D. A., et al. (2002). "Office-Based Treatment of Opioid-Dependent Patients." *New England Journal of Medicine* 347: 817–823.

Fudala, P. J., et al. (2003). "Office-Based Treatment of Opioid Addiction with a Sublingual-Tablet Formulation of Buprenorphine and Naloxone." *New England Journal of Medicine* 349: 949–958.

Goldstein, A. (1994). *Addiction: From Biology to Drug Policy.* New York: Freeman.

Grant, J. E., et al. (2006). "Multicenter Investigation of the Opioid Antagonist Nalmefene in the Treatment of Pathological Gambling." *American Journal of Psychiatry* 163: 303–312.

Hser, Y.-I., et al. (2001). "A 33-Year Follow-Up of Narcotic Addicts." *Archives of General Psychiatry* 58: 503–508.

Johnson, R. E., et al. (2000). "A Comparison of Levomethadyl Acetate, Buprenorphine, and Methadone for Opioid Dependence." *New England Journal of Medicine* 343: 1290–1297.

Jutkiewicz, E. M. (2006). "The Antidepressant-Like Effects of Delta-Opioid Receptor Agonists." *Molecular Interventions* 6: 162–169.

Kakko, J., et al. (2003). "1-Year Retention and Social Function After Buprenorphine-Assisted Relapse Prevention Treatment for Heroin Dependence in Sweden: Randomized, Placebo-Controlled Trial." *Lancet* 361: 662–668.

Kakko, J., et al. (2007). "A Stepped Care Strategy Using Buprenorphine Versus Conventional Methadone Maintenance in Heroin Dependence: A Randomized Controlled Trial." *American Journal of Psychiatry* 164: 797–803.

Katz, N. (2005). "The Impact of Opioids on the Endocrine System." *Pain Management Rounds* 1 (9): 1–6. Available online at www.painmanagementrounds.org.

Kieffer, B. L. (1999). "Opioids: First Lessons from Knockout Mice." *Trends in Pharmacological Sciences* 20: 19–26.

Kraft, M. K., et al. (1997). "Are Supplementary Services Provided During Methadone Maintenance Really Cost-Effective?" *American Journal of Psychiatry* 154: 1214–1219.

Marsch, L. A., et al. (2005). "Comparison of Pharmacological Treatments for Opioid-Dependent Adolescents: A Randomized Controlled Trial." *Archives of General Psychiatry* 62: 1157–1164.

Mason, B. J., et al. (1999). "A Double-Blind, Placebo-Controlled Study of Oral Nalmefene for Alcohol Dependence." *Archives of General Psychiatry* 56: 719–724.

Matthews, E. A., and A. H. Dickenson (2002). "A Combination of Gabapentin and Morphine Mediates Enhanced Inhibitory Effects on Dorsal Horn Neuronal Responses in a Rat Model of Neuropathy." *Anesthesiology* 96: 633–640.

Narita, M., et al. (2001). "Regulations of Opioid Dependence by Opioid Receptor Types." *Pharmacology and Therapeutics* 89: 1–15.

Narita, M., et al. (2006). "Role of Delta-Opioid Receptor Function in Neurogenesis and Neuroprotection." *Journal of Neurochemistry* 97: 1494–1505.

O'Connor, P. G. (2005). "Methods of Detoxification and Their Role in Treating Patients with Heroin Dependence." *Journal of the American Medical Association* 294: 961–963.

Ostermeier, A. M., et al. (2000). "Activation of Mu- and Sigma-Opioid Receptors Causes Presynaptic Inhibition of Glutamatergic Excitation in Neocortical Neurons." *Anesthesiology* 93: 1053–1063.

Pan, Z. Z. (1998). "Mu-Opposing Actions of the Kappa-Opioid Receptor." *Trends in Pharmacological Sciences* 19: 94–98.

Petry, N. M., et al. (1999). "A Comparison of Four Buprenorphine Dosing Regimens in the Treatment of Opioid Dependence." *Clinical Pharmacology and Therapeutics* 66: 306–314.

Price, D. D. (2003). "Central Neural Mechanisms That Interrelate Sensory and Affective Dimensions of Pain." *Molecular Interventions* 2: 392–402.

Resnick, R. B. (2003). "Food and Drug Administration Approval of Buprenorphine-Naloxone for Office Treatment of Addiction." *Annals of Internal Medicine* 138: 360.

Rice, A. S., et al. (2002). "Endocannabinoids and Pain: Spinal and Peripheral Analgesia in Inflammation and Neuropathy." *Prostaglandins, Leukotrienes, and Essential Fatty Acids* 66: 243–256.

Romach, M. K., et al. (1999). "Long-Term Codeine Use Is Associated with Depressive Symptoms." *Journal of Clinical Psychopharmacology* 19: 373–376.

Roth, A. S., et al. (1996). "Naltrexone as a Treatment for Repetitive Self-Injurious Behavior: An Open-Label Trial." *Journal of Clinical Psychiatry* 57: 233–237.

Savage, S. R. (2005). "Critical Issues in Pain and Addiction." *Pain Management Rounds* 2 (9): 1–6. Available on-line at www.painmanagementrounds.org.

Snyder, S. H., and G. W. Pasternak (2003). "Historical Review: Opioid Receptors." *Trends in Pharmacological Sciences* 2: 198–204.

Sproule, B. A., et al. (1999). "Characteristics of Dependent and Nondependent Regular Users of Codeine." *Journal of Clinical Psychopharmacology* 19: 367–372.

Thipphawong, J. B., et al. (2003). "Analgesic Efficacy of Inhaled Morphine in Patients After Bunionectomy Surgery." *Anesthesiology* 99: 693–700.

Torregrossa, M. M., et al. (2006). "Peptic Delta Opioid Receptor Agonists Produce Antidepressant-Like Effects in the Forced Swim Test and Regulate BDND mRNA Expression in Rats." *Brain Research* 1069: 172–181.

Umbricht, A., et al. (1999). "Naltrexone-Shortened Opioid Detoxification with Buprenorphine." *Drug and Alcohol Dependence* 56: 181–190.

Viscusi, E. R., et al. (2004). "Patient-Controlled Transdermal Fentanyl Hydrochloride vs Intravenous Morphine Pump for Postoperative Pain: A Randomized Controlled Trial." *Journal of the American Medical Association* 291: 1222–1341.

White, T., and S. K. Schultz (2000). "Naltrexone Treatment for a 3-Year-Old Boy with Self-Injurious Behavior." *American Journal of Psychiatry* 157: 1574–1580.

Chapter 17

Cannabinoid Agonists and Antagonists

The hemp plant *Cannabis sativa,* commonly called marijuana, grows throughout the world and flourishes in most temperate and tropical regions. Although *cannabinol* and *cannabidiol,* among other components, are present in lesser amounts in cannabis, the major psychoactive ingredient of the marijuana plant is *delta-9-tetrahydrocannabinol* (THC; Figure 17.1). THC is probably responsible also for the side effects and therapeutic effects associated with smoking marijuana.

Names for cannabis products include marijuana, hashish, charas, bhang, ganja, and sinsemilla. *Hashish* and *charas,* which consist of the dried resinous exudates of the female flowers, are the most potent preparations, with a THC content averaging between 10 and 20 percent. *Ganja* and *sinsemilla* refer to the dried material found in the tops of the female plants, where the THC content averages about 5 to 8 percent. *Bhang* and *marijuana* are lower-grade preparations taken from

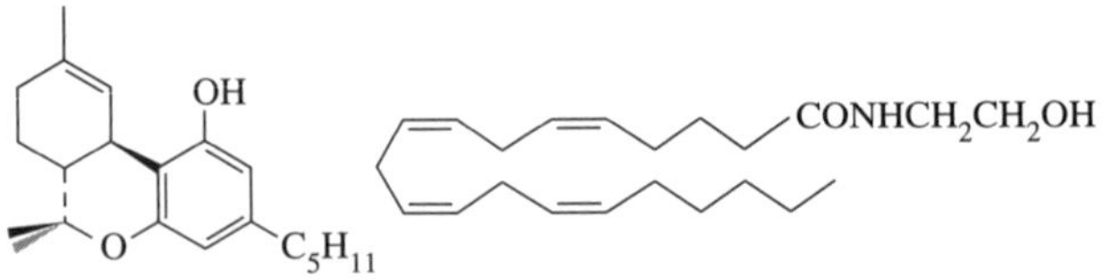

FIGURE 17.1 Structures of delta-9-tetrahydrocannabinol (THC) and anandamide, the endogenous ligand (neurotransmitter) of the cannabinoid receptor.

the dried remainder of the plant, and their THC content varies between 2 to 5 percent, although improved growing, harvesting, and processing techniques have boosted this content considerably, perhaps to as high as 30 percent in hydroponically produced product.

Until about 1990, marijuana was classified according to its behavioral effects, usually as a mild sedative-hypnotic agent with effects similar to low doses of alcohol but without the intoxication. Unlike alcohol, however, higher doses of THC do not depress respiration and are not lethal. THC also produces a unique spectrum of pharmacological effects, including disruption in attention mechanisms, impairment of short-term memory, altered sensory awareness, analgesia, and altered control of motor movements and postural control.

Since the early 1990s, extensive evidence has accumulated to demonstrate that THC binds to specific *cannabinoid receptors* in both the brain (*CB-1 receptors*) and the peripheral nervous system (*CB-2 receptors*). THC mimics the actions of an endogenous cannabinoid (a fatty acid called *anandamide*), which exerts important biological effects of its own. In addition, cannabinoid receptors exist in the brain in quantities that surpass most other G protein-coupled receptors, approaching or exceeding levels observed for the amino acid receptors glutamate and GABA (Felder et al., 2006).

History

The use of *Cannabis sativa* dates from several thousand years ago (Figure 17.2), when it was used as a mild intoxicant; it is somewhat milder than alcohol. It is much less useful for religious and psychedelic experiences than other naturally occurring psychedelic drugs because it produces much less sensory distortion. Over the years, products from *Cannabis sativa* have been claimed to have a wide variety of medical uses, although few persist in native cultures.

Cannabis sativa was introduced into Western cultures probably in the 1850s. During the early 1920s, marijuana was portrayed as being an underground evil and a menace. Because it was claimed that an association existed between marijuana and crime, laws were passed to outlaw its use. By the mid-1930s, marijuana was looked on as a "narcotic" and as a drug responsible for crimes of violence. By 1940, the public was convinced that marijuana was a "killer drug" that (1) induced people to commit crimes of violence, (2) led to heroin addiction, and (3) was a social menace. The emotional campaign against marijuana persists even today, limiting research into the possible medical uses of cannabinoid agonists and antagonists.

Several facts associated with cannabis abuse are disquieting. First, marijuana is the most widely used illicit drug in the United States and

A. The ancient world to the present

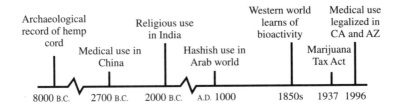

B. Cannabis research developments

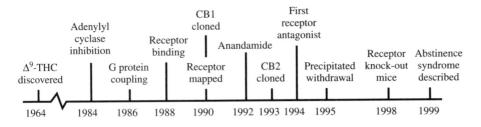

FIGURE 17.2 Two timelines of marijuana history. [Modified from Childers and Breivogel (1998), p. 174.]

the western hemisphere. In 2000, an estimated 76 percent of America's 14.8 million illicit drug users used marijuana alone (59 percent) or in conjunction with other drugs (17 percent). Approximately 6 percent of the population 12 years old and older have used marijuana. Perhaps 5 percent of high school-aged people smoke marijuana daily. Early onset of heavy use is likely to be associated with more severe psychopathology in later years (Brook et al., 2003). Combined alcohol and marijuana use often serves as a marker for later pathology, probably because the substances are used early to self-medicate for psychological distress. Second, a marijuana discontinuation syndrome occurs, although it is probably not as severe as the alcohol withdrawal syndrome. Third, use of marijuana may serve to increase rates of relapse to the use of other drugs such as alcohol, opioids, and stimulants (DeVries et al., 2001).

Since 1996, voters in nine states have approved ballot initiatives to permit the legal use of marijuana for purported medical purposes. Approval of these initiatives signaled the first time since the repeal of the alcohol prohibition amendment some 70 years ago that the public has approved a pullback in the "war on drugs," and these initiatives place state laws in conflict with federal statutes. The medical efficacy of marijuana has been clarified, and evidence is accumulating that marijuana does have medical uses, perhaps most prominently in the relief of certain types of painful conditions. Canada had originally made available medical marijuana, placing the Canadian law in direct conflict with federal statutes in the United States. More recently, Canada approved the use of a product called Sativex, the world's first natural marijuana extract pharmaceutical, to relieve the pain associated with multiple sclerosis. Passage of these Canadian and state initiatives thus raises several issues:

- Should marijuana (or the active drug THC) be made available for medical use throughout the United States, and for what medical uses is THC (or crude marijuana) efficacious?
- Should the U.S. government withhold a therapeutically effective agent (Sativex) from the estimated 350,000 people in the United States with unrelieved pain from multiple sclerosis?
- Should marijuana (or the active drug THC) be made available for recreational use by adults in the United States?
- How should society deal with the use of marijuana by those under the age of 21 years?

Mechanism of Action: Cannabinoid Receptor

THC was isolated from marijuana as its pharmacologically active ingredient (see Figure 17.1) in 1964. Evidence gathered from then until the mid-1980s led to the hypothesis that THC and other cannabinoids act via a pharmacologically distinct set of receptors. In 1986 it was shown that THC inhibits the intracellular enzyme adenylate cyclase and that the inhibition requires the presence of a G protein complex, similar to the opioid receptors discussed in Chapter 16. In about 1990, it was shown that THC does not directly inhibit adenylate cyclase; rather, it acts on a specific receptor in such a way that the enzyme is ultimately inhibited. In 1990 the THC receptor was isolated, sequenced, and cloned. The receptor is a specific G protein-coupled receptor that both inhibits adenylate cyclase and binds THC and other cannabinoids. CB-1 receptors are primarily found on presynaptic nerve terminals and act to inhibit calcium ion flux and facilitate potassium channels. As a result, activation of cannabinoid receptors inhibits the release of other neurotransmitters, primarily the inhibitory neurotransmitter GABA from presynaptic nerve terminals.

Physically, the cannabinoid receptor is a continuous chain of 473 amino acids with seven loops through the cell membrane (Figures 17.3

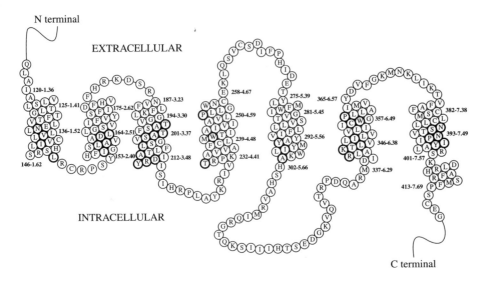

FIGURE 17.3 Two-dimensional representation of the anandamide receptor, a protein consisting of a chain of more than 450 amino acids (the first letter of each amino acid is shown). Like the opioid receptors, the anandamide receptor is a G protein-linked, seven-membrane-spanning structure with three extracellular loops.

and 17.4). As shown by Childers and Breivogel (1998), when THC (or an endogenous endocannabinoid) binds to the cannabinoid receptors, it activates G proteins that act on various effectors, including the second-messenger enzyme adenylate cyclase, to ultimately inhibit GABA release. In 1990, the identification of a naturally occurring ligand (an endocannabinoid) that binds to the cannabinoid receptor and thus might function as a natural THC remained to be demonstrated. In the search for this ligand, Devane and coworkers (1992) first isolated an arachidonic acid derivative named *anandamide* (see Figure 17.1), which not only bound to the cannabinoid receptor but also produced cannabinoidlike pharmacological effects.

Many additional reports since then demonstrated that anandamide produces behavioral, hypothermic, and analgesic effects that parallel those caused by psychotropic cannabinoids. Anandamide is a weaker agonist than is THC and has a shorter half-life. It exhibits the essential criteria required to be classified as the endogenous ligand at cannabinoid receptors. Shen and Thayer (1999) demonstrated that THC acts as a partial agonist at hippocampal glutamate-releasing neurons to "reduce, but not totally block, excitatory transmission" (p. 8). From this statement, we can conclude that both THC and anandamide function as partial agonists that are unable to fully activate cannabinoid receptors at maximally effective concentrations.

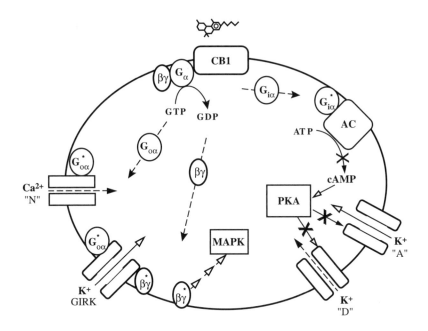

FIGURE 17.4 Several proposed signal transduction mechanisms of cannabinoid receptors. After THC (or anandamide) binds (*top*), the CB1 receptor activates G proteins, which in turn act on various effectors including adenylate cyclase (AC), calcium (Ca^2), and mitogen-activated protein kinase (MAPK). Inhibition of adenylate cyclase and subsequent decreases in cAMP decrease activation of cAMP-dependent protein kinase (PKA), which leads to decreased potassium (K^+) channel fluxes. Stimulatory effects are shown by open arrows and inhibitory effects by filled arrows. The open or closed states of the channels and X's over some arrows reflect the final effects of cannabinoid agonists. [From Childers and Breivogel (1998), p. 179.]

There are huge numbers of cannabinoid receptors in the brain, perhaps 10 to 20 times the number of opioid receptors and perhaps more than any other type of receptor. Anandamide, as a partial agonist, activates perhaps only 50 percent of available receptors; THC activates only about 20 percent. In fact, THC is probably effective not because of any inherent efficacy but because of the tremendous number of receptors for it in the brain. Even in the spinal cord, cannabinoid receptors are expressed in sensory nociceptive cells located in the dorsal root ganglion, from whence the receptors are carried by axoplasmic flow both to peripheral sensory nerve endings and to nerve terminals in the dorsal horn of the spinal cord (Hohmann and Herkenham, 1999a, 1999b).

As can be seen in Figure 17.1, anandamide is structurally dissimilar to THC. Thomas and coworkers (1996) constructed three-dimensional pharmacological models of THC and anandamide and demonstrated that in this conformation the molecules are in actuality quite similar (Figure 17.5) and would be predicted to interact with the same receptor.

As the 1990s ended, the first cannabinoid antagonist was synthesized, and mice lacking the cannabinoid receptor were bred and demonstrated no response to cannabinoid drugs. A marijuana discontinuation syndrome has been described (Smith, 2002), and cannabinoid antagonists are being used to study the discontinuation syndrome and to develop clinical uses in treating obesity and drug craving.

Cannabinoid receptors are located throughout the brain (Figures 17.6 and 17.7). They are most dense in the cortex, hippocampus, basal

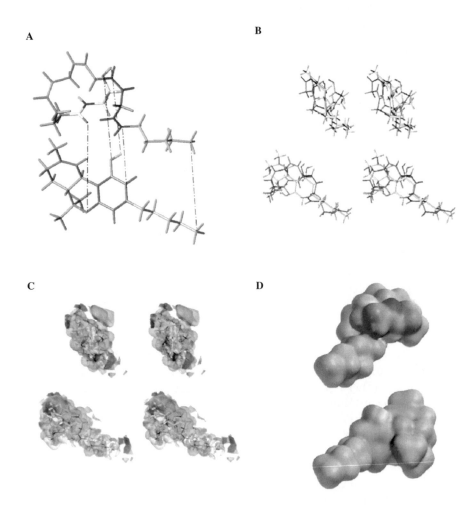

FIGURE 17.5 Several structural comparisons of anandamide and THC. **A.** Stick model showing alignment of the two molecules with dashed lines signifying the five atoms used for superpositioning. **B.** Views of the overlaid structures that predict three-dimensional similarity and thus affinity for the same receptor. **C.** Stereoviews of overlaid structures show nonoverlapping molecular volumes. **D.** Another view of the steric shape and bulk of anandamide (*top*) and THC (*bottom*). [From Thomas et al. (1996), p. 474.]

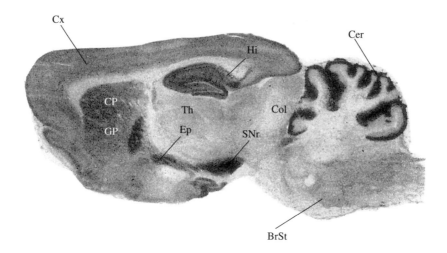

FIGURE 17.6 Autoradiographic binding of potent cannanbinoid-to-cannabinoid receptors in the rat brain. BrSt = brain stem; Cer = cerebellum; Col = colliculi; CP = caudate putamen; Cx = cerebral cortex; Ep = entopeduncular nucleus; GP = globus pallidus; Hi = hippocampus; SNr = substantia nigra; Th = thalamus.

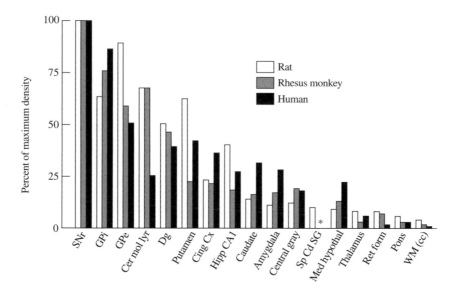

FIGURE 17.7 Relative densities of cannabinoid receptors across brain structures in rat, rhesus monkey, and human. Cer mol lyr = cerebellum, molecular layer; Cing Cx = cingulate cortex; Dg = dentate gyrus; GPe = external globus pallidus; GPi = internal globus pallidus; Hipp CA1 = hippocampal field CA1; Med hypothal = medial hypothalamus; Ret form = reticular formation; SNr = substantia nigra; Sp Cd SG = substantia gelatinosa of spinal cord (*only rat measured); WM (cc) = white matter of corpus callosum.

ganglia, cerebellum, and spinal cord. This distribution is consistent with the effects of cannabinoids on memory, cognition, movement, and nociception (pain relief) (Felder et al., 2006). The large numbers in the basal ganglia and cerebellum reflect the movement and postural controls that are affected by smoking marijuana. Binding of THC to receptors in the cerebral cortex, especially the frontal cortex, probably mediates at least some of the psychoactive effects of the drug, including distortions of the sense of time, sound, color, and taste; alterations in the ability to concentrate; and production of a dreamlike state. Cannabinoid receptors in the hippocampus may account for THC-induced disruption of memory, memory storage, and coding of sensory input. Because brain-stem structures do not bind cannabinoids, THC does not affect basal body functions, including respiration. The absence of cannabinoid–anandamide receptors in the brain stem explains the relative nonlethality of THC.

In 1994 Lynn and Herkenham studied the peripheral effects of cannabinoids and reported cannabinoid receptors outside the brain of a slightly different type (CB-2) than those found in the brain (CB-1 receptors). Originally thought to be located only on specific components of the lymphoid system, they are also located in the heart and in body tissues involved in inflammatory and pain responses.

Farquhar-Smith and Rice (2003) reported on the effects of anandamide on inflammatory responses mediated by the cannabinoid-2 receptors and immune cells. They noted that in the periphery, certain immune cells coexpress cannabinoid-2 receptors as well as a receptor for a protein called nerve growth factor. The researchers found that anandamide (and another synthetic cannabinoid agonist) blocked nerve growth factor-induced painful and inflammatory responses and that this peripheral analgesic/anti-inflammatory response of anandamide is independent of CNS effects involving cannabinoid-1 receptors (which have additional and independent analgesic involvement).

Pharmacokinetics

Most marijuana available in the United States has a THC content that does not exceed 8 percent, although some products contain much higher amounts. THC is usually administered in the form of a hand-rolled marijuana cigarette. Thus, if a marijuana cigarette contains 1.5 grams of plant material with a THC content of about 5 percent, the cigarette contains approximately 75 milligrams of THC. In general, about one-fourth to one-half of the THC present in a marijuana cigarette is actually available in the smoke. Thus, if a cigarette contains 75 milligrams of THC, about 25 milligrams are available in the smoke. In practice, the amount of THC absorbed into the bloodstream as a result of the social smoking of one marijuana cigarette is probably in the range of 5 to 10 milligrams. The absorption of THC from the smoking of marijuana is rapid and complete.

Besides administration by smoking, marijuana can be taken orally, and one THC preparation, dronabinol (Marinol), has been available for oral use since the mid-1980s. Taken orally, onset is delayed and "first-pass metabolism" hinders the drug from reaching significant plasma concentration (Huestis, 2005). Taken orally in therapeutic amounts (for appetite stimulation), plasma concentrations of both THC and its active metabolite (11-hydroxy-delta-9-THC) never exceeded 6.1 nanograms of drug per milliliter of plasma and never persisted beyond 15 hours after oral intake (Goodwin et al., 2006). The levels of inactive metabolite (carboxy-THC, or THCCOOH) were detectable for about 40 hours in plasma, longer in urine (Gustafson et al., 2004).

The behavioral effects of THC in smoked marijuana occur almost immediately after smoking begins and correspond with the rapid attainment of peak concentrations in plasma (Figure 17.8). A "high" is experienced with plasma concentrations of THC of about 5 to 10 nanograms of drug per milliliter of plasma. Unless more is smoked, the effects seldom last longer than 2 to 3 hours. Peak blood levels of THC of 50 to 100 nanograms per milliliter occur about 10 minutes after initiation of smoking cigarettes containing 1.75 percent and 3.55

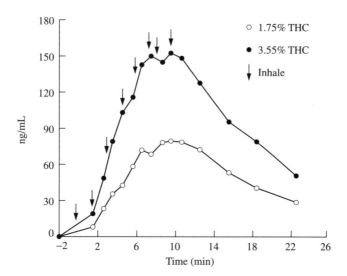

FIGURE 17.8 Mean plasma concentrations of total THC for smoked marijuana and infused THC on days 1 and 22. One marijuana cigarette was smoked from 0 to 15 minutes and was followed by intravenous infusion from 15 to 65 minutes, as indicated by arrows. Results from day 22 were obtained after daily smoking of marijuana and suggest that tolerance failed to develop. [From M. Perez-Reyes et al., "The Pharmacological Effects of Daily Marijuana Smoking in Humans," *Pharmacology Biochemistry and Behavior* 40 (1991), p. 693.]

percent THC, respectively. Within 2 hours, levels fall below 5 nano-grams per milliliter and then decline slowly.

Once THC is absorbed, it is distributed to the various organs of the body, especially those that have significant concentrations of fatty ma-terial. Thus, THC readily penetrates the brain; the blood-brain barrier does not appear to hinder its passage. Similarly, THC readily crosses the placental barrier and reaches the fetus. THC is almost completely metabolized by hepatic cytochrome P450 enzymes to its active metabolite, 11-hydroxy-delta-9-THC, which is subsequently converted to the inactive metabolite THCCOOH, which is then excreted in the urine (Figure 17.9).

Much of the THC taken into the body is stored in body fat, from which it is slowly released. This maintains very low amounts in blood for a considerable time after drug use ceases. The levels achieved with slow release from fat stores are thought to be very low and clinically without significant effect. In frequent users, THC can be detected in plasma for up to 6 days after smoking cannabis, usually less than 1 day in infrequent users (Huestis, 2002). Therefore, THC can actually per-sist in the body for several days to about 2 weeks, longer in chronic smokers and obese smokers. Such a delay tends to prolong and inten-sify the activity of subsequently smoked marijuana, forming a type of "reverse tolerance" to the drug, where the persistent low levels are po-tentiated by subsequently smoked THC cigarettes.

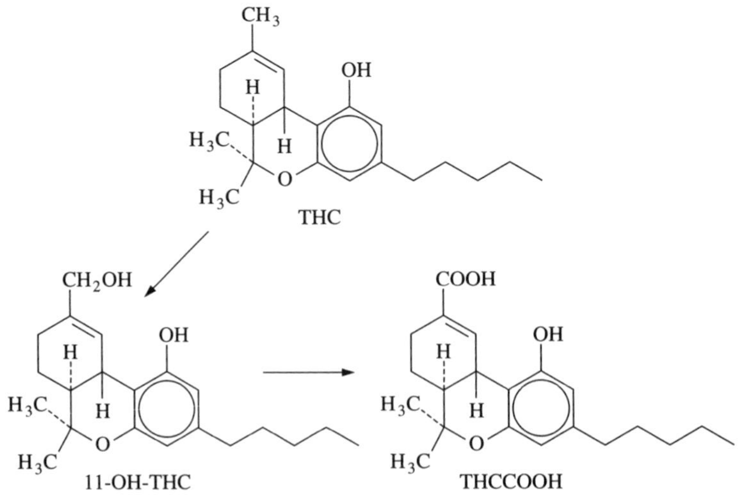

FIGURE 17.9 Major metabolic route for delta-9-tetrahydrocannabinol (THC), including its active metabolite (11-OH-THC) and its primary inactive metabolite (11-nor-9-carboxy-delta-9-tetrahydrocannabinol, or "carboxy-THC").

Like most psychoactive drugs, only minute quantities of active THC are found in the urine of people who use the drug. Therefore, urine testing for THC focuses primarily on identification of its metabolite, carboxy-THC. Carboxy-THC is only slowly excreted; its half-life in urine varies from about 30 hours to 60 hours (Huestis and Cone, 1998), even longer in obese people. Chronic smokers, even if they smoke only two to three times weekly, have persistently positive urine tests for carboxy-THC. A heavy smoker who stops smoking may test positive for carboxy-THC in urine for about a month after cessation. Thus, a positive urinalysis can indicate either recent use or use that occurred several weeks earlier. In addition, a positive urine test does not necessarily mean that a person was under the influence of marijuana at the time the urine specimen was collected; there may be little or no correlation between the presence of carboxy-THC in urine and the presence of a pharmacologically significant amount of THC in the blood.

Pharmacological Effects

THC produces a unique syndrome of behavioral effects, including analgesia, cognitive alterations, and euphoria. Mice lacking the cannabinoid receptor have increased mortality rates, lose body weight, are less active, and have lower than normal pain thresholds. THC and anandamide are analgesic at spinal, brain-stem, and peripheral sites, especially against the pain resulting from persistent inflammation or neuropathic pain (Farquar-Smith and Rice, 2001; Rice et al., 2002). The analgesic action of cannabinoids is similar to but distinct from the action of the opioids such as morphine (Burns and Ineck, 2006).

Effects on the Central Nervous System

In rodents, THC potentiates the analgesic action of morphine, increasing morphine's potency; this action is blocked by cannabinoid antagonists. As discussed, cannabinoid receptors are present in both the peripheral and central terminals of afferent nociceptive neurons. Thus THC can exert analgesic effects by modulating sensory input from peripheral sites of tissue injury and by reducing the release of nociceptive neurotransmitters in the dorsal horn of the spinal cord. THC therefore exerts important analgesic actions in the brain, the spinal cord, and the periphery at the site of tissue injury.

As stated, in late 2005 Canada approved the use of a product called Sativex, the world's first natural marijuana extract pharmaceutical, to relieve the pain associated with multiple sclerosis. Sativex is a cannabis-based pharmaceutical product containing THC and cannabidiol in a 1:1 mixure, delivered in an oromucosal (mouth) spray, similar to asthma inhaler devices. Each spray delivers 2.7 milligrams of

THC and 2.5 milligrams of cannabidiol. At a daily dose of 8 to 12 sprays, a total daily intake of about 22 to 32 millligrams per day of THC and 20 to 30 milligrams per day of cannabidiol are achieved. The efficacy of this product in treating the pain associated with multiple sclerosis has been reviewed by Barnes (2006), Iskedjian and colleagues (2007), and Wade and colleagues (2004, 2006).

Besides analgesia, THC also exerts a variety of other effects in animals and in man. THC decreases body temperature, calms aggressive behavior, potentiates the effects of barbiturates and other sedatives, blocks convulsions, and depresses reflexes. In primates, specifically, THC decreases aggression, decreases the ability to perform complex behavioral tasks, seems to induce hallucinations, and appears to cause temporal distortions. THC causes monkeys to increase the frequency of their social interactions. High doses can depress ovarian function, lower the concentration of female sex hormones, decrease ovulation, and possibly decrease sperm production. Finally, THC can disrupt appetite regulation, inducing overeating in rats exposed to anandamide, which provides evidence for the involvement of a central cannabinoid system in the normal control of eating (Kirkham, 2005). Clinically, THC can be used as an appetite stimulant, useful in wasting diseases such as cancer and AIDS (Berry and Mechoulam, 2002). However, a recent, well-controlled study found that THC was little better than placebo in stimulating appetite in adults with advanced cancer (Cannabis-in-Cachexia-Study-Group, 2006).

The CNS effects of THC vary with dose, route of administration, experience of the user, vulnerability to psychoactive effects, and the setting in which administration happens. In general, the senses may be enhanced and the perception of time is usually altered. Users report an increased sense of well-being, mild euphoria, relaxation, and relief from anxiety. The subjective effects include dissociation of ideas. Illusions and hallucinations occur infrequently. The effect sought after by most users is the "high" and "mellowing out." This effect is described as different from the stimulant high and the opioid high. The effects vary with dose, but the typical marijuana smoker experiences a high that lasts about two hours. During this time, there is impairment of cognitive functions, perception, reaction time, learning, and memory. Impairment of coordination and divided attention have been reported to persist for several hours beyond the perception of the high. These impairments have obvious implications for the operation of a motor vehicle and performance in the workplace or at school.

One of the major deleterious effects of the acute use of marijuana in humans is the short-term disruption of memory and cognition; THC impairs all stages of memory including encoding, consolidation, and retrieval in humans (Ranganathan and D'Souza, 2006). Memory impairments can be attenuated by cannabinoid antagonists, which implies that THC- and anandamide-induced memory disruption is mediated by cannabinoid receptors, not by any indirect sedative mechanism.

During the period of intoxication, there is a modest degree of memory impairment; amnesia, similar to the blackout seen with high-dose alcohol ingestion, is not observed and there are only minimal degradations in behavioral performance on attention tasks. Very heavy use, however, is associated with reduced performance on tests measuring memory, executive functioning, psychomotor speed, and manual dexterity (Bolla et al., 2002). Hart and coworkers (2001) studied people who smoked an average of 24 marijuana cigarettes per week and found that although marijuana increased the time smokers required to complete complex tasks, it had no effect on measures of cognitive flexibility, mental calculation, and reasoning.

Fried and coworkers (2002) followed a group of youths from birth through the age of use of marijuana, thus having the advantage of evaluating them before initiation of drug use. Current marijuana use was associated in a dose-related fashion with a decline in IQ scores. Current heavy users showed decreases averaging 4.1 points compared to gains in IQ points for light current users, former users, and nonusers. Therefore, only subjects who were heavy users (five or more joints smoked per day) showed reductions in IQ, and smoking any amount did not appear to have a long-term negative impact on global intelligence. Bolla and coworkers (2002) noted the persistence of neurocognitive deficits in very heavy users after 28 days of abstinence.

In total, data appear to indicate that heavy marijuana smoking is associated with acute effects detrimental to cognitive functioning. Effects can be detected for at least 1 month following discontinuation of heavy use, and only minimal effects are likely to persist following a 30-day period of abstinence. THC is certainly not a "dementing drug" as are ethanol or the benzodiazepines.

Herning and coworkers (2005) provide a possible explanation of persistent cognitive deficits during the month following abstinence from the drug. They note that acute use of marijuana is associated with increases in cerebral blood flow (which follows reductions in the resistance of blood vessels and can lower blood pressure and cause dizziness). The opposite is observed in recently abstinent chronic THC users: cessation of THC use is associated with increases in blood vessel resistance and reductions in cerebral blood flow, reducing blood flow to the brain. Herning and coworkers then demonstrate that the increased blood vessel resistance with reduction in cerebral blood flow persists for at least one month during abstinence. Blood flow reductions correlate with observed cognitive deficits.

At very high doses, acute depressive reactions, acute panic reactions, and mild paranoia have been observed, probably brought on by drug-induced alterations in perception; some panic responses may follow the feeling of a loss of mental control. Several surveys indicate that 50 to 60 percent of marijuana users have reported at least one anxiety experience. Only at massive doses of THC do delusions, paranoia, hallucinations, confusion and disorientation, depersonalization, altered sensory perception, and loss of insight occur, and these reactions are unusual and generally do not last long.

Marijuana can impair the ability to focus attention and filter out irrelevant information. Users demonstrate weakness in attention and synthetic skills, difficulty making subtle distinctions in relevance and memory, decreased psychospatial skills, poor mental representations of the environment, and poor routines of daily life. These impairments are associated with feelings of alienation and that life is not under control and lacks meaning. With cessation of drug use and with initiation of psychological treatment, users demonstrate improvement in cognitive functioning within 14 days of abstinence and function normally at the end of six weeks of therapy.

Kouri and coworkers (1995) studied cohorts of heavy versus occasional marijuana smokers in a college population. By objective measurement of psychiatric functioning (diagnosed DSM disorders), the two groups were indistinguishable. They differed, however, in the level of use of other drugs: one-third of heavy marijuana users displayed a history of some form of substance abuse or dependence (Tables 17.1 and 17.2).

TABLE 17.1 Lifetime substance use among heavy versus occasional marijuana smokers

	Heavy smokers (n = 45) n (%)	Occasional smokers (n = 44) n (%)
SUBJECTS WHO HAD EVER USED		
Hallucinogens	44 (98)	23 (42)[c]
Hallucinogens >10 times	36 (80)	5 (11)[c]
Cocaine	32 (71)	8 (18)[c]
Cocaine >10 times	20 (44)	0[c]
Inhalants	11 (24)	3 (7)[a]
Stimulants	14 (31)	7 (16)
Sedative-hypnotics	27 (60)	7 (16)[c]
Opioids	12 (27)	1 (2)[b]
Any of the above	45 (100)	26 (59)[c]
SUBJECTS CURRENTLY USING		
Cigarettes ≥1 pack/day	17 (38)	5 (11)[b]
Alcohol >10 drinks/week	17 (38)	9 (20)

Significance of differences between groups: [a]p < .05; [b]p < .01; [c]p < .001.

TABLE 17.2 Lifetime diagnoses of substance abuse and dependence in heavy versus occasional marijuana smokers

	Heavy smokers (n = 45) n (%)	Occasional smokers (n = 44) n (%)
SUBSTANCE		
Cannabis	45 (100)	0
Alcohol	11 (24)	5 (11)
Cocaine	6 (13)	0
Hallucinogens	3 (7)	0
Sedative-hypnotics	1 (2)	0
Polysubstance	2 (4)	0
ANY SUBSTANCE OTHER THAN CANNABIS[a]	15 (33)	5 (11)

[a]Total for heavy users is less than the sum of the individual diagnoses because some subjects reported more than one form of substance abuse or dependence.
Significance of differences: cannabis, $p < .001$; cocaine, $p = .03$; any substance other than cannabis, $p = .01$.

To understand the behavioral attractiveness of marijuana, Gardner and Lowinson (1991) reviewed marijuana's interactions with brain reward systems, particularly in the dopamine-mediated, medial forebrain bundle projection. They stated:

> Acute enhancement of brain reward mechanisms appears to be the single essential commonality of abuse-prone drugs, and the hypothesis that recreational and abused drugs act on these brain mechanisms to produce the subjective reward that constitutes the "high" or "rush" or "hit" sought by drug users is, at present, the most compelling hypothesis available on the neurobiology of recreational drug use and abuse. (p. 571)

More recently, other authors have expanded on the behavioral rewarding effects of both anandamide and THC, concluding that both activate the mesolimbic dopaminergic reward system (nucleus accumbens and ventral tegmentum) where such other drugs as ethanol, stimulants, opioids, and nicotine are thought to act, although probably through a different mechanism (Solinas et al., 2006; Zangen et al., 2006; Gardner, 2005). The implication is an involvement of the cannabinoid system in drug addiction (Maldonado et al., 2006; Vigano et al., 2005). Indeed, as we will see later, cannabinoid antagonists possess potent antiaddictive properties and will lead to exciting therapeutic possibilities in the treatment of alcohol, drug, and nicotine addiction.

The major acute side effects associated with marijuana use are dose-related extensions of its recreational uses: sedation, altered motor coordination, impaired cognition, and reduced short-term memory. Marijuana impairs a person's ability to drive an automobile safely, much as alcohol does. At present, a blood concentration of THC of about 2 nanograms per milliliter or higher is associated with impairment in the ability to drive an automobile (Ramaekers et al., 2004, 2006). Huestis (2002) discussed the correlation of the amount of THC in blood and its detrimental effects on driving:

> Recent exposure (6–8 hours) and possible impairment have been linked to plasma THC concentrations in excess of 2–3 ng/ml. There is some suggestion that 1.6 ng/ml THC in whole blood may indicate possible impairment. This correlates well with the suggested concentration of plasma THC, due to the fact that THC in hemolized blood is approximately one-half the concentration of plasma THC. Interpretation is further complicated by residual THC and THCCOOH concentrations found in blood of frequent cannabis users. In general, it is suggested that chronic cannabis smokers may have residual plasma THC concentrations of less than 2 ng/ml 23 hours after smoking cannabis. (p. 31)

It has been hypothesized that cannabis use in susceptible adolescents and young adults may be a contributory cause of schizophreniform psychosis. "This contributory causal relation is biologically plausible because psychotic disorders involve disturbances in the dopamine neurotransmitter systems with which the cannabinoid system interacts" (Degenhardt and Hall, 2006, p. 556). Further, "It is most plausible that cannabis use precipitates schizophrenia in individuals who are vulnerable because of a personal or family history of schizophrenia" (Degenhardt and Hall, 2006, p. 556). DiForti and coworkers (2007) stated: "Cannabis use in adolescence increases the risk of later schizophrenia-like psychosis, especially in genetically vulnerable individuals" (p. 228).

In a study by Kristensen and Cadenhead (2007) of 48 young people at risk for developing a psychotic disorder, at one-year follow-up, 6 of the 48 (12.5 percent) made the transition to psychosis. Of 32 subjects who had no cannabis use or minimal cannabis use, one subject (3.1 percent) converted to psychosis; of 16 subjects who met criteria for cannabis use or dependence, 5 (31.3 percent) converted to psychosis. Nicotine use was also associated with later conversion. With the prevalence of substance misuse high in young people with early psychosis (51 percent), and with much of the substance misuse being cannabis and alcohol misuse (33 percent and 35 percent, respectively), early intervention to reduce substance misuse may prevent or delay conversion to psychosis (Addington and Addington, 2007; Archie et al, 2007).

The association between cannabis use and early psychosis is complex. As stated by D'Souza (2007):

> There is renewed interest in the long-recognized association between cannabinoids and psychosis. . . . Cannabinoids can induce acute transient psychotic symptoms or an acute psychosis in some individuals. What makes some individuals vulnerable to cannabinoid-induced psychosis is unclear. Cannabinoids can also exacerbate psychosis in individuals with an established psychotic disorder, and these exacerbations may last beyond the period of intoxication. . . . On the other hand, the large majority of individuals exposed to cannabinoids do not experience psychosis or develop schizophrenia and the rates of schizophrenia have not increased commensurate with the increase in rates of cannabis use. Similar to smoking and lung cancer, it is more likely that cannabis exposure is a component cause that interacts with other factors, for example, genetic risk, to "cause" schizophrenia. . . . Further work is necessary to identify those factors that place individuals at higher risk for cannabinoid-related psychosis, to identify the biological mechanisms underlying the risks and to further study whether CB1 receptor dysfunction contributes to the pathophysiology of psychotic disorders. (p. 289)

Hermann and coworkers (2007) discuss a possible mechanism that might underlie the increased risk of early psychosis in susceptible persons.

Effects on the Cardiovascular System

A marked increase in heart rate and a mild increase in blood pressure are two commonly observed physiological effects of THC. During periods of intoxication, the combined effect can increase the workload (increasing oxygen requirements) of the heart and simultaneously reduce blood flow to the heart muscle. Ischemia of the heart can follow, perhaps similar to that seen during exercise. Although the increased heart rate could be a problem for people with cardiovascular disease, dangerous physical reactions to marijuana are almost unknown. There is no association of marijuana use with cardiovascular disease hospitalizations or mortality (Jones, 2002; Sidney, 2002). By extrapolation from animal experiments, the ratio of lethal to effective (intoxicating) dose is estimated to be on the order of thousands to one. Interestingly, peripheral cannabinoid-2 receptors in the heart function in an intrinsic defense of the heart against potentially fatal ischemic attacks (Bouchard et al., 2003). This protective effect of cannabinoids may eventually be an important therapeutic intervention in the prevention of heart attacks.

Blood vessels of the cornea can dilate, which results in bloodshot eyes that can be observed in someone who has just smoked marijuana.

Pulmonary Effects

The gaseous and particulate components of both marijuana and tobacco smoke provide some insights into the potential for marijuana to cause pulmonary damage. With the exception of the presence of THC in marijuana and nicotine in tobacco, both inhalants are remarkably similar; marijuana smoke contains more tars and many of the same carcinogenic compounds identified in tobacco smoke. A single marijuana cigarette may be more harmful than a single tobacco cigarette because more tar is inhaled and retained from marijuana. Also, molecular alterations of lung tissues can be demonstrated, showing evidence of bronchial irritation and inflammation. Recent studies, however, have failed to demonstrate significant associations between marijuana smoking and lung cancer after adjusting for tobacco use (Mehra et al., 2006). Tashkin (2005) noted that tobacco smoking but not marijuana smoking is associated with a decline in lung function; marijuana use was not associated with smoking-related cancers. Aldington and coworkers (2007) recently documented that while marijuana smoking can cause dose-related increases in airway obstruction (an asthmalike effect), its long-term use was not associated with the development of emphysema.

Effects on the Immune System

As noted earlier, cannabinoid-2 receptors are found primarily in the immune system. Long-term marijuana use is associated with a degree of immunosuppression, which might be thought to potentially render the smoker susceptible to infections or disease. Although data in this area are controversial and implications have not been proved, marijuana smoking in some circumstances may partially suppress immunity. The clinical significance of this occurrence is not known, but it should be noted that other depressant drugs, such as alcohol, barbiturates, benzodiazepines, and anticonvulsants, share this immunosuppressive action.

Because both the spleen and the lymphocytes (white blood cells) are important to the body's immune response, they have been investigated to determine how they are affected by cannabinoids. Zhu and coworkers (2000) reported that THC is capable of promoting tumor growth by inhibiting a specific mediator of cancer immunity, exerted via the cannabinoid-2 receptors. The implications of such actions and the physiological role of anandamide in immunomodulation are unknown. To put the immunosuppressive action of marijuana in perspective, in humans marijuana-induced immune suppression is subtle and in most cases insignificant. At this time, little evidence points to cannabinoid-induced immunosuppression as a causative agent in disease.

Effects on the Reproductive System

Evidence of THC-induced suppression of sexual function and reproduction is controversial. The chronic use of marijuana by males can reduce levels of the hormone testosterone and at the same time reduce sperm formation. Reductions in male fertility and sexual potency, however, have not been reported. In females, the levels of follicle-stimulating hormone and luteinizing hormone are reduced by the use of marijuana. Menstrual cycles can be affected and anovulatory cycles have been reported. All these actions reverse when drug use is discontinued.

Marijuana freely crosses the placenta, so its use probably should be avoided during pregnancy. However, estimated prevalence rates of cannabis use during pregnancy range from 3 percent to more than 20 percent of pregnant women (Little et al., 1998). To date, the only medical risk reasonably ascribed to marijuana use during pregnancy appears to be mild fetal growth retardation and maternal lung damage (both similar to that seen with tobacco smoking). Some authors have postulated subtle neurobehavioral effects on infants born of mothers who were heavy cannabis users during pregnancy, but the true risks are unknown.

One of the greatest risks appears to be the high probability that a pregnant female who smokes marijuana during pregnancy may also use other, more fetotoxic drugs (including nicotine cigarettes). Infants born of marijuana-smoking mothers display mild withdrawal signs, including tremulousness, abnormal responses to stimuli, and neurobehavioral performance deficits (deMoraes-Barros et al., 2006). These signs appear to be transient in nature.

Marijuana exposure in utero had modestly adverse effects on executive functioning in offspring at ages 9 to 12 years. Maternal nicotine cigarette smoking contributed to more problems in offspring than did exposure to marijuana smoke. Richardson and coworkers (2002) noted that at age 10 years, children whose mothers smoked marijuana during pregnancy were significantly impaired in measurements of learning, memory, and impulsivity. Smith and coworkers (2006) postulated that prenatal marijuana exposure may alter neural functioning during visuospatial working memory processing in early adulthood (ages 18 to 22 years).

Mereu and coworkers (2003), in a series of studies in rats exposed prenatally to a cannabinoid agonist, noted that offspring showed increased behavioral activity and decreased memory functioning. These offspring also had lower levels of hippocampal glutamate than did control rats (those not exposed to the cannabinoid agonist in utero). The effects on memory and glutamate occurred in the absence of any external evidence of birth defects. These data strongly argue against the use of marijuana during pregnancy.

Tolerance and Dependence

Consequences of chronic marijuana use include profound behavioral tolerance and withdrawal symptoms on drug cessation (Lichtman and Martin, 2005; Gonzalez et al., 2005). Tolerance appears to result from a cannabinoid-induced down regulation and desensitization of brain cannabinoid receptors.

Until recently, it was generally thought that physical dependence on THC probably did not develop, and if it did, any symptoms were mild and transient. Today, a more extensive literature more clearly defines a marijuana withdrawal syndrome that, by definition, implies that body functioning is altered by marijuana use and that uncomfortable symptoms occur when the drug is withdrawn (Budney and Hughes, 2006; Copersino et al., 2006; Haney, 2005). The withdrawal symptoms, however, are generally thought not to be so severe as to call marijuana (or THC) capable of causing "addiction" or inducing a state of strong physical dependence. People seldom use the drug to avoid withdrawal, although the majority of people who enter treatment for marijuana dependence have difficulty in achieving and maintaining abstinence from the drug.

Withdrawal symptoms consist of a craving for marijuana, restlessness, irritability, agitation, anxiety, depressed mood, reduced food intake, insomnia, sleep disturbances, nausea, and cramping. Aggression, anger, irritability, restlessness, and strange dreams can sometimes be observed, but these symptoms are not always present. Withdrawal symptoms occur in over 50 percent of regular users who discontinue the drug. Symptoms begin within 48 hours after cessation of drug administration and last at least 2 days, more usually about 7 to 10 days and perhaps longer, as EEG changes associated with withdrawal persist for at least 28 days. Withdrawal effects appear similar in type and magnitude to those observed in studies of nicotine withdrawal. In treating people who smoke marijuana, significant withdrawal symptoms should be identified and intervention provided as required, including brief hospitalization, extended residential care, and/or pharmacotherapy, if necessary.

DeWit and coworkers (2000) studied 2729 lifetime marijuana users as part of the larger Ontario Mental Health Supplement program. Early and frequent use was associated with highly persistent use and rapid progression to marijuana-related harm. There was a level of use (100 to 200 times) associated with the elevated risk. Females had a lower threshold for risk (50 to 100 times). The researchers concluded: "Required are preventive programs aimed at delaying the onset of first use as well as harm reduction strategies that encourage cessation or reduced levels of consumption among those already using" (p. 455). However society moves toward or away from marijuana availability for medical or recreational use, availability to youths must be restricted.

Until recently, few treatment programs were oriented solely toward marijuana abuse, as both multidrug dependence and comorbid disease are invariably present. Perhaps the recent recognition of a distinct marijuana withdrawal syndrome may draw more attention to the need for specific programs. Historically, treatments such as psychotherapy can be appropriate for frequent users of marijuana, but the therapy is not for marijuana abuse but for an underlying psychopathology (such as depression), one symptom of which is the abuse of cannabis. Grinspoon and Bakalar (1997) wrote:

> Being attached to cannabis is not so much a function of any inherent psychopharmacologic property of the drug as it is emotionally driven by the underlying psychopathology. Success in curtailing cannabis use requires dealing with that pathology. (p. 204)

Diamond and coworkers (2002), Stephens and coworkers (2002), and French and coworkers (2002) described treatment models for marijuana dependence in adolescents. Models included motivational enhancement therapy, cognitive-behavioral therapy, community reinforcement approaches, and multidimensional family therapy. Most were effective, although adolescents with higher levels of externalizing disorders and internalizing disorders continued to experience more substance abuse problems. Following treatment, relapses are common and to be expected (Moore and Budney, 2003).

Therapeutic Uses of Cannabinoid Agonists

The medical applications of marijuana have been a focus of public and scientific interest for a long time, but until recently there was little scientific basis for establishing medical uses. This situation is now rapidly changing. Dronabinol (Marinol), which is synthetic THC formulated in sesame oil, has been available for more than 10 years for use as an appetite stimulant in patients with AIDS and for use in the treatment of nausea and vomiting associated with chemotherapy in cancer patients. In 1997, Schwartz and coworkers reviewed the use of smoked marijuana and oral dronabinol in this population of patients and compared the THC-containing products with physician-prescribed antiemetic compounds. Traditional antiemetics fared better than did THC in treating chemotherapy-induced nausea and vomiting. Bagshaw (2002) concluded that while cannabinoids have modest antiemetic properties, oral cannabinoids would not be recommended as first-line antiemetics. Cannabinoids may prove effective only for refractory nausea or as an adjunct to other antiemetics. Smoked marijuana was not superior to orally administered drug.

Cannabinoids have very specific analgesic properties; analgesic actions have been well described in animals and employed clinically in the treatment of multiple sclerosis in Canada. The problem has been to separate therapeutic analgesic effects from the intoxicating effects. Russo and Guy (2006) discuss that cannabidiol antagonizes some of the adverse effects of THC including intoxication, sedation, and tachycardia (increased heart rate) while contributing analgesic, antiemetic (antivomiting), and antitumor properties of its own. This property of cannabidiol provides a rational basis for combining cannabidiol with THC for clinical efficacy and safety in the treatment of spasticity, pain, and lower urinary tract symptoms in people with multiple sclerosis. This combination appears to increase clinical efficacy while reducing adverse side effects. To date, this product is not available in the United States. Perhaps a groundswell of demand from similar patients in the United States will result in FDA consideration of Sativex for analgesic use in this country, although to do so, a government prohibition against the medical use of cannabis-based products would have to be rescinded.[1]

Other potential uses of cannabinoids as analgesics include relief of neuropathic pain (Berman et al., 2004; Elmes et al., 2004) and reduction of the needed dose of opioid in combination with morphine or other opioids (Roberts et al., 2006).

Animal studies indicate that our endogenous cannabinoid systems may have a role in the normal day-to-day modulation of pain (Hohmann et al., 2004). For example, Farquhar-Smith and Rice (2001) demonstrated that anandamide reduces pain associated with inflammation of the bladder (suggesting a clinical use of THC in treated interstitial cystitis—painful irritation of the bladder—as well as in other types of visceral pain—pain originating from internal organs). It appears that neuronal cell bodies that produce anandamide reside in the dorsal root ganglion (which lies outside the spinal canal). The gene encoding the

---

[1]One possible way to handle the cannabis prohibition in the face of documented legitimate use is to apply the same scheduling model the FDA used with gamma hydroxybutyrate (Chapter 5). Illicit use could still be classified under Schedule I (high potential for abuse with no medical use), and use of Sativex for treating pain associated with multiple sclerosis could be authorized by giving Sativex a Schedule II or III status.

production of anandamide resides in the nucleus of the cell and stimulates production of the anandamide, which then travels by axoplasmic flow both to the bladder (a peripheral site of action) and to the dorsal horn of the spinal cord (exerting a central analgesic action).

Cannabinoid receptors can be found in both the bladder and the spinal cord. Gardell and coworkers (2002) and Clayton and coworkers (2002) note that the spinal analgesic action of cannabinoids is exerted through action on its own cannabinoid receptors rather than indirectly through actions on opioid receptors. Furthermore, the cannabinoid analgesic system is tonically active as a modulator of pain. The modulating effect on pain is discussed by Lever and Malcangio (2002), Walker and coworkers (2001), and Pertwee (2001). Cannabinoid agonists, like THC, will probably have an important role in modulating visceral and inflammatory pain, providing analgesia, and reducing the necessary quantities of opioids in the control of severe pain.

THC increases appetite in patients with AIDS-related wasting disease. Cannabinoids do stimulate appetite, especially for sweet and palatable foods. In fact, one physiological role of the endogenous cannabinoid system is to maintain the stimulus of appetite; a role of endocannabinoids in obesity can be postulated in reward processes that stimulate appetite (Kirkham and Williams, 2001; Fong and coworkers, 2007).

Cannabinoids and their derivatives have been postulated to possess neuroprotective effects following brain injury. This action is based on the ability of THC to inhibit glutaminergic transmission and reduce reactive oxygen intermediates, which are factors in causing neuronal injury after head injury. One synthetic cannabinoid derivative, dexanabinol, underwent trials as a protective agent after head trauma. Preliminary trials were positive, but a recent double blind trial found that it was not efficacious in the treatment of traumatic brain injury in humans (Maas et al., 2006).

Cannabinoids have been reported to reduce intraoccular pressure and therefore might be clinically useful in the treatment of glaucoma. Results are inconclusive, however, and clinical utility is probably minimal and limited by the side effects discussed earlier in this chapter.

Historical use and anecdotal reports indicate that marijuana might have use as symptomatic and prophylactic therapy for migraine. To date, no randomized clinical trials have been conducted to scientifically study this claim. Nevertheless, self-medication for this use probably will continue as will use for such varied disorders as fibromyalgia, irritable bowel syndrome, and other functional conditions for which documented efficacy of cannabinoid efficacy is minimal (Russo, 2004).

Antidepressant effects have been claimed for marijuana. Also, claims of use in treating intractable hiccups have appeared. However, there is little or no scientific evidence to justify these uses. The acute intoxicant effects of marijuana may contribute to a perception of efficacy. The relatively short duration of effect of THC also would lead to either rapid loss of effect or else a need to continue use. CNS side effects including altered perception, forgetfulness, impaired psychomotor skills, and reduced reaction times also limit clinical utility in cases where efficacy is difficult to demonstrate.

Cannabinoid Antagonists

As discussed, activation of cannabinoid receptors underlies the psychological effects of THC and other cannabinoid agonists. Huestis and coworkers (2001) demonstrated for the first time in humans that a specific antagonist for cannabinoid receptors would produce a dose-dependent blockade of marijuana-induced intoxication and tachycardia. This demonstration led to speculation about potential clinical uses of cannabinoid antagonists. Cannabinoid antagonists might be used to reverse cannabinoid intoxication in people who experience unpleasant reactions to marijuana (for example, panic and psychosis), similar to the use of intravenous naloxone to reverse the effects of opioids (Wilson et al., 2006). This use, however, would probably be infrequent and often unpleasant as it would precipitate a cannabinoid withdrawal syndrome. Antagonists, however, might be useful in people who wish to stop using marijuana, blocking any positive effects should marijuana be used, analogous to the use of oral naltrexone to prevent the effects of subsequently taken opioids (Chapter 15).

Because cannabinoid receptor activation also reduces learning, reduces memory formation, and enhances food intake, other potential uses of cannabinoid antagonists might include enhancement of learning and memory (as in the early stages of dementia) and the treatment of obesity. It is important to note that cannabinoid receptors and opioid receptors are intimately related and overlap in function. Also, cannabinoid receptors have been implicated in opioid-induced reward, suggesting a possible role of cannabinoid antagonists in the treatment of addiction to opioids and perhaps psychostimulants (such as cocaine).

Since THC stimulates appetite, especially for sweet and palatable food (Cota et al., 2003), cannabinoid antagonists might be used in the therapy of obesity and other eating disorders by inhibiting the reward processes that stimulate appetite. In animal studies, cannabinoid antagonists lead to maintenance of weight loss as long as the drug is given; withdrawal leads to increased feeding and significant weight gain (Vickers et al., 2003). Therefore, chronically taken, these receptor antagonists are effective, although the effect disappears when the drug is withdrawn (as are the effects of most drugs for their intended uses). Two cannabinoid antagonists have been described in the literature: MK-0364 and rimonabant. Of these, rimonabant is the best studied, reducing body weight and simultaneously improving cardiovascular risk factors in obese patients (Despres et al., 2005; VanGaal et al., 2005; Pi-Sunyer et al., 2006). At a dose of 20 milligrams per day, rimonabant significantly reduced body weight and lowered blood glucose levels in patients with type 2 diabetes. Other claimed uses include reducing the desire to smoke cigarettes, doubling a smoker's success at quitting cigarettes (Gelfand and Cannon, 2006), reducing alcohol ingestion (Gessa et al., 2005; Economidou et al., 2006; Lopez-Moreno et al., 2007), and reducing opioid and stimulant use (Fattore et al., 2005, 2007).

Rimonabant (Figure 17.10) was approved for clinical use by the European Medicines Agency in June 2006, marketed under the trade name Acomplia in seven European countries (Britain, Denmark, Finland, Ireland, Germany, Austria, and Norway) as well as in Argentina. Currently, the trade name Acomplia is being changed to Zimulti, if and when the drug becomes available in the United States. However approval by the FDA has been delayed, perhaps indefinitely. Such delay followed a June 2007 rejection of the drug by an FDA advisory panel because of concerns about a heightened risk of drug-induced depression and suicidal thoughts. These should not be unexpected as rimonabant reduces the attractiveness of substances associated with positive behavioral effects (sweet foods, cigarettes, alcohol, and drugs of compulsive abuse). Should rimonabant or similar drugs become clinically available in the United States, use may require counseling assistance. Indeed, the manufacturer of rimonabant advises that patients be screened for depression before starting the drug and be reassessed frequently to further curtail potential problems.

Rimonabant (and other cannabinoid antagonists under investigation, Table 17.3) certainly provide exciting insights into brain mechanisms involved in behavioral reward and into the treatment of obesity

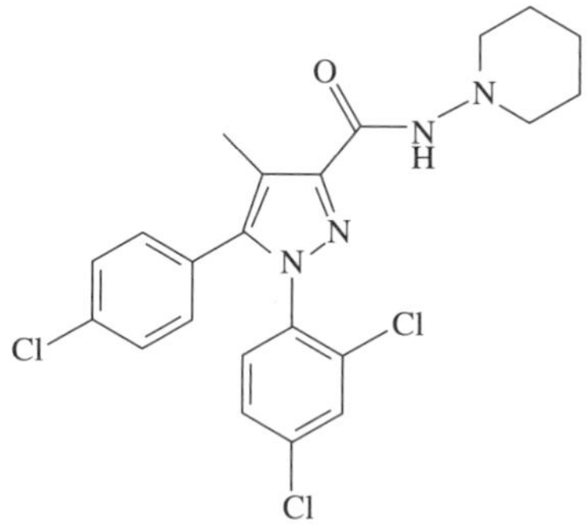

Rimonabant (Acomplia)

FIGURE 17.10 Structure of rimonabant (Acomplia), a cannabinoid antagonist.

TABLE 17.3 CB1 antagonists in clinical development

Drug	Manufacturer	Clinical phase	Study type[a]
Rimonabant	Sanofi-Aventis	III	• Reducing the risk of major cardiovascular events in abdominally obese patients
			• Effects on abdominally obese patients with dyslipidemia
			• Amount and activity of visceral fat in abdominally obese patients with metabolic syndrome
			• Effects on abdominally obese patients with impaired fasting blood glucose with or without other comorbidities
			• Effect on high-density lipoprotein kinetics in patients with abdominal obesity and additional cardiometabolic risk factors
		II	• Reduction of voluntary ethanol drinking
CP-945,598	Pfizer	III	• 2-year weight loss efficacy and safety in obese subjects
			• Long-term study on weight loss and safety in obese subjects
			• Obesity in overweight type 2 diabetic patients
MK-0364	Merck	II	• Weight maintenance in obese subjects
			• Weight loss in obese and overweight subjects
Ave-1625	Sanofi-Aventis	II	• Effects on abdominally obese patients with atherogenic dyslipidemia
Surinaban	Sanofi-Aventis	II	• Efficacy and safety in obese subjects
SLV-319	Solvay Pharmaceuticals Bristol-Myers Squibb	Moved to Phase II	• Smoking cessation

[a] Data at http://www.clinicaltrials.gov

and of drug and alcohol dependence/relapse (Bifulco, 2007). As discussed by Fong and coworkers (2007), only partial occupancy of the cannabinoid receptor is needed for weight loss, and partial occupancy of the receptors was best correlated with reduced food intake and weight loss. Therefore, a "partial agonist" or "weak antagonist" of the receptor might be developed and offer therapeutic potential without the adverse psychological side effects.

STUDY QUESTIONS

1. How are the effects of THC similar to those of the nonselective depressants? How are they dissimilar?

2. How are the effects of THC similar to those of the psychedelic drugs? How are they dissimilar?

3. How does the half-life of THC reflect a person's ability to become intoxicated more easily and with a smaller amount of drug after its repeated use?

4. Discuss some of the concerns and side effects that are associated with varying degrees of THC use by young people.

5. What does THC do to cognition?

6. Are there any long-term effects of marijuana on the brain? The body? Society?

7. Are there any potential long-term effects that might be associated with chronic use of marijuana?

8. Does dependence on marijuana develop? Discuss both views.

9. Discuss the cannabinoid receptor, its location, and its endogenous neurotransmitter.

10. How might a treatment program be organized for people who become dependent on marijuana?

11. What do you think society's response should be to the continued illicit use of marijuana? Should marijuana be legalized for either medical or recreational use? If so, how should it be regulated or restricted?

12. Discuss evidence for or against medical uses of marijuana. If it has medical uses, how might efficacy and societal acceptance be improved?

13. How do you see the future of marijuana and cannabinoid research? What are some of the potential therapeutic uses of cannaboid agonists? Antagonists?

REFERENCES

Addington, J., and D. Addington (2007). "Patterns, Predictors and Impact of Substance Use in Early Psychosis: A Longitudinal Study." *Acta Psychiatrica Scandinavica* 115: 304–309.

Aldington, S., et al. (2007). "The Effects of Cannabis on Pulmonary Structure, Function, and Symptoms." *Thorax*, published online before print, July 31, 2007.

Archie, S., et al. (2007). "Substance Use and Abuse in First-Episode Psychosis: Prevalence Before and After Early Intervention." *Schizophrenia Bulletin*, in press.

Bagshaw, S. M. (2002). "Medical Efficacy of Cannabinoids and Marijuana: A Comprehensive Review of the Literature." *Journal of Palliative Care* 18: 111–122.

Barnes, M. P. (2006). "Sativex: Clinical Efficacy and Tolerability in the Treatment of Symptoms of Multiple Sclerosis and Neuropathic Pain." *Expert Opinions in Pharmacotherapy* 7: 607–615.

Berman, J. S., et al. (2004). "Efficacy of Two Cannabis-Based Medical Extracts for Relief of Central Neuropathic Pain from Brachial Plexus Avulsion: Results of a Randomized Controlled Trial." *Pain* 112: 299–306.

Berry, E. M., and R. Mechoulam (2002). "Tetrahydrocannabinol and Endocannabinoids in Feeding and Appetite." *Pharmacology and Therapeutics* 95: 185–190.

Bifulco, M., et al. (2007). "Rimonabant: Just an Anti-Obesity Drug? Current Evidence on Its Pleiotropic Effects." *Molecular Pharmacology* 71: 1455–1456.

Bolla, K. I., et al. (2002). "Dose-Related Neurocognitive Effects of Marijuana Use." *Neurology* 59: 1337–1343.

Bouchard, J. F., et al. (2003). "Contribution of Endocannabinoids in the Endothelial Protection Afforded by Ischemic Preconditioning in the Isolated Rat Heart." *Life Sciences* 72: 1859–1870.

Brook, J. S., et al. (2003). "Earlier Marijuana Use and Later Problem Behaviors in Colombian Youths." *Journal of the American Academy of Child & Adolescent Psychiatry* 42: 485–492.

Budney, A. J., and J. R. Hughes (2006). "The Cannabis Withdrawal Syndrome." *Current Opinion in Psychiatry* 19: 233–238.

Burns, T. L., and J. R. Ineck (2006). "Cannabinoid Analgesia as a Potential New Therapeutic Option in the Treatment of Chronic Pain." *Annals of Pharmacotherapeutics* 40: 251–260.

Cannabis-In-Cachexia-Study-Group (F. Strasser et al.) (2006). "Comparison of Orally Administered Cannabis Extract and Delta-9-Tetrahydrocannabinol in Treating Patients with Cancer-Related Anorexia-Cachexia Syndrome: A Multicenter, Phase III, Randomized, Double-Blind, Placebo-Controlled Clinical Trial from the Cannabis-In-Cachexia-Study-Group." *Journal of Clinical Oncology* 24: 3394–3400.

Childers, S. R., and C. S. Breivogel (1998). "Cannabis and Endogenous Cannabinoid Systems." *Drug and Alcohol Dependence* 51: 173–187.

Clayton, N. et al. (2002). "CB1 And CB2 Cannabinoid Receptors Are Implicated in Inflammatory Pain." *Pain* 96: 253–260.

Copersino, M. L., et al. (2006). "Cannabis Withdrawal Among Non-Treatment-Seeking Adult Cannabis Users." *American Journal of the Addictions* 15: 8–14.

Cota, D., et al. (2003). "Endogenous Cannabinoid System as a Modulator of Food Intake." *International Journal of Obesity and Related Metabolic Disorders: Journal of the International Association for the Study of Obesity* 27: 289–301.

Degenhardt, L., and W. Hall (2006). "Is Cannabis Use a Contributory Cause of Psychosis?" *Canadian Journal of Psychiatry* 51: 556–565.

DeMoraes-Barros, M. C., et al. (2006). "Exposure to Marijuana During Pregnancy Alters Neurobehavior in the Early Neonatal Period." *Journal of Pediatrics* 149: 781–787.

Despres, J. P., et al. (2005). "Effects of Rimonabant on Metabolic Risk Factors in Overweight Patients with Dyslipidemia." *New England Journal of Medicine* 353: 2121–2134.

Devane, W. A., et al. (1992). "Isolation and Structure of a Brain Constituent That Binds to the Cannabinoid Receptor." *Science* 258: 1946–1949.

DeVries, T. J., et al. (2001). "A Cannabinoid Mechanism in Relapse to Cocaine Seeking." *Nature's Medicine* 7: 1151–1154.

DeWit, D. J., et al. (2000). "The Influence of Early and Frequent Use of Marijuana on the Risk of Desistance and of Progression to Marijuana-Related Harm." *Preventive Medicine* 31: 455–464.

Diamond, G., et al. (2002). "Five Outpatient Treatment Models for Adolescent Marijuana Use: A Description of the Cannabis Youth Treatment Interventions." *Addiction* 97, Supplement 1: S70–S83.

DiForti, M., et al. (2007). "Cannabis Use and Psychiatric and Cognitive Disorders: The Chicken or the Egg?" *Current Opinion in Psychiatry* 20: 228–234.

D'Souza, D. C. (2007). "Cannabinoids and Psychosis." *International Review of Neurobiology* 78: 289–326.

Economidou, D., et al. (2006). "Effect of the Endocannabinoid CB1 Receptor Antagonist SR-141716A on Ethanol Self-Administration and Ethanol-Seeking Behaviour in Rats." *Psychopharmacology* 183: 394–403.

Elmes, S. J., et al. (2004). "Cannabinoid CB2 Receptor Activation Inhibits Mechanically Evoked Responses of Wide Dynamic Range Dorsal Horn Neurons in Naïve Rats and in Rat Models of Inflammatory and Neuropathic Pain." *European Journal of Neuroscience* 20: 2311–2320.

Farquhar-Smith, W. P., and S. Rice (2001). "Administration of Endocannabinoids Prevents a Referred Hyperalgesia Associated with Inflammation of the Urinary Bladder." *Anesthesiology* 94: 507–513.

Farquhar-Smith, W. P., and A. S. C. Rice (2003). "A Novel Neuroimmune Mechanism in Cannabinoid-Mediated Attenuation of Nerve Growth Factor-Induced Hyperalgesia." *Anesthesiology* 99: 1391–1401.

Fattore, L., et al. (2005). "Endocannabinoid System and Opioid Addiction: Behavioural Aspects." *Pharmacology Biochemistry and Behavior* 81: 343–359.

Fattore, L., et al. (2007). "An Endocannabinoid Mechanism in Relapse to Drug Seeking: A Review of Animal Studies and Clinical Perspectives." *Brain Research Reviews* 53: 1–16.

Felder, C. C., et al. (2006). "Cannabinoid Biology: The Search for New Therapeutic Targets." *Molecular Interventions* 6: 149–171.

Fong, T. M., et al. (2007). "Anti-Obesity Efficacy of a Novel Cannabinoid-1 Receptor Inverse Agonist MK-0364 in Rodents." *Journal of Pharmacology and Experimental Therapeutics* 321: 1013–1022

French, M. T., et al. (2002). "The Economic Cost of Outpatient Marijuana Treatment for Adolescents: Findings from a Multi-Site Field Experiment." *Addiction* 97, Supplement 1: S84–S97.

Fried, P., et al. (2002). "Current and Former Marijuana Use: Preliminary Findings of a Longitudinal Study of Effects on IQ in Young Adults." *Canadian Medical Association Journal* 166: 887–891.

Gardell, L. R., et al. (2002). "Dynorphin-Independent Spinal Cannabinoid Antinociception." *Pain* 100: 243–248.

Gardner, E. L. (2005). "Endocannabinoid Signaling System and Brain Reward: Emphasis on Dopamine." *Pharmacology Biochemistry and Behavior* 81: 263–284.

Gardner, E. L., and J. H. Lowinson (1991). "Marijuana's Interaction with Brain Reward Systems: Update 1991." *Pharmacology Biochemistry and Behavior* 40: 571–580.

Gelfand, E. V., and C. P. Cannon (2006). "Rimonabant: A Selective Blocker of the Cannabinoid CB1 Receptors for the Management of Obesity, Smoking Cessation, and Cardiometabolic Risk Factors." *Expert Opinions on Investigational Drugs* 15: 307–315.

Gessa, G. L., et al. (2005). "Suppressing Effect of the Cannabinoid CB1 Receptor Antagonist, SR147778, on Alcohol Intake and Motivational Properties of Alcohol in Alcohol-Preferring sP Rats." *Alcohol and Alcoholism* 40: 46–53.

Gonzalez S., et al. (2005). "Cannabinoid Tolerance and Dependence: A Review of Studies in Laboratory Animals." *Pharmacology Biochemistry and Behavior* 81: 300–318.

Goodwin, R. S., et al. (2006). "Delta-9-Tetrahydrocannabinol, 11-Hydroxy-Delta(9)-Tetrahydrocannabinol and 11-nor-9-Carboxy-Delta(9)-Tetrahydrocannabinol in Human Plasma After Controlled Oral Administration of Cannabinoids." *Therapeutic Drug Monitoring* 28: 545–551.

Grinspoon, L., and J. B. Bakalar (1997). "Marijuana." In J. H. Lowinson, P. Ruiz, R. B. Millman, and J. G. Langrod, eds., *Substance Abuse: A Comprehensive Textbook*, 3rd ed. (pp. 199–206). Baltimore: Williams & Wilkins.

Gustafson, R. A., et al. (2004). "Urinary Pharmacokinetics of 11-nor-9-carboxy-delta9-Tetrahydrocannabinol After Controlled Oral Delta9-Tetrahydrocannabinol Administration." *Journal of Analytical Toxicology* 28: 160–167.

Haney, M. (2005). "The Marijuana Withdrawal Syndrome: Diagnosis and Treatment." *Current Psychiatry Reports* 7: 360–366.

Hart, C. L., et al. (2001). "Effects of Acute Smoked Marijuana on Complex Cognitive Performance." *Neuropsychopharmacology* 25: 757–765.

Hermann, D., et al. (2007). "Dorsolateral Prefrontal Cortex N-Acetylaspartate/Total Creatine (NAA/tCr) Loss in Male Recreational Cannabis Users." *Biological Psychiatry* 61: 1281–1289.

Herning, R. I., et al. (2005). "Cerebrovascular Perfusion in Marijuana Users During a Month of Monitored Abstinence." *Neurology* 64: 488–493.

Hohmann, A. G., and M. Herkenham (1999a). "Cannabinoid Receptors Undergo Axonal Flow in Sensory Nerves." *Neuroscience* 92: 1171–1175.

Hohmann, A. G., and M. Herkenham (1999b). "Localization of Central Cannabinoid CB1 Receptor Messenger RNA in Neuronal Subpopulations of Rat Dorsal Root Ganglia: A Double-Label In Situ Hybridization Study." *Neuroscience* 90: 923–931.

Hohmann, A. G., et al. (2004). "Selective Activation of Cannabinoid CB2 Receptors Suppresses Hyperalgesia Evoked by Intradermal Capsaicin." *Journal of Pharmacology and Experimental Therapeutics* 308: 446–453.

Huestis, M. A. (2002). "Cannabis (Marijuana): Effects on Human Behavior and Performance." *Forensic Science Review* 14: 15–59

Huestis, M. A. (2005). "Pharmacokinetics and Metabolism of the Plant Cannabinoids, Delta9-Tetrahydrocannabinol, Cannabidiol, and Cannabinol." *Handbook of Experimental Pharmacology* 168: 657–690.

Huestis, M. A., and E. J. Cone (1998). "Urinary Excretion Half-Life of 11-Nor-9-Carboxy-Delta9-Tetrahydrocannabinol in Humans." *Therapeutic Drug Monitoring* 20: 570–576.

Huestis, M. A., et al. (2001). "Blockade of Effects of Smoked Marijuana by the CB1Selective Cannabinoid Receptor Antagonist SR141716." *Archives of General Psychiatry* 58: 322–328.

Iskedjian, M., et al. (2007). "Meta-Analysis of Cannabis-Based Treatments for Neuropathic and Multiple Sclerosis-Related Pain." *Current Medical Research Opinions* 23: 17–24.

Jones, R. T. (2002). "Cardiovascular System Effects of Marijuana." *Journal of Clinical Pharmacology* 42, Supplement 11 (November): 58S–63S.

Kirkham, T. C. (2005). "Endocannabinoids in the Regulation of Appetite and Body Weight." *Behavioral Pharmacology* 16: 297–313.

Kirkham, T. C., and C. M. Williams (2001). "Synergistic Effects of Opioid and Cannabinoid Antagonists on Food Intake." *Psychopharmacology* 153: 267–270.

Kouri, E., et al. (1995). "Attributes of Heavy Versus Occasional Marijuana Smokers in a College Population." *Biological Psychiatry* 38: 475–481.

Kristensen, K., and K. S. Cadenhead (2007). "Cannabis Abuse and Risk for Psychosis in a Prodromal Sample." *Psychiatry Research* 151: 151–154.

Lever, I. J., and M. Malcangio (2002). "CB (1) Receptor Antagonist SR141716A Increases Capsaicin-Evoked Release of Substance P from the Adult Mouse Spinal Cord." *British Journal of Pharmacology* 135: 21–24.

Lichtman, A. H., and B. R. Martin (2005). "Cannabinoid Tolerance and Dependence." *Handbook of Experimental Pharmacology* 168: 691–717.

Little, B. B., et al. (1998). "Cannabinoid Use During Pregnancy." In L. C. Gilstrap and B. B. Little, eds., *Drugs and Pregnancy*, 2nd ed. (pp. 413–417). New York: Chapman & Hall.

Lopez-Moreno, J. A., et al. (2007). "The CB1 Cannabinoid Receptor Antagonist Rimonabant Chronically Prevents the Nicotine-Induced Relapse to Alcohol." *Neurobiological Diseases* 25: 274–283.

Lynn, A. B., and M. Herkenham (1994). "Localization of Cannabinoid Receptors and Nonsaturable High-Density Cannabinoid Binding Sites in Peripheral Tissues of the Rat: Implications for Receptor-Mediated Immune Modulation by Cannabinoids." *Journal of Pharmacology and Experimental Therapeutics* 268: 1612–1623.

Maas, A. I., et al. (2006). "Efficacy and Safety of Dexanabinol in Severe Traumatic Brain Injury: Results of a Phase III Randomized, Placebo-Controlled, Clinical Trial." *Lancet Neurology* 5: 38–45.

Maldonado, R., et al. (2006). "Involvement of the Endocannabinoid System in Drug Addiction." *Trends in Neuroscience* 29: 225–232.

Mehra, R., et al. (2006). "The Association Between Marijuana Smoking and Lung Cancer: A Systematic Review." *Archives of Internal Medicine* 166: 1359-1367.

Mereu, G., et al. (2003). "Prenatal Exposure to a Cannabinoid Agonist Produced Memory Deficits Linked to Dysfunction in Hippocampal Long-Term Potentiation and Glutamate Release." *Proceedings of the National Academy of Sciences* 100: 4915–4920.

Moore, B. A., and A. J. Budney (2003). "Relapse in Outpatient Treatment for Marijuana Dependence." *Journal of Substance Abuse Treatment* 25: 85–89.

Pertwee, R. G. (2001). "Cannabinoid Receptors and Pain." *Progress in Neuro-biology* 63: 569–611.

Pi-Sunyer, F. X., et al. (2006). "Effect of Rimonabant, a Cannabinoid-1 Receptor Blocker, on Weight and Cardiometabolic Risk Factors in Overweight or Obese Patients: RIO-North America: A Randomized Controlled Trial." *Journal of the American Medical Association* 295: 761-775.

Ramaekers, J. G., et al. (2004). "Dose Related Risk of Motor Vehicle Crashes After Cannabis Use." *Drug and Alcohol Dependence* 73: 109–119.

Ramaekers, J.G., et al. (2006). "Cognition and Motor Control as a Function of Delta9-THC Concentration in Serum and Oral Fluids: Limits of Impairment." *Drug and Alcohol Dependence* 85: 114–122.

Ranganathan, M., and D. C. D'Souza (2006). "The Acute Effects of Cannabinoids on Memory in Humans: A Review." *Psychopharmacology* 188: 425-444.

Rice, A. S. C., et al. (2002). "Endocannabinoids and Pain: Spinal and Peripheral Analgesia in Inflammation and Neuropathy." *Prostaglandins, Leukotrienes and Essential Fatty Acids* 66: 243–256.

Richardson, G. A., et al. (2002). "Prenatal Alcohol and Marijuana Exposure: Effects on Neuropsychological Outcomes at 10 Years." *Neurotoxicology and Teratology* 24: 309–320.

Roberts, J. D., et al. (2006). "Synergistic Affective Analgesic Interaction Between Delta-9-Tetrahydrocannabinol and Morphine." *European Journal of Pharmacology* 530: 54–58.

Russo, E. B. (2004). "Clinical Endocannabinoid Deficiency (CECD): Can This Concept Explain Therapeutic Benefits of Cannabis in Migraine, Fibromyalgia, Irritable Bowel Syndrome and Other Treatment-Resistant Conditions?" *Neuroendocrinology Letters* 25: 31–39.

Russo, E. B., and G. W. Guy (2006). "The Tale of Two Cannabinoids: The Therapeutic Rationale for Combining Tetrahydrocannabinol and Cannabidiol." *Medical Hypotheses* 66: 234–246.

Schwartz, R. H., et al. (1997). "Marijuana to Prevent Nausea and Vomiting in Cancer Patients: A Survey of Clinical Oncologists." *Southern Medical Journal* 90: 167–172.

Shen, M., and S. A. Thayer (1999). "Delta9-Tetrahydrocannabinol Acts as a Partial Agonist to Modulate Glutamatergic Synaptic Transmission Between Rat Hippocampal Neurons in Culture." *Molecular Pharmacology* 55: 8–13.

Sidney, S. (2002). "Cardiovascular Consequences of Marijuana Use." *Journal of Clinical Pharmacology* 42, Supplement 11: 64S–70S.

Smith, A. M., et al. (2006). "Effects of Prenatal Marijuana on Visuospatial Working Memory: An fMRI Study in Young Adults." *Neurotoxicology and Teratology* 28: 286–295.

Smith, N. T. (2002). "A Review of the Published Literature into Cannabis Withdrawal Symptoms in Human Users." *Addiction* 97: 621–632.

Solinas, M., et al. (2006). "Anandamide Administration Alone and After Inhibition of Fatty Acid Amide Hydrolase (FAAH) Increases Dopamine Levels in the Nucleus Accumbens Shell in Rats." *Journal of Neurochemistry* 98: 408–419.

Stephens, R. S., et al. (2002). "The Marijuana Treatment Project: Rationale, Design and Participant Characteristics." *Addiction* 97, Supplement 1: S109–S124.

Tashkin, D. P. (2005). "Smoked Marijuana as a Cause of Lung Injury." *Monaldi Archives for Chest Disease* 63: 93–100.

Thomas, B. F., et al. (1996). "Structure-Activity Analysis of Anandamide Analogs: Relationship to a Cannabinoid Pharmacophore." *Journal of Medicinal Chemistry* 39: 471–479.

VanGaal, L. F., et al. (2005). "Effects of the Cannabinoid-1 Receptor Blocker Rimonabant on Weight Reduction and Cardiovascular Risk Factors in Overweight Patients: 1-Year Experience from the RIO-Europe Study." *Lancet* 365: 1389–1397.

Vickers, S. P., et al. (2003). "Preferential Effects of the Cannabinoid CB (1) Receptor Antagonist SR 141716 on Food Intake and Body Weight Gain of Obese (fa/fa) Compared to Lean Zucker Rats." *Psychopharmacology* 167: 103–111.

Vigano, D., et al. (2005). "Molecular and Cellular Basis of Cannabinoid and Opioid Interactions." *Pharmacology Biochemistry and Behavior* 81: 360–368.

Wade, D. T., et al. (2004). "Do Cannabis-Based Medical Extracts Have General or Specific Effects on Symptoms in Multiple Sclerosis? A Double-Blind, Randomized, Placebo-Controlled Study on 160 Patients." *Multiple Sclerosis* 10: 339–340.

Wade, D. T., et al. (2006). "Long-Term Use of a Cannabis-Based Medicine in the Treatment of Spasticity and Other Symptoms in Multiple Scherosis." *Multiple Sclerosis* 12: 639–645.

Walker, J. M. et al. (2001). "Cannabinoids and Pain." *Pain Research and Management* 6: 74–79.

Wilson, D. M., et al. (2006). "SR-141716 (Rimonabant) Precipitates Withdrawal in Marijuana-Dependent Mice." *Pharmacology Biochemistry and Behavior* 85: 105–113.

Zangen, A., et al. (2006). "Two Brain Sites for Cannabinoid Reward." *Journal of Neuroscience* 26: 490–4907.

Zhu, L. X., et al. (2000). "Delta-9-Tetrahydrocannabinol Inhibits Antitumor Immunity by a CB2 Receptor-Mediated, Cytokine-Dependent Pathway." *Journal of Immunology* 165: 373–380.

Psychedelic Drugs

This chapter introduces a class of drugs that act on various neuro-transmitters in the CNS to produce visual hallucinations and out-of-body experiences. Their actions are also characterized by marked alterations in cortical functioning, including cognition, perception, and mood (Davis et al., 2002). Because of the wide range of psychological and physiological effects they produce, the single term that might best be used to classify these agents has been debated for a long time. The term *hallucinogen* is used because these agents can, in high enough doses, induce hallucinations. However, that term is somewhat inappropriate because illusory phenomena and perceptual distortions are more common than are true hallucinations. The term *psychoto-mimetic* has also been used because of the alleged ability of these drugs to mimic psychoses or induce psychotic states. However, most of these drugs do not produce the same behavioral patterns that are observed in people who experience psychotic episodes. A descriptive term, such as *phantasticum* or *psychedelic*, has also been used, to imply that these agents all have the ability to alter sensory perception. Drugs such as MDMA that exhibit a blend of stimulant and hallucinogenic actions have been referred to as *entactogens*. In this chapter the term *psychedelic* is used because it allows for more flexibility in grouping together a disparate array of effects into a quantifiable and recognizable syndrome.

A psychedelic drug can be defined as any agent that causes alterations in perception, cognition, and mood as its primary psychobiological actions in the presence of an otherwise clear sensorium. This definition separates the pure psychedelic drugs from other substances

606

that can cause altered states of thinking and perception, such as *poisons* that affect the mind (not discussed in this book) and *deliriants* (such as ethyl alcohol and the inhalants of abuse) that primarily produce clouding of consciousness, impaired cognition, and amnesia. This chapter covers the true psychedelics, mixed psychedelic-stimulant drugs ("club drugs"), and certain other abused deliriants such as scopolamine, phencyclidine, ketamine, and dextromethorphan.

Many psychedelic agents occur in nature; others are synthetically produced. Naturally occurring psychedelic drugs have been inhaled, ingested, worshipped, and reviled since prehistory, and many are available in the United States and throughout the world (Halpern, 2004). Many are viewed as having magical or mystical properties. Prior to the 1960s, most Americans were barely aware of their existence. During the late 1960s and the 1970s, however, some people advocated their use to enhance perception, expand reality, promote personal awareness, and stimulate or induce comprehension of the spiritual or supernatural. These drugs heighten awareness of sensory input, often accompanied by both an enhanced sense of clarity and diminished control over what is experienced. Frequently, there is a feeling that one part of the self seems to be a passive observer, while another part of the self participates and receives the vivid and unusual sensory experiences. In this state, the slightest sensation may take on profound meaning. With the advent of organic chemistry, many of these psychedelic drugs have been chemically identified and many derivatives synthesized.

Most psychedelic drugs structurally resemble one of four neurotransmitters: acetylcholine, two catecholamines (norepinephrine and dopamine), and serotonin. These structural similarities lead to three of the five classes for categorizing psychedelic drugs (Table 18.1): *anticholinergic, catecholaminelike,* and *serotoninlike psychedelics.* The fourth and fifth classes of psychedelic drugs are the *glutaminergic NMDA receptor antagonist*s (the two psychedelic anesthetics as well as dextromethorphan) and the *opioid kappa receptor agonist* salvinorin A. The *deliriants* do not produce hallucinations or profound sensory distortion in doses below intoxicating doses; therefore they are not thought of as psychedelic drugs.

Scopolamine: An Anticholinergic Psychedelic

Scopolamine (Figure 18.1), an acetylcholine receptor blocker (antagonist), is the classic example of an anticholinergic drug with psychedelic properties. Because it binds to acetylcholine receptors but is devoid of intrinsic activity, scopolamine blocks the access of acetylcholine to its receptors—hence the term *anticholinergic.* This term

TABLE 18.1 Classification of psychedelic drugs

• ANTICHOLINERGIC PSYCHEDELIC DRUG
Scopolamine
• CATECHOLAMINELIKE PSYCHEDELIC DRUGS
Mescaline
DOM, MDA, DMA, MDMA (ecstasy), TMA, MDE
Myristin, elemicin
• SEROTONINLIKE PSYCHEDELIC DRUGS
Lysergic acid diethylamide (LSD)
Dimethyltryptamine (DMT)
Psilocybin, psilocin, bufotenine
Ololiuqui
Harmine
• GLUTAMINERGIC NMDA RECEPTOR ANTAGONISTS
Phencyclidine (Sernyl)
Ketamine (Ketalar)
Dextromethorphan
• OPIOID KAPPA RECEPTOR AGONIST
Salvinorin A

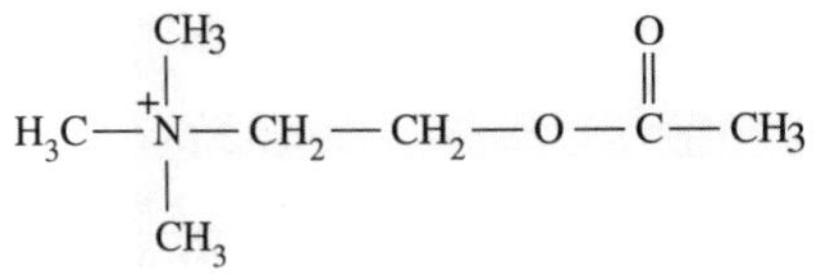
Acetylcholine

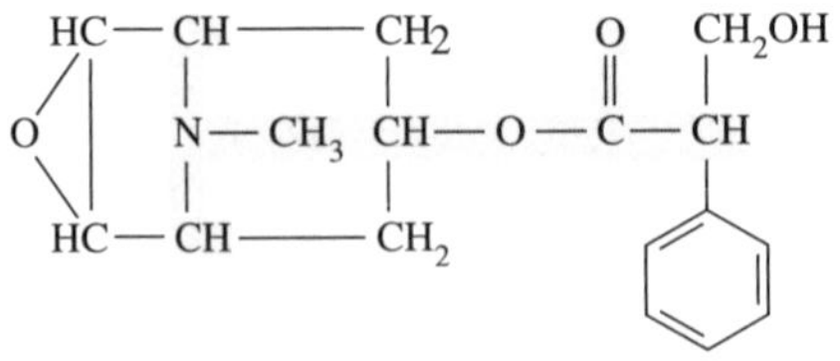
Scopolamine

FIGURE 18.1 Structural formulas of acetylcholine (a chemical transmitter) and the anticholinergic psychedelic scopolamine, which acts by blocking acetylcholine receptors. The shaded portion of each molecule illustrates structural similarities, which presumably contribute to receptor fit.

implies a constellation of effects, including dry mouth, blurred vision, increased heart rate, and urinary retention. Because scopolamine (unlike the closely related drug atropine) crosses the blood-brain barrier and reaches the brain, it causes sedation, amnesia, and delirium. Medically, scopolamine is found in some travel-sickness products including motion-sickness skin patches.

Historical Background

The history of scopolamine is long and colorful (Holzman, 1998). The drug is distributed widely in nature, found in especially high concentrations in the plants *Atropa belladonna* (belladonna, or deadly nightshade), *Datura stramonium* (Jamestown weed, jimsonweed, stinkweed, thorn apple, or devil's apple), *Mandragora officinarum* (mandrake), and *Datura inoxia* (moonflower). Both professional and amateur poisoners of the Middle Ages frequently used deadly nightshade as a source of poison. In fact, the plant's name, *Atropa belladonna*, is derived from Atropos, one of the three Fates, who supposedly cut the thread of life. Belladonna means "beautiful woman," which refers to the drug's ability to dilate the pupils when it is applied topically to the eyes (eyes with widely dilated pupils were presumably a mark of beauty). Accidental ingestion of berries from *Datura* has even been associated with the incapacitation of whole armies, for example, the defeat of Marc Antony's army in 36 B.C. and the defeat of British soldiers by settlers in the rebellion known as Bacon's Revolution near Jamestown, Virginia, in 1676 (hence the name Jamestown weed).

Scopolamine-containing plants have been used and misused for centuries. For example, the delirium caused by scopolamine may have persuaded certain people that they could fly—and that they were witches (associated with the Halloween customs involving flying witches). Marijuana and opium preparations from the Far East were once fortified with material from *Datura stramonium*. Today, cigarettes made from the leaves of *Datura stramonium* and *Atropa belladonna* are smoked occasionally to induce intoxication. Throughout the world, leaves of plants that contain atropine or scopolamine are still used to prepare intoxicating beverages.

Pharmacological Effects

As introduced, scopolamine acts on the peripheral nervous system to produce an anticholinergic syndrome consisting of dry mouth, reduced sweating, dry skin, increased body temperature, dilated pupils, blurred vision, tachycardia, and hypertension. Scopolamine in the CNS functions as a deliriant and intoxicant. Low doses produce drowsiness, mild euphoria, profound amnesia, fatigue, delirium, mental confusion, dreamless sleep, and loss of attention. Rather than expanding consciousness, awareness, and insight, scopolamine clouds consciousness and produces amnesia; it does not expand sensory perception. The amnesia produced is quite intense. As doses of scopolamine increase, psychiatric symptoms include restlessness, excitement, hallucinations, euphoria, and disorientation (DeFrates et al., 2005).

In higher and much more toxic doses, a behavioral state that resembles a toxic psychosis occurs. Delirium, mental confusion, stupor, coma, and respiratory depression dominate. While scopolamine intoxication can convey a sense of excitement and loss of control to the user, the clouding of consciousness and the reduction in memory of the episode render scopolamine rather unattractive as a psychedelic drug. It is probably more appropriate to refer to it as a somewhat dangerous intoxicant, amnestic, and deliriant. Scopolamine is classically stated to make one "hot as a hare, blind as a bat, dry as a bone, red as a beet, and mad as a hen." Typically, sensorium and psychosis usually clear within 36 to 48 hours.

Catecholaminelike Psychedelics

Norepinephrine and dopamine receptors are important sites of action for a large group of psychedelic drugs that are structurally similar to both catecholamine neurotransmitters and the amphetamines (Figure 18.2). They differ structurally from the normal neurotransmitters by the addition of one or more methoxy ($-OCH_3$) groups to the phenyl ring structure. These methoxy groups, varied as they are, confer psychedelic properties on top of their amphetaminelike psychostimulant properties. Methoxylated amphetamine derivatives include mescaline, DOM (also called STP), MDA, MDE, MDMA (ecstasy), MMDA, DMA, and certain drugs that are obtained from nutmeg (myristin and elemicin).

As would be predicted from their structures, catecholamine psychedelics exert amphetaminelike psychostimulant actions, presumably on dopaminergic neurons. They can enhance energy, endurance, sociability, and sexual arousal (Kalant, 2001). However, their psychedelic actions are probably ultimately exerted by augmentation of serotonin neurotransmission—probably as agonists at postsynaptic serotonin 5-HT$_{2A}$ receptors. This action would account for their LSD-like effects. The combination of catecholamine and serotonin actions points to a complex interaction between dopamine and serotonin and explains their intermediate position between stimulants and (LSD-like) hallucinogens. As mentioned at the beginning of this chapter, such agents constitute a rather distinct class of psychedelic agents called *entactogens*, which takes an intermediate position between stimulants and hallucinogens.

As early as the late 1960s, most psychedelics were known to produce a remarkably similar set of effects, including enhanced emotional

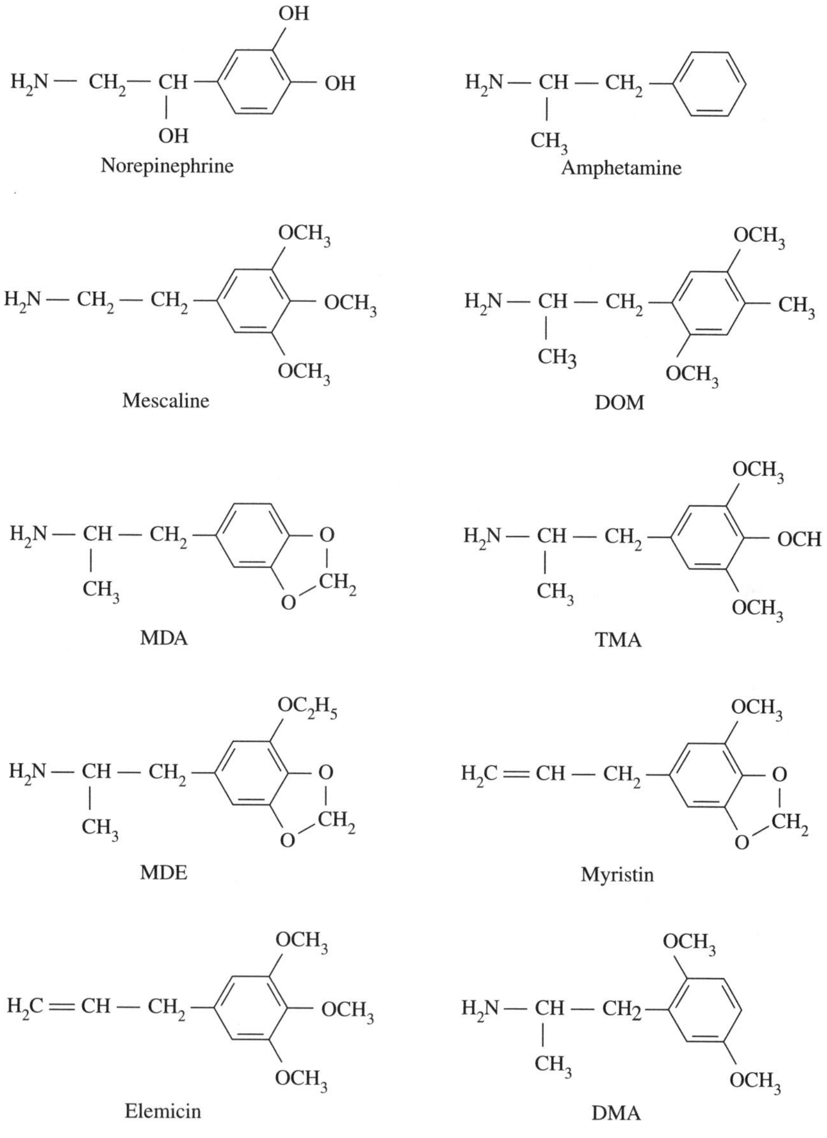

FIGURE 18.2 Structural formulas of norepinephrine (a chemical transmitter), amphetamine, and eight catecholaminelike psychedelic drugs. These eight drugs are structurally related to norepinephrine and are thought to exert their psychedelic actions by altering the transmission of nerve impulses at norepinephrine and serotonin synapses in the brain.

responses; sensory-perceptual distortion; altered perceptions of colors, sounds, and shapes; complex hallucinations; dreamlike feelings; depersonalization; and somatic effects (tingling skin, weakness, tremor, and so on). During the 1980s, it was noted that psychedelic drugs produce marked alterations in brain serotonin. As serotonin receptors were characterized in the early 1990s, it became clear that LSD was a serotonin receptor agonist and that the catecholaminelike psychedelics functioned ultimately as indirectly acting serotonin agonists. Today, the focus of attention has been on activation of a subgroup of the 5-HT_2 receptors, specifically the 5-HT_{2A} receptor. These psychedelics can therefore be safely classified as *mixed dopamine and serotonin agonists* (an *entantogen*).

Mescaline

Peyote (*Lophophora williamsii*) is a common plant in the southwestern United States and in Mexico. It is a spineless cactus that has a small crown, or "button," and a long root. When the plant is used for psychedelic purposes, the crown is cut from the cactus and dried into a hard brown disk. This disk, which is frequently referred to as a "mescal button," is later softened in the mouth and swallowed. The psychedelic chemical in the button is mescaline.

Historical Background.   The use of peyote extends back perhaps 5000 years or more in North America; the cactus was used in the religious rites of the Aztecs and other Mexican and North American Indians (El-Seedi et al., 2005). Currently, peyote is legally available for use in the religious practice of the Native American Church of North America, whose members regard peyote as sacramental. The use of peyote for religious purposes is not considered to be abuse, and peyote is seldom abused by members of the Native American Church. Today, the federal government and 23 states permit its sacramental use.

Pharmacological Effects.   Early research on the peyote cactus led in 1896 to the identification of mescaline as its pharmacologically active ingredient. After the chemical structure of mescaline was elucidated in 1918, the compound was produced synthetically. Because of its structural resemblance to norepinephrine, a wide variety of synthetic mescaline derivatives have now been synthesized, and all have methoxy ($-OCH_3$) groups or similar additions on their benzene rings (see Figure 18.2). Methoxylation of the benzene ring apparently adds psychedelic properties to the drug, presumably due to increased affinity and full agonist activity at the 5-HT_{2A} receptor subtype.

When taken orally, mescaline is rapidly and completely absorbed, and significant concentrations are usually achieved in the brain within 1 to 2 hours. Between 3.5 and 4 hours after drug intake, mescaline produces an acute psychotomimetic state, with prominent effects on the visual system. The effects of a single dose of mescaline persist for approximately 10 hours. The drug does not appear to be metabolized before it is excreted. In functional brain imaging using SPECT, mescaline produced in healthy volunteers a "hyperfrontal" pattern with an emphasis on the right hemisphere, which was correlated with mescaline-induced psychotomimetic psychopathology. Current literature indicates that in Native American populations, illicit peyote use for intoxication is uncommon (Fickenscher et al., 2006) and not associated with severe residual psychological or cognitive deficits (Halpern et al., 2005).

Interest in mescaline focuses on the fact that it produces unusual psychic effects and visual hallucinations. The usual oral dose (5 milligrams per kilogram) in the average normal subject causes anxiety, sympathomimetic effects, hyperreflexia of the limbs, tremors, and visual hallucinations that consist of brightly colored lights, geometric designs, animals, and occasionally people; color and space perception is often concomitantly impaired, but otherwise the sensorium is normal and insight is retained. The psychotic effects are mainly concerned with the dissolution of ego boundaries, visual hallucinations, and dimensions of boundlessness, often mixed with anxious passivity experiences.

Synthetic Amphetamine Derivatives

DOM, MDA, DMA, MDE, TMA, AMT, 5-MeO-DIPT, and MDMA are structurally related to mescaline and methamphetamine (see Figure 18.2) and, as might be expected, produce similar effects. They have moderate behavioral stimulant effects at low doses, but as with LSD, psychedelic effects dominate as doses increase. These derivatives are considerably more potent and more toxic than mescaline.

DOM, MDA, MDE, and TMA. DOM (dimethoxymethamphetamine) has effects that are similar to those of mescaline; doses of 1 to 6 milligrams produce euphoria, which is followed by a 6- to 8-hour period of hallucinations. DOM is 100 times more potent than mescaline but much less potent than LSD. The use of DOM is associated with a high incidence of overdose (because it is potent and street doses are poorly controlled). Acute toxic reactions are common; they consist of tremors that may eventually lead to convulsive movements, prostration, and even death. Because toxic reactions are common, the use of DOM is not widespread.

MDA (methylenedioxyamphetamine), *DMA* (dimethoxymethylamphetamine), *MDE* (methylenedioxyethylamphetamine, or Eve), *TMA* (trimethoxyamphetamine), and other structural variations of amphetamine are encountered as "designer psychedelics." MDA is also a metabolite of MDMA and much of MDMA's effect may be due to the presence of MDA. In general, the pharmacological effects of these drugs resemble those of mescaline and LSD; they reflect the mix of catecholamine and serotonin interactions. Side effects and toxicities (including fatalities) are similar to those of MDMA. MDA is sometimes represented as MDMA; when this occurs, MDA is more lethal in lower doses and its effects are longer lasting than those of MDMA.

AMT and 5-MeO-DIPT. In April 2003, the Drug Enforcement Administration (DEA) designated alpha-methyltryptamine (AMT) and 5-methoxydiisopropyltryptamine (5-MeO-DIPT, or Foxy) as Schedule I substances under the Controlled Substances Act. This classification for these new "designer" psychedelics implies high abuse potential with no therapeutic usefulness. Administered orally, both drugs cause hallucinations, mood elevation, nervousness, insomnia, and pupilary dilation. AMT is of slow onset (3 to 4 hours) after oral administration and prolonged duration (12 to 24 hours). It is also a potent reuptake inhibitor of norepinephrine, dopamine, and serotonin (Nagai et al., 2007). Foxy is of more rapid onset (20 to 30 minutes) and shorter duration (3 to 6 hours). These new drugs are popular at dance raves.

MDMA. MDMA (methylenedioxymethamphetamine, also called ecstasy, XTC, X, E, and Adam) resembles MDA in structure but may be less hallucinogenic, inducing a less extreme sense of disembodiment and visual distortion. MDMA is a potent and selective serotonin neurotoxin both in animals and in humans. The dysfunction is related to dose and duration of use. Reneman and coworkers (2001) verified the neurotoxicity of MDMA on serotonin neurons, adding that women might be more susceptible than men and that although the effects on serotonin neurons might be reversible with time, detrimental effects on memory function might be long-lasting (a year or more). Thomasius and coworkers (2005) reported that cognitive deficits can persist for at least 5 months and may reflect MDMA-induced serotonergic neurotoxicity.

Kalant (2001) summarized persistent MDMA-induced psychiatric problems:

- Impairments in memory, both verbal and visual
- Impairments in decision making
- Greater impulsivity and lack of self-control
- Panic attacks following withdrawal
- Recurrent paranoia, depersonalization, and flashbacks
- Depression, sometimes resistant to treatment with other than SSRI-type antidepressants

Therefore, repeated use of ecstasy is associated with sleep, mood, and anxiety disturbances, elevated impulsiveness, memory deficits, and attention problems, which may persist for up to two years after cessation. Kuypers and Ramaekers (2005), however, while documenting the memory deficits during MDMA intoxication, failed to document residual memory impairments following drug intoxication. Schilt and coworkers (2007) performed a prospective study on 118 ecstasy-naive volunteers, of whom 58 started using ecstasy and 60 remained ecstasy-naive. They found that even a first low cumulative dose of ecstasy (1.5 tablets) was associated with significant declines in verbal memory. Although theirs was a short-term study, they stated that long-term negative consequences could not be excluded.

Sprague and coworkers in 1998 developed a hypothesis stating that MDMA induces a sequence of events that results in serotonergic neurotoxicity:

1. MDMA induces an acute release of serotonin and dopamine.
2. This release is followed by depletion of intraneuronal serotonin stores.
3. Released serotonin activates postsynaptic serotonin-2 receptors located on GABA intraneurons, resulting in decreased GABAergic neurotransmission and increased dopamine release and synthesis.
4. The excessive amounts of dopamine are transported into depleted serotonin nerve terminals.
5. The dopamine is broken down by the enzyme monoamine oxidase located in the serotonin terminals.
6. This breakdown results in free-radical formation and selective degeneration of serotonin axons, nerve terminals, and reuptake transporter proteins.

Although this hypothesis has not been verified, PET scan studies of human users suggest memory impairment, reduced serotonin transporter binding, and ultimately the destruction of presynaptic serotonin transporter.

Despite generally positive emotional effects of single uses at raves, "somatic" effects can be significant. Two examples are dramatic increases in blood pressure and body temperature, increases that are generally well tolerated by young users but undesirable in people with cardiovascular disease. Other somatic effects include jaw clenching, suppressed appetite, restlessness, insomnia, impaired gait, and restless legs. Adverse sequelae after 24 hours include lack of energy and appetite, fatigue, restlessness, difficulty concentrating, and brooding.

TABLE 18.2 Patterns of drug use of 329 ecstasy users

Drug class	Ever used (%)	Used in last 6 months (%)	No. days used in last 6 months (median)[a]
Ecstasy	100	100	10
Alcohol	99.1	93.6	24
Cannabis	98.8	92.1	48
Amphetamine	94.2	81.8	10
LSD	93.3	68.1	4
Tobacco	85.4	74.8	180
Amyl nitrate	75.4	46.5	3
Cocaine	61.4	40.7	2
Nitrous oxide	61.1	35.3	4
Benzodiazepines	56.8	43.2	5.5
MDA	50.5	31.3	3
Other opiates	32.0	20.7	3
Heroin	30.1	17.3	12
Antidepressants	23.1	13.4	6
Ketamine	18.2	10.0	4
Ethyl chloride	10.0	5.8	2
Methadone	7.3	2.7	20
Anabolic steroids	4.3	1.5	20
GHB	2.7	1.8	1.5
Other drugs[b]	—	5.2	2

[a]Among those who had used.
[b]Other drugs included hallucinogenic mushrooms, DMT, and PCP.
From L. Topp et al., "Ecstasy Use in Australia: Patterns of Use and Associated Harm," *Drug and Alcohol Dependence* 55 (1999), p. 108.

Concern about MDMA is increasing as use of this "club drug"[1] increases around the world, especially at dance clubs and raves. As shown in Table 18.2. MDMA use is usually part of a polydrug pattern of use. Users of MDMA can exhibit physical, psychological, financial, relationship, and occupational problems occurred as a result of ecstasy use. Twenty percent of users have received treatment for an ecstasy-related problem, and 15 percent required formal treatment.

[1]Ecstasy, gamma hydroxybutyrate (GHB, Chapter 5), ketamine/phencyclidine (discussed later in this chapter), and methamphetamine (Chapter 13) are four examples of club drugs that are increasing in popularity with young people. Ecstasy is a psychostimulant/hallucinogen (an entactogen), GHB is a sedative/amnestic, ketamine and phencyclidine are dissociative anesthetics, and methamphetamine is a psychostimulant.

MDMA is potentially a very dangerous drug for human use: abuse of MDMA may lead to severe toxicities, including fatalities. When it is used during periods of intense activity, such as skiing and dancing at raves, symptoms include hyperthermia, tachycardia, disorientation, dilated pupils, convulsions, rigidity, breakdown of skeletal muscle, kidney failure, cardiac arrhythmias, and death (Hall and Henry, 2006). The pathology for these serious effects is unclear, although it may represent induction of a fatal syndrome called "malignant hyperthermia." MDMA may precipitate malignant hyperthermia in susceptible people and this response could be blocked by a drug called dantrolene (Duffy and Ferguson, 2007). It is hoped that, should an MDMA-intoxicated, hyperthermic patient be taken to an emergency room in time, dantrolene would be administered and a life saved. Despite these consequences, the intense euphoric high promotes continued use.

Within recent years, a new series of MDMA-related drugs have entered the illicit market. For example, 2,5-dimethoxy-4-propylthiophenethylamine (Schifano et al., 2005) is known as Blue Mystic, 2C-T-7, T7, Tripstay, and Tweety-Bird Mescaline; 4-bromo-2,5-dimethoxyphenethylamine is known as 2C-B, Nexus, 2s, Toonies, Bromo, Spectrum, and Venus. These drugs produce hallucinogenic actions with the side effects of nausea, anxiety, panic attacks, and paranoid ideation (Schifano et al., 2005; Fantegrossi et al., 2005; Theobald and Maurer, 2007). Toxicities specific to these derivatives have not yet been summarized although they are certainly cause for concern.

Myristin and Elemicin

Nutmeg and mace are common household spices sometimes abused for their hallucinogenic properties. Myristin and elemicin, the pharmacologically active ingredients in nutmeg and mace, are responsible for the psychedelic action. Ingestion of large amounts (1 to 2 teaspoons—5 to 15 grams—usually brewed in tea) may, after a delay of 2 to 5 hours, induce feelings of unreality, confusion, disorientation, impending doom, depersonalization, unreality, and euphoria, and visual hallucinations and acute psychotic reactions. Considering the close structural resemblance of myristin and elemicin to mescaline (see Figure 18.2), these psychedelic actions are not unexpected. Ingestion of nutmeg, however, produces many unpleasant side effects, including vomiting, nausea, and tremors. After nutmeg or mace has been taken to produce its psychedelic action, the side effects usually dissuade users from trying these agents a second time. Extremely unpleasant reactions may occur, but deaths are infrequent.

Serotoninlike Psychedelics

The serotoninlike psychedelic drugs include *lysergic acid diethylamide* (LSD), *psilocybin* and *psilocin*, *dimethyltryptamine* (DMT), and *bufotenine* (Figure 18.3). Because of their structural resemblance to each

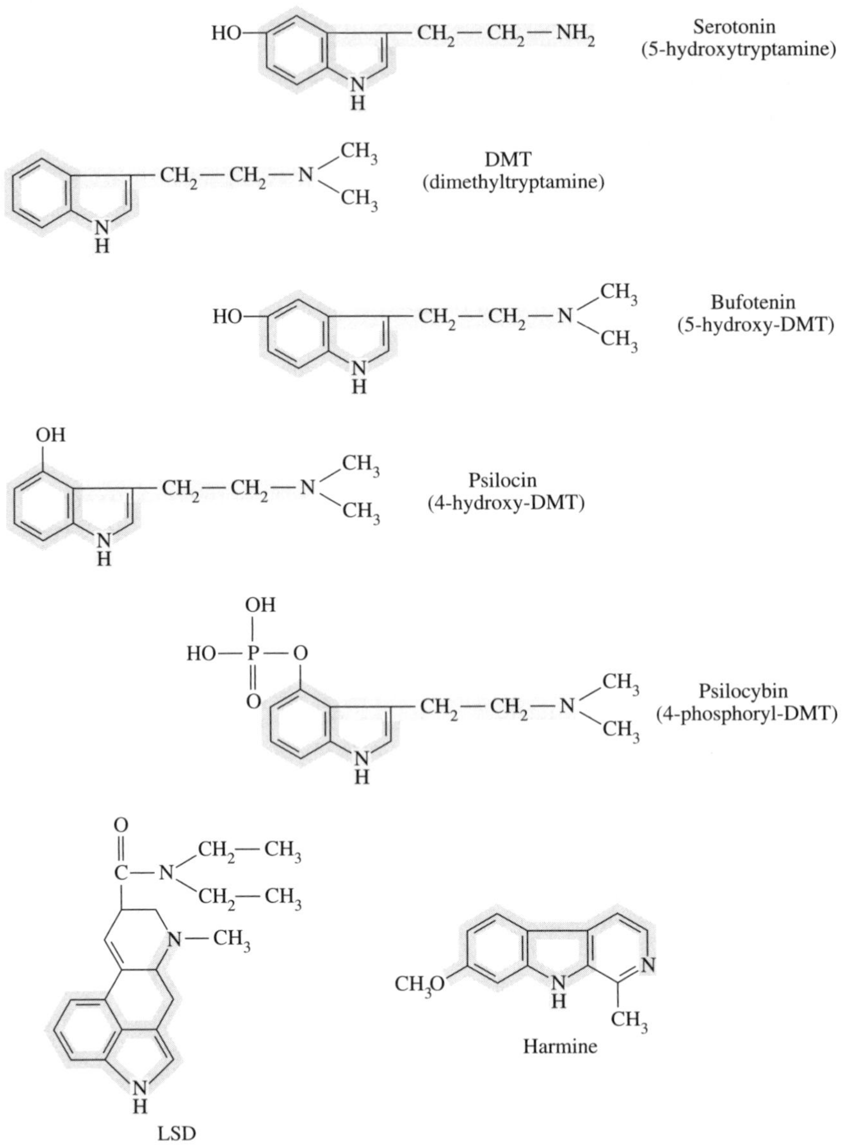

FIGURE 18.3 Structural formulas of serotonin (a chemical transmitter) and six serotoninlike psychedelic drugs. These six drugs are structurally related to serotonin (as indicated by the shading) and are thought to exert their psychedelic actions through alterations of serotonin synapses in the brain. Although LSD is structurally much more complex than serotonin, the basic similarity of the two molecules is apparent.

other and to serotonin, it has been presumed that these agents somehow exert their effects through interactions at serotonin synapses, especially the 5-HT_2 receptor, and this effect seems to be the case.

Almaula and coworkers (1996) first mapped the binding site for LSD on the 5-HT_{2A} receptor and correlated the binding with receptor activation. Ebersole and coworkers (2003) confirmed their results. LSD activation of the medial prefrontal cortex and anterior cingulated cortex is mediated by 5-HT_{2A} receptors, areas involved in the production of hallucinations. In addition to LSD, both DMT and bufotenine act as partial agonists at 5-HT_{2A} receptors. With all this focus of agonist action on serotonin receptors, a major question remains unanswered: Why does serotonin itself not induce psychotomimetic effects? In particular, psychotomimetic effects are seldom seen after administration of SSRI-type antidepressants; although the serotonin syndrome and the behavioral activations that are sometimes seen with SSRI therapy may be a reflection of such action.

Regardless of receptor mechanisms, serotonin psychedelics do produce a characteristic psychedelic syndrome, with disturbances in thinking, illusions, elementary and complex visual hallucinations, and impaired ego functioning. One speculation about the process by which hallucinogens manifest their impressive alterations of mood, perception, and thought is that the pontine (dorsal) raphe, a major center of serotonin activity, serves as a filtering station for incoming sensory stimuli. It screens the flood of sensations and perceptions, eliminating those that are unimportant, irrelevant, or commonplace. A drug like LSD may disrupt the sorting process, allowing a surge of sensory data and an overload of brain circuits. Dehabituation, in which the familiar becomes novel, is noted under LSD. Dehabituation may be caused by indirectly lowering the sensory gates by inhibition of the raphe activity.

Lysergic Acid Diethylamide

During the mid-1960s and early 1970s, lysergic acid diethylamide (LSD) became one of the most remarkable and controversial drugs known. In doses that are so small that they might even be considered infinitesimal, LSD induces remarkable psychological change in a person, enhancing self-awareness and altering internal reality, while causing relatively few alterations in the general physiology of the body.

Historical Background. LSD was first synthesized in 1938 by Albert Hofmann, a Swiss chemist, as part of an organized research program to investigate possible therapeutic uses of compounds obtained from ergot, a natural product derived from a fungus (*Claviceps purpurea*). Early pharmacological studies of LSD in animals failed to reveal anything unusual; the psychedelic action was neither sought nor expected. Thus, LSD remained unnoticed until 1943, when Hofmann had an unusual experience:

> In the afternoon of 16 April, 1943, . . . I was seized by a peculiar sensation of vertigo and restlessness. Objects, as well as the shape of my associates in the laboratory, appeared to undergo optical changes. I was unable to concentrate on my work. In a dreamlike state I left for home, where an irresistible urge to lie down overcame me. I drew the curtains and immediately fell into a peculiar state similar to drunkenness, characterized by an exaggerated imagination. With my eyes closed, fantastic pictures of extraordinary plasticity and intensive color seemed to surge toward me. After two hours, this state gradually wore off. (Hofmann, 1994, p. 80)

Hofmann correctly hypothesized that his experience resulted from the accidental ingestion of LSD. To further characterize the experience, Hofmann self-administered what seemed to be a minuscule oral dose (only 0.25 milligram). We now know, however, that this dose is about ten times the dose required to induce psychedelic effects in most people. As a result of this miscalculation, his response was quite spectacular:

> After 40 minutes, I noted the following symptoms in my laboratory journal: slight giddiness, restlessness, difficulty in concentration, visual disturbances, laughing. . . . Later, I lost all count of time. I noticed with dismay that my environment was undergoing progressive changes. My visual field wavered and everything appeared deformed as in a faulty mirror. Space and time became more and more disorganized and I was overcome by a fear that I was going out of my mind. The worst part of it [was] that I was clearly aware of my condition. My power of observation was unimpaired. . . . Occasionally, I felt as if I were out of my body. I thought I had died. My ego seemed suspended somewhere in space, from where I saw my dead body lying on the sofa. . . . It was particularly striking how acoustic perceptions, such as the noise of water gushing from a tap or the spoken word, were transformed into optical illusions. I then fell asleep and awakened the next morning somewhat tired but otherwise feeling perfectly well. (p. 80)

The first North American study of LSD in humans was conducted in 1949, and during the 1950s large quantities of LSD were distributed to scientists for research purposes. A significant impetus for researching was the notion that the effects of LSD might constitute a model for psychosis, which would provide some insight into the biochemical and physiological processes of mental illness and its treatment (Dyck, 2005). Some therapists tried LSD as an adjunct to psychotherapy to help patients verbalize their problems and gain some insight into the underlying causes, but it did not prove to be an effective treatment.

Pharmacokinetics. LSD is usually taken orally, and it is rapidly absorbed by that route. Usual doses range from about 25 micrograms to more than 300 micrograms. Because the amounts are so small, LSD is often added to other substances, such as squares of paper, the backs of stamps, or sugar cubes, which can be handled more easily. LSD is absorbed within about 60 minutes, reaching peak blood levels in about 3 hours. It is distributed rapidly and efficiently throughout the body; it diffuses easily into the brain and readily crosses the placenta. The largest amounts of LSD in the body are found in the liver, where the drug is metabolized before it is excreted to 2-oxo-3-hydroxy-LSD. The usual duration of action is 6 to 8 hours.

Because of its extreme potency, only minuscule amounts of LSD can be detected in urine, although the metabolite is present in concentrations 16 to 43 times greater than that of LSD. Thus, conventional urine-screening tests are inadequate to detect LSD. When the use of LSD is suspected, urine is collected (up to 30 hours after ingestion) and an ultrasensitive radioimmunoassay is performed to verify the presence of the drug.

Physiological Effects. Although the LSD experience is characterized by its psychological effects, subtle physiological changes also occur. A person who takes LSD may experience a slight increase in body temperature, dilation of the pupils, slightly increased heart rate and blood pressure, increased levels of glucose in the blood, and dizziness, drowsiness, nausea, and other effects that, although noticeable, seldom interfere with the psychedelic experience.

LSD is known to possess a low level of toxicity; the effective dose is about 50 micrograms while the lethal dose is about 14,000 micrograms. These figures provide a therapeutic ratio of 280, making the drug a remarkably nonlethal compound. This calculation does not include any fatal accidents or suicides that occur when a person is intoxicated by LSD. In fact, most deaths attributed to LSD result from accidents, homicides, or suicide. The use of LSD during pregnancy is certainly unwise, although a distinct fetal LSD syndrome has not been described.

Psychological Effects. The psychological effects of LSD are intense. At doses of 25 to 50 micrograms, pupillary dilation and a glassy-eyed appearance may be noticed. These effects are accompanied by alterations in perception, thinking, emotion, arousal, and self-image. Time is slowed or distorted, sensory input intensified. Cognitive alterations include enhanced power to visualize previously seen or imagined objects and decreased vigilance and logical thought. Visual alterations are the most characteristic phenomenon; they typically include colored lights, distorted images, and vivid and fascinating images and shapes. Colors can be heard and sounds may be seen. The loss of boundaries and the fear of fragmentation create a need for a structuring or supporting environment and experienced companions. During the "trip," thoughts and memories can emerge under self-guidance, sometimes to the user's distress. Mood may be labile, shifting from depression to gaiety, from elation to fear. Tension and anxiety may mount and reach panic proportions. The LSD-induced psychedelic experience typically occurs in three phases:

1. The *somatic phase* occurs after absorption of the drug and consists of CNS stimulation and autonomic changes that are predominantly sympathomimetic in nature.

2. The *sensory* (or perceptual) *phase* is characterized by sensory distortions and pseudohallucinations, which are the effects desired by the drug user.

3. The *psychic phase* signals a maximum drug effect, with changes in mood, disruption of thought processes, altered perception of time, depersonalization, true hallucinations, and psychotic episodes. Experiencing this phase is considered a "bad trip."

Tolerance and Dependence.   Tolerance of both the psychological and physiological alterations induced by LSD readily and rapidly develops, and cross-tolerance occurs between LSD and other psychedelics. Tolerance is lost within several days after the user stops taking the drug.

Physical dependence on LSD does not develop, even when the drug is used repeatedly for a prolonged period of time. In fact, most heavy users of the drug say that they ceased using LSD because they tired of it, had no further need for it, or had enough. Even when the drug is discontinued because of concern about bad trips or about physical or mental harm, few withdrawal signs are exhibited. Laboratory animals do not self-administer LSD.

Adverse Reactions and Toxicity.   The adverse reactions attributed to LSD generally fall into five categories:

- Chronic or intermittent psychotic states
- Persistent or recurrent major affective disorder (for example, depression)
- Exacerbation of preexisting psychiatric illness
- Disruption of personality or chronic brain syndrome, known as "burnout"

- Posthallucinogenic perceptual disorder (flashbacks characterized by the periodic hallucinogenic imagery months or even years after the immediate effect of LSD has worn off)

Unpleasant experiences with LSD are relatively frequent and may involve an uncontrollable drift into confusion, dissociative reactions, acute panic reactions, a reliving of earlier traumatic experiences, or an acute psychotic hospitalization. Prolonged nonpsychotic reactions have included dissociative reactions, time and space distortion, body image changes, and a residue of fear or depression stemming from morbid or terrifying experiences under the drug. With the failure of usual defense mechanisms, the onslaught of repressed material overwhelms the integrative capacity of the ego, and a psychotic reaction results.

It appears that LSD-induced disruption of long-established patterns of adapting may be a lasting or semipermanent effect of the drug. In other words, our neocortex modulates awareness of our surroundings and filters a high proportion of incoming information before it can be processed, allowing through only the amount of information that is necessary for survival. LSD works to open this filter, so an increased amount of somatosensory data is processed with a corresponding increase in what is deemed important. Thus, LSD reduces a person's normal ability to control emotional reactions, and drug-induced alterations in perception can become so intense that they overwhelm the ability to cope.

One unique characteristic of LSD and LSD-like substances is the recurrence of some of the symptoms that appeared during the intoxication after the immediate effect of the hallucinogen has worn off. These symptoms are mainly visual and the terms *flashback* and *hallucinogen persisting perception disorder* (HPPD) are used fairly interchangeably. However, a flashback is usually a short-term, nondistressing, spontaneous, recurrent, reversible, and benign condition accompanied by a pleasant affect. In contrast, HPPD is a generally long-term, distressing, spontaneous, recurrent, pervasive, either slowly reversible or irreversible, nonbenign condition accompanied by an unpleasant dysphoric affect.

Treatment of flashbacks and HPPD has been symptomatic. Case reports note the success of benzodiazepines as well as other drugs, but there is no consensus on appropriate therapy and no specific treatment. One of the new atypical antipsychotic drugs with serotonin 2 blocking activity (Chapter 9) may be a reasonable choice to treat acute LSD toxicity.

Other Serotoninlike Hallucinogens

DMT. DMT (dimethyltryptamine) is a short-acting, naturally occurring psychedelic compound that can be synthesized easily and that structurally is related to serotonin. DMT produces LSD-like effects in the user, and like LSD it is a partial agonist at serotonin 5-HT$_2$ receptors. Widely used throughout much of the world, DMT is an active ingredient of various types of South American plants, such as *Virola calophylla* and *Mimosa hostilis*. Used by itself, DMT is snorted or smoked, often in a marijuana cigarette.

Ayahuasca (also called *hoasca*) is a psychoactive beverage that, as a tea, has been drunk for centuries in religious, spiritual, and medicinal contexts by Amazon Indians in the rain forest areas of South America. Two principal ingredients of ayahuasca are harmine (a substance that is a potent MAO inhibitor) and DMT. Administered orally to 15 healthy volunteers, DMT produced prominent thought disorders and inappropriate affective reactions (for example, paranoia) rather than the negative schizophrenic reactions characteristic of ketamine (Gouzoulis-Mayfrank et al., 2005). Effects had an onset of about 30 to 60 minutes, peaked at 1 to 2 hours, and persisted for about 3 to 4 hours. In most cases, effects (changes in perceptual, affective, cognitive, and somatic spheres) are well tolerated, but disorientation, paranoia, and anxiety can be displayed. In religious ceremonial use, such reactions are unusual (Gable, 2007).

In 1994, Strassman and coworkers conducted controlled investigations of DMT in "highly motivated," experienced hallucinogen users. Administered intravenously (0.04 to 0.4 milligram per kilogram of body weight), onset of action occurred within 2 minutes and was negligible at 30 minutes. DMT elevated blood pressure, heart rate, and temperature, dilated pupils, and increased body endorphin and hormone levels. The psychedelic threshold dose was 0.2 milligram per kilogram of body weight; lower doses were primarily "affective and somaesthetic." Hallucinogenic effects included a rapidly moving, brightly colored visual display of images. Auditory effects were less common. "Loss of control," associated with a brief but overwhelming "rush," led to a dissociated state, where euphoria alternated or coexisted with anxiety. These effects completely replaced subjects' previously ongoing mental experience and were more vivid and compelling than dreams or waking awareness.

Thus, DMT produces intense visual hallucinations, intoxication, and often a loss of awareness of the user's surroundings. When DMT is injected, smoked, or taken as a snuff, after the 30-minute period of effect the user returns to normal feelings and perceptions—thus the nicknames "lunch-hour drug," "businessman's lunch," and "businessman's LSD." Administered with an MAO inhibitor (as the ayahuasca tea), it is absorbed orally and has a longer duration of action.

Bufotenine. Bufotenine (5-hydroxy DMT, or dimethylserotonin), like LSD and DMT, is a potent serotonin agonist hallucinogen with an affinity for several types of serotonin receptors. The name bufotenine comes from the name for a toad of the genus *Bufo*, whose skin and glandular secretions supposedly produce hallucinogenic effects when ingested. Toad secretions have been used since ancient times for a variety of mythological and medicinal purposes involving magical, shamanic, or occult uses for casting spells and for divination.

After subcutaneous injection to rats, the half-life of bufotenine is about 2 hours, with MAO responsible for metabolism. Mechanistically, bufotenine is an agonist of serotonin 5-HT$_2$ receptors, as are other serotonin psychedelics.

Bufotenine is not found in the bodies of normal people. However, it can be produced in an alternate and unusual pathway for the metabolic breakdown of serotonin. Indeed, some have attempted to correlate the presence of bufotenine in urine with various psychiatric disorders, although this theory is not generally accepted.

Psilocybin. Psilocybin (4-phosphoryl-DMT) and psilocin (4-hydroxy-DMT) are two psychedelic agents that are found in many species of mushrooms that belong to the genera *Psilocybe, Panaeolus, Copelandia,* and *Conocybe.* As Figure 18.3 (page 618) shows, the only difference between psilocybin and psilocin is that psilocybin contains a molecule of phosphoric acid. After the mushroom has been ingested, phosphoric acid is enzymatically removed from psilocybin, thus producing psilocin, the active psychedelic agent. Psilocybin is a potent hallucinogen that exerts such action through an agonist effect at serotonin 5-HT$_{2A}$ and 5-HT$_{1A}$ receptors, similar to the effects of other serotonin psychedelics. Psilocybin administration (about 0.25 milligram per kilogram of body weight, orally) produces changes in mood, disturbances in thinking, illusions, complex visual hallucinations, and impaired ego functioning, similar to the effects produced by LSD.

Psilocybin-containing mushrooms grow throughout much of the world, including the northwestern United States. Psilocin and psilocybin are approximately 1/200 as potent as LSD, they peak in about 2 hours, and their effects last about 6 to 10 hours. Unlike DMT, psilocin and psilocybin are absorbed effectively when taken orally; the mushrooms are eaten raw to induce psychedelic effects.

There is great variation in the concentration of psilocybin and psilocin among the different species of mushrooms, as well as significant differences among mushrooms of the same species. For example, the usual oral dose of *Psilocybe semilanceata* (liberty caps) may consist of 10 to 40 mushrooms, while the dose for *Psilocybe cyanescens* may be only 2 to 5 mushrooms. Also, some extremely toxic species of mushrooms are not psychoactive, but they bear a superficial resemblance to the mushrooms that contain psilocybin and psilocin. Because the effects of psilocybin so closely resemble those produced by LSD, the "psilocybin" sold illicitly may be LSD, and ordinary mushrooms laced with LSD may be sold as "magic mushrooms."

Although the psychedelic effects of *Psilocybe mexicana* are part of Indian folklore, *Psilocybe* intoxication was not described until 1955, when Gordon Wasson, a New York banker, traveled through Mexico. He mingled with native tribes and was allowed to participate in a *Psilocybe* ceremony, in which he consumed the magic mushroom. Wasson said:

> It permits you to travel backward and forward in time, to enter other planes of existence, even to know God. . . . Your body lies in the darkness, heavy as lead, but your spirit seems to soar and leave the hut, and with the speed of thought to travel where it listeth, in time and space, accompanied by the shaman's singing. . . . At least you know what the ineffable is, and what ecstasy means. Ecstasy! The mind harks back to the origin of that word. For the Greeks, *ekstasis* meant the flight of the soul from the body. Can you find a better word to describe this state? (Crahan, 1969, p. 17).

Some view psilocybin intoxication as inducing a schizophrenialike psychosis, even capable of inducing a *hallucinogen persisting perceptual disorder* (Espiard et al., 2005). Others have proposed usefulness in studying the neurobiological basis of cognition and consciousness (Hasler et al., 2004) as well as time perception and timing performance (Wittmann et al., 2007). Moreno and coworkers (2006) proposed psilocybin as potentially useful in resistant obsessive-compulsive disorder.

Ololiuqui. Ololiuqui is a naturally occurring hallucinogen in morning glory seeds that is used by Central and South American Indians as an intoxicant and as a hallucinogen. The drug is used ritually for spiritual communication, as are extracts of most plants that contain psychedelic drugs. The use of ololiuqui seeds in Central and South America was first described by the sixteenth-century Spanish explorer Francisco Hernandez de Cordoba, who is said to have reported, "When the priests wanted to commune with their Gods, they ate ololiuqui seeds and a thousand visions and satanic hallucinations appeared to them."

The seeds were analyzed in Europe by Albert Hofmann, the discoverer of LSD, who identified several ingredients, one of which was lysergic acid amide (not lysergic acid diethylamide, LSD). The lysergic acid amide that Hofmann identified is approximately one-tenth as active as LSD as a psychoactive agent. However, considering the extreme potency of LSD, lysergic acid amide is still quite potent.

Side effects of ololiuqui include nausea, vomiting, headache, increased blood pressure, dilated pupils, and sleepiness. These side effects are usually quite intense and serve to limit the recreational use of ololiuqui. Ingestion of a hundred or more seeds produces sleepiness, distorted perception, hallucinations, and confusion. Flashbacks have been reported, but they are infrequent.

Harmine. Harmine is a psychedelic agent that is obtained from the seeds of *Peganum harmala*, a plant native to the Middle East, and from *Banisteriopsis caapi* of the South American tropics. Intoxication by harmine is usually accompanied by nausea and vomiting, sedation, and finally sleep. The psychic excitement users experience consists of visual distortions that are similar to those induced by LSD. Harmine probably acts through dopaminergic mechanisms as an MAO inhibitor (Chapter 7) (Iurlo et al., 2001). As discussed earlier, harmine is one of the ingredients in ayahuasca.

Glutaminergic NMDA Receptor Antagonists

Phencyclidine and Ketamine

Phencyclidine (PCP, angel dust) and ketamine (Figure 18.4) are referred to as psychedelic anesthetics because they were first developed as amnestic and analgesic drugs for use in anesthesia; later it was found that they also produced a psychedelic or dissociative state of being. These two drugs are structurally unrelated to the other psychedelic agents, and their psychedelic effects are unique: they do not involve actions on serotonin, acetylcholine, or dopamine neurons.

Phencyclidine was developed in 1956 and was briefly used as an anesthetic in humans before being abandoned because of a high incidence of psychiatric reactions, including agitation, excitement, delirium, disorientation, and hallucinatory phenomena (considered undesirable in the surgical patient!). The altered perception, disorganized thought, suspiciousness, confusion, and lack of cooperation that were exhibited resembled a schizophrenic state that consisted of both positive and negative symptoms. In fact both phencyclidine and ketamine can induce symptoms that are almost indistinguishable from those associated with schizophrenia (Murray, 2002). Phencyclidine is still used as a veterinary anesthetic, primarily as an immobilizing agent.

Ketamine (Ketalar) structurally resembles phencyclidine and was developed shortly after the prominent psychedelic properties of phencyclidine were identified. Introduced in 1960, ketamine induces a phencyclidinelike anesthetic state in low doses, with fewer bothersome

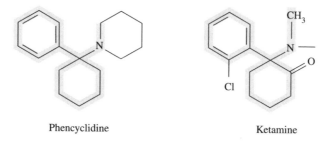

Phencyclidine   Ketamine

FIGURE 18.4 Structural formulas of the psychedelic anesthetic drugs phencyclidine and ketamine.

psychiatric side effects. The anesthetic state is characterized by amnesia and analgesia, combined with maintenance of blood pressure and respiration. Ketamine is occasionally used as anesthesia in patients who cannot tolerate the cardiovascular depressant effects of other anesthetics. Ketamine causes psychiatric reactions similar to but not as severe as those caused by PCP, including brief, reversible positive and negative schizophrenialike symptoms. Both PCP and ketamine can exacerbate psychosis in schizophrenia.

Abuse of phencyclidine and ketamine began in the mid-1960s (Morris et al., 2005; Wolff and Winstock, 2006). Today, abuse of phencyclidine and ketamine persists, with periodic resurgences in popularity. Phencyclidine is the more commonly abused of the two and has appeared in the form of powders, tablets, leaf mixtures, and "rock" crystals. It is commonly sold as crystal, angel dust, hog, PCP, THC, cannabinol, or mescaline. When phencyclidine is sold as crystal or angel dust (terms also used for methamphetamine), the drug is usually in concentrations that vary between 50 and 90 percent. When it is purchased under other names or in concoctions, the amount of phencyclidine falls to between 10 and 30 percent; the typical street dose is about 5 milligrams. Phencyclidine can be eaten, snorted, or injected, but it is most often smoked, sprinkled on tobacco, parsley, or marijuana. Frequently, phencyclidine is sold as a club drug, although its pharmacology is entirely distinct from other club drugs such as ecstasy or GHB. As a club drug PCP is an analgesic/anesthetic/amnestic/psychedelic.

Pharmacokinetics. PCP is well absorbed whether taken orally or smoked. When it is smoked, peak effects occur in about 15 minutes, when about 40 percent of the dose appears in the user's bloodstream. Oral absorption is slower; maximum blood levels are reached about 2 hours after the drug has been taken. The elimination half-life is about 18 hours but ranges from about 11 to about 51 hours. A positive urine assay for PCP is assumed to indicate that PCP was used within the previous week. Because false-positive test results are common, a positive assay requires secondary confirmation.

Mechanism of Action. Phencyclidine and ketamine both exert their psychotomimetic, analgesic, amnestic actions and schizophrenic actions primarily as a result of binding as noncompetitive antagonists of the N-methyl-D-aspartate (NMDA)/glutamate receptors. Several lines of evidence now implicate involvement of NMDA receptor dysfunction in the pathophysiology of schizophrenia (Chapter 9). Adler and coworkers (1999) conducted a neuropsychological comparison of normal volunteers to whom ketamine was administered, and patients with schizophrenia (Figure 18.5). As can be seen, the ketamine-induced thought disorder is not dissimilar to that seen in patients

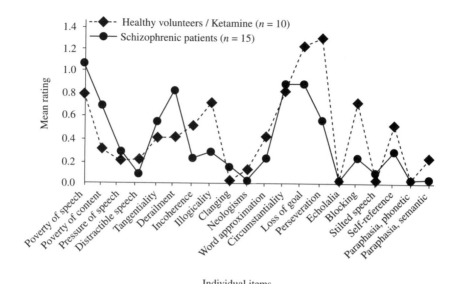

Individual items

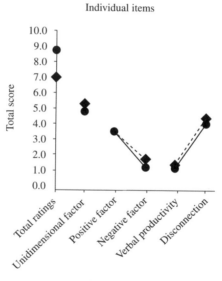

Total and factors

FIGURE 18.5 Comparison of total, factor, and individual item scores for the assessment of thought, language, and communication of 10 healthy volunteers with ketamine-induced thought disorder and 15 patients with schizophrenia (schizophrenic patients were ketamine-free). [From Adler et al. (1999), p. 1647.]

with schizophrenia, providing support for the involvement of NMDA receptor dysfunction in the disease.[2] Although acute doses of PCP and ketamine can induce a toxic psychosis, repeated doses induce a more persistent schizophrenic symptomatology, including psychosis, hallucinations, flattened affect, delusions, formal thought disorder, cognitive dysfunction, and social withdrawal.

Phencyclidine and ketamine inhibit NMDA receptors by two mechanisms: (1) blockade of the open channel by occupying a site within the channel in the receptor protein (as discussed earlier for phencyclidine) and (2) reduction in the frequency of NMDA channel opening by drug binding to a second attachment site on the outside of the receptor protein. As noted, PCP and ketamine are powerful analgesic drugs. The mechanism seems to be twofold: these two drugs (1) activate NMDA-glutamate receptors in the spinal cord and (2) activate descending analgesic pathways, pathways that appear to involve norepinephrine and dopamine. Ketamine and PCP have complex interactions with dopamine in the CNS, interactions that probably are involved in both the schizophrenic and the analgesic actions of these drugs (Balla et al., 2003).

Psychological Effects. Phencyclidine (and ketamine) dissociates individuals from themselves and their environment. It induces an unresponsive state with intense analgesia and amnesia, although the subject's eyes remain open (with a blank stare); the subject may even appear to be awake. When not used under controlled conditions, phencyclidine in low doses produces mild agitation, euphoria, disinhibition, or excitement in a person who appears to be grossly drunk and exhibits a blank stare. The subject may be rigid and unable to speak. In many cases, however, the subject is communicative but does not respond to pain.

PCP acutely induces a psychotic state in which subjects become withdrawn, autistic, negativistic, and unable to maintain a cognitive set; they manifest concrete, impoverished, idiosyncratic, and bizarre responses to questions. People under the influence of PCP exhibit profound alterations of higher emotional functions affecting judgment and cognition.

---

[2]The NMDA/PCP receptor complex has a molecular weight of 203,000 and is composed of four membrane-spanning polypeptides (molecular weights of 67,000, 57,000, 46,000, and 33,000), which cluster together to form an ion channel that resembles the benzodiazepine-GABA receptor. In the NMDA/PCP receptor complex, however, the drug-binding site (the PCP receptor) is located within the lumen of the ion channel. Attachment of PCP to the receptor occludes the channel and inhibits calcium ion influx when the transmitter (glutamate) attaches to its receptor on the outer surface.

High doses of phencyclidine induce a state of coma or stupor. However, abusers tend to titrate their dose to maximize the intoxicant effect while attempting to avoid unconsciousness. Blood pressure usually becomes elevated, but respiration does not become depressed. The patient may recover from this state within 2 to 4 hours, although a state of confusion and cognitive poverty may last for 8 to 72 hours. The disruption of sensory input by PCP causes unpredictable exaggerated, distorted, or violent reactions to environmental stimuli. These reactions are augmented by PCP-induced analgesia and amnesia. Massive oral overdoses, involving up to 1 gram of street-purchased phencyclidine, result in prolonged periods of stupor or coma. This state may last for several days and may be marked by intense seizure activity, increased blood pressure, and a depression of respiration that is potentially lethal. Following this stupor, a prolonged recovery phase, marked by confusion and delusions, may last as long as 2 weeks. In some people, this state of confusion may be followed by a psychosis that lasts from several weeks to a few months.

Side Effects and Toxicity. The course of recovery from a PCP-induced psychotic state is variable for reasons that are poorly understood. The intoxicated state may lead to severe anxiety, aggression, panic, paranoia, and rage. A user can also display violent reactions to sensory input, leading to such problems as falls, drowning, burns, driving accidents, and aggressive behavior. Self-inflicted injuries and injuries sustained while physical restraints are applied are frequent, and the potent analgesic action contributes to the absence of response to pain. Respiratory depression, generalized seizure activity, and pulmonary edema have all been reported.

PCP is the only psychedelic drug self-administered by monkeys as well as by humans. By inference, phencyclidine seems to stimulate brain reward areas and therefore places the user at risk of compulsive abuse despite negative health consequences.

Treatment of Intoxication. Therapy for PCP intoxication is aimed at reducing the systemic level of the drug, keeping the patient calm and sedated, and preventing any of several severe adverse medical effects. It involves the following:

- Minimization of sensory inputs by placing the intoxicated person in a quiet environment
- Oral administration of activated charcoal, which can bind any PCP present in the stomach and intestine and prevent its reabsorption
- Precautionary physical restraint to prevent self-injury
- Sedation with either a benzodiazepine (such as lorazepam) for agitation or an atypical antipsychotic agent for psychosis.

Hyperthermia, hypertension, convulsions, renal failure, and other medical consequences should be treated as necessary by medical experts. PCP-induced psychotic states may be long-lasting, especially in people with a history of schizophrenia.

Dextromethorphan

Dextromethorphan (DXM) is both an analgesic drug and a drug of abuse. As an analgesic, it potentiates the pain-relieving action of morphine and other opioids (Chapter 16). As a drug of abuse, it is a common ingredient in more than 140 varieties of over-the-counter cough and cold medicines; high doses produce hallucinations. Because of this effect and ready availability, abuse has rapidly increased, especially in adolescents (Schwartz, 2005; Bryner et al., 2006). The hallucinations follow from high-dose DXM-induced NMDA receptor blockade, an action similar to that produced by PCP and ketamine. DXM and its metabolite dextrorphan (DXO) can substitute for PCP and exert PCP-like effects. Indeed, the active metabolite DXO may be responsible for many of the high-dose effects of DXM (Miller, 2005). In cough and cold preparations, such as various Coricidin products, Robitussin DM, Vicks 44, Tylenol DM (and many others), ingestion of DXM is referred to as "roboing," "dexing," "robo-tripping," or "robo-copping." Symptoms associated with intoxication include tachycardia, hypertension, sleepiness, agitation, disorientation, slurred speech, hallucinations, altered mental status, and tremor. Acute psychotic reactions have occasionally been reported.

Salvinorin A

Salvia divinorum (magic mint, diviner's sage), a member if the mint family of perennial herbs, is a psychoactive plant that has been used for curing and for divination in traditional spiritual practices by the Mazatec peoples of Oaxaca, Mexico, for many centuries. More recently, young people in Mexico have smoked the dried leaves of the plant as a marijuana substitute. *Salvia* also grows in California and other parts of the United States as well as in other countries. *Salvia* has been used as a short-acting, legal hallucinogen for several years because neither the "magic mint" nor its active compound are banned (yet!). *Salvia* is comparable in hallucinogenic efficacy to other hallucinogens such as psilocybin-containing mushrooms. In use, the fresh leaves of the plant are moistened and chewed as a quid and kept in the mouth. Alternatively, the dried leaves are smoked in the manner of marijuana or cocaine free base. The fresh leaves may also be eaten raw or prepared as an aqueous solution. The mint is essentially inactive if taken orally; the compound is effective when smoked in doses of 200 to 500 micrograms of active drug. Thus, *Salvia* contains the most potent naturally occurring hallucinogen thus far isolated (Vortherms and Roth, 2006; Vortherms et al., 2007).

The main active ingredient of *Salvia divinorum* is a novel compound called *salvinorin A*. The molecular structure and mechanism of action of salvinorin A are distinct from all other naturally occurring hallucinogens (such as DMT, psilocybin, and mescaline) as well as synthetic hallucinogens such as LSD and ketamine (Figure 18.6). Salvinorin A is reported to induce an intense hallucinatory experience in humans, with a typical duration of action of several minutes to an hour or so. Bucheler and coworkers (2005) describe this state as "a short-lived inebriant state with intense, bizarre feelings of depersonalization" (p. 1).

Roth and coworkers (2002) studied the molecular binding profile of salvinorin A at a large number (50) of cloned human G protein receptors, channels, and transporters known to be involved in psychopharmacology. Salvinorin A was active at only one receptor, the kappa opioid receptor, on which it exerted an agonist action. Salvinorin A had no action at the serotonin 5-HT$_{2A}$ receptor, which is the principal molecular target responsible for the actions of classical hallucinogens such as LSD (Figure 18.7). Salvinorin A can therefore now be classified as a *kappa opioid agonist*, the first naturally occurring compound to exhibit such an action. Roth and coworkers (2002) speculated that because of this action, kappa opioid receptors (see Chapter 16) may play a role in the regulation of human perception, and they suggest that kappa opioid antagonists (the opposite of salvinorin A) could represent a novel class of drugs with beneficial activity in diseases in which alterations in perception are predominant. Vortherms and Roth (2006) expanded on these ideas.

In a case report, Hanes (2001) reported on one patient with severe depression unrelieved by traditional antidepressant medications. This

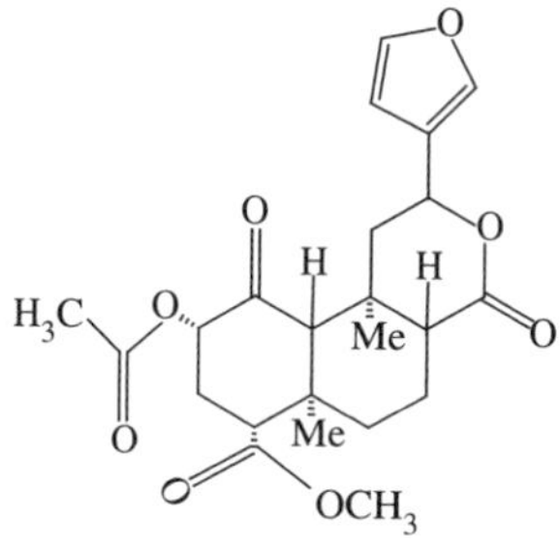

FIGURE 18.6 Structure of salvinorin A, the active drug in *Salvia divinorum*.

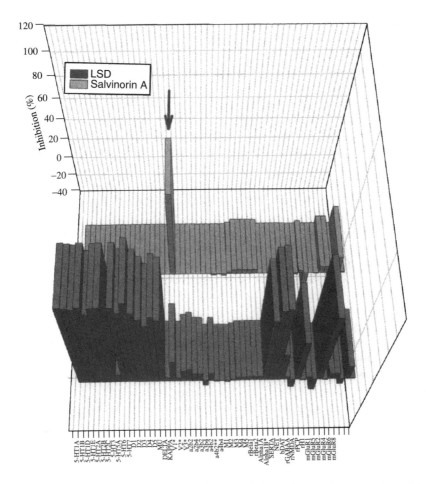

FIGURE 18.7 Large-scale screening of LSD and salvinorin A against many cloned G protein-type receptors. LSD binds to many receptors, especially those involving serotonin. Salvinorin A binds specifically to the kappa opioid receptor and is classified pharmacologically as a specific kappa opioid agonist. [From Roth et al. (2002), p. 11937.]

person obtained *Salvia* through a mail order house. She chewed two or three leaves at a time three times per week and claimed total remission of depressive symptoms. Continued use was accompanied by continued effectiveness, "engendering a kind of psychospiritual awakening, characterized by the discovery of her sense of self, greater self-confidence, increased feelings of intuitive wisdom, and connectedness to nature" (p. 634). However, as a kappa agonist, the drug has the potential to induce (rather than relieve) depressivelike reactions. Vortherms and Roth (2006) discuss this effect as well as its potent analgesic actions. Further information on *Salvia* may be found at www.wikipedia.org/wiki/Salvia_divinorum.

STUDY QUESTIONS

1. What is a psychedelic drug?
2. What differentiates a psychedelic drug from a behavioral stimulant? Discuss from both structural and behavioral viewpoints.
3. List the four classes of psychedelic drugs presented in this chapter.
4. Differentiate between mescaline and LSD.
5. How does LSD exert psychedelic actions?
6. What is the psychedelic syndrome?
7. What are some of the problems associated with LSD use?
8. How does phencyclidine work? Discuss the state of psychosis it produces.
9. What properties characterize the clinical usefulness of phencyclidine and ketamine?
10. Discuss the therapeutic and abuse potentials of dextromethorphan.
11. Compare salvinorin A with other psychedelic drugs.

REFERENCES

Adler, C. M. et al. (1999). "Comparison of Ketamine-Induced Thought Disorder in Healthy Volunteers and Thought Disorder in Schizophrenia." *American Journal of Psychiatry* 156: 1646–1649.

Almaula, N., et al. (1996). "Mapping the Binding Site Pocket of the Serotonin 5-Hydroxytryptamine$_{2A}$ Receptor." *Journal of Biological Chemistry* 271: 14672–14675.

Balla, A. et al. (2003). "Subchronic Continuous Phencyclidine Administration Potentiates Amphetamine-Induced Frontal Cortex Dopamine Release." *Neuropsychopharmacology* 28: 34–44.

Bryner, J. K. et al. (2006). "Dextromethorphan Abuse in Adolescence: An Increasing Trend: 1999–2004." *Archives of Pediatric and Adolescent Medicine* 160: 1217–1222.

Bucheler, R. et al. (2005). "Use of Nonprohibited Hallucinogenic Plants: Increasing Relevance for Public Health? A Case Report and Literature Review on the Consumption of Salvia Divinorum (Diviner's Sage)." *Pharmacopsychiatry* 38: 1–5.

Crahan, M. E. (1969). "God's Flesh and Other Pre-Columbian Phantastica." *Bulletin of the Los Angeles County Medical Association* 99: 17.

Davis, K. L. et al., eds. (2002). *Psychopharmacology—The Fifth Generation of Progress*. Philadelphia: Lippincott, Williams & Wilkins.

DeFrates, L. J. et al. (2005). "Antimuscarinic Intoxication Resulting from the Ingestion of Moonflower Seeds." *Annals of Pharmacotherapy* 39: 173–176.

Duffy, M. R., and C. Ferguson (2007). "Role of Dantrolene in Treatment of Heat Stroke Associated with Ecstasy Ingestion." *British Journal of Anaesthesia* 98: 148–149.

Dyck, E. (2005). "Flashbacks: Psychiatric Experimentation with LSD in Historical Perspective." *Canadian Journal of Psychiatry* 50: 381–388.

Ebersole, B. J. et al. (2003). "Molecular Basis of Partial Agonism: Orientation of Indoleamine Ligands in the Binding Pocket of the Human Serotonin 5-HT$_{2A}$ Receptor Determines Relative Efficacy." *Molecular Pharmacology* 63: 36–43.

El-Seedi, H. R. et al. (2005). "Prehistoric Peyote Use: Alkaloid Analysis and Radiocarbon Dating of Archaeological Specimens of Lophophora from Texas." *Journal of Ethnopharmacology* 101: 238–242.

Espiard, M. L., et al. (2005). "Hallucinogen Persisting Perceptual Disorder after Psilocybin Consumption: A Case Study." *European Psychiatry* 20: 458–460.

Fantegrossi, W. E., et al. (2005). "Hallucinogen-Like Actions of 2,5-Dimethoxy-4-(n)-Propylthiophenethylamine (2C-T-7) in Mice and Rats." *Psychopharmacology* 181: 496–503.

Fickenscher, A., et al. (2006). "Illicit Peyote Use Among American Indian Adolescents in Substance Abuse Treatment: A Preliminary Investigation." *Substance Use and Misuse* 41: 1139–1154.

Gable, R. S. (2007). "Risk Assessment of Ritual Use of Oral Dimethyltryptamine (DMT) and Harmala Alkaloids." *Addiction* 102: 24–34.

Gouzoulis-Mayfrank, E., et al. (2005). "Psychological Effects of (s)-Ketamine and N,N-Dimethyltryptamine (DMT): A Double-Blind, Cross-Over Study in Healthy Volunteers." *Pharmacopsychiatry* 38: 301–311.

Hall, A. P., and J. A. Henry (2006). "Acute Toxic Effects of 'Ecstasy' (MDMA) and Related Compounds: Overview of Pathophysiology and Clinical Management." *British Journal of Anaesthesia* 96: 678–685.

Halpern, J. H. (2004). "Hallucinogens and Dissociative Agents Naturally Growing in the United States." *Pharmacology and Therapeutics* 102: 131–138.

Halpern, J. H., et al. (2005). "Psychological and Cognitive Effects of Long-Term Peyote Use Among Native Americans." *Biological Psychiatry* 58: 624–631.

Hanes, K. R. (2001). "Antidepressant Effects of the Herb *Salvia divinorum*: A Case Report." *Journal of Clinical Psychopharmacology* 21: 634–635.

Hasler, F., et al. (2004). "Acute Psychological and Physiological Effects of Psilocybin in Healthy Humans: A Double-Blind, Placebo-Controlled Dose-Effect Study." *Psychopharmacology* 172: 145–156.

Hofmann, A. (1994). "Notes and Documents Concerning the Discovery of LSD." *Agents and Actions* 43: 79–81.

Holzman, R. S. (1998). "The Legacy of Atropos, the Fate Who Cut the Thread of Life." *Anesthesiology* 89: 241–249.

Iurlo, M., et al. (2001). "Effects of Harmine on Dopamine Output and Metabolism in Rat Striatum: Role of Monoamine Oxidase-A Inhibition." *Psychopharmacology* 159: 98–104.

Kalant, H. (2001). "The Pharmacology and Toxicology of 'Ecstasy' (MDMA) and Related Drugs." *Canadian Medical Association Journal* 165: 917–928.

Kuypers, K. P., and Ramaekers, J. G. (2005). "Transient Memory Impairment After Acute Dose of 75 mg 3,4-Methylene-Dioxymethamphetamine." *Journal of Psychopharmacology* 19: 633–639.

Miller, S. C. (2005). "Dextromethorphan Psychosis, Dependence and Physical Withdrawal." *Addiction Biology* 10: 325–327.

Moreno, F. A., et al. (2006). "Safety, Tolerability, and Efficacy of Psilocybin in 9 Patients with Obsessive-Compulsive Disorder." *Journal of Clinical Psychiatry* 67: 1735–1740.

Morris, B. J., et al. (2005). "PCP: From Pharmacology to Modeling Schizophrenia." *Current Opinions in Pharmacology* 5: 101–106.

Murray, J. B. (2002). "Phencyclidine (PCP): A Dangerous Drug, but Useful in Schizophrenia Research." *Journal of Psychology* 136: 319–327.

Nagai, F., et al. (2007). "The Effects of Non-Medically Used Psychoactive Drugs on Monoamine Neurotransmission in Rat Brain." *European Journal of Pharmacology* 559: 132–137.

Reneman, L., et al. (2001). "Cortical Serotonin Transporter Density and Verbal Memory in Individuals Who Stopped Using 3,4-Methylenedioxymethamphetamine (MDMA or 'Ecstasy')." *Archives of General Psychiatry* 58: 901–906.

Roth, B. L., et al. (2002). "Salvinorin A: A Potent Naturally Occurring Nonnitrogenous Opioid Selective Agonist." *Proceedings of the National Academy of Sciences* 99: 11934–11939.

Schifano, F., et al. (2005). "New Trends in the Cyber and Street Market of Recreational Drugs? The Case of 2C-T-7 ("Blue Mystic")." *Journal of Psychopharmacology* 19: 675–679.

Schilt, T., et al. (2007). "Cognition in Novice Ecstasy Users with Minimal Exposure to Other Drugs." *Archives of General Psychiatry* 64: 728–736.

Schwartz, R. H. (2005). "Adolescent Abuse of Dextromethorphan." *Clinical Pediatrics* 44: 565–568.

Sprague, J. E., et al. (1998). "An Integrated Hypothesis for the Serotonergic Axonal Loss Induced by 3,4-methylenedioxymethamphetamine." *Neurotoxicology* 19: 427–441.

Strassman, R. J., et al. (1994). "Dose-Response Study of N,N-dimethyltryptamine in Humans. II: Subjective Effects and Preliminary Results of a New Rating Scale." *Archives of General Psychiatry* 51: 98–108.

Takeda, N., et al. (1995). "Bufotenine Reconsidered as a Diagnostic Indicator of Psychiatric Disorders." *NeuroReport* 6: 2378–2380.

Theobald, D. S., and H. H. Maurer (2007). "Identification of Monoamine Oxidase and Cytochrome P450 Isoenzymes Involved in the Deamination of Phenethylamine-Derived Designer Drugs (2C-Series)." *Biochemical Pharmacology* 73: 287–297.

Thomasius, R., et al. (2005). "Mental Disorders in Current and Former Heavy Ecstasy (MDMA) Users." *Addiction* 100: 1310–1319.

Vortherms, T. A., and B. L. Roth (2006). "Salvinorin A: From Natural Product to Human Therapeutics." *Molecular Interventions* 6: 257–265.

Vortherms, T. A., et al (2007). "Differential Helical Orientations Among Related G Protein-Coupled Receptors Provide a Novel Mechanism for Selectivity: Studies with Salvinorin A and the κ-Opioid Receptor." *Journal of Biological Chemistry* 282: 146–156.

Wittmann, M., et al. (2007). "Effect of Psilocybin on Time Perception and Temporal Control of Behaviour in Humans." *Journal of Psychopharmacology* 21: 50–64.

Wolff, K., and Winstock, A.R. (2006). "Ketamine: From Medicine to Misuse." *CNS Drugs* 20: 199–218.

Special Topics in Psychopharmacology

Three topics remain to be discussed in this book. Chapter 19 discusses the use of herbal medicines both as agents to treat various psychological disorders and as potential substances of abuse. Included are discussions of St. John's wort, kava, ephedrine, and other substances that affect the brain or behavior.

Chapter 20 is devoted to presentation of anabolic-androgenic steroids. Although some steroids have legitimate medical uses, they are widely used and abused by athletes and nonathletes and by young people and the elderly. Although their use is associated with the development of muscle mass, they carry significant risks and toxicities.

The last chapter, Chapter 21, is devoted to a general discussion of important topics related to drug abuse. Discussed are modern theories of addiction, drug dependence, and risk of relapse, theories of the pharmacological basis of treatment, and philosophies of education about drugs.

Chapter 19

Herbal Medicines for Psychological Disorders

Many drugs derived from natural plant sources are covered elsewhere in this book (Table 19.1). Covered here are herbal products with CNS effects that are otherwise not covered in the book. Often, these herbals are heavily promoted and used for the treatment of various psychological disorders. Promotion of some herbals may be warranted. For others, regulation may be needed should widespread use become a societal problem.

In this chapter the focus is on herbal medicines that are used to treat psychiatric symptoms or disorders, herbal medicines that produce changes in mood, thinking, or behavior as a side effect, and herbal medicines that interact with psychiatric medications (Wong et al., 1998). A special edition of the *Physicians' Desk Reference* is devoted to herbal medicines, although it does not contain critical analysis of potential or claimed efficacy (*PDR for Herbal Medicines*, Third Edition, 2004). Each herb discussed in this chapter presumably contains an active ingredient that accounts for its clinical use. In some instances, the presumed active ingredient has not been conclusively identified, so discussion is oriented to the plant material and the safety, side effects, drug interactions, and efficacy in treating symptoms or diagnoses (Table 19.2, pp. 642–643).

The efficacy of many herbal medications is difficult to evaluate due to incomplete knowledge of active ingredients, absence of standardization, different purities, and so on. The final composition of a plant product varies according to what part of the plant is used, where it was grown, what time of year it was grown or harvested, the reputations of the grower, processor, packager, marketer, promoter, and so on. The

TABLE 19.1 Some of the naturally occurring psychoactive drugs already covered in this book

Drug	Chapter	Used in therapeutics	Drug of abuse
Cocaine	13	Rarely	Yes
Caffeine	14	Occasionally	Probably
Nicotine	14	No	Yes
Lithium	8	Yes	No
Morphine	16	Yes	Yes
Codeine	16	Yes	Yes
Tetrahydrocannabinol	17	Rarely	Yes
Scopolamine	18	Occasionally	Occasionally
Mescaline	18	No	Yes
Myristicin/Elemicin	18	No	Yes
Psilocybin/Psilocin	18	No	Yes
Dimethyltryptamine	18	No	Yes
Bufotenine	18	No	Yes
Ololiuqui	18	No	Yes
Harmine	18	No	Yes
Omega-3 fatty acids	8	Possibly	No
Khat	13	No	Yes

widespread, largely unregulated availability and promotion of herbal products is not new. Herbals have been used from the time of Hippocrates, and patent medicines were widely promoted in the United States until the early part of the twentieth century. Federal regulations in the 1920s severely restricted the sale and nonprescription use of such products, most of which contained large amounts of alcohol as well as "natural" drugs such as cocaine and opium.

The passage of the Dietary Supplement Health Education Act of 1994 severely restricted the Food and Drug Administration's ability to exert control over herbal products. Thus, since 1994, any product can be labeled a "supplement" as long as the product makes no claim to effect a cure for a disease. Thus, a manufacturer cannot claim that a product "alleviates depression"; the manufacturer can claim that it "promotes emotional balance." An herbal product cannot be claimed to alleviate the signs and symptoms of Alzheimer's disease; rather, it "enhances mental sharpness." Even though some herbal products can have significant adverse neuropsychiatric reactions (Pies, 2000), manufacturers must demonstrate neither safety nor efficacy. Promotion of many herbals addresses the fact that fatigue, headache, insomnia, depression, and anxiety—the symptoms and complaints most often underappreciated and untreated by medical doctors—are the most common reasons patients cite for seeking treatment from alternative practitioners.

St. John's Wort

St. John's wort, *Hypericum perforatum,* is named after St. John the Baptist because it blooms around his feast day (June 24) and exudes a red color symbolic of his blood. It has many constituents with biological activity, including naphthodianthrones, flavonoids, and xanthones. *Hypericin* (Figure 19.1) (and possibly *pseudohypericin* and/or *hyperforin*) is generally considered to be the active ingredient, and dosage of the herb is based on its presumed hypericin content (Wurglics and Schubert-Zsilavecz, 2006). The term hypericin is from the Greek *hyper* and *eikon,* and it means "to overcome an apparition"; the ancients believed in its ability to ward off evil spirits (O'Hara et al., 1998).

Draves and Walker (2003) analyzed the summed total of hypericin and pseudohypericin in commercially available St. John's wort preparations. The percentage of drug relative to the claimed amount varied from 0 to 108 percent for capsules and from 31 to 80 percent for tablets. Only two products had an amount within 10 percent of the label amount. Tinctures (alcohol extracts) varied from 0 to 118 percent of the label amount. On average, most labels overstated the amount by a factor of almost 2 (they thus contained only 50 percent of the labeled amount).

Indications

St. John's wort is licensed in Germany for the treatment of anxiety, depression, and insomnia. In the United States, no claims of effectiveness in treating these disorders may be made; St. John's wort is sold only as a dietary supplement, perhaps to promote emotional balance.

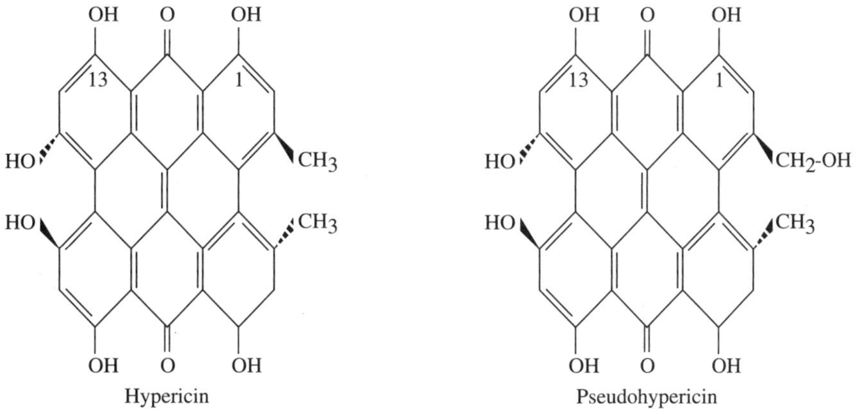

FIGURE 19.1 Structural formulas of hypericin and pseudohypericin.

TABLE 19.2 Herbal remedies commonly used to treat psychiatric symptoms*

Herb	Common usage	Quality of evidence category†	Adverse effects	Cautions/ contraindications	Drug interactions
Black cohosh	Menopause symptoms	I	GI upset (rare), headaches, CV depression	Pregnancy, lactation	Hormonal treatments (theoretical)
	PMS	II			
	Dysmenorrhea	III			
German chamomile	Insomnia	III	Allergy (rare)	Allergy to sunflower family of plants	None reported
	Anxiety	III			
Evening primrose	Schizophrenia	IV	None reported	Mania, epilepsy	Phenothiazines, NSAIDs, corticosteroids., ß blockers, anticoagulants
	ADHD	IV			
	Dementia	IV			
Ginkgo	"Cerebrovascular insufficiency" symptoms	I	Headache, GI upset	Pregnancy, lactation, potential bleeding (e.g., PUD)	Anticoagulants
	Dementia	I			
Hops	Insomnia	III	Allergy, menstrual irregularity	Depression, pregnancy, lactation	Sedative-hypnotics, alcohol (both theoretical)
Kava	Insomnia	III	Scaling of skin on extremities	Pregnancy, lactation	Benzodiazepines, alcohol
	Anxiety	III			
	Seizures	IV			
Lemon balm	Insomnia	IV	None reported	Thyroid disease, pregnancy, lactation	CNS depressants, thyroid medications
	Anxiety	III			

TABLE 19.2 Herbal remedies commonly used to treat psychiatric symptoms* *(continued)*

Herb	Common usage	Quality of evidence category[†]	Adverse effects	Cautions/ contraindications	Drug interactions
Passion flower	Insomnia Anxiety	III] III]	Hypersensitivity vasculitis, sedation	Pregnancy, lactation	Insufficient data
Skullcap	Insomnia Anxiety	IV] IV]	Sedation, confusion, seizures	Pregnancy, lactation	Insufficient data
St. John's wort	Depression	I	Photosensitivity, GI upset, sedation, anticholinergic	CV disease, pregnancy. lactation, pheochromocytoma	Drugs that interact with MAOIs
Valerian	Insomnia Anxiety	III] III]	Sedation	Pregnancy, lactation	CNS depressants

*PMS = premenstrual syndrome; GI = gastrointestinal; CV = cardiovascular; ADHD = attention deficit with hyperactivity disorder; NSAIDs = nonsteroidal anti-inflammatory drugs; PUD = peptic ulcer disease; CNS = central nervous system; MAOIs = monoamine oxidase inhibitors.
[†]Quality of evidence: I = evidence from at least two properly randomized controlled trials; II = evidence from well-designed trials without randomization; III = opinions of respected authorities based on clinical experience, descriptive studies, or reports of expert committees; IV = insufficient evidence to warrant conclusions about efficacy or safety.

From Wong et al. (1998), Table 1.

Much less studied is the use of St. John's wort for the treatment of anxiety disorders, in spite of the fact that patients with anxiety disorders are among the most likely to self-medicate using alternative treatments. Kobak and coworkers (2005a) conducted a double-blind, placebo-controlled study of St. John's wort in 60 patients with obsessive-compulsive disorder without evidence of depression. In a 12-week study, 17.9 percent of St. John's wort-treated patients and 16.7 percent of placebo-treated patients exhibited clinical response (reductions in the Yale-Brown Obsessive-Compulsive scales); the results failed to support the use of St. John's wort for OCD. Similarly, the same authors (Kobak et al., 2005b) reported lack of efficacy in the treatment of social anxiety disorder. These well-conducted studies report results opposite to those of less-controlled or case-study reports of efficacy in certain anxiety disorders.

Pharmacokinetics

Hypericin has been shown to be absorbed following oral administration, with peak blood levels achieved in about 5 hours (Figure 19.2). Hypericin has an elimination half-life of about 25 hours; it thus achieves steady-state concentrations in the brain in about 4 to 6 days (Figure 19.3). Only about 15 to 20 percent of the administered hypericin reaches the central circulation and is available systemically. Of all the alkyloids in *Hypericum perforatum*, only hypericin appears to be detectable in brain tissue (Wurglics and Schubert-Zsilavecz, 2006). Whether hypericin is metabolized, how it is metabolized, what its metabolites are, and how it is excreted are unknown.

St. John's wort contains bioflavonoids, one of which is *quercitin*. Quercitin inhibits the drug-metabolizing enzyme CYP-1A2. Hyperforin is a potent inhibitor of CYP-2D6 and CYP-2C9 (Obach, 2000). The use of St. John's wort could therefore result in numerous adverse interactions when combined with other drugs. For example, it may reduce the effectiveness of codeine (blocking conversion to morphine) and increase the blood levels of caffeine and several psychoactive medications, including tricyclic antidepressants and antipsychotic drugs. St. John's wort has also been reported to induce certain hepatic drug-metabolizing enzymes, increasing the activity of CYP-3A4, for example, and thus reducing the levels in the blood of certain cardiac and anti-inflammatory medicines. As stated by Markowitz and coworkers (2003):

> A 14-day course of St. John's wort significantly induced the activity of CYP-3A4. This suggests that long-term administration of St. John's wort may result in diminished clinical effectiveness or increased dosage requirements for all CYP-3A4 substrates, which represent at least 50 percent of all marketed medications. (p. 1500)

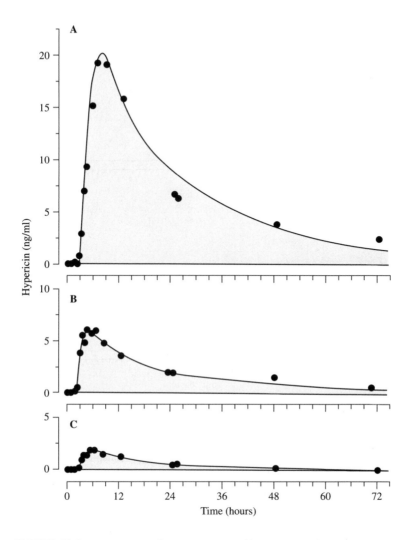

FIGURE 19.2 Time course of concentration of hypericin in plasma in three subjects after receiving a single dose of (A) 300 milligrams, (B) 900 milligrams, or (C) 1800 milligrams. [From B. Staffeldt et al., "Pharmacokinetics of Hypericin and Pseudohypericin After Oral Intake of the *Hypericum perforatum* Extract LI 160 in Healthy Volunteers," *Journal of Geriatric Psychiatry and Neurology* 7 (1994), Supplement 1, p. S49.]

A. Hypericin

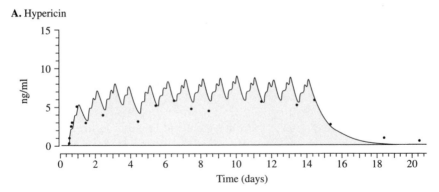

B. Pseudohypericin

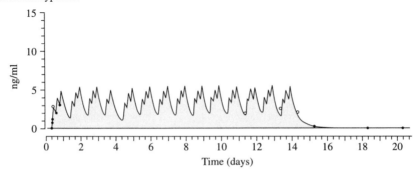

FIGURE 19.3 Time course of concentrations of (**A**) hypericin and (**B**) pseudohypericin in a subject taking one 300-milligram tablet of hypericum extract three times daily for 14 days. [From B. Staffeldt et al., "Pharmacokinetics of Hypericin and Pseudohypericin After Oral Intake of the *Hypericum perforatum* Extract LI 160 in Healthy Volunteers," *Journal of Geriatric Psychiatry and Neurology* 7 (1994), Supplement 1, p. S50.]

Pharmacodynamics

The mechanism of action of hypericin and hypericum extracts is unclear. Initially, it was thought that inhibition of monoamine oxidase (Chapter 7) increased the levels of norepinephrine, epinephrine, and dopamine. This would certainly account for the antidepressant action of St. John's wort. However, although MAO inhibition can be demonstrated in vitro at high concentrations, the effect is too weak to account for clinical efficacy. Other reports hypothesize a hypericin-induced blockade of the presynaptic reuptake of serotonin, norepinephrine, and dopamine. Kasper and coworkers (2006), reviewing the work of others, stated:

> Experimental investigations have provided evidence that serotonin receptor expression is markedly reduced during treatment with hypericum extract, ultimately leading to enhanced synaptic availability of serotonin and norepinephrine. (p. 14)

Evidence for this statement is relatively weak. Other reported effects of hypericum extract include binding to GABA receptors, benzodiazepine receptors, and glutaminergic NMDA-type receptors (Wong et al., 1998).

Recently, Sanchez-Reus and coworkers (2007) reported in studies of rats that a standardized extract of *Hypericum perforatum* exerted an antioxidant action, perhaps protecting neurons from oxidative damage. If correct, St John's wort might be indicated for depressed elderly patients with degenerative disorders exhibiting elevated oxidative stress status.

Clinical Efficacy

As early as 1996, Linde and coworkers conducted a meta-analysis of the clinical efficacy of St. John's wort for depression. They concluded that over a period of two to four weeks of treatment, hypericum extract was superior to placebo. However, data were less than convincing, and in 1998 Wong and coworkers concluded:

> Overall, there are inadequate data regarding long-term use and efficacy in severe depression. There are concerns regarding the standardization and quality control of commercial preparations. Clearly, more research is needed to address these shortcomings in the literature. (p. 1033)

Kim and coworkers (1999) conducted a similar meta-analysis. In a total of 651 patients, they concluded: *"Hypericum perforatum* was more effective than placebo and similar in effectiveness to low-dose tricyclic antidepressants in the short-term treatment of mild to moderately severe depression" (p. 532). However, they were careful to state that "serious questions remain regarding the research design of the studies analyzed."

Philipp and coworkers (2000) reported that hypericum extract (1 gram per day) was comparable in efficacy to imipramine (100 milligrams per day) and superior to placebo. Commenting, Linde and Berner (2000) noted that the study "confirms the existing evidence that hypericum extract is more effective than placebo in mild and moderately severe depression." Linde and Berner added, however, that the dose of hypericum was high, the dose of imipramine was low, and the superiority of both drug treatments over placebo was "not impressive," with placebo responses being quite robust.

In 2001, Sheldon and coworkers conducted the first large-scale, multicentered, randomized, double-blind, placebo-controlled trial of St. John's wort extract and placebo in the treatment of major depression. In this study, St. John's wort (900 to 1200 milligrams per day) was no more effective than placebo (Figure 19.4). In 2002, results were reported of a multicentered, randomized, double-blind, placebo-controlled trial of St. John's wort extract versus both placebo and sertraline (an SSRI-type antidepressant) in the treatment of major

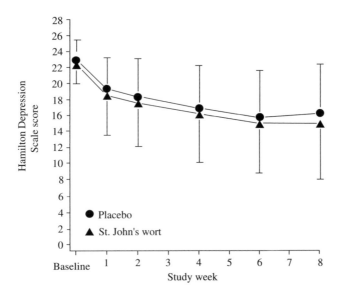

FIGURE 19.4 Effects of St. John's wort and placebo on the Hamilton Rating Scale for Depression over 8 weeks of study. [From Sheldon et al. (2001), p. 1983.]

depression (Hypericum Depression Trial Study Group, 2002). Neither St. John's wort nor sertraline was superior to placebo (Figure 19.5). The researchers concluded:

> This study fails to support the efficacy of *H. perforatum* in moderately severe major depression . . . the complete absence of trends suggestive of efficacy for *H. perforatum* is noteworthy. (p. 1807)

Findling and coworkers (2003) conducted an 8-week, open-label trial of St. John's wort (dosed to 900 milligrams per day) in 33 youths (mean age 10.5 years) with major depression. Twenty-five met the criteria for a positive response. The researchers stated that controlled trials in youths appear to be indicated.

More recent studies have continued to examine the clinical efficacy of St. John's wort. Anghelescu and coworkers (2006) compared hypericum extract (HE) with paroxetine (Paxil) in moderate to severe depression. The Hamilton Depression Scale scores were reduced by HE from 25 to 4 and by paroxetine from 25 to 5. Overall, 81 percent of HE-treated patients and 71 percent of paroxetine-treated patients achieved remission. Overall, the efficacies were very much higher than reported elsewhere (see the results of the STAR*D study in Chapter 7).

Kasper and coworkers (2006) reported that HE was superior to placebo in a 6-week, placebo-controlled study of patients with mild to moderate depression (Figure 19.6). Moreno and coworkers

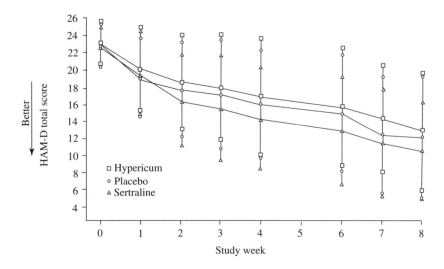

FIGURE 19.5 Effects of St. John's wort, sertraline, and placebo on the Hamilton Rating Scale for Depression over 8 weeks of study. Graphed values are means with vertical bars extending to one standard deviation. [From Hypericum Depression Trial Study Group (2002), p. 1811.]

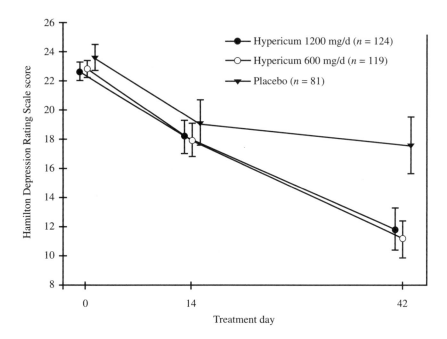

FIGURE 19.6 Change in mean total Hamilton Rating Scale for Depression score of patients suffering a major depressive episode over a 6-week treatment period with hypericum extract (600 or 1200 milligrams per day) or placebo. Means and standard deviations are shown. [From Kasper et al. (2006), Figure 2).

(2006), in a double-blind study, reported that HE was less effective than was either fluoxetine (Prozac) or placebo in treating mild to moderate depression.

Gastpar and coworkers (2006) compared HE and citalopram (Celexa) in moderate depression. They demonstrated the "noninferiority" of HE compared with citalopram and a superiority of HE over placebo. Overall, 54 percent of HE-treated patients, 55 percent of citalopram-treated patients, and 39 percent of placebo-treated patients responded positively.

Randlov and coworkers (2006) reported that HE was effective in treating nondysthymic patients with mild to moderate depression. It was ineffective in patients with comorbid depression and dysthymia or in patients with dysthymia alone.

In summary, have we learned anything more than we knew several years ago? Data are unclear. Perhaps hypericum extract has some efficacy in mild to moderate depression, an effect that may be comparable to that achieved by standard pharmacological agents, even though such effects are not "robust." Hypericum extract does not appear to be effective in treating either anxiety disorders or dysthymia.

Side Effects

The real and potential side effects of St. John's wort are not insignificant. The extract has been shown to cause photosensitivity, especially in fair-skinned people who take large doses. Fortunately, the effect is reversible, usually within a few days. There are also several reports of St. John's wort precipitating a hypomanic state when used either with or without other antidepressant drugs. Used with SSRI-type antidepressants, a serotonin syndrome can occur. Other usually mild side effects include sedation, lethargy, and gastrointestinal upset. The potential for involvement in potentially serious drug interactions was discussed earlier.

St. John's wort, at least until proved safe, should not be used during pregnancy or with other psychoactive agents. Klier and coworkers (2006) found little adverse effect of St. John's wort on the breast-feeding infants of mothers taking the product; very low levels of the herbal were found in breast milk of the mother and the plasma of the infant.

Since St. John's wort induces the CYP-450 enzymes that metabolize oral contraceptives, there has been some concern about unwanted pregnancies; however, to date, this has not been a clinical problem. Pfunder and coworkers (2003) noted no evidence of ovulation during low-dose oral contraceptive therapy, although women treated with St. John's wort experienced more intracycle bleeding episodes.

Ginkgo

The ginkgo tree (*Ginkgo biloba*) is one of the oldest deciduous tree species on earth. The extract of ginkgo is referred to as *EGb-760* and is one of the most popular plant extracts used in Europe to alleviate symptoms associated with a range of cognitive disorders, including dementia. In the United States, the extract can be promoted not to treat cognitive dysfunctions but, for example, to provide "mental sharpness," provide antioxidant protection, maintain healthy circulatory perfusion, and so on. Purported medical indications for use include dementia, chronic cerebrovascular insufficiency (insufficient blood flow to the brain), and "brain protection."

The active ingredients in ginkgo extracts are not completely known. The standardized commercial preparation contains 24 percent ginkgo flavonoids and 6 percent terpenoids. As noted in the discussion of St. John's wort, flavonoids inhibit CYP-1A2 and create drug interactions with many medications (Bressler, 2005).

Flavonoids and terpenoids are antioxidants that scavenge free radicals that have been implicated as the mediators of the cellular damage observed in Alzheimer's disease. Ginkgolide B (a terpenoid) inhibits a platelet-activating factor, interfering with platelet aggregation and slowing blood clotting (as does aspirin). This antiplatelet action by itself provides therapeutic effectiveness by limiting abnormal clot formation in small arteries (as aspirin does). Adversely, it may increase the tendency to bleed and it potentiates the actions of other blood thinners (again, as does aspirin). Presumed antioxidant effects have not been convincingly demonstrated for ginkgo or to correlate well with efficacy in treating cognitive dysfunction.

Pharmacokinetics

Taken orally, *Ginkgo biloba* extracts appear to be readily absorbed, although blood levels of any of the substances found in the extract have not been reported. Concentrations of ginkgo flavonoids peak in plasma at 2 to 3 hours after ingestion. The mechanism of elimination of these substances from the body is not known. It is also not known whether any of the flavonoids or terpenoids are metabolized before excretion. The half-life is thought to be about 5 hours.

Pharmacodynamics

The EGb-761 extract of ginkgo contains several compounds that are thought by some people to act on unidentified processes involved in the homeostasis of inflammation and oxidative stress, presumably providing membrane protection and neurotransmission modulation. EEG studies (Itil et al., 1996) demonstrate an activating effect with increased alpha wave activity, indicative of increased alertness and perhaps of improved cognitive performance (perhaps similar to the effects of caffeine on the EEG).

Clinical Efficacy

Most early studies on ginkgo extract were too poorly conducted to merit conclusions, despite a general conclusion that ginkgo may produce modest improvement in memory loss in patients severely affected with Alzheimer's disease (LeBars et al., 1997). O'Hara and coworkers (1998) stated that while statistically significant, such modest effects are of uncertain clinical benefit.

Oken and coworkers (1998) reviewed 50 studies on *Ginkgo biloba* for neurological disorders and concluded that patients function slightly better than those taking placebo. Wong and coworkers (1998) concluded that there is no clear evidence of efficacy in the treatment of depression, impotence, or brain injury. Van Dongen and colleagues (2000) reported on a 24-week study of EGb 761 in 214 elderly patients in the Netherlands. Ginkgo had no positive effects as a treatment for older people with mild to moderate dementia or age-related memory impairment. The authors' meticulous attention to detail sets a new standard for the study of herbal preparations.

In 2002, Solomon and coworkers conducted a 6-week, randomized, placebo-controlled trial of the effects of ginkgo on 220 patients over the age of 60 years to assess drug effects on memory function. The authors found that ginkgo had no beneficial effects on standard neuropsychological tests of learning, memory, attention, or concentration. They concluded that "ginkgo, when taken following the manufacturer's instructions, provides no measurable benefit in memory or related cognitive function" (p. 835).

In contrast to the results provided by Solomon and coworkers, Mix and Crews (2002) performed a nearly identical set of memory and cognitive experiments in 262 people aged 60 years or older. These authors reported modest improvements in memory and cognition, evaluated both objectively and subjectively. The herbal has been shown to be ineffective in the treatment of either tinnitus or acute mountain sickness.

To summarize, ginkgo may have modest effects on cognitive functioning associated with cerebrovascular impairments (cases where blood flow to the brain is impaired, as in atherosclerotic vascular disease). This potential benefit can be accounted for solely by the herbal's action to reduce the "stickiness" of blood platelets (an action identical to that exerted by aspirin).

Side Effects and Precautions

Side effects of ginkgo include headache and gastrointestinal upset, but they are mild and infrequent. Headache is the most common and can be minimized by starting with a low dose and increasing it gradually. It is important to note that gingko blocks platelet function and increases bleeding time testing, increases spontaneous bleeding, causes interaction with aspirin and other anticoagulants, and has resulted in cases of spontaneous intracranial hemorrhage (Bent et al., 2005). Safety in pregnancy and during lactation has not been established; Dugoua and coworkers (2006) advise that ginkgo preparations be used with caution during pregnancy, especially around the time of delivery where its antiplatelet action may put the fetus/newborn at risk of hemorrhage

Kava

Preparations made from the roots of kava (*Piper methysticin*) have been used for ceremonial and social purposes by the peoples of the South Pacific for thousands of years. Captain James Cook first described kava in the account of his voyage in 1768. Scientific study was not conducted until the early days of pharmacology and pharmacognosy in 1886.

Kava is used by the Oceanic peoples as an antianxiety drug, similar to our use of ethyl alcohol. Kava induces relaxation, improves social interaction, promotes sleep, and plays an important role in the sociocultural life of the islanders of the South Pacific. At higher doses, kava produces sleep and stupor, again like alcohol. Standardized extracts of kava have been widely used in Western countries for the therapy of anxiety, tension, restlessness, and insomnia.

Chemistry

Many agents in kava exhibit pharmacological activity. Most interest centers on the kava lactones, found in the fat-soluble portions of the plant root. Other compounds in kava contribute to efficacy, and the sedative activity of a crude preparation exceeds that of extracted kava lactones. However, as the kava lactone content of the root varies from 3 to 20 percent, preparations standardized for kava lactone content are preferred to crude preparations.

Pharmacokinetics

When taken as the extract, kava lactones appear to be well absorbed; they are not as well absorbed when the isolated substances are taken. Little is known about the distribution, metabolism, and excretion of the ingredients.

Pharmacodynamics

The mechanism of action of ingredients in kava is poorly elucidated. Kava pyrones appear to bind to various GABA receptors or to the benzodiazepine-binding site, a likely action since kava produces effects similar to those produced by the benzodiazepines and alcohol. A kava lactone has been shown to block sodium channels, an anestheticlike effect. Kava has been shown in animals to be an anticonvulsant and a muscle relaxant and to be neuroprotective (much as are benzodiazepines and barbiturates). The EEG alterations induced by kava resemble those induced by benzodiazepines. Therefore, one can hypothesize that kava's action should closely resemble that of ethyl alcohol and the traditional sedative-hypnotic compounds.

Clinical Effects

At a dose of up to 70 milligrams of kava lactone, an anxiolytic effect is thought to occur. At higher doses (125 to 210 milligrams), drowsiness, sedation, and a feeling of intoxication are produced. In Oceanic cultures, doses of 250 milligrams are consumed, often more than once, and inebriation is quite rapidly induced. Recent studies, however, could not document any antianxiety efficacy (Jacobs et al., 2005; Connor et al., 2006).

Side Effects and Complications

Side effects of kava are generally mild and include drowsiness, nausea, muscle weakness, blurred vision, and (with chronic use) yellow skin discoloration. Since kava is a sedative/intoxicant, it should not be combined with alcohol, benzodiazepines, barbiturates, THC, or other CNS depressants. Kava should not be taken before driving or operating machinery.

Campo and coworkers (2002) reported a case of fulminant liver failure (requiring liver transplantation) in a 14-year-old girl. Since this report, other cases of hepatotoxicity have been reported and the herbal has been banned in several Western countries, such as Germany, France, Switzerland, Austria, and Canada. It continues to be sold in the United States, despite evidence of adverse hepatic toxicity (Lim et al., 2007).

Since kava is an intoxicant (Perez and Holmes, 2005), it is interesting that barbiturates and benzodiazepines are restricted to prescription use, alcohol has age restrictions, marijuana is illegal, but kava is freely available in the United States. Its chief deterrents to more widespread use as an alcohollike intoxicant is its expense and its potential for causing serious liver damage.

Ephedrine (Ma-Huang)

Ephedrine is the naturally occurring psychoactive drug found in *Ephedra sinica,* also called ma-huang. The medicinal parts are the young canes collected in autumn and the dried rhizome with roots. Ephedrine is a potent psychostimulant that acts by releasing the body's own stores of the catecholamine neurotransmitters, epinephrine (adrenaline), norepinephrine, and dopamine.

Pharmacologically, ephedrine closely resembles the amphetamines, although the duration of action of ephedrine is considerably shorter. Because of this, ephedrine-containing products should not be considered as metabolic supplements, dietary supplements, or any other designation implying that it is not a drug.

Deaths from ephedrine now number in the dozens. The adrenaline and other catecholamines released by ephedrine increase blood pressure, heart rate, the force of cardiac contraction, and cardiac output of blood. Cardiac arrhythmias can be serious and potentially fatal. Like amphetamines, ephedrine temporarily reduces appetite, is a cardiovascular stimulant, and is a psychostimulant. Its disadvantages, however, far outweigh any therapeutic utility. In athletics, ephedrine is a "doping" substance. Numerous drug interactions occur and many are serious and potentially fatal. Several herbal preparations contain both ephedrine and caffeine: this is a combination that should be avoided because caffeine increases the cardiovascular toxicity of ephedrine. In April 2004, the FDA, in response to 155 deaths and dozens of heart attacks and strokes, initiated a ban on the sale of ephedrine-containing products as too dangerous for use. It was the U.S. government's first ban of a purported dietary supplement.

Other Herbals That Act on the CNS

A variety of other herbals have been used to treat signs and symptoms of CNS dysfunction. A few are described here. Complete descriptions may be found in the *PDR for Herbal Medicines* (2004) and in the review by Wong and coworkers (1998).

Valerian (*Valeriana officalis*) has a long history of use as a mild sedative and as an anxiolytic as well as an antidepressant. The mechanism behind its action is obscure; some data indicate that it may affect GABA receptors, thus acting as a type of mild benzodiazepine. GABA itself is a component of valerian, leading some people to state that valerian is a source of naturally occurring GABA, which it is. The problem is that GABA only very poorly crosses the blood-brain barrier, and it is unlikely that this source of GABA affects the CNS.

Reported side effects of valerian include liver toxicity, headache, excitability, and uneasiness. There are potential drug interactions between valerian and SSRI-type antidepressants, perhaps precipitating a serotonin syndrome (Chapter 7). Nevertheless, valerian may produce CNS depression similar to that produced by benzodiazepines. There is no evidence to indicate that valerian is superior to existing sedative-hypnotic agents for the treatment of insomnia. The safety of valerian during pregnancy has not been delineated, so valerian probably should not be used by pregnant women. Valerian would be expected to potentiate the effects of other CNS depressants, such as ethyl alcohol, and caution is warranted. Valerian should not be taken before driving or in other situations when alertness is required. The usual precautions that apply to other sedatives apply to valerian. As does St. John's wort, valerian contains quercitin; this substance inhibits the drug-metabolizing enzyme CYP-1A2 and can possibly result in clinically significant drug interactions.

German chamomile (*Matricaria recutita*) is used to treat mild insomnia and anxiety. The herb contains flavinoids that are postulated to have affinity for the benzodiazepine receptor and perhaps for a histamine receptor, either perhaps inducing a sedative effect. No controlled clinical trials have investigated these properties.

Evening primrose (*Oenothera biennis*) has been promoted for the treatment of schizophrenia and ADHD, but little scientific evidence or cultural tradition backs up the claims. Primrose contains an omega-3 fatty acid called gamma-linolenic acid, which is felt to be the active ingredient. Objective research reporting efficacy is lacking.

Hops (*Humulus lupulus*) are used in the brewing industry as a component in beer. Hops also have a long history of use as a sedative-hypnotic agent. No clinical studies support the use of hops as a single agent to treat either insomnia or anxiety. Used as a sedative, drug interactions occur, especially potentiation of the effects of other sedatives such as alcohol and benzodiazepines. Use of hops should be avoided in depression, in pregnancy, and during lactation.

Lemon balm (*Melissa officinalis*), *passion flower* (*Passiflora incarnata*), and *skullcap* (*Scutellaria laterifolia*) are all thought to possess CNS sedative properties and are promoted for use as sedatives and anxiolytics. Data on efficacy are lacking, as is information on active ingredients and mechanisms of action. As sedatives, the usual precautions apply, including those concerning drug interactions and cognitive and motor impairments.

Conclusions

Over the next few years, additional studies relating to the safety, efficacy, and drug interactions associated with herbals will undoubtedly be conducted. Until then, caution is warranted: patients should tell prescribing physicians of their use of herbal medications, and most herbals should probably be avoided in pregnancy until they can be proven safe.

Although significant numbers of children and adolescents are receiving one or more herbal medications, studies of these compounds in this age population are unavailable. Some youths purchase the drugs themselves, as the drugs are easily available, relatively inexpensive, and widely advertised or endorsed by their peers. Other young people may be dosed by their parents in attempts to medicate such disorders as ADHD, depression, anxiety, or insomnia. Reasonable medical practitioners recognize that few data exist to support the use of herbals in the treatment of psychiatric disorders in children. Until such evidence becomes available, these agents probably should not be administered to children, especially for long periods of time or in the presence of other medications.

Particularly troubling are unregulated promotions of herbal and herballike preparations via the internet. These products are promoted with appealing and convincing advertising that is attractive to young people. Caution is warranted.

STUDY QUESTIONS

1. Describe the recent legislation changing the herbal industry. How has it helped society? How has it hurt?

2. List some of the herbals discussed in other chapters in this book. Which of them should be more freely available? Defend your answer.

3. What is hypericin? Describe its pharmacokinetics. What is the evidence for its efficacy?

4. What is ginkgo? What are its claimed actions? What evidence is there for efficacy to improve memory? For other uses?

5. What is kava? Does it have therapeutic potential? Does it have abuse potential? What drug does it appear to most resemble? Should there be legal restrictions on its use? Defend your answer.

6. What is ma-huang? What is its active ingredient? Does it have a potential for abuse? Might it induce toxicity? Should its use be regulated? Defend your answer.

7. What in valerian might result in drug interactions?

8. Are there any unaddressed concerns about the use of herbals during pregnancy or by women who might become pregnant? What about in breast-feeding women?

REFERENCES

Anghelescu, I. G., et al. (2006). "Comparison of Hypericum Extract WS 5570 and Paroxetine in Ongoing Treatment After Recovery from an Episode of Moderate to Severe Depression: Results from a Randomized Multicenter Study." *Pharmacopsychiatry* 39: 213–219.

Bent, S., et al. (2005). "Spontaneous Bleeding Associated with *Ginkgo biloba*: A Case Report and Systematic Review of the Literature." *Journal of General Internal Medicine* 20: 657–661.

Bressler, R. (2005). "Herb-Drug Interactions: Interactions Between *Ginkgo biloba* and Prescription Medications." *Geriatrics* 60: 30–33.

Campo, J. V., et al. (2002). "Kava-Induced Fulminant Hepatic Failure." *Journal of the American Academy of Child & Adolescent Psychiatry* 41: 631.

Connor, K. M., et al. (2006). "Kava in Generalized Anxiety Disorder: Three Placebo-Controlled Trials." *International Clinical Psychopharmacology* 21: 249–253.

Draves, A. H., and S. E. Walker (2003). "Analysis of the Hypericin and Pseudo-hypericin Content of Commercially Available St. John's Wort Preparations." *Canadian Journal of Clinical Pharmacology* 10: 114–118.

Dugoua, J. J., et al. (2006). "Safety and Efficacy of Ginkgo (*Ginkgo biloba*) During Pregnancy and Lactation." *Canadian Journal of Clinical Pharmacology* 13: e277–e284.

Findling, R. L., et al. (2003). "An Open-Label Pilot Study of St. John's Wort in Juvenile Depression." *Journal of the American Academy of Child & Adolescent Psychiatry* 42: 908–914.

Gastpar, M., et al. (2006). "Comparative Efficacy and Safety of a Once-Daily Dosage of Hypericum Extract STW3-VI and Citalopram in Patients with Moderate Depression: A Double-Blind, Randomized, Multicentre, Placebo-Controlled Study." *Pharmacopsychiatry* 39: 66-75.

Hypericum Depression Trial Study Group (2002). "Effect of *Hypericum perforatum* (St. John's Wort) in Major Depressive Disorder: A Randomized Controlled Trial." *Journal of the American Medical Association* 287: 1807–1814.

Itil, T. M., et al. (1996). "Central Nervous System Effects of *Ginkgo biloba*, a Plant Extract." *American Journal of Therapeutics* 3: 63–73.

Jacobs, B. P., et al. (2005). "An Internet-Based Randomized, Placebo-Controlled Trial of Kava and Valerian for Anxiety and Insomnia." *Medicine* 84: 197–207.

Kasper, S., et al. (2006). "Superior Efficacy of St. John's Wort Extract WS 5570 Compared to Placebo in Patients with Major Depression: A Randomized, Double-Blind, Placebo-Controlled, Multi-Center Trial." *BMC Medicine* 23 (4):14.

Kim, H. L., et al. (1999). "St. John's Wort for Depression." *Journal of Nervous and Mental Disease* 187: 532–539.

Klier, C. M., et al. (2006). "St. John's Wort (*Hypericum perforatum*) and Breastfeeding: Plasma and Breast Milk Concentratons of Hyperforin for 5 Mothers and 2 Infants." *Journal of Clinical Psychiatry* 67: 305–309.

Kobak, K. A., et al. (2005a). "St. John's Wort Versus Placebo in Obsessive-Compulsive Disorder: Results from a Double-Blind Study." *International Clinical Psychopharmacology* 20: 299–304.

Kobak, K. A., et al. (2005b). "St. John's Wort Versus Placebo in Social Phobia: Results from a Placebo-Controlled Pilot Study." *Journal of Clinical Psychopharmacology* 25: 51–58.

LeBars, P. L., et al. (1997). "A Placebo-Controlled, Double-Blind, Randomized Trial of an Extract of *Ginkgo biloba* for Dementia." *Journal of the American Medical Association* 278: 1327–1332.

Lim, S. T., et al. (2007). "Effects of Kava Alkaloid, Pipermethystine, and Kavalactones on Oxidative Stress and Cytochroma P450 in F-344 Rats." *Toxicological Sciences,* published online Feb. 27.

Linde, K., and M. Berner (2000). "Commentary: Has Hypericum Found Its Place in Antidepressant Treatment?" *British Medical Journal* 319: 1534–1539.

Linde, K., et al. (1996). "St. John's Wort for Depression—An Overview and Meta-Analysis of Randomized Clinical Trials." *British Medical Journal* 313: 253–258.

Markowitz, J. S., et al. (2003). "Effect of St. John's Wort on Drug Metabolism by Induction of Cytochrome P450 3A4 Enzyme." *Journal of the American Medical Association* 290: 1500–1504.

Mix, J. A., and W. D. Crews (2002). "A Double-Blind, Placebo-Controlled, Randomized Trial of *Ginkgo biloba* Extract Egb 761 in a Sample of Cognitively Intact Older Adults: Neuropsychological Findings." *Human Psychopharmacology* 17: 267–277.

Moreno, R. A., et al. (2006). "*Hypericum perforatum* Versus Fluoxetine in the Treatment of Mild to Moderate Depression: A Randomized Double-Blind Trial in a Brazilian Sample." *Revista Brasileira Psiquiatria* 28: 29–32.

Obach, R. S. (2000). "Inhibition of Human Cytochrome P450 Enzymes by Constituents of St. John's Wort, an Herbal Preparation Used in the Treatment of Depression." *Journal of Pharmacology and Experimental Therapeutics* 294: 88–95.

O'Hara, M. A., et al. (1998). "A Review of Twelve Commonly Used Medicinal Herbs." *Archives of Family Medicine* 7: 523–536.

Oken, B. S., et al. (1998). "The Efficacy of *Ginkgo biloba* on Cognitive Function in Alzheimer's Disease." *Archives of Neurology* 55: 1409–1415.

PDR for Herbal Medicines, 3rd ed. (2004). Montvale, NJ: Medical Economics Company.

Perez, J., and J. F. Holmes. (2005). "Altered Mental Status and Ataxia Secondary to Acute Kava Ingestion." *Journal of Emergency Medicine* 28: 49–51.

Pfunder, A., et al. (2003). "Interaction of St. John's Wort with Low-Dose Oral Contraceptive Therapy: A Randomized Controlled Trial." *British Journal of Clinical Pharmacology* 56: 683–690.

Philipp, M., et al. (2000). "Hypericum Extract Versus Imipramine or Placebo in Patients with Moderate Depression: Randomized Multicentre Study of Treatment for Eight Weeks." *British Medical Journal* 319: 1534–1539.

Pies, R. (2000). "Adverse Neuropsychiatric Reactions to Herbal and Over-the-Counter 'Antidepressants.'" *Journal of Clinical Psychiatry* 61: 815–820.

Randlov, C., et al. (2006). "The Efficacy of St. John's Wort in Patients with Minor Depressive Symptoms or Dysthymia—A Double-Blind Placebo-Controlled Study." *Phytomedicine* 13: 215–221.

Sanchez-Reus, M. I., et al. (2007). "Standardized *Hypericum perforatum* Reduces Oxidative Stress and Increases Gene Expression of Antioxidant Enzymes on Rotenone-Exposed Rats." *Neuropharmacology* 52: 606–616.

Sheldon, R. C., et al. (2001). "Effectiveness of St. John's Wort in Major Depression: A Randomized Controlled Trial." *Journal of the American Medical Association* 285: 1978–1986.

Solomon, P. R., et al. (2002). "Ginkgo for Memory Enhancement: A Randomized Controlled Trial." *Journal of the American Medical Association* 288: 835–840.

van Dongen, M., et al. (2000). "The Efficacy of Ginkgo for Elderly People with Dementia and Age-Associated Memory Impairment: New Results of a Randomized Clinical Trial." *Journal of the American Geriatric Society* 48: 1183–1194.

Wong, A. H. C., et al. (1998). "Herbal Remedies in Psychiatric Practice." *Archives of General Psychiatry* 55: 1033–1044.

Wurglics, M., and M. Schubert-Zsilavecz (2006). *"Hypericum perforatum:* A 'Modern' Herbal Antidepressant: Pharmacokinetics of Active Ingredients." *Clinical Pharmacokinetics* 45: 449–468.

Chapter 20

Anabolic Steroids

Anabolic steroids and *anabolic-androgenic steroids* are familiar terms for synthetic substances related to the naturally occurring male sex hormone testosterone. Anabolic steroids have both muscle-building (anabolic) and masculinizing effects and are therefore used to enhance athletic performance and appearance (Bahrke and Yesalis, 2004). Illicit use is a common practice among adolescents and adults, both male and female, athletes and nonathletes. It may not be surprising that 55 percent of 27-year-old male and 10 percent of 24-year-old female bodybuilders use anabolic steroids, but it may be surprising that the prevalence of anabolic steroid injection in college athletics may be as high as 20 percent and anabolic steroid use in high schools has been estimated as high as 6 percent for males and 2.5 percent for females.[1] Elliott and coworkers (2007) reported that prior or ongoing anabolic steroid use was reported by 5.3 percent of female high school students— not confined to adolescent girls in competitive athletics—and was an indicator of a cluster of other health-related behaviors such as illicit drug use, early sexual activity, and daily feelings of hopelessness or sadness.

More than 1 million Americans have used anabolic steroids illicitly either to improve athletic performance or to improve personal appearance, and more than 50 percent are age 26 years or older; the prevalence of use of anabolic steroids is equal in both athletes and nonathletes. Lifetime use is 4.9 percent for males and 2.4 percent for females, and the numbers are likely to increase.

---

[1]Pallesen et al. (2006) in a Norwegian study recently quotes lifetime prevalence for use at 3.6 percent for males and 0.6 percent for females with mean age of about 17 years.

In both athletes and nonathletes, anabolic steroids promote increased muscle mass and enhance physical strength, endurance, physical appearance, and athletic performance. The use of the testosterone precursor *androstenedione* by baseball home run record holder Mark McGwire focused even more attention on steroid use by athletes. In the year 2003, the previously undetectable anabolic steroid *tetrahydrogestrinone* incited a furor in the media when high-profile professional athletes admitted to using this muscle-building, performance-enhancing drug. Subsequently, in March 2004 the U.S. Food and Drug Administration classified this drug as an illegal substance. Tests are now available to detect the drug in urine.

As well as illicit use, anabolic steroids have well-recognized uses in prescription medicine. Uses of these agents include the treatment of delayed puberty and the prevention of weight loss in renal failure patients undergoing hemodialysis and in males with HIV (AIDS)-related weight loss. Rabkin and coworkers (2000) studied the effects of weekly injections of testosterone in 70 males with symptomatic HIV illness. The majority reported improved libido and energy, improvements in mood, and increases in muscle mass. More recently, anabolic steroid use has been shown to positively affect mood, muscle mass, and strength, while reducing morbidity and mortality in older men.

Much of the controversy over anabolic steroid use, medical and illicit, involves the documented health risks associated with steroid use as well as the possibly unfair advantage a performance-enhancing drug offers the competitive athlete. Also, adolescent nonathletes who use steroids as cosmetic enhancers place themselves at risk for long-term health problems, and they also may suffer from serious body self-image problems that should be attended to (Kanayama et al., 2006).

Testosterone is the primary male sex hormone. Normally, the levels of testosterone in the body are tightly regulated by a negative feedback system involving the testes (where testosterone is synthesized), the hypothalamus, and the pituitary gland (Figure 20.1). When the plasma level of testosterone falls, cells in the hypothalamus (which has receptors sensitive to the circulating amount of testosterone) sense the decrease and begin producing a releasing factor called *gonadotropin-releasing factor* (GRF). GRF circulates in blood to the pituitary gland and stimulates the pituitary to produce and release *follicle-stimulating hormone* (FSH) and *luteinizing hormone* (LH). In turn, FSH and LH act on the testes to induce both spermatogenesis (the production of sperm) and synthesis and release of testosterone. (A similar process in the female regulates fertility.)

As testosterone levels in blood increase, the hypothalamus decreases its production of GRF, the pituitary decreases production of FSH and LH, the testes decrease production of testosterone and sperm, and the process repeats. Administering anabolic steroids overwhelms this system; abnormally high levels of steroids shut off production of GRF, FSH,

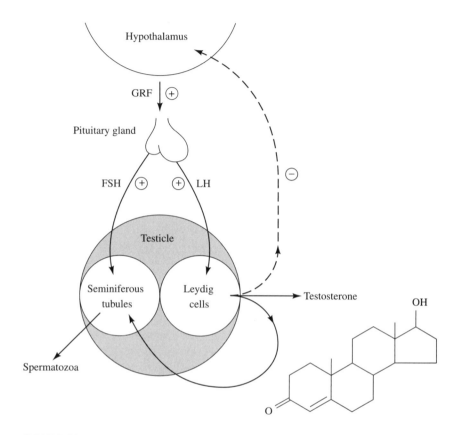

FIGURE 20.1 Hormonal regulation of male fertility. The brain (hypothalamus and pituitary gland) is involved in the control of fertility. However, fertility in the male is not subject to periodic cycling as it is in the female. The structure of naturally occurring testosterone is shown. GRF = gonadotropin-releasing factor; FSH = follicle-stimulating hormone; LH = luteinizing hormone. Solid arrows = stimulation; dashed arrows = inhibition.

LH, and testosterone and shut off the process of spermatogenesis. Therefore, anabolic steroids (1) block the normal process that regulates testosterone, male fertility, and spermatogenesis, (2) exert peripheral hormone actions to increase muscle mass and produce a more masculine appearance, and (3) exert central effects that increase aggression.

Mechanism of Action

The structures of testosterone and several synthetically produced anabolic steroids are illustrated in Figure 20.2. The structures of two related substances, androstenedione, thought to be a precursor to testosterone,

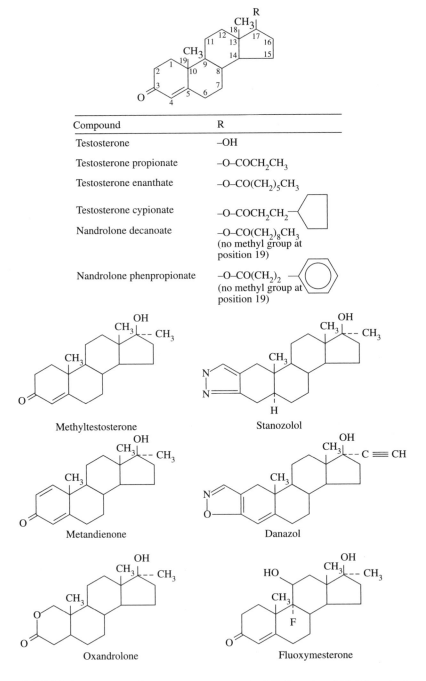

FIGURE 20.2 Structures of some common parenteral (*left*) and oral (*right*) anabolic-androgenic steroids. [From S. E. Lucas, "Current Perspectives on Anabolic-Androgenic Steroid Abuse," *Trends in Pharmacological Sciences* 14 (1993), p. 62.]

and dehydroepiandrosterone (DHEA), an androgen released by the adrenal glands, are not included in Figure 20.2 because, as stated by Yesalis and Bahrke (2002),

> Androstenedione is an anabolic-androgenic steroid used to increase blood testosterone levels for purposes of increasing strength, lean body mass, and sexual performance. However, there is no research indicating androstenedione or its related compounds significantly increase strength and/or lean body mass by increasing testosterone levels. . . . Dehydroepiandrosterone (DHEA) is a weak androgen also used to elevate testosterone levels. DHEA is also advertised as an anti-obesisty and anti-aging supplement capable of improving libido, vitality, and immunity levels. However, research demonstrates that DHEA supplementation does not increase serum testosterone concentrations or increase strength in men and it may have virilizing effects in women. (p. 246)

Bahrke and Yesalis reiterated this statement about DHEA in 2004: "DHEA supplementation does not increase serum testosterone concentrations or increase strength in men, and may actually increase testosterone levels in women, thus producing a virilizing effect" (p. 614).

All anabolic steroids differ from each other not so much in structure as in their resistance to metabolic degradation by liver enzymes. After oral administration, testosterone is effectively absorbed from the intestine. Following absorption, it is rapidly transported in the blood to the liver, where it is immediately metabolized. As a result, little testosterone reaches the systemic circulation. Administered by injection, some of this first-pass metabolism is blunted, and it is the metabolic product androstanolone that is most active as an anabolic substance. Structural modification of the testosterone molecule reduces this rapid metabolic breakdown and thus improves the effectiveness of both oral and intramuscular administration.

Not all anabolic steroids are illicit substances. Testosterone and some related steroids are used for specific therapeutic uses, including testosterone replacement in hypogonadal males, the treatment of certain blood anemias, and severe muscle loss following trauma, HIV, and renal dialysis. In malnourished males with severe pulmonary disease (chronic obstructive pulmonary disease), 27 weeks of oral androgen therapy increased lean body mass and muscle mass even though endurance capacity was not changed (Ferreira et al., 1998). Therefore, in states of malnutrition, anabolic steroid therapy increases muscle mass, an effect that hopefully reduces mortality and improves quality of life. In the United States, oxandrolone (Oxandrin) is FDA-approved as adjunctive therapy to promote weight gain after weight loss following extensive surgery, chronic infection, or severe trauma, for some patients who without definite pathophysiological reasons fail to gain or maintain normal weight to offset the protein catabolism associated with long-term use of corticosteroids, and for the relief of bone pain frequently accompanying osteoporosis. In these unusual situations, anabolic steroids are clinically indicated.

The mechanism of action of testosterone and the various anabolic steroids is quite well understood. Testosterone is synthesized principally in a specialized type of cell (the Leydig cell) of the testes (see Figure 20.1) under the influence of GRF released from the hypothalamus, which stimulates the synthesis and release of LH from the pituitary gland; LH acts on the Leydig cells to stimulate testosterone production.

Once in the bloodstream, testosterone (or an anabolic steroid) passes through the cell walls of its target tissues and attaches to steroid receptors in the cytoplasm of the cell (Figure 20.3). This hormone receptor complex is carried into the nucleus of the cell and attaches to the nuclear material (the DNA). A process of genetic transcription follows, and new messenger RNA is produced. Translation of this RNA results in the production of specific new proteins that leave the cell and mediate the biological functions of the hormone. Thus, the effects of anabolic steroids on target cells are mediated by intracellular receptors and the synthesis of new proteins. The increased levels of circulating testosterone (or anabolic steroid) exert a negative feedback effect on the hypothalamus, inhibiting further stimulation of testosterone release.

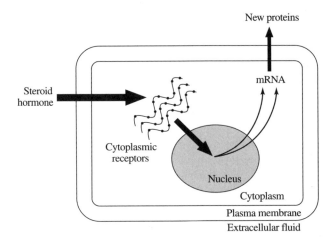

FIGURE 20.3 Mechanism of action of steroid hormones on cells. The hormone passes through the cell wall of its target tissue and binds to steroid receptors in the cytoplasm. The hormone-receptor complex moves into the nucleus and binds to sites on the chromatin, which is transcribed to give specific messenger RNA (mRNA). The mRNA is translated into specific new proteins that mediate the function of the hormone. [From S. E. Lucas, "Current Perspectives on Anabolic-Androgenic Steroid Abuse," *Trends in Pharmacological Sciences* 14 (1993), p. 63.]

Effects

People use anabolic steroids for many reasons. Steroids are used to improve athletic performance because they increase body muscle and reduce body fat. Both competitive bodybuilders and other athletes take advantage of this effect, using either the steroids themselves or their precursors. Nonathletes use anabolic steroids to achieve a desired shape when they have a skewed perception of their body habitus. These people do not recognize the breadth of the effects of these agents on the body, the brain, and behavior.

Effects on Athletic Performance

Because testosterone and anabolic steroids increase protein synthesis, they increase muscle mass and strength and produce a more masculine appearance. The assumption that this is what happens has been around for decades, but a 1996 report by Bhasin and coworkers was the first to demonstrate that supraphysiological doses of testosterone, with or without strength training, increase fat-free mass, muscle size, and strength in normal men. As shown in Figure 20.4, exercise alone or testosterone alone produced increases in strength, triceps and quadriceps size, and fat-free mass. The combination of testosterone and exercise produced additive increases. Despite these beneficial effects of testosterone, the authors concluded:

> Our results in no way justify the use of anabolic-androgenic steroids in sports, because, with extended use, such drugs have potentially serious adverse effects on the cardiovascular system, prostate, lipid metabolism, and insulin sensitivity. Moreover, the use of any performance-enhancing agent in sports raises serious ethical issues. (p. 6)

Hartgens and coworkers (2002) studied the increased muscle fiber size in experienced male athletes. Compared with controls, polydrug regimens of anabolic steroids at supratherapeutic dosages increased the size of deltoid muscle fibers in experienced strength-trained athletes, while a therapeutic dose of an anabolic steroid (nandrolone) did not exert any effect. In rats trained to lift weights, anabolic steroids enhance the rate of protein synthesis, enhance work capacity, and reduce fatigue (Tamaki et al., 2001).

Thus, anabolic steroids increase both the size and the strength of the athlete and so improve performance in athletic activities that require size, strength, and endurance. They have no positive effects on aerobic performance (Haupt, 1993). Therefore, athletes who depend on aerobic energy expenditure (for example, long-distance runners) benefit less from anabolic steroids than do athletes who depend on

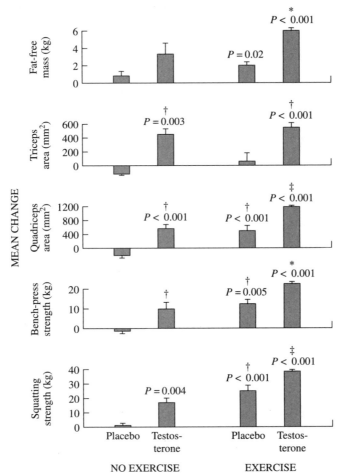

FIGURE 20.4 Changes from baseline in mean (±SE) fat-free mass, triceps, and quadriceps cross-sectional areas, and muscle strength in the bench press and squatting exercises over 10 weeks of treatment with testosterone. The *P* values shown are for the comparison between the change indicated and a change of zero. The asterisks indicate that $P < 0.05$ for the comparison between the change indicated and that in either no-exercise group; the daggers indicate $P < 0.05$ for the comparison between the change indicated and that in the group assigned to placebo with no exercise; the double daggers indicate that $P < 0.05$ for the comparison between the change indicated and the changes in all three other groups. [From Bhasin et al. (1996), p. 6.]

bulk size and short bursts of energy expenditure (football and baseball players and sprint runners, for example).

Anabolic steroids exert effects through anticatabolic, anabolic, and motivational effects on the athlete. Table 20.1 summarizes the constellation of effects and side effects. In the *anticatabolic effect*, the anabolic steroids block the action of natural cortisone, which normally functions

Table 20.1 Effects of anabolic-androgenic steroids

Positive effects
    Transient increase in muscular size and strength
    Treatment of catabolic states
        Trauma
        Surgery
Adverse Effects
    Cardiovascular
        Increase in cardiac risk factors
        Hypertension
        Altered lipoprotein fractions
        Increase in LDL/HDL ratio
        Reported strokes/myocardial infarctions
    Hepatic effects associated with oral compounds
        Elevated liver enzymes
        Peliosis hepatis (greater than 6 months' use)
        Liver tumors
            Benign
            Malignant (greater than 24 months' use)
    Reproductive system effects
        In males
            Decreased testosterone production
                Abnormal spermatogenesis
                Transient infertility
                Testicular atrophy
        In females
            Altered menstruation
    Endocrine effects
        Decreased thyroid function
    Immunological effects
        Decreased immunoglobulins IgM/IgA/IgC
    Musculoskeletal effects
        Premature closure of bony growth centers
        Tendon degeneration
            Increased risk of tendon tears
    Cosmetic
        In males
            Gynecomastia
            Testicular atrophy
            Acne
            Acceleration of male-pattern baldness
        In females
            Clitoral enlargement
            Acne
            Increased facial/body hair
            Coarsening of the skin
            Male-pattern baldness
            Deepened voice
    Psychological
        Risk of habituation
        Severe mood swings
        Aggressive tendencies
        Psychotic episodes
        Depression
        Reports of suicide
    Legislation
        Classified as Schedule III controlled substance

From Haupt (1993), p. 471.

to increase energy stores during periods of stress and training. Cortisone makes energy stores available by breaking down proteins into their constituent amino acids. Carried to excess, muscle wasting can occur. This action is blocked by the anabolic steroids. The anticatabolic action may be the major mechanism by which these drugs increase body mass.

The *anabolic effects* follow both the synthesis of new protein in muscle cells and steroid-induced release of endogenous growth hormone. However, the doses commonly used by athletes are 10 to 200 times the therapeutic dosage for testosterone deficiency. These doses often stack, or pyramid, several drugs, even combining oral and injectable substances, over several weeks (Galloway, 1997).

In the female athlete, anabolic steroids exert the same anabolic and anticatabolic effects found in male athletes. However, these drugs also induce in females masculinizing and related effects, including increases in facial and body hair, lowered voice, enlarged clitoris, coarser skin, and menstrual cycle cessation or irregularity. Cessation of steroid use results in a variable and often incomplete reversal of the altered functions. Tuiten and colleagues (2000) administered sublingual testosterone to eight healthy females and evaluated its effects on sexual arousal. Testosterone achieved maximal plasma levels in 15 minutes, returning to baseline levels by 90 minutes. At about 4.5 hours, significant increases in arousal and genital responsiveness occurred. Alterations in "central" hormonal mechanisms were postulated to account for the discrepancy between plasma levels and physiological responses.

Effects on Physical Appearance

Anabolic steroids are widely used (and abused) by young male (usually noncompetitive) athletes who take them to develop the muscular physique considered fashionable. As many as 250,000 to 500,000 young adult males may take steroids. Regardless of the exact number, a significant number of teenagers and young adults, primarily male, use supraphysiological doses of anabolic steroids to give them more muscle strength and a more powerful, masculine appearance. Unlike competitive athletes who often choose to terminate drug use when competition ends, nonathlete youths may continue to take steroids to maintain the cosmetic effect. As stated by Schwerin and coworkers (1996):

> Physique and physical appearance are ever important in how people are viewed in their social environment. With these come the spoils: social acceptance, admiration, and opportunity. To a certain extent, an attractive physique is related to enhanced self-esteem and perceived social competence. . . . Sometimes the drive reaches an unhealthy extreme . . . taking the form of anorexia, bulimia, and anabolic steroid use. (p. 1)

Furthermore,

> Anabolic steroid users present an appearance of healthfulness,
> strength, "sex appeal," and physical attractiveness. Other illicit drugs
> do not present such an image of healthfulness. . . . It may be this con-
> tradiction of increased steroid use leading to increased appearance of
> healthfulness and physical attractiveness which may allow the seri-
> ousness of steroid use to remain underappreciated. . . . Anabolic
> steroids are the only addictive substance over the short to middle
> term that enhances a user's physical appearance and whose purpose
> is to allow the user to work harder and longer (though stimulants
> share the latter characteristic). (pp. 6–7)

Effects in Middle-Aged and Elderly Males

Recently, attention has been focused on aging males who use anabolic steroids in an attempt to maintain muscle mass, reduce fat tissue, and delay aging. This group includes aging actors as well as
men who utilize specialized medical clinics to combine steroid use
with exercise and weight training. Testosterone levels and muscle
mass do decline with age, with loss of muscle mass and absolute
numbers of muscle fibers, a doubling of fat mass, and a decrease in
bone mineral density by 0.3 percent per year after age 35 (Moretti et
al., 2005). Testosterone can inhibit the accumulation of fat tissue,
restore the lost muscle mass, and maintain bone mineral density in
elderly men.

Bashin and coworkers (2005) demonstrated that healthy men
aged 60 to 75 with normal serum testosterone levels are as responsive to exogenous testosterone as are younger men (Figure 20.5),
although high doses were associated with a high frequency of adverse side effects, such as dangerously increased levels of hemoglo-
bin (greater than 54 percent), leg edema, kidney problems, and
prostate cancer.

Jankowska and coworkers (2006) studied the levels of testosterone, DHEA, and an insulinlike growth factor in elderly men with
moderate to severe chronic heart failure. They noted that age-
related decline of these three circulating anabolic hormones is associated with increased morbidity and mortality (Figure 20.6). Three-year
survival rates in these patients were 83 percent in those with no hormone deficiencies, 74 percent in those with one hormone deficiency,
and 55 percent and 27 percent, respectively, for men with two or
three hormone deficiencies. Malkin and coworkers (2006) determined that testosterone replacement in men with chronic heart failure resulted in improved health and functional capacity. Therefore,
it appears that in middle-aged and elderly male patients with physical

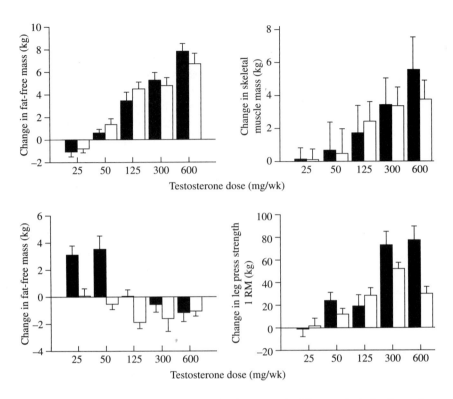

FIGURE 20.5 Changes from baseline in fat-free mass (in kilograms), skeletal muscle mass (in kilograms), total fat mass (in kilograms), and leg press strength (measured as the one-repetition maximum) following weekly intramuscular doses of testosterone enanthate (Delatestryl) at doses of 25, 50, 125, 300, and 600 milligrams per injection. Open bars = results from healthy young men ages 18–35 years. Dark bars = results from healthy older men ages 60–75 years. Results demonstrate increased fat-free mass, increased skeletal muscle mass, increased strength, and reduced total body fat mass in both young and older men. The 300- and 600-milligram doses are supraphysiological and the best balance between positive improvements and adverse effects was achieved at the dosage of 125 milligrams per week. [From S. Bhasin et al. (2005), Figure 4.]

dysfunction associated with chronic illness or aging, testosterone or other anabolic hormones can induce meaningful improvements in physical function and patient-important outcomes (Bhasin et al., 2006). Whether these data should be applied to normally functioning aging males through treatment in "antiaging" clinics is currently the subject of much debate. Positive outcomes may be offset by the side effects to be discussed next, including the possibility of developing steroid-induced cancers and personality changes. Of

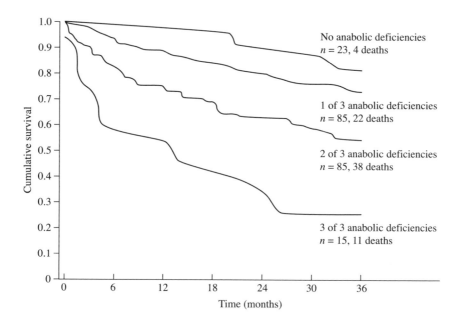

FIGURE 20.6 Graded relationship between the number of endocrine impairments and age-related survival in men (mean age 63 years) with chronic heart failure. All deaths over the 3-year period were cardiovascular in causation (related to the chronic heart failure). See the text for details. [From Jankowska et al. (2006), Figure 3.]

additional consideration in the elderly taking these substances are increases in hematocrit and in the possibility of developing prostate cancer.

Side Effects

Controversies in professional sports such as baseball, football, cycling, and wrestling clearly demonstrate that not only is the use of anabolic steroids beneficial in promoting muscle growth, it also entails significant risks. The risks include aggressive behaviors, cancers, gonadal atrophy, and early onset of atherosclerosis.

Endocrine Effects

Males taking anabolic steroids experience a hypogonadal state, which is characterized by atrophy of the testicles, impaired production of sperm, and infertility, causing reduced libido and impotence (Torres-Calleja et al., 2001). In addition, gynecomastia (enlargement of the breasts in males) may occur and may require surgical treatment (Babigian and Silverman, 2001). In females, puberty is delayed and estrous cyclicity is adversely affected. These effects are usually reversible within a few months after cessation of drug use.

Cardiovascular Effects

Adverse effects of anabolic steroids on the cardiovascular system have been of concern, and reports of fatal myocardial infarctions (heart attacks) occurring in users of anabolic steroids implicate arteriosclerosis-induced coronary artery disease as a cause of death. Thus, analysis of the potential correlation between anabolic steroids and arteriosclerosis is important. The effect of these steroids on blood cholesterol as a predisposing factor to atherosclerotic coronary artery disease must be considered. Cholesterol is of two types: "bad" cholesterol (low-density lipoprotein cholesterol, or LDL) and "good" cholesterol (high-density lipoprotein cholesterol, or HDL). Decreasing HDL and increasing LDL are strongly correlated with an increased risk of coronary artery disease.

All anabolic steroids induce a reduction in serum HDL cholesterol and an elevation in LDL cholesterol. This effect suggests that people taking these drugs are at greater risk of developing atheromatous plaques within arteries, which places them at increased risk of coronary artery disease. This condition can be expressed as myocardial infarctions, thromboembolic disease (blood clots and emboli), strokes, and hypertension. The actual risk of cardiovascular disease is unknown, largely because of the young age of users, their relatively lean or muscular physiques, and the intermittent pattern of drug use. Once young users become adults, it can be determined whether using anabolic steroids during their earlier years harmed them. Hartgens and coworkers (2002), Heriex and Kuipers (2003), and Karila and coworkers (2003) review the cardiovascular effects of the anabolic steroids and propose several models to explain their toxicity, including new information on drug-induced hypertrophy of the left ventricular muscle. Sudden cardiac deaths during abuse of anabolic steroids is being increasingly reported (Fineschi et al., 2007).

Effects on the Liver

The use of oral anabolic steroid preparations has been associated with a risk of liver disorders, especially jaundice and tumors. Increases in the blood levels of liver enzymes, indicative of possible liver dysfunction, are quite common among steroid users. Such adverse effects appear to resolve within a year after cessation of drug use. Hepatitis is also common, perhaps as a result of reusing needles (Parkinson and Evans, 2006). In addition, several dozen cases of liver carcinomas of unusual types have been reported. The incidence of developing these potentially fatal carcinomas is estimated to be 1 to 3 percent within two to eight years of exposure to drugs.

Psychological Effects

Anabolic steroids are centrally acting drugs, involved in the regulation of sexuality, aggression, cognition, emotion, and personality. Thus, drug-induced increases in aggression, competitiveness, and combativeness can be predicted in people who use large doses of these drugs. It is now well established that areas of the brain that influence mood and judgment contain steroid receptors and that sharp fluctuations in the levels of steroid hormones have important psychological effects.

The *motivational* and *behavioral effects* are profound: athletes taking anabolic steroids often develop very aggressive personalities, a condition nicknamed "roid rage." For some sports, such as football, the enhancement of combativeness can be desirable. But for most purposes, the adverse behavioral effects associated with anabolic steroids are detrimental. These effects include anger, violent feelings, irritability, forgetfulness, and distractibility (Daly et al., 2003). Clearly, users of anabolic steroids tend to be less in control of their aggression, and increases in aggression are reported by 60 percent of steroid users. However, it is unclear whether steroid use causes aggression or whether aggressive people are attracted to steroid use. The prevalence of extreme cases of violence and behavioral disorders seems to be low (National Institute on Drug Abuse, 2003).

Pope and colleagues (2000) conducted a six-week trial of testosterone in 56 males, increasing the weekly dose to 600 milligrams. Their goal was to assess drug effects on mood and aggression. Doses of up to 300 milligrams per week produced few psychiatric effects; doses of 500 to 600 milligrams per week produced prominent effects in some of the men. Under these "laboratory" conditions, 84 percent exhibited minimal psychiatric effects, 12 percent became mildly hypomanic, and 4 percent became markedly hypomanic or manic. Two participants withdrew when they became "alarmingly" hypomanic and aggressive. From these results it appears that in small and unpredictable numbers of users, high doses of anabolic steroids may produce marked signs of mania and/or aggression. This report is perhaps the first to quantify these effects and provide statistics on the possible numbers of users who might be expected to display these symptoms. Why some of the men were markedly and dangerously affected while the majority were not is unknown.

Kanayama and coworkers (2003) interviewed 223 male substance abusers admitted to a substance abuse program. Twenty-nine men (13 percent) reported prior steroid use (only 4 of these men were identified on the physicians' referral forms). Among 88 men who listed opioids as their drug of choice, 22 (25 percent) acknowledged steroid use. Only 7 of the remaining 135 men in the program admitted to steroid use. Many of the opioid-dependent men (who were also steroid abusers) received their opioids from the same person who sold them the injectable steroids. Four of the 29 men with steroid abuse histories (17 percent) reported severe aggressiveness or violence during their periods of steroid use.

Pagonis and coworkers (2006) studied 320 athletes, 50 percent of whom were active users of anabolic steroids. In this well-controlled, 13-month study, extent of steroid use was tightly correlated with increases in all psychometric measures of hostility. As early as 1993, Haupt had stated:

> Athletes taking anabolic steroids suffer some degree of personality change that may range from simple mood swings to a psychosis requiring hospitalization for treatment. A Jekyll-and-Hyde personality is common, where even the slightest provocation can cause an exaggerated, violent, and often uncontrolled response. The users of anabolic steroids often suffer disturbed personality relationships that may include separations from family and friends and even divorce. Arrest records are not uncommon. Fortunately these psychological effects are reversible when the steroids are discontinued, but the social scars may be permanent, (p. 470)

Klotz and coworkers (2006, 2007) updated these earlier findings of steroid-induced aggression and concluded that use of anabolic steroids in certain predisposed people might increase the commission of violent crimes, especially if the use of the steroids is combined with the use of other illicit substances. Galloway (1997) added that about 50 percent of interviewed weightlifters experienced depression and an even higher percentage experienced paranoid thoughts and some psychotic behaviors, experiences consistent with the studies discussed earlier.

Physical Dependence

Physical dependence is characterized by withdrawal symptoms when a drug is removed. Withdrawal from large doses of anabolic steroids can be accompanied by moderate to severe psychological depression, fatigue, restlessness, insomnia, loss of appetite, and decreased libido. Other withdrawal symptoms that have been reported include drug craving, headache, dissatisfaction with body image, and suicidal ideation (Brower, 2002). Despite these observations, no defined psychiatric withdrawal syndrome has been described; withdrawal psychosis or bipolar illness has not been reported, although depression is commonplace.

Abuse and Treatment

The use of anabolic steroids for athletic or cosmetic purposes constitutes drug abuse because abuse persists despite recognized, unavoidable side effects and negative consequences for the physical and psychological health of the user. The mechanisms responsible for dependence are largely unknown and may be psychological and/or physiological.

Testosterone is the most potent hormonal determinant of physical and behavioral masculinization. It has been implicated for decades in the stimulation of sexual behavior, as well as in the activation of dominance and aggressive behaviors in male primates, including humans. The attraction to the use of supraphysiological doses of testosterone derivatives is strong, with significant numbers of young people succumbing to their attractiveness.

As with all other psychoactive drugs, treatment of steroid dependence requires drug abstinence, treatment of any signs of withdrawal, and maintenance of abstinence. Behavioral and cognitive approaches are possible treatment tools (Kanayama et al., 2006). Supportive therapy, including reassurance, education, and counseling, remains the mainstay of treatment. Antidepressants may be indicated when dependency is complicated by major depression. A physician trained in endocrinology can best prescribe other therapies for hormonal alterations.

One societal response to the use of anabolic steroids has been to ban their use in athletics and institute antidoping testing procedures (Green, 2006). Since the beginning of organized competition, athletes have tried to gain every possible advantage over their competitors. Sometimes this competitive edge is gained fairly by training harder or developing new and improved methods. Sometimes, however, athletes seek an advantage by using substances that affect the body in ways that can improve athletic performance.

The National Collegiate Athletic Association (NCAA) and the United States Olympic Committee (USOC) have declared the use of anabolic steroids illegal, not only because of their ability to artificially increase muscle mass and competitiveness but also because of their serious and sometimes permanent side effects. As early as 1996, Olivier argued in favor of the ban, stating that these drugs not only harm the user but create a climate of subtle coercion toward their use by others, as well as placing others (for example, partners of steroid users) at risk of violence from users while they are on the drug. Olivier concluded:

> I have argued that prohibition of harmful practices is justified by potential harm to others (rather than just to one's self). One must bear in mind the powerful effects of subtle coercion and influence and the consequent limitations placed on choice. So, on the grounds that it is wrong to harm others or to coerce them into potentially harmful situations,

> this paper takes issue with sports libertarians who claim that banning performance-enhancing substances is an unjustified paternalistic action that violates the principle of autonomy. (p. S45)

Education has to be the mainstay of anabolic steroid abuse prevention, especially since the drugs initially promote a healthier, masculine appearance as well as increasing muscle mass and strength. But simply telling young people about the harmful effects of steroids is not enough; in fact scare tactics are not only ineffective but can be counterproductive, since young people know about professional athletes who have used them successfully. Some programs that have had demonstrable success use a combination of approaches.

Goldberg and coworkers (1996, 2000), for example, first designed and tested a team-based, educational interventional program to reduce the intent of male adolescent athletes to use steroids. Termed the Adolescents Training and Learning to Avoid Steroids (ATLAS) program, it was initially conducted with 702 football players in 31 high schools. Seven weekly classroom sessions, seven weekly weight room sessions, and one evening parent session led to increased understanding of anabolic steroid effects, greater belief in personal vulnerability to the adverse consequences of steroids, improved drug refusal skills, less belief in steroid-promoting media messages, increased belief in the team as an information source, improved perception of athletic abilities and strength-training self-efficacy, improved nutritional and exercise behaviors, and reduced intentions to use steroids.

In 2004, the same researchers (Elliot et al., 2004, 2006) developed and evaluated a similar program, the Athletes Targeting Healthy Exercise and Nutrition Alternatives (ATHENA), to prevent young female high school athletes from disordered eating and body-shaping drug use. This intervention is a scripted, coach-facilitated, peer-led, eight-session program incorporated into a team's usual training activities. The ATHENA program has reduced ongoing and new use of diet pills and body-shaping substance use (amphetamines, anabolic steroids, and sport supplements). As a result of these programs, the Anabolic Steroid Control Act of 2004 states that monetary grants will be available to combat steroid abuse. The bill calls for $15 million per year from 2005 to 2010 to be spent on anabolic steroid prevention with preference given to programs based on the ATLAS and ATHENA models. The ATHENA research found that twice as many female nonathletes as female athletes used steroids; the researchers attributed this finding to a desire to look thin yet fit. This observation deserves additional research and treatment recommendations.

The abuse of anabolic steroids by athletes, bodybuilders, and body-conscious people poses a special challenge to society. Perhaps the desire of adolescents and young adults to take steroids has been fostered largely by our societal fixations on winning and physical appearance. Thus, successful intervention must go beyond education, counseling, law enforcement, and drug testing to changing the social environment that subtly encourages steroid abuse.

Professional sports have certainly fostered the notion that steroid use may be acceptable as long as the goal is to win athletic competitions. Perhaps most notorious is major league baseball, which only in 2004 began testing for anabolic steroid use (many baseball players have acknowledged steroid use); however, penalties are less than stringent and allow for some positive tests. Testing in professional basketball is more stringent (perhaps because anabolic steroids are of less use in athletes who need prolonged endurance). Professional football bans steroid use. Professional hockey does not have a mandatory drug-testing policy and tests only players already in the league's substance abuse aftercare program. Players who seek help the first time are neither exposed nor suspended. As long as professional athletics "allows" the abuse of anabolic steroids, the example will pass to both fans and younger athletes.

Finally, the use/abuse of anabolic steroids to "delay aging" in middle-aged males is likely to increase and may develop into an interesting public debate.

STUDY QUESTIONS

1. What are androgenic-anabolic steroids?

2. How do androgenic-anabolic steroids affect body functions?

3. How do steroids increase muscle mass?

4. Describe the similarities and differences between dependence on anabolic steroids and dependence on the more traditional drugs of abuse.

5. Describe the two groups of people who are the most frequent users of anabolic steroids. How are they similar? How are they different?

6. Describe the anticatabolic, anabolic, and motivational effects of anabolic steroids.

7. What are the side effects associated with use of anabolic steroids?

8. What are the psychological effects associated with use of anabolic steroids?

9. How might the misuse of anabolic steroids be prevented?

WEB SITES FOR ADDITIONAL INFORMATION ON ANABOLIC STEROIDS

www.steroidabuse.org

www.nida.nih.gov/ResearchReports/Steroids/AnabolicSteroids.html

www.steroidabuse.gov

www.ohsu.edu.edu/hpsm/atlas.html

www.ohsu.edu.edu/hpsm/athena.html

www.cenegenics.com

REFERENCES

Babigian, A., and R. T. Silverman (2001). "Management of Gynecomastia Due to Use of Anabolic Steroids in Bodybuilders." *Plastic and Reconstructive Surgery* 107: 240–242.

Bahrke, M. S., and C.E. Yesalis (2004). "Abuse of Anabolic Androgenic Steroids and Related Substances in Sport and Exercise." *Current Opinions in Pharmacology* 4: 614–620.

Bhasin, S., et al. (1996). "The Effects of Supraphysiologic Doses of Testosterone on Muscle Size and Strength in Normal Men." *New England Journal of Medicine* 335: 1–7.

Bhasin, S., et al. (2005). "Older Men Are as Responsive as Young Men to the Anabolic Effects of Graded Doses of Testosterone on the Skeletal Muscle." *Journal of Clinical Endocrinology & Metabolism* 90: 678–688.

Bhasin, S., et al. (2006). "Drug Insight: Testosterone and Selective Androgen Receptor Modulators as Anabolic Therapies for Chronic Illness and Aging." *Nature Clinical Practice Endocrinology & Metabolism* 2: 146–159.

Brower, K. J. (2002). "Anabolic Steroid Abuse and Dependence." *Current Psychiatry Reports* 4: 377–387.

Daly, R. C., et al. (2003). "Neuroendocrine and Behavioral Effects of High-Dose Anabolic Steroid Administration in Male Normal Volunteers." *Psychoneuroendocrinology* 28: 317–331.

Elliot, D. L., et al. (2004). "Preventing Substance Use and Disordered Eating: Initial Outcomes of the ATHENA (Athletes Targeting Healthy Exercise and Nutrition Alternatives) Program." *Archives of Pediatrics & Adolescent Medicine* 158: 1043–1049.

Elliot, D. L., et al. (2006). "Definition and Outcome of a Curriculum to Prevent Disordered Eating and Body-Shaping Drug Use." *Journal of School Health* 76: 67–73.

Elliot, D. L., et al. (2007). "Cross-Sectional Study of Female Students Reporting Anabolic Steroid Use." *Archives of Pediatrics & Adolescent Medicine* 161: 572–577.

Ferreira, I. M., et al. (1998). "The Influence of Six Months of Oral Anabolic Steroids on Body Mass and Respiratory Muscles in Undernourished COPD Patients." *Chest* 114: 19–28.

Fineschi, V., et al. (2007). "Sudden Cardiac Death During Anabolic Steroid Abuse: An Internet Survey of Drug Utilization." *International Journal of Legal Medicine* 121: 48–53.

Galloway, G. P. (1997). "Anabolic Steroids." In J. H. Lowinson, P. Ruiz, R. B. Millman, and J. G. Langrod, eds., *Substance Abuse: A Comprehensive Textbook*, 3rd ed. (pp. 380–395). Baltimore: Williams & Wilkins.

Goldberg, L., et al. (1996). "Effects of a Multidimensional Anabolic Steroid Prevention Intervention: The Adolescents Training and Learning to Avoid Steroids (ATLAS) Program." *Journal of the American Medical Association* 276: 1555–1562.

Goldberg, L., et al. (2000). "The Adolescents Training and Learning to Avoid Steroids Program: Preventing Drug Use and Promoting Health Behaviors." *Archives of Pediatrics & Adolescent Medicine* 154: 332–338.

Green, G. A. (2006). "Doping Control for the Team Physician: A Review of Drug Testing Procedures." *American Journal of Sports Medicine* 34: 1690–1698.

Hartgens, F., et al. (2002). "Misuse of Androgenic-Anabolic Steroids and Human Deltoid Muscle Fibers: Differences Between Polydrug Regimens and Single Drug Administration." *European Journal of Applied Physiology* 86: 233–239.

Haupt, H. A. (1993). "Anabolic Steroids and Growth Hormone." *American Journal of Sports Medicine* 21: 468–474.

Heriex, A., and H. Kuipers (2003). "Prospective Echocardiographic Assessment of Androgenic-Anabolic Steroids: Effects on Cardiac Structure and Function in Strength Athletes." *International Journal of Sports Medicine* 24: 344–351.

Jankowska, E. A., et al. (2006). "Anabolic Deficiency in Men with Chronic Heart Failure: Prevalence and Detrimental Impact on Survival." *Circulation* 114: 1829–1837.

Kanayama, G., et al. (2003). "Past Anabolic-Androgenic Steroid Use Among Men Admitted for Substance Abuse Treatment: An Underrecognized Problem?" *Journal of Clinical Psychiatry* 64: 156–160.

Kanayama, G., et al. (2006). "Body Images and Attitudes Toward Male Roles in Anabolic-Androgenic Steroid Users." *American Journal of Psychiatry* 163: 697–703.

Karila, T. A., et al. (2003). "Anabolic Androgenic Steroids Produce Dose-Dependent Increase in Left Ventricular Mass in Power Athletes, and This Effect Is Potentiated by Concomitant Use of Growth Hormone." *International Journal of Sports Medicine* 24: 337–343.

Klotz, F., et al. (2006). "Criminality Among Individuals Testing Positive for the Presence of Anabolic Androgenic Steroids." *Archives of General Psychiatry* 63: 1274–1279.

Klotz, F., et al. (2007). "Violent Crime and Substance Abuse: A Medico-Legal Comparison Between Deceased Users of Anabolic Androgenic Steroids and Abusers of Illicit Drugs." *Forensic Science International* 166: in press.

Malkin, C. J., et al. (2006). "Testosterone Therapy in Men with Moderate Severity Heart Failure: A Double-Blind, Randomized, Placebo-Controlled Trial." *European Heart Journal* 27: 57–64.

Moretti, C., et al. (2005). "Androgens and Body Composition in the Aging Male." *Journal of Endocrinological Investigation* 28 (3 Supplement): S56–S64.

National Institute on Drug Abuse (2003). "Anabolic Steroid Abuse." Research Report Series. NIH publication 00–3721.

Olivier, S. (1996). "Drugs in Sport: Justifying Paternalism on the Grounds of Harm." *American Journal of Sports Medicine* 24: S43–S45.

Pagonis, T. A., et al. (2006). "Psychiatric Side Effects Induced by Supraphysiological Doses of Combinations of Anabolic Steroids Correlate to the Severity of Abuse." *European Psychiatry* 21: 551–562.

Pallesen, S., et al. (2006). "Anabolic Steroid Use in High School Students." *Substance Use and Misuse* 41: 1705–1717.

Parkinson, A. B., and N. A. Evans (2006). "Anabolic Androgenic Steroids: A Survey of 500 Users." *Medicine & Science in Sports & Exercise* 34: 644–651.

Pope, H. C., et al. (2000). "Effects of Supraphysiologic Doses of Testosterone on Mood and Aggression in Normal Men: A Randomized Controlled Trial." *Archives of General Psychiatry* 57: 133–140.

Rabkin, J. G., et al. (2000). "A Double-Blind, Placebo-Controlled Trial of Testosterone Therapy for HIV-Positive Men with Hypogonadal Symptoms." *Archives of General Psychiatry* 57: 141–147.

Schwerin, M. J., et al. (1996). "Social Physique Anxiety, Body Esteem, and Social Anxiety in Bodybuilders and Self-Reported Anabolic Steroid Users." *Addictive Behaviors* 21: 1–8.

Tamaki, T., et al. (2001). "Anabolic Steroids Increase Exercise Tolerance." *American Journal of Physiology—Endocrinology and Metabolism* 280: E973–E981.

Torres-Calleja, J., et al. (2001). "Effect of Androgenic Anabolic Steroids on Sperm Quality and Serum Hormone Levels in Adult Male Body Builders." *Life Sciences* 68: 1769–1774.

Tuiten, A., et al. (2000). "Time Course of Effects of Testosterone Administration on Sexual Arousal in Women." *Archives of General Psychiatry* 57: 149–153.

Yesalis, C. E., and M. S. Bahrke (2002). "Anabolic-Androgenic Steroids and Related Substances." *Current Sports Medicine Report* 1: 246–252.

Chapter 21

Topics in Drug Abuse

Drug abuse has been a societal problem for thousands of years, ever since grain was fermented (ethyl alcohol) and natural substances were found that produced euphoria (cocaine), relieved pain (morphine), or produced altered states of consciousness for divination (psilocybin, mescaline). As history suggests, as long as these drugs persist in society (and they will!), their use will be associated with compulsive use and abuse as well as with dependency and addiction. This chapter reviews the mechanisms responsible for producing compulsive drug abuse and dependency. It also reviews the literature on the current concepts of treatment of dependency and abuse. The individual drugs discussed in their own chapters are brought together in a chapter devoted to general concepts that apply to all drugs of abuse.

Historical and Current Perspectives

In all of recorded history, every society has used drugs to produce alterations in mood, thought, feeling, or behavior or to provide temporary alterations in reality. Moreover, some people have always digressed from social custom with respect to the time, the amount, and the situation in which drugs are used. Abuse of psychoactive drugs has always produced problems for the person taking the drug, for those in direct contact with the user, and for society at large.

Alcohol is the classic psychoactive drug used throughout history primarily for recreational purposes, but it is not the only such agent. Naturally occurring substances are used to alleviate anxiety, produce relaxation, provide relief from boredom, communicate with the gods, alleviate pain, and/or increase strength or work tolerance. In most cultures, only very few naturally occurring substances have been available and their use has been closely monitored, so just a relatively small minority of people have abused them. Today, patterns of abuse differ considerably from traditional patterns:

- Virtually all the naturally occurring psychoactive and psychedelic drugs ever identified are available at one time (now) and in one culture (ours).

- In most cases, the pharmacologically active ingredient in each natural product has been isolated, identified, often synthesized, and then made available to those who desire it.

- Organic chemistry has made possible synthetic derivatives of naturally occurring drugs. In many cases, the synthetic derivatives magnify the psychoactive potency of the natural substance 100 times or more.

- Users have adopted new methods of drug delivery, starting with the invention of the hypodermic syringe in the 1860s, and new drugs, the most recent of which are crack cocaine, ice methamphetamine, and "designer" derivatives of both fentanyl and mescaline. These developments have markedly increased the delivered dose, decreased the time to onset of drug action, and increased both the potency and the toxicity of these agents compared with their naturally occurring counterparts.

As in past decades, caffeine, nicotine, and ethyl alcohol are the addictive drugs used by the vast majority of people. Caffeine use is nearly universal; 90 percent of Americans over the age of 11 use the drug at least once weekly. Thankfully, little harm seems to follow. Nicotine and alcohol are the next most widely used and abused addictive drugs, and their economic toll on lives, productivity, and health are enormous. In fact, legitimate manufacturers of legal or prescription substances find ways to make them more concentrated and powerful, from increasing the nicotine content in cigarettes and increasing the amount of caffeine in energy drinks to popularizing alcoholic beverages of high alcohol content and making stronger opioid analgesic products without limiting the potential for misuse. The probability that an American living today has a drug abuse or dependence disorder is 36 percent for nicotine, 14 percent for alcohol, and 4 percent for marijuana (now the most commonly used illicit drug).

Extent of the Drug Problem

The total yearly economic costs of substance abuse are estimated at $427 billion: alcohol abuse makes up $175 billion of this amount, substance abuse $114 billion, and cigarette smoking $138 billion. A 2002 national survey on drug use and health (U.S. Department of Health and Human Services, 2003) noted that 22 million Americans suffered from dependence on or abuse of drugs, alcohol, or both. There were 19.5 million Americans (8.3 percent of the population age 12 or older) who currently used drugs, 54 million who participated in binge drinking in the previous 30 days, and 15.9 million who were heavy drinkers. Almost 8 million people (3.3 percent of the total population age 12 or older) needed treatment for a diagnosable drug problem, and 18.6 million (7.9 percent of the population age 12 or older) needed treatment for a serious alcohol problem. Yet only 1.4 million people received specialized substance abuse treatment for an illicit drug problem and 1.5 million received treatment for an alcohol problem. Over 94 percent of people with substance abuse disorders who do not receive treatment do not believe they needed treatment.

The 2002 Department of Health and Human Services survey reported that marijuana was the most commonly used illicit drug. Over 14 million Americans, one-third of whom used it on 20 or more days in the previous month, smoked it. There was a continuing decline in the yearly number of adolescents initiating use of marijuana, with 1.7 million new users in youth ages 12 to 17 years in the year 2002. At any given time in 2002, about 2 million people used cocaine, of whom "hard core" crack cocaine users numbered over 500,000. Hallucinogens were used by 1.2 million people, half of them users of ecstasy. There were about 160,000 current heroin users. Among young adults ages 18 to 26 years, the use of crystal methamphetamine is increasing (Iritani et al., 2007).

In a 2006 survey of eighth-, tenth-, and twelfth-grade students, past month use of illicit drugs had dropped from 19 percent to 15 percent over a five-year period (U.S. Department of Health and Human Services, 2006). By contrast, abuse of prescription opioid narcotics had markedly increased. Over all age groups, prescription drug abuse is about to exceed the use of street substances such as heroin, cocaine, and ecstasy. The number of Americans abusing prescription drugs nearly doubled, from 7.8 million people in 1992 to 15.1 million in 2003. Among prescription drugs, the opioids oxycodone (OxyContin) and hydrocodone (Vicodin or generic equivalents) were widely used by college students in 2005. An estimated 1.9 million people ages 12 or older had used the painkiller OxyContin at least once.

Substance abuse is related to age. Current illicit drug use is highest among people ages 18 to 25 years, 20 percent of whom use such drugs. Second-highest users are people ages 12 to 17; 11 percent use drugs. Third are people age 26 and older—only 5.8 percent use drugs. Binge drinking and driving under the influence of drugs and alcohol affect millions. Initiation to drug and alcohol abuse begins almost universally before the age of 21 years; most occurs in the 14- to 16-years range. Although some people who develop a substance abuse disorder in adulthood do not expose themselves to recreational drugs until after the age of 21 years, it is unusual, Should these people develop a problem with dependence, they are much more successfully treatable than are people who initiate drug use in the early teenage years. The age of first exposure is an important predictor and estimate of the likelihood of developing both a substance abuse problem and a need for treatment for illicit drug abuse problems. Whether initial use of a drug represents self-medication for an underlying mental health disorder or whether it represents a progression in drug experimentation is not clear. Based on current estimates of early-age drug exposure, substance abuse treatment needs will increase by 57 percent by the year 2020. To stem this tide of substance dependence, early-age initiation to alcohol, cigarettes, and marijuana must be curbed.

In September 2003, the Institute of Medicine of the National Academy of Sciences published and presented to the U.S. Congress a report addressing underage drinking (National Academy of Sciences, Institute of Medicine, 2003). The report detailed the economic cost of the problem ($53 billion per year) and the causes of underage drinking, and it presented a comprehensive societal strategy for reducing underage drinking. In July 2007, U. S. Surgeon General Kennith Moritsugu issued three action guides aimed at assisting parents, communities, and educators in preventing problems associated with underage drinking.[1]

Substance abuse is also related to mental health (Havassy et al., 2004). Over 23 percent of people with a serious mental health problem were dependent on or abused alcohol or illicit drugs compared with 8 percent of people without mental illness. Of adults with substance dependence, over 20 percent had serious mental illness compared with 7 percent of adults who were not dependent on or abusing drugs or alcohol. This comorbidity of substance abuse with diagnosable mental health disorders argues strongly for a combined approach to both problems. In other words, people being seen for a mental health disorder must be evaluated and treated (if necessary) for substance dependence, and vice versa.

Nosology and Psychopathology of Substance Abuse

Published in 2000 in its revised fourth edition, the *Diagnostic and Statistical Manual of Mental Disorders* (DSM-IV-TR) (American Psychiatric Association, 2000) presents commonly accepted criteria for what constitutes substance dependence and substance abuse (Table 21.1). The two substance use disorders involve maladaptive patterns of substance use,

---

[1]The guidelines are available at www.stopalcoholabuse.gov. Also newly available is a five-step prevention guide aimed at assisting communities plan, implement, and evaluate strategies aimed at reducing underage drinking. This guide may be obtained at www.rand.org/pubs/technical_reports/TR403.

TABLE 21.1 DSM-IV criteria for substance dependence or abuse

CRITERIA FOR SUBSTANCE DEPENDENCE:

A maladaptive pattern of substance use, leading to clinically significant impairment or distress, as manifested by three (or more) of the following, occurring at any time in the same 12-month period:

(1) tolerance, as defined by either: (a) need for markedly increased amounts of the substance to achieve intoxication or desired effect; (b) markedly diminished effect with continued use of the same amount of substance

(2) withdrawal, as manifested by either: (a) the characteristic withdrawal syndrome for the substance; (b) the same (or a closely related) substance is taken to relieve or avoid withdrawal symptoms

(3) the substance is often taken in larger amounts or over a longer period than was intended

(4) there is a persistent desire or unsuccessful efforts to cut down or control substance use

(5) a great deal of time is spent in activities necessary to obtain the substance, use the substance, or recover from its effects

(6) important social, occupational, or recreational activities are given up or reduced because of substance use

(7) the substance use is continued despite knowledge of having a persistent or recurrent physical or psychological problem that is likely to have been caused or exacerbated by the substance

CRITERIA FOR SUBSTANCE ABUSE:

A. A maladaptive pattern of substance use leading to clinically significant impairment or distress, as manifested by one (or more) of the following occurring within a 12-month period:

(1) recurrent substance use resulting in a failure to fulfill major role obligations at work, school, or home

(2) recurrent substance use in situations in which it is physically hazardous

(3) recurrent substance-related legal problems

(4) continued substance use despite having persistent or recurrent social or interpersonal problems caused or exacerbated by the effects of the substance

B. The symptoms have never met the criteria for Substance Dependence for this class of substance.

Adapted from American Psychiatric Association (2000), pp. 181–183.

leading to clinically significant impairments or distress. The distinctions between abuse and dependence are listed in the table and discussed by Cami and Farre (2003).

Approximately one-third of people addicted to an illicit drug or alcohol have a diagnosed *comorbid* (Axis I) psychiatric disorder, a situation covered by the term *dual diagnosis*. This term is one of convenience, used to capture the concept that many patients have a substance use disorder in addition to another psychiatric disorder (Goldsmith, 1999). The epidemiology of this comorbidity is striking. Of people with a lifetime diagnosis of schizophrenia, 47 percent have met criteria for substance abuse or dependence; of those with an anxiety disorder, 23.7 percent; obsessive-compulsive disorder, 32.8 percent; bipolar disorder, 50 percent; and depression, 32 percent—with distribution equal for males and females. Jacobsen and coworkers (2001) and Kilpatrick and coworkers (2003) review the complex interactions between substance abuse and PTSD. Hasin and coworkers (2002) discuss the interactive effects of major depression on the remission and relapse of substance use and dependence. Skodol and coworkers (1999) noted that close to 60 percent of subjects with substance abuse disorders had personality disorders, including borderline personality disorder, antisocial personality disorder, and conduct disorder. Leshner (1997) stated:

> Comorbidity is reality! Estimates vary by disorder, but more than 50 percent of people with mental disorders have also been found to abuse drugs, including alcohol; there is also a widespread belief that many mentally ill people who abuse drugs may be actually attempting to medicate themselves. We do not know if this is actually true, but the sequence of onset between the mental disorder and substance use favors the hypothesis for many patients. . . . Many of our causative models ignore the almost inevitability of comorbidity or at best treat it superficially. Worse, many of our treatment approaches ignore comorbidity or insist that mental and addictive disorders be treated separately. (p. 692)

There are serious deficiencies in the diagnosis and provision of services for patients with dual or comorbid illnesses. Making the correct diagnosis is a pivotal component in the successful treatment of dual-diagnosis patients. It is important to maintain a high level of suspicion of the existence of dual disorders and to gather information about the patient from as many sources as possible. A key clinical issue is that the underlying psychiatric disorder and the substance use disorder must be treated concomitantly, and the dual-diagnosis program should include pharmacotherapy, psychoeducation, behavioral intervention, skills training, and case management. It is essential that both diseases be addressed simultaneously, with appropriate communication and coordination among the treatment providers (prescribers and nonprescribers).

Drugs as Behavioral Reinforcers: Neurobiology of Drug Dependence

It was not demonstrated until 1969 that an underlying predisposition to drug dependence was not necessary for intravenously administered drugs to serve as behavioral reinforcers. It was shown that a variety of drugs could produce self-administration behaviors in animals. Thus, reinforcing effects of drugs were shown to be a property of the drug, not of the person. This observation was revolutionary in that era (Bergman and Paronis, 2006). Subsequently, it was shown that the reinforcing effects of drugs (and presumably their "addictive" potentials) were receptor-related phenomena; they were dose-related and could be antagonized by selective receptor blockers, and they did not occur in animals selectively bred to lack certain specific receptors.

Today, the prevailing view is that drugs and other reinforcers act, at least partly, through common brain mechanisms involved in motivated behaviors. Also, the reinforcing strength of self-administered drugs is highly sensitive to both pharmacological and environmental manipulations. Therefore, current therapies have often been aimed at manipulating the pharmacological environment (for example, through use of receptor antagonists or partial receptor agonists) and through environmental manipulations (for example, removal from drug-relapsing cues). Pharmacological manipulations ultimately involve medications that may reduce relapse to drug-taking behaviors (Bergman and Paronis, 2006). A new perspective today is describing addiction as a pathology of learning and memory; it is a chronic brain disease involving two neurobiological phases:

1. The development of addiction is a form of overlearning that is promoted by drugs that elicit the release of large, supraphysiological amounts of dopamine into frontal cortical, basal forebrain, and limbic brain regions.

2. Expression of drug-seeking behaviors (relapse) results from activation of the overlearned drug associations that drive the behavior in a matter that is difficult to regulate. This phase is probably linked to altered cortical and basal forebrain glutaminergic drive into the limbic system (amygdala, ventral tegmentum, and nucleus accumbens) (Volkow et al., 2005; Kalivas and Volkow, 2005; Kalivas et al., 2006).

Kalivas and Volkow (2005) present a hypothesis for the development of drug dependence with long-term propensity to relapse. They begin by stating that the primary behavioral pathology in drug addiction is the overpowering motivational strength and decreased ability to control the desire to obtain and use drugs. Drug-induced dopamine release is certainly crucial for the initial reward effect and

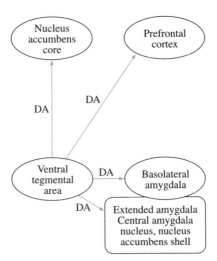

FIGURE 21.1 Neural circuitry mediating the activation of goal-directed behavior. Dopaminergic projections (DA) from the ventral tegmental area to the amygdala, nucleus accumbens, and prefrontal cortex signal the circuit to initiate a rewarding and adaptive-behavioral response to a motivating event, such as a drug. [Modified from Kalivas and Volkow (2005), Figure 1.]

transition to addiction. As shown in Figure 21.1, the dopaminergic projections from the ventral tegmental area causes release of dopamine throughout a reward circuit involving the nucleus accumbens, prefrontal cortex, and amygdala. The projections, over time, facilitate cellular changes that establish learned associations with drug and reward.[2]

Dopamine thus serves two functions: it initiates the reward experience, and (2) it promotes learning (through neuroplasticity) that predisposes to relapse. Kalivas and Volkow call this phenomenon *end-stage addiction* (an overwhelming desire to obtain the drug); it involves glutaminergic projections (Figure 21.2) as a final common pathway for relapse as initiation of drug seeking. Although dopamine release in the nucleus accumbens is required for a drug "high" and for the initiation of addiction, repeated use causes recruitment of the frontal cortex and

---

[2]Russo and coworkers (2007) demonstrated that, in rats, morphine self-administration resulted in reductions in dopamine neuron size, associated with decreased morphine-induced reward, reflecting possible development of dependency and tolerance. Reductions in reward and neuronal size lasted at least 2 weeks following drug removal but returned to normal within a month, consistent with the behavior of human addicts who enter detoxification programs to restore their drug responsiveness at lower doses.

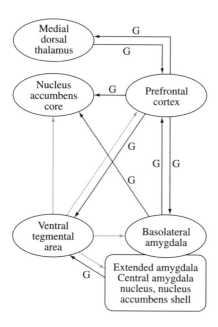

FIGURE 21.2 Dopamine-mediated projections from the ventral tegmentum to the amygdala, prefrontal cortex, and nucleus accumbens (light arrows from Figure 21.1) facilitate neuroplastic changes in glutamate neurons and their axon projections (dark arrows) that establish learned associations with the event. G = glutamate. [Modified from Kalivas and Volkow (2005), Figure 1.]

its glutaminergic learned efferents to the accumbens. Thus, a switch from dopamine-based reward to glutamate-based learned behaviors reveals that the development of addiction with long-term propensity to relapse occurs in a chronological sequence resulted from cellular learning and learning-based responses (Figure 21.3).

Vulnerability to relapse endures for years and results from equally enduring cellular changes in glutamate neurons in the frontal cortex. These glutaminergic projections from the frontal cortex to the nucleus accumbens appear to be the final common pathway for eliciting drug seeking and may represent new target sites for the development of medications that may be used to ameliorate craving and relapse.

Thus, learned behaviors occur because of glutaminergic inputs from the prefrontal cortex to the nucleus accumbens. Stress involves regions of the amygdala and dopaminergic projections to the prefrontal cortex, whereas association cues activate dopaminergic pathways to the amygdala that, in turn, has glutaminergic projections to the prelimbic cortex and nucleus accumbens (Kalivas et al., 2006). Cocaine and the amphetamines, as examples, activate input directly into the prelimbic cortex, accounting for their potent "addictive" properties.

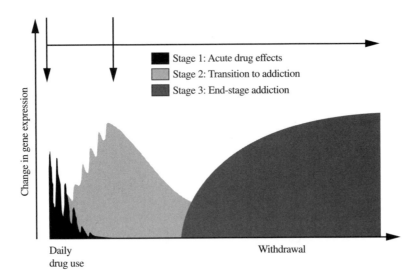

FIGURE 21.3 Three stages of addiction. Stage 1: Acute drug effects result from release of dopamine in the ventral tegmentum and dopaminergic afferents to the amygdala, nucleus accumbens, and prefrontal cortex. Stage 2: Neuroadaptions mediating the transition from recreational drug use to addiction endure for a finite period after discontinuation of drug use and initiate changes in gene protein expression that emerge during withdrawal. Stage 3: Onset of end-stage addiction with desire to obtain drug. Includes craving, relapse, and reduced ability to suppress drug seeking. [Modified from Kalivas and Volkow (2005), Figure 4.]

Other dependence-producing substances (for example, opioids and marijuana) act indirectly but nevertheless activate the same systems.

Relapse (reinstatement of drug seeking after a period without drug) can be readily demonstrated in animals (Figure 21.4) when one of several things happens: (1) presentation of an environmental stimulus previously associated with receipt of drug, (2) direct administration of the drug itself, or (3) exposure to a stressor. From this occurrence, the methods of behavioral treatments for relapse prevention become obvious.

Role of Dopamine in Drug Reward

We now have an idea about how drug dependency develops: drugs that are prone to compulsive abuse activate brain mechanisms involved in reward and positive reinforcement by increasing the level of dopamine in the frontal cortical nucleus accumbens system. Increased dopamine in the nucleus accumbens is the key in mediating the initial rewarding effects (or positive reinforcement) of drugs of abuse. For example, alcohol and morphine do not have rewarding effects in mice that lack the dopamine-2 receptor. In humans, cocaine and methylphenidate

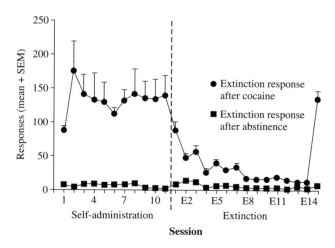

FIGURE 21.4 Development and extinction phases of addiction in an animal model. Animals were trained for 12 days to self-administer cocaine in response to a lever press (black circles). At the vertical dashed line, the animals underwent extinction training (no drug with lever press) for 14 days. At the end of this phase, the animals were presented with a cue that accompanied cocaine administration in the training stage (mild stressor or cocaine). Cue or drug overcame extinction and resulted in lever pressing even though no drug was delivered ("reinstatement" of drug seeking). In "placebo" animals (black squares) to whom no cocaine was administered even in response to lever press, presentation of a "cue" at day E14 did not result in drug-seeking behavior. [Modified from Kalivas et al. (2006), Figure 1, p. 340.]

(Ritalin) increase dopamine levels in the brain, an effect associated with euphoria and pleasurable experiences. People with the lowest control dopamine levels have the greatest pleasure responses to cocaine. Subjects with the highest control dopamine levels experience less pleasurable responses to cocaine, and some even experience dysphoric responses.

Nucleus Accumbens

As discussed, specific circuits in the brain are dedicated to the neural mediation of reward and pleasure (Pierce and Kumaresan, 2006). As early as 1992, Koob stated:

Dopamine forms a critical link for all reward, including opiates and sedative/hypnotics. While open to multiple neurotransmitter inputs and outputs, this view still holds a centrist position for dopamine in all reward. An emphasis on multiple independent neurochemical elements, . . . places the focus on the nucleus accumbens and its circuitry as an important, perhaps critical, substrate for drug reward. (p. 181)

Childress and coworkers (1999) pointed out that during craving (Kalivas and Volkow's end-stage addiction), the user is gripped by a visceral emotional state, experiences a highly focused incentive to act, and is unencumbered by the memory of negative consequences of drug taking. Sensory cues, even more than food or reinforcing drugs, activate the frontal cortical glutaminergic projections to the accumbens. Nucleus accumbens dopamine then becomes involved in responsiveness to conditioned stimuli and the activational aspects of motivation (Salamone et al., 2003). If a drug is not administered after the cue increases dopamine, dopamine drops and dysphoria follows (an unfulfilled cue). The fall in dopamine is proposed to initially increase the drive to obtain the drug.

With extinction, the user becomes extremely vulnerable to cues (see Figure 21.4). In both adolescents and adults who have an alcohol use disorder, brain activation to alcohol-related cues is greater than in people who do not have an alcohol use problem. Youth who drink more per month and who have more desire to drink have the greatest degree of brain activation to cues (Tapert et al., 2003). This finding is a major reason for some of the recommendations of the 2003 Institute of Medicine report to make alcohol advertising less appealing to underage youth who might be excessively vulnerable to it. Relapse prevention is also a major goal of both pharmacological and behavioral therapies of drug dependency (Witkiewitz and Marlatt, 2004; Lingford-Hughes et al., 2004, 2006; Lingford-Hughes and Nutt, 2003).

Dopamine and Withdrawal

Reductions in brain dopamine, especially in the mesolimbic circuitry, are observed in the early stages (perhaps several months) of abstinence from drugs of abuse. These reductions are associated with reduced levels of dopamine receptors and in the size of dopamine neurons, which slowly recover over a period of abstinence (Russo et al., 2007). This period of a hypodopaminergic state leads to drug craving and an increased risk of relapse. Reinitiating drug use increases dopamine levels and provides relief from withdrawal and craving, as would be predicted.

Since replacement of dopamine activity reduces the symptoms of withdrawal and the associated drug craving, might there be a way to replace dopamine or reduce receptor sensitivity to dopamine to reduce the risk of relapse? Although there are no dopamine receptor blockers (aside from antipsychotic drugs) or partial dopamine receptor agonists, replacement of illicit drug with prescription dopaminergic agonists is one possibility. Currently, the only agent available for clinical use is bupropion (Wellbutrin, Zyban), a dopamine reuptake inhibitor that has proved effective in the treatment of nicotine dependency and has been used as an adjunct to contingency management relapse prevention therapies to psychostimulant dependency (Dwoskin et al., 2006; Poling et al., 2006).

Other Neurotransmitter Systems Involved in Reward: Modulators of Dopaminergic Activity

No brain system works in isolation. The dopaminergic reward system in the nucleus accumbens is under the control of many other neurotransmitter systems (Cami and Farre, 2003). Discussion of three of these systems follows.

Opioids

Chapter 16 discussed the pharmacology of the opioids and the receptors on which they act. Activation of the mu receptors increases dopamine in the nucleus accumbens, and mice lacking mu receptors do not exhibit a reward response to morphine. The rewarding action of mu receptors underlies the action of naltrexone in treating alcohol dependence (Chapter 4). This usefulness is thought to be a consequence of naltrexone's ability to block the actions of endorphins that are released by drinking alcohol and that mediate pleasure.

Conversely, activation of kappa receptors reduces activity in the nucleus accumbens. Kappa agonist opioids are not behaviorally rewarding, and their administration can result in a dysphoric response. Similarly, experimental delta receptor antagonists reduce alcohol self-administration. Therefore, increased delta activity should play a role in positive reinforcement.

Glutamate

Glutamate is the brain's major excitatory neurotransmitter and, as stated, is involved in projection from the frontal cortex to the nucleus accumbens. These neurons therefore project to the mesolimbic reward system and affect thought, affect, behavioral reward, and addiction. The NMDA-type glutamate receptors have been implicated in dependence associated with nicotine, ethanol, benzodiazepines, and marijuana. Antagonists of these same NMDA receptors inhibit responsiveness to stimulants such as cocaine and the amphetamines and the development of opioid dependence. Memantine, a nonpsychedelic NMDA antagonist that is used in the treatment of moderate to severe dementia (Chapter 11), attenuates naloxone-precipitated withdrawal (Bisaga et al., 2001). Glutamate receptors are proposed to be involved in cocaine self-administration (McFarland et al., 2003).

During ethanol withdrawal, increases in activity in NMDA-type glutamate receptors are observed, along with increases in glutamate release. The increases in glutamate activity are thought to be involved in alcohol withdrawal seizures and in the loss of neurons during long-term alcoholism with repeated detoxifications. Acamprosate (Campral; Chapter 4) is an NMDA antagonist approved for use in treating alcoholism. Perhaps acamprosate therapy should be initiated with the onset of ethanol detoxification (Lingford-Hughes and Nutt, 2003), although the same can be said for initiation of therapy with anticonvulsant mood stabilizers such as topiramate (Topamax; Chapter 8).

Cannabinoid Antagonists

As discussed in Chapter 17, cannabinoid receptors and opioid receptors are remarkably similar, and cannabinoid-opioid interactions are important in current concepts of addiction and drug reward mechanisms. It is now widely recognized that cannabinoids act on brain reward mechanisms in strikingly similar fashion to other drugs of abuse (Mechoulam and Parker, 2003). Cannabinoids are capable of increasing endorphin synthesis or release, and opioid antagonists, such as naloxone, can block some of the effects of THC as well as inducing withdrawal in THC-dependent animals. In mice lacking cannabinoid receptors, the rewarding and withdrawal responses to morphine (but not cocaine) are reduced. Therefore, cannabinoid CB-1 receptors are involved in dependence not only on THC but on opioids such as morphine. The cannabinoid antagonist rimonabant will probably be an effective antirelapse agent; it blocks relapses to sweet and fattening foods, nicotine cigarettes, ethanol, and other drugs of abuse (Lallemand and deWitte, 2006; Fattore et al., 2007; Beardsley and Thomas, 2005). As discussed in Chapter 17, rimonabant is being withheld from the U.S. market because of concerns over drug-induced depression and suicidal behaviors. Should this problem be resolved, rimonabant or related drugs under development will probably have a prominent role in the future treatment of drug dependence, smoking cessation, obesity, and diabetes.

Drug Availability

Over the years, laws have been passed to limit the availability of certain drugs and to punish drug users deemed dangerous to themselves or to society. When these laws are strictly enforced, they can reduce drug use by people who fear reprisal, but aggressive legislation does not control the development of drug dependency after administration of a drug of abuse, nor does it reduce the rates of relapse to previous patterns of abuse. It only makes addictive drugs more expensive and more difficult to obtain. This is true whether or not the person seeks the drug as self-medication for psychological distress, as relief for physical or psychological pain, or as anything else. Moreover, legislation often fails to address the legally available drugs that cause the greatest amount of harm to people and society—ethanol, nicotine, and prescription medications. Legalization of currently illegal drugs (for example, THC) is not likely to solve drug abuse problems, and it is politically unlikely that legalization will happen. The Marijuana Policy Project (www.prohibitioncosts.org) discusses budgetary costs of marijuana prohibition at length. Modest alteration in the status of currently illegal drugs, if properly implemented, could solve much of the drug traffic-related crime problem. However, it would do little to solve the substance abuse problem, especially the major part of it caused by tobacco, alcohol, and prescription abuse.

Besides legislation, other traditional techniques for reducing drug abuse include education and developing negative attitudes toward drugs in both users and potential users. Such efforts have brought limited results,[3] although the antianabolic steroid intervention programs (ATLAS and ATHENA) described in Chapter 20 are encouraging. Perhaps it is time to take a public health approach to the problem of drug abuse, an approach that attempts to minimize danger to the individual and society. The primary goal of this approach is to reduce the use and abuse of all the recreational mood-altering drugs to a level of safe, pleasurable use consistent with centuries-old human experience, while minimizing to the greatest degree possible their harmful effects on individuals, the family, and society as a whole.

A second major goal is the elimination of the use of alcohol, cigarettes, and marijuana by people under the age of 21 years. Given a historical perspective of human use of psychoactive drugs, these are reasonable social goals. The first step is to agree on the need to implement them, and the second step is implementation of measures to achieve them. The 2003 report of the National Academy of Sciences Institute of Medicine on underage drinking is an important start, especially if it serves to reduce advertising intended as an ethanol cue to susceptible youth.

Addiction as a Chronic, Relapsing Illness

In past years, success of treatment programs for substance abuse has often been measured by the percentage of people who, after detoxification, remain drug-free, or abstinent from drug use. Relapse to drug use has been considered as treatment failure, and people have often been lost to treatment following relapse. With so much dependent on the success of treatment, efforts have traditionally involved costly residential treatment programs aimed at drug detoxification. These programs were usually followed by a "graduation" ceremony that recognized those who completed the detoxification program and were preparing to make the transition from the residential program to the "real

---

[3]See Caudill et al. (2007) for discussion of the limited efficacy of college fraternity-based peer-to-peer programs to limit binge drinking by underage college males.

world." Unfortunately, the time course of such programs only models the time period for dopaminergic neurons to recover (Russo et al., 2007), returning to a time period of increased drug responsiveness and entering the period that Kalivas and Volkow (2005) called end-stage addiction, or the prolonged period of learning-caused overwhelming desire to use the drug.

As discussed elsewhere in this book, one of the goals of pharmacotherapy of drug dependence (on alcohol, cocaine, opioids, marijuana, and so on) is the long-term prevention of craving and relapse, recognizing that relapses can and probably will occur. Therefore, the great need in addiction treatment involves treating drug dependence as a chronic disease, subject to inevitable relapses and setbacks. Medically, this viewpoint is no different than viewing chronic illnesses such as hypertension, diabetes, asthma, thyroid deficiency, and so on as chronic diseases. In those situations, relapses occur periodically, often involving noncompliance with prescribed medicines or necessary life-style changes. When relapses occur, the physician counsels the patient, usually in brief periods of counseling, and therapy is started over again. These lapses are considered not treatment failures but merely temporary lapses or setbacks. The long-term goals are to help the patient with chronic illness maintain as healthy and productive a life and lifestyle as possible. As examples, the long-term consequences of diabetes or hypertension may be unavoidable, but if they are addressed early, a productive life-style can be maintained for as long as possible. The same should hold true for the treatment of drug dependence. Imagine treating diabetes as a 28-day disease. This is no different than treating drug abuse with a 28-day stint in a rehabilitation facility, often with no follow-up therapy. Certainly this kind of program would not work for diabetes; why should it be expected to work for drug dependence?

Positive treatment outcomes should not be measured by abstinence alone but should involve such factors as family life, employment, and decreased involvement with the criminal justice system. Treatment of drug dependence should involve the same standards of success used to measure the effectiveness of treatment of chronic medical illnesses, where periodic relapses and noncompliance with therapy and medications are common and expected. In essence, this is a disease management model for addiction treatment that requires that success be measured in incremental improvements and that relapses be considered as temporary setbacks, not total failures.

Relapse rates for drug dependence are about the same as relapse rates during the treatment of chronic medical illnesses, ranging from 90 percent for very brief relapses to 50 percent for major setbacks. In essence, periodic relapses are a part of the lifelong management of chronic illnesses. Treatment is therefore prolonged, usually lifelong, and outcomes are measured by incremental improvements in the patient's life. The potential for relapse is part of chronic disease.

If we adopt the model of substance dependence, or addiction, as a chronic illness, the model of prolonged residential treatment is inappropriate. As with the treatment of chronic medical illnesses, brief therapeutic interventions are appropriate and effective. Here we do not mean only one intervention, or two, or several. We mean lifelong, continuing treatment, like the treatment of a patient with diabetes or hypertension. Although each intervention may be brief, the patient is engaged in the system for life (Stout, 2002). Interventions in drug abuse treatment would undoubtedly include regular patient-medical personnel visits. Mental health personnel as well as support groups such as Alcoholics Anonymous would be involved. Family support therapy would also be essential.

Another reason for bringing treatment of addictive diseases into the medical mainstream is the fact that many, if not most, people with substance dependence also suffer from comorbid disorders such as major depression, dysthymia, bipolar illness, schizophrenia, or anxiety disorders. Personality disorders, such as antisocial personality disorder, are also frequently encountered. Unless comorbid illnesses are controlled and control is maintained, relapse is probable. Pharmacological and behavioral treatment for both substance dependence and comorbid illnesses can and must occur together.

One example of an advance in this direction was the passage in the year 2000 of legislation that allows a physician to treat opioid dependence in an office setting; the practitioner can now prescribe Schedule III drugs (for example, Suboxone) for this purpose (Chapter 16). Many opioid-dependent people are now being treated in a medical clinic rather than in a methadone clinic. People dependent on other drugs may fall into this medical model should rimonabant become commercially available in this country (Beardsey and Thomas, 2005; Bifulco et al., 2007).

Major factors that may inhibit a move to treating substance dependence as a chronic medical illness include the following:

- Lack of availability of physicians trained in the treatment of substance dependence and its associated comorbid illnesses
- Lack of established relationships between prescribers of psychotherapeutic medications and personnel trained to diagnose and treat mental/behavioral disorders
- Poor financial reimbursement from insurance companies for long-term mental health treatment
- Poor support from local, state, and federal governments to adequately fund this model of care

Each of these factors can be overcome. It only needs commitment from all involved.

In July 2003, the New Freedom Commission on Mental Health presented its report on the mental health changes that need to be made in the United States. The report calls for a transformation of mental health care, bringing mental health care into the mainstream of society. The commission's vision statement was as follows:

> We envision a future when everyone with a mental illness will recover, a future when mental illness can be prevented or cured, a future when mental illness can be detected early, and a future when everyone with a mental illness at any stage of life has access to effective treatment and supports—essentials for living, working, learning, and participating fully in the community. (p. 1)

Drug Education

Drug education and dependency treatment programs must consider the extent of a person's behavioral and physiological involvement with psychoactive drugs. Although educational programs may be useful approaches, formal treatment programs are necessary for people who are compulsive abusers or addicts.

One approach to drug education is to teach the pharmacology of psychoactive drugs, as this book does. Even though this approach can be seen as providing directions for taking drugs, it can also be seen as providing accurate information for people to use in examining and modifying their own risk-taking behavior and thus making the informed decisions necessary to lead a healthy life in the community.

No program of drug education can guarantee to reduce the use of psychoactive drugs. A drug education program can, however, teach people the beneficial and harmful effects of a given drug (whether licit or illicit). Education may limit experimentation by some people. It will not dissuade those already involved in drugs, nor will it dissuade those who seek pharmacological relief from their own psychiatric symptoms or disorders. In other words, it will not dissuade self-prescription for symptom relief.

To alter the behavior of youths requires both education and examples set by teachers, peers, parents, and the whole community, including government officials. Three measures are necessary:

1. Basic information—truthful information—has to be imparted to generate motivation for behavior change. Only honest, straightforward, and full information about the health risks of the addictive drugs will meet this requirement.

2. The means for behavior change have to be provided. Many techniques have proved effective, especially teaching children how to

resist peer pressure. It is important to promote a redefinition of drug-using peers as not "cool."

3. Methods for reinforcing the new behaviors have to be employed. This means that children need recognition, praise, and other rewards for not using drugs. Emphasis on how drugs detract from a healthy body and an attractive appearance, for example, appeals to adolescents' interest in athletics as well as to their developing sexuality and their striving for intimate peer relationships.

In essence, this approach is directed toward building self-esteem in a drug-free environment. Although praiseworthy, the approach works best for young people least likely to abuse drugs. The Project ALERT program has been demonstrated to be an effective method for reducing drug use in middle school students (Ellickson et al., 2003). Project ALERT seeks to motivate students against using drugs and give them the skills to translate motivation into effective resistance behavior.

Prevention of drug abuse in young people requires adults to be willing to set a consistent example by responsibly using or minimizing their own use of psychoactive drugs. In addition, legislation must be consistent and in agreement with accepted, documented scientific evidence. This action is particularly important regarding cigarettes and alcohol. The casualness with which these drugs are used and promoted, distributed, and sold demonstrates both ignorance of and societal hypocrisy about the use of addicting drugs.

Treatment Issues

In past years, many people equated physical dependence with addiction. In older views, the defining problem of addiction was physical dependence, implying that fear of withdrawal following drug removal was the engine driving addictive substance use. Detoxification was seen as the principal treatment for addiction: free the addicted person from the clutches of the drug by assisting him or her through withdrawal and the grip of the addiction was broken. It is not surprising that treatment focused on detoxification, often in a clinical, residential, or hospital setting. Even today, detoxification is often a primary goal of addiction treatment. But physical dependence (as defined by existence of a withdrawal syndrome with drug removal) is not equated with "addiction," as study of the effects of the serotonin-type antidepressants makes clear. None would argue that these drugs are prone to compulsive abuse or are "addicting," yet a well-characterized, multifaceted withdrawal syndrome can follow cessation of their use (Chapter 7).

A twenty-first century view of addiction treatment followed the observation that most people who go through detoxification eventually relapse to drug use. Early focus was on drug-induced reward rather than on drug withdrawal as the engine driving addiction. Clearly, the positive aspects of the drug experience support drug self-administration. The reinforcing properties of drugs are powerful motivational forces that the subjects prefer to natural reinforcers. Thus, drug reinforcement becomes the unifying feature of drug abuse and dependence. Drug abstinence is then viewed as a behavioral and physical state induced by the absence of the drug of abuse to which the addict has adapted. It is behaviorally reinforcing to reverse the abstinence state by the readministration of a drug (relapse is behaviorally reinforcing). The state of abstinence is, therefore, not a return to "normal," as presumed by old models of addiction and withdrawal. Abstinence is characterized by a mental state of apathy, boredom, depression, malaise, anhedonia, and craving for relief. The person needs the drug to feel normal. Thus, relapse is driven both by the negative reinforcement of abstinence and the positive reinforcement of the drug.

As discussed earlier, researchers are now looking beyond the rather simplistic concepts of reward and withdrawal as the engines driving addiction. Not all people who experiment with drugs develop a substance abuse disorder; risk factors become an important predisposing variable to the expression of the genetically influenced, complex, chronic, and relapsing disease that we call "addiction" or "substance dependence." In adolescents, there are several broad classes of risk factors for the development of substance use disorders, including parent and family risk factors, peer-related risk factors, individual risk factors (including biogenetic variables), and community risk factors. Just as the focus cannot be solely on the drug of dependence and its rewarding and withdrawal effects as the principal factors driving abuse of the drug, neither can the focus be only on pharmacotherapy for treatment of an addiction. Focusing on physical brain changes is not adequate; addicts have to be able to handle later exposure to craving-eliciting cues in the environment and need rehabilitation to either learn or relearn social skills or job skills. Moreover, it is likely that combined behavioral and pharmacological treatments will be truly synergistic, not just complementary in nature.

Comprehensive treatment does work (Marwick, 1998), and it can be provided in a cost-effective manner (Shepard et al., 1999). In general, regular outpatient treatment programs are the most cost-effective, and long-term residential treatment programs provide little extra benefit at a fivefold increase in expenses. Any reasonable treatment strategy—even 5 to 10 minutes of physician counseling on several visits—is more effective than no treatment. Friedman and coworkers (1998) summarized the techniques that can be used to manage adults recovering from substance abuse problems (Table 21.2). They presented a practical

TABLE 21.2 Relapse prevention strategies in the primary care setting

Identify patients in recovery
Establish a supportive patient-physician relationship
Schedule regular follow-up
Mobilize family support
Facilitate involvement in 12-step recovery groups
Help recovering patients recognize and cope with relapse precipitants and craving
Advise recovering patients to develop a plan to manage early relapse
Facilitate positive lifestyle changes
Manage depression, anxiety, and other comorbid conditions
Consider adjunctive pharmacotherapy
Collaborate with addiction specialty professionals

From Friedman et al. (1998), p. 1228.

approach to the support of a substance-free life-style, centering on patients who are early into recovery and at the highest risk of relapse, although many of the principles also apply to longer-term recovery.

Pharmacotherapy of Substance Use Disorders

It must be acknowledged that medications have limited usefulness in most cases of substance use disorders; they should be used to augment psychosocial therapies. Despite this limitation, pharmacological treatment options for people with substance use disorders are many:

- Use a substitute drug to ameliorate or reduce the intensity of any withdrawal effects or to reduce the risk of relapse to illicit drug use.

- Substitute a "legal," usually medically prescribed, longer-acting agonist for an illicit one to ameliorate some of the acute withdrawal effects, maintain an agonistic effect, and reduce craving and relapse (so-called relapse prevention pharmacology).

- Treat the substance abuse with a receptor antagonist so that taking the illicit drug will be without effect.

- Treat comorbid psychiatric disorders with appropriate psychotherapeutic agents.

Complete details of the use of specific pharmacological agents to manage dependence on specific drugs of abuse can be found in the chapters devoted to specific drugs of abuse (benzodiazepines, alcohol, opioids, cannabinoids, nicotine, psychostimulants, and so on). In 2004, the British Association for Psychopharmacology (Lingford-Hughes et al., 2004) published extensive guidelines that primarily focus on the pharmacological management of all major substances of abuse and their comorbidity with psychiatric disorders. The guidelines provide a comprehensive review of evidence-based treatments and are highly recommended to all mental health practitioners who treat people with substance abuse disorders and psychological comorbidities.

STUDY QUESTIONS

1. What is meant when a particular drug is called a "behavioral reinforcer"?

2. Why might the evaluation of drug-reinforcing properties in animals be valuable in the assessment of human experiences?

3. Is a propensity for abusing drugs caused by a psychopathological process in the user, or is it a property of the particular drug?

4. On a physiological level, what might explain the lack of self-reinforcing action of phenothiazines or antidepressants?

5. What is the mechanism that underlies the behavioral reinforcing properties of abused drugs?

6. List several key principles that underlie a positive approach toward drug education.

7. Where has drug education failed? How might drug education be used successfully?

8. What is the relationship between age of first use of drugs and development of a substance use disorder? What are the limitations to this relationship?

9. List, from most harmful to least harmful, the classes of psychoactive drugs presented in this book. Defend your ranking.

10. Should certain drugs be more readily available? How should legislation be directed?

11. Are current efforts to limit cigarette smoking likely to prove successful? How should we change our approach?

12. Where should alcohol education be aimed? Defend your position.

REFERENCES

American Psychiatric Association (2000). *Diagnostic and Statistical Manual of Mental Disorders*, 4th ed., text revision (DSM-IV-TR). Washington, DC: American Psychiatric Association.

Beardsey, P. M., and B. F. Thomas (2005). "Current Evidence Supporting a Role of Cannabinoid CB1 Receptor (CB1R) Antagonists as Potential Pharmacotherapies for Drug Abuse Disorders." *Behavioral Pharmacology* 16: 275–296.

Bergman, J., and C. A. Paronis (2006). "Measuring the Reinforcing Strength of Abused Drugs." *Molecular Interventions* 6: 273–284.

Bifulco, M., et al. (2007). "Rimonabant: Just an Anti-Obesity Drug? Current Evidence on its Pleiotropic Effects." *Molecular Pharmacology* 71: 1445–1456.

Bisaga, A., et al. (2001). "The NMDA Antagonist Memantine Attenuates the Expression of Opioid Physical Dependence in Humans." *Psychopharmacology* 157: 1–10.

Cami, J., and M. Farre (2003). "Drug Addiction." *New England Journal of Medicine* 349: 975–986.

Caudill, B. D., et al. (2007). "Alcohol Risk-Reduction Skills Training in a National Fraternity: A Randomized Intervention Trial with Longitudinal Intent-to-Treat Analysis." *Journal of Studies on Alcohol and Drugs* 68: 399–409.

Childress, A. R., et al. (1999). "Limbic Activation During Cue-Induced Cocaine Craving." *American Journal of Psychiatry* 156: 11–18.

Dwoskin, L. P., et al. (2006). "Review of the Pharmacology and Clinical Profile of Bupropion, an Antidepressant and Tobacco Use Cessation Agent." *CNS Drug Reviews* 12: 178–207.

Ellickson, P. L., et al. (2003). "New Inroads in Preventing Adolescent Drug Use: Results from a Large-Scale Trial of Project ALERT in Middle Schools." *American Journal of Public Health* 93: 1830–1836.

Fattore, L., et al. (2007). "An Endocannabinoid Mechanism in Relapse to Drug Seeking: A Review of Animal Studies and Clinical Perspectives." *Brain Research Reviews* 53: 1–16.

Friedman, P. D., et al. (1998). "Management of Adults Recovering from Alcohol and Other Drug Problems." *Journal of the American Medical Association* 279: 1227–1231.

Goldsmith, R. J. (1999). "Overview of Psychiatric Comorbidity: Practical and Theoretical Considerations." *Psychiatric Clinics of North America* 22: 331–349.

Hasin, D., et al. (2002). "Effects of Major Depression on Remission and Relapse of Substance Dependence." *Archives of General Psychiatry* 59: 375–380.

Havassy, B. E., et al. (2004). "Comparisons of Patients with Comorbid Psychiatric and Substance Use Disorders: Implications for Treatment and Service Delivery." *American Journal of Psychiatry* 161: 139–145.

Iritani, B. J., et al. (2007). "Crystal Methamphetamine Use Among Young Adults in the USA." *Addiction* 102: 1102–1113.

Jacobsen, L. K., et al. (2001). "Substance Use Disorders in Patients with Posttraumatic Stress Disorder: A Review of the Literature." *American Journal of Psychiatry* 158: 1184–1190.

Kalivas, P. W., and N. D. Volkow (2005). "The Neural Basis of Addiction: A Pathology of Motivation and Choice." *American Journal of Psychiatry* 162: 1403–1413.

Kalivas, P. W., et al. (2006). "Animal Models and Brain Circuits in Drug Addiction." *Molecular Interventions* 6: 339–344.

Kilpatrick, D. K., et al. (2003). "Violence and Risk of PTSD, Major Depression, Substance Abuse/Dependence, and Comorbidity: Results from the National Survey of Adolescents." *Journal of Consulting and Clinical Psychology* 71: 692–700.

Koob, G. F. (1992). "Drugs of Abuse: Anatomy, Pharmacology, and Function of Reward Pathways." *Trends in Pharmacologic Sciences* 13: 177–182.

Lallemand, F., and P. DeWitte. (2006). "SR147778, a CB1Cannabinoid Receptor Antagonist, Suppresses Ethanol Preference in Chronically Alcoholized Wistar Rats." *Alcohol* 39: 125–134.

Leshner, A. I. (1997). "Drug Abuse and Addiction Treatment Research: The Next Generation." *Archives of General Psychiatry* 54: 691–694.

Lingford-Hughes, A., and D. Nutt. (2003). "Neurobiology of Addiction and Implications for Treatment." *British Journal of Psychiatry* 182: 97–100.

Lingford-Hughes, A., et al. (2004). "Evidence-Based Guidelines for the Pharmacological Management of Substance Misuse, Addiction and Comorbidity: Recommendations from the British Association for Psychopharmacology." *Journal of Psychopharmacology* 18: 293–335.

Lingford-Hughes, A., et al. (2006). "Imaging Alcohol Cue Exposure in Alcohol Dependence Using a PET 150-H2O Paradigm: Results from a Pilot Study." *Addiction Biology* 11: 107–115.

Marwick, C. (1998). "Physician Leadership on National Drug Policy Finds Addiction Treatment Works." *Journal of the American Medical Association* 279: 1149–1150.

McFarland, K., et al. (2003). "Prefrontal Glutamate Release into the Core of the Nucleus Accumbens Mediates Cocaine-Induced Reinstatement of Drug-Seeking Behavior." *Journal of Neuroscience* 23: 3531–3537.

Mechoulam, R., and L. Parker. (2003). "Cannabis and Alcohol: A Close Friendship." *Trends in Pharmacological Sciences* 24: 266–268.

National Academy of Sciences, Institute of Medicine (2003). *Reducing Underage Drinking: A Collective Responsibility*. Washington DC: National Academic Press.

New Freedom Commission on Mental Health (2003, July). *Achieving the Promise: Transforming Mental Health Care in America: Final Report*. U.S. Department of Health and Human Services Publication SMA-03-3832. Rockville, MD.

Pierce, R. C., and V. Kumaresan (2006). "The Mesolimbic Dopamine System: The Final Common Pathway for the Reinforcing Effect of Drugs of Abuse?" *Neuroscience Biobehavioral Reviews* 30: 215–238.

Poling, J., et al. (2006). "Six-Month Trial of Bupropion with Contingency Management for Cocaine Dependence in a Methadone-Maintained Population." *Archives of General Psychiatry* 63: 219–228.

Russo, S. J., et al. (2007). "IRS2-Akt Pathway in Midbrain Dopamine Neurons Regulates Behavioral and Cellular Responses to Opiates." *Nature Neuroscience* 10: 93–99.

Salamone, J. D., et al. (2003). "Nucleus Accumbens Dopamine and the Regulation of Effort in Food-Seeking Behavior: Implications for Studies of Natural Motivation, Psychiatry, and Drug Abuse." *Journal of Pharmacology and Experimental Therapeutics* 305: 1–8.

Shepard, D. S., et al. (1999). "Cost-Effectiveness of Substance Abuse Services: Implications for Public Policy." *Psychiatric Clinics of North America* 22: 385–400.

Skodol, A. E., et al. (1999). "Axis II Comorbidity of Substance Use Disorders Among Patients Referred for Treatment of Personality Disorders." *American Journal of Psychiatry* 156: 733–738.

Stout, R. (2002, October). "Treatment Failure Is the First Step to Success." *Brown University Digest of Addiction Theory and Application*, p. 8.

Tapert, S. F., et al. (2003). "Neural Response to Alcohol Stimuli in Adolescents with Alcohol Use Disorder." *Archives of General Psychiatry* 60: 727–735.

U.S. Department of Health and Human Services (2003). "National Survey on Drug Use and Health, 2002." Washington, DC: USDHHS Substance Abuse and Mental Health Services Administration.

U.S. Department of Health and Human Services (2006). "National Youth Risk Behavior Survey: 1991–2005." Washington, DC: Centers for Disease Control and Prevention. Available at www.cdc.gov.yrbss.

Volkow, N. D., et al. (2005). "Activation of Orbital and Medial Prefrontal Cortex by Methylphenidate in Cocaine-Addicted Subjects but Not in Controls: Relevance to Addiction." *Journal of Neuroscience* 25: 3932–3939.

Witkiewitz, K., and G. A. Marlatt (2004). "Relapse Prevention for Alcohol and Drug Problems: That Was Zen, This Is Tao." *American Psychologist* 59: 224–235.

Abstinence syndrome   State of altered behavior that follows cessation of drug administration.

Acetylcholine   Neurotransmitter in the central and peripheral nervous systems.

Additive effect   Increased effect that occurs when two drugs that have similar biological actions are administered. The net effect is the sum of the independent effects exerted by the drugs.

Adenosine   Chemical neuromodulator in the CNS, primarily at inhibitory synapses.

Adenylate cyclase   Intracellular enzyme that catalyzes the conversion of cyclic AMP to adenosine monophosphate.

Affective disorder   Type of mental disorder characterized by recurrent episodes of mania, depression, or both.

Agonist   Drug that attaches to a receptor and produces actions that mimic or potentiate those of an endogenous transmitter.

Aldehyde dehydrogenase   Enzyme that carries out a specific step in alcohol metabolism: the metabolism of acetaldehyde to acetate. This enzyme may be blocked by the drug disulfiram (Antabuse).

Alzheimer's disease   Progressive neurological disease that occurs primarily in the elderly. It is characterized by a loss of short-term memory and intellectual functioning. It is associated with a loss of function of acetylcholine neurons.

Amphetamine   Behavioral stimulant.

Anabolic steroid   Testosteronelike drug that acts to increase muscle mass and produces other masculinizing effects.

Anandamide   Endogenous chemical compound that attaches to cannabinoid receptors in the CNS and to specific components of the lymphatic system.

Anandamide receptor   Receptor to which anandamide and tetrahydrocannabinol bind.

Anesthetic   Sedative-hypnotic compound used primarily in doses capable of inducing a state of general anesthesia that involves both loss of sensation and loss of consciousness.

Antagonist   Drug that attaches to a receptor and blocks the action of either an endogenous transmitter or an agonistic drug.

Anticonvulsant   Drug that blocks or prevents epileptic convulsions. Some anticonvulsants (for example, carbamazepine and valproic acid) are also used to treat certain nonepileptic psychiatric disorders.

Antidepressant   Drug that is useful in treating mentally depressed patients but does not produce stimulant effects in nondepressed persons. Subdivided into several categories.

Antipsychotic   Drug that has the ability to calm psychotic states and make the psychotic patient more manageable. Two classes are defined: classical antipsychotics and atypical (or new generation) antipsychotics.

Anxiolytic   Drug used to relieve the symptoms associated with defined states of anxiety. Classically, the term refers to the benzodiazepines and related drugs.

Attention deficit/hyperactivity disorder (ADHD)   Learning and behavioral disability characterized by reduced attention span and hyperactivity.

Atypical antipsychotic   Drug that ameliorates the symptoms of schizophrenia without necessarily causing abnormal motor movements. Also used in the treatment of mania.

Autonomic nervous system   Portion of the peripheral nervous system that controls, or regulates, the visceral, or automatic, functions of the body, such as heart rate and blood pressure.

Barbiturates   Class of chemically related sedative-hypnotic compounds that share a characteristic six-membered ring structure.

Basal ganglia   Part of the brain that contains vast numbers of dopamine-containing synapses. Forms part of the extrapyramidal system. Parkinson's disease follows dopamine loss in this structure.

Benzodiazepines   Class of chemically related sedative-hypnotic agents of which chlordiazepoxide (Librium) and diazepam (Valium) are examples.

Bipolar disorder   Affective disorder characterized by alternating bouts of mania and depression. Also called *manic-depressive illness.*

Blackout   Period of time during which a person may be awake but memory is not imprinted. It frequently occurs in people who have consumed excessive alcohol or to whom have been administered (or who have taken) large doses of sedative drugs.

Brain syndrome, organic   Pattern of behavior induced when neurons are either reversibly depressed or irreversibly destroyed. Behavior is characterized by clouded sensorium, disorientation, shallow and labile affect, and impaired memory, intellectual function, insight, and judgment.

Brand name   Unique name licensed to one manufacturer of a drug. Contrasts with *generic name,* the name under which any manufacturer may sell a drug.

Caffeine   Behavioral and general cellular stimulant found in coffee, tea, cola drinks, and chocolate.

Caffeinism   Habitual use of large amounts of caffeine.

Cannabis sativa   Hemp plant; contains marijuana.

Carbidopa   Drug that inhibits the enzyme dopa decarboxylase, allowing increased availability of dopa within the brain. Contained in Sinemet.

Central nervous system (CNS)   Brain and spinal cord.

Cirrhosis   Serious, usually irreversible liver disease. Usually associated with chronic excessive alcohol consumption.

Clonidine (Catapres)   Antihypertensive useful in ameliorating the symptoms of narcotic withdrawal.

Cocaine   Behavioral stimulant.

Codeine   Sedative and pain-relieving agent found in opium. Structurally related to morphine but less potent; constitutes approximately 0.5 percent of the opium extract.

Comorbid disorder   Psychiatric disorder that coexists with another psychiatric disorder (for example, multisubstance abuse in a patient with a major depressive disorder).

Convulsant   Drug that produces convulsions by blocking inhibitory neurotransmission.

COX inhibitors   Aspirinlike analgesic drugs that produce their actions by inhibiting the enzyme cyclooxygenase. Two variants of the enzyme occur: COX-1 and COX-2. Some drugs are specific for COX-2; others are nonspecific inhibitors.

Crack   Street name for a smokable form of potent, concentrated cocaine.

Cross-dependence   Condition in which one drug can prevent the withdrawal symptoms associated with physical dependence on a different drug.

Cross-tolerance   Condition in which tolerance of one drug results in a lessened response to another drug.

Delirium tremens (DTs)   Syndrome of tremulousness with hallucinations, psychomotor agitation, confusion and disorientation, sleep disorders, and other associated discomforts, lasting several days after alcohol withdrawal.

Dementia   General designation for nonspecific mental deterioration.

Detoxification   Process of allowing time for the body to metabolize and/or excrete accumulations of drug. Usually a first step in drug abuse evaluation and treatment.

Differential diagnosis   Listing of all possible causes that might explain a given set of symptoms.

Dimethyltryptamine (DMT)   Psychedelic drug found in many South American plants.

Disinhibition   Physiological state of the central nervous system characterized by decreased activity of inhibitory synapses, which results in a net excess of excitatory activity.

Dopamine transporter   Presynaptic protein that binds synaptic dopamine and transports the neurotransmitter back into the presynaptic nerve terminal.

Dose-response relation   Relation between drug doses and the response elicited at each dose level.

Drug Chemical substance used for its effects on bodily processes.

Drug absorption Mechanism by which a drug reaches the bloodstream from the skin, lungs, stomach, intestinal tract, or muscle.

Drug administration Procedures through which a drug enters the body (oral administration of tablets or liquids, inhalation of powders, injection of sterile liquids, and so on).

Drug dependence State in which the use of a drug is necessary for either physical or psychological well-being.

Drug interaction Modification of the action of one drug by the concurrent or prior administration of another drug.

Drug misuse Use of any drug (legal or illegal) for a medical or recreational purpose when other alternatives are available, practical, or warranted or when drug use endangers either the user or others with whom he or she may interact.

Drug receptor Specific molecular substance in the body with which a given drug interacts to produce its effect.

Drug tolerance State of progressively decreasing responsiveness to a drug.

DSM-IV, DSM-IV-TR *Diagnostic and Statistical Manual of Mental Disorders,* Fourth Edition, published by the American Psychiatric Association in 1994. The Text Revision of the Fourth Edition was published in 2000.

Dual-action antidepressants Antidepressant drugs that act by inhibiting the active presynaptic reuptake of norepinephrine and serotonin.

Electroconvulsive therapy (ECT) Nonpharmacological treatment used for major depression.

Endorphin Naturally occurring protein that causes endogenous morphine-like activity.

Enkephalin Naturally occurring protein that causes morphinelike activity.

Enzyme Large organic molecule that mediates a specific biochemical reaction in the body.

Enzyme induction Increased production of drug-metabolizing enzymes in the liver, stimulated by certain drugs that increase the rate at which the body can metabolize them. It is one mechanism by which pharmacological tolerance is produced.

Epilepsy Neurological disorder characterized by an occasional, sudden, and uncontrolled discharge of neurons.

Fetal alcohol syndrome Symptom complex of congenital anomalies, seen in newborns of women who ingested high doses of alcohol during critical periods of pregnancy.

G protein Specific intraneuronal protein that links transmitter-induced receptor alterations with intracellular second-messenger proteins or with adjacent ion channels.

Gamma aminobutyric acid (GABA) Inhibitory amino acid neurotransmitter in the brain.

Generic name Name that identifies a specific chemical entity (without describing the chemical). Often marketed under different brand names by different manufacturers.

Glutamic acid Excitatory amino acid neurotransmitter.

Hallucinogen Psychedelic drug that produces profound distortions in perception.

Harmine Psychedelic agent obtained from the seeds of *Peganum harmala*.

Hashish Extract of the hemp plant (*Cannabis sativa*) that has a higher concentration of THC than does marijuana.

Heroin Semisynthetic opiate produced by a chemical modification of morphine.

Hypothalamus Structure located at the base of the brain, above the pituitary gland.

Hypoxia State of relative lack of oxygen in the tissues of the body and the brain.

Ice Street name for a smokable, free-base form of potent, concentrated methamphetamine.

Levodopa Precursor substance to the transmitter dopamine; useful in ameliorating the symptoms of Parkinson's disease.

Limbic system Group of brain structures involved in emotional responses and emotional expression.

Lithium Alkali metal effective in the treatment of mania and depression.

Lysergic acid diethylamide (LSD) Semisynthetic psychedelic drug.

Major tranquilizer Drug used in the treatment of psychotic states.

Mania Mental disorder characterized by an expansive emotional state, elation, hyperirritability, excessive talkativeness, flights of ideas, and increased behavioral activity.

MAO See **Monoamine oxidase.**

Marijuana Mixture of the crushed leaves, flowers, and small branches of both the male and female hemp plant (*Cannabis sativa*).

Mescaline Psychedelic drug extracted from the peyote cactus.

Minor tranquilizer Sedative-hypnotic drug promoted primarily for use in the treatment of anxiety.

Mixed agonist-antagonist Drug that attaches to a receptor, producing weak agonistic effects but displacing more potent agonists, precipitating withdrawal in drug-dependent persons.

Monoamine oxidase (MAO) Enzyme capable of metabolizing norepinephrine, dopamine, and serotonin to inactive products.

Monoamine oxidase inhibitor (MAOI) Drug that inhibits the activity of the enzyme monoamine oxidase.

Mood stabilizer Drug used in the treatment of bipolar illness. Examples are lithium and any of the neuromodulator anticonvulsants.

Morphine Major sedative and pain-relieving drug found in opium; composed of approximately 10 percent of the crude opium exudate.

Muscarine Drug extracted from the mushroom *Amanita muscaria* that directly stimulates acetylcholine receptors.

Myristin Psychedelic agent obtained from nutmeg and mace.

Neuromodulator Antiepileptic drug used to treat bipolar illness, aggressive disorders, chronic pain, and a variety of other disorders.

Neurotransmitter Endogenous chemical released by one neuron that alters the electrical activity of another neuron.

Nicotine Behavioral stimulant found in tobacco.

Norepinephrine-specific reuptake inhibitor See **Selective norepinephrine reuptake inhibitor.**

Off-label Term applied to the clinical use of a drug for an indication other than that for which the drug was approved by the U.S. Food and Drug Administration. Use is usually justified by medical literature, even though formal USDA approval for the use was not sought by the manufacturer of the drug. The manufacturer is not permitted to promote a drug for an off-label use.

Ololiuqui Psychedelic drug obtained from the seeds of the morning glory plant.

Opioid Natural or synthetic drug that exerts actions on the body similar to those induced by morphine, the major pain-relieving agent obtained from the opium poppy (*Papaver somniferum*).

Opium Crude resinous exudate from the opium poppy. Contains morphine and codeine as active opioids.

Parkinson's disease Disorder of the motor system characterized by involuntary movements, tremor, and weakness.

Partial agonist Drug that binds to a receptor, contributing only part of the action exerted by the endogenous neurotransmitter or producing a submaximal receptor response. Buprenorphine (in Suboxone) is an example.

Peptide Chemical composed of a chain-link sequence of amino acids.

Peyote Cactus that contains mescaline.

Pharmacodynamics Study of the interactions of a drug and the receptors responsible for the action of the drug in the body.

Pharmacokinetics Study of the factors that influence the absorption, distribution, metabolism, and excretion of a drug.

Pharmacology Branch of science that deals with the study of drugs and their actions on living systems.

Phencyclidine (Sernyl, PCP) Psychedelic surgical anesthetic; acts by binding to and inhibiting ion transport through the NMDA-glutamate receptors.

Phenothiazine Class of chemically related compounds useful in the treatment of psychosis.

Physical dependence State in which the use of a drug is required for a person to function normally. Physical dependence is revealed by withdrawing the drug and noting the occurrence of withdrawal symptoms (abstinence syndrome). Characteristically, withdrawal symptoms can be terminated by readministration of the drug.

Placebo   Pharmacologically inert substance that may elicit a significant reaction largely because of the mental set of the patient or the physical setting in which the drug is taken.

Potency   Measure of drug activity expressed in terms of the amount required to produce an effect of given intensity. Potency varies inversely with the amount of drug required to produce this effect—the more potent the drug, the lower the amount required to produce the effect.

Psilocybin   Psychedelic drug obtained from the mushroom *Psilocybe mexicana*.

Psychedelic   Drug that can alter sensory perception.

Psychoactive drug   Chemical substance that alters mood or behavior as a result of alterations in the functioning of the brain.

Psychological dependence   Compulsion to use a drug for its pleasurable effects. Dependence may lead to a compulsion to misuse a drug.

Psychopharmacology   Branch of pharmacology that deals with the effects of drugs on the nervous system and behavior.

Psychopharmacotherapy   Clinical treatment of psychiatric disorders with drugs.

Psychotherapy   Nonpharmacological treatment of psychiatric disorders utilizing a wide range of modalities from simple education and supportive counseling to insight-oriented, dynamically based therapy.

Receptor   Location in the nervous system at which a neurotransmitter or drug binds to exert its characteristic effect. Most receptors are members of genetically encoded families of specialized proteins.

Reye's syndrome   Rare CNS disorder that occurs in children; associated with aspirin ingestion.

Risk-to-benefit ratio   Arbitrary assessment of the risks and benefits that may accrue from administration of a drug.

Schizophrenia   Debilitating neuropsychiatric illness associated with disturbances in thought, perception, emotion, cognition, relationships, and psychomotor behavior.

Scopolamine   Anticholinergic drug that crosses the blood-brain barrier to produce sedation and amnesia.

Second messenger   Intraneuronal protein that, when activated by an excitatory G protein, initiates the neuronal response to the initial neurotransmitter attachment to an extracellular receptor.

Sedative-hypnotic   Chemical substance that exerts a nonselective general depressant action on the nervous system.

Selective norepinephrine reuptake inhibitor (SNRI)   Drug that blocks the active presynaptic transporter for norepinephrine. Clinically used to treat ADHD, depression, and other disorders, including seasonal affective disorder.

Selective serotonin reuptake inhibitor (SSRI)   Second-generation antidepressant drug.

Serotonin (5-hydroxytryptamine, 5-HT) Synaptic transmitter in both the brain and the peripheral nervous system.

Serotonin syndrome Clinical syndrome resulting from excessive amounts of serotonin in the brain. The syndrome can follow use of excessive doses of SSRIs, and it is characterized by extreme anxiety, confusion, and disorientation.

Serotonin withdrawal syndrome Clinical syndrome that can follow withdrawal or cessation of SSRI therapy. The syndrome is characterized by mental status alterations, severe flulike symptoms, and feelings of tingling or electrical shock in the extremities.

Side effect Drug-induced effect that accompanies the primary effect for which the drug is administered.

Substance P Protein neurotransmitter that regulates affective behavior, increasing the perception of pain. Substance P antagonists exhibit analgesic and antidepressant actions.

Tardive dyskinesia Movement disorder that appears after months or years of treatment with neuroleptic (antipsychotic) drugs. It usually worsens with drug discontinuation. Symptoms are often masked by the drugs that cause the disorder.

Teratogen Chemical substance that induces abnormalities of fetal development.

Testosterone Hormone secreted from the testes that is responsible for the distinguishing characteristics of the male.

Tetrahydrocannabinol (THC) Major psychoactive agent in marijuana, hashish, and other preparations of hemp (*Cannabis sativa*).

Therapeutic drug monitoring (TDM) Process of correlating the plasma level of a drug with therapeutic response.

Tolerance Clinical state of reduced responsiveness to a drug; can be produced by a variety of mechanisms, all of which require increased doses of drug to produce an effect once achieved by lower doses.

Toxic effect Drug-induced effect either temporarily or permanently deleterious to any organ or system of an animal or person. Drug toxicity includes both the relatively minor side effects that invariably accompany drug administration and the more serious and unexpected manifestations that occur in only a small percentage of patients who take a drug.

INDEX